Makers of the Western Tradition
PORTRAITS FROM HISTORY
Second Edition

J. KELLEY SOWARDS, editor

Makers of the Western Tradition

PORTRAITS FROM HISTORY
Second Edition

St. Martin's Press   New York

Cover design and illustrations: Rus Anderson

ISBN: 0-312-50613-9

ACKNOWLEDGMENTS

AKHENATON: "Hymn to Aton" from "Egyptian Hymns and Prayers," translated by
John A. Wilson, in *Ancient Near Eastern Texts Relating to the Old Testament,* 3rd
edition, with Supplement, edited by James B. Pritchard. Omission of footnotes.
Copyright © 1969 by Princeton University Press. Reprinted by permission of
Princeton University Press. From *The Dawn of Conscience* by James Henry
Breasted. Copyright 1933 by James Henry Breasted. Reprinted by permission of
Charles Scribner's Sons. From *Ikhnaton: Legend and History* by F. J. Giles. Re-
printed by permission of the Hutchinson Publishing Group Ltd.
KING DAVID: Excerpts from the *Revised Standard Version Bible.* Reprinted by permis-
sion of the National Council of the Churches of Christ. From *Kingship and the
Gods: A Study of Ancient Near Eastern Religion as the Integration of Society and
Nature* by Henri Frankfort. Copyright 1948 by The University of Chicago Press.
Reprinted by permission of The University of Chicago Press. From *Archaeology
in the Holy Land,* 3rd edition, by Kathleen M. Kenyon. Copyright © Kathleen M.
Kenyon 1960, 1965, 1970 in London, England. Reprinted by permission of Praeger
Publishers, Inc. and Ernest Benn Limited.
SOCRATES: From *The Clouds* by Aristophanes, translated by William Arrowsmith.
Copyright © 1962 by William Arrowsmith. Reprinted by arrangement with The
New American Library, Inc., New York, New York. From "The Apology" from
The Dialogues of Plato, translated by Benjamin Jowett, 3rd edition, 1892. Also
published by Random House in 1937. Reprinted by permission of Oxford University
Press. From "The Image of Socrates" from *Heroes and Gods* by Moses Hadas and
Morton Smith, Volume Thirteen, Religious Perspectives, edited by Ruth Nanda
Anshen. Copyright © 1965 by Moses Hadas and Morton Smith.
ALEXANDER THE GREAT: "The Ancient Sources" from *The Campaigns of Alexander
by Arrian,* translated by Aubrey de Sélincourt (Penguin Classics, Revised Edition,
1971). © the Estate of Aubrey de Sélincourt 1958. From *The Geography of Strabo,*
translated by Horace Leonard Jones. "The Loeb Classical Library" published by
Harvard University Press and William Heinemann, Ltd., 1917. From *Plutarch's
Moralia,* translated by Frank Cole Babbitt. "The Loeb Classical Library" published
by Harvard University Press and William Heinemann, Ltd., 1936. From *Plutarch's
Lives,* translated by Bernadotte Perrin. "The Loeb Classical Library" published by
Harvard University Press and William Heinemann, Ltd. 1919. From "Alexander
the Great and the Unity of Mankind" by W. W. Tarn, published in *The British
Academy Proceedings,* 19 (1933). Reprinted by permission of The British Academy.
Excerpts from "W. W. Tarn and the Alexander Ideal" by Richard A. Todd, published in *The Historian,* 27 (1964), 48–55. Reprinted by permission of the author
and *The Historian.*
JULIUS CAESAR: From *The Lives of the Twelve Caesars by Seutonius,* edited by Joseph
Gavorse. Copyright 1931 and renewed 1959 by Modern Library, Inc. Reprinted by
permission of Random House, Inc. From Ronald Syme, *The Roman Revolution*
published in 1939; reprinted by permission of Oxford University Press.
AUGUSTINE: From *The Confessions of St. Augustine,* translated by Rex Warner. Copyright © 1963 by Rex Warner. Reprinted by permission of The New American
Library, Inc., New York, New York. From *Augustine of Hippo: A Biography* by
Peter Brown. Originally published by the University of California Press, 1967; reprinted by permission of The Regents of the University of California and Faber
and Faber Ltd. From *Thought and Letters in Western Europe, A.D. 500 to 900* by
M.L.W. Laistner. Copyright 1931 by M.L.W. Laistner; revised edition, Methuen &
Co. Ltd. and Cornell University Press, 1957. Used by permission of Cornell Uni-
versity Press.

To my parents, in love and gratitude

Preface

Are men and women able to force change upon history by their own skill and wits, their nerve and daring? Are they capable of altering its course by their own actions? Or are they hopelessly caught up in the grinding process of great, impersonal forces over which they have no real control?

Historians, like theologians, philosophers, and scientists, have long been fascinated by this question. People in every age have recognized great forces at work in their affairs, whether they perceived those forces as supernatural and divine, climatological, ecological, sociological, or economic. Yet obviously at least a few individuals—Alexander, Charlemagne, Napoleon, Hitler—were able to seize the opportunity of their time and compel the great forces of history to change course. Still other individuals—Moses, Jesus, Copernicus, Darwin, Einstein—were able, solely by the power of their thought or their vision, to shape the history of their period and of all later time more profoundly than the conquerors or military heroes could do.

The purpose of this book is to examine the careers and the impact of several figures who significantly influenced the history of Western civilization, or who embodied much that is significant about the periods in which they lived, and at the same time to introduce the student to the chief varieties of historical interpretation. Few personalities or events stand without comment in the historical record; contemporary accounts and documents, the so-called original sources, no less than later studies, are written by people with a distinct point of view and interpretation of what they see. Problems of interpretation are inseparable from the effort to achieve historical understanding.

The readings in this book have been chosen for their inherent interest and their particular way of treating their subject. Typically, three or four selections are devoted to each figure. The first selection is usually an autobiographical or contemporary biographical account; in a few instances, differing assessments by contemporaries are included. Next, a more or less orthodox interpretation is presented; it is often a selection from the "standard work" on the figure in question. The final selection offers a more recent view, which may reinforce the standard interpretation, revise it in the light of new evidence, or dissent from it completely. In some cases, two very different recent views are set side by side.

A book of this size cannot hope to include full-length biographies of all the individuals studied. Instead, each chapter focuses on an important interpretative issue. In some chapters, the figure's relative historical importance is at issue; in others, the significance of a major point mooted in the sources; in still others, the general meaning of the figure's career, as debated in a spread of interpretative positions. In every chapter, it is hoped, the problem examined is interesting and basic to an understanding of the figure's place in history.

Note to the Second Edition

The second edition was undertaken after some three years' experience with the book, both in my own classes and in those of colleagues across the country. Many of these colleagues generously responded to a questionnaire about the book and its usefulness to them, and on the basis of their suggestions as well as my own reactions after using it, revisions were made. In some instances only a single selection in a chapter was changed; in others whole chapters were deleted and totally different historical personalities were substituted. And in still other chapters the consensus was that no changes should be made. It is my sincere hope that the book is improved in its usefulness for teachers and students alike.

J.K.S.

Contents

Makers of the Western Tradition

PORTRAITS FROM HISTORY
Second Edition

Akhenaton:
The Heretic King

With the enormous distance in time that separates us from ancient Egypt
and the Near East, the scale of individual human size is reduced
nearly to the point of oblivion. Even the greatest kings and conquerors,
high priests, viziers, queens and "chief wives" tend to be reduced to
lists of properties and exploits, names without substance or dimension.

For Egypt in particular the problem is compounded by the fact
that the Egyptian culture tended to stress timelessness and eternity rather
than history or individuals. The Egyptians had no continuous chronology.
The names of successive pharaohs and their identifying epithets were
often run together, overlapped, and sometimes blandly falsified
in records and inscriptions. The great modern British Egyptologist Sir
Alan Gardiner, speaking of this maddening anonymity of Egyptian
history, notes however that "in one case only, that of Akhenaten
towards the end of Dyn. XVIII, do the inscriptions and reliefs bring us
face to face with a personality markedly different from that of
all his predecessors." [1]

This is the famous "heretic king," the most intriguing figure in
Egyptian history.

[1] Sir Alan Gardiner, *Egypt of the Pharaohs* (Oxford: Oxford University Press;
1st ed., 1961; 1972), p. 55. The reader will note the first of several variations in the
spelling of Akhenaton in this passage. Hieroglyphics did not write the vowels and
there were consonant sounds we do not have. Hence considerable latitude in render-
ing names is to be expected.

1

A Hymn to Aton

*There is no contemporary biographical account of this remarkable ruler,
nor should we expect to find one. But what is more intriguing,
conscious efforts apparently were made to obliterate every trace of him
and of his reign. His name was systematically hacked out of official
inscriptions and omitted from king lists. Even the genealogical lines, so
important to Egyptian royal continuity, were altered. But a handful
of inscriptions did remain, the most substantial being the* Long Hymn to
Aton, *from the tomb of one of Akhenaton's successors, Eye. Part of
this inscription follows below. The hymn may not have been actually
composed by Akhenaton, although he certainly may have written
it. Nor is it about him. Rather, it is a hymn to the god Aton, the disk
of the sun, to whom Akhenaton subordinated all the other myriad of
Egyptian gods, "sole god, like whom there is no other!" This was the
apostasy of "the heretic king." This was the offense that seems to
have created the animus toward Akhenaton, unique in Egyptian
history.*

THOU APPEAREST beautifully on the horizon of heaven
Thou living Aton, the beginning of life!
When thou art risen on the eastern horizon,
Thou has filled every land with thy beauty.
Thou art gracious, great, glistening, and high over every land;
Thy rays encompass the lands to the limit of all that thou hast made:
As thou art Re, thou reachest to the end of them;
(Thou) subduest them (for) thy beloved son.

. . . .

When thou settest in the western horizon,
The land is in darkness, in the manner of death.
Every lion is come forth from his den;
All creeping things, they sting.
Darkness *is a shroud,* and the earth is in stillness,
For he who made them rests in his horizon.

At daybreak, when thou arisest on the horizon,
When thou shinest as the Aton by day,
Thou drivest away the darkness and givest thy rays.

. . . .

All the world, they do their work.

All beasts are content with their pasturage;
Trees and plants are flourishing.
The birds which fly from their nests,
Their wings are (stretched out) in praise to thy *ka*.
All beasts spring upon (their) feet.
Whatever flies and alights,
They live when thou hast risen (for) them.
The ships are sailing north and south as well,
For every way is open at thy appearance.
The fish in the river dart before thy face;
Thy rays are in the midst of the great green sea.

. . . .

How manifold it is, what thou hast made!
They are hidden from the face (of man).
O sole god, like whom there is no other!
Thou didst create the world according to thy desire,
Whilst thou wert alone:
All men, cattle, and wild beasts,
Whatever is on earth, going upon (its) feet,
And what is on high, flying with its wings.

The countries of Syria and Nubia, the *land* of Egypt,
Thou settest every man in his place,
Thou suppliest their necessities:
Everyone has his food, and his time of life is reckoned.
Their tongues are separate in speech,
And their natures as well;
Their skins are distinguished,
As thou distinguishest the foreign peoples.
Thou makest a Nile in the underworld,
Thou bringest it forth as thou desirest
To maintain the people (of Egypt)
According as thou madest them for thyself,
The lord of all of them, wearying (himself) with them,
The lord of every land, rising for them,
The Aton of the day, great of majesty.

. . . .

Thou art in my heart,
And there is no other that knows thee
Save thy son Nefer-kheperu-Re Wa-en-Re,
For thou hast made him well-versed in thy plans and in thy strength.

The world came into being by thy hand,
According as thou hast made them.
When thou hast risen they live,

When thou settest they die.
Thou art lifetime thy own self,
For one lives (only) through thee.
Eyes are (fixed) on beauty until thou settest.
All work is laid aside when thou settest in the west.
(But) when (thou) risest (again),
[*Everything is*] made to flourish for the king, . . .
Since thou didst found the earth
And raise them up for thy son,
Who came forth from thy body:
the King of Upper and Lower Egypt, . . . Akh-en-Aton, . . . and
the Chief Wife of the King . . . Nefert-iti, living and youthful for-
ever and ever.

The Dawn of Conscience
JAMES H. BREASTED

*It was largely this hymn to Aton, so obviously similar in sentiment, even
in phrasing, to Psalm 104 of the Hebrew Old Testament, that intrigued
James H. Breasted and started him on his search to piece together the
story of Akhenaton, "the world's first monotheist."*

*Breasted was the pioneer figure in American Egyptology. He almost
singlehandedly created the Oriental Institute of the University of Chicago
in 1919, held the first chair of Egyptology in the United States,
and by his popular books, articles, and lectures was largely responsible
for the great vogue of things Egyptian in America in the 1920s and
1930s. But despite his other interests, Breasted kept returning in
fascination to Akhenaton. Here in brief is the story he recreated.*

*The pharaohs of the Eighteenth Dynasty had been a strong line of kings
who aggressively pushed Egyptian influence into western Asia to form
the Egyptian "empire" and who asserted their rights and powers
in Egypt with equal force. One of the strongest of these kings was
Amenhotep III. About 1380 B.C. the throne passed to his young and
immature son, who took the name Amenhotep IV and who, despite
his frail health, might have successfully continued his father's vigorous*

*policies. Instead, he became a religious revolutionary, promoting the
worship of his own private deity, Aton, at the expense of the other gods.
The young pharaoh in effect changed the state religion of Egypt
and in the process mortally offended the entrenched interests of the
powerful priesthoods, in particular the priests of Amon, who had come to
be regarded as the chief of the gods and the special tutelary god of
the pharaoh. His devotion to Aton led Amenhotep to change his own
regnal name—further offending Amon, whose name was part of his
own—to Akhenaton, meaning "Spirit of the Aton." He even abandoned
the site of the court at Thebes, where the worship of Amon particularly
flourished, and built a new capital city at Tell el-Amarna, which
he called Akhetaton, "Horizon of Aton." Akhenaton's attention was
riveted upon the service of his god. He was interested in nothing else,
neither the administration of his state nor the maintenance of his empire.*

In James H. Breasted's most famous book, suggestively titled The
Dawn of Conscience, *the story of Akhenaton is continued.*

ON A MOMENT'S reflection, such fundamental changes as these suggest
what an overwhelming tide of inherited thought, custom, and tradition had
been diverted from its channel by the young king who was guiding this
revolution. It is only as this aspect of his movement is clearly discerned
that we begin to appreciate the power of his remarkable personality. Before his time religious documents were commonly attributed to ancient
kings and wise men, and the power of a belief lay chiefly in its claim to
remote antiquity and the sanctity of immemorial custom. Until Ikhnaton
the history of the world had largely been merely the irresistible drift of
tradition. The outstanding exception was the great physician-architect, Imhotep, who introduced stone architecture and built the first stone masonry
pyramidal tomb of the Thirtieth Century B.C. Otherwise men had been but
drops of water in the great current. With the possible exception of Imhotep,
Ikhnaton was the first individual in history. Consciously and deliberately,
by intellectual process he gained his position, and then placed himself
squarely in the face of tradition and swept it aside. He appeals to no myths,
to no ancient and widely accepted versions of the dominion of the gods, to
no customs sanctified by centuries—he appeals only to the present and
visible evidences of his god's dominion, evidences open to all, and as for
tradition wherever it had left material manifestations of other gods in
records which could be reached, he endeavoured to annihilate it. A policy
so destructive was doomed to encounter fatal opposition. . . .

Here had been a great people, the onward flow of whose life, in spite of
its almost irresistible momentum, had been suddenly arrested and then
diverted into a strange channel. Their holy places had been desecrated,
the shrines sacred with the memories of thousands of years had been

closed up, the priests driven away, the offerings and temple incomes confiscated, and the old order blotted out. Everywhere whole communities, moved by instincts flowing from untold centuries of habit and custom, returned to their holy places to find them no more, and stood dumfounded before the closed doors of the ancient sanctuaries. On feast days, sanctified by memories of earliest childhood, venerable halls that had resounded with the rejoicings of the multitudes, as we have recalled them at Siut, now stood silent and empty; and every day as the funeral processions wound across the desert margin and up the plateau to the cemetery, the great comforter and friend, Osiris, the champion of the dead in every danger, was banished, and no man dared so much as utter his name. Even in their oaths, absorbed from childhood with their mothers' milk, the involuntary names must not be suffered to escape the lips; and in the presence of the magistrate at court the ancient oath must now contain only the name of Aton. All this to them was as if the modern man were asked to worship X and swear by Y. Groups of muttering priests, nursing implacable hatred, must have mingled their curses with the execration of whole communities of discontented tradesmen—bakers who no longer drew a livelihood from the sale of ceremonial cakes at the temple feasts; craftsmen who no longer sold amulets of the old gods at the temple gateway; hack sculptors whose statues of Osiris lay under piles of dust in many a tumbled-down studio; cemetery stone-cutters who found their tawdry tombstones with scenes from the Book of the Dead banished from the necropolis; scribes whose rolls of the same book, filled with the names of the old gods, or even if they bore the word god in the plural, were anathema; actors and priestly mimes who were driven away from the sacred groves on the days when they should have presented to the people the "passion play," and murmuring groups of pilgrims at Abydos who would have taken part in this drama of the life and death and resurrection of Osiris; physicians deprived of their whole stock in trade of exorcising ceremonies, employed with success since the days of the earliest kings, two thousand years before; shepherds who no longer dared to place a loaf and a jar of water under yonder tree, hoping thus to escape the anger of the goddess who dwelt in it, and who might afflict the household with sickness in her wrath; peasants who feared to erect a rude image of Osiris in the field to drive away the typhonic demons of drought and famine; mothers soothing their babes at twilight and fearing to utter the old sacred names and prayers learned in childhood, to drive away from their little ones the lurking demons of the dark. In the midst of a whole land thus darkened by clouds of smouldering discontent, this marvellous young king, and the group of sympathisers who surrounded him, set up their tabernacle to the daily light, in serene unconsciousness of the fatal darkness that enveloped all around and grew daily darker and more threatening.

    In placing the movement of Ikhnaton against a background of popular discontent like this, and adding to the picture also the far more immediately

dangerous secret opposition of the ancient priesthoods, the still uncon-
quered party of Amon, and the powerful military group, who were disaffected by the king's peace policy in Asia and his lack of interest in imperial administration and maintenance, we begin to discern something of
the powerful individuality of this first intellectual leader in history. His reign
was the earliest attempt at a rule of ideas, irrespective of the condition and
willingness of the people upon whom they were to be forced. . . .

And so the fair city of the Amarna plain arose, a fatuous Island of the
Blest in a sea of discontent, a vision of fond hopes, born in a mind fatally
forgetful that the past cannot be annihilated. The marvel is that such a man
should have first arisen in the East, and especially in Egypt, where no man
except Ikhnaton possessed the ability to forget. Nor was the great Mediterranean World which Egypt now dominated any better prepared for an
international religion than its Egyptian lords. The imperial imagination of
Ikhnaton reminds one of that of Alexander the Great, a thousand years
later, but it was many centuries in advance of his own age. . . .

The fall of the great revolutionary is shrouded in complete obscurity.
The immediate result of his fall was the restoration of Amon and the old
gods whom the Amonite priesthood forced upon Ikhnaton's youthful and
feeble son-in-law, Tutenkhamon. The old régime returned. . . . In the
great royal lists recording on the monuments the names of all the past
kings of Egypt, the name of Ikhnaton never appears; and when under later
Pharaohs, it was necessary in a state document to refer to him, he was
called "the criminal of Akhetaton."

Ikhnaton, Legend and History
F. J. GILES

*It was inevitable that such an unequivocal and dramatic view as
Breasted's would attract critics. And those critics have found bases for
their objections not only in the materials Breasted used and in his rein-
terpretation of them but in substantial materials that have come to light
in more recent years. Among these finds was the discovery at Amarna
of an almost intact cache of diplomatic correspondence, some three
hundred fifty pieces, written on clay tablets and in cuneiform, including*

*letters from the Hittite kings and other peoples of Syria-Palestine and
western Asia. The discovery of even more Hittite records at the site of
Bogazkoy in Turkey produced further information on aspects of
Akhenaton's reign.*

*The tomb of Akhenaton's successor, Tutankamen, was discovered in
1922, probably the most sensational of all archaeological finds, for it is the
only Egyptian royal tomb yet discovered that has not been rifled by
tomb robbers. Breasted was among those who celebrated this discovery.
But the analysis of the tomb furnishings and inscriptions extended beyond
Breasted's time and continues today to produce important information
relative to the Aton cult.*

*But perhaps more important than any single find, the continuing patient
work of Egyptologists, archaeologists, linguists, and other scholars in
studying, restudying, reclassifying, and comparing the material of old and
new discoveries has produced a rather more complicated story about
the events at Amarna and some cautious reservations about Akhenaton
and his religious revolution.*

*The striking affinities between the hymn to Aton and the Old Testament
remain. But James B. Pritchard, in* Ancient Near Eastern Texts Relating
to the Old Testament *and in his more recent* The Ancient Near East,
Supplementary Texts and Pictures Relating to the Old Testament [2]—*as
well as other scholars—has shown that the uniqueness of those affinities is
considerably lessened by the discovery, both in the Near East and Egypt,
of hundreds of other parallel sources, even a hymn to Aton's great rival
Amon, that reveal the same exalted spirituality and seeming monotheism
of the Aton hymn. It has even been suggested that the apparent
monetheism of the Aton worship was no more than a mode of addressing
any number of major Egyptian gods both before and after Akhenaton's
supposed religious revolution. John A. Wilson, for example, believes
that* "this is an adequate explanation of the similarity between the Aton
hymn and the 104th Psalm. Hymns of this kind were current after the fall
of Akh-en-aton, so that when Hebrew religion had reached a point
where it needed a certain mode of expression it could find in another
literature phrases and thoughts which would meet the need." [3]
*Wilson also argues against the lofty monotheism of Akhenaton: at best, it
was a henotheism—the ranking of the other gods below the new chief
god Aton and thus simply a displacement of Amon; at worst, a selfish
bigotry in which Akhenaton reserved the worship of Aton to himself and
his family and was in turn worshipped as a god and the "prophet" of
Aton by all other lesser folk.*

*Many critics have called attention to the highly unusual, even grotesque,
artistic depiction of Akhenaton (found only at Amarna) and have raised*

---

[2] (Princeton: Princeton University Press, 1969).

[3] John A. Wilson, *The Culture of Ancient Egypt* (Chicago: University of Chicago
Press; 1st. ed., 1951; 1956), p. 229.

questions about the physical and mental competence of the king. The
British Egyptologist Cyril Aldred, in his Akhenaten Pharaoh of Egypt—
a New Study,[4] *denies that there was anything at all revolutionary in the*
social and political character of Akhenaton's reign.

Much of this cumulative scholarship is reflected in a book by F. J.
Giles, Ikhnaton, Legend and History. *Giles is one of the most insistent*
critics of the Breasted tradition, which, he claims, has created "a wholly
legendary Ikhnaton, a kind of pre-Christian Christian in whose life and
teachings scholars have found the germ of ideal Western morality." [5]
His book has been called "a debunking book." [6] *And it is certainly that.*
But it is also the most piquant, if not the most persuasive, recasting
of the Akhenaton story we now have.

Here is the story as Giles tells it.

BEFORE APPROACHING the major historical problems of the era, it is useful to turn for a moment to Ikhnaton himself and his environment.

We know him to have been the son of Amenhotep III and Queen Tiy
from inscriptions on the Theban tomb of the official Heruef and from
the funerary shrine which he presented to his mother. Probably he was
their oldest son, and though it could be that an elder brother had died
in childhood, it is more likely that he was from his youth the crown prince
and heir to the throne of Egypt. This is in itself somewhat unusual, since
Tiy could not have been the royal heiress, that is, the daughter of the
preceding king.

Ikhnaton was apparently raised in Thebes and was extremely influenced
by and interested in religious questions, especially the worship of the
Aton, a cult which was increasing in importance during his formative
years.

As soon as he was old enough he married a woman of uncertain origin
named Nofretiti, and by his ninth regnal year had six daughters by her.
His wife stood in the same relationship to him as had Tiy to Amenhotep
III. She is shown at his side on all kinds of state occasions, her name was
very frequently inscribed alongside his, and intimate scenes of their life
together—at meals, enjoying their leisure, on journeys, and in company
with their children—are depicted on the tombs of the Akhetaton necropolis
to such an extent that these form far more a record of the existence of
the royal family than of their owners.

Of the royal princesses the eldest, Meritaton, married Smenkhkare, the
heir to the throne; the second, Meketaton, died before the end of her

---

4 (New York: McGraw-Hill, 1968).
5 F. J. Giles, *Ikhnaton, Legend and History* (London: Hutchinson, 1970), p. 6.
6 By E. P. Uphill in the *Journal of Egyptian Archaeology,* 57 (1971), 219. But
Uphill also finds the book "well done" and one that "opens new vistas."

father's reign; and a third, Ankhsenpaaton, married Tutankhamen, possibly the next in line of succession to Smenkhkare. Nothing definite is known of the other three. . . . For us it is sufficient that, by Egyptian standards, Ikhnaton was at his accession either mature, or almost so, a married man, at least once and perhaps twice a father, and certainly not a boy. . . .

. . . At his accession the young king was known as Neferkheperure (Uanre usually present) Amenhotep the Divine King of Thebes, but by the fifth year of his reign he had changed his name to Neferkheperure Uanre Ikhnaton, by which he is generally known to us and which he retained until the end of his reign.

Ikhnaton was intimately concerned with the Aton cult as it developed during his lifetime, and a number of the strange features of the belief may have been his own idea. . . . In the fourth year of his reign, as he declared on the boundary stele set up to mark the city limits, Ikhnaton began to build his new capital of Akhetaton. It was not ready for permanent occupation until four more years had passed, which perhaps explains the relatively few uses of the early form of the full name of the Aton in the city. Here the king lived out the major remaining portion of his reign. Here he built his tomb, here he sought to be buried, and here he still may lie in a tomb yet undiscovered.

Varied scenes of life in the city during its brief heyday are shown on the wall reliefs in the tombs of the nobles of the court. We see the great temple of Aton, open to the rays of the sun, the great court filled with offering tables, and we stand, as if among his subjects, looking up at the great window of appearances from which the king with his family would reward his servants. . . .

The plan of the major buildings of Akhetaton may well have altered from time to time as its royal creator's ideas evolved, and the atelier of the royal sculptor would certainly have been kept busy producing enough decorative statuary and relief to keep up with the royal building.

Much has been written about the so-called revolutionary art style of Amarna. True, Egyptian art had always maintained a stiff and rigid canon of conventions—in which the peculiar Egyptian notion of perspective is important—when portraying the human figure, but we must at the same time remember that by far the greater part of their surviving pictorial art was originally designed for use in tomb or temple, and hence had a religious significance. Even at a very early period the portrayal of animals had always been more natural than that of the human figure, and it is just this treatment of human beings which is to a certain extent changed in the Amarna style. In the paintings, statuary and relief of Akhetaton, and to a very limited extent outside the city proper, the royal family and once in a while members of its entourage, are depicted naturalistically. In pose they are relaxed, they lounge and lean and slouch; all of this is anomalous in religious or semi-religious art. The person of the king is specially treated: the usual portrayal is more or less distorted and at time verges on a malignant caricature, as in the case of the colossal statues from Karnak. His head is enlarged and he is shown with a long, hanging jaw. His belly is pendulous and bloated, and his thighs very fat and feminine, and the lower part of his legs spindle-shanked. If Egyptian art has any historical value whatever, as I am sure it has, then this strange portrayal of Ikhnaton must have some origin in his actual physical condition. The art work, however, tends to exaggerate. This is shown particularly because this series of deformities is, as it were, catching. Nofretiti and her daughters are shown in a similar fashion, as is Smenkhkare. Such a great concatenation of gross malformity is a genetic absurdity, and stems from a kind of honorific transposition, whereby it is regarded as desirable for a subject to resemble his monarch even in that which is loathsome. . . .

. . . After the notion that Ikhnaton succeeded to the throne as a child has been disposed of, it becomes less improbable that the so-called Atonist heresy was his work alone. Nevertheless, there are enough references to the Aton, coming from the years before Ikhnaton's reign, to make careful investigation of his primary responsibility for Aton worship necessary.

There follows a lengthy passage in which Giles sifts the evidence—the Amarna letters, inscriptional material, temples and tombs and papyri—and puts together a substantial case on two points. First he argues for a long period of joint rule by Amenhotep III and Akhenaton at the beginning of the latter's reign, followed by a regency exercised by his mother, Queen Tiy, and, at the end of his reign, another regency with the Pharaoh Smenkhkare. Secondly he argues that the Aton worship was routinely practiced both before and after the "Amarna revolution" and was honored by the regents as well as by Akhenaton.

. . . The reign of Ikhnaton now takes shape as being two-thirds spent in a co-regency with Amenhotep III, after whose death Queen Tiy was apparently regent for her son. Then followed a short period of sole rule by Ikhnaton, and the last part of the reign was passed in a co-regency with his son-in-law.

The co-regency with Amenhotep III, from the evidence of the late Aton names used on the doubly inscribed objects, lasted at least nine years. The Gurob Papyri suggest approximately twelve years as the shortest period that will fit the chronology. This second figure agrees with my interpretation of the durbar depicted in the tombs of Huya and Meryre II at Amarna, as either the celebration of the start of Ikhnaton's sole rule, or the funeral and deification of Amenhotep III. The docket on the Amarna letter which Gardiner would read 2, actually must be read 12, and the presence of Ikhnaton in Thebes might well be in connection with the obsequies of Amenhotep III. The period when Tiy apparently held power could only be that immediately succeeding the death of her husband. Its duration is uncertain, but anything more than an outside limit of six months would make the period of Ikhnaton's sole rule very short indeed. We do not know how much longer Smenkhkare reigned after the graffito in the tomb of Pere was written, nor at what period in the year 17 Ikhnaton's reign ended, but late in the year 14 seems the most likely time at which the co-regency with Smenkhkare began. Thus Ikhnaton ruled alone two years, if the above figures are approximately accurate, and two and a half years if the figures are both erroneous to the largest extent possible in the existing circumstances.

Certainly the persecution of the Amen cult and the erasing of the names of other gods as well, which extended in a few cases even to the erasure of the plural noun "gods," could not have taken place while Amenhotep III was alive, since until his death he was building Luxor, a large temple to Amen. Besides, the shrine Ikhnaton presented to Tiy, which was certainly produced after the year 9 on his order by his own workmen, originally contained the Amen name of Amenhotep III. Tiy, in her steles to the Osiris Amenhotep III, used her husband's Amen name so that this policy was not a feature of her regency. By his third year Smenkhkare had a temple in Thebes, in which a scribe of the divine offerings of Amen officiated. Thus, the only period left at which the fanatical Atonism of the reign could have broken out was the period of Ikhnaton's sole rule, the two years between the latter part of years 12 and 14.

The fact is, then, that out of a reign of seventeen years, Ikhnaton ruled only between two and two and a half years by himself. The most obvious conclusion is that Ikhnaton was incompetent to rule. This was recognised by Amenhotep III, and by Tiy and the court officials after the death of the old king, and it resulted in the earliest possible opportunity being taken to put another ruler on the throne with Ikhnaton. This theory is corroborated by the fact that it was during the sole rule of Ikhnaton that such an outbreak of fanatical religious frenzy occurred, wherein workmen were travelling around Egypt chiselling gods' names out of inscriptions. The pictures of Ikhnaton, if they correspond in any way to his actual condition, certainly point in the same direction, for such a badly deformed body might indicate the presence of some mental abnormality as well.

It is scarcely reasonable to assume that Amenhotep III elevated his son to the co-regency knowing that he was completely incompetent to rule, hence if Ikhnaton was actually mentally deranged, he probably became so after his appointment as co-regent, his condition deteriorating to a point at which he could no longer be allowed to rule. It is possible that his father was aware of this, and let Akhetaton be built as a place where Ikhnaton might be kept out of trouble, and left him there hoping that his state of health might improve. It may also be that the Egyptians suffered a mad king as long as they were able, but finally for the safety of their state they had to remove him.

With all of this information in mind, it is possible now to attempt an explanation for the co-regency. We have already seen the extraordinary influence of Queen Tiy, and that she must have possessed quite a command over her husband's affections in order to achieve the position she did. Her origins were well known, indeed Amenhotep III published them far and wide, and there is no possibility whatever that she was the royal heiress, so that, in Egyptian eyes, her children would have no right to the throne. However, because of the affection which he held for his wife, Amenhotep III quite naturally wished that the son of their marriage might succeed him. To this end he elevated Ikhnaton to a position of power long before there was any question of his own health failing. He recognised that, despite his own wishes, the claims of Tiy's children were invalid by custom, and that if he died before Ikhnaton had grasped the reigns of power very firmly, some other prince might be accepted instead of the son whom he wished to succeed him. . . .[7]

. . . Until recently most scholars were very reluctant to admit that the Aton cult had any real historical background before the reign of Ikhnaton. An article of Marianne and Jean Doresse in 1941–2 was the first discussion in detail of the history of the cult, and even today there is no study of the surviving traces of the Aton cult after the Amarna period, or of the extent of its distribution throughout Egypt during that period.

At one time it was thought to have links with western Asia and particularly with the Mitannian sun cult, but there was no definite supporting evidence from either inside or outside Egypt, except rather improbable theories about the Asiatic ancestry of Queen Tiy or Nofretiti. Queen Tiy's father is alleged to have been a western Asiatic on no evidence whatever, and Nofretiti has been thought to be the Mitannian princess sent by Tushratta to Amenhotep III shortly before the latter's death. Mitannian, Babylonian and other princesses were taken in marriage by the king of Egypt, but such alliances would probably be political, the ladies having little influence with their husband.

Moreover, neither the nature nor the literature of the cult shows signs of foreign elements. It is true that the word "Adon" in Hebrew meant "lord" but such a comparison is of very little value since Hebrew appears as a literary language long after this period, and even parallels between the Aton hymns and Hebrew religious literature may well be the result of Egyptian influence on the Hebrews whose familiarity with the older culture is known.

It is enough to say here that the word Aton has an eminently respectable Egyptian history going back at least to the Middle Kingdom, and to mention that the title of the Amarna high priest "greatest of seers" is borne also by the high priests of Re at Heliopolis and at Southern On, whether

[7] Although there were relatively few reigning queens in Egyptian history, the claim to the throne passed through the female rather than the male line and thus a Pharaoh whose mother had been a "commoner" had a defective title.—Ed.

the latter be identified with Hermonthis or Thebes. It is interesting, also, that the name of the Aton in its early form in Ikhnaton's reign is compounded with that of Re Harakhte. The Aton temple as preserved at Amarna and in pictorial form in the necropolis there is similar in appearance and structure to the sun temples of older times, and the sun hymns of the Aton are very similar to older sun hymns. The house of the benben (shrine) of the Aton temples in Amarna and Thebes is parallel to similar structures in sun temples. The Mnevis bull was held sacred at Amarna as it was in Heliopolis. It is also worth mention that the fanaticism of the Aton cult was not directed against the solar gods. Worship of the Aton was closely connected with, if not an offshoot from, that of Re.

From the earliest to the latest times there was a particular link between the monarch and the Re cult, the kings almost invariably compounding their praenomen with Re, and the cult figuring to a large extent in the royal burial rites. In the Fifth Dynasty it became pre-eminent throughout Egypt, a pre-eminence to some extent lost by the start of the Middle Kingdom, but still leaving the cult a very powerful church. The Amen cult, perhaps wishing to take advantage of this established reputation, made a syncretic identification between Amen and Re, and Amen is very frequently called Amen-Re. Which cult derived the most benefit from this association is not clear. The Amen priesthood may have regarded the connection as necessary, because of the particular attachment of the king to the Re cult, which manifested itself especially in the Atonist fanaticism under Ikhnaton, but it may well have been a factor in royal policy since the beginning of the dynasty, either because of the close connection of the Re cult with the burial ritual, or as a means of fostering the interests of the king in Lower Egypt where it was the most important church.

It is possible to trace the god Aton back to the Middle Kingdom. References exist from the early Eighteenth Dynasty, but as yet no monuments have been discovered which are connected directly or indirectly with the Aton church apparatus before the reign of Amenhotep III. It is arguable that if the Aton cult were the private religion of the monarch, as it appears to have been at the time of Ikhnaton, references to it would not need to be very numerous. In addition, both Amenhotep II and Thutmose IV had close connections with Lower Egypt, Amenhotep II having been born there and Thutmose IV recording on the "Dream Stele" a prophecy received while he was living in Lower Egypt that he would be king.

It is certainly conceivable, if not probable, that the kings might have played one cult against another, but this idea can be overworked since all the kings concerned constructed portions of Karnak, and Amenhotep III probably constructed more buildings in honour of Amen than any previous king.

On balance, it would seem that the fanaticism of Ikhnaton resulted more from a disordered brain than policy. The Egyptian king was always considered a god and an incarnation of god, but it is worth considering whether Ikhnaton might not have taken this idea literally where other more stable monarchs took it figuratively. In other words, he identified himself with the Aton whose high priest he became at the beginning of his reign, considering himself Egypt's paramount god, and attempted to destroy the worship of all the gods except those connected with Aton (that is himself). If all the data were available it might prove that too much emphasis has been given to his destruction of the name of Amen. He made an effort to destroy the names of other gods than the Theban Triad: Amen, Mut and Khonsu, and these may only have received the most attention because Thebes was a most important centre, because a relatively large number of Amen buildings have survived from this period, and because the Amen cult was probably, except for that of Re, the most powerful in Egypt. We have also seen that Ikhnaton did not destroy the names of the gods over a long period of time, such a policy only being put into practice over a two-year period, from the death of Amenhotep III until the elevation of Smenkhkare as co-regent.

To see the end of the Amarna period as the triumph of the Amen cult is a mistake, for the Amarna period was a complete disaster not only for the Amen cult but for Thebes. Never again did the city enjoy the position which it had held until the reign of Ikhnaton. Where Tutankhamen (for the latter part of his reign) and Eye made their headquarters is not definitely known. Haremhab, the so-called violent proponent of Amen, probably spent much of his time in Lower Egypt, and the Nineteenth Dynasty which succeeded him seemed to regard Thebes as no more than a religious centre. From this I venture to argue that the role of the Amen cult in this situation may have been overemphasised. The Amarna revolt was neither against the power of the Amen priesthood nor against Thebes, and its end was no triumph for either. . . .

. . . Material dealing with the Aton cult after the end of the reign of Ikhnaton is very scanty, but it does exist. Bouriant noted, though without adducing evidence, that both Eye and Tutankhamen added to the Aton temple in Thebes, but a full report of this Theban material is as yet not published.

Nevertheless, the fact that Tutankhamen did not change his name from Tukankhaton until quite some time after his accession, indicates that he, or more likely his advisers, were still interested in the new cult. The royal residence was not removed from Akhetaton to Thebes until the reign had well started, and in the tomb of Tutankhamen a number of objects inscribed in the Atonist fashion were found. However, except for Bouriant's statement, no evidence of Aton buildings of this reign exists, unless the remark that the Kawa temple of Tutankhamen was first planned as an Aton structure, and only later changed to an Amen temple, be literally correct. In the inscriptions of this temple the phrase "rule what the Aton encircles" occurs, and a noble who calls himself "a child of the court, the overseer of the southern countries, fan bearer on the king's right,"

Khay, uses the epithet "the chosen one of the Aton" on a stele. . . .

Other miscellaneous items include the dual reading cartouche ring of Tutankhamen found by Petrie; a peculiar stele of Pareemheb, a Heliopolitan priest, which was originally a normal Amarna product showing Ikhnaton and a daughter but was usurped for the reigning king, Haremhab, though the sun disc with hands—symbol of the Aton—is left untouched; and the frequent writing, in the Ramesside manuscripts of the Book of the Dead of the word of Aton with the divine determinative and, on occasion, a cartouche. It is also worth noting that Kawa in Nubia was known as late as the reign of the Nubian king Aspelta in the sixth century B.C. as Pergematon.

Yet it is noticeable that after Ikhnaton the Atonists were no longer fanatical. In almost all of the quoted examples the name of Amen appears as well as that of Aton, and it is obvious that at least by the reign of Haremhab the cult apparatus of the Aton has disappeared. There seems, however, to have been no attempt to destroy the emblem of the god, although there was undoubted enmity on the part of some against Ikhnaton. By the reign of Haremhab the buildings which were erected to the Aton had become handy sources of stone for filling between wall spaces or other such purposes. Whatever officially fostered pro-Aton party had existed between the reigns of Amenhotep II and Tutankhamen had largely died out by the time of Haremhab's death.

It should be stressed, however, that the decline of the Aton cult did not result in the triumph of Amen, since even though Atonism disappeared as a popular religion—though probably not as an article of worship—Amenism never recovered the pre-eminent position it had enjoyed during the first three-quarters of the Eighteenth Dynasty. The kings from Haremhab onward had their main royal residence in Lower Egypt, Thebes ceasing to be the major administrative headquarters of the government, and becoming only a religious centre.

What the disappearance of Atonism from the records signifies is as much of a mystery as its original appearance. If my idea that it was an attempt to construct an empire-wide religion from above has any merit, then its disappearance was a consequence of the failure of a policy of religious nationalism. Since it seems, from what traces remain, that the cult was constructed for personal or political purposes by the rulers rather than evoked as a response to some particular religious need, its disappearance for all practical purposes was not surprising. . . .

. . . The idea that Iknaton, through innate pacifism and devotion to his religion, allowed his empire in Asia to collapse derives directly from an interpretation of the Tell el Amarna letters. It is easy enough when reading them to find the material on which this view is based, but even a cursory examination shows that grounds exist, perhaps far better grounds, for an entirely different interpretation. . . . [For example] in his final letter written towards the end of Ikhnaton's reign, [the Babylonian king]

Burnaburiash objects to the Egyptian king sending an escort of five chariots to fetch the Babylonian princess who is being given to him in marriage. This is not the protest of a father anxious for his daughter's safety on a long and dangerous route through hostile territory; the ground of his objection is simply that five chariots constitutes insufficient pomp and circumstance for the transport of a future queen of Egypt. It is evident that he considers the country safe enough for a small expedition to cross from Egypt to Babylon, and also for the letters themselves to be sent from one court to the other. Nowhere, either in the letters of Burnaburiash or those of other kings, is there any mention of marauding tribes, such as those Khabiru or SA-GAZ peoples to whom various princes subject to Egypt, notably Abdi Hilba, the ruler of Jerusalem, refer. . . .

Only two letters are preserved from the king of the Hittites: one is directed to Ikhnaton, but the other is too badly broken for either salutation or context to provide a clue to the addressee. However, both indicate that relations between the two states have been uniformly good for some time, and the second refers in unambiguous terms to an alliance.

The letters from Alashia and to (as well as perhaps from) Arzawa contain little positive information for the general conditions of the period, but it is interesting to see that Amenhotep's habit of diplomacy by matrimony extended as far as Arzawa. One letter from Alashia gives advice that no treaties should be made by Egypt with the Hittites or the land of Sankhar, but this is an isolated comment with no further references. With both these powers—Alashia and Arzawa—communication would have to be by sea, and transit seems to have been unhindered by hostilities here also.

In short, except for the remarks of Tushratta in what was obviously the earliest of his letters to Amenhotep III, there is no reference in the surviving royal letters indicating a state of war among any of the current great powers. All countries in correspondence with Egypt seem simply to have been in competition for gifts of gold, and the period seems to have been one of unparalleled prosperity with no hint of a collapsing Egyptian Empire. . . .

We also learn from this material that the frontier of the Egyptian hegemony in Western Asia at the end of the reign of Tutankhamen remained the same as when the scene opened on the Tell el Amarna letters. This, of course, lays the ghost of the second part of the Amarna legend: the king can no longer be seen as a pacifist, who spent his time in Amarna composing hymns while his empire fell to pieces. . . .

Suggestions for Further Reading

FOR ALL THE antiquity of its subject, the Akhenaton controversy is essentially a modern one, a continuing dispute among Egyptologists about nearly everything connected with the so-called Amarna period of Eighteenth Dynasty Egyptian history and its central figure. F. J. Giles, whose *Ikhnaton, Legend and History* (London: Hutchinson, 1970) is excerpted in this chapter, represents one view. The British archaeologist Cyril Aldred, in the *Akhenaten—A New Study* (New York: McGraw-Hill, 1968), represents a radically different one. Although Aldred's book is in a series on popular archaeology, it is nevertheless somewhat technical. Students may prefer a further popularization of his views in the work of Joy Collier, *King Sun, In Search of Akhenaten* (London: Ward Lock, 1970), also published under the title *The Heretic Pharaoh* (New York: John Day, 1970). Also dissenting from the Giles view is Donald B. Redford, *History and Chronology of the Eighteenth Dynasty of Egypt, Seven Studies* (Toronto: University of Toronto Press, 1967). The last three of the seven deal with Akhenaton and, while somewhat difficult and detailed, illuminate the way Egyptologists come to their conclusions and the grounds for their often considerable disagreements—excellent reading in parallel with Giles. Much easier to read is Eléanore Bille-De Mot, *The Age of Akhenaten*, tr. Jack Lindsay (New York and Toronto: McGraw-Hill, 1966), which deals interestingly as well with Akhenaton's queen, Nefrititi. The Pulitzer Prize-winning novelist Allen Drury has written a novel dealing with Akhenaton, *A God Against the Gods* (New York: Doubleday, 1976) and one about his successor, Tutankamen, *Return to Thebes* (New York: Doubleday, 1977). They are both first-rate historical novels, dealing with the perennial problems of political power and based upon respectable research.

For the larger setting of the Akhenaton problem, three works by outstanding American, British, and French Egyptologists can be recommended. John A. Wilson, *The Burden of Egypt, An Interpretation of Ancient Egyptian Culture* (Chicago: University of Chicago Press, 1951), republished under the title *The Culture of Ancient Egypt* (Chicago: Phoenix, 1971), while somewhat dated in its research, is still valuable for its insights and an eminently readable book. More up-to-date and equally readable is Sir Alan Gardiner, *Egypt of the Pharaohs, An Introduction* (London and New York: Oxford University Press, 1972 [1961]) which also treats the Amarna period more centrally. Pierre Montet, *Lives of the Pharaohs* (Cleveland and New York: World Publishing Co., 1968) is, with its biographical organization, the most popularly conceived of the

three. Finally, to understand more fully the profound nature of Akhenaton's religious revolt, students should read Henri Frankfort, *Ancient
Egyptian Religion, An Interpretation* (New York: Columbia University
Press, 1948; republished by Harper Torchbooks, 1961), a popular but
authoritative essay, and very readable.

King David:
"The Lord's Anointed"

In dealing with Akhenaton we noted the fact—on which there is some degree of consensus—that he is the earliest "individual" we can find in human history. If we take "history" in a slightly broader sense and view the Bible as a species of history, this is not quite true. The Hebrew religion was, from an early time, a religion moving through history and seeing history as the record of God's relationship with his special people, "the sons of Abraham, Isaac, and Jacob."

The history that the Hebrews recorded is admittedly a parochial one, dealing almost exclusively with its own subject and touching only in the most superficial fashion the histories of the "great peoples" of the ancient Near East with whom the Hebrews came in contact. But it does reveal a series of strongly marked protohistorical, even mythohistorical, figures; we find not only Abraham, Isaac, and Jacob but also—at the point where myth and protohistory edge into history—the most interesting and fully rounded personality in the Old Testament, King David.

The Biblical David

*The story of David is found in the Old Testament books of I and II Samuel
and the opening verses of I Kings. The story is very old, preserved in
the religiohistorical tradition from the time of the events themselves,
shortly after the year 1000 B.C., and probably first written down when
the monarchy had finally fallen and the kingdom itself had been swept
away, Israel caught up in the advance of the brutal Assyrians in 722 B.C.
and Judah "carried away captive" to Babylon in 586 B.C. It was a time
of despair, a time when the Hebrew priests and scribes looked back
with longing to the age of their hero-king David, when God had been
gracious to them. David thus took on a special significance in Hebrew
history, which he was never to lose. And it is in terms of this special
significance and unique character of David, as well as against the backdrop
of historic events, that we must examine the story of the founder of
Israel's holy monarchy.*

*The story of David is rich in anecdote and detail. One need only recall
his single combat with the Philistine champion Goliath, or his coming
by night to Saul's camp, standing by the head of the sleeping king,
and sparing his life. The character of David is developed with equal
richness. David's response when he heard that Saul and Jonathan had died
in battle against the Philistines on Mount Gilboa is described in
II Samuel 1:17–27, from the* Revised Standard Version Bible.

DAVID LAMENTED with this lamentation over Saul and Jonathan his son,
and he said it should be taught to the people of Judah; behold, it is written
in the Book of Jashar. He said:

> "Thy glory, O Israel, is slain upon thy high places!
>   How are the mighty fallen!
> Tell it not in Gath,
>   publish it not in the streets of Ash'kelon;
> lest the daughters of the Philistines rejoice,
>   lest the daughters of the uncircumcised exult.
>
> "Ye mountains of Gilbo'a,
>   let there be no dew or rain upon you,
>   nor upsurging of the deep!
> For there the shield of the mighty was defiled,
>   the shield of Saul, not anointed with oil.

"From the blood of the slain,
   from the fat of the mighty,
the bow of Jonathan turned not back,
   and the sword of Saul returned not empty.

"Saul and Jonathan, beloved and lovely!
   In life and in death they were not divided;
they were swifter than eagles,
   they were stronger than lions.

"Ye daughters of Israel, weep over Saul,
   who clothed you daintily in scarlet,
   who put ornaments of gold upon your apparel.

"How are the mighty fallen
   in the midst of the battle!

"Jonathan lies slain upon thy high places.
I am distressed for you, my brother Jonathan;
very pleasant have you been to me;
   your love to me was wonderful,
   passing the love of women.

"How are the mighty fallen,
   and the weapons of war perished!"

*The preceding passage, one of the finest lyric passages of the Old
Testament, reveals David the singer, the lyre-player, the psalmist. But the
passage contrasts sharply with the account of how David ordered the
execution of the messenger who had come to report that he had helped
Saul end his life on the battlefield, even though the man pleaded that
he acted only out of mercy for the old, wounded king. But that did not
matter to David, "for your mouth has testified against you, saying
'I have slain the Lord's anointed.'" (II Sam. 1:16). Nor is this the only
such contradiction of character in the story of David. The incident
of Uriah the Hittite and David's desire for his handsome wife Bathsheba
is an account of the king's human weakness. In another instance, we hear
the plaint for David's dead rebel son Absalom that his battle commander,
the rough and outspoken Joab, finds so hard to understand.
   Despite the rich and varied detail that makes David live so vividly
for us, the emphasis in the account of II Samuel is less upon the man
than upon his special relationship—and the special relationship of the
monarchy—with God. David stood very close to the beginning of the
monarchy itself. It was, after all, less than a generation since the scattered*

tribes of Hebrews, presided over by their "judges" and halted in their uneven conquest of their promised land, had turned to the aged prophet Samuel and asked him to "appoint for us a king to govern us like all the nations," "to go out before us and fight our battles." (I Sam. 8:4–6). Samuel had appointed Saul, to be succeeded by David. But the choice both of Saul and of David had not been Samuel's; he was simply the vehicle of God's will. As a learned, modern German critic has put it, ". . . the king set over the people of God must be a man of God's grace, called by him and a real instrument in his hand. . . . Only the man 'on whom the spirit of the Lord shall rest' (Isa. 11:2) can really be the king in Israel. . . . Only he who allows God to be wholly king, and who is therefore himself completely obedient, can be king over the people of God." [1]

The special character of David as the instrument of God's will is stressed from the beginning of the biblical narrative. When, following God's direction, Samuel hesitated to choose the young shepherd boy David, God told him, "The Lord sees not as man sees. Anoint him; for this is he." (I Sam. 16:12).

David brought his people together in victory over the Philistines; he captured Jerusalem and established his capital there, calling it "the city of David."

. . . David became greater and greater, for the LORD, the God of hosts, was with him.

And Hiram king of Tyre sent messengers to David, and cedar trees, also carpenters and masons who built David a house. And David perceived that the LORD had established him king over Israel, and that he had exalted his kingdom for the sake of his people Israel. . . .

Now when the king dwelt in his house, and the LORD had given him rest from all his enemies round about, the king said to Nathan the prophet, "See now, I dwell in a house of cedar, but the ark of God dwells in a tent." And Nathan said to the king, "Go, do all that is in your heart; for the LORD is with you."

But that same night the word of the LORD came to Nathan, "Go and tell my servant David, 'Thus says the LORD: Would you build me a house to dwell in? I have not dwelt in a house since the day I brought up the people of Israel from Egypt to this day, but I have been moving about in a tent for my dwelling. In all places where I have moved with all the people of Israel, did I speak a word with any of the judges of Israel, whom I commanded to shepherd my people Israel, saying, "Why have you not built me a house of cedar?" ' Now therefore thus you shall say to my servant David, 'Thus says the LORD of hosts, I took you from the pasture, from following the sheep, that you should be prince over my people Israel; and I have been

---

[1] Hans Wilhelm Herzberg, *I & II Samuel, A Commentary*, J. S. Bowden, trans. (Philadelphia: Westminster Press, 1964), pp. 133–134.

with you wherever you went, and have cut off all your enemies from before you; and I will make for you a great name, like the name of the great ones of the earth. And I will appoint a place for my people Israel, and will plant them, that they may dwell in their own place, and be disturbed no more; and violent men shall afflict them no more, as formerly, from the time that I appointed judges over my people Israel; and I will give you rest from all your enemies. Moreover the LORD declares to you that the LORD will make you a house. When your days are fulfilled and you lie down with your fathers, I will raise up your offspring after you, who shall come forth from your body, and I will establish his kingdom. He shall build a house for my name, and I will establish the throne of his kingdom for ever. I will be his father, and he shall be my son. When he commits iniquity, I will chasten him with the rod of men, with the stripes of the sons of men; but I will not take my steadfast love from him, as I took it from Saul, whom I put away from before you. And your house and your kingdom shall be made sure for ever before me; your throne shall be established for ever.' " In accordance with all this vision, Nathan spoke to David.

Then King David went in and sat before the LORD, and said, "Who am I, O Lord GOD, and what is my house, that thou hast brought me thus far? And yet this was a small thing in thy eyes, O Lord GOD; thou hast spoken also of thy servant's house for a great while to come, and hast shown me future generations, O Lord GOD! And what more can David say to thee? For thou knowest thy servant, O Lord GOD! Because of thy promise, and according to thy own heart, thou has wrought all this greatness, to make thy servant know it. Therefore thou art great, O LORD God; for there is none like thee, and there is no God besides thee, according to all that we have heard with our ears. What other nation on earth is like thy people Israel, whom God went to redeem to be his people, making himself a name, and doing for them great and terrible things, by driving out before his people a nation and its Gods? And thou didst establish for thyself thy people Israel to be thy people for ever; and thou, O LORD, didst become their God. And now, O LORD God, confirm for ever the word which thou has spoken concerning thy servant and concerning his house, and do as thou hast spoken; and thy name will be magnified for ever, saying, 'The LORD of hosts is God over Israel,' and the house of thy servant David will be established before thee. For thou, O LORD of hosts, the God of Israel, hast made this revelation to thy servant, saying, 'I will build you a house'; therefore thy servant has found courage to pray this prayer to thee. And now, O Lord GOD, thou art God, and thy words are true, and thou hast promised this good thing to thy servant; now therefore may it please thee to bless the house of thy servant, that it may continue for ever before thee; for thou, O Lord GOD, hast spoken, and with thy blessing shall the house of thy servant be blessed for ever."

As David grew "old and advanced in years," his servants sought of him, "who should sit on the throne of my lord the king after him?"

Then King David answered, "Call Bathshe'ba to me." So she came into the king's presence, and stood before the king. And the king swore, saying, "As the LORD lives, who has redeemed my soul out of every adversity, as I swore to you by the LORD, the God of Israel, saying, 'Solomon your son shall reign after me, and he shall sit upon my throne in my stead'; even so will I do this day." Then Bathshe'ba bowed with her face to the ground, and did obeisance to the king, and said, "May my lord King David live for ever!"

King David said, "Call to me Zadok the priest, Nathan the prophet, and Benai'ah the son of Jehoi'ada." So they came before the king. And the king said to them, "Take with you the servants of your lord, and cause Solomon my son to ride on my own mule, and bring him down to Gihon; and let Zadok the priest and Nathan the prophet there anoint him king over Israel; then blow the trumpet, and say, 'Long live King Solomon!'

You shall then come up after him, and he shall come and sit upon my throne; for he shall be king in my stead; and I have appointed him to be ruler over Israel and over Judah." And Benai'ah the son of Jehoi'ada answered the king, "Amen! May the LORD, the God of my lord the king, say so. As the LORD has been with my lord the king, even so may he be with Solomon, and make his throne greater than the throne of my lord King David."

Kingship and the Gods
HENRI FRANKFORT

We turn now from the ancient scriptural account of King David to modern scholarship and the work of one of the most eminent of Near Eastern scholars, Henri Frankfort (d. 1954). Although Frankfort was European-born and trained, he spent most of his career at the University of Chicago as Field Director and Research Professor of Oriental Archaeology. But Henri Frankfort's real talent was his ability to move beyond the stones and shards of ancient material culture to speculate—as his great Chicago predecessor James H. Breasted had done—on the nature of ancient Near Eastern thought, ancient philosophical and religious beliefs, and the substance they gave to the forms of ancient institutions such as kingship.

One of Frankfort's most provocative books in this respect is Kingship and the Gods. *In this book he argues that the ancient Near Eastern peoples considered kingship to be the very basis of civilization. "Only savages could live without a king" to bring security, peace, and justice. And yet the ancient Egyptians and Mesopotamians regarded kingship as a religious, rather than a political, institution. These peoples "experienced human life as part of a widely spreading network of connections that reached beyond the local and the national communities into the hidden depths of nature, the powers that rule nature." [2] The king was the necessary link between the dangerous and potentially destructive power of nature—that is, the gods—and human survival. As either chief priest (as he was in Mesopotamia) or fellow god of the gods themselves (as he was in Egypt), it was the king who maintained the rituals necessary to secure the continued benefactions of the gods. The maintenance of life itself was in the hands of the king.*

At first glance this view would seem to concur, to a large extent, with what we have already seen of David and the ancient Hebrew monarchy. But Henri Frankfort does not agree.

THE ANCIENT Near East knew a third kind of king. In addition to the god incarnate who was Pharaoh and the chosen servant of the gods who ruled Mesopotamia, we find a hereditary leader whose authority derived from descent and was originally coextensive with kinship. This is a more primitive kind of monarchy, a product rather of nature than of man, based on the facts of consanguinity, not on any conception of man's place in the universe. Yet it was the equal of the Egyptian and Mesopotamian institutions in that it formed an integral part of the civilizations in which it occurred. For the type of rulership we are now to discuss is found among people who acknowledged kinship above every other bond of loyalty and whose coherence derived from a shared nomadic past rather than from what they had achieved as a settled community. It is found, significantly, in the peripheral regions of the ancient Near East where autochthonous civilization was feeble. Palestine and Syria, Anatolia and Persia, were overrun by foreign peoples on many occasions, and, furthermore, the newcomers succeeded in taking charge. In this respect the contrast between the peripheral regions and the centers of the ancient Near East is striking. Foreigners could rise to power in Egypt, but on condition that they were completely assimilated. When large groups of immigrants—Amorites, Kassites, Aramaeans—were absorbed by Mesopotamia, they insinuated themselves in the traditional fabric of Mesopotamian culture which henceforth determined their behavior. But the peripheral regions lacked cultural individuality, and once immigrants had asserted their power their mastery

[2] Henri Frankfort, *Kingship and the Gods, A Study of Ancient Near Eastern Religion as the Integration of Society and Nature* (Chicago: University of Chicago Press, 1948), p. 3.

was complete. The Philistines and Hebrews put their stamp on Palestine; Hittites, Mitanni, Medes, and Persians on other peripheral regions.

The position of these new arrivals was anomalous. They brought with them hereditary tribal institutions, such as rulership based on descent. But settling in civilized lands, they faced problems for which their nomadic existence had not prepared them. . . .

Our knowledge of Hittite, Syrian, and Persian kingship is so incomplete that we cannot pass beyond generalities. But we know more about the Hebrew monarchy. This was also based upon descent but possessed a peculiar character of its own which makes it an effective foil for the material we have discussed in this book; for the Hebrews, though in the Near East, were only partly of it. Much is made nowadays of Canaanite and other Near Eastern elements in Hebrew culture. . . . But it should be plain that the borrowed features in Hebrew culture, and those which have foreign analogies, are least significant. In the case of kingship they are externalities, the less important since they did not affect the basic oddness of the Hebrew institution. If kingship counted in Egypt as a function of the gods, and in Mesopotamia as a divinely ordained political order, the Hebrews knew that they had introduced it on their own initiative, in imitation of others and under the strain of an emergency. When Ammonite oppression was added to the Philistine menace, the people said: "Nay; but we will have a king over us; that we also may be like all the nations; and that our king may judge us, and go out before us, and fight our battles" (I Sam. 8:19–20).

If the Hebrews, like the Mesopotamians, remembered a kingless period, they never thought that "kingship descended from heaven." Hence the Hebrew king did not become a necessary bond between the people and the divine powers. On the contrary, it was in the kingless period that the people had been singled out by Yahweh and that they had been bound, as a whole, by the Covenant of Sinai. It was said in the Law: "Ye are the children of the Lord your God: . . . and the Lord hath chosen thee to be a peculiar people unto himself, above all the nations that are upon earth" (Deut. 14:1–2). Moses said to Pharaoh: "Thus saith the Lord, Israel is my son, even my firstborn: and I say unto thee, Let my son go, that he may serve me" (Exod. 4:22–23). For the service of God was part of the Covenant, which the people must keep even though it imposes a moral obligation which man's inadequacy makes forever incapable of fulfilment: "Now therefore, if you will obey my voice indeed, and keep my covenant, then ye shall be a peculiar treasure unto me above all people: for all earth is mine: And ye shall be unto me a kingdom of priests and an holy nation" (Exod. 19:5–6).

The conviction of the Hebrews that they were a chosen people is the one permanent, as it is the most significant, feature in their history. The tenacity of the Hebrew struggle for existence in the sordid turmoil of the Levant was rooted in the consciousness of their election. This animated the leaders of the people, whether they were kings like David and Hezekiah, or prophets opposing kings in whom belief in the unique destiny of Israel had been compromised. But this intimate relationship between the Hebrew people and their god ignored the existence of an earthly ruler altogether. Hebrew tradition, vigorously defended by the great prophets and the post-Exilic leaders, recognized as the formative phase of Hebrew culture the sojourn in the desert when Moses, the man of God, led the people and gave them the law. Kingship never achieved a standing equal to that of institutions which were claimed—rightly or wrongly—to have originated during the Exodus and the desert wandering.

The antecedents of Saul's kingship were known. The settlement in Canaan left the tribal divisions intact, and the Book of Judges shows the varying ranges of power to which individual chieftains might aspire. . . .

The tribesmen recognized the bond of blood alone, and it was exceedingly difficult to envisage a loyalty surpassing the scope of kinship. Nevertheless, when the separate tribes were threatened with extinction or enslavement, Saul was made king over all. Samuel anointed Saul, thereby expressing Yahweh's approval of the initiative of the people who had in any case sought advice from the seer. But royalty received little sanctity from this involvement. It is true that David shrank from buying personal immunity at the price of laying hands "upon the Lord's anointed" (I Sam. 24:10); but such scruples are perhaps more revealing for David's character than for the esteem in which kingship was held among the Hebrews. And the tragic sequel of Saul's history proves how little Yahweh's initial approval protected office and officeholder. In fact, once kingship had been established, it conformed to the tribal laws which treat relatives as one, for better or for worse. Saul's "house" was exterminated by David (II Sam., chap. 21) on Yahweh's orders. David's "house" was promised lasting dominion by Yahweh through the mouth of the prophet Nathan (see below). It is very significant that in actual fact the Davidian dynasty was never dethroned in Judah. But David belonged to Judah; and when Solomon died and his son Rehoboam was ill advised and refused to alleviate the burdens imposed by Solomon's splendor, ten of the tribes refused to acknowledge him: "So when all Israel saw that the king hearkened not unto them, the people answered the king, saying, What portion have we in David? neither have we an heritance in the son of Jesse: to your tents O Israel: now see to thine own house, David" (I Kings 12:16). No voice was raised to decry the rejection of David's grandson as an impious act. On the contrary, even David, Yahweh's favorite, had been confirmed in his rulership by the elders of all the tribes who, in accepting him, began by acknowledging their consanguinity:

> Then came all the tribes of Israel to David unto Hebron, and spake, saying, Behold we are thy bone and thy flesh. . . . So all the elders of Israel came to the king to Hebron, and King David made a league with them in Hebron before the Lord: and they anointed David king of Israel [II Sam. 5:1, 3]).

In the light of Egyptian, and even Mesopotamian, kingship, that of the Hebrews lacks sanctity. The relation between the Hebrew monarch and his people was as nearly secular as is possible in a society wherein religion is a living force. The unparalleled feature in this situation is the independence, the almost complete separation, of the bonds which existed between Yahweh and the Hebrew people, on the one hand, and between Yahweh and the House of David, on the other. Yahweh's covenant with the people antedated kingship. His covenant with David concerned the king and his descendants, but not the people. Through Nathan, Yahweh promised David:

> I will set up thy seed after thee. . . . I will be his father, and he shall be my son. If he commits iniquity, I shall chasten him with the rod of men, and with the stripes of the children of men: But my mercy shall not depart from him, as I took it from Saul, whom I put away before thee. And thine house and thy kingdom shall be established for ever before thee: thy throne shall be established for ever [II Sam. 7:12–16].

Only in later times, when this promise was made the foundation of Messianic expectations, did the people claim a share in it. As it was made, it was as simple and direct a pledge to David as the earlier divine promises had been to the Patriarchs (e.g., Gen. 15:18–21). It committed Yahweh solely to maintain the greatness of the House of David. It can be argued that this implied the greatness of the Hebrew people, or at least of Judah; but the conclusion is not inevitable. Nowhere else in the Near East do we find this dissociation of a people from its leader in relation to the divine; with the Hebrews we find parallelism while everywhere else we find coincidence. In the meager information about Hebrew ritual it has been attempted to find indications that the king fulfilled a function not unlike that of contemporary rulers. But even if we take an exceptional and apparently simple phrase, "[Solomon] sat on the throne of the Lord as king, instead of David, his father" (I Chron. 29:23), we need only compare this with the corresponding phrases "throne of Horus" or "throne of Atum" to realize that the Hebrew expression can only mean "throne favored by the Lord," or something similar. The phrase confirms what the account of Saul's elevation and David's scruples showed in the first place —namely, that there is interplay between the king's person and sancity, as there was a connection between the king's fate and the national destiny. But these relations were not the nerve center of the monarchy, as they were in Egypt and Mesopotamia, but rather cross-currents due to the religious orientation of Hebrew society; and their secondary nature stands out most clearly when we consider the functions of the Hebrew king.

The Hebrew king normally functioned in the profane sphere, not in the sacred sphere. He was the arbiter in disputes and the leader in war. He was emphatically not the leader in the cult. The king created the conditions which made a given form of worship possible: David's power allowed him to bring the Ark to Jerusalem; Solomon's riches enabled him to build the temple; Jeroboam, Ahab, Manasseh, and others had idols made and arranged for "groves" and "high places" for the cult of the gods of fertility. But the king played little part in the cult. He did not, as a rule, sacrifice; that was the task of the priests. He did not interpret the divine will; that, again, was the task of the priests, who cast lots for an oracle. Moreover, the divine intentions were sometimes made known in a more dramatic way when prophets—men possessed—cried, "Thus saith the Lord." These prophets were often in open conflict with the king precisely because the secular character of the king entitled them to censor him.

The predominant accusation of the prophets against the kings was faithlessness to Yahweh, a "seduction" of his chosen people (e.g., II Kings 21:9–11) so that they followed the ways of the gentiles. Said the prophet Jehu in the name of Yahweh to Baasha, king of Israel: "Forasmuch as I exalted thee out of the dust, and made thee prince over my people Israel; and thou hast walked in the way of Jeroboam, and hast made my people Israel to sin, to provoke me to anger with their sins" (I Kings 16:2). Such accusations recur with monotonous regularity throughout the Books of Kings. Most rulers "did evil in the sight of the Lord"; and we cannot discuss Hebrew kingship without considering this evil which seems to have attached to it. If the kings seduced the people, we must admit, in the light of the Egyptian and Mesopotamian evidence, that they offered the people something eminently desirable. The keeping of Yahweh's covenant meant relinquishing a great deal. It meant, in a word, sacrificing the greatest good ancient Near Eastern religion could bestow—the harmonious integration of man's life with the life of nature. The biblical accounts stress the orgiastic joys of the Canaanite cult of natural powers; we must remember that this cult also offered the serene awareness of being at one with the universe. In this experience ancient oriental religion rewarded its devotees with the peace of fulfilment. But the boon was available only for those who believed that the divine was immanent in nature, and Hebrew religion rejected precisely this doctrine. The absolute transcendence of God is the foundation of Hebrew religious thought. God is absolute, unqualified, ineffable, transcending every phenomenon, the one and only cause of all existence. God, moreover, is holy, which means that all values are ultimately his. Consequently, every concrete phenomenon is devaluated. We have discussed elsewhere this austere transcendentalism of Hebrew thought, which denied the greatest values and the most cherished potentialities of contemporary creeds, and have offered an explanation of its origin. Here we must point out that it bereft kingship of a function which it exercised all through the Near East, where its principal task lay in the maintenance of the harmony with the gods in nature. And so we observe—now for the third time—the inner logic and consistency of ancient Near Eastern thought. We have described the peculiar nature of Hebrew kingship, starting from its relation to the people and their past; it would have appeared with the same characteristics if we had taken our stand on Hebrew theology. The transcendentalism of Hebrew religion prevented kingship from

assuming the profound significance which it possessed in Egypt and Mesopotamia. It excluded, in particular, the king's being instrumental in the
integration of society and nature. It denied the possibility of such an
integration. It protested vehemently—in the persons of the great prophets
—that attempts by king and people to experience that integration were
incompatible with their avowed faithfulness to Yahweh. To Hebrew
thought nature appeared void of divinity, and it was worse than futile to
seek a harmony with created life when only obedience to the will of the
Creator could bring peace and salvation. God was not in sun and stars,
rain and wind; they were his creatures and served him (Deut. 4:19; Psalm
19). Every alleviation of the stern belief in God's transcendence was
corruption. In Hebrew religion—and in Hebrew religion alone—the ancient
bond between man and nature was destroyed. Those who served Yahweh
must forego the richness, the fulfilment, and the consolation of a life which
moves in tune with the great rhythms of earth and sky. There were no
festivals to celebrate it. No act of the king could promote it. Man remained
outside nature, exploiting it for a livelihood, offering its first-fruits as a
sacrifice to Yahweh, using its imagery for the expression of his moods;
but never sharing its mysterious life, never an actor in the perennial cosmic
pageant in which the sun is made "to rise on the evil and on the good"
and the rain is sent "on the just and the unjust."

   Kingship, too, was not, for the Hebrews, anchored in the cosmos.
Except by way of contrast, it has no place in a "study of ancient Near
Eastern religion as an integration of society and nature." The Hebrew
king, as every other Hebrew, stood under the judgment of God in an alien
world, which—as the dying David knew (II Sam. 23:3–4)—seems friendly
only on those rare occasions when man proves not inadequate: "He that
ruleth over men must be just, ruling in the fear of God. And he shall be
as the light of the morning, when the sun riseth, even a morning without
clouds; as the tender grass, springing out of the earth by clear shining
after rain."

The Evidence of Archaeology
KATHLEEN M. KENYON

*The most significant omission in the biblical account of the Davidic
monarchy, and even in Frankfort's brilliant conceptualization, is the*

setting in which the events of David's reign occurred. The scriptural record mentions some peoples, like the Ammonites, the Amalekites, and the Moabites, about whom we have virtually no other records, and others, like the Philistines and the Hittites, for whom we are only now beginning to gain substantial information. It cites battles and events and persons with an easy familiarity that seems to reflect an accurate history. But in the parallel records, admittedly fragmentary, of the other contemporary peoples, there is not a shred of evidence to verify any of the events that loom so large in the narrative of Samuel, nor is there mention of any name that could be equated to Saul or David or even Solomon. To fill the gap we must turn to another kind of reconstruction, that of modern archaeology, to see what we can tell about the setting of the Hebrew monarchy, the contemporary physical and political world, the other peoples of Palestine, and the way men lived.

For that purpose we sample the work of one of the foremost contemporary Near Eastern archaeologists, Dr. Kathleen M. Kenyon, who won such well-deserved acclaim for the excavations at Jericho. The following excerpts are from her Archaeology in the Holy Land.

. . . ARCHAEOLOGY HAS NOT yet given us a clear picture of the Philistines, for none of their important cities has as yet been sufficiently excavated for any generalisations as to Philistine or non-Philistine traits to be made. . . .

Such exact evidence as there is suggests that an initial settlement on the coast was followed by a more gradual conquest of towns farther inland, up to the edge of the central ridge, which they never settled, though in the 11th century B.C. they exercised some degree of suzerainty over the Israelites there. The evidence comes from the relation of the appearance of the Philistine pottery to the termination of the 13th century Cypriot and Mycenaean imports, which has been described above and which must be ascribed to the disruption of trade caused by the movements of the Peoples of the Sea. . . .

Thus the area of Philistine occupation was a limited one, though ultimately their political control extended considerably beyond this. For a hundred years or so they lived side by side with their Canaanite and Israelite predecessors. As has already been said, there is no archaeological evidence to decide which sites belong to which of these two groups. It is only on historical grounds, for instance the mention of the people Israel by Merneptah, that we know in fact that the Israelites were by now firmly established in the land, in two groups, divided by the Canaanite wedge round Jerusalem.

Our fullest evidence concerning non-Philistine areas at this period does, however, come from sites which were certainly not Israelite, notably

Megiddo. There is actually no mention in the Bible of when this important city came to be part of Israel. It is included in the list of those that remained under the Canaanites in the initial conquest, while it was Israelite by the time of Solomon. It may well be that it came under Israelite control during the 11th century, during much of which period the site was unoccupied, and therefore no particular importance was attached to the fact. . . .

All the sites so far described lie outside the area at this period occupied by the Israelites. It must in fact be admitted that we know tantalisingly little about the early Israelite settlements. The reason for this is partly owing to the limitations of archaeological evidence, partly owing to the limitations of the culture of the Israelites themselves.

The archaeological limitations arise from the fact that the area in which these settlements lie is the hill country. Sites in such districts do not present the same thick deposits of successive strata as do the sites in the plains. The buildings are naturally constructed of stone, which is readily available all over the area. As a result, when buildings of one period decay, their walls are apt to be dismantled and the stones re-used in their successors. Thus instead of the ruins being buried intact beneath a mass of collapsed mud-brick, the usual material for the superstructure in the plains, they are disturbed and destroyed to the very base of the walls. The story of the successive phases is thus very much more difficult to deduce. The excavation of the great site of Gezer, for instance, carried out before modern refinements of archaeological technique had been introduced, did little to give us a detailed picture of its history, since the buildings could not be ascribed to definite periods. The same drawback applies to the results of the excavation of many other sites in the hill country.

The character of the settlements is the second factor which limits our information. The period is undoubtedly that in which the national consciousness of the Israelites is developing greatly. The biblical narrative shows how the groups were gradually combining together, with tentative efforts at temporal unification under the Judges and the stronger spiritual link of a national religion, with the high priest at times exercising temporal power. It is during these centuries that the groups allied by race, but differing in the manner and time of their settlement in Palestine, . . . must have come to combine their ancestral traditions together under the influence of the Yahwehistic religion, and to believe that all their ancestors took part in the Exodus. The nation was thus emerging, but its culture was as yet primitive. Its settlements were villages, its art crude, and the objects of everyday use homely and utilitarian. . . .

For something like a hundred years the Philistines and the Israelites lived side by side, the Philistines in the rich coastal plain, the Israelites in the more barren hill country. About 1080 B.C. the Philistines began trying to extend their control over the hill country, and this is the period of oppression by the Philistines of which the Bible gives such a vivid account. The period was one of oppression, but it was also one that gave a stimulus towards nationhood. Saul, leading a revolt which started about 1030 B.C., became the acknowledged leader of the whole country in the struggle, and though his success was varying, and marred by quarrels with the religious leaders and with David, and terminated by defeat on Mount Gilboa, it was on the foundations of the unity that he achieved that David was able to establish the free and united kingdom of Israel. . . .

The united kingdom of Israel had a life span of only three-quarters of a century. It was the only time in which the Jews were an important political power in western Asia. Its glories are triumphantly recorded in the Bible, and the recollection of them profoundly affected Jewish thought and aspirations. Yet the archaeological evidence for the period is meagre in the extreme.

After the disaster on Mount Gilboa, when the bodies of Saul and Jonathan were exhibited as trophies at Beth-shan, the Philistines set up two vassal kingdoms, with David as ruler at Hebron and Ishbaal in the north. In between the two lay Jerusalem, still occupied by the Canaanite tribe of Jebusites. But David, though he had taken refuge with the Philistines when Saul had turned against him, was not prepared to continue as a vassal now that his old leader was dead. He succeeded in defeating Ishbaal, apparently without intervention by the Philistines, thus reuniting the kingdom of Saul, and he threw off the Philistine overlordship. He then achieved the crucial success of capturing Jerusalem.

The control of Jerusalem was essential to the control of a united Palestine, as it lies on the central ridge which is the only convenient route north and south through the hill country. . . .

The previous lack of cohesion among the Israelites is well illustrated by the fact that this Canaanite enclave had been allowed to persist in their midst for centuries. Without its possession, political unity was impossible. Once it was secured, the great period of Israelite history begins. But the effect of the long division of the Israelites into two groups, added to that of probable difference of origin between the northern and southern tribes, was permanent and contributed to the renewed division into Israel and Judah at the end of the 10th century B.C. . . .

The capture of Jerusalem is to be dated c.995 B.C. By it, David's position was assured. His growing power inevitably aroused the hostility of the Philistines. Their defeats at Baal-Perazim and Rephaim caused their withdrawal once more to the coastal plain, and they ceased to be a permanent menace. But though David now started on a policy of expansion, he never annexed Philistia. It may be conjectured that Egypt, in spite of its weakness at this time, gave sufficient support to deter him. The coastal plain in fact never became part of the Israelite domain, and the Philistines reappear in the 8th and 7th centuries B.C. as an independent group.

David followed up his success against the Philistines by attacking other ancient enemies. The various "oppressors" were now oppressed in their turn. Moab, Ammon, Edom, were all subjugated, and the most surprising

expansion is the defeat of the Aramaeans and the annexation of Damas-
cus. The Israelites thus controlled a large part of the country from the
Euphrates to the borders of Egypt, though the Phoenician towns on the
Syrian coast remained independent.

This unification and expansion inevitably brought about a revolution in
the culture of the country. The people of simple hill villages, united in
reality only by religious ties, became part of an organised kingdom. The
transfer of the religious centre to Jerusalem established a combined political and religious focus, and strengthened the monarch at the expense
of the priesthood. The international contacts of the Israelites were opened
up for the first time. Instead of being circumscribed within their limited
area, they were brought into touch with the main currents of civilisation
of the period. In particular, they were brought into touch with the Phoeni-
cians. Recent archaeological research in Syria and the adjacent countries
has shown that Phoenicia at this time had a highly developed civilisation,
manifesting itself in fine buildings and a distinctive (though eclectic
rather than original) art, and a remarkable development in literature, as
well as in the trading and colonising ventures for which they have long
been famous. Research in Palestine is beginning to show how strong
Phoenician influence was in the process which began under David, which
was in fact the civilising of Israel.

This process was indeed begun under David, but he only provided the
groundwork for the great developments under Solomon. There is little in
the record, either literary or archaeological, to show that much progress
towards civilisation was made during David's reign. For Solomon's reign
there is considerable literary evidence, but not much archaeological.
Many attempts have been made to reconstruct on paper the Temple Solomon built at Jerusalem on the hill north of Ophel. Finds on other sites
make it easier to understand the description and to visualise some of the
details, but the area of the Temple and that of the extension of the city
under the Israelites lie beneath modern Jerusalem, beyond the reach of
the archaeologist's spade.

Suggestions for Further Reading

THE PRIMARY account of King David is, of course, I and II Samuel and
the first part of I Kings in the Old Testament, and students are encour-

aged to read the entire story. There are many versions and editions of the Bible, but students will find particularly attractive *The Bible Designed To Be Read as Living Literature,* ed. Ernest S. Bates (New York: Simon and Schuster, 1937) and *The Modern Reader's Bible,* ed. Richard G. Moulton (New York: Macmillan, 1924) because of their organization and format. *The Dartmouth Bible,* ed. R. B. Chamberlain and Herman Feldman (Boston: Houghton Mifflin, 1950), *The Oxford Annotated Bible,* and the appropriate sections of vols. 2 and 3 of *The Interpreter's Bible* (New York and Nashville: Abingdon-Cokesbury Press, 1953–1954) have exhaustive and useful notes. Useful too is the brief section on the David monarchy in Harold H. Watts, *The Modern Reader's Guide to the Bible* (New York: Harper, 1949), with its emphasis upon literary rather than biblical criticism. There is also an attractive, solidly researched historical novel by Laurence Chambers Chinn, *The Unanointed* (New York: Crown, 1959), featuring as its central character David's friend Joab.

The greatest modern authority on the history and archaeology of Palestine is William Foxwell Albright. His most famous book is *From the Stone Age to Christianity, Monotheism and the Historical Process* (Baltimore: Johns Hopkins University Press, 1940), reprinted in a revised second edition by Anchor, 1957; chs. 4 and 5 are especially useful for the early monarchy. More recent and popular is his *The Biblical Period from Abraham to Ezra, an Historical Survey* (New York: Harper Torchbooks, 1963 [1949]), chs. 3–6. Somewhat more specialized but still very readable is his revised edition of *Archaeology and the Religion of Israel* (Baltimore: Johns Hopkins University Press, 1968), ch. 4. For one of the neighboring people of the ancient Hebrews, students should find useful John Gray, *The Canaanites* (New York: Praeger, 1964), a first-class popularization and updating of scholarship, an attractive book in an attractive and authoritative series. Students may also wish to read any of the several specialized essays in *The Biblical Archaeologist Reader,* vol. 3, ed. E. F. Campbell, Jr., and David N. Freedman (New York: Doubleday Anchor, 1970). H. and H. A. Frankfort, John A. Wilson, Thorkild Jacobsen, and William A. Irwin, *The Intellectual Adventure of Ancient Man, An Essay on Speculative Thought in the Ancient Near East* (Chicago: University of Chicago Press, 1946), is a famous book, a pioneering work in the intellectual history of the ancient Near East; students should see especially chs. 10–12.

Recommended finally is *The Cambridge History of the Bible,* vol. I, *From the Beginnings to Jerome,* ed. P. R. Ackroyd and C. F. Evans (Cambridge, England: Cambridge University Press, 1970), a fascinating book about the Bible as a book.

The Image of Socrates:
Man or Myth?

By the lifetime of Socrates, in the late fifth century B.C., Greek civilization was almost at an end. This historic civilization was centered in Socrates' own city of Athens, which Pericles proudly called "the school of Hellas." But that magnificent city, which has so captivated our imagination, was widely regarded by her fellow city-states as a threat to their own independence—and with more than a little justification.

This threat led to the great Peloponnesian War, so vividly recounted in the pages of Socrates' contemporary, the historian Thucydides. Athens and her subject states were set against her arch-rival Sparta and Sparta's allies, the Peloponnesian League. It was a long, costly, and enervating war of almost thirty years' duration. And Athens finally lost it. She was humiliated, forced to accept her enemies' terms, and stripped of her subject states, her wealth, her navy. The buoyant optimism that had earlier characterized the city was one of the prime casualties of the war, along with confidence in her institutions and even in many of the presuppositions of her public life and private morality. It is in the backwash of these events that we must seek the life, and the death, of Socrates.

Socrates was surely the most famous Athenian of his age. Yet despite that fame, the facts of his life remain stubbornly vague. He was not a public official; hence we do not have archival records to rely on. And though he is a famous figure in literature, he actually wrote nothing

39

himself to which we can refer. There are scattered references to him
in Aristotle; a substantial (though prosaic) account in the works of
Xenophon, who knew him; and, of course, the principal source of our
information about him, the dialogues of the great philosopher Plato,
who was Socrates' adoring pupil and disciple and made him the main
character in most of his dialogues. And there are references and anecdotes
from a considerable number of near contemporary accounts of Socrates
that have been preserved, although the original sources are now lost.

What we know about Socrates is this. He was born an Athenian citizen
about 470 B.C. His family belonged to the class of small artisans;
his mother was a midwife and his father a stone mason. Socrates himself
followed his father's trade. Rather late in life he married Xanthippe,
and they had three sons, two of them still very young at the time of their
father's death. Like most able-bodied Athenians of his time, Socrates
was a veteran of the Peloponnesian War and even served with some
distinction. On two occasions he seems to have held office on the large
civic boards and commissions that carried on the business of the city.
But generally he avoided public life. From a number of surviving
descriptions and portrait busts we know what Socrates looked like—small
and bald and ugly, anything but the Greek ideal of physical beauty.
And we also know that he spent most of his time going about the city,
trailed by a delighted and curious crowd of bright young aristocrats,
asking often embarrassing questions of people who interested him, usually
public officials and men of substance and position. This practice was
to the detriment of his own family and his own trade. Socrates was
a poor man.

The Clouds
ARISTOPHANES

*The preceding bare account of Socrates is supplemented—one must
almost say contradicted—by a single additional source,* The Clouds
*of Aristophanes. This work is of considerable value in that it is the only
really substantial account of Socrates by a mature contemporary. Even
Plato, our principal source of information, was forty years younger
than Socrates, knew him only as an old man, and wrote* The Dialogues
many years after Socrates' death. The Clouds *is, of course, not a biography.
It is a play, by the greatest of Greek comic dramatists, in which Socrates
is not only one of its chief characters but also the object of its satire.*

*Aristophanes was a conservative, and his plays are a catalog of his
objections to the management of the war and public policy, the state
of literature and philosophy, the subversion of the stern old virtues "of our
forefathers," and the "new morality" that he saw about him. In*
The Clouds *he accused Socrates of being a professional teacher who
received, nay extracted, money for his "lessons"—which was not true.
He denounced him as a cynical, opportunistic atheist—which was also
apparently not the case. He attributed to him an expert competence
in natural philosophy—which was highly unlikely. And in what was perhaps
the most unfounded of all his charges, he portrayed Socrates as being
the chief of the Sophists.*

*The Sophists were a school of professional teachers, then very popular
in Athens, who taught young men of wealth and position (usually for
substantial fees) the techniques of public life, mostly logic and oratorical
persuasion. The Sophists also tended to a flexible morality in which
success was to be preferred to virtue, victory to either morality or
philosophic consistency. It is a more than Socratic irony that Socrates
should have been depicted as one of them, for it was squarely against
the Sophists and their moral relativism that he had taken his stand. The
whole point of his life, the reason he engaged other people in his famous
questioning and endured their animosity, the entire "Socratic method"
was an attempt to make people understand that there are moral absolutes,
unchanging abstract principles of conduct to which they must ultimately
resort.*

*Why Aristophanes portrayed Socrates in this fashion we do not know.
Perhaps he genuinely believed that Socrates was a Sophist. Or perhaps
he knew the truth but simply did not care, and made use of Socrates'*

*notoriety in Athens to score his own point about the scandalous decline
of education and what he regarded as philosophic quackery.*

*In any event, the play is cruel, mean, and malicious, but it is also
outrageously funny. And it gives us a view, however hostile, of the historic
Socrates.*

The Clouds *opens in the house of Strepsiades, a foolish old farmer,
whose son's extravagant passion for racehorses—his name is even
Pheidippides, "lover of horses"—has piled up so many debts that the old
man is faced with ruin. One night, unable to sleep, Strepsiades decides
to enroll the boy in the Sophist's school down the street. He calls it
the "Thinkery." But Pheidippides will have nothing to do with "those
filthy charlatans you mean—those frauds, those barefoot pedants with
the look of death. Chairephon and that humbug, Sokrates."*

*The old man then decides to go to the school himself. He kicks on the
door, and a student-doorman answers. As they stand at the door, the
student extols the wisdom of his master Socrates, citing a number of
examples, not the least of which is Socrates' resolution of the problem
of how the gnat hums. "According to him, the intestinal tract of the gnat
is of puny proportions, and through this diminutive duct the gastric gas
of the gnat is forced under pressure down to the rump. At that point
the compressed gases, as through a narrow valve, escape with a whoosh,
thereby causing the characteristic tootle or cry of the flatulent gnat."*

*Strepsiades is suitably impressed. "Why, Thales himself was an amateur
compared to this! Throw open the Thinkery! Unbolt the door and let
me see this wizard Sokrates in person. Open up! I'm MAD for education!"
And Strepsiades enters the school.*

STREPSIADES

      Look: who's that dangling up there in the basket?

STUDENT

Himself.

STREPSIADES

      Who's Himself?

STUDENT

            Sokrates.

STREPSIADES

              SOKRATES!
Then call him down. Go on. Give a great big shout.

STUDENT

Hastily and apprehensively taking his leave.

Er . . . *you* call him. I'm a busy man.

Exit Student.

STREPSIADES

O Sokrates!

No answer from the basket.

Yoohoo. Sokrates!

SOKRATES

From a vast philosophical height.

Well, creature of a day?

STREPSIADES

What in the world are you doing up there?

SOKRATES

Ah, sir,
I walk upon the air and look down upon the sun
from a superior standpoint.

STREPSIADES

Well, I suppose it's better
that you sneer at the gods from a basket up in the air
than do it down here on the ground.

SOKRATES

Precisely. You see,
only by being suspended aloft, by dangling
my mind in the heavens and mingling my rare thought
with the ethereal air, could I ever achieve strict
scientific accuracy in my survey of the vast empyrean.
Had I pursued my inquiries from down there on the ground,
my data would be worthless. The earth, you see, pulls down
the delicate essence of thought to its own gross level.

As an afterthought.

Much the same thing happens with watercress.

STREPSIADES

Ecstatically bewildered.

                                        You don't say?
Thought draws down . . . delicate essence . . . into
watercress. O dear little Sokrates, please come down.
Lower away, and teach me what I need to know!

Sokrates is slowly lowered earthwards.

SOKRATES

                                        What subject?

STREPSIADES

Your course on public speaking and debating techniques.
You see, my creditors have become absolutely ferocious.
You should see how they're hounding me. What's more,
Sokrates, they're about to seize my belongings.

SOKRATES

                                        How in the
world could you fall so deeply in debt without realizing it?

STREPSIADES

How? A great, greedy horse-pox ate me up, that's how.
But that's why I want instruction in your second Logic,
you know the one—the get-away-without-paying argument.
I'll pay you *any* price you ask. I swear it.
By the gods.

SOKRATES

            By the gods? The gods, my dear simple fellow,
are a mere expression coined by vulgar superstition.
We frown upon such coinage here.

STREPSIADES

                        What do *you* swear by?
Bars of iron, like the Byzantines?

SOKRATES

Tell me, old man,
would you honestly like to learn the truth, the *real* truth,
about the gods?

STREPSIADES

By Zeus, I sure would. The *real* truth. . . .

[*At this point the chorus of clouds enters, singing.*]

STREPSIADES

Holy Zeus, Sokrates, who were those ladies that sang
that solemn hymn? Were they heroines of mythology?

SOKRATES

No, old man.
Those were the Clouds of heaven, goddesses of men of
leisure and philosophers. To them we owe our repertoire of
verbal talents: our eloquence, intellect, fustian, casuistry,
force, wit, prodigious vocabulary, circumlocutory skill—

.   .   .   .

[*The leader of the chorus greets them.*]

KORYPHAIOS

Hail, superannuated man!
Hail, old birddog of culture!

To Sokrates.

And hail to you, O Sokrates,
high priest of poppycock!
Inform us what your wishes are.
For of all the polymaths on earth, it's you we most prefer—

.   .   .   .

sir, for your swivel-eyes, your barefoot swagger down the
street, because you're poor on our account and terribly
affected.

STREPSIADES

Name of Earth, what a voice! Solemn and holy and awful!

SOKRATES

These are the only gods there are. The rest are but figments.

STREPSIADES

Holy name of Earth! Olympian Zeus is a figment?

SOKRATES

Zeus?
     What Zeus?
            Nonsense.
                  There is no Zeus.

STREPSIADES

                      No Zeus?
Then *who* makes it rain? Answer me that.

SOKRATES

                    Why, the Clouds,
of course.
       What's more, the proof is incontrovertible.
                    For instance,
have you ever yet seen rain when you didn't see a cloud?
But if your hypothesis were correct, Zeus could drizzle
   from an empty sky
while the clouds were on vacation.

STREPSIADES

                By Apollo, you're right. A pretty
   proof.
And to think I always used to believe the rain was just Zeus
pissing through a sieve.
             All right, *who* makes it thunder?
Brrr. I get goosebumps just saying it.

SOKRATES

                The Clouds again,
of course. A simple process of Convection.

STREPSIADES

                 I admire you,
but I don't follow you.

SOKRATES

     Listen. The Clouds are a saturate water-solution.

Tumescence in motion, of necessity, produces precipitation. When these distended masses collide—*boom!*
Fulmination.

STREPSIADES

But who makes them move before they collide? Isn't that Zeus?

SOKRATES

Not Zeus, idiot. The Convection-principle!

STREPSIADES

Convection? That's a new one.
Just think. So Zeus is out and Convection-principle's in. Tch, tch.
But wait: you haven't told me who makes it thunder.

SOKRATES

But I just *finished* telling you! The Clouds are water-packed; they collide with each other and explode because of the pressure.

STREPSIADES

Yeah?
And what's your proof for *that?*

SOKRATES

Why, take yourself as example.
You know that meat-stew the vendors sell at the Pana-thenaia? [1] How it gives you the cramps and your stomach starts to rumble?

STREPSIADES

Yes, by Apollo! I remember. What an awful feeling! You feel sick and your belly churns and the fart rips loose like thunder. First just a gurgle, *pappapax;* then louder, *pappa-PAPAXapaX,* and finally like thunder, *PAPAPAPAXA-PAXAPPAPAXapap!*

SOKRATES

Precisely.
First think of the tiny fart that your intestines make.

[1] The quadrennial festival of Athena, the patron goddess of Athens.—ED.

Then consider the heavens: their infinite farting is thunder.
For thunder and farting are, in principle, one and the same.

[*Strepsiades is convinced and is initiated into Socrates' school. But, alas, he is incapable of learning the subtleties Socrates sets out to teach him and is contemptuously dismissed from the school. Then the leader of the chorus suggests that he fetch his son to study in his place. A splendid idea! As Strepsiades drags his son on to the scene, Pheidippides protests.*]

PHEIDIPPIDES

But Father,
what's the matter with you? Are you out of your head?
Almighty Zeus, you must be mad!

STREPSIADES

"Almighty Zeus!"
What musty rubbish! Imagine, a boy your age.
still believing in Zeus!

PHEIDIPPIDES

What's so damn funny?

STREPSIADES

It tickles me when the heads of toddlers like you
are still stuffed with such outdated notions. Now then,
listen to me and I'll tell you a secret or two
that might make an intelligent man of you yet.
But remember: you mustn't breathe a word of this.

PHEIDIPPIDES

A word of what?

STREPSIADES

Didn't you just swear by Zeus?

PHEIDIPPIDES

I did.

STREPSIADES

Now learn what Education can do for *you:*
Pheidippides, there is no Zeus.

PHEIDIPPIDES

There is no Zeus?

STREPSIADES

No Zeus. Convection-principle's in power now.
Zeus has been banished.

PHEIDIPPIDES

                              Drivel!

STREPSIADES

                                        Take my word for it,
it's absolutely true.

PHEIDIPPIDES

                    Who says so?

STREPSIADES

                              Sokrates.
And Chairephon too. . . .

PHEIDIPPIDES

Are you so far gone on the road to complete insanity
you'd believe the word of those charlatans?

STREPSIADES

                                        Hush, boy.
For shame. I won't hear you speaking disrespectfully
of such eminent scientists and geniuses. And, what's more,
men of such fantastic frugality and Spartan thrift,
they regard baths, haircuts, and personal cleanliness
generally as an utter waste of time and money—whereas
you, dear boy, have taken me to the cleaner's so many times,
I'm damn near washed up. Come on, for your father's sake,
go and learn.

[*Some time later*]
*Enter Strepsiades from his house, counting on
his fingers.*

STREPSIADES

Five days, four days, three days, two days, and then
that one day of the days of the month
I dread the most that makes me fart with fear—
the last day of the month, Duedate for debts,
when every dun in town has solemnly sworn
to drag me into court and bankrupt me completely.

And when I plead with them to be more reasonable—
"But PLEASE, sir. Don't demand the whole sum now.
Take something on account. I'll pay you later."—
they snort they'll never see the day, curse me
for a filthy swindler and say they'll sue.
                                        Well,
let them. If Pheidippides has learned to talk,
I don't give a damn for them and their suits.
                                        Now then,
a little knock on the door and we'll have the answer.

He knocks on Sokrates' door and calls out.

Porter!
        Hey, porter!

Sokrates opens the door.

SOKRATES
                        Ah, Strepsiades. Salutations.

STREPSIADES
Same to you, Sokrates.

He hands Sokrates a bag of flour.

                        Here. A token of my esteem.
Call it an honorarium. Professors always get honorariums.

Snatching back the bag.

But wait: has Pheidippides learned his rhetoric yet—. . . .

SOKRATES

Taking the bag.

He has mastered it.

STREPSIADES
                        O great goddess Bamboozle!

SOKRATES
Now, sir, you can evade any legal action you wish to.

[*But instead of help with his creditors, Strepsiades gets a very different kind of treatment from his son.*]

With a bellow of pain and terror, Strepsiades plunges out of his house, hotly pursued by Pheidippides with a murderous stick.

STREPSIADES

OOOUUUCH!!!
        HALP!
                For god's sake, help me!

Appealing to the Audience.

                                 Friends!
Fellow-countrymen! Aunts! Uncles! Fathers! Brothers!
To the rescue!
            He's beating me!
                   Help me!
                        Ouuch!
O my poor head!

          Ooh, my jaw!

To Pheidippides.
                —You great big bully,
Hit your own father, would you?

PHEIDIPPIDES

               Gladly, Daddy.

STREPSIADES

You hear that? The big brute *admits* it.

PHEIDIPPIDES

                  Admit it? Hell,
I *proclaim* it. . . .
            Would a logical demonstration
convince you?

STREPSIADES

       A logical demonstration? You mean to tell me
you can *prove* a shocking thing like that?

PHEIDIPPIDES

                              Elementary, really.
What's more, you can choose the logic. Take your pick.
Either one.

STREPSIADES

                    Either *which?*

PHEIDIPPIDES

                    Either *which?* Why,
Socratic logic or pre-Socratic logic. Either logic.
Take your pick.

STREPSIADES

                    Take my pick, damn you? Look,
who do you think paid for your shyster education anyway?
And now you propose to convince *me* that there's nothing
wrong in whipping your own father?

PHEIDIPPIDES

                              I not only propose it:
I propose to *prove* it. Irrefutably, in fact. Rebuttal
is utterly inconceivable. . . .

[*Phedippides then "proves" that since his father beat him as a child "for
your own damn good" "because I loved you," then it is only "a fortiori"
logic that the father be beaten by the son, since "old men logically deserve
to be beaten more, since at their age they have clearly less excuse for the
mischief that they do."*]

*There is a long tense silence as the full force of this
crushing argument takes its effect upon Strepsiades.*

STREPSIADES

                              What?
                              But how . . .?
                                   Hmm,
by god, you're right!

To the Audience.

                    —Speaking for the older generation,
gentlemen, I'm compelled to admit defeat. The kids have
proved their point: naughty fathers should be flogged. . . .

[*But this arrogance is too much, logic or no logic, for Strepsiades.*]

STREPSIADES

       O Horse's Ass, Blithering Imbecile,
Brainless Booby, Bonehead that I was to ditch the gods
for Sokrates!

He picks up Pheidippides' stick and savagely
smashes the potbellied model of the Universe in front
of the Thinkery. He then rushes to his own house
and falls on his knees before the statue of Hermes.

       —Great Hermes, I implore you!

[*Strepsiades and his slave set fire to the Thinkery and he beats the choking,*
sputtering Socrates and his pallid students off the stage.]

The Apology
PLATO

In 399 B.C., twenty-five years after The Clouds, *Socrates stood before*
the great popular court of Athens. He was accused of much the same
charges that had been leveled at him by Aristophanes, specifically "that
Socrates is a doer of evil, who corrupts the youth; and who does not
believe in the gods of the state, but has other new divinities of his own."
The charges were brought by three fellow Athenians, Meletus, Lycon, and
Anytus. Although only one of the accusers, Anytus, was a man of any
importance, and he only a minor political figure, the charges carried
the death penalty if the court so decided. Indeed, this was the intent
of the accusers.
    The man, now seventy years old, who rose to speak in his own defense
was not the pettifogging buffoon of The Clouds. *Perhaps that man never*
really existed. By the same token, did the speaker at the trial ever
exist? The trial is Socrates', but the account of it is Plato's. The Apology,
from The Dialogues of Plato, *is the "defense" of Socrates at his trial.*

HOW YOU, O Athenians, have been affected by my accusers, I cannot tell; but I know that they almost made me forget who I was—so persuasively did they speak; and yet they have hardly uttered a word of truth. But . . . first, I have to reply to the older charges and to my first accusers, and then I will go on to the later ones. For of old I have had many accusers, who have accused me falsely to you during many years; and I am more afraid of them than of Anytus and his associates, who are dangerous, too, in their own way. But far more dangerous are the others, who began when you were children, and took possession of your minds with their falsehoods, telling of one Socrates, a wise man, who speculated about the heaven above, and searched into the earth beneath, and made the worse appear the better cause. The disseminators of this tale are the accusers whom I dread; for their hearers are apt to fancy that such enquirers do not believe in the existence of the gods. And they are many, and their charges against me are of ancient date, and they were made by them in the days when you were more impressible than you are now—in childhood, or it may have been in youth—and the cause when heard went by default, for there was none to answer. And hardest of all, I do not know and cannot tell the names of my accusers; unless in the chance case of a Comic poet. . . .

I dare say, Athenians, that some one among you will reply, 'Yes, Socrates, but what is the origin of these accusations which are brought against you; there must have been something strange which you have been doing? All these rumours and this talk about you would never have arisen if you had been like other men: tell us, then, what is the cause of them, for we should be sorry to judge hastily of you.' Now I regard this as a fair challenge, and I will endeavour to explain to you the reason why I am called wise and have such an evil fame. . . .

. . . I will refer you to a witness who is worthy of credit; that witness shall be the God of Delphi—he will tell you about my wisdom, if I have any, and of what sort it is. You must have known Chaerephon; he was early a friend of mine. . . . Well, Chaerephon, as you know, was very impetuous in all his doings, and he went to Delphi and boldly asked the oracle to tell him whether—as I was saying, I must beg you not to interrupt —he asked the oracle to tell him whether any one was wiser than I was, and the Pythian prophetess answered, that there was no man wiser. Chaerephon is dead himself; but his brother, who is in court, will confirm the truth of what I am saying.

Why do I mention this? Because I am going to explain to you why I have such an evil name. When I heard the answer, I said to myself, What can the god mean? and what is the interpretation of his riddle? for I know that I have no wisdom, small or great. What then can he mean when he says that I am the wisest of men? And yet he is a god, and cannot lie; that would be against his nature. After long consideration, I thought of a method of trying the question. I reflected that if I could only find a man wiser than myself, then I might go to the god with a refutation in my hand. I should say to him, 'Here is a man who is wiser than I am; but you said that I was the wisest.' Accordingly I went to one who had the reputation of wisdom, and observed him—his name I need not mention; he was a politician whom I selected for examination—and the result was as follows: When I began to talk with him, I could not help thinking that he was not really wise, although he was thought wise by many, and still wiser by himself; and thereupon I tried to explain to him that he thought himself wise, but was not really wise; and the consequence was that he hated me, and his enmity was shared by several who were present and heard me. So I left him, saying to myself, as I went away: Well, although I do not suppose that either of us knows anything really beautiful and good, I am better off than he is,—for he knows nothing, and thinks that he knows; I neither know nor think that I know. In this latter particular, then, I seem to have slightly the advantage of him. Then I went to another who had still higher pretensions to wisdom, and my conclusion was exactly the same. Whereupon I made another enemy of him, and of many others besides him. . . .

This inquisition has led to my having many enemies of the worst and most dangerous kind, and has given occasion also to many calumnies. And I am called wise, for my hearers always imagine that I myself possess the wisdom which I find wanting in others: but the truth is, O men of Athens, that God only is wise, and by his answer he intends to show that the wisdom of men is worth little or nothing; he is not speaking of Socrates, he is only using my name by way of illustration, as if he said, He, O men, is the wisest, who, like Socrates, knows that his wisdom is in truth worth nothing. And so I go about the world, obedient to the god, and search and make enquiry into the wisdom of any one, whether citizen or stranger, who appears to be wise; and if he is not wise, then in vindication of the oracle I show him that he is not wise, and my occupation quite absorbs me, and I have no time to give either to any public matter of interest or to any concern of my own, but I am in utter poverty by reason of my devotion to the god.

There is another thing:—young men of the richer classes, who have not much to do, come about me of their own accord; they like to hear the pretenders examined, and they often imitate me, and proceed to examine others; there are plenty of persons, as they quickly discover, who think they know something, but really know little or nothing; and then those who are examined by them instead of being angry with themselves are angry with me: This confounded Socrates, they say; this villainous misleader of youth—and then if somebody asks them, Why, what evil does he practise or teach? they do not know, and cannot tell; but in order that they may not appear to be at a loss, they repeat the ready-made charges which are used against all philosophers about teaching things up in the clouds and under the earth, and having no gods and making the worse appear the better cause. . . .

Turning to the formal charges against him, Socrates dismisses them almost contemptuously, returning to the main charges as he sees them and his life-long "argument" with his city and its citizenry.

And now, Athenians, I am not going to argue for my own sake, as you may think, but for yours, that you may not sin against the God by condemning me, who am his gift to you. For if you kill me you will not easily find a successor to me, who, if I may use such a ludicrous figure of speech, am a sort of gadfly, given to the state by God; and the state is a great and noble steed who is tardy in his motions owing to his very size, and requires to be stirred into life. I am that gadfly which God has attached to the state, and all day long and in all places am always fastening upon you, arousing and persuading and reproaching you. You will not easily find another like me, and therefore I would advise you to spare me. I dare say that you may feel out of temper (like a person who is suddenly awakened from sleep), and you think that you might easily strike me dead as Anytus advises, and then you would sleep on for the remainder of your lives, unless God in his care of you sent you another gadfly. When I say I am given to you by God, the proof of my mission is this:—if I had been like other men, I should not have neglected all my own concerns or patiently seen the neglect of them during all these years, and have been doing yours, coming to you individually like a father or elder brother, exhorting you to regard virtue; such conduct, I say, would be unlike human nature. If I had gained anything, or if my exhortations had been paid, there would have been some sense in my doing so; but now, as you will perceive, not even the impudence of my accusers dares to say that I have ever exacted or sought pay of any one; of that they have no witness. And I have a sufficient witness to the truth of what I say—my poverty. . . .

The jury returns the verdict of guilty.

There are many reasons why I am not grieved, O men of Athens, at the vote of condemnation. I expected it, and am only surprised that the votes are so nearly equal; for I had thought that the majority against me would have been far larger; but now, had thirty votes gone over to the other side, I should have been acquitted. And I may say, I think, that I have escaped Meletus. I may say more; for without the assistance of Anytus and Lycon, any one may see that he would not have had a fifth part of the votes, as the law requires, in which case he would have incurred a fine of a thousand drachmae.

And so he proposes death as the penalty. . . .

Some one will say: Yes, Socrates, but cannot you hold your tongue, and then you may go into a foreign city, and no one will interfere with you? Now I have great difficulty in making you understand my answer to this. For if I tell you that to do as you say would be a disobedience to the God, and therefore that I cannot hold my tongue, you will not believe that I am serious; and if I say again that daily to discourse about virtue, and of those other things about which you hear me examining myself and others, is the greatest good of man, and that the unexamined life is not worth living, you are still less likely to believe me. Yet I say what is true, although a thing of which it is hard for me to persuade you. Also, I have never been accustomed to think that I deserve to suffer any harm. Had I money I might have estimated the offence at what I was able to pay, and not have been much the worse. But I have none, and therefore I must ask you to proportion the fine to my means. Well, perhaps I could afford a mina, and therefore I propose that penalty: Plato, Crito, Critobulus, and Apollodorus, my friends here, bid me say thirty minae, and they will be the sureties. Let thirty minae be the penalty; for which sum they will be ample security to you. . . .

Socrates is condemned to death.

And now, O men who have condemned me, I would fain prophesy to you; for I am about to die, and in the hour of death men are gifted with prophetic power. And I prophesy to you who are my murderers, that immediately after my departure punishment far heavier than you have inflicted on me will surely await you. Me you have killed because you wanted to escape the accuser, and not to give an account of your lives. But that will not be as you suppose: far otherwise. For I say that there will be more accusers of you than there are now; accusers whom hitherto I have restrained: and as they are younger they will be more inconsiderate with you, and you will be more offended at them. If you think that by killing men you can prevent some one from censuring your evil lives, you are mistaken; that is not a way of escape which is either possible or honourable; the easiest and the noblest way is not to be disabling others, but to be improving yourselves. This is the prophecy which I utter before my departure to the judges who have condemned me.

Friends, who would have acquitted me, I would like also to talk with you about the thing which has come to pass, while the magistrates are busy, and before I go to the place at which I must die. Stay then a little, for we may as well talk with one another while there is time. You are my friends, and I should like to show you the meaning of this event which has happened to me. O my judges—for you I may truly call judges—I should like to tell you of a wonderful circumstance. Hitherto the divine faculty of which the internal oracle [2] is the source has constantly been in the habit of opposing me even about trifles, if I was going to make a slip or error in any matter; and now as you see there has come upon me that which may be thought, and is generally believed to be, the last and worst evil. But the oracle made no sign of opposition, either when I was leaving my house in the morning, or when I was on my way to the court, or while I was speaking, at anything which I was going to say; and yet I have often been stopped in the middle of a speech, but now in nothing I either said or did touching the matter in hand has the oracle opposed me. What do I take to be the explanation of this silence? I will tell you. It is an intimation that what has happened to me is a good, and that those of us who think that death is an evil are in error. For the customary sign would surely have opposed me had I been going to evil and not to good. . . .

Wherefore, O judges, be of good cheer about death, and know of a certainty, that no evil can happen to a good man, either in life or after death. He and his are not neglected by the gods; nor has my own approaching end happened by mere chance. But I see clearly that the time had arrived when it was better for me to die and be released from trouble; wherefore the oracle gave no sign. For which reason, also, I am not angry with my condemners, or with my accusers; they have done me no harm, although they did not mean to do me any good; and for this I may gently blame them.

Still I have a favour to ask them. When my sons are grown up, I would ask you, O my friends, to punish them; and I would have you trouble them, as I have troubled you, if they seem to care about riches, or anything, more than about virtue; or if they pretend to be something when they are really nothing,—then reprove them, as I have reproved you, for not caring about that for which they ought to care, and thinking that they are something when they are really nothing. And if you do this, both I and my sons will have received justice at your hands.

The hour of departure has arrived, and we go our ways—I to die, and you to live. Which is better God only knows.

---

[2] This was Socrates' famous "daimon," more than a conscience, less perhaps than a separate "in-dwelling" god, but, as he claimed, at least a guiding voice.—ED.

Socrates: A Modern Perspective
MOSES HADAS AND MORTON SMITH

*Which Socrates are we to choose? Is it even possible to reconstruct the
real man from either the idealized, "gospel"-like account of Plato or the
malicious parody of Aristophanes, or from both together? Two distinguished American professors, Moses Hadas (d. 1966) and Morton Smith,
do not think so. They state their case in the following selection from their
book* Heroes and Gods, Spiritual Biographies in Antiquity.

AS SURELY AS the figure of Achilles is the paradigm for heroic epic, so
surely is Socrates the paradigm for aretalogy.[3] He is manifestly the point of
departure for the development of the genre after his time, but he is also
the culmination of antecedent development. It is likely that the historical
Achilles (assuming there was one) was both more and less than Homer's
image of him, but even if he was exactly as the image represents him, without it he could never have served posterity as a paradigm. Nor could
Socrates have served posterity except through the image Plato fashioned.
It is not, strictly speaking, a developed aretalogy that Plato presents; that
is to say, he does not provide a single systematic account of a career that
can be used as a sacred text. Indeed, Plato's treatment made it impossible
for others to elaborate the image plausibly or to reduce it to a sacred text.
But the whole image, full and consistent and unmistakable, is presupposed
in every Platonic dialogue which contributes to it. Undoubtedly the historical Socrates was an extraordinarily gifted and devoted teacher, and his
image does undoubtedly reflect the historical figure, but the image clearly
transcends the man, and the image is the conscious product of Plato's art.

Because of Plato, and only Plato, Socrates' position in the tradition of
western civilization is unique. Other fifth-century Greeks have won admiration bordering on adulation for high achievement in various fields, but
only Socrates is completely without flaw; the perfect image leaves no
opening for impugning his wisdom or temperance or courage or wholehearted devotion to his mission. We might expect that a dim figure out of
the imperfectly recorded past, an Orpheus or Pythagoras or even Em-
pedocles, might be idealized, but Socrates lived in the bright and merciless
light of a century that could ostracize Aristides, deny prizes to Sophocles,

[3] The worship of, or reverence for, nobility or virtue; from the Greek *areté*,
"virtue."—ED.

throw Pericles out of office. Perhaps the nearest approach to Plato's idealization of Socrates is Thucydides' idealization of Pericles; some critics have thought that Thucydides' main motive in writing his history was to glorify Pericles. But Thucydides never claimed for Pericles the kind of potency that Plato suggests for Socrates, and on the basis of Thucydides' own history the world has accepted Pericles as a farseeing but not preternaturally gifted or wholly successful statesman. Only in the case of Socrates has the idealized image effaced the reality.

What makes Plato's share in the idealization obvious is the existence of parallel accounts of Socrates that are less reverent. Plato's reports are indeed the fullest: the larger part of his extensive writings purports to be an exposition of Socrates' thought. But there are other witnesses. . . . In the *Clouds* of Aristophanes, Socrates is the central figure, and the boot is on a different foot, for it was produced in 423, when Socrates was not yet fifty and therefore in the prime of his career but not yet shielded by the extraordinary eminence later bestowed upon him. Nor was Aristophanes' comedy the only caricature of Socrates. Also in 423 a comic Socrates figured in a play of Amipsias and two years later in one of Eupolis. These poets, it must be remembered, were dealing with a personality that was familiar to them and also, perhaps more important, to their audiences.

The caricature, certainly Aristophanes' and presumably the others' also, is of course grossly unfair: Socrates did not meddle with natural science or receive pay for his teaching, as the *Clouds* alleges he did: the most carping critic could not question his probity. The very absurdity of the charges and the topsy-turvy carnival atmosphere of the festival eliminated the possibility of rancor; in the *Symposium,* of which the fictive date is a decade after the presentation of the *Clouds,* Plato represents Aristophanes and Socrates as consorting on the friendliest of terms. And yet it is plain that Aristophanes' large audience was not outraged by the frivolous treatment of a saint, and in the *Apology,* which Socrates is presumed to have pronounced at his defense twenty-five years later, the point is made that the caricature had seriously prejudiced the public against Socrates. To some degree, then, the caricature is a significant corrective to later idealization. . . .

Really to know where the truth lies, . . . we should have his actual words or a public record of his deeds, but Socrates wrote nothing and was not, like Pericles, a statesman. The image is therefore not subject to correction on the basis of his own works. Aristophanes also deals harshly with Euripides, but we have Euripides' own plays to read, so that the caricature tells us more of Aristophanes than it does of Euripides. Isocrates wrote an encomium of Evagoras and Xenophon of Agesilaus, but the praise of these statesmen carries its own corrective. Of Socrates we know, or think we know, much more than of those others—what he looked like,

how he dressed and walked and talked, and most of all, what he thought
and taught. . . .

Actually the only significant datum in the inventory which is beyond
dispute is that Socrates was condemned to death in 399 B.C. and accepted
his penalty when he might have evaded it. The magnanimity of this act
no one can belittle; it is enough to purify and enhance even a questionable
career, and it is certainly enough to sanctify a Socrates. For Plato it clearly
marked a decisive turn, as he himself records in his autobiographical
Seventh Epistle. For him it undoubtedly crystallized the image of Socrates
that fills the early dialogues. . . . All of Plato's earlier dialogues, and the
more plainly in the degree of their earliness, are as much concerned with
the personality of Socrates as with his teachings. His pre-eminence in
reason, his devotion to his mission, his selfless concern for the spiritual
welfare of his fellow men, the purity of his life, even his social gifts, are
made prominent. The *Apology,* quite possibly the earliest of the Socratic
pieces, is concerned with the man and his personal program, not his
doctrines. Here he is made to present, without coyness or swagger or
unction, his own concept of his mission to sting men, like a gadfly, to self-
examination and to serve as midwife to their travail with ideas. The
Apology also illustrates the devotion of his disciples to Socrates and the
surprisingly large proportion of his jurors who were willing to acquit him.
Again, in the short early dialogues, which are mainly concerned with questioning common misconceptions of such abstract nouns as "piety" or
"friendship," it is the man as defined by his program, not the abstract
doctrine, that is being presented. In the great central group—*Protagoras,
Gorgias, Symposium, Republic*—the proportion of doctrinal content is
larger, but the doctrine requires the personality of Socrates to make it
plausible. The moral significance of education may emerge from the rather
piratical dialectic in the *Protagoras,* but the argument takes on special
meaning from Socrates' wise and tender treatment of the eager and youthful disciple who is enamored of Protagoras' reputation. That it is a worse
thing for a man to inflict than to receive an injury and that a good man
is incapable of being injured is the kind of doctrine which absolutely requires that its promulgator be a saint, as Socrates is pictured in the *Gorgias;*
on the lips of a lesser man it would be nothing more than a rhetorical
paradox. A great weight of individual prestige must similarly be built up
to enable a man to enunciate the grand scheme of the *Republic,* and the
occasional playfulness of the tone only emphasizes the stature of the individual who enunciates it. People too earth-bound to recognize such
stature, like Thrasymachus in Book I, can only find the whole proceeding
absurd. And only from a man whose special stature was recognized could
the vision of Er be accepted as other than an old wives' tale.

In the *Symposium* more than in other dialogues the individuality of
Socrates is underscored. It is not a trivial matter, for establishing the

character of Socrates, that he could be welcome at a party of the fashionable wits of Athens, could get himself respectably groomed for the occasion, and engage in banter with his fellow guests without compromising his spiritual ascendancy one whit. We hear incidentally of his absolute bravery in battle and his disregard of self in the service of a friend, of his extraordinary physical vitality that enabled him to stand all night pondering some thought while his fellow soldiers bivouacked around him to watch the spectacle, of how he could lose himself in some doorway in a trance and so make himself late for his appointment until he had thought through whatever was on his mind. The subject of the *Symposium* is love, and love had been conceived of, in the series of speeches praising it, in a range from gross homosexuality to romantic attachment, to a cosmic principle of attraction and repulsion, to Socrates' own concept . . . of an ascent to union with the highest goodness and beauty. . .

But it is in the *Phaedo* that Socrates comes nearest to being translated to a higher order of being. In prison, during the hours preceding his death, Socrates discourses to his devoted followers on the most timely and timeless of all questions, the immortality of the soul. The *Phaedo* is the most spiritual and the most eloquent of all dialogues; the account of Socrates' last moments is surely the second most compelling passion in all literature. If Plato's object was to inculcate a belief in immortality, there are of course sound practical reasons for giving the spokesman of the doctrine extraordinary prestige. In such an issue it is the personality of the teacher rather than the cogency of his arguments that is most persuasive. . . .

But the saintliness with which Socrates is endowed in the *Phaedo* seems more than a mere device to promote belief in the immortality of the soul. If belief is being inculcated, it is belief in Socrates, not in immortality. Only an occasional reader of the *Phaedo* could rehearse its arguments for immortality years or months after he had laid the book down; the saintliness of Socrates he can never forget. It is his image of Socrates rather than any specific doctrine that Plato wished to crystallize and perpetuate. From the tenor of all his writing it is clear that Plato believed that the welfare of society depended upon leadership by specially endowed and dedicated men. Ordinary men following a prescribed code would not do. Indeed, Plato conceived of his own effectiveness as teacher in much the same way; in the autobiographical *Seventh Epistle* he tells us that no one could claim to have apprehended his teachings merely from study of his writings: long personal contact with a master spirit is essential.

In the centuries after Plato the images of certain saintly figures who, like Socrates, had selflessly devoted themselves to the spiritual improvement of the community and had accepted the suffering, sometimes the martyrdom, these efforts entailed, played a considerable role in the development of religious ideas and practices. In some cases the image may have masked a character negligible or dishonest, and the men who created and exploited the image may have done so for selfish motives; but in some cases, surely, the man behind the image was a devoted teacher whose disciples embroidered his career in good faith into a kind of hagiology [4] that they then used for moral edification. Whatever the motivation, there can be little doubt that the prime model for the spiritual hero was Socrates. . . .

Suggestions for Further Reading

BECAUSE THE STRIKING figure of Socrates exists in a powerful literary and philosophic tradition and yet has almost no historical foundation, there is a nearly irresistible urge to create a "historical Socrates," which has produced a number of biographical or semibiographical works on him. The preeminent modern account is A. E. Taylor, *Socrates* (New York: Anchor, 1953 [1933]), in which the great British Platonist argues that the striking figure of Socrates as derived from Plato's dialogues is essentially an accurate historical account. The book is clear and readable as well as authoritative. An almost equally good account is Jean Brun, *Socrates,* tr. Douglas Scott (New York: Walker, 1962), in which the author, writing for young people, simplifies and sorts out the leading elements in the traditional view of Socrates—i.e. the Delphic dictum "Know thyself," Socrates' "in-dwelling Daimon," and the Socratic irony. At the other extreme are Alban D. Winspear and Tom Silverberg, *Who Was Socrates?* (New York: Russell and Russell, 1960 [1939]), and Norman Gulley, *The Philosophy of Socrates* (London and New York: Macmillan and St. Martin's, 1968). Winspear and Silverberg argue—not entirely convincingly—for a complete revision of the tradition and make Socrates evolve in the course of his career from a democratic liberal to an aristocratic conservative. And Gulley argues for the rejection of Plato's view of Socrates as a skeptic and agnostic in favor of a more constructive role for Socrates in ancient philosophy. Laszlo Versényi, *Socratic Humanism* (New Haven, Conn.: Yale University Press, 1963), while not going as far as Gulley, does advocate a separation between the often paired Socrates and Plato in favor of tying Socrates more closely to the sophists, especially Protagoras and Gorgias. Students should find especially inter-

---

[4] Veneration of a saint or saints.—ED.

esting Alexander Eliot, *Socrates, A Fresh Appraisal of the Most Celebrated Case in History* (New York: Crown, 1967). It is less a fresh appraisal than a popular and extremely readable review of Socrates' background, life, and the evidence brought to his trial. The second part of the book is what the author calls "a free synthesis" of all the Platonic dialogues touching on the trial and death of Socrates—essentially a new, dramatic dialogue account in fresh, modern English.

Of somewhat larger scope is the important scholarly work of Victor Ehrenberg, *The People of Aristophanes, A Sociology of Old Attic Comedy* (New York: Schocken, 1962 [1943]), a study not only of the characters in the plays but also of the audiences; see especially ch. 10, on religion and education, for Socrates. Of larger scope still is T. B. L. Webster, *Athenian Culture and Society* (Berkeley and Los Angeles: University of California Press, 1973), a superb analysis of the linkage between the culture of Athens and its society—the background to an understanding of the place of Socrates in that society and culture. For this sort of analysis, students may prefer Rex Warner, *Men of Athens* (New York: Viking, 1972), a brilliant popularization which sees Socrates as the end product as well as the victim of fifth-century Athenian culture.

The standard work on the system of Athenian government is A. H. M. Jones, *Athenian Democracy* (Oxford, England: Oxford University Press, 1957), which should be updated by reference to W. R. Connor, *The New Politicians of Fifth Century Athens* (Princeton, N.J.: Princeton University Press, 1971).

"The Problem" of Alexander the Great

If Alexander had simply been a successful conqueror, no matter how
stupefying his conquests, there would really be no "Alexander problem."
But, from his own lifetime, there lingered about Alexander the sense
that there was something more to him, that he was "up to something,"
that he had great, even revolutionary, plans. The conviction of manifest
destiny that Alexander himself felt so strongly contributed to this,
as did his instinct for the unusual, the cryptic, the dramatic in political
and religious, as well as in strategic and military, decisions. But
most of all, his death at age thirty-three, in the year 323 B.C.—his
conquests barely completed and his schemes for the future only hinted
at or imperfectly forecast—led the ancient writers to speculate about the
questions, "What if Alexander had lived on?" "What plans would his
imperial imagination have conceived?" and to sift and resift every
scrap of information available—and to invent a few that were not!

The problem of the ancient sources themselves has added greatly to the
difficulty of interpretation. And this is surely ironic. Alexander's own
sense of his destiny made him unusually sensitive to the need for keeping
records of his deeds. A careful log or diary was maintained, but it
exists today only in the most useless fragments, if indeed the "fragments"
in question even came from that record. Alexander's staff included at
least two scholar-secretaries to keep records. One was Callisthenes,
the nephew of Alexander's old friend and tutor Aristotle. The other was

the scientist-philosopher Aristobulus. Callisthenes subsequently fell out with Alexander and was either executed or disgraced, and, while nothing of his work remains, it was clearly the basis for a strongly anti-Alexander tradition that flourished particularly in the old states, like Athens, of the Greek homeland. But the records of Aristobulus, who was apparently much closer to Alexander and much more favorable to him, are also lost. Ptolemy, one of Alexander's most trusted generals and later the founder of the Hellenistic monarchy in Egypt, wrote a detailed memoir, but this did not survive either.

Later ancient writers like Diodorus and Plutarch, Curtius and Justin did know these sources and used them. But of the accounts of Alexander surviving from antiquity, the best one is that of the Greek writer Arrian, of the second century—thus over four hundred years removed from his sources! Furthermore, while Arrian's account is our fullest and most detailed and is based scrupulously on his sources, it is terribly prosaic: we miss precisely what we most want to have, some sense of the "why" of Alexander. In spite of Arrian's devotion to his subject, he tends to tell the story—mainly the military side of it at that —without significant comment. And where we would like to have him analyze, he moralizes instead.

Modern scholars have continued to be fascinated by the puzzle of what Alexander was "up to," and none more than William W. Tarn (d. 1957). Tarn was one of those brilliant English "amateurs" of independent means and equally independent views who have contributed so uniquely to scholarship in a score of fields. He was a lawyer by profession, but he devoted most of his scholarly life—more than half a century—to Greek history. Tarn practically invented Hellenistic scholarship, that is, the study of the post-Alexandrian period in the history of Greek civilization. He authored numerous books and studies, beginning with his "Notes on Hellenism in Bactria and India," which appeared in the *Journal of Hellenic Studies* for 1902, through his first important book, *Antigonos Gonatas* (1913), to *Hellenistic Civilization* (1928), *Hellenistic Military and Naval Developments* (1930), *The Greeks in Bactria and India* (1938), and chapters in the first edition of the *Cambridge Ancient History* (1924–1929).

Since the springboard of the Hellenistic age was Alexander, Tarn devoted special attention to him. He adopted the stance of a scholar-lawyer, in a sense, taking Alexander as his "client" and setting out to make a case for the defense. And Alexander was badly in need of such defense. The trend of modern scholarship before Tarn had been to view Alexander as an archtyrant, arbitrary and megalomaniac, a drunken murderer, and the oppressor of Greek political freedom and philosophic independence—a view derived ultimately from the Callisthenes tradition of antiquity.

Tarn was brilliantly successful in turning opinion around in his defense of Alexander, so much so that the "traditional" view of Alexander today is still essentially that created by Tarn. His authority has been so great that it has even affected the way in which we interpret the ancient sources themselves, whether they seem to be "for" or "against" Tarn's case.

The Ancient Sources:
Arrian, Eratosthenes, and Plutarch

*In the first selection of this chapter, we present the five "proof texts"
on which Tarn built his defense of Alexander: one from Arrian, one from
Eratosthenes (preserved in Strabo), and three from Plutarch.*

This passage, from The Life of Alexander the Great *by Arrian,
took place near the end of Alexander's incredible journey of conquest.
In 324 B.C. Alexander assembled his Macedonian troops at Opis in
Mesopotamia and announced that he proposed to discharge and send home,
with lavish rewards, all those who were disabled or overage. But, instead
of gratitude, a smoldering resentment surfaced, and the entire Macedonian
force began to clamor to be sent home. Arrian attributes the resentment
to Alexander's "orientalizing," his adoption of Persian dress and customs,
and his attempt to incorporate Persians and other peoples in his army.
This had offended the Macedonians' stubborn pride and sense of
exclusiveness, and they now threatened a mutiny. Alexander was furious.
After having the ringleaders arrested, he addressed the Macedonians
in a passionate, blistering speech, reminding them of their own accomplishments, as well as his, and of what he had done for them. Alexander's
speech had a profound effect upon the Macedonians, as did the plans,
immediately put into effect, for reorganizing the army in the event that
they defected. But instead of deserting, the Macedonians repented.*

ALEXANDER, THE MOMENT he heard of this change of heart, hastened out
to meet them, and he was so touched by their grovelling repentance and
their bitter lamentations that the tears came into his eyes. While they continued to beg for his pity, he stepped forward as if to speak, but was anticipated by one Callines, an officer of the mounted Hetaeri, distinguished
both by age and rank. "My lord," he cried, "what hurts us is that you
have made Persians your kinsmen—Persians are called 'Alexander's kinsmen'—Persians kiss you. But no Macedonian has yet had a taste of this
honour."

"Every man of you," Alexander replied, "I regard as my kinsman, and
from now on that is what I shall call you."

Thereupon Callines came up to him and kissed him, and all the others
who wished to do so kissed him too. Then they picked up their weapons

and returned to their quarters singing the song of victory at the top of their voices.

To mark the restoration of harmony, Alexander offered sacrifice to the gods he was accustomed to honour, and gave a public banquet which he himself attended, sitting among the Macedonians, all of whom were present. Next them the Persians had their places, and next to the Persians distinguished foreigners of other nations; Alexander and his friends dipped their wine from the same bowl and poured the same libations, following the lead of the Greek seers and the Magi. The chief object of his prayers was that Persians and Macedonians might rule together in harmony as an imperial power. It is said that 9,000 people attended the banquet; they unanimously drank the same toast, and followed it by the paean of victory.

After this all Macedonians—about 10,000 all told—who were too old for service or in any way unfit, got their discharge at their own request.

Eratosthenes of Cyrene, who lived about 200 B.C., was head of the great Library of Alexandria and one of the most learned men of antiquity. But his works exist only in fragments and in citations in the writings of others, such as the following, from The Geography *by the Greek scientist Strabo, of the first century B.C.*

Now, towards the end of his treatise—after withholding praise from those who divide the whole multitude of mankind into two groups, namely, Greeks and Barbarians, and also from those who advised Alexander to treat the Greeks as friends but the Barbarians as enemies—Eratosthenes goes on to say that it would be better to make such divisions according to good qualities and bad qualities; for not only are many of the Greeks bad, but many of the Barbarians are refined—Indians and Arians, for example, and, further, Romans and Carthaginians, who carry on their governments so admirably. And this, he says, is the reason why Alexander, disregarding his advisers, welcomed as many as he could of the men of fair repute and did them favours—just as if those who have made such a division, placing some people in the category of censure, others in that of praise, did so for any other reason than that in some people there prevail the law-abiding and the political instinct, and the qualities associated with education and powers of speech, whereas in other people the opposite characteristics prevail! And so Alexander, not disregarding his advisers, but rather accepting their opinion, did what was consistent with, not contrary to, their advice; for he had regard to the real intent of those who gave him counsel.

Two of the Plutarch passages are from his essay "On the Fortune of Alexander," which is one of the pieces comprising the collection known as the Moralia.

Moreover, the much-admired *Republic* of Zeno, the founder of the Stoic sect, may be summed up in this one main principle: that all the inhabitants of this world of ours should not live differentiated by their respective rules of justice into separate cities and communities, but that we should consider all men to be of one community and one polity, and that we should have a common life and an order common to us all, even as a herd that feeds together and shares the pasturage of a common field. This Zeno wrote, giving shape to a dream or, as it were, shadowy picture of a well-ordered and philosophic commonwealth; but it was Alexander who gave effect to the idea. For Alexander did not follow Aristotle's advice to treat the Greeks as if he were their leader, and other peoples as if he were their master; to have regard for the Greeks as for friends and kindred, but to conduct himself toward other peoples as though they were plants or animals; for to do so would have been to cumber his leadership with numerous battles and banishments and festering seditions. But, as he believed that he came as a heaven-sent governor to all, and as a mediator for the whole world, those whom he could not persuade to unite with him, he conquered by force of arms, and he brought together into one body all men everywhere, uniting and mixing in one great loving-cup, as it were, men's lives, their characters, their marriages, their very habits of life. He bade them all consider as their fatherland the whole inhabited earth, as their stronghold and protection his camp, as akin to them all good men, and as foreigners only the wicked; they should not distinguish between Grecian and foreigner by Grecian cloak and targe, or scimitar and jacket; but the distinguishing mark of the Grecian should be seen in virtue, and that of the foreigner in iniquity; clothing and food, marriage and manner of life they should regard as common to all, being blended into one by ties of blood and children.

After dwelling on the wisdom of Alexander in affecting a mixed Graeco-Macedonian and Persian costume, Plutarch continues.

For he did not overrun Asia like a robber nor was he minded to tear and rend it, as if it were booty and plunder bestowed by unexpected good fortune. . . . But Alexander desired to render all upon earth subject to one law of reason and one form of government and to reveal all men as one people, and to this purpose he made himself conform. But if the deity that sent down Alexander's soul into this world of ours had not recalled him quickly, one law would govern all mankind, and they all would look toward one rule of justice as though toward a common source of light. But as it is, that part of the world which has not looked upon Alexander has remained without sunlight.

The passage from the famous "Life of Alexander" in Plutarch's Lives deals with an incident early in Alexander's career, after his conquest of Egypt—his journey across the desert to the oracle of Ammon at Siwah.

When Alexander had passed through the desert and was come to the place of the oracle, the prophet of Ammon gave him salutation from the god as from a father; whereupon Alexander asked him whether any of the murderers of his father had escaped him.[1] To this the prophet answered by bidding him be guarded in his speech, since his was not a mortal father. Alexander therefore changed the form of his question, and asked whether the murderers of Philip had all been punished; and then, regarding his own empire, he asked whether it was given to him to become lord and master of all mankind. The god gave answer that this was given to him, and that Philip was fully avenged. Then Alexander made splendid offerings to the god and gave his priests large gifts of money. . . . We are told, also, that he listened to the teachings of Psammon [2] the philosopher in Egypt, and accepted most readily this utterance of his, namely, that all mankind are under the kingship of God, since in every case that which gets the mastery and rules is divine. Still more philosophical, however, was his own opinion and utterance on this head, namely that although God was indeed a common father of all mankind, still, He made peculiarly His own the noblest and best of them.

Alexander the Great and the Unity of Mankind
W. W. TARN

We turn now to the thesis that W. W. Tarn built in defense of Alexander. He had begun to develop his characteristic view in a number of journal articles and anticipated it in fairly complete form in his contributions to the 1927 edition of the Cambridge Ancient History. *He was later*

[1] Alexander had come to the throne of Macedonia upon the murder of his father, Philip II, in 336 B.C.—ED.
[2] This is the only reference in antiquity to such a person.—ED.

to state it most completely in his monumental two-volume Alexander
the Great *(Cambridge: Cambridge University Press, 1948). But
the most succinct statement of the Tarn thesis is that contained in his
Raleigh Lecture on History, read before the British Academy in 1933.
It is entitled "Alexander the Great and the Unity of Mankind."*

WHAT I AM going to talk about is one of the great revolutions in human
thought. Greeks of the classical period, speaking very roughly, divided
mankind into two classes, Greeks and non-Greeks; the latter they called
barbarians and usually regarded as inferior people, though occasionally
some one, like Herodotus or Xenophon, might suggest that certain barbarians possessed qualities which deserved consideration, like the wisdom
of the Egyptians or the courage of the Persians. But in the third century B.C.
and later we meet with a body of opinion which may be called univer-
salist; all mankind was one and all men were brothers, or anyhow ought
to be. Who was the pioneer who brought about this tremendous revolution
in some men's way of thinking? Most writers have had no doubt on that
point; the man to whom the credit was due was Zeno, the founder of the
Stoic philosophy. But there are several passages in Greek writers which, *if*
they are to be believed, show that the first man actually to think of it was
not Zeno but Alexander. This matter has never really been examined;
some writers just pass it over, which means, I suppose, that they do not
consider the passages in question historical; others have definitely said
that it is merely a case of our secondary authorities attributing to Alexander
ideas taken from Stoicism. I want to consider to-day whether the passages in question are or are not historical and worthy of credence; that is,
whether Alexander was or was not the first to believe in, and to contemplate, the unity of mankind. This will entail, among other things, some
examination of the concept which Greeks called Homonoia, a word which
meant more than its Latin translation, Concord, means to us; it is more
like Unity and Concord, a being of one mind together, or if we like the
phrase, a union of hearts; ultimately it was to become almost a symbol of
the world's longing for something better than constant war. For convenience
of discussion I shall keep the Greek term Homonoia.

Before coming to the ideas attributed to Alexander, I must sketch very
briefly the background against which the new thought arose, whoever was
its author; and I ought to say that I am primarily talking throughout of
theory, not of practice. It may be possible to find, in the fifth century, or
earlier, an occasional phrase which looks like a groping after something
better than the hard-and-fast division of Greeks and barbarians; but this
comes to very little and had no importance for history, because anything
of the sort was strangled by the idealist philosophies. Plato and Aristotle
left no doubt about their views. Plato said that all barbarians were enemies

by nature; it was proper to wage war upon them, even to the point of
enslaving or extirpating them. Aristotle said that all barbarians were slaves
by nature, especially those of Asia; they had not the qualities which entitled them to be free men, and it was proper to treat them as slaves. His
model State cared for nothing but its own citizens; it was a small aristocracy
of Greek citizens ruling over a barbarian peasantry who cultivated the
land for their masters and had no share in the State—a thing he had seen
in some cities of Asia Minor. Certainly neither Plato nor Aristotle was
quite consistent; Plato might treat an Egyptian priest as the repository of
wisdom, Aristotle might suggest that the constitution of Carthage was
worth studying; but their main position was clear enough, as was the impression Alexander would get from his tutor Aristotle.

There were, of course, other voices. Xenophon, when he wanted to
portray an ideal shepherd of the people, chose a Persian king as shepherd
of the Persian people. And there were the early Cynics. But the Cynics
had no thought of any union or fellowship between Greek and barbarian;
they were not constructive thinkers, but merely embodied protests against
the vices and follies of civilization. When Diogenes called himself a cos-
mopolite, a horrible word which he coined and which was not used again
for centuries, what he meant was, not that he was a citizen of some imaginary world-state—a thing he never thought about—but that he was not a
citizen of any Greek city; it was pure negation. And the one piece of Cynic
construction, the ideal figure of Heracles, labouring to free Greece from
monsters, was merely shepherd of a *Greek* herd till after Alexander, when
it took colour and content from the Stoics and became the ideal benefactor
of humanity. All that Xenophon or the Cynics could supply was the figure
of an ideal shepherd, not of the human herd, but of some national herd.

More important was Aristotle's older contemporary Isocrates, because
of his conception of Homonoia. The Greek world, whatever its practice,
never doubted that in theory unity in a city was very desirable; but though
the word Homonoia was already in common use among Greeks, it chiefly
meant absence of faction-fights, and this rather negative meaning lasted in
the cities throughout the Hellenistic period, as can be seen in the numerous
decrees in honour of the judicial commissions sent from one city to another, which are praised because they tried to compose internal discord.
There was hardly a trace as yet of the more positive sense which Homonoia
was to acquire later—a mental attitude which should make war or faction
impossible because the parties were at one; and Isocrates extended the application of the word without changing its meaning. He took up a suggestion
of the sophist Gorgias and proposed to treat the whole Greek world as one
and the futile wars between city and city as faction fights—to apply Homonoia to the Greek race. For this purpose he utilized Plato's idea that the
barbarian was a natural enemy, and decided that the way to unite Greeks
was to attack Persia; "I come," he said, "to advocate two things: war
against the barbarian, Homonoia between ourselves." But somebody had

to do the uniting; and Isocrates bethought him of the Cynic Heracles, benefactor of the Greek race, and urged King Philip of Macedonia, a descendant of Heracles, to play the part. But if Philip was to be Heracles and bring about the Homonoia of the Greek world, the way was being prepared for two important ideas of a later time; the essential quality of the king must be that love of man, φιλανθρωπία,[3] which had led Heracles to perform his labours, and the essential business of the king was to promote Homonoia; so far this only applied to Greeks, but if its meaning were to deepen it would still be the king's business. The actual result of all this, the League of Corinth [4] under Philip's presidency, was not quite what Isocrates had dreamt of.

This then was the background against which Alexander appeared. The business of a Macedonian king was to be a benefactor of Greeks to the extent of preventing inter-city warfare; he was to promote Homonoia among Greeks and utilize their enmity to barbarians as a bond of union; but barbarians themselves were still enemies and slaves by nature, a view which Aristotle emphasized when he advised his pupil to treat Greeks as free men, but barbarians as slaves.

I now come to the things Alexander is supposed to have said or thought; and the gulf between them and the background I have sketched is so deep that one cannot blame those who have refused to believe that he ever said or thought anything of the sort. There are five passages which need consideration: one in Arrian; one from Eratosthenes, preserved by Strabo; and three from Plutarch, one of which, from its resemblance to the Strabo passage, has been supposed by one of the acutest critics of our time to be taken in substance from Eratosthenes,[5] and as such I shall treat it. The passage in Arrian says that, after the mutiny of the Macedonians at Opis and their reconciliation to Alexander, he gave a banquet to Macedonians and Persians, at which he prayed for Homonoia and partnership in rule between these two peoples. What Eratosthenes says amounts to this. Aristotle told Alexander to treat Greeks as friends, but barbarians like animals; but Alexander knew better, and preferred to divide men into good and bad without regard to their race, and thus carried out Aristotle's real intention. For Alexander believed that he had a mission from the deity to harmonize men generally and be the reconciler of the world, mixing men's lives and customs as in a loving cup, and treating the good as his kin, the bad as strangers; for he thought that the good man was the real Greek and the bad man the real barbarian. Of the two Plutarch passages, the first says that his intention was to bring about, as between mankind generally, Homonoia and peace and fellowship and make them all one people; and the other,

[3] Literally "philanthropy."—ED.
[4] The league Philip formed after defeating the Greek states at Chaeronea in 338 B.C.—ED.
[5] The reference is to the German scholar E. Schwarz.—ED.

which for the moment I will quote without its context, makes him say that God is the common father of all men.

It is obvious that, wherever all this comes from, we are dealing with a great revolution in thought. It amounts to this, that there is a natural brotherhood of all men, though bad men do not share in it; that Homonoia is no longer to be confined to the relations between Greek and Greek, but is to unite Greek and barbarian; and that Alexander's aim was to substitute peace for war, and reconcile the enmities of mankind by bringing them all— all that is whom his arm could reach, the peoples of his empire—to be of one mind together: as men were one in blood, so they should become one in heart and spirit. That such a revolution in thought did happen is unquestioned; the question is, was Alexander really its author, or are the thoughts attributed to him those of Zeno or somebody else? . . .

"To try to answer that question," Tarn follows with a long and complex analysis of Homonoia and kingship in Graeco-Roman history, leading to the universalism of the late Roman empire.

The belief that it was the business of kings to promote Homonoia among their subjects without distinction of race thus travelled down the line of kingship for centuries; but the line, you will remember, had no beginning, for nobody will suppose that it began with writers so obscure as Diotogenes and Pseudo-Ecphantus. It must clearly have been connected with some particular king at the start, and that king has to be later than Isocrates and Philip and earlier than Diotogenes and Demetrius. It would seem that only one king is possible; we should have to postulate Alexander at the beginning of the line, even if there were not a definite tradition that it *was* he. This means that Plutarch's statement, that Alxeander's purpose was to bring about Homonoia between men generally—that is, those men whom his arm could reach—must be taken to be true, unless some explicit reason be found for disbelieving it; and I therefore now turn to the Stoics, in order to test the view that the ideas attributed to him were really taken from Stoicism. . . . We have seen that it was the business of kings to bring about Homonoia; but this was not the business of a Stoic, because to him Homonoia had already been brought about by the Deity, and it existed in all completeness; all that was necessary was that men should see it. . . .

This is the point I want to make, the irreconcilable opposition between Stoicism and the theory of kingship, between the belief that unity and concord existed and you must try and get men to see it, and the belief that unity and concord did not exist and that it was the business of the rulers of the earth to try and bring them to pass. . . . Consequently, when Eratosthenes says that Alexander aspired to be the harmonizer and reconciler of the world, and when Plutarch attributes to him the intention of bringing about fellowship and Homonoia between men generally—those men whom his arm reached—then, wherever these ideas came from, they were not Stoic; between them and Stoicism there was a gulf which nothing could bridge. This does not by itself prove that Alexander held these ideas; what it does do is to put out of court the only alternative which has ever been seriously proposed, and to leave the matter where I left it when considering the theory of kingship, that is, that there is a strong presumption that Alexander *was* their author. . . .

Before leaving Stoicism, I must return for a moment to Zeno's distinction of the worthy and the unworthy; for Alexander, as we saw, is said to have divided men into good and bad, and to have excluded the bad from the general kinship of mankind and called them the true barbarians. Might not *this* distinction, at any rate, have been taken from Stoicism and attributed to him? The reasons against this seem conclusive, apart from the difficulty of discarding a statement made by so sound and scientific a critic as Eratosthenes. First, no Stoic ever equated the unworthy class with barbarians; for to him there were no barbarians.

. . . Secondly, while the unworthy in Zeno, as in Aristotle, are the majority of mankind, Alexander's "bad men" are not; they are, as Eratosthenes says, merely that small residue everywhere which cannot be civilized. One sees this clearly in a story never questioned, his prayer at Opis, when he prayed that the Macedonian and Persian races (without exceptions made) might be united in Homonoia. And thirdly, we know where the idea comes from: Aristotle had criticized some who said that good men were really free and bad men were really slaves (whom he himself equated with barbarians), and Alexander is in turn criticizing Aristotle; as indeed Eratosthenes says, though he does not quote this passage of Aristotle. The matter is not important, except for the general question of the credibility of Eratosthenes, and may conceivably only represent that period in Alexander's thought when he was outgrowing Aristotle; it does not conflict, as does Zeno's conception of the unworthy, with a general belief in the unity of mankind. . . .

There is just one question still to be asked; whence did Zeno get his universalism? Plutarch says that behind Zeno's dream lay Alexander's reality; and no one doubts that Alexander was Zeno's inspiration, but the question is, in what form? Most writers have taken Plutarch to mean Alexander's *empire;* but to me this explains nothing at all. One man conquers a large number of races and brings them under one despotic rule; how can another man deduce from this that distinctions of race are immaterial and that the universe is a harmony in which men are brothers? It would be like the fight between the polar bear and the parallelepiped. The Persian kings had conquered and ruled as large an empire as Alexander, including many Greek cities; why did Darius never inspire any one with similar theories? It does seem to me that what Plutarch really means is not Alexander's empire but Alexander's ideas; after all, the frequent references in antiquity to Alexander as a philosopher, one at least of which is contemporary, must mean *something*. Zeno's inspiration, then, was Alexander's idea of the unity of mankind; and what Zeno himself did was to carry this idea to one of its two logical conclusions. Judging by his prayer at Opis for the Homonoia of Macedonians and Persians, Alexander, had he lived, would have worked through national groups, as was inevitable in an empire like his, which comprised many different states and subject peoples; Theophrastus,[6] who followed him, included national groups in his chain of progress towards world-relationship. But Zeno abolished all distinctions of race, all the apparatus of national groups and particular states, and made his world-state a theoretic whole. His scheme was an inspiration to many; but in historical fact it was, and remained, unrealizable. But Alexander's way, or what I think was his way, led to the Roman Empire being called one people. I am not going to bring in modern examples of these two different lines of approach to world-unity, but I want to say one thing about the Roman Empire. It has been said that Stoic ideas came near to realization in the empire of Hadrian and the Antonines, but it is quite clear, the moment it be considered, that this was not the case; that empire was a huge national state, which stood in the line of kingship and was a partial realization of the ideas of Alexander. When a Stoic *did* sit on the imperial throne, he was at once compelled to make terms with the national state; to Marcus Aurelius, the Stoic world-state was no theoretic unity, but was to comprise the various particular states as a city comprises houses. And there is still a living reality in what he said about himself: "As a man I am a citizen of the world-state, but as the particular man Marcus Aurelius I am a citizen of Rome."

I may now sum up. We have followed down the line of kingship the theory that it was the business of a king to promote Homonoia among his subjects—all his subjects without distinction of race; and we have seen that this theory ought to be connected at the start with some king, who must be later than Philip and earlier than Demetrius; and there is a definite tradition which connects the origin of the theory with Alexander. We have further seen that the intention to promote Homonoia among mankind, attributed in the tradition to Alexander, is certainly not a projection backwards from Stoicism, or apparently from anything else, while it is needed to explain certain things said by Theophrastus and done by Alexarchus.[7] Lastly, we have seen the idea of the kinship or brotherhood of mankind appearing suddenly in Theophrastus and Alexarchus; their common source can be no one but Alexander, and again tradition supports this. Only one conclusion from all this seems possible: the things which, in the tradition, Alexander is supposed to have thought and said are, in substance, true. He did say that all men were sons of God, that is brothers, but that God

---

6 The philosopher-scientist who followed Aristotle as head of his school.—ED.

7 A minor Macedonian princeling, following Alexander, who set up his small state apparently on the model of Alexander's ideas.—ED.

made the best ones peculiarly his own; he did aspire to be the harmonizer and reconciler of the world—that part of the world which his arm reached; he did have the intention of uniting the peoples of his empire in fellowship and concord and making them of one mind together; and when, as a beginning, he prayed at Opis for partnership in rule and Homonoia between Macedonians and Persians, he meant what he said—not partnership in rule only, but true unity between them. I am only talking of theory, not of actions; but what this means is that he was the pioneer of one of the supreme revolutions in the world's outlook, the first man known to us who contemplated the brotherhood of man or the unity of mankind, whichever phrase we like to use. I do not claim to have given you exact proof of this; it is one of those difficult borderlands of history where one does not get proofs which could be put to a jury. But there is a very strong presumption indeed that it is true. Alexander, for the things he *did,* was called The Great; but if what I have said to-day be right, I do not think we shall doubt that this idea of his—call it a purpose, call it a dream, call it what you will— was the greatest thing about him.

Tarn and the Alexander Ideal
RICHARD A. TODD

Tarn's case for Alexander was brilliant and persuasive. But a new generation of scholars has begun to question both the defense and the defender. Nor is this a matter of superficial revisionism. It is much more fundamental. Tarn's case just will not hold up: the underpinnings of his sources will not support it. And the case is not helped by the fact that, in pursuit of his defense, Tarn often mistranslated key passages in his sources, misdirected or distorted their sense, and grafted his own idealism upon his ideal Alexander.

Ernst Badian, probably Tarn's most effective critic among this generation's scholars, has called the Alexander of Tarn's vision a "phantom" that "has haunted the pages of scholarship" for "a quarter of a century." [8]

[8] Ernst Badian, "Alexander the Great and the Unity of Mankind," *Historia,* 7 (1958), 425.

*The criticism of Tarn has for the most part been presented in heavily
documented, detailed, and technical works well beyond the skill of
most nonspecialists. There is, however, a balanced and thoughtful
summary of this growing body of criticism in the essay "W. W. Tarn
and the Alexander Ideal" by the young American classical historian
Richard A. Todd.*

IN ADDITION to many learned books and articles, the great Hellenistic historian, Sir William Woodthorpe Tarn, also wrote a tale for his daughter,
The Treasure of the Isle of Mist. When in this story the reformed villain
Jeconiah asks for a fairy-tale to learn, the doctor in charge of his case
advises, "If you can't find a fairy-tale, try him with a history book; he'll
never know the difference." A certain scholar has recently said nearly as
much about one of Tarn's own history books:

> Tarn was the most distinguished exponent . . . of an attitude that has
> made the serious study of Alexander's reign from the point of view of
> political history not only impossible but (to many students) almost in-
> conceivable. . . . It is not the business of the historian to envelop a
> successful military leader in an aureole of romantic idealisation. . . .[9]

It is true that the vivid imagination and the high idealism present in
Tarn's fairy-tale are the very qualities in his historical works that have contributed most to their success and which have at the same time detracted
somewhat from the stature of his writings as examples of sound scholarship.
There are other qualities of Tarn's mind, however, which carry him far
beyond the mere historical romancer. One of these is what F. E. Adcock
calls "the judgment and acumen of his legal training."

Tarn was not a "professional" historian. That is, he never took a degree
in history nor found it necessary to become a college or university instructor.
After Eton he studied Greek philosophy at Trinity College, Cambridge,
and then went into law. It was only after the breakdown of his health in
1905 (at the age of 36) that he decided to devote his life to the study of
Hellenistic history. . . .

We fancy we can see the lawyer behind the technique and style of Tarn
the historian—he masters the evidence and, making every fact obey his
command, marshals all in defence of his proposition with the zeal of one
who knows his cause is just. Even the more minute questions of Hellenistic
history, the oarage of the Greek warship, for example, or the wife of
Philip V, call forth the same vigor and conviction as do the larger ones. A
friend once remarked to C. Bradford Welles that reading Tarn was "like

[9] E. Badian, "The Death of Parmenio," *Transactions of the American Philological
Association,* XCI (1960), 324.

walking over glass solidified on the surface, through which you can see and feel the hot and molten masses below." His intense partisanship, though it often arrayed an army of scholars against him, is one of the most attractive features of his writing, for when he touches one of the many insignificant and unrelated facts of which Hellenistic history is principally made, it becomes important and alive, as does every individual resurrected by him. How successful a lawyer Tarn might have become had he persisted in that career is evident from his famous defence of Alexander the Great.[10] So brilliant was the case he made out for Alexander's innocence that only recently have scholars [11] dared to revive the old charges of tyranny, megalomania, and unprincipled murder, for which, indeed, there has always been ample evidence, though that could be variously interpreted. . . .

That Tarn should be best known for his portrait of Alexander the Great is probably just, for his Alexander seems to lie at the heart of his thinking; the image is reflected throughout his works. The examination of this motif, therefore, should tell us a great deal about Tarn the historian. This selection from the concluding pages of volume I of *Alexander the Great* is the climax of his vision:

> Aristotle's State had still cared nothing for humanity outside its own borders; the stranger must still be a serf or an enemy. Alexander changed all that. When he declared that all men were alike sons of one Father, and when at Opis he prayed that Macedonians and Persians might be partners in the commonwealth and that the people of his world might live in harmony and in unity of heart and mind, he proclaimed for the first time the unity and brotherhood of mankind. . . . Above all, Alexander inspired Zeno's vision of a world in which all men should be members one of another, citizens of one State without distinction of race or institutions, subject only to and in harmony with the Common Law immanent in the Universe, and united in one social life not by compulsion but only by their own willing consent, or (as he put it) by Love. . . .[12]

It may be Tarn's admiration for Alexander that has warped his estimate of Alexander's opponent, the Persian king Darius. Tarn's verdict on Darius, "He may have possessed the domestic virtues; otherwise he was a poor type of despot, cowardly and inefficient," [13] is a clever statement of the Macedonian point of view, but it fails to allow for the bias of our Greek sources, at best hostile to Darius, at their worst merely repeating the propaganda with which Alexander encouraged his troops.

[10] In *Proceedings of the British Academy* for 1933 and *Alexander the Great* (2 vols.; Cambridge, 1948).

[11] Principally E. Badian: *Historia, 1958; Classical Quarterly,* VIII (1958), 156; *TAPhA,* XCI (1960), 324ff.

[12] *Alexander the Great,* I, 147-148.

[13] *Ibid.,* 58.

How central the vision of Alexander is to Tarn's thought may be seen from the frequency with which he measures other historical figures by Alexander standards, turning up brotherhood and unity in the most surprising places. There is probably some justice in his view of the Macedonian king, Antigonos Gonatas,[14] whom Tarn believes to have been the first king to regard himself as the servant of his people, for he was a close friend of Zeno the Stoic, and very well may have said to his son, "Do you not understand, boy, that *our* kingship is a noble servitude?"

But flashes of the idealized Alexander image are seen also in other less likely rulers, the Greek kings of Bactria and India, for instance, who, after Alexander, maintained themselves in power in the East for some two centuries—by the usual royal methods, most scholars have thought. Tarn's judgment is different. The rule of the second-century (B.C.) king, Demetrius, he believes to have been

> a partnership of Greek and Indian; he was not to be a Greek king of Indian subjects, but an Indian king no less than a Greek one, head of both races. . . . It has already been shown that Demetrius was consciously copying Alexander; but in this matter his inspiration was not the Alexander who had cut his blood-stained way to the Beas but the Alexander who had imagined something better, the man who had prayed at Opis for a joint rule of the Macedonian and the Persian, the man whom Eratosthenes had called "reconciler of the world," and who had dreamt of a union of peoples in a human brotherhood.[15]

Knowing little of Demetrius of Bactria, we might give him the benefit of the doubt, but the evidence is really quite fanciful which Tarn uses in his attempt to put the Egyptian king Ptolemy IV, Philopator, in the Alexander tradition—the king Polybius describes as "absorbed in unworthy intrigues, and senseless and continuous drunkennesses. . . ." In a very questionable manner, dreams of brotherhood are deduced from Philopator's Dionysus worship:

> He must have learned from his tutor Eratosthenes that other races beside Greeks were of the human brotherhood; and very possibly, deceived by the current identification of Dionysus' name Sabazius with the Jewish Sabaoth, he thought of uniting Jews and Greeks in Dionysus worship as Ptolemy I had tried to unite Greeks and Egyptians in the worship of Sarapis; and as Sarapis, being Osiris-Apis, could also be equated with Dionysus, Philopator may have dreamt a dream, no unworthy one, of a universal religion which, while promising immortality to its initiates, should reconcile the three chief races in his composite empire. . . .[16]

[14] *Antigonos Gonatas* (Oxford, 1913), 256.
[15] *The Greeks in Bactria and India* (2nd ed.; Cambridge, 1951), 181.
[16] *Cambridge Ancient History*, VII, 727.

Finally, none other than the last Cleopatra has been made Alexander's heir:

> In her relations with the native Egyptians she seems to stand close to Alexander; and in some way she had won their confidence. One reason may have been that she could speak to them in their own language, a thing unique among monarchs of Macedonian blood; but much more important, probably, was her sympathetic attitude toward the native religion, which had laid its spell upon her. Alexander had sacrificed to Apis, but she went further; she began her reign by going to Upper Egypt, to the very center of the old disaffection, and in person at the head of her fleet and of the burghers and priests of Thebes and Hermonthis, escorted a new Buchis bull to his home. . . .[17]

A reading of Tarn's fairy-tale, *The Treasure of the Isle of Mist,* helps us to understand why he chooses to find in the Hellenistic world so much good will among kings, for the treasure which the girl Fiona (his own daughter) seeks and finds is not a material one, but rather an apprehension of his own high idealism. It is the discovery that fame is a battered trumpet, that Aphrodite's girdle gives unpopularity with beauty, that the iron sceptre means both kingly power and exile, and that better than all of these, or any other treasure, is the joy of forgiving one's enemies. Finally, the girl discovers, this act of forgiveness can change the old sinner Jeconiah into a marvel of childlike virtue. That the author of such a book should look for brotherhood and unity wherever he might hope to find it —in the ancient as well as in the modern world—is not surprising.

Does Tarn's idealism mean also optimism? In other words, does he see the course of history as the story of progress, like Macaulay, or does he see brotherhood and unity as rarely occurring, heroic but hopeless ideals lost on a selfish world—more like Carlyle, whose appreciation for the hero in history he certainly shares? The closest approach to an answer to this question will be found in the last sentences of his Alexander book. Alexander's ideal, in the hero's own day, is described as only a "hopeless dream," but its apprehension by later generations shows it not entirely futile:

> There is certainly a line of descent from his prayer at Opis, through the Stoics and one portion of the Christian ideal, to that brotherhood of all men which was proclaimed, though only proclaimed, in the French Revolution. The torch Alexander lit for long only smouldered; perhaps it still only smoulders to-day; but it never has been, and never can be, quite put out.[18]

But this was written in 1926. A later note to this passage (probably about 1948) shows more hesitancy. "I have left the latter part of this

[17] *Ibid.,* **X,** 36.
[18] *Alexander the Great,* I, 148.

paragraph substantially as written in 1926. Since then we have seen new and monstrous births, and are still moving in a world not realised; and I do not know how to rewrite it." The prospect for realization of Tarn's ideal of brotherhood can hardly have brightened the remaining years of his life.

Tarn's defence of Alexander was brilliant, but the case is once again going against him. If the present trend continues, Alexander seems likely to fall from his recent place near heaven to the lowest circle of hell. The critics are probably more right than wrong. The realities of power politics in the ancient world left little scope for the kind of idealism that Tarn wished to find. This admission, however, hardly detracts from the magnitude of his achievement. More than any other historian it is he who has clothed with flesh the dry bones of Hellenistic history.

Suggestions for Further Reading

AS IS OFTEN THE CASE, the classical sources for the biography of Alexander are among the most lively and entertaining works about him, especially Plutarch and Arrian. Plutarch's Life of Alexander from his *Parallel Lives of Noble Greeks and Romans* (available in several editions) is, like the rest of the biographical sketches in this famous book, a gossipy and charming account, containing most of the familiar anecdotes associated with Alexander. Arrian's work, the most substantial of the ancient sources, despite a certain stuffiness and lack of analytical daring, is solidly based on more contemporary sources now long lost—particularly Ptolemy's journal and the work of Aristobulus. And it contains the best and most detailed account of Alexander's conquests. See the excellent modern translation by Aubrey de Sélincourt, *Arrian's Life of Alexander the Great* (Harmondsworth, England: Penguin, 1958).

The views of W. W. Tarn summarized in the excerpted passage above from his Raleigh Lecture on History, "Alexander the Great and the Unity of Mankind," are spelled out in greater detail in the chapters he wrote on Alexander and his age—chs. 12–15 of the *Cambridge Ancient History*, vol. 6 (Cambridge, England: Cambridge University Press, 1927), and in his larger *Alexander the Great*, 2 vols. (Cambridge, England: Cambridge

University Press, 1948), based on the account in *Cambridge Ancient History* but expanded and updated.

Tarn's most bitter critic is Ernst Badian, who chose to challenge Tarn in particular for the views expressed in his Raleigh Lecture. Badian's article, with the same title, "Alexander the Great and the Unity of Mankind," appeared in *Historia*, 7 (1958), 425–444, and is reprinted in *Alexander the Great, the Main Problems*, ed. G. T. Griffith (New York: Barnes and Noble, 1966). This article is highly specialized, closely reasoned, and contains long passages in Greek; but it is very important and, despite the difficulties of the text, the argument can be clearly followed even by the nonspecialist. Peter Green, *Alexander the Great* (New York: Praeger, 1970), is a modern general account of Alexander's career in the same critical tradition as Badian. Two other modern works that deal more with the conquests than the conqueror are Peter Bamm, *Alexander the Great, Power as Destiny*, tr. J. M. Brownjohn (New York: McGraw-Hill, 1968), and Sir Mortimer Wheeler, *Flames over Persepolis, Turning Point in History* (New York: Morrow, 1968), the latter of particular interest because of Wheeler's expert knowledge of Near Eastern and Indian archaeology. The most balanced and readable modern general account of Alexander is still probably A. R. Burn, *Alexander the Great and the Hellenistic Empire* (London: The English Universities Press, 1947).

Finally, Alexander is the subject of two first-rate historical novels by Mary Renault, *Fire from Heaven* (New York: Pantheon, 1969) and *The Persian Boy* (New York: Pantheon, 1972), the first carrying the story through Alexander's childhood to his accession to the throne of Macedonia, the second recounting his conquests as narrated by the Persian boy-eunuch Bagoas, Alexander's companion and lover. Renault has also produced a nonfiction account, fully as readable as her novels, and based on the meticulous research she prepared for them, *The Nature of Alexander* (New York: Pantheon, 1975).

Julius Caesar:
The Colossus that
Bestrode the Narrow World

Unlike Alexander, who conquered the world "as a boy" and was dead at thirty-three, Julius Caesar reached a mature age without achieving astonishing success. He did have considerable experience as a political faction leader, but in the judgment of most of his contemporaries he was not likely to be a world conqueror of Alexander's stamp. And yet, in 49 B.C., when Caesar was fifty years old, a series of events began to unfold that would make him one of the great conquerors of world history and set him alongside Alexander in the estimation of scholar and schoolboy alike.

For the past ten years, Caesar had been building a military reputation with his successful campaigns in Gaul, Britain, and along the Rhine frontier, but always with an eye on events in the city of Rome and the Roman senate, where he had a personal interest in the fierce contest among cliques and factions that dominated senatorial politics in the last years of the Roman Republic. As the year 49 B.C. approached, Caesar's proconsular authority in Gaul was running out. He demanded that he be permitted to stand *in absentia* for the consulship for the following year—neither an unprecedented nor unreasonable demand. Caesar attempted to negotiate with his old ally, the great general Pompey, perhaps to prolong their alliance. But Pompey, his own military reputation threatened by Caesar's growing prestige, and relentlessly pressured by Caesar's enemies in the senate, refused him and joined with the senate in demanding that

Caesar surrender his military command and return to Rome as a private citizen to stand for the consulship. But to do so would have meant his death or proscription. Thus, in January of 49 B.C., Caesar took the fateful step into open revolution, leading a token force across the Rubicon, the little stream that separated his Gallic province from peninsular Italy.

For nearly a century the Roman constitution had been progressively subverted by a succession of extralegal expedients to legitimize the authority of one strong man after another, one faction after another— whether the prolonged consulships of Marius, the perpetual dictatorship of Sulla, or the triumviral authority that Caesar himself had held with Pompey and Crassus. Such practices, as well as a pervasive disenchant- ment with the self-serving senatorial oligarchy, had created broad support in Rome and in Italy for a policy of change, even revolutionary change. Caesar's popular reputation attracted that support as he marched south toward Rome. Even Pompey's legions in Spain declared for Caesar. Pompey and his remaining allies fled to Greece, where they were pursued by Caesar under vast emergency authority readily granted by an overawed senate, and were defeated at Pharsalus. In the next four years, Caesar moved through Asia Minor and Syria, Egypt, North Africa, and Spain and encircled the Mediterranean with his conquests, giving the final rough form to the greatest empire of antiquity.

It was at this point that the plot to assassinate Caesar was formed and carried out on the Ides of March of the year 44 B.C.

Caesar and Alexander beg for comparison, despite the many dis- similarities in their lives. Plutarch, the greatest of ancient biographers, paired them in his *Parallel Lives of Noble Greeks and Romans,* and almost every other ancient writer who speculates upon the meaning of Caesar's career suggests comparison with Alexander. The obvious basis for the comparison is, of course, the military parallel and the fact that Caesar, like Alexander, seized his time and wrenched it so violently that the direction of world events was fundamentally changed. But equally important, both men were cut off before their schemes for a civil order could be realized. There was about Caesar, as about Alexander, an aura of things to come, of unfulfilled dreams even more astounding than his conquests. Thus the question again intrigues us, "What would Caesar have accomplished had he lived on?"

In one important respect Caesar differs radically from Alexander—in our sources of information about him. As we saw in the last chapter, all the contemporary works that dealt with the career of Alexander have been lost, and the best surviving account of him was written some four hundred years after he died. Not so with Caesar. He lived during the most heavily documented period in ancient history, a time when we know more about the people and events at the center of the world's stage than we will know again for more than a thousand years. We have Caesar's own considerable volume of writings. We have the works of his

great senatorial contemporary Cicero. We have the writings of poets
and essayists and narrative historians. But despite the abundance of
material and the wealth of detail about Julius Caesar, a clear and convincing picture of the man—what he was and what he might have
become—eludes us, precisely because, as Shakespeare's Cassius says in
Julius Caesar, ". . . he doth bestride the narrow world like a colossus,"
because his dominating personality, his overweening amibition, and his
striking accomplishments made it nearly impossible for his contemporaries
to be objective about him. His own writings are propagandistic, and
the writings of Cicero, his often bitter and vindictive opponent, and
Sallust, his partisan, are obviously biased. The accounts of both Pollio
and Livy exist only in epitomes or in traces in others' works. For our
best account of Caesar, we must reach down into the imperial period that
followed his own brilliant "golden age of Latin literature," to one of
the writers of "the silver age," the biographer Suetonius.

The Life of Caesar
SUETONIUS

The choice of Suetonius is a good one on a number of counts. Although he has been charged with a journalistic style and mentality and with too great a fondness for scandal, rumor, and portent, the late imperial Historia Augusta, *for what it is worth, refers to him as having written* vere, *"truly," and a great modern Roman historian calls him "far and away the best authority" on Caesar.*[1] *Unlike his contemporary Plutarch, Suetonius was not a moralist using biography as a source of example. Nor was he a deliberate partisan: the factionalism of Caesar's age was long dead. Suetonius was interested only in writing a plain, straightforward account of the men and events that were his subject. And, like Arrian, he turned to archival sources for his information. The book in which his biography of Caesar appears,* The Lives of the Twelve Caesars, *was begun when Suetonius was still in the imperial civil service of the Emperor Hadrian. It is clear that he had access to archival records, now long lost, as well as to literary sources, and that he followed his sources carefully. His biography of Caesar was apparently a part of the book done before Suetonius left the imperial service in about A.D. 120 and thus is especially well documented with records and sources.*

And yet, in an important sense, Suetonius was the captive of those very sources he followed so scrupulously. For even though Suetonius was more than a century removed from his sources, the hostility toward Caesar that these records expressed is clearly reflected in Suetonius's writing. Despite his fascination and admiration for Caesar, Suetonius's basic assessment is that Caesar's arrogance and his flaunting of the republican tradition led to his murder: "He abused his powers and was justly slain."

Even after the Civil War and the furious activity of the years 48–44 B.C., Suetonius tells us, Caesar was full of plans for beautifying the city of Rome, opening libraries, draining the Pomptine marshes, building new highways, constructing a canal through the Isthmus of Corinth, and waging war against both the Dacians and the Parthians.

---

[1] Sir Ronald Syme, in a review of Matthias Gelzer's *Caesar der Politiker und Staatsmann* in *Journal of Roman Studies,* 34 (1944), 95.

ALL THESE ENTERPRISES and plans were cut short by his death. But before I speak of that, it will not be amiss to describe briefly his personal appearance, his dress, his mode of life, and his character, as well as his conduct in civil and military life.

He is said to have been tall of stature, with a fair complexion, shapely limbs, a somewhat full face, and keen black eyes; sound of health, except that towards the end he was subject to sudden fainting fits and to nightmare as well. He was twice attacked by the falling sickness during his campaigns. He was somewhat overnice in the care of his person, not only keeping the hair of his head closely cut and his face smoothly shaved, but, as some have charged, even having superfluous hair plucked out. His baldness was a disfigurement which troubled him greatly, since he found that it was often the subject of the gibes of his detractors. Because of it he used to comb forward his scanty locks from the crown of his head, and of all the honors voted him by the Senate and people there was none which he received or made use of more gladly than the privilege of wearing a laurel wreath at all times. . . .

It is admitted by all that he was much addicted to women, as well as very extravagant in his intrigues with them, and that he seduced many illustrious women, among them Postumia, wife of Servius Sulpicius, Lollia, wife of Aulus Gabinius, Tertulla, wife of Marcus Crassus, and even Gnaeus Pompey's wife Mucia. . . .

He had love affairs with Queens, too, including Eunoe the Moor, wife of Bogudes, on whom, as well as on her husband, he bestowed many splendid presents, as Naso writes. But his greatest favorite was Cleopatra, with whom he often feasted until daybreak, and he would have gone through Egypt with her in her state-barge almost to Aethiopia, had not his soldiers refused to follow him. Finally he called her to Rome and did not let her leave until he had laden her with high honors and rich gifts, and he allowed her to give his name to the child which she bore. . . .

That he drank very little wine not even his enemies denied. There is a saying of Marcus Cato that Caesar was the only man who undertook to overthrow the state when sober. Even in the matter of food Gaius Oppius tells us that he was so indifferent, that once when his host served stale oil instead of fresh, and the other guests would have none of it, Caesar partook even more plentifully than usual, that he might not seem to charge his host with carelessness or lack of manners.

But his abstinence did not extend to pecuniary advantages, either when in command of armies or when in civil office. For we have the testimony of some writers that when he was Proconsul in Spain, he not only begged money from the allies, to help pay his debts, but also attacked and sacked some towns of the Lusitanians, although they did not refuse his terms and opened their gates to him on his arrival. In Gaul he pillaged shrines and temples of the Gods filled with offerings, and oftener sacked towns for the sake of plunder than for any fault. . . .

He was highly skilled in arms and horsemanship, and of incredible powers of endurance. On the march he headed his army, sometimes on horseback, but oftener on foot, bareheaded both in the heat of the sun and in rain. He covered great distances with incredible speed, making a hundred miles a day in a hired carriage and with little baggage, swimming the rivers which barred his path or crossing them on inflated skins, and very often arriving before the messengers sent to announce his coming. . . .

He joined battle, not only after planning his movements in advance but on a sudden opportunity, often immediately at the end of a march, and sometimes in the foulest weather, when one would least expect him to make a move. It was not until his later years that he became slower to engage, through a conviction that the oftener he had been victor, the less he ought to tempt fate, and that he could not possibly gain as much by success as he might lose by a defeat. He never put his enemy to flight without also driving him from his camp, thus giving him no respite in his panic. When the issue was doubtful, he used to send away the horses, and his own among the first, to impose upon his troops the greater necessity of standing their ground by taking away that aid to flight. . . .

When his army gave way, he often rallied it single-handed, planting himself in the way of the fleeing men, laying hold of them one by one, even seizing them by the throat and turning them to face the enemy; that, too, when they were in such a panic that an eagle-bearer made a pass at him with the point as he tried to stop him, while another left the standard in Caesar's hand when he would hold him back. . . .

At Alexandria, while assaulting a bridge, he was forced by a sudden sally of the enemy to take to a small skiff. When many others threw themselves into the same boat, he plunged into the sea, and after swimming for two hundred paces, got away to the nearest ship, holding up his left hand all the way, so as not to wet some papers which he was carrying, and dragging his cloak after him with his teeth, to keep the enemy from getting it as a trophy.

He valued his soldiers neither for their personal character nor their fortune, but solely for their prowess, and he treated them with equal strictness and indulgence. . . .

He certainly showed admirable self-restraint and mercy, both in his conduct of the civil war and in the hour of victory. While Pompey threatened to treat as enemies those who did not take up arms for the government, Caesar gave out that those who were neutral and of neither party should be numbered with his friends. He freely allowed all those whom he had made Centurions [2] on Pompey's recommendation to go over to his rival. . . . At the battle of Pharsalus he cried out, "Spare your fellow citizens," and afterwards allowed each of his men to save any one man he pleased of the opposite party. . . .

[2] Centurions were "company grade" officers in the Roman legion.—ED.

Yet after all, his other actions and words so far outweigh all his good qualities that it is thought he abused his power and was justly slain. For not only did he accept excessive honors, such as an uninterrupted consulship, the dictatorship for life, and the censorship of public morals, as well as the forename Imperator,[3] the surname of Father of his Country, a statue among those of the Kings,[4] and a raised couch in the orchestra of the theater. He also allowed honors to be bestowed on him which were too great for mortal man: a golden throne in the House and on the judgment seat; a chariot and litter in the procession at the circus; temples, altars, and statues beside those of the Gods; a special priest, an additional college of the Luperci, and the calling of one of the months by his name. In fact, there were no honors which he did not receive or confer at pleasure.

He held his third and fourth consulships in name only, content with the power of the dictatorship conferred on him at the same time as the consulships. Moreover, in both years he substituted two Consuls for himself for the last three months, in the meantime holding no elections except for Tribunes and plebeian Aediles, and appointing Praefects instead of the Praetors, to manage the affairs of the city during his absence. When one of the Consuls suddenly died the day before the Kalends of January, he gave the vacant office for a few hours to a man who asked for it. With the same disregard of law and precedent he named magistrates for several years to come, bestowed the emblems of consular rank on ten ex-Praetors, and admitted to the House men who had been given citizenship, and in some cases even half-civilized Gauls. He assigned the charge of the mint and of the public revenues to his own slaves, and gave the oversight and command of the three legions which he had left at Alexandria to a favorite boy of his called Rufio, son of one of his freedmen.

No less arrogant were his public utterances, which Titus Ampius records: that the Republic was a name only, without substance or reality; that Sulla did not know his A. B. C. when he laid down his dictatorship; that men ought now to be more circumspect in addressing him, and to regard his word as law. So far did he go in his presumption, that when a soothsayer once announced to him the direful omen that a victim offered for sacrifice was without a heart, he said: "The entrails will be more favorable when I please. It ought not to be taken as a miracle if a beast have no heart."

But it was the following action in particular that roused deadly hatred against him. When the Senate approached him in a body with many highly honorary decrees, he received them before the temple of Venus Genetrix without rising. Some think that when he attempted to get up, he was held back by Cornelius Balbus; others, that he made no such move at all, but

[3] The title *Imperator*, synonymous with conqueror, was that by which troops would hail a victorious commander. It first assumed a permanent and royal character through Caesar's use of it as a prenomen.

[4] Statues of each of the seven Kings of Rome were in the Capitol, to which an eighth was added in honor of Brutus, who expelled the last. The statue of Julius was afterwards raised near them.

on the contrary frowned angrily on Gaius Trebatius when he suggested that he should rise. This action of his seemed the more intolerable, because when he himself in one of his triumphal processions rode past the benches of the Tribunes, he was so incensed because one of their number, Pontius Aquila by name, did not rise, that he cried: "Come then, Aquila, mighty Tribune, and take from me the Republic," and for several days afterwards, he would promise a favor to no one without adding, "That is, if Pontius Aquila will give me leave."

To an insult which so plainly showed his contempt for the Senate he added an act of even greater insolence. After the sacred rites of the Latin Festival, as he was returning to the city, amid the extravagant and unprecedented demonstrations of the populace, some one in the press placed on his statue a laurel wreath with a white fillet tied to it. When Epidius Marullus and Caesetius Flavus, Tribunes of the Commons, gave orders that the ribbon be removed from the crown and the man taken off to prison, Caesar sharply rebuked and deposed them, either offended that the hint at regal power had been received with so little favor, or, as was said, that he had been robbed of the glory of refusing it. But from that time on he could not rid himself of the odium of having aspired to the title of monarch, although he replied to the Commons, when they hailed him as King, "I am Caesar and not King." At the Lupercalia, when the Consul Antony several times attempted to place a crown upon his head as he spoke from the rostra, he put it aside and at last sent it to the Capitol, to be offered to Jupiter Optimus Maximus. Nay, more, the report had spread in various quarters that he intended to move to Ilium or Alexandria, taking with him the resources of the state, draining Italy by levies, and leaving it and the charge of the city to his friends; also that at the next meeting of the Senate Lucius Cotta would announce as the decision of the Fifteen,[5] that inasmuch as it was written in the books of fate that the Parthians could be conquered only by a King, Caesar should be given that title. . . .

More than sixty joined the conspiracy against him, led by Gaius Cassius and Marcus and Decimus Brutus. At first they hesitated whether to form two divisions at the elections in the Campus Martius, so that while some hurled him from the bridge as he summoned the tribes to vote, the rest might wait below and slay him; or to set upon him in the Sacred Way or at the entrance to the theater. When, however, a meeting of the Senate was called for the Ides of March in the Hall of Pompey, they readily gave that time and place the preference.

Now Caesar's approaching murder was foretold to him by unmistakable signs: . . . when he was offering sacrifice, the soothsayer Spurinna warned him to beware of danger, which would come not later than the Ides of March. . . .

Both for these reasons and because of poor health he hesitated for a long

---

[5] The college of fifteen priests who inspected and expounded the Sybilline books.

time whether to stay at home and put off what he had planned to do in the Senate. But at last, urged by Decimus Brutus not to disappoint the full meeting, which had for some time been waiting for him, he went forth almost at the end of the fifth hour. When a note revealing the plot was handed him by some one on the way, he put it with others which he held in his left hand, intending to read them presently. Then, after many victims had been slain, and he could not get favorable omens, he entered the House in defiance of portents, laughing at Spurinna and calling him a false prophet, because the Ides of March were come without bringing him harm. Spurinna replied that they had of a truth come, but they had not gone.

As he took his seat, the conspirators gathered about him as if to pay their respects, and straightway Tillius Cimber, who had assumed the lead, came nearer as though to ask something. When Caesar with a gesture put him off to another time, Cimber caught his toga by both shoulders. As Caesar cried, "Why, this is violence!" one of the Cascas stabbed him from one side just below the throat. Caesar caught Casca's arm and ran it through with his stylus, but as he tried to leap to his feet, he was stopped by another wound. When he saw that he was beset on every side by drawn daggers, he muffled his head in his robe, and at the same time drew down its lap to his feet with his left hand, in order to fall more decently, with the lower part of his body also covered. And in this wise he was stabbed with three and twenty wounds, uttering not a word, but merely a groan at the first stroke, though some have written that when Marcus Brutus rushed at him, he said in Greek, "You too, my child?" All the conspirators made off, and he lay there lifeless for some time, until finally three common slaves put him on a litter and carried him home, with one arm hanging down.

The Heroic Image of Caesar
THEODOR MOMMSEN

Theodor Mommsen (1817–1903) was awarded the Nobel Prize for Literature in 1902, largely for the literary achievement of his monumental, multivolume The History of Rome. *The Nobel citation called him the "greatest . . . master of historical narrative" of his age—a considerable claim in an era that had produced Ranke and Burckhardt, Guizot,*

Grote, Carlyle, and Macaulay. Still, the assertion may be true. Mommsen, a prolific writer, had gained an immense and well-deserved authority, and his massive The History of Rome *was profoundly influential. It was Mommsen who at last placed the study of ancient history on a scientific and critical foundation. And he began and directed the first great critical collection of ancient Latin inscriptions.*

    Like W. W. Tarn, Theodor Mommsen was trained both in classics and in law. His first academic appointment was as professor of law at Leipzig. Then in 1858 he was appointed to the chair of ancient history at the University of Berlin. Throughout his long life, Mommsen was not only a professor but a passionate political activist. He was involved in the Revolution of 1848 and lost his academic post at Leipzig because of it. In the 1870s he was a prominent member of the Prussian Parliament, frequently clashing with Otto von Bismarck. Like many great historians, Mommsen read the past in terms of present politics. Thus his view of Caesar and the late Roman Republic was colored by his profound disillusionment with German political liberalism and an equally profound hatred for Junker conservatism. Julius Caesar became for Mommsen the archetypal strong man who had swept away the broken pieces of a ruined oligarchy and set the rule of the beneficent Roman Empire firmly on its base. While Mommsen has been rightly criticized for the extravagance of his opinions both on Caesar and on the late Roman Republic, his views, though never quite accepted as the "standard" interpretation, did exert a strong influence on modern scholarship until fairly recently.

    Here, from The History of Rome, *is Mommsen's evaluation of Julius Caesar. The prose is old fashioned and florid and the judgments are dated, but there is still some power left in the sweep of Mommsen's portrayal of his "perfect man."*

THE NEW MONARCH of Rome, the first ruler over the whole domain of Romano-Hellenic civilization, Gaius Julius Caesar, was in his fifty-sixth year . . . when the battle at Thapsus [46 B.C.], the last link in a long chain of momentous victories, placed the decision as to the future of the world in his hands. Few men have had their elasticity so thoroughly put to the proof as Caesar—the sole creative genius produced by Rome, and the last produced by the ancient world, which accordingly moved on in the path that he marked out for it until its sun went down. Sprung from one of the oldest noble families of Latium—which traced back its lineage to the heroes of the Iliad and the kings of Rome, and in fact to the Venus-Aphrodite common to both nations—he spent the years of his boyhood and early manhood as the genteel youth of that epoch were wont to spend them. He had tasted the sweetness as well as the bitterness of the cup of fashionable life, had recited and declaimed, had practised literature and made verses in his idle hours, had prosecuted love-intrigues of every sort, and got himself initiated into all the mysteries of shaving, curls, and ruffles pertaining to the toilette-wisdom of the day, as well as into the still more mysterious art of always borrowing and never paying. But the flexible steel of that nature was proof against even these dissipated and flighty courses; Caesar retained both his bodily vigour and his elasticity of mind and of heart unimpaired. In fencing and in riding he was a match for any of his soldiers, and his swimming saved his life at Alexandria; the incredible rapidity of his journeys, which usually for the sake of gaining time were performed by night—a thorough contrast to the procession-like slowness with which Pompeius moved from one place to another—was the astonishment of his contemporaries and not the least among the causes of his success. The mind was like the body. His remarkable power of intuition revealed itself in the precision and practicability of all his arrangements, even where he gave orders without having seen with his own eyes. His memory was matchless, and it was easy for him to carry on several occupations simultaneously with equal self-possession. . . .

Caesar was thoroughly a realist and a man of sense; and whatever he undertook and achieved was pervaded and guided by the cool sobriety which constitutes the most marked peculiarity of his genius. To this he owed the power of living energetically in the present, undisturbed either by recollection or by expectation; to this he owed the capacity of acting at any moment with collected vigour, and of applying his whole genius even to the smallest and most incidental enterprise; to this he owed the many-sided power with which he grasped and mastered whatever understanding can comprehend and will can compel; to this he owed the self-possessed ease with which he arranged his periods as well as projected his campaigns; to this he owed the "marvellous serenity" which remained steadily with him through good and evil days; to this he owed the complete independence, which admitted of no control by favourite or by mistress, or even by friend. It resulted, moreover, from this clearness of judgment that Caesar never formed to himself illusions regarding the power of fate and the ability of man; in his case the friendly veil was lifted up, which conceals from man the inadequacy of his working. Prudently as he laid his plans and considered all possibilities, the feeling was never absent from his breast that in all things fortune, that is to say accident, must bestow success; and with this may be connected the circumstance that he so often played a desperate game with destiny, and in particular again and again hazarded his person with daring indifference. As indeed occasionally men of predominant sagacity betake themselves to a pure game of hazard, so there was in Caesar's rationalism a point at which it came in some measure into contact with mysticism.

Gifts such as these could not fail to produce a statesman. From early youth, accordingly, Caesar was a statesman in the deepest sense of the term, and his aim was the highest which man is allowed to propose to himself—the political, military, intellectual, and moral regeneration of his own deeply decayed nation, and of the still more deeply decayed Hellenic nation intimately akin to his own. The hard school of thirty years' experience changed his views as to the means by which this aim was to be reached; his aim itself remained the same in the times of his hopeless humiliation and of his unlimited plenitude of power, in the times when as demagogue and conspirator he stole towards it by paths of darkness, and in those when, as joint possessor of the supreme power and then as monarch, he worked at his task in the full light of day before the eyes of the world. . . . According to his original plan he had purposed to reach his object, like Pericles and Gaius Gracchus, without force of arms, and throughout eighteen years he had as leader of the popular party moved exclusively amid political plans and intrigues—until, reluctantly convinced of the necessity for a military support, he, when already forty years of age, put himself at the head of an army [59 B.C.]. . . .

The most remarkable peculiarity of his action as a statesman was its perfect harmony. In reality all the conditions for this most difficult of all human functions were united in Caesar. A thorough realist, he never allowed the images of the past or venerable tradition to disturb him; for him nothing was of value in politics but the living present and the law of reason, just as in his character of grammarian he set aside historical and antiquarian research and recognized nothing but on the one hand the living *usus loquendi* and on the other hand the rule of symmetry. A born ruler, he governed the minds of men as the wind drives the clouds, and compelled the most heterogeneous natures to place themselves at his service—the plain citizen and the rough subaltern, the genteel matrons of Rome and the fair princesses of Egypt and Mauretania, the brilliant cavalry-officer and the calculating banker. His talent for organization was marvellous; no statesman has ever compelled alliances, no general has ever collected an army out of unyielding and refractory elements with such decision, and kept them together with such firmness, as Caesar displayed in constraining and upholding his coalitions and his legions; never did regent judge his instruments and assign each to the place appropriate for him with so acute an eye.

He was monarch; but he never played the king. Even when absolute lord of Rome, he retained the deportment of the party-leader; perfectly pliant and smooth, easy and charming in conversation, complaisant towards every one, it seemed as if he wished to be nothing but the first among his peers. Caesar entirely avoided the blunder into which so many men otherwise on an equality with him have fallen, of carrying into politics the military tone of command; however much occasion his disagreeable relations with the senate gave for it, he never resorted to outrages. . . . Caesar was monarch; but he was never seized with the giddiness of the tyrant. He is perhaps the only one among the mighty ones of the earth, who in great matters and little never acted according to inclination or caprice, but always without exception according to his duty as ruler, and who, when he looked back on his life, found doubtless erroneous calculations to deplore, but no false step of passion to regret. There is nothing in the history of Caesar's life, which even on a small scale can be compared with those poetico-sensual ebullitions—such as the murder of Kleitos or the burning or Persepolis—which the history of his great predecessor in the east records. He is, in fine, perhaps the only one of those mighty ones, who has preserved to the end of his career the statesman's tact of discriminating between the possible and the impossible, and has not broken down in the task which for greatly gifted natures is the most difficult of all—the task of recognizing, when on the pinnacle of success, its natural limits. What was possible he performed, and never left the possible good undone for the sake of the impossible better, never disdained at least to mitigate by palliatives evils that were incurable. But where he recognized that fate had spoken, he always obeyed. . . .

Such was this unique man, whom it seems so easy and yet is so infinitely difficult to describe. His whole nature is transparent clearness; and tradition preserves more copious and more vivid information about him than about any of his peers in the ancient world. Of such a personage our conceptions may well vary in point of shallowness or depth, but they cannot be, strictly speaking, different; to every not utterly perverted inquirer the grand figure has exhibited the same essential features, and yet no one has succeeded in reproducing it to the life. The secret lies in its perfection. In his character as a man as well as in his place in history, Caesar occupies a position where the great contrasts of existence meet and balance each other. Of mighty creative power and yet at the same time of the most penetrating judgment; no longer a youth and not yet an old man; of the highest energy of will and the highest capacity of execution; filled with republican ideals and at the same time born to be a king; a Roman in the deepest essence of his nature, and yet called to reconcile and combine in himself as well as in the outer world the Roman and the Hellenic types of culture—Caesar was the entire and perfect man.

Caesar the Politician
RONALD SYME

*The long-time Oxford professor Sir Ronald Syme is probably our leading
ancient historian today. His most important book, and possibly the
outstanding work in Roman history in this generation,[6] is* The Roman
Revolution. *Syme worked on this book through the late 1930s, against
the backdrop of events taking place in Mommsen's Germany, but the
vision of one-man rule was not quite as alluring to him as it had been to
Mommsen. Syme's view of Caesar, however, was not only affected by
the rise of Hitler and the political drift toward World War II. He had
before him an impressive accumulation of scholarly research on the
darker side of the Caesarian monarchy. Eduard Meyer's* Caesars Monarchie
und das Principat des Pompejus *(1919) argues that Caesar aspired
to the establishment of a Hellenistic monarchy in Rome. The second
volume of Jerome Carcopino's* Histoire Romaine *(1936) deals with
Caesar and maintains that, since his youth, Caesar's ambition was
directed toward monarchy.*

*Syme also read the important work of Matthias Gelzer—Die Nobilität
der Römischen Republik (1912) and Caesar der Politiker und
Staatsmann (1921)—which prompted him to examine some of the same
ground, the social and political setting in which Caesar lived and
died. Syme, like Gelzer, was especially interested in the senatorial
oligarchy. The "Roman Revolution" of his title, he argues, occurred
when this oligarchy lost its power to a new social group composed of
people from all parts of Italy, even the provinces. And he saw Caesar as
the political genius who began the revolution that he could not then control.*

*Syme insists that Caesar be judged—as he was murdered— "for what
he was, not for what he might become," be that an oriental despot
or a Hellenistic monarch. What Caesar was was a Roman aristocrat
whose brilliance and luck enabled him to surpass his fellow aristocrats.
The key event leading to his assassination was not his arrogance, which was
common to his class and station, and not even his high-handedness
in subverting the republic; it was the Caesarian dictatorship, prolonged
first for ten years and then, in January of 44 B.C., for life, that was
intolerable to the senatorial nobility and the cause of his murder.*

The following, from The Roman Revolution, *is Syme's analysis of
Caesar.*

[6] Cf. the review, for example, of Michael Ginsburg in *American Historical Review*, 46 (1940), 108.

THE CONQUEST of Gaul, the war against Pompeius and the establishment of the Dictatorship of Caesar are events that move in a harmony so swift and sure as to appear pre-ordained; and history has sometimes been written as though Caesar set the tune from the beginning, in the knowledge that monarchy was the panacea for the world's ills, and with the design to achieve it by armed force. Such a view is too simple to be historical.

Caesar strove to avert any resort to open war. Both before and after the outbreak of hostilities he sought to negotiate with Pompeius. Had Pompeius listened and consented to an interview, their old *amicitia* might have been repaired. With the nominal primacy of Pompeius recognized, Caesar and his adherents would capture the government—and perhaps reform the State. Caesar's enemies were afraid of that—and so was Pompeius. After long wavering Pompeius chose at last to save the oligarchy. Further, the proconsul's proposals as conveyed to the Senate were moderate and may not be dismissed as mere manoeuvres for position or for time to bring up his armies. Caesar knew how small was the party willing to provoke a war. As the artful motion of a Caesarian tribune had revealed, an overwhelming majority in the Senate, nearly four hundred against twenty-two, wished both dynasts to lay down their extraordinary commands. A rash and factious minority prevailed.

The precise legal points at issue in Caesar's claim to stand for the consulate in absence and retain his province until the end of the year 49 B.C. are still matters of controversy. If they were ever clear, debate and misrepresentation soon clouded truth and equity. The nature of the political crisis is less obscure. Caesar and his associates in power had thwarted or suspended the constitution for their own ends many times in the past. Exceptions had been made before in favour of other dynasts; and Caesar asserted both legal and moral rights to preferential treatment. In the last resort his rank, prestige and honour, summed up in the Latin word *dignitas,* were all at stake: to Caesar, as he claimed, "his *dignitas* had ever been dearer than life itself." Sooner than surrender it, Caesar appealed to arms. A constitutional pretext was provided by the violence of his adversaries: Caesar stood in defence of the rights of the tribunes and the liberties of the Roman People. But that was not the plea which Caesar himself valued most—it was his personal honour.

His enemies appeared to have triumphed. They had driven a wedge between the two dynasts, winning over to their side the power and prestige of Pompeius. They would be able to deal with Pompeius later. It might not come to open war; and Pompeius was still in their control so long as he was not at the head of an army in the field. Upon Caesar they had thrust the choice between civil war and political extinction. . . .

Caesar was constrained to appeal to his army for protection. At last the enemies of Caesar had succeeded in ensnaring Pompeius and in working the constitution against the craftiest politician of the day: he was declared a public enemy if he did not lay down his command before a certain day. By invoking constitutional sanctions against Caesar, a small faction misrepresented the true wishes of a vast majority in the Senate, in Rome, and in Italy. They pretended that the issue lay between a rebellious proconsul and legitimate authority. Such venturesome expedients are commonly the work of hot blood and muddled heads. The error was double and damning. Disillusion followed swiftly. Even Cato was dismayed. It had confidently been expected that the solid and respectable classes in the towns of Italy would rally in defence of the authority of the Senate and the liberties of the Roman People, that all the land would rise as one man against the invader. Nothing of the kind happened. Italy was apathetic to the war-cry of the Republic in danger, sceptical about its champions. . . .

Caesar, it is true, had only a legion to hand: the bulk of his army was still far away. But he swept down the eastern coast of Italy, gathering troops, momentum and confidence as he went. Within two months of the crossing of the Rubicon he was master of Italy. Pompeius made his escape across the Adriatic carrying with him several legions and a large number of senators, a grievous burden of revenge and recrimination. The enemies of Caesar had counted upon capitulation or a short and easy war.

They had lost the first round. Then a second blow, quite beyond calculation: before the summer was out the generals of Pompeius in Spain were outmanoeuvred and overcome. Yet even so, until the legions joined battle on the plain of Pharsalus, the odds lay heavily against Caesar. Fortune, the devotion of his veteran legionaries and the divided counsels of his adversaries secured the crowning victory. But three years more of fighting were needed to stamp out the last and bitter resistance of the Pompeian cause in Africa and in Spain.

"They would have it thus," said Caesar as he gazed upon the Roman dead at Pharsalus, half in patriot grief for the havoc of civil war, half in impatience and resentment. They had cheated Caesar of the true glory of a Roman aristocrat—to contend with his peers for primacy, not to destroy them. His enemies had the laugh of him in death. Even Pharsalus was not the end. His former ally, the great Pompeius, glorious from victories in all quarters of the world, lay unburied on an Egyptian beach, slain by a renegade Roman, the hireling of a foreign king. Dead, too, and killed by Romans, were Caesar's rivals and enemies, many illustrious consulars. Ahenobarbus fought and fell at Pharsalus, and Q. Metellus Scipio ended worthy of his ancestors; while Cato chose to fall by his own hand rather than witness the domination of Caesar and the destruction of the Free State.

That was the nemesis of ambition and glory, to be thwarted in the end. After such wreckage, the task of rebuilding confronted him, stern and thankless. Without the sincere and patriotic co-operation of the governing class, the attempt would be all in vain, the mere creation of arbitrary power, doomed to perish in violence. . . .

Under these unfavourable auspices, a Sulla but for *clementia,* a Gracchus but lacking a revolutionary programme, Caesar established his Dictator-ship. His rule began as the triumph of a faction in civil war: he made it his task to transcend faction, and in so doing wrought his own destruction. A champion of the People, he had to curb the People's rights, as Sulla had done. To rule, he needed the support of the *nobiles,* yet he had to curtail their privileges and repress their dangerous ambitions.

In name and function Caesar's office was to set the State in order again (*rei publicae constituendae*). Despite odious memories of Sulla, the choice of the Dictatorship was recommended by its comprehensive powers and freedom from the tribunician veto. Caesar knew that secret enemies would soon direct that deadly weapon against one who had used it with such dexterity in the past and who more recently claimed to be asserting the rights of the tribunes, the liberty of the Roman People. He was not mis-taken. Yet he required special powers: after a civil war the need was patent. The Dictator's task might well demand several years. In 46 B.C. his powers were prolonged to a tenure of ten years, an ominous sign. A gleam of hope that the emergency period would be quite short flickered up for a moment, to wane at once and perish utterly. In January 44 B.C. Caesar was voted the Dictatorship for life. About the same time decrees of the Senate ordained that an oath of allegiance should be taken in his name. Was this the measure of his ordering of the Roman State? Was this a *res publica constituta*?

It was disquieting. Little had been done to repair the ravages of civil war and promote social regeneration. For that there was sore need, as both his adherents and his former adversaries pointed out. From Pompeius, from Cato and from the oligarchy, no hope of reform. But Caesar seemed different: he had consistently advocated the cause of the oppressed, whether Roman, Italian or provincial. He had shown that he was not afraid of vested interests. But Caesar was not a revolutionary. . . .

[He] postponed decision about the permanent ordering of the State. It was too difficult. Instead, he would set out for the wars again, to Mace-donia and to the eastern frontier of the Empire. At Rome he was hampered: abroad he might enjoy his conscious mastery of men and events, as before in Gaul. Easy victories—but not the urgent needs of the Roman People.

About Caesar's ultimate designs there can be opinion, but no certainty. The acts and projects of his Dictatorship do not reveal them. For the rest, the evidence is partisan—or posthumous. No statement of unrealized inten-tions is a safe guide to history, for it is unverifiable and therefore the most attractive form of misrepresentation. The enemies of Caesar spread ru-mours to discredit the living Dictator: Caesar dead became a god and a myth, passing from the realm of history into literature and legend, declama-tion and propaganda. . . .

Yet speculation cannot be debarred from playing round the high and momentous theme of the last designs of Caesar the Dictator. It has been supposed and contended that Caesar either desired to establish or had actually inaugurated an institution unheard of in Rome and unimagined there—monarchic rule, despotic and absolute, based upon worship of the ruler, after the pattern of the monarchies of the Hellenistic East. Thus may Caesar be represented as the heir in all things of Alexander the Macedonian and as the anticipator of Caracalla, a king and a god incarnate, levelling class and nation, ruling a subject, united and uniform world by right divine.

This extreme simplification of long and diverse ages of history seems to suggest that Caesar alone of contemporary Roman statesmen possessed either a wide vision of the future or a singular and elementary blindness to the present. But this is only a Caesar of myth or rational construction. . . .

If Caesar must be judged, it is by facts and not by alleged intentions. As his acts and his writings reveal him, Caesar stands out as a realist and an opportunist. In the short time at his disposal he can hardly have made plans for a long future or laid the foundation of a consistent government. Whatever it might be, it would owe more to the needs of the moment than to alien or theoretical models. More important the business in hand; it was expedited in swift and arbitrary fashion. Caesar made plans and decisions in the company of his intimates and secretaries: the Senate voted but did not deliberate. As the Dictator was on the point of departing in the spring of 44 B.C. for several years of campaigning in the Balkans and the East, he tied up magistracies and provincial commands in advance by placing them, according to the traditional Roman way, in the hands of loyal partisans, or of reconciled Pompeians whose good sense should guarantee peace. For that period, at least, a salutary pause from political activity: with the lapse of time the situation might become clearer in one way or another. . . .

At the moment it was intolerable: the autocrat became impatient, annoyed by covert opposition, petty criticism and laudations of dead Cato. That he was unpopular he well knew. "For all his genius, Caesar could not see a way out," as one of his friends was subsequently to remark. And there was no going back. To Caesar's clear mind and love of rapid decision, this brought a tragic sense of impotence and frustration—he had been all things and it was no good. He had surpassed the good fortune of Sulla Felix and the glory of Pompeius Magnus. In vain—reckless ambition had ruined the Roman State and baffled itself in the end. Of the melancholy that descended upon Caesar there stands the best of testimony—"my life has been long enough, whether reckoned in years or in renown." The words were remembered. The most eloquent of his contemporaries did not disdain to plagiarize them.

The question of ultimate intentions becomes irrelevant. Caesar was slain for what he was, not for what he might become. . . .

It is not necessary to believe that Caesar planned to establish at Rome a "Hellenistic Monarchy," whatever meaning may attach to that phrase. The Dictatorship was enough. The rule of the *nobiles,* he could see, was an anachronism in a world-empire; and so was the power of the Roman plebs when all Italy enjoyed the franchise. Caesar in truth was more conservative and Roman than many have fancied; and no Roman conceived of government save through an oligarchy. But Caesar was being forced into an autocratic position. It meant the lasting domination of one man instead of the rule of the law, the constitution and the Senate; it announced the triumph soon or late of new forces and new ideas, the elevation of the army and the provinces, the depression of the traditional governing class. Caesar's autocracy appeared to be much more than a temporary expedient to liquidate the heritage of the Civil War and reinvigorate the organs of the Roman State. It was going to last—and the Roman aristocracy was not to be permitted to govern and exploit the Empire in its own fashion. The tragedies of history do not arise from the conflict of conventional right and wrong. They are more august and more complex. Caesar and Brutus each had right on his side. . . .

Without a party a statesman is nothing. He sometimes forgets that awkward fact. If the leader or principal agent of a faction goes beyond the wishes of his allies and emancipates himself from control, he may have to be dropped or suppressed. . . .

When Caesar took the Dictatorship for life and the sworn allegiance of senators, it seemed clear that he had escaped from the shackles of party to supreme and personal rule. For this reason, certain of the most prominent of his adherents combined with Republicans and Pompeians to remove their leader. The Caesarian party thus split by the assassination of the Dictator none the less survived, joined for a few months with Republicans in a new and precarious front of security and vested interests led by the Dictator's political deputy until a new leader, emerging unexpected, at first tore it in pieces again, but ultimately, after conquering the last of his rivals, converted the old Caesarian party into a national government in a transformed State. The composition and vicissitudes of that party, though less dramatic in unity of theme than the careers and exploits of the successive leaders, will yet help to recall the ineffable complexities of authentic history.

Suggestions for Further Reading

AS IN THE CASE of Alexander, the ancient sources for the life of Julius Caesar are among the liveliest and most entertaining accounts of him. Students are encouraged to read the rest of Suetonius' sketch beyond what is excerpted in this chapter. They are also encouraged to read Plutarch's Life of Caesar, which, as we have noted, he wrote to be compared with his Life of Alexander. Plutarch and Suetonius between them give us most of the anecdotal matter commonly associated with Caesar. We have in addition, as also noted above, the considerable volume of Caesar's own writings in several attractive modern editions, *The Gallic War*, tr. and ed. Moses Hadas (New York: Modern Library, 1957), tr. J. Warrington (New York: Heritage, 1955), and tr. S. A. Handford (Baltimore: Penguin, 1965); and *The Civil War*, ed. and tr. Jane F. Mitchell (Baltimore: Penguin, 1967). We also have references to Caesar scattered throughout the works of such contemporaries as Cicero and Sallust.

Caesar has always been a fascinating figure, and there are an impossibly large number of biographies of him. Two recent ones can be especially recommended to students. Probably the best brief biography is J. P. V. D. Balsdon, *Julius Caesar and Rome* (London: The English Universities Press, 1967), an authoritative work by an established authority, another in the excellent "Teach Yourself History Library" series. Students may prefer the somewhat larger and more lavish Michael Grant, *Caesar* (London: Weidenfeld and Nicolson, 1974), in the "Great Lives" series; it is interesting and readable as well as authoritative, another book by one of the best modern popularizers of ancient history.

There are also many books dealing with Caesar's era and the late Roman republic. One of the best of these, and one that combines the account of the man and the era, is Matthias Gelzer, *Caesar, Politician and Statesman*, tr. Peter Needham (Cambridge, Mass.: Harvard University Press, 1968). Despite its relentlessly prosaic quality, it is an important interpretive work by a great German scholar, stressing Caesar as a political figure of genius and paralleling the views of Sir Ronald Syme, which are represented in this chapter. A somewhat broader account, still considered a standard work by many authorities, is that of F. E. Adcock in chs. 15–17 in vol. 9 of the *Cambridge Ancient History* (Cambridge, England: Cambridge University Press, 1932). Also recommended are R. E. Smith, *The Failure of the Roman Republic* (Cambridge, England: Cambridge University Press, 1955); the somewhat more detailed Erich S. Gruen, *The*

Last Generation of the Roman Republic (Berkeley: University of California Press, 1974); and the now famous small study by Lily Ross Taylor, *Party Politics in the Age of Caesar* (Berkeley: University of California Press, 1975 [1949]).

Finally, two special studies are recommended, the attractive small book by F. E. Adcock, *Caesar as Man of Letters* (Cambridge, England: Cambridge University Press, 1956), and Gen. John F. C. Fuller, *Julius Caesar: Man, Soldier, and Tyrant* (New Brunswick, N.J.: Rutgers University Press, 1965), a lively, opinionated, and somewhat debunking book by a great military historian about Caesar as a less-than-brilliant general.

Augustine:
The Thinking Man's Saint

The historian Edward Gibbon capsulized the rise of Christianity in
this dramatic sentence: "A pure and humble religion gently insinuated
itself into the minds of men, grew up in silence and obscurity, derived
new vigor from opposition, and finally erected the triumphant banner of
the Cross on the ruins of the Capitol." [1] While modern historians may
quarrel with one aspect or another of Gibbon's views, most agree
that by the mid-fourth century Christianity was the dominant spiritual
force in the Roman Empire. The public policy of persecution had been
replaced by toleration and then endorsement; and since Constantine
every emperor, save the much maligned Julian "the Apostate"
(361–363), had been at least nominally Christian. The church as an
institution had taken form, and its officials were people of importance,
from one end of the empire to the other. It was at long last both
fashionable and profitable to be Christian; and men of position and
substance adopted the faith.

It is thus not surprising that a bright, well-educated, and ambitious
young man of the late fourth century should have been attracted to
Christianity. What is unusual is that he wrote a sensitive, detailed account
of the experience of his conversion, entitled the *Confessions*. This work
is all the more valuable, for the man who wrote it went on to become
the most important theologian of the early church and one of the most
influential thinkers in human history—St. Augustine.

[1] *Decline and Fall of the Roman Empire*, Ch. XV.1.

The Confessions
ST. AUGUSTINE

The Confessions *is a remarkable book. A modern critic has called it ". . . one of the truest, frankest, and most heart-lifting autobiographies ever written."* [2] *For us, however, its "heart-lifting" inspirational quality— and surely it was written to impart just that quality—will be of less interest than its fascinating revelation of the process by which a tough-minded intellectual, examining his own life, was brought not only to embrace Christianity but to make it the very center of his being. No document has ever laid open that process more candidly or more searchingly than the* Confessions.

Aurelius Augustinus was born at Tagaste in Roman North Africa in 354, of a not-uneducated pagan father and a devoutly Christian mother. Signs of intellectual precocity led his father to send the boy to school at an early age and at considerable financial sacrifice. He was trained first at the nearby town of Madaura and then at the great city of Carthage, the capital and the intellectual and trade center of Roman Africa. Augustine was studying to be a professional rhetorician. And neither the program nor its aims—the study of eloquence for the sake of persuasion—had changed in centuries. When he finished his schooling, Augustine became a teacher of rhetoric. He also became a member of the Manicheans, a sect particularly strong in North Africa that taught a form of radical dualism as its principal spiritual-intellectual doctrine. Though he remained a Manichean for some nine years, Augustine was also attracted to astrology; he was impressed with Cicero's urbane, academic skepticism; he studied Aristotle and Plato and the fashionable Neoplatonism; and he sampled and rejected the Christian Bible. Without fully realizing it, his search for belief was beginning.

By this time Augustine had become a teacher in his native Tagaste, had taken a wife, and had fathered a son. He then obtained a teaching position in Carthage and was becoming a well-known rhetorician and philosopher when, in 383 at the age of twenty-nine, he went to teach in Rome. Within a year, he heard of a position as master of rhetoric to the great city of Milan, which in these declining years of the Roman empire had come to overshadow the old capital as the center of imperial government in the West. It was an important position; Augustine competed for it, delivering a public oration, and was awarded the post.

[2] Stewart Perowne, *The End of the Roman World* (New York: Crowell, 1967), p. 143.

*It was in Milan that Augustine came under the influence of one of
the most powerful figures in the early church, St. Ambrose, the Bishop
of Milan, who, as Augustine says, "received me as a father." The process
of conversion was under way. But it was to be neither an easy nor a
painless process. For such a man as Augustine had hard intellectual
questions to ask of any faith.*

Let St. Augustine himself continue the story.

I BEGAN TO love him at first not as a teacher of the truth (for I had quite
despaired of finding it in your Church) but simply as a man who was kind
and generous to me. I used to listen eagerly when he preached to the
people, but my intention was not what it should have been; I was, as it
were, putting his eloquence on trial to see whether it came up to his
reputation, or whether its flow was greater or less than I had been told.
So I hung intently on his words, but I was not interested in what he was
really saying and stood aside from this in contempt. I was much pleased
by the charm of his style, which, although it was more learned, was still,
so far as the manner of delivery was concerned, not so warm and winning
as the style of Faustus.[3] With regard to the actual matter there was, of
course, no comparison. Faustus was merely roving around among Manichaean fallacies, while Ambrose was healthily teaching salvation. But
salvation is far from sinners of the kind that I was then. Yet, though I
did not realize it, I was drawing gradually nearer.

For although my concern was not to learn what he said but only to hear
how he said it (this empty interest being all that remained to me, now that
I had despaired of man's being able to find his way to you), nevertheless,
together with the language, which I admired, the subject matter also, to
which I was indifferent, began to enter into my mind. Indeed I could not
separate the one from the other. And as I opened my heart in order to
recognize how eloquently he was speaking it occurred to me at the same
time (though this idea came gradually) how truly he was speaking. . . .

By this time my mother had joined me. Her piety had given her strength
and she had followed me over land and sea, confident in you throughout
all dangers. In the perils of the sea it was she who put the fresh heart into
the sailors although as a rule it is for the sailors to reassure the passengers
who are inexperienced on the high seas. But she promised them that they
would get safely to land because you had promised this to her in a vision.
She found me in grave danger indeed, my danger being that of despairing
of ever discovering the truth. I told her that, though I was not yet a

[3] A famous Manichean preacher. Augustine had eagerly anticipated hearing him
but was disappointed when he did. From this point his break with Manicheanism
began.—ED.

Catholic Christian, I was certainly no longer a Manichaean; but she showed no great signs of delight, as though at some unexpected piece of news, because she already felt at ease regarding that particular aspect of my misery; she bewailed me as one dead, certainly, but as one who would be raised up again by you; she was in her mind laying me before you on the bier so that you might say to the widow's son: *"Young man, I say unto thee, Arise,"* and he should revive and begin to speak and you should give him to his mother. So her heart was shaken by no storm of exultation when she heard that what she had daily begged you with her tears should happen had in so large a part taken place—that I was now rescued from falsehood, even though I had not yet attained the truth. She was indeed quite certain that you, who had promised her the whole, would give her the part that remained, and she replied to me very calmly and with a heart full of confidence that she believed in Christ that, before she departed from this life, she would see me a true Catholic. . . .

I was not yet groaning in prayer for you to help me. My mind was intent on inquiry and restless in dispute. I considered Ambrose himself, who was honored by people of such importance, a lucky man by worldly standards; only his celibacy seemed to me rather a burden to bear. But I could neither guess nor tell from my own experience what hope he had within him, what were his struggles against the temptations of his exalted position, what solace he found in adversity; nor could I tell of that hidden mouth of his (the mouth of his heart), what joys it tasted in the rumination of your bread. And he on his side did not know of the turmoil in which I was or the deep pit of danger before my feet. I was not able to ask him the questions I wanted to ask in the way I wanted to ask them, because I was prevented from having an intimate conversation with him by the crowds of people, all of whom had some business with him and to whose infirmities he was a servant. And for the very short periods of time when he was not with them, he was either refreshing his body with necessary food or his mind with reading. When he was reading, his eyes went over the pages and his heart looked into the sense, but voice and tongue were resting. Often when we came to him (for no one was forbidden to come in, and it was not customary for visitors even to be announced) we found him reading, always to himself and never otherwise; we would sit in silence for a long time, not venturing to interrupt him in his intense concentration on his task, and then we would go away again. We guessed that in the very small time which he was able to set aside for mental refreshment he wanted to be free from the disturbance of other people's business and would not like to have his attention distracted. . . . But I needed to find him with plenty of time to spare if I was to pour out to him the full flood of agitation boiling up inside me, and I could never find him like this. Yet every Sunday I listened to him rightly preaching to the people the word of truth, and I became more and more sure that all those knots of cunning calumny which, in their attacks on the holy books, my deceivers had tied could be unraveled. In particular I discovered that the phrase "man, created by Thee, after Thine own image" was not understood by your spiritual children, whom you have made to be born again by grace through the Catholic mother, in such a way as to mean that you are bounded by the shape of a human body. And although I had not the faintest or most shadowy notion about what a spiritual substance could be, nevertheless with a kind of pleasant shame I blushed to think of how for all these years I had been barking not against the Catholic faith but against figments of carnal imaginations. . . .

. . . So I was both confounded and converted, and I was glad, my God, that your only Church, the body of your only son—that Church in which the name of Christ had been put upon me as an infant[4]—was not flavored with this childish nonsense and did not, in her healthy doctrine, maintain the view that you, the Creator of all things, could be, in the form of a human body, packed into a definite space which, however mighty and large, must still be bounded on all sides. . . . But it was the same with me as with a man who, having once had a bad doctor, is afraid of trusting himself even to a good one. So it was with the health of my soul which could not possibly be cured except by believing, but refused to be cured for fear of believing something falser. So I resisted your hands, for it was you who prepared the medicines of faith and applied them to the diseases of the world and gave them such potency. . . .

And I, as I looked back over my life, was quite amazed to think of how long a time had passed since my nineteenth year, when I had first become inflamed with a passion for wisdom and had resolved that, when once I found it, I would leave behind me all the empty hopes and deceitful frenzies of vain desires. And now I was in my thirtieth year, still sticking in the same mud, still greedy for the enjoyment of things present, which fled from me and wasted me away, and all the time saying: "I shall find it tomorrow. See, it will become quite clear and I shall grasp it. Now Faustus will come and explain everything. What great men the Academics are! Is it true that no certainty can possibly be comprehended for the direction of our lives? No, it cannot be. We must look into things more carefully and not give up hope. And now see, those things in the Scriptures which used to seem absurd are not absurd; they can be understood in a different and perfectly good way. I shall take my stand where my parents placed me as a child until I can see the truth plainly. But where shall I look for it? And when shall I look for it? Ambrose has no spare time; nor have I time for reading. And where can I find the books? From where can I get them and when can I get them? Can I borrow them from anybody? I must arrange fixed periods of time and set aside certain hours for the health of my soul.

4 Though he had not been baptized as a child, he had apparently been at least nominally Christian, through his mother's influence—ED.

A great hope has dawned. The Catholic faith does not teach the things I thought it did and vainly accused it of teaching. The learned men of that faith think it quite wrong to believe that God is bounded within the shape of a human body. Why then do I hesitate to knock, so that the rest may be laid open to me? My pupils take up all my time in the morning. But what do I do for the rest of the day? Why not do this? But, if I do, how shall I find time to call on influential friends whose support will be useful to me? When shall I prepare the lessons for which my pupils pay? When shall I have time to relax and to refresh my mind from all my pre-occupations? . . . As I became more unhappy, so you drew closer to me. Your right hand was ready, it was ready to drag me out of the mud and to wash me; but I did not know. And there was nothing to call me back from that deeper gulf of carnal pleasure, except the fear of death and of judgment to come, and this, whatever the opinions I held from time to time, never left my mind. . . .

Now my evil abominable youth was a thing of the past. I was growing into manhood, and the older I was the more discreditable was the emptiness of my mind. I was unable to form an idea of any kind of substance other than what my eyes are accustomed to see. I did not think of you, God, in the shape of a human body. From the moment when I began to have any knowledge of wisdom I always avoided that idea, and I was glad that I had found the same view held in the faith of our spiritual mother, your Catholic Church. But how else I was to think of you, I did not know. . . .

As to me, I would certainly say and I firmly believed that you—our Lord, the true God, who made not only our souls but our bodies, and not only our souls and bodies but all men and all things—were undefilable and unalterable and in no way to be changed, and yet I still could not understand clearly and distinctly what was the cause of evil. Whatever it might be, however, I did realize that my inquiry must not be carried out along lines which would lead me to believe that the immutable God was mutable; if I did that, I should become myself the very evil which I was looking for. And so I pursued the inquiry without anxiety, being quite certain that what the Manichees said was not true. I had turned against them with my whole heart, because I saw that in their inquiries into the origin of evil they were full of evil themselves; for they preferred to believe that your substance could suffer evil rather than that their substance could do evil. . . . So I thought of your creation as finite and as filled with you, who were infinite. And I said: "Here is God, and here is what God has created; and God is good and is most mightily and incomparably better than all these. Yet He, being good, created them good, and see how He surrounds them and fills them. Where, then, is evil? Where did it come from and how did it creep in here? What is its root and seed? Or does it simply not exist? In that case why do we fear and take precautions against something that does not exist? Or if there is no point in our fears, then our fears themselves are an evil which goads and tortures the heart for no good reason—and all the worse an evil if there is nothing to be afraid of and we are still afraid. Therefore, either there is evil which we fear or else the fact that we do fear is evil. Where then does evil come from, seeing that God is good and made all things good? Certainly it was the greater and supreme Good who made these lesser goods, yet still all are good, both the creator and his creation. Where then did evil come from? Or was there some evil element in the material of creation, and did God shape and form it, yet still leave in it something which He did not change into good? But why? Being omnipotent, did He lack the power to change and transform the whole so that no trace of evil should remain? Indeed why should He choose to use such material for making anything? Would He not rather, with this same omnipotence, cause it not to exist at all? Could it exist against His will? Or, supposing it was eternal, why for so long through all the infinite spaces of time past did He allow it to exist and then so much later decide to make something out of it? Or, if He did suddenly decide on some action, would not the omnipotent prefer to act in such a way that this evil material should cease to exist, and that He alone should be, the whole, true, supreme, and infinite Good? Or, since it was not good that He who was good should frame and create something not good, then why did He not take away and reduce to nothing the material that was evil and then Himself provide good material from which to create all things? For He would not be omnipotent if He could not create something good without having to rely on material which He had not Himself created."

These were the kind of thoughts [5] which I turned over and over in my unhappy heart, a heart overburdened with those biting cares that came from my fear of death and my failure to discover the truth. Yet the faith of your Christ, our Lord and Saviour, professed in the Catholic Church, remained steadfastly fixed in my heart, even though it was on many points still unformed and swerving from the right rule of doctrine. But, nevertheless, my mind did not abandon it, but rather drank more and more deeply of it every day.

By this time too I had rejected the fallacious forecasts and impious ravings of the astrologers. . . .

But then, after reading these books of the Platonists which taught me to seek for a truth which was incorporeal, I came to see your *invisible things, understood by those things which are made*. I fell back again from this point, but still I had an apprehension of what, through the darkness

---

[5] The long and complex foregoing discussion of "the problem of evil" relates, on the one hand, to Augustine's rejection of Manicheanism, which explained evil by identifying it with matter, and, on the other, to his own important speculations on the problem of free will and predestination.—ED.

of my mind, I was not able to contemplate; I was certain that you are and that you are infinite, yet not in the sense of being diffused through space whether infinite or finite: that you truly are, and are always the same, not in any part or by any motion different or otherwise: also that all other things are from you, as is proved most certainly by the mere fact that they exist. On all these points I was perfectly certain, but I was still too weak to be able to enjoy you. I talked away as if I were a finished scholar; but, if I had not sought the way to you in Christ our Saviour, what would have been finished would have been my soul. For I had begun to want to have the reputation of a wise man; my punishment was within me, but I did not weep; I was merely puffed up with my knowledge. Where was that charity which builds from the foundation of humility, the foundation which is Christ Jesus? Humility was not a subject which those books would ever have taught me. Yet I believe that you wanted me to come upon these books before I made a study of your Scriptures. You wanted the impression made by them on me to be printed in my memory, so that when later I had become, as it were, tamed by your books (your fingers dressing my wounds), I should be able to see clearly what the difference is between presumption and confession, between those who see their goal without seeing how to get there and those who see the way which leads to that happy country which is there for us not only to perceive but to live in. For if I had been first trained in your Scriptures and by my familiarity with them had found you growing sweet to me, and had then afterward come upon these books of the Platonists, it is possible that they might have swept me away from the solid basis of piety; or, even if I had held firmly to that healthy disposition which I had imbibed, I might have thought that the same disposition could be acquired by someone who had read only the Platonic books.[6]

So I most greedily seized upon the venerable writings of your spirit and in particular the works of the apostle Paul. In the past it had sometimes seemed to me that he contradicted himself and that what he said conflicted with the testimonies of the law and the prophets; but all these difficulties had now disappeared; I saw one and the same face of pure eloquence and learned *to rejoice with trembling*. Having begun, I discovered that everything in the Platonists which I had found true was expressed here, but it was expressed to the glory of your grace. . . .

Augustine, convinced now on the intellectual plane, retires to a garden with his friend Alypius, who had accompanied him from Africa—and the controversy "in my heart" begins.

[6] This is a reference to the Neoplatonic writings that Augustine had again taken up with renewed interest. These works had long been esteemed by the Christians as being an aid to faith. Notice that they are so regarded by Augustine.—ED.

So went the controversy in my heart—about self, and self against self. And Alypius stayed close by me, waiting silently to see how this strange agitation of mine would end.

And now from my hidden depths my searching thought had dragged up and set before the sight of my heart the whole mass of my misery. Then a huge storm rose up within me bringing with it a huge downpour of tears. So that I might pour out all these tears and speak the words that came with them I rose up from Alypius (solitude seemed better for the business of weeping) and went further away so that I might not be embarrassed even by his presence. This was how I felt and he realized it. No doubt I had said something or other, and he could feel the weight of my tears in the sound of my voice. And so I rose to my feet, and he, in a state of utter amazement, remained in the place where we had been sitting. I flung myself down on the ground somehow under a fig tree and gave free rein to my tears; they streamed and flooded from my eyes, an *acceptable sacrifice to Thee*. And I kept saying to you, not perhaps in these words, but with this sense: *"And Thou, O Lord, how long? How long, Lord; wilt Thou be angry forever? Remember not our former iniquities."* For I felt that it was these which were holding me fast. And in my misery I would exclaim: "How long, how long this 'tomorrow and tomorrow'? Why not now? Why not finish this very hour with my uncleanness?"

So I spoke, weeping in the bitter contrition of my heart. Suddenly a voice reaches my ears from a nearby house. It is the voice of a boy or a girl (I don't know which) and in a kind of singsong the words are constantly repeated: "Take it and read it. Take it and read it." At once my face changed, and I began to think carefully of whether the singing of words like these came into any kind of game which children play, and I could not remember that I had ever heard anything like it before. I checked the force of my tears and rose to my feet, being quite certain that I must interpret this as a divine command to me to open the book and read the first passage which I should come upon. For I had heard this about Antony[7]: he had happened to come in when the Gospel was being read, and as though the words read were spoken directly to himself, had received the admonition: *Go, sell that thou hast, and give to the poor, and thou shalt have treasure in heaven, and come and follow me.* And by such an oracle he had been immediately converted to you.

So I went eagerly back to the place where Alypius was sitting, since it was there that I had left the book of the Apostle when I rose to my feet. I snatched up the book, opened it, and read in silence the passage upon which my eyes first fell: *Not in rioting and drunkenness, not in chambering and wantonness, not in strife and envying: but put ye on the Lord Jesus*

---

[7] The Egyptian desert hermit, St. Anthony. Augustine and his friends had only recently heard the whole miraculous story of St. Anthony from a mutual friend who had visited them. Thus it was much in his mind.—ED.

Christ, and make not provision for the flesh in concupiscence. I had no wish to read further; there was no need to. For immediately I had reached the end of this sentence it was as though my heart was filled with a light of confidence and all the shadows of my doubt were swept away.

A New Look
at the Confessions
PETER BROWN

What does modern scholarship have to say about this book, which has fascinated readers for more than fifteen hundred years? There is no better work for such an examination than the well-received, recent critical biography of Augustine by the young Oxford scholar Peter Brown.

Peter Brown treats the Confessions *as a source for the understanding of Augustine's inner self, his emotional disposition and intellectual growth. But Brown also has a synoptic view of the vast scholarship on this work, as on every writing of Augustine, and that scholarship is brought to bear in his conclusions about the* Confessions.

WANDERING, TEMPTATIONS, sad thoughts of mortality and the search for truth: these had always been the stuff of autobiography for fine souls, who refused to accept superficial security. Pagan philosophers had already created a tradition of "religious autobiography" in this vein: it will be continued by Christians in the fourth century, and will reach its climax in the *Confessions* of S. Augustine.

Augustine, therefore, did not need to look far to find an audience for the *Confessions*. It had been created for him quite recently, by the amazing spread of asceticism in the Latin world. The *Confessions* was a book for the *servi Dei,* for the "servants of God," it is a classic document of the tastes of a group of highly sophisticated men, the *spiritales,* the "men of the spirit." It told such men just what they wanted to know about—the course of a notable conversion; it asked of its readers what they made a habit of asking for themselves—the support of their prayers. It even contained moving appeals to the men who might join this new élite: to the austere Manichee and the pagan Platonist, still standing aloof from the crowded basilicas of the Christians. . . .

The *Confessions* is very much the book of a man who had come to regard his past as a training for his present career. Thus, Augustine will select as important, incidents and problems that immediately betray the new bishop of Hippo. He had come to believe that the understanding and exposition of the Scriptures was the heart of a bishop's life. His relations with the Scriptures, therefore, come to form a constant theme throughout the *Confessions*. His conversion to the Manichees, for instance, is now diagnosed, not in terms of a philosophical preoccupation with the origin of evil, but as a failure to accept the Bible. We see Ambrose through the eyes of a fellow-professional: we meet him as a preacher and exegete, facing the Christian people in the basilica, not as the connoisseur of Plotinus.[8] Augustine remembered how, in his early days in Milan, he had seen the distant figure of Ambrose as a bishop, from the outside only. Now a bishop himself, he will ensure that he will not be seen in this way: he will tell his readers exactly how he still had to struggle with his own temptations; and in the last three books of the *Confessions,* as he meditates on the opening lines of the book of *Genesis,* he will carry his readers with him into his thoughts as he, also, sat in his study, as he had once seen Ambrose sit, wrapt in the silent contemplation of an open page. . . .

The *Confessions,* therefore, is not a book of reminiscences. They are an anxious turning to the past. The note of urgency is unmistakable. "Allow me, I beseech You, grant me to wind round and round in my present memory the spirals of my errors. . . ."

It is also a poignant book. In it, one constantly senses the tension between the "then" of the young man and the "now" of the bishop. The past can come very close: its powerful and complex emotions have only recently passed away; we can still feel their contours through the thin layer of new feeling that has grown over them. . . .

Augustine had been forced to come to terms with himself. The writing of the *Confessions* was an act of therapy. The many attempts to explain the book in terms of a single, external provocation, or of a single, philosophical *idée fixe,* ignore the life that runs through it. In this attempt to find himself, every single fibre in Augustine's middle age grew together with every other, to make the *Confessions* what it is. . . .

The *Confessions* are a masterpiece of strictly intellectual autobiography. Augustine communicates such a sense of intense personal involvement in the ideas he is handling, that we are made to forget that it is an exceptionally difficult book. Augustine paid his audience of *spiritales* the great (perhaps the unmerited) compliment of talking to them, as if they were as

---

[8] The third-century Alexandrian scholar who really created Neoplatonism. He was a great favorite of St. Ambrose.

steeped in Neo-Platonic philosophy as himself. His Manichaean phase, for instance, is discussed in terms of ideas on which the Platonists regarded themselves as far in advance of the average thought of their age, the ideas of a "spiritual" reality, and of the omnipresence of God. . . .

It is often said that the *Confessions* is not an "autobiography" in the modern sense. This is true, but not particularly helpful. Because, for a Late Roman man, it is precisely this intense, autobiographical vein in the *Confessions,* that sets it apart from the intellectual tradition to which Augustine belonged.

It is more important to realize that the *Confessions* is an autobiography in which the author has imposed a drastic, fully-conscious choice of what is significant. The *Confessions* are, quite succinctly, the story of Augustine's "heart," or of his "feelings"—his *affectus.* An intellectual event, such as the reading of a new book, is registered only, as it were, from the inside, in terms of the sheer excitement of the experience, of its impact on Augustine's feelings: of the *Hortensius* of Cicero, for instance, he would never say "it changed my views" but, so characteristically, "it changed my way of feeling"—*mutavit affectum meum.*

The emotional tone of the *Confessions* strikes any modern reader. The book owes its lasting appeal to the way in which Augustine, in his middle-age, had dared to open himself up to the feelings of his youth. Yet, such a tone was not inevitable. Augustine's intense awareness of the vital role of "feeling" in his past life had come to grow upon him. . . .

Seeing that Augustine wrote his *Confessions* "remembering my wicked ways, thinking them over again in bitterness," it is amazing how little of this bitterness he has allowed to colour his past feelings. They are not made pale by regret: it is plainly the autobiography of a man who, even as a schoolboy, had known what it was to be moved only by "delight," to be bored by duty, who had enjoyed fully what he had enjoyed: " 'One and one is two, two and two is four,' this was a hateful jingle to me: and the greatest treat of all, that sweet illusion—the Wooden Horse full of armed men, Troy burning and the very ghost of Creusa.". . .

Augustine analyses his past feelings with ferocious honesty. They were too important to him to be falsified by sentimental stereotypes. It is not that he had abandoned strong feeling: he merely believed it possible to transform feelings, to direct them more profitably. This involved scrutinizing them intently. . . .

The *Confessions* are one of the few books of Augustine's, where the title is significant. *Confessio* meant, for Augustine, "accusation of oneself; praise of God." In this one word, he had summed up his attitude to the human condition: it was the new key with which he hoped, in middle age, to unlock the riddle of evil.

The Age of Augustine:
The Pagan-Christian Tradition
M. L. W. LAISTNER

*While the searing, intensely personal conversion experience of Augustine
was clearly unique—and would have been unique for such a man in
any age—both Augustine and the church he finally came to embrace
were the end products of a long and complex accommodation that
we must examine in order to set both the man and the institution in
the age to which they belonged.*

*The earliest converts to Christianity were, if not "slaves and
outcasts," at least humble men, like its earliest preachers, the "weak and
simple apostles." But Christianity did not remain simple. In the course
of the second and third centuries—perhaps even earlier—the flourishing
new cult attracted in increasing numbers men who were the products
of the schools of rhetoric and philosophy that had been established
in every city of the empire. As it fought its way to recognition, Christianity
had to answer the philosophic questions posed by both its antagonists
and its converts. In this inherent conflict between the fanatic spiritualism
of early Christianity and the logical rationalism of the classical
philosophic tradition lay one of the gravest problems the early church
had to face. The problem manifested itself in the form of doctrinal
disputes so bitter and prolonged that they threatened the very existence
of the church. But out of the debates that roiled about these controversies,
the church gradually developed its doctrine. And in the process, the
disparate elements of the pagan intellectual tradition and the Christian
spiritual tradition were reconciled. Augustine played a major role in
that process, combining in himself the disparate elements of the
accommodation.*

*To put the age of Augustine in perspective, we turn to the work of
the great modern Anglo-American scholar M. L. W. Laistner (d. 1959).
Laistner devoted most of his impressive scholarship to the problem of the
transmission of the classical intellectual tradition to the Middle Ages.
Augustine and the age of Augustine were crucial to that process. The
following selection is from the last and one of the best of Laistner's
books,* Thought and Letters in Western Europe A.D. 500 to 900.

THE POLICY OF religious toleration adopted by Constantine and Licinius radically altered the position of the Christian minorities in the Empire. The communities of the Faithful, which for three centuries had been either illicit organizations, or, even when tolerated by the highest authority, were without legal status, now came into the category of permitted associations. The Christians, who hitherto had always been liable to suffer individually or in groups because of occasional outbursts of popular hostility in the several provinces of the Roman world, and in whose lives for sixty years (251–311) a precarious toleration had alternated with rigorous persecution by the imperial Government, could now live in and by their faith without let or hindrance. Moreover, if religious differences provoked disturbances of the peace, the Christians could, if wronged, claim the redress under the law that was the right of all citizens, whatever their religious beliefs. Within less than a decade from 313 the Church had secured from the emperor the right to corporate ownership of property, and like other lawful associations, could receive testamentary bequests. As a result the wealth of the Church grew with remarkable swiftness. Even if nothing further had developed from these changes they would have been noteworthy enough; actually the fourth century witnessed a transformation which deserves to be called revolutionary. With the exception of Julian, all the emperors from Constantine I were Christian rulers. The adherents of a religion which was not only permitted but fostered by the imperial family increased with such rapidity that at the death of Theodosius I in A.D. 395 the Christians in the Empire were in a marked majority. . . .

Long before 313 the ecclesiastical organization had travelled a long way from the simple system of the primitive Church. The democratic election of elders by each congregation had been gradually superseded, as a purely parochial arrangement no longer sufficed for a steadily expanding body, by a monarchic method of government which developed side by side with the growth of a more elaborate hierarchy. In the fourth century this evolution became more rapid than before. The Church which waxed so quickly in size and authority began to derive inspiration from the civil law of the Empire for her own purposes. From this and from the decisions of councils and synods, over and above the authority of the Bible and tradition handed down from Apostolic times, there developed, slowly but steadily, the impressive body of canon law. So, too, in the matter of administration: the organization of the temporal State seems to have served as a model for the ecclesiastical. . . .

The transmutation of a despised cult into a State religion was not effected without moral and spiritual loss. All too often worldliness and love of the good things of this life contrasted glaringly with the lofty ethics of the primitive Christian communities, even as they gave the lie to the efficacy of the Church's teaching whose moral standards had not been lowered. Not less painful is the effect produced by contemplating the disunion and

often rancorous quarrels in the Christian body as a whole, and their concomitant religious intolerance. . . .

The attitude of Christian thinkers to pagan education and literature,
which brought in its train the problem how best to instruct the children
of Christians, is a question of some complexity. . . . When Christianity
early in the fourth century became "a lawful religion," there would indeed
have been no danger or illegality in the establishment of specifically
Christian schools; but there were nevertheless in practice very real difficulties to overcome, especially in the western half of the Empire. Although
the Latin Church by then could boast of Tertullian, Cyprian, Victorinus of
Pettau, Arnobius, and Lactantius, their writings were not suitable as
school-books. There were no treatises on grammar, rhetoric, or any of
the liberal arts save those by pagan authors; and, while there was no
danger to orthodoxy in declensions, conjugations, and, in short, the rules
of idiomatic language and composition, the illustrations from literature
which were sown broadcast through the more popular text-books of grammar and rhetoric were from infidel prose writers and poets. At every turn
the Christian boy or youth was familiarized with pagan mythology, and
with aspects of pagan literature and thought which the leaders of the
Church were bound to disapprove. Thus there existed a dilemma from
which there was no escape for those who were willing to seek a compromise.

The extreme attitude in the earlier period is well exemplified by Tertullian who fiercely attacked pagan letters. His famous aphorism, "the philosophers are the patriarchs of the heretics," illustrates the danger to which,
in his view, well-to-do Christians were exposed if they were subjected to
the higher education of the day. He would have liked, too, to forbid Christians to teach the literature of the heathen; yet he was bound to advise
sending children to school. This could only mean handing them over to
the *litterator* or *grammaticus,* in other words, giving them the same education as their pagan contemporaries. How far the safeguard which he
advocates, that the young should first have received some religious instruction at home, was effective, it would be rash to surmise. And in at least
one passage Tertullian admits that the study of philosophy might have some
value and that ignorance can be more dangerous than knowledge. . . .

Both Jerome and Augustine had pondered more deeply on educational
theory and practice, and on the place of non-Christian literature in a
scheme of Christian education. Both men had enjoyed the best secular
education available in their day, Jerome in Rome, Augustine at Madaura
and in Carthage, whose schools were reputed amongst the best in the
Empire. Both again were experienced teachers. . . .

Augustine, like Jerome, had passed with distinction through the schools
of the *grammaticus* and *rhetor;* but unlike his older contemporary, he was
himself for a decade a teacher of rhetoric in Africa, in Rome, and finally

in Milan. From several of his works it is possible to ascertain with some distinctness his earlier and his later views on the education of a Christian. He himself has recorded the profound impression left upon his youthful mind—he was nineteen years old at the time—by the study of Cicero's *Hortensius.* The purpose of this treatise, which has not survived, was to serve as an introduction to the study of philosophy (and, more particularly, to Cicero's own works in this field), and at the same time to combat prevailing misconceptions about the value of philosophical speculations. The effect of its perusal on the young Augustine was far-reaching. It was an antidote to the one-sided rhetorical training which had hitherto fallen to his lot. It started that deep admiration for Cicero which remained with him to the end of his life. It gave a new direction to his intellectual activity by leading him to some interest in science and to a study of philosophy, particularly Neoplatonism. The steadily deepening understanding which came to him from constant application to these subjects ultimately caused him to reject the Manichaean heresy to which he had adhered for a few years. The treatise, *De ordine,* composed in 386 at Cassiciacum near Milan, a retreat to which he had withdrawn with a few friends after his conversion to the orthodox Faith, is a dialogue having as its theme the order existing in the Universe, and the position and significance of evil therein. The existence of order and method throughout the Universe is illustrated incidentally from divers human examples, amongst others from the liberal arts. As one would expect from a Ciceronian and an ex-teacher, his attitude is liberal and even enthusiastic. . . .

But Augustine's most elaborate contribution to educational theory is the long treatise, *De doctrina Christiana.* . . .

There are many passages in the *De doctrina Christiana* which show Augustine striving for some mean between practical necessity and orthodoxy. He deserves all credit for being the first to write a comprehensive guide for the education of the Christian teacher; a book, moreover, which became a standard work in the Middle Ages. At the same time those parts which deal with the liberal arts, in which the standard of attainment regarded as needful is still elementary, reflect the low level to which the intellectual life of the later Empire had declined. One may also wonder whether, if he had completed his encyclopedia of the liberal arts, the treatment of each subject and the standard aimed at would have been more exacting; and whether such a work would have been able to displace the older pagan treatises in the monasteries and Christian schools of the earlier Middle Ages. In Books II and III Augustine is fain to admit the need of the liberal arts but, like other Christian thinkers before him, he urges that their study should cease as early as possible; and science—he is thinking particularly of astronomy—is dangerous because it may lead the student to belief in astrology which was so prevalent during the later Empire. In Book IV, written a year before the *Retractations,* he tries to prove that there is no necessity for profane literature in training the Christian preacher or orator, because the Scriptures provide all necessary material for illustration. . . . [But] what did Augustine himself do in composing Book IV of the *De doctrina Christiana?* He adapted Cicero's *Orator* to Christian needs, even as the first Latin treatise on Christian ethics, Ambrose's *De officiis,* was modelled on Cicero's dialogue of the same name. Augustine took his illustrations from Christian authors, but the framework of the whole is closely modelled on the *Orator.* Thus the love and admiration for Rome's greatest orator was never quenched in Augustine's heart. And the noble and impressive chapters which conclude the *De doctrina Christiana* (IV, 28 and 29) are the utterance not of a narrow doctrinaire but of a man who can recognize and welcome truth wheresoever he may find it.

Suggestions for Further Reading

ST. AUGUSTINE WAS not only an important and influential thinker, he was also a prolific writer, and students are encouraged to read more extensively in his works—certainly to read further in *The Confessions* and at least to try the book generally considered Augustine's most influential work, *The City of God.* Both works are available in a number of editions. For *The City of God,* because of its size and complexity, students may prefer St. Augustine, *The City of God, An Abridged Version,* tr. Gerald G. Walsh, D. B. Zema, Grace Monahan, and D. J. Honan, ed. and intro. V. J. Bourke (New York: Doubleday, 1958). For a further sampling *An Augustine Reader,* ed. John J. O'Meara (New York: Doubleday, 1973) or *Basic Writings of St. Augustine,* ed. Whitney J. Oates, 2 vols. (New York: Random House, 1948) are recommended.

There is a wilderness of interpretive and explanatory writing about Augustine and his thought, most of it recondite in the extreme, but there are some useful aids. The most readily available and one of the most generally useful is *A Companion to the Study of St. Augustine,* ed. Roy W. Battenhouse (New York: Oxford University Press, 1955). A more strictly theological guide of the same sort is Eugène Portalié, *A Guide to the Thought of St. Augustine,* intro. V. J. Bourke, tr. R. J. Bastian (Chicago: Regnery, 1960), the republication and translation of a famous essay from a French dictionary of Catholic theology at the turn of the century.

Equally orthodox but more lively and readable is Etienne Gilson, *The Christian Philosophy of St. Augustine*, tr. L. E. M. Lynch (New York: Random House, 1960), a standard work of interpretation by the greatest Catholic authority on medieval philosophy. More specifically, students can read from a well-selected series of modern critical essays, *Saint Augustine, His Age, Life and Thought* (Cleveland and New York: Meridian, 1969).

Of a more biographical nature is Frederik van der Meer, *Augustine the Bishop* (London and New York: Sheed and Ward, 1961), a classic work dealing in great detail essentially with Augustine as Bishop of Hippo, the city, its people, the area, and the controversies that involved its famous bishop. Three of those controversies—the Manichaean, the Donatist, and the Pelagian—are examined in considerable detail in Gerald Bonner, *St. Augustine of Hippo, Life and Controversies* (Philadelphia: Westminster Press, 1963).

There is no lack of books dealing with the historical setting of Augustine and Augustinianism or with late antiquity and the early Middle Ages. Two of the old standard works are still among the best: Ferdinand Lot, *The End of the Ancient World and the Beginnings of the Middle Ages*, tr. Philip and Mariette Leon (New York: Barnes and Noble, 1953 [1931]), and Samuel Dill, *Roman Society in the Last Century of the Western Empire* (London: Macmillan, 1898). One of the best recent accounts of the rise of Christianity within late Roman antiquity is R. A. Markus, *Christianity in the Roman World* (New York: Scribners, 1974). Finally, students will find useful (if somewhat heavyweight) a fundamental work of reference, A. H. M. Jones, *The Later Roman Empire 284–602, A Social, Economic, and Administrative Survey*, 2 vols. (Norman: University of Oklahoma Press, 1964).

Charlemagne
and the First Europe

The world of late Roman antiquity that had shaped the mind and spirit of St. Augustine was already, even in his own lifetime, crumbling under the impact of the Germanic barbarian invasions. His great reflection on history, *The City of God,* was written in response to the fall of the city of Rome to the Visigoths in 410, and as he lay dying in the year 430 his own episcopal city of Hippo was under siege by the Vandals. Within another century, the Roman political order in the west had disappeared completely, to be replaced by a number of regional barbarian kingdoms under their German tribal chiefs. The Roman world had entered irretrievably upon what an earlier generation of historians was fond of calling "the Dark Ages."

Though the darkness was by no means as pervasive as scholars once thought, the early Middle Ages were a time of great dislocation, surely one of the two or three most important periods of transition in the history of western civilization—for the product of the transition was nothing less than what some historians have called "the first Europe."

It was a Europe no longer classical and imperial, no longer a vast free-trade network of cities governed by a centralized system and ruled by a common law. It was a Europe from which long distance trade had disappeared, to be replaced by an economic localism. It was a Europe of equally localized culture, in which the common classical tradition was maintained by an ever dwindling minority of educated people, with an

131

ever decreasing sophistication. Most, virtually all, of those educated
were professional churchmen, for, perhaps most important of all, the first
Europe was a Christian Europe.

The great Frankish king Charlemagne (768–814) was, by all accounts
and from whatever interpretive viewpoint we choose to see him, the
pivotal figure in this first Europe. The Franks were one of the barbarian
Germanic tribes that succeeded to the broken pieces of the western
empire. By a combination of luck, talent, and timing, they had come to be
the leading power among their fellow barbarians. Their position was
enhanced by Charlemagne's immediate predecessors, his grandfather
Charles Martel and his father, Pepin, who established the claim of his
house to the Frankish kingdom. Frankish supremacy was assured by
Charlemagne's dramatic conquests, which brought most of continental
western Europe—save only Moslem Spain south of the Ebro River,
southern Italy, and the barbarian fringes of the Scandinavian North—
under his rule.

Charlemagne's imperial rule was epitomized in his resumption of the
ancient imperial title. On Christmas day of the year 800, in the church
of St. Peter in Rome, Pope Leo III crowned Charlemagne as "Emperor
of the Romans." No one had claimed this exalted title in more than
three hundred years, and no barbarian king had ever before presumed
to such a dignity. Charlemagne continued to bear his other titles, so
we are not sure precisely how he himself saw his imperial role—whether it
was an "umbrella" title over his many different dominions, a Christian
symbol for "the temporal sword," or simply "a feather in his cap."
We do know that it involved him in a delicate and complex negotiation
with the other "Emperor of the Romans" in Byzantium, whose rights,
however remotely exercised, Charlemagne's act had encroached upon.
The assumption of the title, moreover, by virtue of the part played by
the pope, was inextricably bound up with the larger role of the church
in the secular affairs of the West.

We cannot be sure what Charlemagne's plans for his empire were,
although he saw to the imperial succession of his son Louis the Pious.
We cannot even be certain of the extent to which Charles was able to
realize the plans he did have, for the records of the time simply do not
tell us.

But however many unanswered questions remain, the records do
contain a precious contemporary account of King Charles, written by his
devoted friend, the Frankish noble Einhard.

The Emperor Charlemagne
EINHARD

*One of the most obvious signs of the barbarism of early medieval Europe
is the scarcity of records. Even more scarce than documentary records
are the literary accounts—the biographies, the memoirs, the formal
histories—that can give flesh and substance to historical figures. Most,
even the greatest, personages of the early Middle Ages remain simply
names, with only a handful of facts (and often doubtful "facts" at that)
attached to them. Fortunately, this is not the case for Charlemagne.
We might wish that Einhard's account had been longer and more detailed,
or that he had included more information about Charles' public policy,
his political motives, his plans for the empire, and the structure of
his reign. But we are lucky to have what we do. Einhard was sensitive
about his modest literary gifts. Indeed, he could not even conceive of a
formal framework for his account; he simply took Suetonius's biography
of Augustus and substituted his own material in the model. But so
indebted was Einhard to Charles, his "lord and foster father," and so
important were his lord's deeds that he chose to record them rather "than
to suffer the most glorious life of this most excellent king, the greatest of
all the princes of his day, and his illustrious deeds, hard for men of
later times to imitate, to be wrapped in the darkness of oblivion."* [1]

Despite its limitations, Einhard's Life of Charlemagne *is an extraordinarily valuable document. It would have been under any circumstances. But
its value is enhanced because Einhard was an intimate of the king and
his family; he had been raised at Charles' court and later was one of
his most trusted councillors. No one was in a better position than Einhard
to write on Charles the Great.*

*After sketching the background of Charles' dynasty and how the
Carolingians (for this is the name historians have given to the house
of* Carolus Magnus*) succeeded to the Frankish throne, how Charles' father,
Pepin, set aside the last of the weak Merovingians with their "vain title
of king," Einhard describes in some detail the wars of conquest that
earned for Charles the title "Charles the Great"—his pacification of
Aquitaine, his conquest of the Lombards and his assumption of the
Lombard crown, his long wars with the pagan Saxons along the eastern
frontier, his unsuccessful attempt to invade Moslem Spain, his successful*

---

[1] *The Life of Charlemagne by Einhard* (Ann Arbor: University of Michigan
Press, 1960), Preface, p. 16. Translated from the *Monumenta Germaniae* by
Samuel Epes Turner.

*quelling of the revolt of Bavaria, and his wars against the Avars along
the Danube, the Danes, and other border peoples. Then Einhard continues:*

SUCH ARE THE wars, most skilfully planned and successfully fought, which
this most powerful king waged during the forty-seven years of his reign.
He so largely increased the Frank kingdom, which was already great and
strong when he received it at his father's hands, that more than double its
former territory was added to it. The authority of the Franks was formerly
confined to that part of Gaul included between the Rhine and the Loire,
the Ocean and the Balearic Sea; to that part of Germany which is inhabited
by the so-called Eastern Franks, and is bounded by Saxony and the Danube,
the Rhine and the Saale—this stream separates the Thuringians from the
Sorabians; and to the country of the Alemanni and Bavarians. By the wars
above mentioned he first made tributary Aquitania, Gascony, and the
whole of the region of the Pyrenees as far as the River Ebro, which rises
in the land of the Navarrese, flows through the most fertile districts of
Spain, and empties into the Balearic Sea, beneath the walls of the city of
Tortosa. He next reduced and made tributary all Italy from Aosta to
Lower Calabria, where the boundary line runs between the Beneventans
and the Greeks, a territory more than a thousand miles long; then Saxony,
which constitutes no small part of Germany, and is reckoned to be twice
as wide as the country inhabited by the Franks, while about equal to it
in length; in addition, both Pannonias, Dacia beyond the Danube, and
Istria, Liburnia, and Dalmatia, except the cities on the coast, which he
left to the Greek Emperor for friendship's sake, and because of the treaty
that he had made with him. In fine, he vanquished and made tributary
all the wild and barbarous tribes dwelling in Germany between the Rhine
and the Vistula, the Ocean and the Danube, all of which speak very much
the same language, but differ widely from one another in customs and dress.
The chief among them are the Welatabians, the Sorabians, the Abodriti, and
the Bohemians, and he had to make war upon these; but the rest, by far
the larger number, submitted to him of their own accord.

He added to the glory of his reign by gaining the good will of several
kings and nations. . . . His relations with Aaron, King of the Persians,[2]
who ruled over almost the whole of the East, India excepted, were so
friendly that this prince preferred his favor to that of all the kings and
potentates of the earth, and considered that to him alone marks of honor
and munificence were due. Accordingly, when the ambassadors sent by
Charles to visit the most holy sepulchre and place of resurrection of our

[2] This was the famous Harun al-Raschid (786–809), not "King of the Persians"
but the Abbasid Caliph of Baghdad, with whom Charles did indeed enjoy good
diplomatic relations. Harun was most likely interested in a possible alliance against
the Byzantine Empire.—ED.

Lord and Savior presented themselves before him with gifts, and made known their master's wishes, he not only granted what was asked, but gave possession of that holy and blessed spot. When they returned, he dispatched his ambassadors with them, and sent magnificent gifts, besides stuffs, perfumes, and other rich products of the Eastern lands. A few years before this, Charles had asked him for an elephant, and he sent the only one that he had. The Emperors of Constantinople, Nicephorus, Michael, and Leo, made advances to Charles, and sought friendship and alliance with him by several embassies; and even when the Greeks suspected him of designing to wrest the empire from them, because of his assumption of the title Emperor, they made a close alliance with him, that he might have no cause of offense. In fact, the power of the Franks was always viewed by the Greeks and Romans with a jealous eye, whence the Greek proverb "Have the Frank for your friend, but not for your neighbor." . . .

He liked foreigners, and was at great pains to take them under his protection. There were often so many of them, both in the palace and the kingdom, that they might reasonably have been considered a nuisance; but he, with his broad humanity, was very little disturbed by such annoyances, because he felt himself compensated for these great inconveniences by the praises of his generosity and the reward of high renown.

Charles was large and strong, and of lofty stature, though not disproportionately tall (his height is well known to have been seven times the length of his foot); the upper part of his head was round, his eyes very large and animated, nose a little long, hair fair, and face laughing and merry. Thus his appearance was always stately and dignified, whether he was standing or sitting; although his neck was thick and somewhat short, and his belly rather prominent; but the symmetry of the rest of his body concealed these defects. His gait was firm, his whole carriage manly, and his voice clear, but not so strong as his size led one to expect. His health was excellent, except during the four years preceding his death, when he was subject to frequent fevers; at the last he even limped a little with one foot. Even in those years he consulted rather his own inclinations than the advice of physicians, who were almost hateful to him, because they wanted him to give up roasts, to which he was accustomed, and to eat boiled meat instead. In accordance with the national custom, he took frequent exercise on horseback and in the chase, accomplishments in which scarcely any people in the world can equal the Franks. He enjoyed the exhalations from natural warm springs, and often practiced swimming, in which he was such an adept that none could surpass him; and hence it was that he built his palace at Aix-la-Chapelle, and lived there constantly during his latter years until his death. He used not only to invite his sons to his bath, but his nobles and friends, and now and then a troop of his retinue or bodyguard, so that a hundred or more persons sometimes bathed with him.

He used to wear the national, that is to say, the Frank, dress—next his skin a linen shirt and linen breeches, and above these a tunic fringed with silk; while hose fastened by bands covered his lower limbs, and shoes his feet, and he protected his shoulders and chest in winter by a close-fitting coat of otter or marten skins. Over all he flung a blue cloak, and he always had a sword girt about him, usually one with a gold or silver hilt and belt; he sometimes carried a jeweled sword, but only on great feastdays or at the reception of ambassadors from foreign nations. He despised foreign costumes, however handsome, and never allowed himself to be robed in them, except twice in Rome, when he donned the Roman tunic, chlamys, and shoes; the first time at the request of Pope Hadrian, the second to gratify Leo, Hadrian's successor. On great feastdays he made use of embroidered clothes and shoes bedecked with precious stones, his cloak was fastened by a golden buckle, and he appeared crowned with a diadem of gold and gems, but on other days his dress varied little from the common dress of the people.

Charles was temperate in eating, and particularly so in drinking, for he abominated drunkenness in anybody, much more in himself and those of his household. . . . Charles had the gift of ready and fluent speech, and could express whatever he had to say with the utmost clearness. He was not satisfied with command of his native language merely, but gave attention to the study of foreign ones, and in particular was such a master of Latin that he could speak it as well as his native tongue; but he could understand Greek better than he could speak it. He was so eloquent, indeed, that he might have passed for a teacher of eloquence. He most zealously cultivated the liberal arts, held those who taught them in great esteem, and conferred great honors upon them. He took lessons in grammar of the deacon Peter of Pisa, at that time an aged man. Another deacon, Albin of Britain, surnamed Alcuin, a man of Saxon extraction, who was the greatest scholar of the day, was his teacher in other branches of learning. The King spent much time and labor with him studying rhetoric, dialectics, and especially astronomy; he learned to reckon, and used to investigate the motions of the heavenly bodies most curiously, with an intelligent scrutiny. He also tried to write, and used to keep tablets and blanks in bed under his pillow, that at leisure hours he might accustom his hand to form the letters; however, as he did not begin his efforts in due season, but late in life, they met with ill success.[3]

He cherished with the greatest fervor and devotion the principles of the Christian religion, which had been instilled into him from infancy. Hence it was that he built the beautiful basilica at Aix-la-Chapelle, which he adorned with gold and silver and lamps, and with rails and doors of solid brass. He had the columns and marbles for this structure brought from Rome and Ravenna, for he could not find such as were suitable elsewhere. . . .

---

[3] What is probably meant here is not that Charles literally could not write but that he could not master the precise and beautiful "book hand," the Carolingian Minuscule, developed by Alcuin for the use of the court copyists.—ED.

He was very forward in succoring the poor, and in that gratuitous generosity which the Greeks call alms, so much so that he not only made a point of giving in his own country and his own kingdom, but when he discovered that there were Christians living in poverty in Syria, Egypt, and Africa, at Jerusalem, Alexandria, and Carthage, he had compassion on their wants, and used to send money over the seas to them. The reason that he zealously strove to make friends with the kings beyond seas was that he might get help and relief to the Christians living under their rule. He cherished the Church of St. Peter the Apostle at Rome above all other holy and sacred places, and heaped its treasury with a vast wealth of gold, silver, and precious stones. He sent great and countless gifts to the popes, and throughout his whole reign the wish that he had nearest at heart was to re-establish the ancient authority of the city of Rome under his care and by his influence, and to defend and protect the Church of St. Peter, and to beautify and enrich it out of his own store above all other churches. Although he held it in such veneration, he only repaired to Rome to pay his vows and make his supplications four times during the whole forty-seven years that he reigned.

When he made his last journey thither, he had also other ends in view. The Romans had inflicted many injuries upon the Pontiff Leo, tearing out his eyes and cutting out his tongue, so that he had been compelled to call upon the King for help. Charles accordingly went to Rome, to set in order the affairs of the Church, which were in great confusion, and passed the whole winter there. It was then that he received the titles of Emperor and Augustus, to which he at first had such an aversion that he declared that he would not have set foot in the Church the day that they were conferred, although it was a great feastday, if he could have foreseen the design of the Pope. He bore very patiently with the jealousy which the Roman emperors showed upon his assuming these titles, for they took this step very ill; and by dint of frequent embassies and letters, in which he addressed them as brothers, he made their haughtiness yield to his magnanimity, a quality in which he was unquestionably much their superior.

It was after he had received the imperial name that, finding the laws of his people very defective (the Franks have two sets of laws, very different in many particulars [4]), he determined to add what was wanting, to reconcile the discrepancies, and to correct what was vicious and wrongly cited in them. However, he went no further in this matter than to supplement the laws by a few capitularies, and those imperfect ones; but he caused the unwritten laws of all the tribes that came under his rule to be compiled and reduced to writing. He also had the old rude songs that celebrate the deeds and wars of the ancient kings written out for transmission to posterity. He began a grammar of his native language. He gave the months names in his own tongue, in place of the Latin and barbarous names by which they were formerly known among the Franks. . . .

[4] The codes of the two Frankish tribes, the Salian and Ripuarian, that had combined to form the nation.—ED.

Toward the close of his life, when he was broken by ill-health and old age, he summoned Louis, King of Aquitania, his only surviving son by Hildegard, and gathered together all the chief men of the whole kingdom of the Franks in a solemn assembly. He appointed Louis, with their unanimous consent, to rule with himself over the whole kingdom, and constituted him heir to the imperial name; then, placing the diadem upon his son's head, he bade him be proclaimed Emperor and Augustus. This step was hailed by all present with great favor, for it really seemed as if God had prompted him to it for the kingdom's good; it increased the King's dignity, and struck no little terror into foreign nations. After sending his son back to Aquitania, although weak from age he set out to hunt, as usual, near his palace at Aix-la-Chapelle, and passed the rest of the autumn in the chase, returning thither about the first of November. While wintering there, he was seized, in the month of January, with a high fever, and took to his bed. As soon as he was taken sick, he prescribed for himself abstinence from food, as he always used to do in case of fever, thinking that the disease could be driven off, or at least mitigated, by fasting. Besides the fever, he suffered from a pain in the side, which the Greeks call pleurisy; but he still persisted in fasting, and in keeping up his strength only by draughts taken at very long intervals. He died January twenty-eighth, the seventh day from the time that he took to his bed, at nine o'clock in the morning, after partaking of the holy communion, in the seventy-second year of his age and the forty-seventh of his reign.

A New Portrait
of the Emperor
HEINRICH FICHTENAU

*We turn now from Einhard's contemporary account of Charlemagne
to the description by the modern Austrian medievalist Heinrich Fichtenau.
It is rather more a reconstruction than a description, for in* The
Carolingian Empire, The Age of Charlemagne, *Fichtenau goes beyond
Einhard's account to the other fragmentary records of Charles' age,
as well as to the best of modern Carolingian scholarship. Fichtenau's*

*work is a careful, even conservative, attempt to set Charlemagne securely
in his age. The result is a distinguished new portrait of the emperor to
set beside that of his adoring friend and subject.*

NO MAN'S STATURE is increased by the accumulation of myths, and nothing
is detracted from genuine historical greatness by the consideration of a
man's purely human side. In order to analyse an epoch it is necessary to
analyse the man who was its centre, who determined its character and who
was, at the same time, shaped and determined by it. It is therefore not mere
curiosity but an endeavour to fulfil the historian's task if we strive to pierce
and get behind the myth that has surrounded the figure of Charles. That
myth has been built up over a period of centuries and has tended to
conjure up in place of a tangible personality, full of vitality, the figure of
a timeless hero.

In the case of Charles—and that alone would justify our beginning with
him—we can even form a picture of his bodily physique. The bodily
appearance of his contemporaries, although we know their names and their
works, remains shadow-like for us to-day. But as far as Charles the Great
is concerned, we are not only in possession of his bodily remains but also
have an exact description of his appearance. It is true that Charles's
biographer Einhard borrowed the terms of his description from Suetonius.
Nevertheless it was possible for him to choose from among the numerous
biographies of the ancient emperors which he found in Suetonius those
expressions which were most applicable to his master. Einhard and his
contemporaries were especially struck by Charles's bodily size. Ever since
the opening of Charles's tomb in 1861 we have known that his actual height
was a full 6 feet 3½ inches. It was therefore not poetic licence when one
of the court-poets, describing the royal hunt, remarked: "The king, with
his broad shoulders, towers above everybody else." . . .

It is a pity that Einhard fails us when he describes Charles's personality,
for his description is entirely conventional. It had to be conventional, for,
although emperors may differ in physical build, they must all have the
same virtues, namely the imperial virtues without which nobody can be a
real emperor. Thus his description of Charles is couched in Aristotelian
and Stoic terms, such as *temperantia, patientia,* and *constantia animi.* And
in so far as Einhard attributed *magnanimitas* and *liberalitas* to Charles,
we can discern a mingling of ancient and Germanic princely ideals. When
the hospitality shown to foreign guests resulted in neglect of considerations
of public economy, Stoic *magnanimitas* was imperceptibly transformed into
Germanic "loftiness of spirit." For Charles "found in the reputation of
generosity and in the good fame that followed generous actions a compensation even for grave inconveniences."

The Stoic traits in Einhard's picture of Charles are, however, by no means insignificant. Many of Charles's counsellors must have drawn his attention to the fact that these traits were ideals that had been appropriate to his imperial predecessors and therefore appropriate for him. People must have appealed again and again to his *clementia,* a Stoic concept subsumed under *temperantia,* when it was a question of preventing the execution of conspirators, of liberating hostages, or of returning property that had been confiscated in punishment for an offence. Stoicism was, after all, allied with Christianity. A Christian ruler had to exercise self-control. If he indulged in *crudelitas* and raged against his enemies he was not far from the very opposite of a good king, the *rex iniquus* or tyrant.

Charles endeavoured in more than one sense to live up to the model of Stoic and Christian self-discipline. He could not tolerate drunkards in his palace. Banquets were held only on important feast days. Fasting, however, he deeply loathed. He often complained that it impaired his health. When he was an old man he conducted a long battle with his physicians who never succeeded in making him eat boiled meat in place of the roast to which he was accustomed. The fact that Einhard incorporated such stories in his biography and that a large number of almost humourous anecdotes, such as were collected later by Notker,[5] were recounted by his own contemporaries, shows that there was a very real difference between the late Roman, and especially the Byzantine, conception of the ruler, on one hand, and the Frankish conception, on the other. Charles did not observe in his court the stiff dignity and the ceremonious distance that became an emperor. In this respect he never modelled himself on anyone; he behaved naturally and revealed his true self.

There is no evidence that Charles ever withdrew from the people around him in order to ponder and work out his plans. He always needed the company of people, of his daughters, of his friends, and even of his menial retinue. He not only invited to his banquets everybody who happened to be about; he also gathered people for the hunt and even insisted that his magnates, his learned friends and his bodyguard were to be present when he was having a bath. The author of a poetical description of palace life at Aix-la-Chapelle refers repeatedly to the noisy bustle in the baths. It seems that Charles was happiest among the din of the hunt or in the midst of the building going on at Aix-la-Chapelle.

Charles was the centre of the whole kingdom—not only because it became him as ruler to be the centre, but also because it suited his temperament. Generally receptive, and approaching both science and scholarship with an open mind, he wanted to feel that he was at the centre of everything. It must have been an easy matter for court scholars, like Theodulf of Orléans, to persuade the king that his intellectual faculties were broader than the Nile, larger than the Danube and the Euphrates, and no less powerful than the Ganges. . . . As a rule the courtiers, and Alcuin

---

[5] A late Carolingian monastic chronicler.—ED.

among them, vied with each other in hiding from the king that there was any difference of quality between the achievements of ancient Christian civilization and their own. A new Rome or Athens was expected to arise in Aix-la-Chapelle, and they were anxious to emphasize their superiority over Byzantium, where government was in the hands of females and theology was riddled with errors. Charles required all the fresh naturalness of his temperament in order to prevent himself from sliding from the realm of practical possibilities into the world of fantastic dreams and illusions in which so many Roman emperors had foundered. . . .

At times Charles's affability, so much praised by Einhard, gave way to surprising explosions of temper. . . . Without a reference to such explosions, however, the portrait of Charles's impulsive and impetuous nature would be incomplete. The king's ire, which made his contemporaries tremble, was quite a different matter. It was part of the Germanic, just as it was of the oriental, conception of a ruler and was contrary to the Stoic ideal. At the beginning of the legend of Charlemagne there stands the figure of the "iron Charles" as his enemies saw him approaching—clad from top to toe in iron, and with an iron soul as well. In confusion they shouted: "Oh, the iron! Woe, the iron!" Not only the king's enemies, however, but also his faithful followers stood in fear of him. Charles's grandson Nithard wrote with approval that Charles had governed the nations with "tempered severity." Charles was able to control the warring men and the centrifugal tendencies of his dominions because the fear of his personal severity made evil men as gentle as lambs. He had the power to make the "hearts of both Franks and barbarians" sink. No amount of official propaganda could produce the same effect as the hardness of Charles's determination. The lack of such determination in Louis, his successor, was among the factors that led to the decay of the empire.

This side of Charles's character, although necessary for the preservation of the kingdom, was well beyond the boundaries laid down by the precepts of Stoicism and of Christianity. Charles himself was probably not aware of this. But Einhard, his biographer, who had much sympathy with both these ideals, felt it deeply. . . . Charles thought of himself as a Christian through and through, but he never managed to transcend the limits of the popular piety of the Franks. . . . He supported needy Christians, even outside the borders of the empire. He sent money to Rome and made four pilgrimages to the papal city. Such were the religious works of Charles as related by his biographer, Einhard. The inner life of the Christian, the regeneration of the soul and the new religious attitude which, at the very time when Einhard was writing, Charles's son, Louis the Pious, was labouring to acquire, are not so much as mentioned. The reason why Einhard is silent about such things is scarcely that he could not find the words to describe them in his model, Suetonius. Charles organized the salvation of his soul as he was wont to organize his Empire. It would have been contrary to his nature, and the most difficult task of all, for him to seek the highest levels of spiritual experience in his own heart. His task as a ruler, as he saw it, was to act upon the world.

We must remember, however, that the world upon which he acted bore little resemblance to the sober and dry reality created by modern commerce and technology. Such modern conceptions were shaped much later, mostly under the impression of Calvinism. They were unknown to Charles, who, for instance, first learnt of the pope's mutilation in distant Rome through a dream. He took it to be one of his duties as a ruler to observe the course of the stars with the greatest of attention, for the approach of misfortune for his kingdom could be foretold from the stars more accurately than from anything else. For this reason the emperor devoted more time and labour to the study of astronomy than to any other of the "liberal arts." If the observation of the stars had been a mere hobby, he would surely have interrupted it while he was devastating the Saxon country with his army. . . .

Charles the Great was not one of those men who have to fight against their times and who, misunderstood by their contemporaries, are appreciated only after their death. He embodied all the tendencies of his own age; he was carried forward by them and, at the same time, moved them forward. It is impossible to describe him except in close conjunction with his friends and the magnates of his land. But for the picture to be complete he must also be shown in the midst of his family. He was surrounded by his children, his wives and the retinue of females, whose numbers and conduct seemed so unbecoming to the puritanism of his successor when he first entered the palace. Such conditions were not peculiar to Charles. It was all part and parcel of Frankish tradition. Charles lived as the head of a clan. The servants were, at least for the purposes of everyday life, included in the clan. As part of the family they enjoyed peace and protection and were, together with their master's blood relations, subject to his authority. Within the framework of the old tribal law, the master ruled his household unconditionally. . . .

In the king's palace there was a constant going and coming. Emigrés from England and from Byzantium rubbed shoulders with foreign ambassadors and all manner of public officials. There must have been, nevertheless, a few fixed key positions in the organization. There was little love lost among the occupants of these positions. For the most part, our sources remain silent on this matter. But now and again we catch a glimpse of the situation. The office of the chamberlain was one of these key positions. It was he who received the people who had come to demand an audience. He decided whether and in what order they were to appear before the king. He also received the annual "donations" of the magnates to the royal treasure which was in his custody. Alcuin considered himself happy to count this man among his friends and emphasized again and again how many envious people and evil counsellors were busy in other places trying to ruin the king.

Alcuin wrote repeatedly that, though the king tried to enforce justice, he was surrounded by predatory men. His judgment was probably no less partisan than that of his opponents who maintained that he himself was ruining the king. . . . Charles's own open and generous nature had never been inclined to inquire too closely into the intrigues and corruptions of his trusted friends and servants.

All things considered, there is little difference between the picture we form of Charles's surroundings and the one we have of his ancestors and of other princes of the period. The only difference was that the imperial household, as in fact the empire itself, was greater, more splendid and therefore also more exposed to danger. As long as its power and splendour were increasing, the cracks in the structure remained concealed. It was the achievement of Charles's own powerful personality to have brought about this rise which, without him, might have taken generations to reach its zenith. His efforts were crowned with success because his whole personality was in tune with the progressive forces active among his people. If this had not been the case, no amount of power concentrated in the hands of the king would have suffered to stamp his countenance upon the age. If this is remembered much of the illusion of well-nigh superhuman achievement, that has inspired both the mediaeval legend of Charlemagne and many modern narratives, is dispelled. What remains is quite enough justification for calling Charles historically great.

A More Somber Light
F. L. GANSHOF

Just as Heinrich Fichtenau represents the tradition of Austrian-German scholarship in modern Carolingian studies, the other great tradition, the Belgian-French, is represented by the Belgian scholar François Louis Ganshof—who has been justly called the dean of Carolingian studies. The passage excerpted below is from an address presented to the Mediaeval Academy of America in 1948. It is in the nature of a summary judgment drawn from a lifetime of patient study and reflection, and has not been materially altered by his continued work of the last thirty years. Ganshof does not really dissent from the portrait created by Fichtenau. But he has always had a penchant for analysis rather than interpretation. He therefore strives to go beyond the limitations of Einhard's biography and other contemporary biographical fragments to describe not so much Charlemagne the man as Charlemagne the statesman. The result is a somewhat somber judgment, dwelling more upon his limitations than his accomplishments. For Ganshof is sharply aware that if Fichtenau sees Charlemagne as the universal father figure of the first Europe,[6] it is of a Europe hardly yet born and due for many turns and reverses before it can realize the promise anticipated in the age of Charlemagne.

We begin just before what Ganshof calls the fifth and last period of Charlemagne's reign.

IT WOULD SEEM that by 792, when Charles was fifty years old, he had acquired experience and wisdom; perhaps, also, the advice of certain counsellors had brought him to understand that moderation is necessary to consolidate the results of victory. One of the deep causes of the Saxon revolt of 792–793 had been the reign of terror of 785, caused especially by the *Capitulatio de partibus Saxoniæ*,[7] to secure the Frankish domination and the authority of the Christian religion. One must mention, also, the ruthlessness shown by the clergy in exacting payment of the tithe. In 797 a more gentle rule was introduced in Saxony by the *Capitulare Saxonicum* and the results of this new policy were favorable. In the Danube countries the methods used were less rigorous than formerly in Saxony.

A feature which at this period seems to have developed strongly was Charles' special care concerning the interests of the church and their close association with the interests of the state. In the capitulary, where dispositions made by the Synod of Frankfurt in 794 were promulgated, regulations of purely political or administrative character are next to those concerning the life of the church, e.g., the measures taken to extend the right of exclusive jurisdiction of the church over the clerics, and those aiming to render the discipline of the higher clergy more strict by reestablishing over the bishops, chiefs of the dioceses, the superior hierarchical office of the metropolitan.

In matters of dogma the Synod of Frankfurt, under the presidency of Charlemagne, had agreed with Pope Hadrian to condemn adoptianism, a christological heresy. Contrary to the advice of the pope, the synod had condemned the worship of images, which had been restored to honor by the decision of a so called œcumenical council of the Eastern Church. Charlemagne had already got his theologians to criticize this worship in

[6] D. A. Bullough, *"Europae Pater:* Charlemagne and His Achievement in the Light of Recent Scholarship," *English Historical Review*, 85 (1970), 59–105.

[7] "The Capitulary on the Saxon Regions." Capitularies were edicts of the crown which had the effect of law and are among the best evidence we have of Charlemagne's paternalistic style of government.—ED.

the *Libri Carolini*. In spite of his reverence for the Holy See, Charlemagne appears to be, far more than the pope, the real head of the church in the West. When Leo III ascended the pontifical throne in 795, on the death of Hadrian, Charles stated precisely their respective positions in a letter which leaves no doubt on the subject. The pope became more or less the first of his bishops.

Alcuin and a few other clerics had developed an idea linked with ancient traditions. To protect the church against many corrupt practices and dangers, the realization of the will of God on earth required the reestablishment in the West of an imperial power that would protect faith and church. Charlemagne, in their eyes, fulfilled the necessary conditions to be that Roman Christian emperor; to be, indeed, an emperor quite different in their minds from the historical Constantine and Theodosius. Favorable circumstances occurred. A revolution in Rome overthrew Pope Leo III in 799 and created an extremely difficult situation which remained confused even after Charles had had the pope reestablished on his throne. Charlemagne not only admired in Alcuin the theologian and the scholar to whom he had entrusted the task of revising the Latin text of the Bible, but he also had confidence in his judgment and was strongly under his influence. It was, I believe, owing to Alcuin that he went to Rome with the idea of putting order into the affairs of the church; it was under the same influence that he accepted there the imperial dignity. Pope Leo III crowned him emperor on 25 December 800.

To give even a short account of the immediate and later effects of this great event would be irrelevant here. I shall merely mention the fifth and last period of the reign of Charlemagne, which began on the day following the coronation. It is a rather incoherent stage of his career. One notices this when trying to distinguish what changes in Charlemagne's conduct could be attributed to the influence of his newly-acquired dignity.

He certainly appreciated his new position. He intended to make the most of it towards Byzantium and he exercised a political and military pressure on the eastern emperor until that Byzantine prince recognized his imperial title in 812. However, in matters of government Charles's attitude was not constant. In 802, shortly after his return from Italy, he appeared to be fully aware of the eminent character of his imperial power. He stated that it was his duty to see that all western Christians should act according to the will of God; he ordered all his subjects to take a new oath of allegiance, this time in his quality of emperor, and he extended the notion of allegiance. He started legislating in the field of private law; he stipulated that the clergy must obey strictly canonical legislation or the Rule of St. Benedict; he reformed the institution of his enquiring and reforming commissioners, the *missi dominici*, to make it more efficient. In spite of all this, when (806) he settled his succession, the imperial dignity appeared to have lost, in his eyes, much of its importance. Unless it were to lose its meaning entirely, the empire was indivisible. Yet Charles foresaw the partition of his states between his three sons, according to the ancient Frankish custom, and took no dispositions concerning the *imperialis potestas*. Doubtless those things that had influenced him a few years earlier were no longer effective and the Roman tradition and Alcuin's influence no longer dominated him. Everything was as if the imperial dignity had been for Charles a very high distinction but a strictly personal one. In the very last years of his reign, however, he seemed again to attach more importance to this dignity and most likely some new influences had altered his mind. His two older sons, Charles and Pepin, being dead, he himself conferred the title of emperor on his son Louis in 813.

During the end of the reign, with the one exception of the Spanish "march," which was enlarged and reinforced (Barcelona was taken in 801), no new territorial acquisition was made, in spite of military efforts often of considerable importance. The campaigns against the Northern Slavs, against Bohemia, against the Bretons of Armorica, and against the duke of Benevento only resulted in the recognition of a theoretical supremacy. Actually, fearful dangers became apparent. The Danes threatened the boundary of Saxony and their fleets devastated Frisia; the Saracen fleets threatened the Mediterranean coasts. The general impression left by the relation of these events is the weakening of the Carolingian monarchy. This impression increases when one examines internal conditions of the empire. In the state as in the church abuses increased; insecurity grew worse; the authority of the emperor was less and less respected. The capitularies, more and more numerous, constantly renewed warnings, orders, and interdictions which were less and less obeyed. Charles had grown old. Until then, his personal interferences and those which he directly provoked, had made up for the deficiencies of a quite inadequate administrative organization in an empire of extraordinary size. The physical and intellectual capacities of Charles were declining; he stayed almost continuously at Aachen, his favorite residence after 794, and he hardly ever left the place after 808. The strong antidote present before was now missing; all the political and social defects revealing a bad government appeared. When Charlemagne died in Aachen on 28 January 814, at the age of seventy-two, the Frankish state was on the verge of decay.

I have tried to describe and characterize briefly the successive phases of Charlemagne's reign. Is it possible to grasp his personality as a statesman? Perhaps. A primary fact that must be emphasized is that—even compared with others of his time—Charlemagne was not a cultivated man. In spite of his thirst for knowledge and his admiration of culture, he was ignorant of all that is connected with intellectual life and he had little gift for abstraction.

But he had a sense for realities, and especially those of power. He knew how one gains power, how one remains in power and how one reaches the highest degrees of superior and supreme power. His attitude towards the imperial dignity revealed this. The conception of the clerics, and especially of Alcuin, for whom that dignity was an ideal magistrature infinitely above the royal power, was quite inaccessible to him. He knew or rather he felt, that the real basis of his power was solely his double royal authority [8] and he refused to omit evidence of this from his titles after the imperial coronation. For him the imperial dignity magnified and glorified the royal authority; it neither absorbed nor replaced it.

Charles had also the sense of what was practicable. Save for the campaign in Spain in 778, he undertook no tasks out of proportion to his means.

Einhard praises the equanimity of Charlemagne, his *constantia*. This was, indeed, a remarkable aspect of his personality. In the two periods of crisis which shook his reign—in 778 and in 792/793—no danger, no catastrophe, could make him give up the tasks he had undertaken or alter his methods of government. The moderation with which he happened to treat his vanquished enemies at certain times was not in contradiction with the constancy of his character. On the contrary. Equanimity implies a clear view of one's plans and one can therefore understand the variations of Charlemagne's attitude towards the imperial dignity, the full significance of which he never really understood.

To have a clear line of conduct and keep to it is one thing, but it is quite another to follow out a complete and detailed program. Charlemagne had, indeed, certain lines of conduct that he followed persistently. The facts presented are sufficient to show this as regards his foreign policy. It is also true as regards political, administrative, and juridical institutions. Charlemagne wanted to improve their efficiency so as to bring about a more complete fulfillment of his wishes and to achieve greater security for his subjects. But one cannot make out a real program in his actions. He resorted to shifts; he adopted and improved what was already existing. This is true of the institution of the *missi,* true also of the royal court of justice, of the royal vassality and of the "immunity." Occasionally he created something new, but without troubling about a general scheme. His reforms were empiric and at times went through several stages of development: as in the case of the organization of the *placita generalia,*[9] which was roughly outlined at the beginning of the reign but did not assume a definite shape until about the year 802, and also the use of writing in recording administrative and juridical matter, prescribed by a series of distinct decisions relating to particular cases.

One must avoid any attempt to credit Charlemagne with preoccupations proper to other times. Because of his efforts to protect *pauperes liberi homines,*[10] for instance, one cannot attribute to him the inaugura-

---

[8] As king of the Franks and of the Lombards.—Ed.

[9] The General Assembly.—Ed.

[10] Impoverished free men.—Ed.

tion of a social policy; nor because he promulgated the *capitulare de villis* [11] can one speak of an economic policy. In both cases he acted on the spur of urgent interests then on hand: free men of modest condition supplied soldiers and the royal manors had to be fit to maintain the court. . . .

This sketch of Charles as a statesman would be distorted if stress was not laid upon his religious concerns. It is indeed hard to draw a line between his religious and his political ideas. His will to govern and to extend his power was inseparable from his purpose to spread the Christian religion and let his subjects live according to the will of God. If something of the "clerical" conception of the empire struck him deeply, it was the feeling that he was personally responsible for the progress of God's Kingdom on earth. But always it was he who was concerned. His piousness, his zeal for the Christian religion were no obstacles to his will to power; in religious matters as in others the pope was nothing more than his collaborator.

One is often tempted to turn Charlemagne into a superman, a far-seeing politician with broad and general views, ruling everything from above; one is tempted to see his reign as a whole, with more or less the same characteristics prevailing from beginning to end. This is so true that most of the works concerning him, save for the beginning and the end of his reign, use the geographical or systematic order rather than a chronological one. The distinctions that I have tried to make between the different phases of his reign may, perhaps, help to explain more exactly the development and effect of Charlemagne's power; they may help us to appreciate these more clearly. Perhaps, also, the features that I have noted bring out the human personality in the statesman and lead to the same results. The account I have given and the portrait I have drawn certainly justify the words which the poet ascribed to Charles in the last verse but one of the *Chanson de Roland*: "Deus" dist li Reis, "si penuse est ma vie." ("O Lord," said the king, "how arduous is my life.")

---

[11] The Capitulary on Manors.—ED.

Suggestions for Further Reading

THE ALMOST unique value of Einhard's biography of Charlemagne is dramatized by the scarcity and poor quality of other contemporary sources. Students can become aware of this contrast by looking even briefly at some of these other materials. There is a life of Charlemagne nearly contemporary with Einhard's, authored by a monk of St. Gall—possibly Notker the Stammerer. But unlike the solid and straightforward narrative of Einhard, the monk's account is disjointed and rambling, filled with legendary matter and scraps of the history of his monastery, and almost totally unreliable. It is available in a good modern edition, *Early Lives of Charlemagne by Eginhard and the Monk of St. Gall,* tr. and ed. A. J. Grant (New York: Cooper Square, 1966). Of the same sort are two somewhat later biographies of the brothers Adalard and Wala, abbots of Corbie, by the monk Radbertus of Corbie, although they contain only a few casual bits of information about Charlemagne, despite the fact that the two abbots were Charlemagne's cousins and both had played prominent roles at court: *Charlemagne's Cousins: Contemporary Lives of Adalard and Wala,* tr. and ed. Allen Cabaniss (Syracuse: Syracuse University Press, 1967). The only other narrative source of any value for the reign of Charlemagne is the Royal Frankish Annals, but they are thin and uncommunicative. They can be read as part of *Carolingian Chronicles, Royal Frankish Annals and Nithard's Histories,* tr. Bernhard W. Scholz with Barbara Rogers (Ann Arbor: University of Michigan Press, 1970). Several of these accounts and other sorts of documentary materials relating to Charlemagne's reign have been collected in a convenient and well-edited series of selections, *The Reign of Charlemagne, Documents on Carolingian Government and Administration,* ed. H. R. Loyn and John Percival (New York: St. Martin's, 1975).

Because of the stature and importance of Charlemagne and despite the problem of the sources, scholars continue to write about him. Many of their works are specialized scholarly studies. Some can be read profitably by beginning students, such as the several essays in Heinrich Fichtenau, *The Carolingian Empire,* excerpted above, or some of the articles of F. L. Ganshof collected in *The Carolingians and the Frankish Monarchy, Studies in Carolingian History,* tr. Janet Sondheimer (Ithaca, N.Y.: Cornell University Press, 1971). There are two excellent modern works, both brief and readable, that treat interesting aspects of Charles' reign: Richard E. Sullivan, *Aix-la-Chapelle in the Age of Charlemagne,* "Centers of Civilization Series" (Norman: University of Oklahoma Press, 1963), focuses on the cultural achievements at Charles' capital, and Jacques Boussard, *The Civilization of Charlemagne,* tr. Frances Partridge (New York: McGraw-Hill, 1968), presents a favorable revisionist interpretation of the Carolingian culture. One of the most important and most readable of the works on this period is Donald Bullough, *The Age of Charlemagne* (New York: Putnam, 1965).

Of the several biographies of Charlemagne, the best, as well as the most exciting and readable, is Richard Winston, *Charlemagne: From the Hammer to the Cross* (New York: Vintage, 1954). A somewhat briefer and less colorful biography but by an established authority is James A. Cabaniss, *Charlemagne,* "Rulers and Statesmen of the World" (Boston: Twayne, 1972).

Henri Pirenne, *Mohammed and Charlemagne*, tr. Bernard Miall (New York: Barnes and Noble, 1958 [1939]), is the masterwork of a great medieval historian and the chief entry in an important medieval scholarly controversy which continues to be of some interest to students of Charlemagne's reign. It has to do with the question of when and how the Middle Ages actually began. Pirenne says not until Charlemagne. The controversy and its chief figures are represented in *The Pirenne Thesis, Analysis, Criticism, and Revision,* ed. Alfred F. Havighurst (Boston: Heath, 1958). Students are also referred to two more recent works which indicate that the Pirenne controversy is still alive: Bryce Lyon, *The Origins of the Middle Ages, Pirenne's Challenge to Gibbon* (New York: Norton, 1972), and Robert S. Lopez, *The Birth of Europe* (New York: Lippincott, 1967).

Peter Abelard:
"The Knight of Dialectic"

By the turn of the twelfth century, the Europe of Charlemagne had been transformed. The downward curve of population had steadied and then begun to climb. There were more knights than there were fiefs for them to hold. They had joined the host of William the Bastard, Duke of Normandy, in his chancy adventure against England in the summer of 1066 in return for promises of land, as a decade earlier others had followed the Norman Guiscards and Hautevilles to Sicily. They swelled the armies of Saxon dukes and German kings in their conquests of eastern Europe and of Spanish Christian kings in the *reconquista* of Spain from the Moslems. And they went off to the crusades, the grandest adventure of an expanding Christendom.

Less sanguinary souls had taken to the roads with backpacks and strings of mules. Commerce began to revive, linking together villages and fortresses that would soon become towns and cities. The urban centers swelled with a growing population.

This bulging, booming, changing Europe had need for the skills of the mind. Schools multiplied—there were monastic schools, cathedral schools, guild schools, notarial schools. And men of learning found themselves thrust into the center of things. "The Renaissance of the twelfth century" was at hand, a revolution in learning and teaching, in the subjects to be taught and the methods of teaching them. It was to produce a renewed interest in the Latin classics, revived study of the ancient

Roman civil law and the codification of the law of the church. It was
to bring a flood of Moslem and Jewish and, ultimately, Greek influences
into the processes of Western thought and within a century to create
medieval scholasticism, with the medieval university as its institutional
setting.

One of the most fascinating, controversial, and important figures of
this world of twelfth-century intellectualism was the scholar-teacher-
philosopher-theologian-poet Peter Abelard (1079–1142). Abelard
is remembered principally for the arrogant rationalism he expounded
among the schoolmen of Paris, Laon, Melun, and Corbeil, and particularly
for his logical textbook *Sic et Non;* for his ill-fated romance with Heloise,
the fair niece of Canon Fulbert; and for Fulbert's terrible vengeance
upon him. But modern scholarship has begun to search beyond the inherited
stereotypes of Abelard as the demon lover and the rationalist-out-of-time,
neither of which can satisfactorily account for the astonishing reputation
that Abelard had among his own contemporaries.

The Story of My Misfortunes
PETER ABELARD

*The building of a kind of legendary Abelard began during his own lifetime
and resulted, in part, from the appearance of Abelard's autobiography,
its stark Latin title* Historia suarum calamitatum *somewhat weakly
translated as* The Story of My Misfortunes. *This remarkable and candid
book had a strange beginning. In 1135 a friend, apparently very close
to Abelard—he calls him "most dear brother in Christ and comrade closest
to me in the intimacy of speech"—appealed to him for consolation in
some sorrow of his own. In response, Abelard wrote him "of the sufferings
which have sprung out of my misfortunes" "so that, in comparing your
sorrows with mine, you may discover that yours are in truth nought, or
at the most but of small account, and so shall you come to bear them
more easily."*

*After describing his home in Brittany and how he had given up his
feudal inheritance and gained the permission of his father to pursue studies,
Abelard continues:*

I CAME AT length to Paris, where above all in those days the art of dialectics
was most flourishing, and there did I meet William of Champeaux, my
teacher, a man most distinguished in his science both by his renown and
by his true merit. With him I remained for some time, at first indeed well
liked of him; but later I brought him great grief, because I undertook to
refute certain of his opinions, not infrequently attacking him in disputation,
and now and then in these debates, I was adjudged victor. Now this, to
those among my fellow students who were ranked foremost, seemed all
the more insufferable because of my youth and the brief duration of my
studies.

Out of this sprang the beginning of my misfortunes, which have followed
me even to the present day; the more widely my fame was spread abroad,
the more bitter was the envy that was kindled against me. It was given out
that I, presuming on my gifts far beyond the warranty of my youth, was
aspiring despite my tender years to the leadership of a school; nay, more,
that I was making ready the very place in which I would undertake this
task, the place being none other than the castle of Melun, at that time a

royal seat. My teacher himself had some foreknowledge of this, and tried to remove my school as far as possible from his own. Working in secret, he sought in every way he could before I left his following to bring to nought the school I had planned and the place I had chosen for it. Since, however, in that very place he had many rivals, and some of them men of influence among the great ones of the land, relying on their aid I won to the fulfillment of my wish; the support of many was secured for me by reason of his own unconcealed envy. From this small inception of my school, my fame in the art of dialectics began to spread abroad, so that little by little the renown, not alone of those who had been my fellow students, but of our very teacher himself, grew dim and was like to die out altogether. Thus it came about that, still more confident in myself, I moved my school as soon as I well might to the castle of Corbeil, which is hard by the city of Paris, for there I knew there would be given more frequent chance for my assaults in our battle of disputation. . . .

To him did I return, for I was eager to learn more of rhetoric from his lips; and in the course of our many arguments on various matters, I compelled him by most potent reasoning first to alter his former opinion on the subject of the universals,[1] and finally to abandon it altogether. Now, the basis of this old concept of his regarding the reality of universal ideas was that the same quality formed the essence alike of the abstract whole and of the individuals which were its parts: in other words, that there could be no essential differences among these individuals, all being alike save for such variety as might grow out of the many accidents of existence. Thereafter, however, he corrected this opinion, no longer maintaining that the same quality was the essence of all things, but that, rather, it manifested itself in them through diverse ways. This problem of universals is ever the most vexed one among logicians, to such a degree, indeed, that even Porphyry,[2] writing in his "Isagoge" regarding universals, dared not attempt a final pronouncement thereon, saying rather: "This is the deepest of all problems of its kind." Wherefore it followed that when William had first revised and then finally abandoned altogether his views on this one subject, his lecturing sank into such a state of negligent reasoning that it could scarce be called lecturing on the science of dialectics at all; it was as if all his science had been bound up in this one question of the nature of universals.

Thus it came about that my teaching won such strength and authority that even those who before had clung most vehemently to my former master, and most bitterly attacked my doctrines, now flocked to my school. . . .

While these things were happening, it became needful for me again to

[1] This is a reference to the most famous and fundamental of all medieval learned controversies, the Nominalist-Realist controversy over the nature of reality and "universal" properties. The Nominalists traced their position ultimately to Aristotle; the Realists, to Plato.—ED.

[2] A third-century Neoplatonic philosopher whose works were important in the transmission of medieval Platonism.—ED.

repair to my old home, by reason of my dear mother, Lucia, for after the conversion of my father, Berengarius, to the monastic life, she so ordered her affairs as to do likewise. When all this had been completed, I returned to France,[3] above all in order that I might study theology, since now my oft-mentioned teacher, William, was active in the episcopate of Châlons. In this field of learning Anselm of Laon, who was his teacher therein, had for long years enjoyed the greatest renown.

I sought out, therefore, this same venerable man, whose fame, in truth, was more the result of long-established custom than of the potency of his own talent or intellect. If any one came to him impelled by doubt on any subject, he went away more doubtful still. He was wonderful, indeed, in the eyes of these who only listened to him, but those who asked him questions perforce held him as nought. He had a miraculous flow of words, but they were contemptible in meaning and quite void of reason. When he kindled a fire, he filled his house with smoke and illumined it not at all. He was a tree which seemed noble to those who gazed upon its leaves from afar, but to those who came nearer and examined it more closely was revealed its barrenness. . . .

It was not long before I made this discovery, and stretched myself lazily in the shade of that same tree. I went to his lectures less and less often, a thing which some among his eminent followers took sorely to heart, because they interpreted is as a mark of contempt for so illustrious a teacher. . . .

Challenged by those "eminent followers" of Anselm, Abelard undertakes to lecture on scripture, at their choice, "that most obscure prophecy of Ezekiel," and carries it off brilliantly—at least in his own opinion.

Now this venerable man of whom I have spoken was acutely smitten with envy, and straightway incited, as I have already mentioned, by the insinuations of sundry persons, began to persecute me for my lecturing on the Scriptures no less bitterly than my former master, William, had done for my work in philosophy. . . .

And so, after a few days, I returned to Paris, and there for several years I peacefully directed the school which formerly had been destined for me, nay, even offered to me, but from which I had been driven out. At the very outset of my work there, I set about completing the glosses on Ezekiel which I had begun at Laon. These proved so satisfactory to all who read them that they came to believe me no less adept in lecturing on

---

[3] Brittany was not yet a part of the royal domain of "France." He means the vicinity of Paris.—ED.

theology than I had proved myself to be in the field of philosophy. . . .
Thus, I, who by this time had come to regard myself as the only philosopher
remaining in the whole world, and had ceased to fear any further disturbance of my peace, began to loosen the rein on my desires, although
hitherto I had always lived in the utmost continence. And the greater
progress I made in my lecturing on philosophy or theology, the more I
departed alike from the practice of the philosophers and the spirit of the
divines in the uncleanness of my life. For it is well known, methinks, that
philosophers, and still more those who have devoted their lives to arousing
the love of sacred study, have been strong above all else in the beauty
of chastity.

Thus did it come to pass that while I was utterly absorbed in pride and
sensuality, divine grace, the cure for both diseases, was forced upon me,
even though I, forsooth, would fain have shunned it. First was I punished
for my sensuality, and then for my pride. . . .

Now there dwelt in that same city of Paris a certain young girl named
Héloïse, the niece of a canon who was called Fulbert. Her uncle's love
for her was equalled only by his desire that she should have the best
education which he could possibly procure for her. Of no mean beauty,
she stood out above all by reason of her abundant knowledge of letters.
Now this virtue is rare among women, and for that very reason it doubly
graced the maiden, and made her the most worthy of renown in the entire
kingdom. It was this young girl whom I, after carefully considering all
those qualities which are wont to attract lovers, determined to unite with
myself in the bonds of love, and indeed the thing seemed to me very easy
to be done. So distinguished was my name, and I possessed such advantages
of youth and comeliness, that no matter what woman I might favour with
my love, I dreaded rejection of none. . . .

Thus, utterly aflame with my passion for this maiden, I sought to
discover means whereby I might have daily and familiar speech with her,
thereby the more easily to win her consent. For this purpose I persuaded
the girl's uncle, with the aid of some of his friends, to take me into his
household—for he dwelt hard by my school—in return for the payment
of a small sum. My pretext for this was that the care of my own household
was a serious handicap to my studies, and likewise burdened me with an
expense far greater than I could afford. Now, he was a man keen in
avarice, and likewise he was most desirous for his niece that her study
of letters should ever go forward, so, for these two reasons, I easily won
his consent to the fulfillment of my wish, for he was fairly agape for
my money, and at the same time believed that his niece would vastly
benefit by my teaching. More even than this, by his own earnest entreaties he fell in with my desires beyond anything I had dared to hope,
opening the way for my love; for he entrusted her wholly to my guidance,
begging me to give her instruction whensoever I might be free from the
duties of my school, no matter whether by day or by night, and to punish

her sternly if ever I should find her negligent of her tasks. In all this the man's simplicity was nothing short of astounding to me; I should not have been more smitten with wonder if he had entrusted a tender lamb to the care of a ravenous wolf. . . .

The inevitable ensued. Heloise became pregnant, and the child was born. Abelard proposed marriage, but Heloise was reluctant for fear of damaging his career. They finally agreed upon a secret marriage. Then, to protect her from the fury of her uncle and her family, Abelard sent her to the convent at Argenteuil where she had been educated as a young girl.

When her uncle and his kinsmen heard of this, they were convinced that now I had completely played them false and had rid myself forever of Héloïse by forcing her to become a nun. Violently incensed, they laid a plot against me, and one night, while I, all unsuspecting, was asleep in a secret room in my lodgings, they broke in with the help of one of my servants, whom they had bribed. There they had vengeance on me with a most cruel and most shameful punishment, such as astounded the whole world, for they cut off those parts of my body with which I had done that which was the cause of their sorrow. This done, straightway they fled, but two of them were captured, and suffered the loss of their eyes and their genital organs. One of these two was the aforesaid servant, who, even while he was still in my service, had been led by his avarice to betray me.

When morning came the whole city was assembled before my dwelling. It is difficult, nay, impossible, for words of mine to describe the amazement which bewildered them, the lamentations they uttered, the uproar with which they harassed me, or the grief with which they increased my own suffering. Chiefly the clerics, and above all my scholars, tortured me with their intolerable lamentations and outcries, so that I suffered more intensely from their compassion than from the pain of my wound. In truth I felt the disgrace more than the hurt to my body, and was more afflicted with shame than with pain. My incessant thought was of the renown in which I had so much delighted, now brought low, nay, utterly blotted out, so swiftly by an evil chance. I saw, too, how justly God had punished me in that very part of my body whereby I had sinned. I perceived that there was indeed justice in my betrayal by him whom I had myself already betrayed; and then I thought how eagerly my rivals would seize upon this manifestation of justice, how this disgrace would bring bitter and enduring grief to my kindred and my friends, and how the tale of this amazing outrage would spread to the very ends of the earth. . . .

I must confess that in my misery it was the overwhelming sense of

my disgrace rather than any ardour for conversion to the religious life
that drove me to seek the seclusion of the monastic cloister. Héloïse had
already, at my bidding, taken the veil and entered a convent. Thus it was
that we both put on the sacred garb, I in the abbey of St. Denis, and she
in the convent of Argenteuil, of which I have already spoken. . . .

*But even in the monastery Abelard could be neither silent nor humble.
His theological writings—in particular a book on the Trinity—led to
his being summoned before a council at Soissons. And though the
condemnation of his work was far from unanimous, the book was
nevertheless condemned, and Abelard himself was forced to cast it into
the flames. He was banished to another monastery, which he was
eventually permitted to leave. He sought out a lonely spot in the forest
near Troyes in Champagne, built a hut, and formed his own monastic
congregation. But even here students came to be taught, and his critics
revived their charges, this time led by the most formidable religious
figure of the century, the great St. Bernard of Clairvaux. And, though
Abelard's account ends before that point, Bernard succeeded in having
him condemned by the church. But Abelard died in 1142 before the
ban could take effect.*

A "Renaissance Man"
of the Twelfth Century
CHARLES HOMER HASKINS

*The classic modern treatment of Abelard is to be found in Charles Homer
Haskins'* The Renaissance of the Twelfth Century, *one of the
outstanding works of modern medieval scholarship. This book was one
of the contributions to the academic controversy in the early part of
this century over the status and conception of the Renaissance. That
dispute has long been over, but Haskins' charming book survives, as
well as his interpretation of Abelard as one of the principal figures
in the construction of a medieval Renaissance.*

Haskins begins his account at the point of Abelard's confrontation with St. Bernard. This is where Abelard himself, as we have seen, left off in the history of his own misfortunes.

"VANITY OF VANITIES, saith the preacher," and St. Bernard was first and foremost a preacher, and a fundamentalist preacher at that. Vain above all to him were pride of intellect and absorption in the learning of this world, and his harshest invectives were hurled at the most brilliant intellect of his age, Abaelard, that "scrutinizer of majesty and fabricator of heresies" who "deems himself able by human reason to comprehend God altogether." Between a mystic like Bernard and a rationalist like Abaelard there was no common ground, and for the time being the mystic had the church behind him. With Abaelard we have another type of autobiography, the intellectual, in that long tale of misfortune which he addressed to an unknown friend under the title of *Historia suarum calamitatum.*

Abaelard, it is true, was a monk and an abbot, but he became such by force of circumstances and not from choice. Even when he retires into the forests of Champagne or the depths of Brittany, he has always one eye on Paris and his return thither; indeed, his *Historia calamitatum* seems to have been written to prepare the way for his coming back, to serve an immediate purpose rather than for posterity. It shows nothing of monastic humility or religious vocation, but, on the contrary, is full of arrogance of intellect and joy of combat, even of the lust of the flesh and the lust of the eyes and the pride of life. Its author was a vain man, vain of his penetrating mind and skill in debate, vain of his power to draw away others' students, vain even of his success with the fair sex—so that he "feared no repulse from whatever woman he might deign to honor with his love"— always sure of his own opinions and unsparing of his adversaries. He relies on talent rather than on formal preparation, venturing into the closed field of theology and even improvising lectures on those pitfalls of the unwary, the obscurest parts of the prophet Ezekiel. He was by nature always in opposition, a thorn in the side of intellectual and social conformity. In the classroom he was the bright boy who always knew more than his teachers and delighted to confute them, ridiculing old Anselm of Laon, whose reputation he declared to rest upon mere tradition, unsupported by talent or learning, notable chiefly for a wonderful flow of words without meaning or reason, "a fire which gave forth smoke instead of light," like the barren fig tree of the Gospel or the old oak of Lucan, mere shadow of a great name. In the monastery of Saint-Denis he antagonized the monks by attacking the traditions respecting their founder and patron saint. Always it is he who is right and his many enemies who are wrong. And, as becomes a history of his misfortunes, he pities himself much. Objectively, the facts of Abaelard's autobiography can in the main be verified from his other writings and the statements of contemporaries. Subjectively, the *Historia calamitatum* confirms itself throughout, if we discern between the bursts of self-confidence the intervals of irresolution and despondency in what he tries to present as a consistently planned career. The prolixity and the citations of ancient authority are of the Middle Ages, as are the particular problems with which his mind was occupied, but the personality might turn up in any subsequent epoch— "portrait of a radical by himself"! Yet, just as Heloise's joy in loving belongs to the ages, Abaelard's joy in learning is more specifically of the new renaissance, of which he is the bright particular star. . . .

In Abaelard . . . we have one of the most striking figures of the mediaeval renaissance. Vain and self-conscious, as we have found him in his autobiography, his defects of temperament must not blind us to his great mental gifts. He was daring, original, brilliant, one of the first philosophical minds of the whole Middle Ages. First and foremost a logician, with an unwavering faith in the reasoning process, he fell in with the dialectic preoccupations of his age, and did more than any one else to define the problems and methods of scholasticism, at least in the matter of universals and in his *Sic et non*. The question of universals, the central though not the unique theme of scholastic philosophy, is concerned with the nature of general terms or conceptions, such as man, house, horse. Are these, as the Nominalists asserted, mere names and nothing more, an intellectual convenience at the most? Or are they realities, as the Realists maintained, having an existence quite independent of and apart from the particular individuals in which they may be for the moment objectified? A mere matter of logical terminology, you may say, of no importance in the actual world. Yet much depends upon the application. Apply the nominalistic doctrine to God, and the indivisible Trinity dissolves into three persons. Apply it to the Church, and the Church ceases to be a divine institution with a life of its own and becomes merely a convenient designation for the whole body of individual Christians. Apply to it the State, and where does political authority reside, in a sovereign whole or in the individual citizens? In this form, at least, the problem is still with us. Practical thinking cannot entirely shake itself free from logic, and, conversely, logic has sometimes practical consequences not at first realized.

The debate respecting universals has its roots in Boethius and Porphyry, but it comes into the foreground with Roscellinus, an extreme Nominalist, condemned in 1092 for tritheism at the instance of Anselm. Against the extreme realism represented in various forms by William of Champeaux, Abaelard maintained a more moderate view, a doctrine which he worked out with his usual brilliancy and which we have just begun to understand with the publication, now proceeding, of his *Glosses on Porphyry*. As here explained, this resembles closely the doctrine of later orthodoxy. In an age, however, when theology was a prime object of attention, the logicians were always under the temptation of applying their dialectic to fundamental problems concerning the nature of God, and it is not surprising to find that Abaelard, like Roscellinus before him, ran into difficulties on the subject of the Trinity, being condemned for heresy at Soissons in 1121 and at Sens in 1141. Such conflicts were inevitable with one of Abaelard's radical temper, who courted opposition and combat. . . .

In another way Abaelard contributed to the formation of scholasticism, namely, in his *Sic et non,* or *Yes* and *No.* True, the method of collecting and arranging passages from the Fathers on specific topics had been used before, as in the *Sentences* of Anselm of Laon, but Abaelard gave it a pungency and a wide popularity which associate it permanently with his name. Like everything he did, it was well advertised. His method was to take significant topics of theology and ethics and to collect from the Fathers their opinions pro and con, sharpening perhaps the contrast and being careful not to solve the real or seeming contradiction. Inerrancy he grants only to the Scriptures, apparent contradictions in which must be explained as due to scribal mistakes or defective understanding; subsequent authorities may err for other reasons, and when they disagree he claims the right of going into the reasonableness of the doctrine itself, of proving all things in order to hold fast that which is good. He has accordingly collected divergent sayings of the Fathers as they have come to mind, for the purpose of stimulating tender readers to the utmost effort in seeking out truth and of making them more acute as the result of such inquiry. "By doubting we come to inquiry, and by inquiry we perceive truth." The propositions cover a wide range of topics and of reading; some are dismissed briefly, while others bring forth long citations. . . . Some . . . , one can almost imagine briefed on either side in modern manuals for the training of debaters. Some such purpose, the stimulating of discussion among his pupils, seems to have been Abaelard's primary object, but the emphasis upon contradiction rather than upon agreement and the failure to furnish any solutions, real or superficial, tended powerfully to expose the weaknesses in the orthodox position and to undermine authority generally.

The Substance of Abelard
DAVID KNOWLES

To Haskins belongs the well-deserved credit, if not for "discovering"
Abelard, at least for giving him a setting in which he can be seen with some
clarity. More recent scholarship, however, has moved beyond the
conception of Abelard as an example of the medieval Renaissance man—
no matter how brilliant, fascinating, and attractive—to the larger question
of his importance as a substantive figure in medieval intellectual history.
Much of this new scholarship is summarized, and some of it anticipated,
by the distinguished British medievalist and ecclesiastical historian
Dom David Knowles in his The Evolution of Medieval Thought.
We turn now to that summary.

UNTIL VERY RECENT years all discussions of Abelard centred upon his alleged heretical and rationalistic teaching. At the present day, as a result both of research among unpublished manuscripts and of critical methods applied to his works, he can be seen as a figure of positive import, as a logician of supreme ability and as the originator of ideas as well as of methods that were to have a long life. Not only is it now possible to grasp more fully than before what Abelard taught and thought, but it has been shown conclusively that throughout his life he was constantly rewriting and reconsidering his works, and that his opinions grew more orthodox and more carefully expressed with the passage of the years.

Was Abelard a rationalist? The question has been variously answered. Eighty years ago, the rationalists of the nineteenth century, Renan among them, saw in Abelard a herald of their enlightenment, and some of the historians of the day agreed with them; such was the opinion of Charles de Rémusat and Victor Cousin, and to their names, with some reserves, may be added the more recent opinion of Maurice de Wulf: "Exaggerating the rights of dialectic in theological matters, Peter Abelard established the relations of theology and philosophy on rationalistic principles." Others, even, have not hesitated to reverse Anselm's motto for Abelard; he would have said: "I understand in order that I may believe." Nevertheless, even at the beginning of this century some of the most distinguished names were found among Abelard's advocates, among them those of Harnack and Portalié, the latter of whom remarks: "In theory at least, Abelard never desired to give a philosophical demonstration of a mystery of the faith; still less did he profess himself a rationalist." This, expressed in various forms, is the almost unanimous verdict of recent scholars—Geyer, Chenu, Grabmann, de Ghellinck, Gilson—and we may agree with the judgment of the last-named of these, that the legend of Abelard the free-thinker has now become an exhibit of the historical curiosity-shop.

Of a truth, Abelard was never a rebel against the authority of the Church, and never a rationalist in the modern sense. He never persisted in teaching what had been censured, even though until censured he may have protested vehemently that he had been misrepresented. Similarly, he never intended that his dialectic should attack or contradict or replace the doctrines of the Church as formulated by tradition. In this, full weight must be given to his words in his *Introduction to Theology:* "Now therefore it remains for us, after having laid down the foundation of authority, to place upon it the buttresses of reasoning." This is unquestionably a genuine expression of his programme, as are also the celebrated and moving words of his letter to Héloise after the condemnation of 1141: "I will never be a philosopher, if this is to speak against St Paul; I would not be an Aristotle, if this were to separate me from Christ. . . . I have set my building on the corner-stone on which Christ has built his Church . . . if the tempest rises, I am not shaken; if the winds rave, I am not fearful. . . . I rest upon the rock that cannot be moved." These are not the words of a deliberate heretic or of a professed rationalist.

There are, in fact, two quite distinct questions. Did Abelard intend to formulate the doctrines of the faith in terms of dialectic, and to establish or invalidate them by this means? And, did Abelard in fact, in his writing and teaching, err from the orthodox teaching of the Church?

As we have seen, the answer to the first question, if it were needful to give it in a single word, would be negative. Such a simple answer, however, does not meet the complexity of the matter. . . . Abelard knew Anselm's work, and though he does not mention his motto, *credo ut intelligam,*[4] would certainly have echoed it, though perhaps on a slightly more superficial level and with more emphasis on the last word. But Abelard, besides having his full share of the contemporary trust in dialectic as the mistress of all truth, had a far greater acquaintance with, and trust in, the current *sprachlogik,* the conviction that just as words and terms and methods could be found to express truth with absolute fidelity, so all speculation, and indeed the nature and modes of acting of things in themselves, must follow and in a sense be modified by, the words and terms used by the skilled dialectician. *A fortiori,* the theological expression of religious truths must conform to dialectical practice; only so could any discussion or explanation of the mysteries of the faith be practicable. This postulate was probably at the root of Berengar's controversy with Lanfranc. It was certainly a prime cause of misunderstanding between Bernard

---

[4] "I believe in order that I might understand."—ED.

and Gilbert de la Porrée. So it was with Abelard. By genius, choice and practice he was a dialectician, and a dialectician he almost always remained. The dogmas of the faith are not for him wells of infinite depth, the reflection in words of luminous supernatural truth. Rather, they are so many propositions or facts thrown, so to say, to the Christian philosopher, upon which he may exercise his ingenuity and to which he can apply no laws but those of logic and grammar. . . .

As to the second question, Abelard was unquestionably technically unorthodox in many of his expressions. Though his opponents, and in particular St Bernard, may have erred in the severity of their attacks and in the universality of their suspicions, and though recent scholarship has shown that some, at least, of his expressions can, in their context, bear an orthodox interpretation, and that Abelard became more, and not less, respectful of tradition as the years passed, yet many of his pronouncements on the Trinity, the Incarnation, and Grace were certainly incorrect by traditional standards and, if carried to their logical issue, would have dangerously weakened the expression of Christian truth. The catalogue of erroneous, or at least of erratic, propositions in his writings drawn up by Portalié sixty years ago cannot be wholly cancelled by explanations of a verbal or logical nature. Error, however, is not always heretical. In the theological controversies of every age there have always been two families among those accused of heresy. There are those who, whatever their professions, are in fact attacking traditional doctrine, and those who, despite many of their expressions have, as we may say, the root of the matter in them . . . and there can be no doubt to which of the families Abelard belongs.

Abelard's genius was versatile, and left a mark on everything he touched. We have already considered his important contribution to logic, and in particular his solution of the problem of universals. In methodology he marked an epoch with his *Sic et non*. This short treatise, composed perhaps in its earliest form *c.* 1122, is perhaps the most celebrated (though not necessarily the most important) of Abelard's contributions to the development of medieval thought; it has in recent years been the occasion of a number of controversies. It consists of a relatively short prologue explaining its purpose and giving rules for the discussion of what follows; then comes a series of texts from Scripture and the Fathers on 150 theological points. The texts are given in groups, and in each case are apparently mutually contradictory. The essence of the work is the exposition of methodical doubt. As Abelard has it, "careful and frequent questioning is the basic key to wisdom," or, as he writes in the same prologue: "By doubting we come to questioning, and by questioning we perceive the truth."

Opinions have been divided as to how far the *Sic et non* is original, how far it is an instrument of scepticism, and what was its influence on the development of scholastic method. It was for long the common opinion

that it was completely original, an innovation with resounding consequences as great in its own field as the invention of the spinning-jenny or
the mechanical reaper in the world of economics. This view, usually held
in conjunction with that which saw in Abelard the first great apostle of
free thought, was convincingly refuted by the researches of Fournier
and Grabmann, who showed that the juxtaposition of seemingly contradictory authorities was already a method in common use in Abelard's day
by compilers of canonical collections, who had not only amassed texts
but given rules for criticism and harmonization. Bernold of Constance and
Ivo of Chartres in particular had employed this technique, and the *Decre-
tum* and *Panormia* of the latter were shown to have furnished Abelard
with some of his quotations from the Fathers.

As regards the primary aim of the *Sic et non,* there have been two views.
Many in the past, Harnack among them, have seen in it an attempt to
undermine tradition by showing its essentially self-contradictory character,
in order to make way for a more rational approach. Others, and among
them the greatest names among historians of medieval thought, have
strenuously opposed this view, seeing in the *Sic et non* simply an exercise
for explaining and harmonizing discrepancies and difficulties in the authorities. This opinion gains additional support from the fact that the work
was never used by his opponents as a stick with which to beat Abelard.
Such a view might well allow that *Sic et non* was a reaction against the
purely traditionalist teaching of the day, and that it was intended to open
a wide new field to dialectic, for which only a few samples were given.

As for the influence of the work upon the schools, the verdict of the
early historians was summary, and Abelard was hailed as the creator of
the scholastic method, and even Denifle in his early days regarded it as
the basis of the method of question and disputation. As we have seen,
all now admit that the borrowing was on Abelard's side. . . .

In theology, the main achievement of Abelard was to discuss and explain, where others merely asserted or proved, and to provide an outline
of the whole field of doctrines. It would seem, indeed, that he was the
first to use the Latin word *theologia* in the sense that is now current in all
European languages; the word had previously borne the connotation familiar in the Greek Fathers and the pseudo-Denis, of the mystical or at
least the expert knowledge of God and His attributes. By giving, in versions of increasing length and scope, an "introduction" or survey of
Christian teaching, Abelard's writings are an important link in the development of the *summa,* the typical medieval survey of theology.

When thus "introducing" his disciples to theology, Abelard met, as he
himself tells us, a genuine demand for an explanation of the mysteries of
the faith, and he gave this explanation with opinions that were often original, and which aimed at being reasonable. Abelard was in many ways a
humanist; he stressed the exemplary purpose of the Incarnation and
Crucifixion at the expense of the redemptive, and minimized the concep-

tion of original sin, regarding it as a penalty rather than a stain and re-garding grace as an assistance rather than as an enablement. He reacted against all legalistic interpretations, such as the opinion that the death or blood of Christ was a discharge of the rights claimed over mankind by the devil. In his Trinitarian theology, which was the head and front of his offending at Soissons and remained a charge at Sens, the principal accusation was that in reaction from the "tritheism" of Roscelin he founded the distinctions within the Godhead upon the traditional "appro-priations" ("power" of the Father, "wisdom" of the Word, and "love" of the Holy Spirit) thereby either reducing them to aspects of the one Godhead (Sabellianism) or, by an exclusive appropriation, limiting the equality of the persons. He was further accused of obscuring the personal union of the divine and human natures in Christ by treating the humanity as something assumed, as it were, as a garment by the divine Son. This, and other questionable propositions, make up an impressive total of erroneous opinions, and although some were due to faulty terminology and others were tacitly dropped from later versions of the same work—for Abelard, resembling other lecturers before and since, was always rewrit-ing and adding precision to his treatises—too much smoke remains to allow the cry of fire to be ignored. Above and through all else was the charge that Abelard left no place in his system for faith. . . .

In yet one more important field, that of ethics, Abelard was destined to leave a durable mark. In his discussion of moral problems in *Scito te ip-sum* [5] he showed his originality in such a way as to be one of the founders of scholastic moral theology. Reacting against the view then current which placed moral goodness solely in the conformity of an act to the declared law of God, and which tended to see sin as the factual transgression of the law, even if unknown or misunderstood (e.g. the obligation of certain degrees of fasting on certain days), Abelard placed goodness wholly in the intention and will of the agent, and saw sin not as the actual transgres-sion of the law, but as a contempt of God the lawgiver. . . . Abelard, in commenting upon the text, "Father, forgive them, for they know not what they do," tended to excuse wholly from sin the agents of the Crucifixion, stressing "they know not what they do" rather than the implicit sin that needed forgiveness. This shocked current susceptibilities, and was one of the charges against him. In another direction his opinions minimized the conception of the law of God and of the absolute ethical goodness of par-ticular actions. Abelard, anticipating with strange exactness the opinions of some fourteenth century "voluntarists," suggested that with God as with man the good depended upon the free choice, and that God might have established canons of morality other than, and even contrary to, those of the Hebrew and Christian revelation.

Look at him how we will, and when full weight has been given to the

[5] "Know thyself."—ED.

impression of restlessness, vanity and lack of spiritual depth given by his
career and some of his writings, Abelard remains, both as a teacher and as
a thinker, one of the half-dozen most influential names in the history of
medieval thought. . . . As a theologian, he was the first to see his subject as a whole, and to conceive the possibility of a survey or synthesis
for his pupils, thus taking an important part in fixing the method of teaching. Finally, and perhaps most significantly, he approached theological and
ethical problems as questions that could be illuminated, explained and
in part comprehended by a carefully reasoned approach, and still more
by a humane, practical attitude which took account of difficulties and of
natural, human feelings, and he endeavoured to solve problems of belief
and conscience not by the blow of an abstract principle, but by a consideration of circumstances as they are in common experience. Abelard
failed to become a much-cited authority by reason of his double condemnation and the attacks of celebrated adversaries, but his ideas lingered
in the minds of his disciples, and many of them came to the surface, un-
acknowledged, in the golden age of scholasticism.

Suggestions for Further Reading

ABELARD'S AUTOBIOGRAPHY, which is excerpted in this chapter and which
took the form of a letter to a friend, is available in another translation
along with seven additional letters exchanged between Abelard and Eloise,
The Letters of Abelard and Eloise, tr. C. K. Scott-Moncrieff (New York:
Knopf, 1926). There are a number of biographical treatments of Abelard.
One of the best is a small and elegant book by Etienne Gilson, *Héloïse
and Abelard*, tr. L. K. Shook (Ann Arbor: University of Michigan Press,
1963 [1951]), in which the great French medievalist retells the familiar
story with scholarship and insight. He also includes an appendix in which
he argues for the authenticity of the letters. R. W. Southern, the distinguished British medievalist, also deals with the letters and some related
topics in a collection of his articles, *Medieval Humanism and Other
Studies* (Oxford, England: Blackwell, 1970). There is a first-rate historical novel by Helen J. Waddell, *Peter Abelard, A Novel* (New York:
Barnes and Noble, 1971 [1933]). J. G. Sikes, *Peter Abelard* (New York:

Russell and Russell, 1965 [1932]), is largely about Abelard's thought rather than about his life and is complex and difficult, as is the more recent detailed documentary study of Abelard's influence, D. E. Luscombe, *The School of Peter Abelard, The Influence of Abelard's Thought in the Early Scholastic Period* (Cambridge, England: Cambridge University Press, 1969), but the latter is an important revisionist work, showing Abelard as less the founder of a distinctive school and more a journey-man critic.

It was, of course, largely Abelard's thought that got him in trouble with the church and with St. Bernard of Clairvaux. Their differences are dealt with in Denis Meadows, *A Saint and a Half: A New Interpretation of Abelard and St. Bernard of Clairvaux* (New York: Devin-Adair, 1963); it is less a new interpretation than an attempt to soften the disagreements between them. A sharper treatment of their differences is to be found in A. Victor Murray, *Abelard and St. Bernard, A Study in Twelfth Century "Modernism"* (New York: Barnes and Noble, 1967). For the church itself in Abelard's time, the best brief general survey of the papacy is G. Barraclough, *The Medieval Papacy* (New York: Harcourt, Brace, 1968). Equally authoritative and readable but more comprehensive for this period is H. Daniel-Rops, *Cathedral and Crusade, Studies of the Medieval Church 1050–1350*, tr. John Warrington (New York: Dutton, 1957). As for the more specific environment of Abelard, the medieval schools, the best and most readable works are still the old classics, Helen Waddell, *The Wandering Scholars* (New York: Holt, 1934 [1927]), Charles Homer Haskins, *The Rise of Universities* (New York: P. Smith, 1940 [1923]), and his *Studies in Medieval Culture* (New York: Ungar, 1958 [1929]). Haskins' notions about the Renaissance of the twelfth century are still being debated: see the review of the literature in C. Warren Hollister (ed.), *The Twelfth-Century Renaissance* (New York: Wiley, 1969); Christopher Brooke, *The Twelfth-Century Renaissance* (New York: Harcourt, Brace, 1969), not so much a revision of Haskins' classic work as an updating and extension; and the graceful and learned work of Sidney R. Packard, *12th Century Europe, An Interpretive Essay* (Amherst: University of Massachusetts Press, 1973).

For the relationship of Abelard to medieval learning and scholasticism, further reading in Dom David Knowles, *The Evolution of Medieval Thought* (New York: Vintage, 1962), is recommended, along with Gordon Leff, *Medieval Thought* (Harmondsworth, England: Penguin, 1958). Two more straightforward surveys are Meyrick H. Carré, *Realists and Nominalists* (London: Oxford University Press, 1946), and F. C. Copleston, *A History of Medieval Philosophy* (New York: Harper & Row, 1972 [1952]).

Finally, students must remember that the towns and schools of the twelfth century were the products of the economic revolution that was sweeping Europe. The best and most comprehensive treatment of the new medieval economic history is *The Cambridge Economic History of Europe*, 2nd ed., vols. 1–3 (Cambridge, England: Cambridge University Press, 1952–1966). Three additional works may also be recommended, one by the American economic historian Robert S. Lopez, *The Commercial Revolution of the Middle Ages, 950–1350* (Englewood Cliffs, N.J.: Prentice-Hall, 1971), and two by French authorities, R. H. Bautier, *The Economic Development of Medieval Europe*, tr. H. Karolyi (New York: Harcourt, Brace, 1971), and Georges Duby, *The Early Growth of the European Economy*, tr. H. B. Clarke (Ithaca, N.Y.: Cornell University Press, 1974).

Eleanor of Aquitaine and the Wrath of God

Eleanor of Aquitaine was one of the most remarkable and important figures in medieval history. In her own right, she was duchess of the vast domain of Aquitaine and countess of Poitou, the wife first of Louis VII of France and then of Henry II of England, the mother of "good King Richard" and "bad King John," patroness of poets and minstrels. Tradition remembers her as beautiful and passionate, headstrong and willful. But beyond that intriguing traditional reputation, she is a figure only imperfectly seen and, ironically enough, seen at all largely through the accounts of her enemies.

The sources of medieval history are scanty at best and tend, moreover, to record men's doings in a preponderantly man's world. Even the greatest of medieval women appear in the records of their time as conveyors of properties and channels for noble blood lines, and we know of them only that they were "good and faithful wives"—or that they were not. So it is with Eleanor. We do not even have a contemporary description of her. Troubadour poets sang rapturously of her "crystal cheeks," her "locks like threads of gold," her eyes "like Orient pearls." One even proclaims,

> Were the world all mine,
> From the sea to the Rhine,
> I'd give it all
> If so be the Queen of England
> Lay in my arms.

In sober fact, we do not know what color her eyes were, nor her hair, whether it was indeed "like threads of gold" or raven black. Even the few pictorial representations we have of her—including her tomb effigy at the Abbey of Fontevrault—are purely conventional.

But Eleanor's part in the great events of her time was real enough. It began with her marriage, at the age of fifteen, to Louis the young king, son of Louis VI (Louis the Fat) of France. Her father, the turbulent Duke William X of Aquitaine, had died suddenly and unexpectedly on pilgrimage to Spain, leaving Eleanor his heiress. And, in feudal law, the disposition of both Eleanor and her fiefs was a matter to be decided by her father's overlord, Louis VI of France. Duke William had been Louis' most intractable vassal, and his death was a priceless opportunity not only to put an end to the contumaciousness of Aquitaine but to tie that large and wealthy duchy to the French realm. Louis decided that the interests of his house were best served by the marriage of Eleanor to his son. And so, it was done. There is no record of how either the young bride or the young groom responded, only an account of the brilliant assemblage that gathered to witness the ceremony in Bordeaux and to accompany the happy couple back by weary stages to Paris. In the course of this journey, the aged King Louis died. His son was now Louis VII, the Duchess Eleanor now queen of France. The year was 1137.

We must not imagine that Eleanor was a very happy bride in those first years of her marriage. Paris was a cold and gloomy northern city, very different from sunny Provence, and the Capetian castles in which she lived were dark and uncomfortable. The king her husband had an inexhaustible thirst for devotion and piety and surrounded himself with ecclesiastical advisors, confessors, theologians, and barren, quibbling scholars, so unlike the more robust and charming practitioners of the *gai savoir* (merry learning) with whom Eleanor had grown up at her father's court. Nor was Louis very happy, for his young wife gave him two daughters and no son, no member of "the better sex" to be groomed for the Capetian throne.

Then word reached Paris of the fall of Edessa in the distant Latin Kingdom of Jerusalem, one of those fortress principalities to secure the Holy Land dating from the first crusade almost half a century before. The resurgence of Moslem power was clearly seen to threaten the Holy Land, and the call for a second crusade went out. The pious King Louis took the cross—to the consternation of his more realistic advisors. And Eleanor insisted upon accompanying him. Whatever Louis and his fellow crusaders may have thought about this matter, Eleanor's position as a great vassal who could summon a substantial host of warriors from her own lands made her support crucial: and her support was contingent upon her going in person. There is a persistent legend that the queen and her ladies decked themselves out as Amazons in anticipation of their role in the coming military adventure.

But the military adventure itself turned into a military disaster. The second crusade was a dismal failure. The French forces of Louis VII were seriously defeated by the Turks, and the German contingent led by the Emperor Conrad III was almost wiped out. Both the French and the Germans accused the Byzantine Greeks of treachery. There were disagreements among the Western knights, and many of them simply abandoned the crusade and returned home. There were divided counsels among those who remained and mistrust between them and the Christian lords of the Eastern principalities. And there were continued military blunders and defeats. Tempers were short, old quarrels flared, new ones commenced.

In this atmosphere, what had apparently been a growing estrangement between King Louis and Queen Eleanor became an open break. Their troubles were aggravated by the boldness and outspokenness of the queen and in particular by her attentions to her handsome uncle, only eight years older than she, Raymond of Poitiers, Prince of Antioch. It may have been no more than an innocent flirtation. But Louis thought otherwise. He brooded not only on his queen's conduct but on her failure to produce a son for him, and his mind turned to divorce, the grounds for which were to be found in consanguinity, a marriage within the prohibited degree of blood relationship, which was the usual legal pretext for the dissolution of feudal marriages no longer bearable or profitable.

Eleanor and the Chroniclers
WILLIAM OF TYRE AND JOHN OF SALISBURY

Eleanor's role in the second crusade is scarcely mentioned by the chroniclers who recorded the deeds of its other leading figures. Odo of Deuil, a monk of the French royal monastery of St. Denis and the chaplain of Louis VII, wrote the most detailed account of Louis' part in the crusade—De profectione Ludovici VII in orientem—but he makes only four passing references to the queen in the entire narrative. Odo clearly had reason to favor the cause of the king his master. And, for one reason or another, so did the few other chroniclers who give any account at all of the estrangement between Louis and Eleanor. The most detailed is that of William Archbishop of Tyre. William is

*generally regarded as the best of all the chroniclers of the crusades, but
he was not present at the time of this crisis and we do not know what
source he used. In any event, he regarded the behavior of the queen
and the resulting breach with her husband as part of a cynical attempt
by Raymond of Antioch to turn the crusade to his own advantage.
Here is the account of William of Tyre.*

FOR MANY DAYS Raymond, prince of Antioch, had eagerly awaited the
arrival of the king of the Franks. When he learned that the king had
landed in his domains, he summoned all the nobles of the land and the
chief leaders of the people and went out to meet him with a chosen escort.
He greeted the king with much reverence and conducted him with great
pomp into the city of Antioch, where he was met by the clergy and the
people. Long before this time—in fact, as soon as he heard that Louis
was coming—Raymond had conceived the idea that by his aid he might
be able to enlarge the principality of Antioch. With this in mind, therefore, even before the king started on the pilgrimage, the prince had sent
to him in France a large store of noble gifts and treasures of great price
in the hope of winning his favor. He also counted greatly on the interest
of the queen with the lord king, for she had been his inseparable companion on his pilgrimage. She was Raymond's niece, the eldest daughter
of Count William of Poitou, his brother.

As we have said, therefore, Raymond showed the king every attention
on his arrival. He likewise displayed a similar care for the nobles and
chief men in the royal retinue and gave them many proofs of his great
liberality. In short, he outdid all in showing honor to each one according
to his rank and handled everything with the greatest magnificence. He felt
a lively hope that with the assistance of the king and his troops he would
be able to subjugate the neighboring cities, namely, Aleppo, Shayzar, and
several others. Nor would this hope have been futile, could he have
induced the king and his chief men to undertake the work. For the arrival
of King Louis had brought such fear to our enemies that now they not
only distrusted their own strength but even despaired of life itself.

Raymond had already more than once approached the king privately
in regard to the plans which he had in mind. Now he came before the
members of the king's suite and his own nobles and explained with due
formality how his request could be accomplished without difficulty and
at the same time be of advantage and renown to themselves. The king,
however, ardently desired to go to Jerusalem to fulfil his vows, and his
determination was irrevocable. When Raymond found that he could not
induce the king to join him, his attitude changed. Frustrated in his ambitious designs, he began to hate the king's ways; he openly plotted
against him and took means to do him injury. He resolved also to deprive

him of his wife, either by force or by secret intrigue. The queen readily assented to this design, for she was a foolish woman. Her conduct before and after this time showed her to be, as we have said, far from circumspect. Contrary to her royal dignity, she disregarded her marriage vows and was unfaithful to her husband.

As soon as the king discovered these plots, he took means to provide for his life and safety by anticipating the designs of the prince. By the advice of his chief nobles, he hastened his departure and secretly left Antioch with his people. Thus the splendid aspect of his affairs was completely changed, and the end was quite unlike the beginning. His coming had been attended with pomp and glory; but fortune is fickle, and his departure was ignominious.

The only other substantial account of the events leading to the divorce of Louis and Eleanor is that of the great twelfth-century ecclesiastic and intellectual, John of Salisbury, in his Historia Pontificalis. *In one respect, John was even further removed from the events than William of Tyre. He had no direct knowledge of the East at all and was, at this time, in Rome on a mission from the see of Canterbury and attached to the papal court. We do not know what source he used for the events in Antioch. It is likely that he is simply repeating the story as he heard it from members of Louis' retinue, for the hostility against Eleanor that already animated Louis' close supporters is clearly present in John's account. It is also possible that the hostility of the account and its strong pro-French bias is related to the later time at which John's work was actually written, about 1163. At this time, John was involved in the growing bitterness between Thomas Becket, whom he supported, and Henry II of England, who had just sent John into exile for his support of Becket. John found refuge in France.*

But in any event, the account in the Historia Pontificalis *is strongly favorable to Louis, even to the extent of ascribing to Eleanor the initiative in the proposal for the divorce.*

IN THE YEAR of grace 1149 the most Christian king of the Franks reached Antioch, after the destruction of his armies in the east, and was nobly entertained there by Prince Raymond, brother of the late William, count of Poitiers. He was as it happened the queen's uncle, and owed the king loyalty, affection and respect for many reasons. But whilst they remained there to console, heal and revive the survivors from the wreck of the army, the attentions paid by the prince to the queen, and his constant, indeed almost continuous, conversation with her, aroused the king's suspicions. These were greatly strengthened when the queen wished to remain behind, although the king was preparing to leave, and the prince made every effort to keep her, if the king would give his consent. And when the king made haste to tear her away, she mentioned their kinship, saying it was not lawful for them to remain together as man and wife, since they were related in the fourth and fifth degrees. Even before their departure a rumour to that effect had been heard in France, where the late Bartholomew bishop of Laon had calculated the degrees of kinship; but it was not certain whether the reckoning was true or false. At this the king was deeply moved; and although he loved the queen almost beyond reason he consented to divorce her if his counsellors and the French nobility would allow it. There was one knight amongst the king's secretaries, called Terricus Gualerancius, a eunuch whom the queen had always hated and mocked, but who was faithful and had the king's ear like his father's before him. He boldly persuaded the king not to suffer her to dally longer at Antioch, both because "guilt under kinship's guise could lie concealed," and because it would be a lasting shame to the kingdom of the Franks if in addition to all the other disasters it was reported that the king had been deserted by his wife, or robbed of her. So he argued, either because he hated the queen or because he really believed it, moved perchance by widespread rumour. In consequence, she was torn away and forced to leave for Jerusalem with the king; and, their mutual anger growing greater, the wound remained, hide it as best they might.

In the next passage, John is on more familiar ground since he was in Rome, a familiar of the curia and of Pope Eugenius III, and perhaps even a witness to some of the events he describes.

In the year of grace eleven hundred and fifty the king of the Franks returned home. But the galleys of the Emperor of Constantinople lay in wait for him on his return, capturing the queen and all who were journeying in her ship. The king was appealed to to return to his Byzantine brother and friend, and force was being brought to bear on him when the galleys of the king of Sicily came to the rescue. Freeing the queen and releasing the king, they escorted them back to Sicily rejoicing, with honour and triumph. This was done by order of the king of Sicily, who feared the wiles of the Greeks and desired an opportunity of showing his devotion to the king and queen of the Franks. Now therefore he hastened to meet him with an ample retinue, and escorted him most honourably to Palermo, heaping gifts both on him and on all his followers; thereafter he travelled with him right across his territory to Ceprano, supplying all his needs on the way. This is the last point on the frontier between the principality of Capua and Campania, which is papal territory.

At Ceprano the cardinals and officials of the church met the king and, providing him with all that he desired, escorted him to Tusculum to the lord pope, who received him with such tenderness and reverence that one would have said he was welcoming an angel of the Lord rather than a mortal man. He reconciled the king and queen, after hearing severally the accounts each gave of the estrangement begun at Antioch, and forbade any future mention of their consanguinity: confirming their marriage, both orally and in writing, he commanded under pain of anathema that no word should be spoken against it and that it should not be dissolved under any pretext whatever. This ruling plainly delighted the king, for he loved the queen passionately, in an almost childish way. The pope made them sleep in the same bed, which he had had decked with priceless hangings of his own; and daily during their brief visit he strove by friendly converse to restore love between them. He heaped gifts upon them; and when the moment for departure came, though he was a stern man, he could not hold back his tears, but sent them on their way blessing them and the kingdom of the Franks, which was higher in his esteem than all the kingdoms of the world.

Eleanor the Queen of Hearts
AMY KELLY

In spite of "the lord pope's" good offices, his tears and his blessing, even his threat of anathema, the estrangement between Louis and Eleanor continued. Louis was adamant, and finally, in the spring of 1152 at a solemn synod in Beaugency on the Loire, Louis' spokesmen argued the case of the consanguinity of their lord and his queen, and the Archbishop of Sens proclaimed their marriage invalid. The Archbishop of Bordeaux, the queen's surrogate, sought only the assurance that her lands be restored. But this had already been arranged, as had all the other details of this elaborate royal charade. Eleanor was not even present. She had already returned to Poitou.

But Eleanor was not destined to reign as a dowager duchess in her own domains. Within two months, she had married Henry, Duke of Normandy. He was not only the Norman duke but also the heir to the fiefs of his father, Geoffrey Plantagenet, Count of Maine and Anjou. These already substantial lands, when joined to those of his new bride, made Henry lord of a nearly solid block of territories that stretched from

the English Channel to the Mediterranean and from Bordeaux to the
Vexin, hardly a day's ride from Paris. At one stroke, Henry of Anjou had
become the greatest feudatory of France, with lands and resources many
times the size of those held by his nominal overlord, King Louis VII. Two
years later, another piece of Henry's inheritance came into his hands.
His mother, Matilda, was the daughter of the English King Henry I and
had never ceased to press the claim of her son to the English throne.
The reign of King Stephen was coming to an end, and he had no surviving
heirs. At his death in 1154, Henry of Anjou claimed his crown, and there
was none to deny him. Eleanor was a queen once more.

But this time, she had a very different king. Henry II was as godless
as Louis had been pious, as flamboyant as Louis had been humble. Where
Louis was stubborn and persistent, Henry was furiously energetic and
decisive. The setting was at hand for one of the classic confrontations of
medieval history that was to stretch into the following generation of the
kings of both France and England.

As for Eleanor, the sources are once more silent. We know that she
produced for Henry the family of sons she had denied to Louis. The eldest,
William, born before the succession to England, died in childhood. But in
1155 came Henry, in 1157, Richard—to be called the Lion-Hearted—
and in 1158, Geoffrey, in 1166 came John, the last of her sons, and there
were by this time two daughters as well. We know that through the early
years of her marriage to Henry, Eleanor was often with him at court
and sometimes presided in his absence, a fact attested by writs and seals.
But her marriage was by no means serene. There were long periods of
separation during which the king was known to be unfaithful. The
incidents of his infidelity had grown more flagrant with the passing years.
At about the time of prince John's birth in 1166, Henry was involved
with a paramour of spectacular beauty, Rosamond Clifford. Their affair
was the object of such celebration by poets, balladeers, and wags alike that
Eleanor may have decided that her bed and her dignity could no longer
endure such an affront. But there may have been other matters at issue.
The queen may have become alarmed at her husband's efforts to substitute
his rule for hers in her dower lands.

In any case, about 1170 she returned to Poitou with her favorite among
her sons, Richard, whom she installed as her heir for the lands of Poitou
and Aquitaine. For the next three or four years she lived in her old
capital of Poitiers, separated from her husband. In these years of self-
imposed exile, Eleanor not only reasserted her rights to her own lands, but
created a center in Poitiers for the practice of the troubadour culture and
l'amour courtois that had long been associated with her family.

The following passage, from Amy Kelly's Eleanor of Aquitaine and the
Four Kings—the book that has come to be regarded as the standard work
on Eleanor—is a brilliant reconstruction of this period of Eleanor's life.

WHEN THE COUNTESS of Poitou settled down to rule her own heritage, she took her residence in Poitiers, which offered a wide eye-sweep on the world of still operative kings. In the recent Plantagenet building program her ancestral city, the seat and necropolis of her forebears, had been magnificently enlarged and rebuilt, and it stood at her coming thoroughly renewed, a gleaming exemplar of urban elegance. The site rose superbly amidst encircling rivers. Its narrow Merovingian area had lately been extended to include with new and ampler walls parishes that had previously straggled over its outer slopes; ancient quarters had been cleared of immemorial decay; new churches and collegials had sprung up; the cathedral of Saint Pierre was enriched; markets and shops of tradesmen and artisans bore witness to renewed life among the *bourgeoisie*; bridges fanned out to suburbs and monastic establishments lying beyond the streams that moated the city. Brimming with sunshine, the valleys ebbed far away below—hamlet and croft, mill and vineyard—to a haze as blue as the vintage. . . .

When Eleanor came in about 1170 to take full possession of her newly restored city of Poitiers and to install her favorite son there as ruling count and duke in her own patrimony, she was no mere game piece as were most feudal women, to be moved like a queen in chess. She had learned her role as *domina* in Paris, Byzantium, Antioch, London, and Rouen, and knew her value in the feudal world. She was prepared of her own unguided wisdom to reject the imperfect destinies to which she had been, as it were, assigned. In this, her third important role in history, she was the pawn of neither prince nor prelate, the victim of no dynastic scheme. She came as her own mistress, the most sophisticated of women, equipped with plans to establish her own assize, to inaugurate a regime dedicated neither to Mars nor to the Pope, nor to any king, but to Minerva, Venus, and the Virgin. She was resolved to escape from secondary roles, to assert her independent sovereignty in her own citadel, to dispense her own justice, her own patronage, and when at leisure, to survey, like the Empress of Byzantium, a vast decorum in her precincts. . . .

The heirs of Poitou and Aquitaine who came to the queen's high place for their vassals' homage, their squires' training, and their courtiers' service, were truculent youths, boisterous young men from the baronial strongholds of the south without the Norman or Frankish sense of nationality, bred on feuds and violence, some of them with rich fiefs and proud lineage, but with little solidarity and no business but local warfare and daredevil escapade. The custom of lateral rather than vertical inheritance of fiefs in vogue in some parts of Poitou and Aquitaine—the system by which lands passed through a whole generation before descending to the next generation—produced a vast number of landless but expectant younger men, foot-loose, unemployed, ambitious, yet dependent upon the reluctant bounty of uncles and brothers, or their own violent exploits.

These wild young men were a deep anxiety not only to the heads of their houses, but to the Kings of France and England and to the Pope in Rome. They were the stuff of which rebellion and schism are made. For two generations the church had done what it could with the problem of their unemployment, marching hordes out of Europe on crusade and rounding other hordes into the cloister.

It was with this spirited world of princes and princesses, of apprentice knights and chatelaines, at once the school and the court of young Richard, that the duchess, busy as she was with the multifarious business of a feudal suzerain, had to deal in her palace in Poitiers. . . .

Eleanor found a willing and helpful deputy to assist her in the person of her daughter by Louis of France, now entrusted to her tutelage, a young woman already well grown, well educated, and apparently well disposed to her mother and to her mother's plans—Marie, Countess of Champagne.

. . . The character of the milieu which Marie appears to have set up in Poitiers suggests a genuine sympathy between the queen and her daughter who had so long been sundered by the bleak fortuities of life. Old relationships were knit up. Something native blossomed in the countess, who shone with a special luster in her mother's court. The young Count of Poitou learned to love particularly his half sister Marie and forever to regard the Poitiers of her dispensation as the world's citadel of valor, the seat of courtesy, and the fountainhead of poetic inspiration. Long after, in his darkest hours, it was to her good graces he appealed. The countess, having carte blanche to proceed with the very necessary business of getting control of her academy, must have striven first for order. Since the miscellaneous and high-spirited young persons in her charge had not learned order from the liturgy nor yet from hagiography, the countess bethought her, like many an astute pedagogue, to deduce her principles from something more germane to their interests. She did not precisely invent her regime; rather she appropriated it from the abundant resources at her hand.

The liberal court of Eleanor had again drawn a company of those gifted persons who thrive by talent or by art. Poets, *conteurs* purveying romance, ecclesiastics with Latin literature at their tongues' end and mere clerks with smatterings of Ovid learned from quotation books, chroniclers engaged upon the sober epic of the Plantagenets, came to their haven in Poitiers. The queen and the countess, with their native poetic tradition, were the natural patrons of the troubadours. It will be seen that the Countess Marie's resources were rich and abundant, but not so formalized as to afford the disciplines for a royal academy nor give substance to a social ritual. The great hall was ready for her grand assize; the expectant court already thronged to gape at its suggestive splendors. . . .

At least one other important source Marie employed. She levied upon the social traditions of her Poitevin forebears. Nostredame relates that in Provence chatelaines were accustomed to entertain their seasonal assemblies with so-called "courts of love," in which, just as feudal vassals brought their grievances to the assizes of their overlords for regulation, litigants in love's thrall brought their problems for the judgment of the ladies. André in his famous work [1] makes reference to antecedent decisions in questions of an amatory nature by "les dames de Gascogne," and the poetry of the troubadours presupposes a milieu in which their doctrines of homage and deference could be exploited. Thus we have in André's *Tractatus* the framework of Ovid with the central emphasis reversed, the Arthurian code of manners, the southern ritual of the "courts of love," all burnished with a golden wash of troubadour poetry learned by the queen's forebears and their vassals in the deep Midi, probably beyond the barrier of the Pyrenees. Marie made these familiar materials the vehicle for her woman's doctrine of civility, and in so doing, she transformed the gross and cynical pagan doctrines of Ovid into something more ideal, the woman's canon, the chivalric code of manners. Manners, she plainly saw, were after all the fine residuum of philosophies, the very flower of ethics. . . .

With this anatomy of the whole corpus of love in hand, Marie organized the rabble of soldiers, fighting cocks, jousters, springers, riding masters, troubadours, Poitevin nobles and debutantes, young chatelaines, adolescent princes, and infant princesses in the great hall of Poitiers. Of this pandemonium the countess fashioned a seemly and elegant society, the fame of which spread to the world. Here was a woman's assize to draw men from the excitements of the tilt and the hunt, from dice and games to feminine society, an assize to outlaw boorishness and compel the tribute of adulation to female majesty. . . .

While the ladies, well-accoutered, sit above upon the dais, the sterner portion of society purged, according to the code, from the odors of the kennels and the highway and free for a time from spurs and falcons, range themselves about the stone benches that line the walls, stirring the fragrant rushes with neatly pointed shoe. There are doubtless preludes of music luring the last reluctant knight from the gaming table, *tensons* or *pastourelles*, the plucking of rotes, the "voicing of a fair song and sweet," perhaps even some of the more complicated musical harmonies so ill-received by the clerical critics in London; a Breton *lai* adding an episode to Arthurian romance, or a chapter in the tale of "sad-man" Tristram, bringing

---

[1] André, simply known as the Chaplain, a scholar of this court whose work *Tractatus de Amore* is referred to here, one of the basic works on medieval chivalry and the courts of love.—ED.

a gush of tears from the tender audience clustered about the queen and the Countess of Champagne.

After the romance of the evening in the queen's court, the jury comes to attention upon petition of a young knight in the hall. He bespeaks the judgment of the queen and her ladies upon a point of conduct, through an advocate, of course, so he may remain anonymous. A certain knight, the advocate deposes, has sworn to his lady, as the hard condition of obtaining her love, that he will upon no provocation boast of her merits in company. But one day he overhears detractors heaping his mistress with calumnies. Forgetting his vow in the heat of his passion, he warms to eloquence in defense of his lady. This coming to her ears, she repudiates her champion. Does the lover, who admits he has broken his pledge to his mistress, deserve in this instance to be driven from her presence?

The Countess of Champagne, subduing suggestions from the floor and the buzz of conference upon the dais, renders the judgment of the areopagus. The lady in the case, anonymous of course, is at fault, declares the Countess Marie. She has laid upon her lover a vow too impossibly difficult. The lover has been remiss, no doubt, in breaking his vow to his mistress, no matter what cruel hardship it involves; but he deserves leniency for the merit of his ardor and his constancy. The jury recommends that the stern lady reinstate the plaintiff. The court takes down the judgment. It constitutes a precedent. Does anyone guess the identity of the young pair whose estrangement is thus delicately knit up by the countess? As a bit of suspense it is delicious. As a theme for talk, how loosening to the tongue!

A disappointed petitioner brings forward a case, through an advocate, involving the question whether love survives marriage. The countess, applying her mind to the code, which says that marriage is no proper obstacle to lovers (*Causa coniugii ab amore non est excusatio recta*), and after grave deliberation with her ladies, creates a sensation in the court by expressing doubt whether love in the ideal sense can exist between spouses. This is so arresting a proposition that the observations of the countess are referred to the queen for corroboration, and all wait upon the opinion of this deeply experienced judge. The queen with dignity affirms that she cannot gainsay the Countess of Champagne, though she finds it admirable that a wife should find love and marriage consonant. Eleanor, Queen of France and then of England, had learned at fifty-two that, as another medieval lady put it, "Mortal love is but the licking of honey from thorns."

Eleanor the Regent
MARION MEADE

*During the years of Eleanor's dalliance at Poitiers, her husband's larger
world had been turned upside down by his quarrel with Thomas Becket.
It had not ended even with the martyrdom of that troublesome prelate at
the altar of Canterbury in 1170. The question of whether Henry ordered
Becket's murder or not—and he probably did not—is quite immaterial.
For he bore its consequences. And its principal consequence was to
give to the French king a priceless justification to move against Henry
and his fiefs. What is more, Henry's own sons were as often as not in
league with the French king. With some of this devil's brood of offspring
Henry had been too hard, with others too soft. And when he favored one,
the others feared and plotted against the favorite of the moment. Even
Henry's proposed disposition of his estates and titles served only to
further their quarrels with each other and with him. These quarrels
reached their first climax in the great rebellion of 1173, in which Henry
the young king, Richard, and Geoffrey were in open alliance with Louis of
France against their father. To the alliance flocked rebellious barons
from Scotland to Aquitaine. Henry charged Eleanor with sedition and
with embittering his sons against him. As the rebellion faltered and then
was quelled, Henry was reconciled, however fitfully, with his sons but not
their mother. With Eleanor, Henry was unyielding. She was imprisoned,
first at Salisbury Castle, later at Winchester and other places, for the next
sixteen years. One must imagine that the captivity was genteel, but it was
nonetheless real. From time to time, she was released for a holiday visit
to court or to participate in some stormy family council.*

*In the last years of her imprisonment two of her sons, Henry and
Geoffrey, had died, but the surviving sons, Richard and John, could still
intrigue against their father. They did so in league with a new and more
dangerous Capetian enemy, Philip II Augustus, the able and energetic
son of Louis VII, who had followed him to the throne in 1180. Henry II's
final years were filled with his sons' rebellion, and he died in 1189
shamed by defeat at their hands. It was only after Henry's death and the
succession of Richard that Eleanor was released from her captivity.*

*With none of her ardor dimmed, the queen, now almost seventy, set
about to serve her favored son, now king at last. While Richard was still on
the Continent, Eleanor assumed the regency and on her own authority
convoked a court at Westminster to demand the oaths of loyalty from the
English feudality to their new king. She then traveled to other centers to
take similar obeisances and to set the affairs of the kingdom in order.*

Her son arrived for an undisputed coronation in the summer of 1189.

But Richard's thoughts in that triumphal summer season were not upon the affairs of England or any of his other lands. He had already taken the cross almost two years before, and the third crusade was about to begin. The Lion-Hearted was to be its greatest hero.

The third crusade, despite Richard's heroics, was as unsuccessful as the second. And, after three years, during which most of his fellow crusaders had declared their vows discharged and returned to their own lands— including his Capetian rival, Philip Augustus—Richard started for home.

We pick up the story of his return—with its delays and betrayals— and of Eleanor's role in it from her most recent biography, by Marian Meade, Eleanor of Aquitaine, A Biography. *Meade's book is broadly revisionist, and the basis of her revisionism is her feminist sympathy. She observes that "the historical record, written to accommodate men" has judged Eleanor ". . . a bitch, harlot, adultress, and monster" and that this is not surprising "for she was one of those rare women who altogether refused to be bound by the rules of proper behavior for her sex; she did as she pleased, although not without agonizing personal struggle" (p. ix). In Meade's account, as in any other account of Eleanor, there is much latitude for interpretation, given the pervasive silence of contemporary chronicles. Meade further argues that even these are "riddled with lies since monks and historians—in the twelfth century one and the same—have always abhorred emancipated women" (p. xi). Meade intends to redress the balance. And she does so, in no part of her account more forcefully than in the following passage.*

IN ENGLAND, Eleanor was expecting her son home for Christmas. All through November and early December companies of Crusaders had begun arriving in the kingdom; in the ports and marketplaces there were firsthand reports of the king's deeds in Palestine and plans for celebrations once he arrived. But the days passed without news, and newly arrived contingents of soldiers expressed astonishment that they had beaten the king home although they had left Acre after Richard. Along the coast, lookouts peered into the foggy Channel in hope of sighting the royal vessel, and messengers waited to race over the frozen roads toward London with the news of the king's landing. Eleanor learned that Berengaria and Joanna[2] had safely reached Rome, but of her son, weeks overdue, there was an alarming lack of information. She held a cheerless Christmas court at Westminster, her apprehension mounting with each day, her silent fears being expressed openly in the ale houses along the Thames: The king had

---

[2] Berengaria was Richard's wife—a Spanish princess he had married, at Eleanor's urging, on his way to the crusade. Joanna was Richard's sister, the widowed Queen of Sicily, whom he had taken under his protection to Palestine.—ED.

encountered some calamity, a storm along the Adriatic coast no doubt, and now he would never return.

Three days after Christmas, the whereabouts of the tardy Richard Plantagenet became known, not at Westminster but at the Cité Palace in Paris. On December 28, Philip Augustus received an astounding letter from his good friend Henry Hohenstaufen, the Holy Roman emperor: [3]

> We have thought it proper to inform your nobleness that while the enemy of our empire and the disturber of your kingdom, Richard, King of England, was crossing the sea to his dominions, it chanced that the winds caused him to be shipwrecked in the region of Istria, at a place which lies between Aquila and Venice. . . . The roads being duly watched and the entire area well-guarded, our dearly beloved cousin Leopold, Duke of Austria, captured the king in a humble house in a village near Vienna. Inasmuch as he is now in our power, and has always done his utmost for your annoyance and disturbance, we have thought it proper to relay this information to your nobleness.

Shortly after the first of the new year, 1193, the archbishop of Rouen was able to send Eleanor a copy of the letter, accompanied by a covering note in which he cited whatever comforting quotations he could recall from Scripture to cover an outrage of this magnitude.

Eleanor's most imperative problem—finding the location where Richard was being held prisoner—she tackled with her usual energy and resourcefulness. From all points, emissaries were dispatched to find the king: Eleanor herself sent the abbots of Boxley and Pontrobert to roam the villages of Bavaria and Swabia, following every lead and rumor; Hubert Walter, bishop of Salisbury, stopping in Italy on his way home from the Crusade, changed course and hastened to Germany; even William Longchamp, the exiled chancellor, set out at once from Paris to trace his master. It was not until March, however, that Richard's chaplain, Anselm, who had shared many of the king's misadventures, arrived in England, and Eleanor was able to obtain authentic details [including the fact that Richard was being held in a remote castle of Durrenstein in Austria].

Treachery was rife not only in Germany but in Paris and Rouen; it even percolated rapidly in the queen's own family. Before Eleanor could take steps to secure Coeur de Lion's release, she was faced with more immediate catastrophes in the form of Philip Augustus and his newest ally, her son John. These two proceeded on the assumption that Richard, king of England, was dead. Or as good as dead. But before Eleanor could take her youngest son in hand, he fled to Normandy, where he declared him-

---

[3] The Plantagenet kings were related by marriage to the great German feudal family, the Welfs, who were the most dangerous rivals to the imperial house of Hohenstaufen. The Angevins, including Richard, had frequently supported the Welfs, hence the emperor's hostility.—ED.

self the king's heir, an announcement the Norman barons greeted with disdain. John did not wait to convince them, proceeding instead to Paris, where he did homage to Philip for the Plantagenet Continental domains and furthermore agreeing to confirm Philip's right to the Vexin.[4] . . . In the meantime, Eleanor, "who then ruled England," had taken the precaution of closing the Channel ports and ordering the defense of the eastern coast against a possible invasion, her hastily mustered home guard being instructed to wield any weapon that came to hand, including their plowing tools.

At this point, Eleanor's dilemma in regard to her sons would have taxed the most patient of mothers. John, returning to England, swaggered about the countryside proclaiming himself the next king of England —perhaps he sincerely believed that Richard would never be released alive—and, never known for his sensitivity, constantly regaled Eleanor with the latest rumors concerning the fate of her favorite son. Her actions during this period indicate clearly that she failed to take John seriously. Although he was twenty-seven, she thought of him as the baby of the family, always a child showing off and trying to attract attention. Her attitude was probably close to that of Richard's when, a few months later, he was informed of John's machinations: "My brother John is not the man to subjugate a country if there is a person able to make the slightest resistance to his attempts." With one hand, Eleanor deftly managed to anticipate John's plots and render him harmless; with the other, she worked for Richard's release. After Easter, the king had been removed from Durrenstein Castle and the hands of Duke Leopold and, after some haggling, had been taken into custody by Leopold's suzerain, the Holy Roman emperor. As the emperor's prisoner, Richard found himself the object of high-level decisions. His death, it was decided, would achieve no useful purpose; rather the arrogant Plantagenets, or what remained of them, should be made to redeem their kin, but at a price that would bring their provinces to their knees: 100,000 silver marks with two hundred hostages as surety for payment. The hostages, it was specified, were to be chosen from among the leading barons of England and Normandy or from their children.

Relieved as Eleanor must have felt to learn that her son could be purchased, she could only have been appalled at the size of the ransom. The prospect of collecting such an enormous sum, thirty-five tons of pure silver, seemed impossible after Henry's Saladin tithe [5] and Richard's great sale before the Crusade.[6] Where was the money to be found? Where were two hundred noble hostages to be located? At a council convened at Saint

---

[4] The Vexin was an area at the juncture of Normandy, Anjou, and the Ile de France, long disputed by the English and French kings.—ED.

[5] A tax that Henry had levied for a crusade, hence called after the great Moslem leader Saladin.—ED.

[6] A sale not only of movable property of the crown but that of such protected folk as foreign and Jewish merchants, and what could be extracted from the nobility.—ED.

Albans on June 1, 1193, she appointed five officers to assist with the dreaded task. During the summer and fall, England became a marketplace to raise the greatest tax in its history. The kingdom was stripped of its wealth: "No subject, lay or clerk, rich or poor, was overlooked. No one could say, 'Behold I am only So-and-So or Such-and-Such, pray let me be excused.' " Barons were taxed one-quarter of a year's income. Churches and abbeys were relieved of their movable wealth, including the crosses on their altars. The Cistercians, who possessed no riches, sheared their flocks and donated a year's crop of wool. Before long, the bars of silver and gold began slowly to pile up in the crypt of Saint Paul's Cathedral under Eleanor's watchful eyes. But not quickly enough to comfort her. Even more painful was the job of recruiting hostages from the great families, their lamentations and pleadings rising like a sulphurous mist all over the kingdom and providing constant agony for the queen.

From Haguenau, where Richard was incarcerated, came a flood of letters to his subjects and most especially to his "much loved mother." He had been received with honor by the emperor and his court, he is well, he hopes to be home soon. He realizes that the ransom will be difficult to raise but he feels sure that his subjects will not shirk their duty; all sums collected should be entrusted to the queen. . . .

It is said that in her anguish she addressed three letters to Pope Celestine III imploring his assistance in securing Richard's release and in her salutation addressed the pontiff as "Eleanor, by the wrath of God, Queen of England." . . . Why, she demands, does the sword of Saint Peter slumber in its scabbard when her son a "most delicate youth," the anointed of the Lord, lies in chains? Why does the pope, a "negligent," "cruel" prevaricator and sluggard, do nothing?

These letters, supposedly written for her by Peter of Blois, are so improbable that it is surprising that many modern historians have accepted them as authentic. While preserved among the letters of Peter of Blois, who is undoubtedly their author—they are characteristic of his style and use his favorite expressions—there is no evidence that they were written for Eleanor or that they were ever sent. Most likely they were rhetorical exercises. No contemporary of Eleanor's mentioned that she wrote to the pope, and not until the seventeenth century were the letters attributed to her. From a diplomatic point of view, they are too fanciful to be genuine; Eleanor, clearheaded and statesmanlike, was never a querulous old woman complaining of age, infirmities, and weariness of life. On the contrary, her contemporaries unanimously credit her with the utmost courage, industry, and political skill. A second point to notice is that the details of the letters misrepresent the facts of Richard's imprisonment. He was never "detained in bonds," and as both she and the pope knew, Celestine had instantly, upon receiving news of Richard's capture, excommunicated Duke Leopold for laying violent hands on a brother Crusader; he had threatened Philip Augustus with an interdict if he trespassed upon Plantagenet territories; and he had menaced the English with interdict should they fail to collect the ransom. Under the circumstances, Celestine had done all he could. In the last analysis, the letters must be viewed as Peter of Blois's perception of Eleanor's feelings, a view that may or may not be accurate.

In December 1193, Eleanor set sail with an imposing retinue of clerks, chaplains, earls, bishops, hostages, and chests containing the ransom. By January 17, 1194, the day scheduled for Richard's release, she had presented herself and the money at Speyer, but no sooner had they arrived than, to her amazement, Henry Hohenstaufen announced a further delay. He had received letters that placed an entirely new light on the matter of the king's liberation. As the gist of the problem emerged, it seemed Philip Augustus and John Plantagenet had offered the emperor an equivalent amount of silver if he could hold Coeur de Lion in custody another nine months, or deliver him up to them. These disclosures, and Henry's serious consideration of the counteroffer, provoked horror from the emperor's own vassals, and after two days of argument, Henry relented. He would liberate Richard as promised if the king of England would do homage to him for all his possessions, including the kingdom of England. This request, a calculated humiliation, would have made Richard a vassal of the Holy Roman emperor, a degradation that the Plantagenets were hard put to accept. Quick to realize the meaninglessness, as well as the illegality, of the required act, Eleanor made an on-the-spot decision. According to Roger of Hovedon, Richard, "by advice of his mother Eleanor, abdicated the throne of the kingdom of England and delivered it to the emperor as the lord of all." On February 4, the king was released "into the hands of his mother" after a captivity of one year six weeks and three days.

Seven weeks later, on March 12, the king's party landed at Sandwich and proceeded directly to Canterbury, where they gave thanks at the tomb of Saint Thomas. By the time they reached London, the city had been decorated, the bells were clanging furiously, and the Londoners ready to give a rapturous welcome to their hero and champion. Her eldest son "hailed with joy upon the Strand," Eleanor looked in vain for the remaining male member of her family, but the youngest Plantagenet was nowhere to be found. Once Richard's release had been confirmed, he had fled to Paris upon Philip Augustus's warning that "beware, the devil is loose." . . .

According to the chronicles, "the king and John became reconciled through the mediation of Queen Eleanor, their mother." In the circumstances, it seemed the safest course as well as the wisest. There was no doubt in Eleanor's mind that the boy, now twenty-eight, could not be held responsible for his actions, that he was, as Richard of Devizes termed him, "light-minded." But at that moment, he was the last of the Plantagenets. With luck, Richard might reign another twenty-five years or more. Who was to say that he would not produce an heir of his own? Thus the queen must have reasoned in the spring of 1194 when her son, after so many adversities, had come home to her.

Suggestions for Further Reading

SEVERAL OF THE general works listed for the last chapter will also be useful for this one since Abelard and Eleanor of Aquitaine were both figures of the twelfth century. But, as we have seen, despite her importance and inherent interest there are virtually no contemporary source materials for Eleanor. Thus, whether hostile or sympathetic, the treatments of Eleanor have had to be not so much biographies as life-and-times books. This is true even of the best modern works. Two of them, Amy Kelly, *Eleanor of Aquitaine and the Four Kings* (Cambridge, Mass.: Harvard University Press, 1950), and Marion Meade, *Eleanor of Aquitaine, A Biography* (New York: Hawthorn, 1977), are excerpted in this chapter, and students are encouraged to read further in them. Two additional works are also recommended: Curtis H. Walker, *Eleanor of Aquitaine* (Chapel Hill: University of North Carolina Press, 1950), and Regine Pernoud, *Eleanor of Aquitaine*, tr. P. Wiles (New York: Coward-McCann, 1967), both well written, lively, and fast moving. *Eleanor of Aquitaine, Patron and Politician,* ed. Wm. W. Kibler (Austin: University of Texas Press, 1976), is a series of specialized papers on aspects of Eleanor's life and reign.

Of Eleanor's contemporaries, the best, most comprehensive, and up-to-date work on Henry II is W. L. Warren, *Henry II* (London: Eyre Methuen, 1973). Somewhat less intimidating are the smaller but entirely competent Richard Barber, *Henry Plantagenet* (Totowa, N.J.: Rowman and Littlefield, 1964), and John Schlight, *Henry II Plantagenet*, "Rulers and Statesmen of the World" (New York: Twayne, 1973). Probably the best biography of Richard I is Philip Henderson, *Richard Coeur de Lion, A Biography* (New York: Norton, 1959), but students are also encouraged to read James A. Brundage, *Richard Lion Heart* (New York: Scribners, 1974), largely a study of Richard as soldier and crusader and a tough, realistic work. The standard work on John is Sidney Painter, *The Reign of King John* (Baltimore: Johns Hopkins University Press, 1949). W. J. Warren, *King John* (New York: Norton, 1961), is a somewhat revisionist treatment of John showing him as a hard-working monarch and more the victim than the causer of his troubles—but he still is a far from attractive figure. For Eleanor's French royal contemporaries see R. Fawtier, *The Capetian Kings of France*, tr. Lionel Butler and R. J. Adam (London: Macmillan, 1960). There are a handful of studies of important nonroyal figures whose lives intertwined with Eleanor's: Sidney Painter, *William Marshall, Knight Errant, Baron, and Regent of England* (Baltimore: Johns Hopkins University Press, 1933); Charles

R. Young, *Hubert Walter, Lord of Canterbury and Lord of England* (Durham, N.C.: Duke University Press, 1968); and a number of books on the durable subject of Henry and Becket—the best are Richard Winston, *Thomas Becket* (New York: Knopf, 1967), a tough, skeptical, but solidly source-based work; Dom David Knowles, *Thomas Becket* (London: A. and C. Black, 1970), a scrupulously objective account by a great ecclesiastical historian, but, naturally, most occupied with the arguments of Thomas and the church; and finally, Alfred L. Duggan, *My Life for My Sheep* (New York: Coward-McCann, 1955), a lively novelized account by an experienced historical novelist.

Two special topics relate to Eleanor throughout her life—chivalry and courtly love and the crusades. Both have been much studied and written about. On chivalry and courtly love, see two excellent and well-written background works—John C. Moore, *Love in Twelfth-Century France* (Philadelphia: University of Pennsylvania Press, 1972), and Jack Lindsay, *The Troubadours and Their World of the Twelfth and Thirteenth Centuries* (London: Frederick Muller, 1976), and two equally interesting ones dealing with the actual operation of knightly chivalry as well as its romanticized literary aspects—Sidney Painter, *French Chivalry, Chivalric Ideas and Practices in Medieval France* (Baltimore: Johns Hopkins University Press, 1940), and the more comprehensive Richard Barber, *The Knight and Chivalry* (New York: Scribners, 1970). The standard work on the crusades is now *The History of the Crusades* (Philadelphia: University of Pennsylvania Press, 1955–1962), a great multiauthored work under the general editorship of Kenneth M. Setton: vol. 1, *The First Hundred Years*, ed. M. W. Baldwin, and vol. 2, *The Later Crusades, 1189–1311*, ed. R. L. Wolff. Steven Runciman, *A History of the Crusades*, 3 vols. (Cambridge, England: Cambridge University Press, 1951–1954), may, however, still be the best account. Students may prefer Zoé Oldenbourg, *The Crusaders,* tr. Anne Carter (New York: Pantheon, 1966), somewhat less successful than her famous historical novels but still excellent and exciting.

The Meaning
of Dante

The ambitious title of this chapter does not announce a new breakthrough
in Dante scholarship. It refers instead to the sampling of views
presented here from the incredible volume of writing that has been done
in an attempt to determine what Dante means—as historical figure,
as historical symbol, or as a symbol of eternal truths. The need to
"interpret" Dante in order to discover his meaning arises in part from
the great complexity and range of his work and its seeming obscurity to
many modern readers and in part from the contradictory rather than
conforming nature of Dante himself.

In his youth Dante fought for the Guelf cause and was a functionary
of Guelf Florence. As a mature exile he reviled his city—"ingrato
popolo maligno"—revived classical Ghibellinism, made an unlikely hero
of the Emperor Henry VII, and lodged Pope Boniface VIII in hell!
Although he remained a layman, Dante was as learned in theology as
any clerical theologian of his time. He wrote a book defending the
use of the vernacular, but he wrote it in Latin, *De Vulgari Eloquentia,*
and then chose to write his greatest work, *The Divine Comedy,* in the
vernacular Italian.

The problem of interpreting Dante is further complicated by the nature
of our information about him. Dante was reticent and prickly, stiff,
aloof, and secretive about himself, and, as a result, few of the routine
facts of his life were recorded. We have, of course, the great corpus

of his work, which even contains, in the *Vita Nuova,* what one scholar has called "one of the great spiritual autobiographies of all time." But Dante himself leaves many important questions unanswered, and his contemporaries are not much more helpful. In spite of the fact that Dante was the most famous poet of his time, with an international reputation and following, he had no contemporary biographer. The earliest life of Dante appeared some half century after his death, written by his fellow Florentine, Giovanni Boccaccio.

The Life of Dante
BOCCACCIO

Boccaccio (1313–1375), like Dante earlier, was one of the most celebrated literary figures of his own generation. Yet his Vita di Dante *is, in many respects, an unsatisfactory biography. The humanist Leonardo Bruni, who wrote a short sketch of Dante still another generation later, found it so. He took Boccaccio to task for his failure to collect the physical evidence about Dante's life and the recollections of contemporaries while they were still available. He criticized him for dwelling on the poet rather than the man. But Boccaccio, a poet himself, was much more interested in this aspect of his subject. We owe to Boccaccio the first body of serious, systematic Dante criticism, as well as the earliest biography. Indeed, Boccaccio was drawn to Dante in many ways and for many reasons, not the least of which was that Boccaccio was a master of the Italian language second only to Dante among its early literary users.*

But the generation gap between Dante and Boccaccio was also an important factor. For, unlike Dante, Boccaccio clearly lived across whatever line we may use to separate the Middle Ages from the Renaissance. Moreover, he was not only "in" but "of" the early Renaissance. He was a friend and disciple of Petrarch, "the Father of Humanism," and, while he did not share his master's snobbish disdain for the vernacular, he adopted a great many of his other notions and prejudices. One of these was a propensity to see the age in which he lived as a new age—"novus ordo saeculorum"—rather sharply set off from the barbaric period of the recent past, which later humanists would contemptuously dub "the Middle Ages," "the Dark Ages," or "the Gothic Age." And in his enthusiasm for Dante, Boccaccio tended to carry him across into his own new age, to view him as the first "modern" poet who had rescued literary art from the darkness, obscurity, and ignorance in which it had languished since antiquity.

We turn now to Boccaccio's account from The Life of Dante.

. . . I AM GOING to record the banishment of that most illustrious man, Dante Alighieri, an ancient citizen and born of no mean parents, who merited as much through his virtue, learning, and good services as is adequately shown and will be shown by the deeds he wrought. If such deeds had been done in a just republic, we believe they would have earned for him the highest rewards.

O iniquitous design! O shameless deed! O wretched example, clear proof of ruin to come! Instead of these rewards there was meted to him an unjust and bitter condemnation, perpetual banishment with alienation of his paternal goods, and, could it have been effected, the profanation of his glorious renown by false charges. The recent traces of his flight, his bones buried in an alien land, and his children scattered in the houses of others, still in part bear witness to these things. If all the other iniquities of Florence could be hidden from the all-seeing eyes of God, should not this one suffice to provoke his wrath upon her? Yea, in truth. . . .

But inasmuch as we should not only flee evil deeds, albeit they seem to go unpunished, but also by right action should strive to amend them, I, although not fitted for so great a task, will try to do according to my little talent what the city should have done with magnificence, but has not. For I recognize that I am a part, though a small one, of that same city whereof Dante Alighieri, if his merits, his nobleness, and his virtue be considered, was a very great part, and that for this reason I, like every other citizen, am personally responsible for the honors due him. Not with a statue shall I honor him, nor with splendid obsequies—which customs no longer hold among us, nor would my powers suffice therefor—but with words I shall honor him, feeble though they be for so great an undertaking. Of these I have, and of these will I give, that other nations may not say that his native land, both as a whole and in part, has been equally ungrateful to so great a poet. . . .

This special glory of Italy was born in our city in the year of the saving incarnation of the King of the universe 1265, when the Roman Empire was without a ruler owing to the death of the [Emperor] Frederick, and Pope Urban the Fourth was sitting in the chair of Saint Peter. The family into which he was born was of a smiling fortune—smiling, I mean, if we consider the condition of the world that then obtained. I will omit all consideration of his infancy—whatever it may have been—wherein appeared many signs of the coming glory of his genius. But I will note that from his earliest boyhood, having already learned the rudiments of letters, he gave himself and all his time, not to youthful lust and indolence, after the fashion of the nobles of to-day, lolling at ease in the lap of his mother, but to continued study, in his native city, of the liberal arts, so that he became exceedingly expert therein. And as his mind and genius ripened with his years, he devoted himself, not to lucrative pursuits, whereto every one in general now hastens, but, with a laudable desire for perpetual fame, scorning transitory riches, he freely dedicated himself to the acquisition of a complete knowledge of poetic creations and of their exposition by rules of art. In this exercise he became closely intimate with Virgil, Horace, Ovid, Statius, and with every other famous poet. And not only did he delight to know them, but he strove to imitate them in lofty song, even as his works demonstrate, whereof we shall speak at the proper time. . . .

. . . . And to the end that no region of philosophy should remain un-

visited by him, he penetrated with acute genius into the profoundest depths
of theology. Nor was the result far distant from the aim. Unmindful of
heat and cold, vigils and fasts, and every other physical hardship, by
assiduous study he grew to such knowledge of the Divine Essence and of
the other Separate Intelligences as can be compassed here by the human
intellect. And as by application various sciences were learned by him
at various periods, so he mastered them in various studies under various
teachers. . . .

Studies in general, and speculative studies in particular—to which, as
has been shown, our Dante wholly applied himself—usually demand solitude, remoteness from care, and tranquility of mind. Instead of this
retirement and quiet, Dante had, almost from the beginning of his life
down to the day of his death, a violent and insufferable passion of love, a
wife, domestic and public cares, exile, and poverty, not to mention those
more particular cares which these necessarily involve. The former I deem
it fitting to explain in detail, in order that their burden may appear the
greater.

In that season wherein the sweetness of heaven reclothes the earth with
all its adornments, and makes her all smiling with varied flowers scattered
among green leaves, the custom obtained in our city that men and women
should keep festival in different gatherings, each person in his neighbor-
hood. And so it chanced that among others Folco Portinari, a man held
in great esteem among his fellow-citizens, on the first day of May gathered
his neighbors in his house for a feast. Now among these came the afore-
mentioned Alighieri, followed by Dante, who was still in his ninth year;
for little children are wont to follow their fathers, especially to places of
festival. And mingling here in the house of the feast-giver with others of
his own age, of whom there were many, both boys and girls, when the first
tables had been served he boyishly entered with the others into the games,
so far as his tender age permitted.

Now amid the throng of children was a little daughter of the aforesaid
Folco, whose name was Bice, though he always called her by her full
name, Beatrice. She was, it may be, eight years old, very graceful for her
age, full gentle and pleasing in her actions, and much more serious and
modest in her words and ways than her few years required. Her features
were most delicate and perfectly proportioned, and, in addition to their
beauty, full of such pure loveliness that many thought her almost a little
angel. She, then, such as I picture her, or it may be far more beautiful,
appeared at this feast to the eyes of our Dante; not, I suppose, for the
first time, but for the first time with power to inspire him with love. And
he, though still a child, received the lovely image of her into his heart with
so great affection that it never left him from that day forward so long as
he lived.

Now just what this affection was no one knows, but certainly it is true
that Dante at an early age became a most ardent servitor of love. . . .

Forsaking, therefore, all other matters, with the utmost solicitude he went wherever he thought he might see her, as if he were to attain from her face and her eyes all his happiness and complete consolation.

O insensate judgment of lovers! who but they would think to check the flames by adding to the fuel? Dante himself in his *Vita Nuova* in part makes known how many and of what nature were the thoughts, the sighs, the tears, and the other grievous passions that he later suffered by reason of this love, wherefore I do not care to rehearse them more in detail. This much alone I do not wish to pass over without mention, namely, that according as he himself writes, and as others to whom his passion was known bear witness, this love was most virtuous, nor did there ever appear by look or word or sign any sensual appetite either in the lover or in the thing beloved; no little marvel to the present world, from which all innocent pleasure has so fled, and which is so accustomed to have the thing that pleases it conform to its lust before it has concluded to love it, that he who loves otherwise has become a miracle, even as a thing most rare.

If such love for so long season could interrupt his eating, his sleep, and every quietness, how great an enemy must we think it to have been to his sacred studies and to his genius? Certainly no mean one, although many maintain that it urged his genius on, and argue for proof from his graceful rimed compositions in the Florentine idiom, written in praise of his beloved and for the expression of his ardors and amorous conceits. But truly I should not agree with this, unless I first admitted that ornate writing is the most essential part of every science—which is not true.

As every one may plainly perceive, there is nothing stable in this world, and, if anything is subject to change, it is our life. A trifle too much cold or heat within us, not to mention countless other accidents and possibilities, easily leads us from existence to non-existence. Nor is gentle birth privileged against this, nor riches, nor youth, nor any other worldly dignity. Dante must needs experience the force of this general law by another's death before he did by his own. The most beautiful Beatrice was near the end of her twenty-fourth year when, as it pleased Him who governs all things, she left the sufferings of this world, and passed to the glory that her virtues had prepared for her.

. . . By her departure Dante was thrown into such sorrow, such grief and tears, that many of those nearest him, both relatives and friends, believed that death alone would end them. They expected that this would shortly come to pass, seeing that he gave no ear to the comfort and consolation offered him. The days were like the nights, and the nights like the days. Not an hour of them passed without groans, and sighs, and an abundant quantity of tears. His eyes seemed two copious springs of welling water, so that most men wondered whence he received moisture enough for his weeping. . . .

In Dante's time the citizens of Florence were perversely divided into two factions, and by the operations of astute and prudent leaders each party was very powerful, so that sometimes one ruled and sometimes the other, to the displeasure of its defeated rival. . . .

Dante decided, then, to pursue the fleeting honor and false glory of public office. Perceiving that he could not support by himself a third party, which, in itself just, should overthrow the injustice of the two others and reduce them to unity, he allied himself with that faction which seemed to him to possess most of justice and reason—working always for that which he recognized as salutary to his country and her citizens. But human counsels are commonly defeated by the powers of heaven. Hatred and enmities arose, though without just cause, and waxed greater day by day; so that many times the citizens rushed to arms, to their utmost confusion. They purposed to end the struggle by fire and sword, and were so blinded by wrath that they did not see that they themselves would perish miserably thereby.

After each of the factions had given many proofs of their strength to their mutual loss, the time came when the secret counsels of threatening Fortune were to be disclosed. Rumor, who reports both the true and the false, announced that the foes of Dante's faction were strengthened by wise and wonderful designs and by an immense multitude of armed men, and by this means so terrified the leaders of his party that she banished from their minds all consideration, all forethought, all reason, save how to flee in safety. Together with them Dante, instantly precipitated from the chief rule of his city, beheld himself not only brought low to the earth, but banished from his country. Not many days after this expulsion, when the populace had already rushed to the houses of the exiles, and had furiously pillaged and gutted them, the victors reorganized the city after their pleasure, condemning all the leaders of their adversaries to perpetual exile as capital enemies of the republic, and with them Dante, not as one of the lesser leaders, but as it were the chief one. Their real property was meanwhile confiscated or alienated to the victors.

This reward Dante gained for the tender love which he had borne his country! . . .

In such wise, then, Dante left that city whereof not only he was a citizen, but of which his ancestors had been the rebuilders. . . .

Boccaccio recounts Dante's exile and his wandering from court to court, city to city, and his hopes for a restoration of order in Italy dashed by the death of the Emperor Henry VII.

Since all hope, though not the desire, of ever returning to Florence was gone, Dante continued in Ravenna several years, under the protection of its gracious lord. And here he taught and trained many scholars in poetry, and especially in the vernacular, which he first, in my opinion, exalted and made esteemed among us Italians, even as Homer did his tongue among the Greeks, and Virgil his among the Latins. Although the vulgar tongue is supposed to have originated some time before him, none thought or dared to make the language an instrument of any artistic matter, save in the numbering of syllables, and in the consonance of its endings. They employed it, rather, in the light things of love. Dante showed in effect that every lofty subject could be treated of in this medium, and made our vulgar tongue above all others glorious.

But even as the appointed hour comes for every man, so Dante also, at or near the middle of his fifty-sixth year, fell ill. And having humbly and devoutly received the sacraments of the Church according to the Christian religion, and having reconciled himself to God in contrition for all that he, as a mortal, had committed against His pleasure, in the month of September in the year of Christ 1321, on the day whereon the Exaltation of the Holy Cross is celebrated by the Church, not without great sorrow on the part of the aforesaid Guido and in general of all the other citizens of Ravenna, he rendered to his Creator his weary spirit. . . .

Our poet was of moderate height, and, after reaching maturity, was accustomed to walk somewhat bowed, with a slow and gentle pace, clad always in such sober dress as befitted his ripe years. His face was long, his nose aquiline, and his eyes rather large than small. His jaws were large, and the lower lip protruded beyond the upper. His complexion was dark, his hair and beard thick, black, and curled, and his expression ever melancholy and thoughtful.

Our poet, in addition . . . was of a lofty and disdainful spirit. On one occasion a friend, moved by entreaties, labored that Dante might return to Florence—which thing the poet desired above all else—but he found no way thereto with those who then held the government in their hands save that Dante should remain in prison for a certain time, and after that be presented as a subject for mercy at some public solemnity in our principal church, whereby he should be free and exempt from all sentences previously passed upon him. But this seemed to Dante a fitting procedure for abject, if not infamous, men and for no others. Therefore, notwithstanding his great desire, he chose to remain in exile rather than return home by such a road. O laudable and magnanimous scorn, how manfully hast thou acted in repressing the ardent desire to return, when it was only possible by a way unworthy of a man nourished in the bosom of philosophy! . . .

This glorious poet composed many works during his lifetime, an orderly arrangement of which would, I think, be fitting, in order that his works may not be attributed to some one else, and that the works of another may not be ascribed to him.

In the first place, while his tears still flowed for the death of Beatrice, in his twenty-sixth year or thereabouts, he brought together in a little volume, entitled *Vita Nuova,* certain marvelously beautiful pieces in rime, like sonnets and canzoni, which he had previously written at various times.

Before each one he wrote in order the causes that had led him to compose it, and after each one he placed its divisions. Although in his maturer years he was greatly ashamed of this little book, nevertheless, if his age be considered, it is very beautiful and pleasing, especially to the common people.

. . . Having long premeditated what was to be done, in his thirty-fifth year he began to put into effect what he had before deliberated upon, namely, to censure and reward the lives of men according to the diversity of their merits. And inasmuch as he saw that life was of three sorts—the vicious life, the life of departing from vice and advancing toward virtue, and the virtuous life—he admirably divided his work, which he entitled *Commedia,* into three books, in the first of which he censured the wicked and in the last rewarded the good. The three books he again divided into cantos, and the cantos into rhythms (*ritmi*), as may be plainly seen. He composed it in rime and in the vernacular with such art, and in so wonderful and beautiful an order, that there has yet been none who could justly find any fault therewith.

The Historical Dante
HENRY OSBORN TAYLOR

Although at the present time Dante is usually considered to be at least a transitional figure between the Middle Ages and the Renaissance, historians have traditionally viewed him as the summation of all the trends and tendencies of the Middle Ages. No one exemplifies this interpretive approach better than the American medievalist Henry Osborn Taylor (d. 1941). Taylor's most important book was his massive, brilliant, and original The Mediaeval Mind, *still one of the standard works in medieval intellectual history. The following selection is from the chapter on Dante, subtitled "The Mediaeval Synthesis," in which Dante is seen as bringing together all the strands of medieval thought and temperament.*

. . . [DANTE] IS NOT merely mediaeval; he is the end of the mediaeval development and the proper issue of the mediaeval genius.

Yes, there is unity throughout the diversity of mediaeval life; and Dante is the proof. For the elements of mediaeval growth combine in him, demonstrating their congruity by working together in the stature of the full-grown mediaeval man. When the contents of patristic Christianity and the surviving antique culture had been conceived anew, and had been felt as well, and novel forms of sentiment evolved, at last comes Dante to possess the whole, to think it, feel it, visualize its sum, and make of it a poem. He had mastered the field of mediaeval knowledge, diligently cultivating parts of it, like the Graeco-Arabian astronomy; he thought and reasoned in the terms and assumptions of scholastic (chiefly Thomist-Aristotelian) philosophy; his intellectual interests were mediaeval; he felt the mediaeval reverence for the past, being impassioned with the ancient greatness of Rome and the lineage of virtue and authority moving from it to him and thirteenth-century Italy and the already shattered Holy Roman Empire. He took earnest joy in the Latin Classics, approaching them from mediaeval points of view, accepting their contents uncritically. He was affected with the preciosity of courtly or chivalric love, which Italy had made her own along with the songs of the Troubadours and the poetry of northern France. His emotions flowed in channels of current convention, save that they overfilled them; this was true as to his early love, and true as to his final range of religious and poetic feeling. His was the emotion and the cruelty of mediaeval religious conviction; while in his mind (so worked the genius of symbolism) every fact's apparent meaning was clothed with the significance of other modes of truth.

Dante was also an Italian of the period in which he lived; and he was a marvellous poet. One may note in him what was mediaeval, what was specifically Italian, and what, apparently, was personal. This scholar could not but draw his education, his views of life and death, his dominant inclinations and the large currents of his purpose, from the antecedent mediaeval period and the still greater past which had worked upon it so mightily. His Italian nature and environment gave point and piquancy and very concrete life to these mediaeval elements; and his personal genius produced from it all a supreme poetic creation.

The Italian part of Dante comes between the mediaeval and the personal, as species comes between the genus and the individual. The tremendous feeling which he discloses for the Roman past seems, in him, specifically Italian: child of Italy, he holds himself a Latin and a direct heir of the Republic. Yet often his attitude toward the antique will be that of mediaeval men in general, as in his disposition to accept ancient myth for fact; while his own genius appears in his beautifully apt appropriation of the Virgilian incident or image; wherein he excels his "Mantuan" master, whose borrowings from Homer were not always felicitous. Frequently the specifically Italian in Dante, his yearning hate of Florence, for example, may scarcely be distinguished from his personal temper; but its civic bitterness is different from the feudal animosities or promiscuous rages which were more generically mediaeval. . . .

Again, Dante's arguments in the *De monarchia* seem to be those of an Italian Ghibelline. Yet beyond his intense realization of Italy's direct succession to the Roman past, his reasoning is scholastic and mediaeval, or springs occasionally from his own reflections. The Italian contribution to the book tends to coalesce either with the general or the personal elements. . . .

The *De vulgari eloquentia* illustrates the difference between Dante accepting and reproducing mediaeval views, and Dante thinking for himself. . . . And in the *De Vulgari Eloquentia,* as in the *Convivio,* Dante is deeply conscious of the worth of the Romance vernacular. . . .

Certainly the *Convivio* gives evidence touching the writer's mental processes and the interests of his mind. Except for its lofty advocacy of the *volgare* and its personal apologetic references, it contains little that is not blankly mediaeval. . . . [A] significant phrase may be drawn from it: "Philosophy is a loving use of wisdom (*uno amoroso uso di sapienza*) which chiefly is in God, since in Him is utmost wisdom, utmost love, and utmost actuality." A loving use of wisdom—with Dante the pursuit of knowledge was no mere intellectual search, but a pilgrimage of the whole nature, loving heart as well as knowing mind, and the working virtues too. This pilgrimage is set forth in the *Commedia,* perhaps the supreme creation of the Middle Ages, and a work that by reason of the beautiful affinity of its speech with Latin, exquisitely expressed the matters which in Latin had been coming to formulation through the mediaeval centuries.

The *Commedia* (*Inferno, Purgatorio, Paradiso*) is a *Summa,* a *Summa salvationis,* a sum of saving knowledge. It is such just as surely as the final work of Aquinas is a *Summa theologiae.* But Aquinas was the supreme mediaeval theologian-philosopher, while Dante was the supreme theologian-poet; and with both Aquinas and Dante, theology includes the knowledge of all things, but chiefly of man in relation to God. Such was the matter of the *divina scientia* of Thomas, and such was the subject of the *Commedia,* which was soon recognized as the *Divina Commedia* in the very sense in which Theology was the divine science. The *Summa* of Thomas was *scientia* not only in substance, but in form; the *Commedia* was *scientia,* or *sapientia,* in substance, while in form it was a poem, the epic of man the pilgrim of salvation. . . . The *Commedia* rested upon the entire evolution of the Middle Ages. Therein had lain its spiritual preparation. To be sure it had its casual forerunners (*precursori*): narratives, real or feigned, of men faring to the regions of the dead. But these signified little; for everywhere thoughts of the other life pressed upon men's mind: fear of it blanched their hearts; its heavenly or hellish messengers had been seen, and not a few men dreamed that they had walked within those gates and witnessed clanging horrors or purgatorial pain. Heaven had been more rarely visited.

Dante gave little attention to any so-called "forerunners," save only two, Paul and Virgil. The former was a warrant for the poet's reticence as to the manner of his ascent to Heaven; the latter supplied much of his scheme of Hell. . . .

One observes mediaeval characteristics in the *Commedia* raised to a higher power. The mediaeval period was marked by contrasts of quality and of conduct such as cannot be found in the antique or the modern age. And what other poem can vie with the *Commedia* in contrasts of the beautiful and the loathsome, the heavenly and the hellish, exquisite refinement of expression and lapses into the reverse, love and hate, pity and cruelty, reverence and disdain? These contrasts not only are presented by the story; they evince themselves in the character of the author. Many scenes of the *Inferno* are loathsome: Dante's own words and conduct there may be cruel and hateful or show tender pity; and every reader knows the poetic beauty which glorifies the *Paradiso,* renders lovely the *Purgatorio,* and ever and anon breaks through the gloom of Hell.

Another mediaeval quality, sublimated in Dante's poem, is that of elaborate plan, intended symmetry of composition, the balance of one incident or subject against another. And finally one observes the mediaeval inclusiveness which belongs to the scope and purpose of the *Commedia* as a *Summa* of salvation. Dante brings in everything that can illuminate and fill out his theme. Even as the *Summa* of St. Thomas, so the *Commedia* must present a whole doctrinal scheme of salvation, and leave no loopholes, loose ends, broken links of argument or explanation.

The substance of the *Commedia,* practically its whole content of thought, opinion, sentiment, had source in the mediaeval store of antique culture and the partly affiliated, if not partly derivative, Latin Christianity. The mediaeval appreciation of the Classics, and of the contents of ancient philosophy, is not to be so very sharply distinguished from the attitude of the fifteenth or sixteenth, nay, if one will, the eighteenth, century, when the *Federalist* in the young inchoately united States, and many an orator in the revolutionary assemblies of France, quoted Cicero and Plutarch as arbiters of civic expediency. Nevertheless, if we choose to recognize deference to ancient opinion, acceptance of antique myth and poetry as fact, unbounded admiration for a shadowy and much distorted ancient world, as characterizing the mediaeval attitude toward whatever once belonged to Rome and Greece, then we must say that such also is Dante's attitude, scholar as he was; and that in his use of the Classics he differed from other mediaeval men only in so far as above them all he was a poet. . . .

Yet however universally Dante's mind was solicited by the antique matter and his poet's nature charmed, he was profoundly and mediaevally Christian. The *Commedia* is a mediaeval Christian poem. Its fabric, springing from the life of earth, enfolds the threefold quasi-other world of damned, of purging, and of finally purified, spirits. It is dramatic and doctrinal. Its drama of action and suffering, like the narratives of Scripture, offers literal fact, moral teaching, and allegorical or spiritual significance. The doctrinal contents are held partly within the poem's dramatic action and partly in expositions which are not fused in the drama. Thus, whatever else it is, the poem is a *Summa* of saving doctrine, which is driven home by illustrations of the sovereign good and abysmal ill coming to man under the providence of God. One may perhaps discern a twofold purpose in it, since the poet works out his own salvation and gives precepts and examples to aid others and help truth and righteousness on earth. The subject is man as rewarded or punished eternally by God—says Dante in the letter to Can Grande.[1] This subject could hardly be conceived as veritable, and still less could it be executed, by a poet who had no care for the effect of his poem upon men. Dante had such care. But whether he, who was first and always a poet, wrote the *Commedia* in order to lift others out of error to salvation, or even in order to work out his own salvation,—let him say who knows the mind of Dante. No divination, however, is required to trace the course of the saving teaching, which, whether dramatically exemplified or expounded in doctrinal statement, is embodied in the great poem; nor is it hard to note how Dante drew its substance from the mediaeval past.

Dante's Relevance Today
PHILIP MC NAIR

In our truncated search for "the meaning of Dante" we have examined that meaning as seen by the fourteenth-century Florentine poet and littérateur Boccaccio and the early twentieth-century American historian Henry Osborn Taylor. Boccaccio expressed the view that Dante was (or should be) the great preceptor of his ungrateful mother city, Taylor that he is the exemplification of the medieval mind. We turn now to a third view, in an essay by the Cambridge Italian scholar Philip McNair —"Dante's Relevance Today," one of the many works on Dante published in 1965 to commemorate the seven hundredth anniversary of the poet's birth. McNair finds the relevance of Dante today (and every day) in the fact that Dante, more than any other poet or most philosophers, deals "with the things which affect us most—and these things do not alter from one millennium to another"—things such as God, grace, sin, love, justice, and human nature.

"Poeta nascitur non fit"[2] is a well-worn tag, and a true one; and that is why the birth of a supreme poet is supremely worth celebrating. Last

---

[1] Can Grande della Scala, the Lord of Verona, to whom Dante dedicated part of the *Commedia*. Dante wrote a letter to Can Grande explaining the meaning of the poem.—ED.

[2] "Poets are born, not made."—ED.

year it was Shakespeare; this year it is Dante: and the conjunction of these two great names could hardly be happier, for in the words of the late T. S. Eliot: "Dante and Shakespeare divide the modern world between them; there is no third" (Weimar's objection overruled).[3]

"The modern world"—Eliot said—and at first blush "modern" may seem quite the wrong word to use when talking about Dante. Shakespeare, after all, stands closer to us by three centuries and half-a-dozen revolutions in taste and outlook, such as the Renaissance and the Reformation. But a cursory glance at *The Divine Comedy* discovers a medieval world reflected in a medieval mind. We are back in a pre-Copernican cosmology with God at the circumference and Satan at the centre, exploring a three-storeyed universe crammed with scholastic bric-à-brac and Christian myths. . . .

But dip deeper into Dante and we find how curiously relevant he is today—far more so than Virgil, for instance, or Homer, or practically any other poet who wrote before Shakespeare. Perhaps "perennial" is a better word than "modern," for, like the *philosophia perennis* [4] which it reflects, his poem just goes on applying to the human situation year after year and from age to age. Dante is 700 years old this summer, yet he is still the most topical poet for a cosmonaut floating in space to read; and seven centuries from now, when the science-fiction of his *Comedy* has come true, the men who contemplate this world from the stars will not have outsoared the shadow of his genius or exhausted the meaning of his poem.

Dante's relevance today stems from the fact that he is one of the most engaged writers of all time, as well as one of the most engaging. In commemorating him it is all too easy to slip into superlatives, and say that he is the poet "with the mostest" (most understanding, most insight, most vision, and so on); but surely we may make the modest claim that in the *Comedy*, despite its medieval structure, Dante is dealing with the things which affect us most—and these things do not alter from one millennium to another. God, grace, sin, love, justice, and human nature have not changed since Moses knew them. Dante's total involvement in them is best explained in terms of his purpose in writing the poem at all.

Apart from the basic urge which every poet feels to express himself, Dante's particular poetic reason for projecting the *Comedy* seems to have been his desire to measure up to an exacting challenge, to stretch his technique to breaking-point in doing what no other poet had ever done before—to pioneer in the vernacular, indeed in language itself. . . .

But Dante is more than a poet and his *Comedy* more than a poem. His prime purpose in writing is missionary and prophetic, and concerns the state of the world, the redemption of mankind. You do not have to

---

[3] A reference to the claim for similar stature for the German author Goethe.—ED.
[4] Eternal philosophy.—ED.

read very far to know that he is not out simply to entertain—"A funny thing happened to me in the dark wood"—although reading him *is* tremendous fun. His aim, says that problematic letter to Cangrande della Scala, "is to rescue those living in this life from a state of misery and bring them to a state of bliss." It is, of course, the same end proposed by the Christian Gospel, and springs from the same realism about sin and damnation: in fact this led one nineteenth-century Pope to dub the *Divine Comedy* the "Fifth Gospel." But Dante is less an evangelist than a prophet.

If poets are born and not made, prophets are called by God and fitted by experience. Dante is robustly conscious of his call, but that is his own private affair and inscrutable. What falls under our survey is his experience as a man among men, and the most important thing that happened to him —apart from being born a poet in 1265—was banishment from his native Florence in January 1302, unjustly charged with injustice in the form of political corruption. Important, because it made him brood on justice: not only in his own life, but also in the history of the world. His exile from Florence is due to Man's injustice, but Man's exile from paradise is due to the justice of God. What then is this Divine Justice? How does it operate? And how does it square with God's love?

Here we have one of the *Comedy's* central themes which must be seen against the dark background of human injustice. God's in His heaven, but all is *not* right with the world. Fallen Man is unjust because sin in him has disturbed the balance between reason and desire and warped his will. When we reach the poem's end we find Dante's *disio* and his *velle* [5] harmonized by the Divine Love which keeps the solar system in equilibrium. But the first note he strikes is the reality of sin. He begins with his own predicament—astray in a dark wood, having left the right road—and little by little reveals that this is the predicament of Man, of human nature, of every human institution. Florence is astray, Italy is astray, the papacy is astray, and so is the empire; the entire world is astray through sin, and therefore Dante is called to write "*in pro del mondo che mal vive.*" [6] Karl Vossler described the *Comedy* as the whole course of a religious conversion, but it is more than that: it is the whole programme of the world's redemption to God from sin. Dante sees himself not only as a sinner being saved, but in some sense as an agent of the salvation of others. This accounts for the fact that at times his tone is positively Messianic, for we have no evidence that he underrated his mission.

For Dante, as for all prophets, *hora novissima, tempora pessima sunt.* [7] The end of the world is at hand, the number of the Elect is almost complete, nearly all the seats in heaven are already taken. But his prophetic

---

[5] "Desire" and "ambition."—ED.
[6] "On behalf of the world that lives in evil."—ED.
[7] The most recent times are the worst.—ED.

burden is not Bunyanesque; he does not suggest fleeing from the wrath
to come, or abandoning the world to its doom. He does not even "look
for new heavens and a new earth, wherein dwelleth righteousness"; he
looks rather for a regeneration of this earth, for the coming of the Kingdom of God. The point of his allegory of hell, purgatory, and heaven is
not so much pie-in-the-sky as the reorganization of this world in love and
justice. . . .

It seems to me that Dante might have pictured hell in one of two ways:
either like a concentration camp, with Satan as its commandant, in which
sinners are at the mercy of a power more evil than themselves; or like a
penitentiary, in which a just government exacts retributive punishment
for sin. Following Christ and the Church, he has chosen the second way
in his *Inferno*, where Divine Justice is seen as Vengeance. This is never
stressed more starkly than in the Third Ring of the Seventh Circle, where
the violent against God suffer the inexorable rain which falls in broad
flakes of fire upon them in a slow downward drift "as Alpine snows in
windless weather fall."

But God's justice is not only punitive. In purgatory, the "Mount where
Justice probes us," it sets the desire of the repentant toward their purging
pains as once that desire was set on sin. In heaven it rewards the blessed
with the vision of God. But it is also active in the history of the world for
Man's good and salvation. Here Dante's most distinctive idea is that
Divine Justice master-minded the rise and rule of the Roman Empire
"che 'l buon mondo feo." [8] In fact, this is one of his key concepts, discussed in detail in the *Monarchia*, and informing the *Comedy* from beginning to end. . . .

Of course Dante, like all political thinkers, starts out from the existing
situation in his own day, dominated by the two great institutions of the
empire and the papacy, yet menaced by the rising power of French
nationalism and the emergence of city-states like Florence. But with a
prophet's mind he argues back to God's purpose behind Rome's two suns
—her *due soli*—and with a prophet's eye he sees their destiny in God's
salvation, when Man has attained his *duo ultima*—his two supreme ends of
temporal and eternal happiness. For God's plan of salvation is one and
indivisible, and Dante's study of history has taught him how dovetailed that
immense operation of love and justice is: David contemporary with Aeneas;
Christ, the Son of David, contemporary with Augustus, the son of Aeneas;
the Roman Pope, Christ's Vicar, the complement of the Roman Emperor,
Augustus Caesar's successor. And not only is there a developed parallelism
in Dante's mind, which condemns Judas to the same fate as Brutus and
Cassius, but also an ingenious interaction which provides the legal basis
of his soteriology.[9]

[8] "that the good world might come about."—ED.
[9] Doctrine of salvation.—ED.

For the Roman Emperor is the fount of Roman law, and is declared *de jure* the governing power in the world by God Himself in two great acts of Divine Vengeance. God willed that His Son should be born under the *Pax Romana* and suffer under Pontius Pilate, Caesar's Procurator. Thereby He willed that the Roman Emperor should perform a crucial function in the Atonement; for it was by the authority of Tiberius Caesar that God avenged the sin of Adam in the crucifixion of Christ, in whom the whole human race was vicariously punished to satisfy Divine Justice. But having avenged Man's sin in Christ's death under Tiberius, Justice avenged Christ's death upon the Jews by the destruction of Jerusalem under Titus. This devious doctrine is propounded to Dante in the Heaven of Mercury by no less an authority than the Emperor Justinian, who, inspired by *il primo amore* and *la viva giustizia*,[10] traces the course of Rome's rise to world dominion in a panoramic unfolding of history from the divine standpoint. But the sweep and scope of his review is capped by Beatrice, who takes his cryptic words on divine vengeance and explains them to Dante in one of the most impressive expositions of the Atonement to be found in non-canonical literature.

Echoing the Anselmian [11] doctrine of satisfaction, Beatrice proves how the justice and the love of God meet in the cross, where divine vengeance is exhausted and divine compassion expressed. Ruined by his fall, Adam's helpless race lay sick for many a century until it pleased the Word of God to descend and unite Man's estranged nature to Himself "with the sole act of His eternal love." The love that is the life of the Trinity, that binds the leaves of the volume of the universe together, the love that moves the sun and the other stars, that moved Beatrice to seek out Virgil on Dante's behalf—it is this primal eternal love that was kindled in the Virgin's womb and bore our nature to judicial execution on the cross.

In that Man was punished, the penalty was just; in that God suffered, it was outrageously *unjust*. Why God should take this way to redeem His creature "is buried from the eyes of all whose wit is not matured within Love's flame." But—Beatrice explains—if Man were to be saved at all, one of two fords must be passed: either God of His sole courtesy must remit the debt, or Man of himself must make satisfaction for his sin. . . .

What the love and justice of God mean to the sinner saved by grace is witnessed throughout the *Purgatorio* and *Paradiso* as Dante's mind and heart are conformed to the pleasure of God. To take one instance, it is seen in Manfred,[12] whom we meet at the mountain's foot. He repented at the point of death, but died excommunicate. His dead body was cast out of the kingdom of Naples, but his undying soul was received into the Kingdom of God. Why? Because weeping he gave himself up to Him

---

10 "The first love" and "the living justice."—Ed.
11 St. Anselm of Canterbury, medieval theologian (d. 1109).—Ed.
12 The son and successor of Emperor Frederick II.—Ed.

Who willingly pardons. Horrible though he confessed his sins to be, "Infinite Goodness has such wide arms that she accepts all who turn to her." The bishop and the pope who banned his corpse had read only the one face of God, His inexorable justice; but Manfred saw the face of everlasting love. God receives him because Christ has borne the penalty of his sins; but the laws of the kingdom still operate even though Manfred is forgiven, and Justice excludes him from purgatory until thirty times the period of his presumption is fulfilled.

Although Dante can write movingly about the wide arms of Infinite Goodness and the two faces of God, His justice and His love, it is disappointing to find that to the end of the *Comedy* his God remains strangely impersonal. Consummate poet though he is, Dante's greatest omission is his failure to portray Christ, the very personification of the justice and the love of God. Only three times do we glimpse Him in heaven, but although He is the Incarnate Word on no occasion does He speak. . . .

In the *Divine Comedy* we see the unveiled mystery and the radiant hosts, the uncreated light and the vision of God; but we do not see the Lamb, without Whose sacrifice we could not see heaven at all.

Suggestions for Further Reading

DANTE IS, first and foremost, a poet—one of the two or three greatest of all time—and students ought to sample his poetry, no matter how difficult, abstruse, or philosophical it may seem. Dante's greatest work, *The Divine Comedy*, is available in many translations, but students will probably be most pleased with the contemporary verse translation by the popular poet-critic John Ciardi, *The Inferno* (New Brunswick, N.J.: Rutgers University Press, 1954), *The Purgatorio* (New York: New American Library, 1961), and *The Paradiso* (New York: New American Library, 1970). It is not entirely faithful to the letter (more so to the spirit) of the original but it is a lively, often earthy, and always entertaining effort. Somewhat less successful is Dorothy L. Sayers' translation, *The Comedy of Dante Alighieri, the Florentine*, 3 vols. (Harmondsworth, England: Penguin, 1955–1973), which attempts the almost impossible task of duplicating

Dante's interlocking three-line rhyme scheme. The translation suffers from it in places, but it is generally readable; the long introduction and critical notes are, however, first class and an enormous help. For a sampling of Dante's other writings, the most convenient work is *The Portable Dante*, ed. Paolo Milano (New York: Viking, 1968), with the complete text of the *Divine Comedy* and *Vita Nuova* and excerpts from his other verse and Latin prose works. Two conventional guides to the *Divine Comedy* are *Companion to the Divine Comedy*, ed. C. S. Singleton (Cambridge, Mass.: Harvard University Press, 1975), and *A Concordance to the Divine Comedy of Dante Alighieri*, ed. Ernest Hatch Wilkins and Thomas G. Bergin (Cambridge, Mass.: Harvard University Press, 1965).

There is an enormous literature of Dante criticism, much of it as difficult and obscure as the poet himself. A handful of works, however, can be recommended for beginning students. The most readable and among the most sensible are two collections of essays by Dorothy L. Sayers, *Introductory Papers on Dante* (New York: Barnes and Noble, 1969 [1954]), and *Further Papers on Dante* (New York: Harper, 1957). Thomas G. Bergin is one of the world's great authorities on Dante, and three of his books are so clear and readable that they can be recommended even to those with little or no prior exposure to Dante—*Dante* (Boston: Houghton Mifflin, 1965); *Perspectives on the Divine Comedy* (New Brunswick, N.J.: Rutgers University Press, 1967); and *A Diversity of Dante* (New Brunswick, N.J.: Rutgers University Press, 1969). Two older famous books of Dante criticism are also recommended: Erich Auerbach, *Dante, Poet of the Secular World*, tr. Ralph Manheim (Chicago: University of Chicago Press, 1961 [1929]), and Etienne Gilson, *Dante and Philosophy*, tr. David Moore (New York: Harper, 1963 [1949]).

Most of the foregoing books deal not only with Dante the poet but also with his life and times. The following works deal more explicitly with the man and his age. The most authoritative modern biography of Dante is by the great Italian Dante scholar Michele Barbi, *Life of Dante*, tr. and ed. Paul G. Ruggiers (Berkeley and Los Angeles: University of California Press, 1954 [1933]). The more bulky and comprehensive Karl Vossler, *Mediaeval Culture: An Introduction to Dante and His Times*, tr. Wm. C. Lawton (New York: Harcourt, Brace, 1929), is also a standard work. Highly recommended is Domenico Vittorini, *The Age of Dante* (Westport, Conn.: Greenwood Press, 1975 [1957]), which can serve as a corrective to the views of Vossler and Henry Osborn Taylor (excerpted in this chapter), in that Vittorini ties Dante into the new scholarly views on the early Renaissance.

Leonardo da Vinci: Universal Man of the Renaissance

While scholars may still argue whether Dante belongs in the Renaissance or the Middle Ages, there is no question where Leonardo da Vinci belongs. More than any other figure, he is commonly regarded as the exemplar of that uniquely Renaissance ideal *uomo universale,* the universal man.

Leonardo, the spoiled, loved, and pampered illegitimate son of a well-to-do Florentine notary, was born in 1452 at the very midpoint of Florence's magnificent Renaissance century, the Quattrocento. The boy grew up at his father's country home in the village of Vinci. His precocious genius and his talent for drawing led his father to apprentice Leonardo to the artist Verrocchio in Florence. While Verrocchio is best remembered as a sculptor, it should be noted that he was, like most Florentine artists of his time, a versatile master of other artistic crafts, and that his *bottega*—like Ghiberti's earlier or Michelangelo's later— was not only a lively school of craftsmanship and technique but a place where people gathered to gossip and talk over on a wide range of subjects. Here the young Leonardo's multiple talents bloomed.

At the age of twenty Leonardo was admitted to the painters' guild and soon after set up his own shop and household. He was well enough received and commissions came his way. But, for reasons that are not entirely clear, he seems not to have been marked for the lavish patronage of the Medici family—as were so many of his fellow artists—or of

215

any other great Florentine houses. The fashion of the moment preferred those artists like Alberti and Botticelli who mingled learned humanism with their art and could converse in Latin with the humanists, poets, and philosophers who dominated the intellectual scene in Florence. But Leonardo knew no Latin. His education consisted only of apprenticeship training and beyond that a hodge-podge of self-instruction directed to his own wide-ranging interests, in some areas profound and original, in others hopelessly limited and naive. It is also possible that Leonardo may simply have set himself apart from the circle of his fellow artists and their patrons. There are hints of alienation and jealousy and even a vaguely worded reference to a homosexual charge against him that was brought before a magistrate and then dropped. But it is most likely that Leonardo's own restless curiosity was already carrying him beyond the practice of his art.

In 1482 Leonardo left Florence for Milan and the court of its lord, Ludovico Sforza, one of the most powerful princes of Italy. In the letter Leonardo wrote commending himself to Ludovico, which has been preserved, he described himself as a military architect, siege and hydraulic engineer, ordnance and demolition expert, architect, sculptor, and painter; he ended the letter, "And if any one of the above-named things seems to anyone to be impossible or not feasible, I am most ready to make the experiment in your park, or in whatever place may please your Excellency, to whom I commend myself with the utmost humility." [1] Humility indeed! The universal man had declared himself.

Leonardo spent the next seventeen years—the most vigorous and productive of his life—at the court of Milan. He painted *The Last Supper* for the Dominican Convent of Santa Maria delle Grazie. He conceived and created the model for what might well have been the world's greatest equestrian statue; but the statue, memorializing Ludovico Sforza's father, the old soldier-duke Francesco, was never cast, and the model was destroyed. In addition, Leonardo created gimcrackery for court balls and fetes—costumes, jewelry, scenery, engines, floats, spectacles. But increasingly he was occupied with studies of a bewildering variety of subjects. The notebooks he kept reveal drawings and notes on the flight of birds and the possibility of human flight; military engineering, tanks, submarines, exploding shells, rapid-firing artillery pieces, and fortifications; bold schemes for city planning and hydraulic engineering; plans for machinery of every sort, pulleys, gears, self-propelled vehicles, a mechanical clock, and a file cutter; detailed studies of plant, animal, and human anatomy that go well beyond the needs of an artist; a complete treatise on painting and another on the comparison of the arts. Despite the fact that much of this

[1] Quoted in E. G. Holt (ed.), *A Documentary History of Art* (New York: Doubleday, 1957), vol. I, pp. 273–275.

body of work—including a treatise on perspective that was reputed to be far in advance of other such works—was scattered and lost, some seven thousand pages have survived, all written in a code-like, left-handed, mirror script.

Leonardo's handwriting is of particular interest, for it is indicative of a special side of his nature—almost obsessively secretive, aloof, touchy and suspicious of others. These qualities are part of the traditional image of Leonardo that has been passed down to us, beginning with his earliest biography, by his younger contemporary Vasari.

In Praise of Leonardo
GIORGIO VASARI

Giorgio Vasari (1511–1574) was himself something of a universal man. He was an artist of more than middling ability who worked all over Italy. He was also a respected man of affairs, the familiar of popes, princes, and dignitaries, as well as artists and scholars. But his most important achievement was his book Lives of the Most Eminent Painters, Sculptors & Architects from Cimabue until our own Time, *the first edition published in Florence in 1550. Wallace K. Ferguson has called it "a masterpiece of art history." [2] In fact, the book is more than a masterpiece of art history, for it virtually created the concept of art history itself.*

Vasari introduces "our present age" with his treatment of Leonardo. But this biography, despite its extravagant praise of Leonardo's genius, is seriously limited. Vasari had access to many of Leonardo's notes, even some that we no longer have. But he was most familiar with the art and artists of Tuscany. It is clear that he had not actually seen several of Leonardo's most important works, in Milan and elsewhere. And much of the information he provided on Leonardo's life was nothing more than current rumor or gossip about him. Vasari, furthermore, was himself a pupil and lifelong admirer of Leonardo's great contemporary Michelangelo (1475–1564), and it was Vasari's thesis that the whole tradition of Italian art reached its fulfillment in Michelangelo. It

[2] In *The Renaissance in Historical Thought: Five Centuries of Interpretation* (Boston: Houghton Mifflin, 1948), 60.

might be recalled also that Michelangelo despised Leonardo; they had at least one nasty quarrel. And Michelangelo was fond of saying that Leonardo was a technically incompetent craftsman, who could not complete the projects he began. Whether by design or not, this charge became the main line of criticism in Vasari's biography of Leonardo, and it has persisted alongside Leonardo's reputation as an enigmatic genius.

We look now at Vasari's account from Lives of the Most Eminent Painters, Sculptors & Architects.

THE GREATEST GIFTS are often seen, in the course of nature, rained by celestial influences on human creatures; and sometimes, in supernatural fashion, beauty, grace, and talent are united beyond measure in one single person, in a manner that to whatever such an one turns his attention, his every action is so divine, that, surpassing all other men, it makes itself clearly known as a thing bestowed by God (as it is), and not acquired by human art. This was seen by all mankind in Leonardo da Vinci, in whom, besides a beauty of body never sufficiently extolled, there was an infinite grace in all his actions; and so great was his genius, and such its growth, that to whatever difficulties he turned his mind, he solved them with ease. In him was great bodily strength, joined to dexterity, with a spirit and courage ever royal and magnanimous; and the fame of his name so increased, that not only in his lifetime was he held in esteem, but his reputation became even greater among posterity after his death.

Truly marvellous and celestial was Leonardo, the son of Ser Piero da Vinci; and in learning and in the rudiments of letters he would have made great proficience, if he had not been so variable and unstable, for he set himself to learn many things, and then, after having begun them, abandoned them. Thus, in arithmetic, during the few months that he studied it, he made so much progress, that, by continually suggesting doubts and difficulties to the master who was teaching him, he would very often bewilder him. He gave some little attention to music, and quickly resolved to learn to play the lyre, as one who had by nature a spirit most lofty and full of refinement; wherefore he sang divinely to that instrument, improvising upon it. Nevertheless, although he occupied himself with such a variety of things, he never ceased drawing and working in relief, pursuits which suited his fancy more than any other. Ser Piero, having observed this, and having considered the loftiness of his intellect, one day took some of his drawings and carried them to Andrea del Verrocchio, who was much his friend, and besought him straitly to tell him whether Leonardo, by devoting himself to drawing, would make any proficience. Andrea was astonished to see the extraordinary beginnings of Leonardo, and urged Ser Piero that he should make him study it; wherefore he arranged with Leonardo that he should enter the workshop of Andrea, which Leonardo did with the greatest willingness in the world. And he practised not one branch of art only, but all those in which drawing played a part; and having an intellect so divine and marvellous that he was also an excellent geometrician, he not only worked in sculpture, making in his youth, in clay, some heads of women that are smiling, of which plaster casts are still taken, and likewise some heads of boys which appeared to have issued from the hand of a master; but in architecture, also, he made many drawings both of ground-plans and of other designs of buildings; and he was the first, although but a youth, who suggested the plan of reducing the river Arno to a navigable canal from Pisa to Florence. He made designs of flour-mills, fulling-mills, and engines, which might be driven by the force of water: and since he wished that his profession should be painting, he studied much in drawing after nature. . . . He was continually making models and designs to show men how to remove mountains with ease, and how to bore them in order to pass from one level to another; and by means of levers, windlasses, and screws, he showed the way to raise and draw great weights, together with methods for emptying harbours, and pumps for removing water from low places, things which his brain never ceased from devising; and of these ideas and labours many drawings may be seen, scattered abroad among our craftsmen; and I myself have seen not a few. . . .

He was so pleasing in conversation, that he attracted to himself the hearts of men. And although he possessed, one might say, nothing, and worked little, he always kept servants and horses, in which latter he took much delight, and particularly in all other animals, which he managed with the greatest love and patience; and this he showed when often passing by the places where birds were sold, for, taking them with his own hand out of their cages, and having paid to those who sold them the price that was asked, he let them fly away into the air, restoring to them their lost liberty. For which reason nature was pleased so to favour him, that, wherever he turned his thought, brain, and mind, he displayed such divine power in his works, that, in giving them their perfection, no one was ever his peer in readiness, vivacity, excellence, beauty, and grace.

It is clear that Leonardo, through his comprehension of art, began many things and never finished one of them, since it seemed to him that the hand was not able to attain to the perfection of art in carrying out the things which he imagined; for the reason that he conceived in idea difficulties so subtle and so marvellous, that they could never be expressed by the hands, be they ever so excellent. And so many were his caprices, that, philosophizing of natural things, he set himself to seek out the properties of herbs, going on even to observe the motions of the heavens, the path of the moon, and the courses of the sun. . . .

He began a panel-picture of the Adoration of the Magi, containing many beautiful things, particularly the heads, which was in the house of Amerigo Benci, opposite the Loggia de' Peruzzi; and this, also, remained unfinished, like his other works.

It came to pass that Giovan Galeazzo, Duke of Milan, being dead, and

Lodovico Sforza raised to the same rank, in the year 1494,[3] Leonardo was summoned to Milan in great repute to the Duke, who took much delight in the sound of the lyre, to the end that he might play it: and Leonardo took with him that instrument which he had made with his own hands, in great part of silver, in the form of a horse's skull—a thing bizarre and new—in order that the harmony might be of greater volume and more sonorous in tone; with which he surpassed all the musicians who had come together there to play. Besides this, he was the best improviser in verse of his day. The Duke, hearing the marvellous discourse of Leonardo, became so enamoured of his genius, that it was something incredible: and he prevailed upon him by entreaties to paint an altar-panel containing a Nativity, which was sent by the Duke to the Emperor.

He also painted in Milan, for the Friars of S. Dominic, at S. Maria delle Grazie, a Last Supper, a most beautiful and marvellous thing; and to the heads of the Apostles he gave such majesty and beauty, that he left the head of Christ unfinished, not believing that he was able to give it that divine air which is essential to the image of Christ.[4] This work, remaining thus all but finished, has ever been held by the Milanese in the greatest veneration, and also by strangers as well; for Leonardo imagined and succeeded in expressing that anxiety which had seized the Apostles in wishing to know who should betray their Master. . . .

While he was engaged on this work, he proposed to the Duke to make a horse in bronze, of a marvellous greatness, in order to place upon it, as a memorial, the image of the Duke.[5] And on so vast a scale did he begin it and continue it, that it could never be completed. And there are those who have been of the opinion (so various and so often malign out of envy are the judgments of men) that he began it with no intention of finishing it, because, being of so great a size, an incredible difficulty was encountered in seeking to cast it in one piece; and it might also be believed that, from the result, many may have formed such a judgment, since many of his works have remained unfinished. But, in truth, one can believe that his vast and most excellent mind was hampered through being too full of desire, and that his wish ever to seek out excellence upon excellence, and perfection upon perfection, was the reason of it. "Tal che l' opera fosse ritardata dal desio," [6] as our Petrarca has said. And, indeed, those who saw the great model that Leonardo made in clay vow that they have never seen a more beautiful thing, or a more superb; and it was preserved until the French came to Milan with King Louis of France, and broke it all to pieces.[7] Lost, also, is a little model of it in wax, which was

[3] The date was actually 1482.—ED.

[4] The head of Christ was finished, along with the rest of the painting. Vasari was repeating gossip and had not seen the work.—ED.

[5] Rather of the Duke's father, Francesco, the founder of the Sforza dynasty.—ED.

[6] "So that the work was retarded by the very desire of it."—ED.

[7] Louis XII of France. The incident of the model's destruction took place during the French occupation of Milan in 1499.—ED.

held to be perfect, together with a book on the anatomy of the horse made by him by way of study.

He then applied himself, but with greater care, to the anatomy of man, assisted by and in turn assisting, in this research, Messer Marc' Antonio della Torre, an excellent philosopher, who was then lecturing at Pavia, and who wrote of this matter; and he was one of the first (as I have heard tell) that began to illustrate the problems of medicine with the doctrine of Galen, and to throw true light on anatomy, which up to that time had been wrapped in the thick and gross darkness of ignorance. And in this he found marvellous aid in the brain, work, and hand of Leonardo, who made a book drawn in red chalk, and annotated with the pen, of the bodies that he dissected with his own hand, and drew with the greatest diligence; wherein he showed all the frame of the bones; and then added to them, in order, all the nerves, and covered them with muscles; the first attached to the bone, the second that hold the body firm, and the third that move it; and beside them, part by part, he wrote in letters of an ill-shaped character, which he made with the left hand, backwards; and whoever is not practised in reading them cannot understand them, since they are not to be read save with a mirror. . . .

With the fall of Ludovico Sforza and the French occupation of Milan in 1499, the artist returned to Florence.

Leonardo undertook to execute, for Francesco del Giocondo, the portrait of Monna Lisa, his wife; and after toiling over it for four years, he left it unfinished; and the work is now in the collection of King Francis of France, at Fontainebleau. In this head, whoever wished to see how closely art could imitate nature, was able to comprehend it with ease; for in it were counterfeited all the minutenesses that with subtlety are able to be painted. . . .

By reason, then, of the excellence of the works of this divine craftsman, his fame had so increased that all persons who took delight in art—nay, the whole city of Florence—desired that he should leave them some memorial, and it was being proposed everywhere that he should be commissioned to execute some great and notable work, whereby the commonwealth might be honoured and adorned by the great genius, grace and judgment that were seen in the works of Leonardo. And it was decided between the Gonfalonier [8] and the chief citizens, the Great Council Chamber having been newly built . . . and having been finished in great haste, it was ordained by public decree that Leonardo should be given some beautiful work to paint; and so the said hall was allotted to him by Piero Soderini, then Gonfalonier of Justice. Whereupon Leonardo, determining to execute this work, began a cartoon in the Sala del Papa, an apartment

[8] The title of the chief magistrate of Florence.—ED.

in S. Maria Novella, representing the story of Niccolò Piccinino,[9] Captain of Duke Filippo of Milan; wherein he designed a group of horsemen who were fighting for a standard, a work that was held to be very excellent and of great mastery, by reason of the marvellous ideas that he had in composing that battle. . . . It is said that, in order to draw that cartoon, he made a most ingenious stage, which was raised by contracting it and lowered by expanding. And conceiving the wish to colour on the wall in oils, he made a composition of so gross an admixture, to act as a binder on the wall, that, going on to paint in the said hall, it began to peel off in such a manner that in a short time he abandoned it, seeing it spoiling.[10] . . .

He went to Rome with Duke Giuliano de' Medici, at the election of Pope Leo,[11] who spent much of his time on philosophical studies, and particularly on alchemy; where, forming a paste of a certain kind of wax, as he walked he shaped animals very thin and full of wind, and, by blowing into them, made them fly through the air, but when the wind ceased they fell to the ground. . . .

He made an infinite number of such follies, and gave his attention to mirrors; and he tried the strangest methods in seeking out oils for painting, and varnish for preserving works when painted. . . . It is related that, a work having been allotted to him by the Pope, he straightway began to distil oils and herbs, in order to make the varnish; at which Pope Leo said: "Alas! this man will never do anything, for he begins by thinking of the end of the work, before the beginning."

There was very great disdain between Michelagnolo Buonarroti and him, on account of which Michelagnolo departed from Florence, with the excuse of Duke Giuliano, having been summoned by the Pope to the competition for the façade of S. Lorenzo. Leonardo, understanding this, departed and went into France, where the King, having had works by his hand, bore him great affection; and he desired that he should colour the cartoon of S. Anne, but Leonardo, according to his custom, put him off for a long time with words.

Finally, having grown old, he remained ill many months, and, feeling himself near to death, asked to have himself diligently informed of the teaching of the Catholic faith. . . . [He] expired in the arms of the King, in the seventy-fifth year of his age.[12]

---

[9] A mercenary commander who had worked for Florence.—ED.

[10] Michelangelo was assigned a companion panel and also abandoned his work on it before it was completed.—ED.

[11] Pope Leo X, the former Giovanni Cardinal dei Medici.—ED.

[12] Vasari is inaccurate. In the year Leonardo died, 1519, he actually was sixty-seven.—ED.

Leonardo the Scientist
JOHN HERMAN RANDALL, JR.

From Vasari's time to the present, there has clung to the image of Leonardo da Vinci a kind of Faustian quality, linking him to the origins of modern science. Throughout his life, and increasingly from middle age on, Leonardo was preoccupied with technical studies and scientific experiments, often to the detriment of his art. But the judgments of modern scholars on "Leonardo the scientist" are much more varied and more circumspect than those upon "Leonardo the artist."

We turn first to the views of a distinguished philosopher and historian of science, especially medieval and Renaissance science, the long-time Columbia University Professor of Philosophy, John Herman Randall, Jr. This selection is from his article "The Place of Leonardo da Vinci in the Emergence of Modern Science."

LEONARDO WAS NOT himself a scientist. "Science" is not the hundred-odd aphorisms or "pensieri" that have been pulled out of his Codici and collected, by Richter, Solmi, and others. "Science" is not oracular utterances, however well phrased; it is not bright ideas jotted down in a notebook. "Science" is systematic and methodical thought. . . .

"Science" is not just the appeal to experience, though it involves such an appeal, as Leonardo stated in answering those critics who had censured him as a mere empiric: "If I could not indeed like them cite authors and books, it is a much greater and worthier thing to profess to cite experience, the mistress of their masters." "Science" is not the mere rejection of authority, the case for which is well put by Leonardo: "He who argues by citing an authority is not employing intelligence but rather memory." . . .

It is true that during Leonardo's youth—the second half of the Quattrocento—the intellectual influence of the non-scientific humanists had been making for a kind of St. Martin's summer of the "authority" of the ancients, and that his life coincides with this rebirth of an authoritarian attitude toward the past. Leonardo's protests were magnificent, and doubtless pertinent. But they are not enough to constitute "science." "Science" is not merely fresh, first-hand observation, however detailed and accurate.

Above all, "science" is not the intuitions of a single genius, solitary and alone, however suggestive. It is cooperative inquiry, such as had prevailed in the Italian schools from the time of Pietro d'Abano († 1315; his

Conciliator appeared earlier)—and such as was to continue till the time of Galileo—the cumulative cooperative inquiry which actually played so large a part in the emergence of modern science. . . .

In practice, Leonardo always becomes fascinated by some particular problem—he has no interest in working out any systematic body of knowledge. His artist's interest in the particular and the concrete, which inspires his careful, precise and accurate observation, is carried further by his inordinate curiosity into a detailed analytic study of the factors involved. His thought seems always to be moving from the particularity of the painter's experience to the universality of intellect and science, without ever quite getting there. . . .

No evidence has ever been offered that anybody in the sixteenth century capable of appreciating scientific ideas ever saw the Codici of Leonardo. . . . But since the scientific ideas expressed therein were all well-known in the universities of Leonardo's day, and were accessible in much more elaborated form in the books the scientists were reading, there seems to be no "problem" of tracing any presumed "influence" of Leonardo on the development of sixteenth-century scientific thought in Italy.

The *Trattato de la Pittura,* or *Paragone,* was not printed until 1651, but its existence in manuscript form suggests that it had been read much earlier by the Urbino circle. It was put together from various manuscripts of Leonardo by an editor whose identity is not known, but who seems to have been responsible for its systematic organization—an organization which later editors have uniformly tried to improve upon.

With Leonardo's anatomical studies, the story is somewhat different. There is no evidence that Vesalius [13] ever actually saw his drawings; but in view of the marked similarities between them and his own much more systematically planned and organized series of drawings, it is difficult to think that he did not. . . .

Turning now from the things that Leonardo, despite all the adulations of his genius, was clearly not, let us try to state what seems to have been his real genius in scientific matters. During the Renaissance, as a result of the surprising dissolution of the rigid boundaries which had previously kept different intellectual traditions, as it were, in watertight compartments, the many different currents of thought which had long been preparing and strengthening themselves during the Middle Ages managed to come together, and to strike fire. The explanation of this phenomenon can ultimately be only sociological—the breaking down of the fairly rigid boundaries that had hitherto shut off one discipline and one intellectual tradition from another. Whatever its cause, the confluence of many different intellectual traditions in the fertile, all-too-fertile mind of Leonardo renders

---

[13] The Flemish anatomist at the University of Padua who in 1543 published the first modern, scientific descriptive treatise on human anatomy.—ED.

his views an unusually happy illustration of the way in which very diverse intellectual traditions managed during the Renaissance to unite together to create what we now call "modern science."

There is first the "scientific tradition," the careful, intelligent, cooperative and cumulative criticism of Aristotelian physics, which began with William of Ockham.[14] . . . In his reading Leonardo was in touch with this scientific tradition, as Duhem has shown.

There is secondly Leonardo's enthusiasm for mathematics, which goes far beyond its obvious instrumental use. It is very hard to assay the precise sense in which Leonardo thought of mathematics as the alphabet of nature: in this area much work remains to be done. There seems to be in Leonardo no trace of the popular contemporary Pythagoreanism or Platonism. If we examine Leonardo's conception of mathematics as depicted in his drawings, not as inadequately stated in his prose, we find that it differs markedly from the static and very geometrical notion of Dürer.[15] It is movement, not geometrical relations, that Leonardo is trying to capture. There is much in his drawings that suggests a world envisaged in terms of the calculus— like the world of Leibniz [16]—rather than in terms of the purely geometrical vision of the Greek tradition. In his mathematical vision of the world, Leonardo seems to belong to the realm of "dynamic" and "Faustian" attitudes, rather than to the static geometrical perfection of Greek thought.

There is thirdly the tradition of what Edgar Zilsel has called the "superior craftsman"—the man who is not afraid to take an idea and try it out, to experiment with it. . . . As a pupil of Verrocchio [Leonardo] had no fastidious objections to sullying his hands with "experiment." This habit of Leonardo's of descending from the academic cathedra and actually trying out the ideas of which he read had broad repercussions: it is one of the activities of Leonardo that seems to have become generally known, and to have awakened emulation. The consequences of Leonardo's willingness to experiment are to be found in the "practical geometry" of Tartaglia, the greatest of the sixteenth-century Italian mathematicians. Galileo, of course, was in this tradition of the "practical geometers"; he too was an indefatigable inventor. Indeed, Leonardo can fairly claim to belong not to the line of scientists but to the noble tradition of the inventors. . . .

Many of Leonardo's aphorisms treat the matter of the proper intellectual method. He has much to say on the relation between "reason" and "experience," and what he says used to lead commentators to impute to him the anticipation of Francis Bacon's "inductive method"—God save the mark, as though that had anything to do with the method employed by the pioneering scientists of the seventeenth century!

Neither experience alone nor reason alone will suffice. "Those who are enamored of practice without science are like the pilot who boards his ship

[14] The important nominalist philosopher of the early fourteenth century.—ED.

[15] The great German artist, a contemporary of Leonardo.—ED.

[16] The great German philosopher and mathematician of the seventeenth century who shares with Newton the discovery of the calculus.—ED.

without helm or compass, and who is never certain where he is going."
On the other hand, pure reasoning is without avail: "Should you say that
the sciences which begin and end in the mind have achieved truth, that
I will not concede, but rather deny for many reasons; and first, because
in such mental discourse there occurs no experience, without which there is
no certainty to be found."

But Leonardo does not bother to give any precise definition of what
he means by his key terms, "experience," "reason," "certainty," or "truth."
Certainty depends on "experience," but "there is no certainty where one
of the mathematical sciences cannot apply, or where the subject is not
united with mathematics." And—maxim for all inventors!—"Mechanics
is the paradise of the mathematical sciences, because in it they come to
bear their mathematical fruits." . . .

These aphorisms as to the relation between reason and experience are
no doubt rhetorically effective. But we have only to compare such vague
utterances with the very detailed analyses of precisely the same methodological relation which were being carried out at this very time in the
Aristotelian schools of the Italian universities to realize the difference between an artist's insights and the scientist's analysis.

Leonardo was above all else the anatomist of nature. He could see, and
with his draughtsmanship depict clearly, the bony skeleton of the world—
the geological strata and their indicated past. He could also see everywhere
nature's simple machines in operation—in man and in the non-human world
alike. . . .

As a genuine contributor, then, to the descriptive sciences, Leonardo
reported with his pencil fundamental aspects of nature the great machine—
in anatomy, geology, and hydrostatics. As a writer rather than as a graphic
reporter, Leonardo shows himself an extremely intelligent reader. But he
was clearly never so much the scientist as when he had his pencil in hand,
and was penetrating to the mechanical structure of what he was observing.

Leonardo the Technologist
LADISLAO RETI

*A substantial group of modern scholars agrees with Randall. Some,
however, do not. In the following selection, we will sample the views of
one of them, Ladislao Reti, an historian of science and medicine and
an authority on Leonardo's scientific and technical manuscripts. Reti not
only attaches more importance to Leonardo's scientific work than does
Randall; he vigorously denies Randall's charges that Leonardo failed
to exhibit a sustained, systematic body of scientific thought; that he stood
alone outside the tradition of science; that he failed to develop a
methodological terminology; and that he failed to influence the evolution
of science beyond his own time. But most of all, Reti disputes Randall's
view that science is abstract conception. Rather, he takes the position that
science must be the accumulation of particular observations and
applications. Reti views "Leonardo the scientist" as "Leonardo the
technologist," and he insists that a technologist of such brilliance and
inventiveness as Leonardo cannot be so readily dismissed. "The greatest
engineer of all times" surely deserves a place in the history of science.*

VARIED AS LEONARDO'S interests were, statistical analysis of his writings
points to technology as the main subject. As was acutely pointed out by
Bertrand Gille in a recent book, judging by the surviving original documents, Leonardo's métier was rather an engineer's than an artist's.

However we may feel about this opinion, it is disturbing to take an
inventory of Leonardo's paintings, of which no more than half a dozen are
unanimously authenticated by the world's leading experts.

Contrast this evident disinclination to paint with the incredible toil and
patience Leonardo lavished on scientific and technical studies, particularly
in the fields of geometry, mechanics, and engineering. Here his very indulgence elicited curious reactions from his contemporaries and in the
minds of his late biographers. They regretted that a man endowed with such
divine artistic genius should waste the precious hours of his life in such
vain pursuits. And, of course, as the well-known episodes of his artistic
career testify, this exposed him not only to criticism but also to serious
inconveniences.

But were Leonardo's nonartistic activities truly marginal?

Documentary evidence proves that every official appointment refers to him not only as an artist but as an engineer as well.

At the court of Ludovico il Moro he was *Ingeniarius et pinctor*.[17] Cesare Borgia called him his most beloved *Architecto et Engengero Generale*.[18] When he returned to Florence he was immediately consulted as military engineer. . . . Louis XII called him *nostre chier et bien amé Léonard da Vincy, nostre paintre et ingenieur ordinaire*.[19] Even in Rome, despite the pope's famous remark on hearing of Leonardo's experiments with varnishes preparatory to beginning an artistic commission, Leonardo's duties clearly included technical work, as is documented by three rough copies of a letter to his patron Giuliano de' Medici. Nor was his position different when he went to France at the invitation of Francis I. The official burial document calls him *Lionard de Vincy, noble millanois, premier peinctre et ingenieur et architecte du Roy, mescanichien d'Estat, et anchien directeur du peincture du Duc de Milan.*[20]

We can thus see that Leonardo had a lively interest in the mechanical arts and engineering from his earliest youth, as evidenced by the oldest drawing in the Codex Atlanticus, to the end of his industrious life. Thousands of his drawings witness to it, from fleeting sketches (though always executed with the most uncanny bravura) to presentation projects finished in chiaroscuro wash. Often these sketches and drawings are accompanied by a descriptive text, comments, and discussion.

The drawings and writings of Leonardo on technical matters, though scattered throughout the notebooks and especially in the Codex Atlanticus (a true order probably never existed nor did the author attempt to make one), represent an important and unique source for the history of technology. . . .

It is far from my intention and beyond my possibilities to discuss Leonardo's technology as a whole on this occasion. Enough is said when we remember that there is hardly a field of applied mechanics where Leonardo's searching mind has left no trace in the pages of his notebooks. To illustrate Leonardo's methods I shall limit myself to discussing some little-known aspects of how he dealt with the main problem of technology, the harnessing of energy to perform useful work.

At the time of Leonardo the waterwheel had been improved and in some favored places wind was used to grind corn or pump water. But the main burden of human industry still rested on the muscle power of man or animal. Little thought was given to how this should be used. Animals were

[17] Engineer and painter.—ED.

[18] Architect and Engineer-General.—ED.

[19] Our dear and well-loved Leonardo da Vinci, our painter and engineer ordinary.—ED.

[20] Leonardo da Vinci, Milanese nobleman, first painter and engineer and architect of the King, state technician, and former director of painting of the Duke of Milan.—ED.

attached to carts or traction devices; fortunately collar harness was already in use, multiplying by five the pulling strength of the horse. Men worked tools by hand, turned cranks, or operated treadmills. Of course, power could be gained, sacrificing time, with the help of levers, screws, gears, and pulleys. Little attention was given to the problems of friction, strength of materials, and to the rational development of power transmission. At least this is the picture suggested by studying the few manuscripts that precede Leonardo, devoted to technological matters.

Leonardo's approach was fundamentally different. He firmly believed that technological problems must be dealt with not by blindly following traditional solutions but according to scientific rules deduced from observation and experiment.

When Leonardo searched for the most efficient ways of using the human motor, the force of every limb, of every muscle, was analyzed and measured. Leonardo was the first engineer who tried to find a quantitative equivalent for the forms of energy available.

In MS H (written *ca.* 1494) on folios 43*v* and 44*r* (figs. 1 and 2) there are two beautiful sketches showing the estimation of human muscular effort with the help of a dynamometer. The force is measured in pounds which represent the lifting capacity of the group of muscles under scrutiny. In figure 1 no less than six different cases covering the whole body are examined, while in figure 2 Leonardo tries to compare the force of the arm in different positions and points of attachment. Between the last two draw-

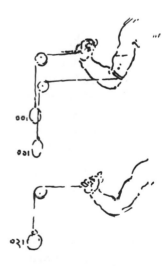

Figure 1
MS H, fol. 43*v*.

Figure 2
MS H, fol. 44*r*.

ings a diagram shows the arm as a compound lever. In many other instances Leonardo compares the human body with a mechanical system, anticipating Borelli. We shall see one of them on folio 164*r*, *a* of the Codex Atlanticus. . . .

The interest of Leonardo in the maximum efficiency of muscle power is understandable. It was the only motor he could have used in a flying machine; a project that aroused his ambition as early as the year 1488 and in which he remained interested till the end of his life.

The efficiency of the human motor depends not only on its intrinsic strength but also on the ways the force is applied. Indeed, what is the greatest strength a man can generate, without the help of mechanical devices like levers, gears, or pulleys? In a very interesting passage of MS A, folio 30*v* (fig. 3), Leonardo answers the question:

A man pulling a weight balanced against himself (as in lifting a weight with the help of a single block) cannot pull more than his own weight. And if he has to raise it, he will raise as much more than his weight, as his strength may be more than that of another man. The greatest force a man can apply, with equal velocity and impetus, will be when he sets his feet on one end of the balance and then leans his shoulders against some stable support. This will raise, at the other end of the balance, a weight equal to his own, and added to that, as much weight as he can carry on his shoulders.

Masterly executed marginal sketches illustrate the three different cases. The problem has been already touched on folio 90*v* of MS B, where the following suggestion is made beside a similar sketch: "See at the mill how much is your weight, stepping on the balance and pressing with your shoulders against something."

But Leonardo was always anxious to integrate theory with application. His own advice was: "When you put together the science of the motions of water, remember to include under each proposition its application and use, in order that this science may not be useless" (MS F, fol. 2*v*).

I should like to select, among many, a few cases in which Leonardo demonstrates the usefulness of his rules. One of them is pile driving for foundation work or the regulation of river banks. The simplest pile-driving machine consists of a movable frame, provided with a drop hammer raised by men pulling at a rope provided with hand lines. After being raised, the hammer is released by a trigger. The operation is repeated until the pile has been sunk to the necessary depth. In Belidor's classic treatise we may see the figure of this age-old device (fig. 4).

Leonardo, often engaged in architectural and hydraulic projects, obviously had a more than theoretical interest in the operation. . . .

As for the practical improvements, I should like to present a group of notes on this subject, from the Leicester Codex, folio 28*v*, which so far

Figure 3
MS A, fol. 30v.

Figure 4
Belidor, *Architecture Hydraulique*,
pt. 2, p. 128, pl. 8.

as I know have never been reproduced, commented upon, or translated.
Marginal drawings (figs. 5 and 6) illustrate the text.

The very best way to drive piles (*ficcare i pali a castello*) is when the
man lifts so much of the weight of the hammer as is his own weight.
And this shall be done in as much time as the man, without burden, is
able to climb a ladder quickly. Now, this man shall put his foot immediately in the stirrup and he will descend with so much weight as his
weight exceeds that of the hammer. If you want to check it thoroughly,
you can have him carry a stone weighing a pound. He will lift so much
weight as is his own on descending from the top of the ladder and the
hammer will raise and remain on top, locked by itself, until the man
dismounts the stirrup and again climbs the ladder. When you unlock
the hammer with a string, it will descend furiously on top of the pile
you want to drive in. And with the same speed the stirrup will rise again

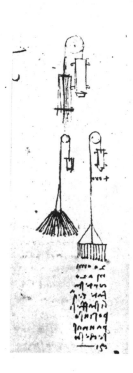

Figure 5
MS Leicester, fol. 28*v*.

Figure 6
MS Leicester, fol. 28*v*.

to the feet of the man. And this shall be done again and again. And if you want to have more men, take several ropes that end in one rope and several ladders to allow the men to reach the top of the ladders at the same time. Now, at a signal from the foreman, they shall put their feet in the stirrups and climb the ladder again. They will rest while descending and there is not much fatigue in climbing the ladders because it is done with feet and hands, and all the weight of the man that is charged on the hands will not burden the feet. But one man shall always give the signal.

Pile driving by raising the hammer by hand is not very useful, because a man cannot raise his own weight if he does not sustain it with his arms. This cannot be done unless the rope he is using is perpendicular to the center of his gravity. And this happens only to one of the men in a crowd who is pulling on the hammer.

We can further observe in the sketches of the Leicester Codex that Belidor's first two improvements had already been considered by Leonardo:

the substitution of a large wheel for the block and use of a capstan or a winch. . . .

A last word on the pile driver of Leonardo. He spoke of a hammer that is locked and unlocked by itself. In the pile driver drawn on folio 289*r, e* of the Codex Atlanticus (fig. 7) we can observe the kind of mechanism Leonardo was hinting at. It is amazing to verify the identity of this device with that of the mentioned, improved pile driver of Belidor (fig. 8). According to the French author, the machine had been invented by Vauloue, a London watchmaker, and used at the construction of the famous Westminster bridge, that is, in 1738–1750. The story is recorded also by Desaguliers. Devices of this type are still used.

Many notes and sketches of Leonardo refer to the construction of canals, a subject that often turns up in the manuscripts. . . .

He began by analyzing the best ways of disposing men to work if this had to be done by hand. For those calculations Leonardo even constructed a kind of chronometer on the nature of which Augusto Marinoni tells us more. Hc filled many sheets, extremely interesting in themselves, with calculations and sketches (e.g., C.A., fol. 210*r, a*), arriving at the conclusion that the only reasonable solution was to mechanize the whole operation.

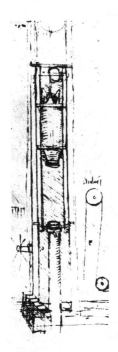

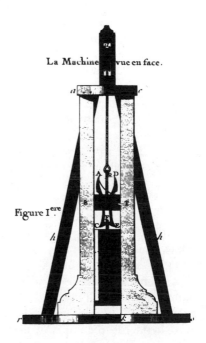

Figure 7
Codex Atlanticus, fol. 289*r, e.*

Figure 8
Belidor, *Architecture Hydraulique.*

It was not only a matter of digging. The excavated material had to be cleared and transported a long way. For this purpose wheeled vehicles were considered next and rejected.

Leonardo did not underestimate wheeled vehicles. He notes that "the cart has the first place among all human inventions, particularly when it has the right proportions, although I have never seen such a one." But a cart is useful only on level ground; on steep runs the weight nullifies the effort of the animal. Besides, "to fill the carts requires more time than needed for the transport itself" (C.A., fol. 164r, a). . . .

The well-known folio 211r, a of the Codex Atlanticus shows the theoretical justification of this statement; less noticed are the beautiful sketches above the main drawing, where the influence of the relative thickness of the axle on the movement is measured by an amazingly modern-looking dynamometer. On folio 340v, d, of the same codex, a similar arrangement is suggested for the measurement of the force required in pulling a four-wheeled vehicle. Leonardo was to use the same type of apparatus to gauge the force of a waterfall (C. Fors. III, fol. 47r) and to determine the power requirement of a grain mill (ibid., fol. 46v), anticipating the classic experiments of Smeaton.

After rejecting wheeled vehicles as unsuitable for excavation work and recognizing that a large and deep canal could not economically be dug by hand, Leonardo examined the possibility of substituting progressive hand shoveling from level to level by excavation machines combined with a system of cranes. Power was again his main concern.

To activate a crane, in addition to a horse-driven capstan, the only transportable motor available at the time would have been a treadmill, a machine that converts muscle power into rotary motion. . . .

Leonardo did not invent the external treadmill; there are older examples as far back as Vitruvius. But he was the first to use the principle rationally and in accordance with sound engineering principles. . . .

However, the increasing size of the complex machines created by the imagination of Leonardo required more power than that which could be supplied by the weight of a few men walking on a treadmill, even admitting the most rational mechanical arrangements. Leonardo was well aware of the situation, and wrote: "There you see the best of all motors, made by the ancient architects, that I cleaned from every fault and reduced to the ultimate perfection, with improvements that were not and could not be in its simple state. But I am still not satisfied and I intend to show a way of quicker motion of more usefulness and brevity" (C.A., fol. 370v, c). . . .

Still, the ultimate perfection had not yet been achieved. There was too much human work in filling and emptying the buckets and, particularly, in the excavation itself, the breaking up and the shoveling of the soil. Let us see how Leonardo the engineer tackled these problems.

Amazingly modern systems for the emptying of the buckets are described and shown on other pages of the Codex Atlanticus. The box is discharged

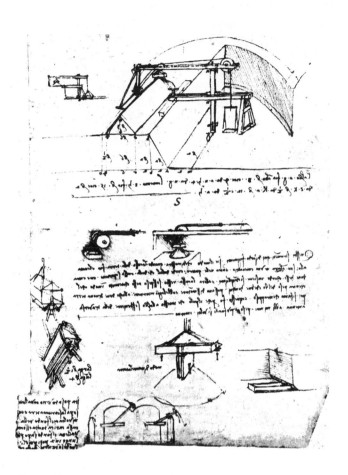

Figure 9
Codex Atlanticus, fol. 363*r*, *a*.

by hitting the ground as in folio 363*r*, *a* (fig. 9), or by releasing the bottom with a string (C.A., fol. 344*r*, *a*), or it is ingeniously overturned with the least possible effort as in folio 294*r*, *a*. As for the mechanization of the excavation itself, Leonardo offered several solutions that command the admiration of the modern engineer. He devised wheeled scrapers that with the aid of a horse could dig and remove the earth. Their design contains all the main features of modern tools (C.A., fols. 294*r*, *a*; 389*r*, *b*; 389*v*, *c*).

Leonardo's aim, however, was total mechanization. He declared emphatically that in the making of canals "the most useful method would be one by which the soil, removed, would jump by itself quickly on the instrument that will transport it" (C.A., fol. 164*r*, *a*; C. Ar., fol. 127*r–v*). . . .

A number of reasonable questions advanced by several authors will be echoed at this point. Those marvelously modern-looking projects of Leonardo, do they have reality or are they to be considered as the unfulfilled dreams of an inventor? Are they original or do they come from a long tradition of engineering experience?

These questions can be answered both ways. Leonardo did find ample inspiration in the deeds and writings of his predecessors in the technical arts, and some of his projects were so advanced that they could not have been carried out, for lack of adequate technical support. Others, even if brilliantly conceived, were based on faulty theories and would not work (e.g., the use of syphons more than 30 feet tall).

There can be no doubt, however, that most of Leonardo's technical ideas were grounded in firm and actual experience, even if the corresponding historical records are meager. His canal-building activity in the Romagnas, while in the service of Cesare Borgia, must have been successful in view of his immediate appointment by the Signoria of Florence in a similar capacity after the downfall of his frightful patron. Leonardo's innovations and inventions in the field of mechanical engineering can be traced in the writings of a number of sixteenth- and seventeenth-century authors, especially Cardan, Besson, Ramelli, Zonca, Castelli, Verantius, De Caus, etc. It is useless to speculate about the fact that Leonardo's manuscripts were hardly accessible to those writers: his technological ideas, like those related to the arts, were already incorporated in the common knowledge of the epoch.

But arts and techniques can be easily lost when genius is not understood and assimilated. The technology of the sixteenth and seventeenth centuries was much inferior to the standards set by Leonardo; only at the end of the seventeenth century was there a renewal that led to the beginning of modern engineering. A thorough study of Leonardo's technical activities and ideas, even if presented in the disorderly state of the mutilated and plundered heritage, points to him, as Feldhaus has correctly remarked, as the greatest engineer of all times.

Suggestions for Further Reading

THERE ARE TWO standard editions of Leonardo's notebooks, Leonardo da Vinci, *Notebooks*, tr. and ed. Edward McCurdy, 2 vols. (London: Cape,

1956), and *The Notebooks of Leonardo da Vinci*, ed. Jean Paul Richter, 2 vols. (New York: Dover, 1970), as well as a small collection of excerpts, Leonardo da Vinci, *Philosophical Diary*, tr. and ed. Wade Baskin (New York: Philosophical Library, 1959). Of the many collections of his artistic works, one of the best is *Leonardo da Vinci* (New York: Reynal, 1956), the catalogue of the comprehensive Milan Leonardo Exposition of 1938.

Two general works on Leonardo can be recommended—*Leonardo da Vinci, Aspects of the Renaissance Genius,* ed. Morris Philipson (New York: Braziller, 1966), a well-selected set of articles and special studies, and Cecil H. M. Gould, *Leonardo: the Artist and the Non-artist* (Boston: New York Graphic Society, 1975). Both these books recognize the two aspects of Leonardo's life and work that are generally dealt with, the scientific and the artistic. Of the works on Leonardo the artist, the best is Kenneth M. Clark, *Leonardo da Vinci, An Account of His Development as an Artist,* rev. ed. (Baltimore: Penguin, 1958); it may well be the best work on him of any sort. For Leonardo's mechanical engineering interests, the pioneer study is Ivor B. Hart, *The Mechanical Investigations of Leonardo da Vinci,* 2nd ed. (Berkeley: University of California Press, 1963 [1925]), and a later work by Hart updating the research, *The World of Leonardo, Man of Science, Engineer, and Dreamer of Flight* (New York: Viking, 1961). For Leonardo's anatomical studies see Elmer Belt, *Leonardo the Anatomist* (New York: Greenwood, 1955).

A special interest in Leonardo was stirred by two works of Sigmund Freud, *Leonardo da Vinci: A Study in Psychosexuality*, tr. A. A. Brill (New York: Random House, 1947), and *Leonardo da Vinci and a Memory of His Childhood,* tr. Alan Tyson (New York: Norton, 1964), in which Freud treated Leonardo as the subject of his most extensive attempt at psychohistory. The works are full of errors and not solidly based on research, but they thrust into the forefront of controversy about Leonardo the questions of his homosexuality and the paralyzing duality of his interests in science and art. There are two later important books in this controversy: Kurt R. Sissler, *Leonardo da Vinci: Psychoanalytic Notes on an Enigma* (New York: International Universities Press, 1961), and Raymond S. Stites, *The Sublimation of Leonardo da Vinci, with a Translation of the Codex Trivulzianus* (Washington: Smithsonian, 1970), the latter a large, detailed, and difficult book but an important revisionist study on Freud's tentative conclusions.

Although its assertions and research are now dated, students may still enjoy a famous historical novel, Dmitrii Merezhkovskii, *The Romance of Leonardo da Vinci,* tr. B. G. Guerney (New York: Heritage, 1938).

For the background to Leonardo's biography and the Renaissance, see Wallace K. Ferguson, *Europe in Transition, 1300–1520* (Boston: Houghton Mifflin, 1962), and Ernst Breisach, *Renaissance Europe, 1300–1517* (New York: Macmillan, 1973).

Martin Luther:
Protestant Saint or
"Devil in the Habit of a Monk"?

On a summer day in the year 1505, a young German law student was returning to the University of Erfurt after a visit home. He was overtaken by a sudden, violent thunderstorm and struck to the ground by a bolt of lightning. Terrified, he cried out, "St. Anne, help me! I will become a monk." Such vows were usually quickly forgotten, but not this one, for the student was Martin Luther, the man who was to bring about the most profound revolution in the history of the Christian faith. Within a matter of weeks, he disposed of his worldly goods, including his law books, and joined the order of the Augustinian Eremites in Erfurt. His father was furious; his friends were dismayed. And historians and theologians since the sixteenth century have speculated about the motives that compelled him. But this is only one of the questions about Martin Luther that have fascinated scholars and made him the subject of more writing than any other figure in European history.

There was seemingly nothing in his youth or adolescence to account for his decision to become a monk. But once that decision was made, Luther was swept by such a tidal wave of religious intensity that it troubled even his monastic superiors. He prayed for hours on end; he subjected himself to such ascetic rigors that he almost ruined his health; and he confessed his sins over and over again. He was assaulted by what one modern scholar has aptly called "the terror of the holy." God was for him a terrible judge, so perfect and so righteous that sinful man could not even begin to deserve anything at His hands but eternal damnation. Martin Luther was beginning his search for "justification," the sense that somehow, against all odds, he might earn God's grace and escape damnation.

The terror of the holy remained, and the monastic life gave Luther no assurance that God's grace was close at hand. But the very religious disquiet that tormented the young monk also caused his superiors to single him out, for this was the stuff that the great figures of religion were made of—St. Francis, St. Bernard, St. Benedict. Moreover, Brother Martin, for all his inner turmoil, was a bright and capable young man and already well educated, a Master of Arts. Soon he was ordained priest. He was sent on a matter of chapter business to Rome. And his education was continued, but now in theology rather than law.

Then the Elector of Saxony, Frederick the Wise, approached the Erfurt Augustinians in search of faculty members for the newly founded university in his capital town of Wittenberg. Brother Martin was sent. In Wittenberg he taught the arts course, worked at his own studies, and assumed more than a fair share of the parish duties. By 1513 he earned his doctor's degree and began to teach theology. As he prepared a series of lectures on the Psalms, he began to gain new understanding of his texts. And then, while he was working out his lectures on the Epistles of St. Paul, he found meaning in the familiar passage from Romans 1:17 that he had never before perceived. "For therein is the righteousness of God revealed from faith to faith: as it is written, the just shall live by faith." Later Luther said, "This passage of Paul became to me a gate to heaven." Here was the "justification" he had sought so long in vain. Man is justified by faith, by the simple act of belief in Christ, in a way that no amount of works, however pious and well intended, no amount of prayers or anguish or penance can insure. Justification by faith was to become the cardinal doctrine of a new religious sect.

But Luther's inward revelation might never have led to a separate sect, much less a Reformation, except for a chain of events external to him. It began with a particularly scandalous sale of indulgences in the neighboring lands of the Archbishop of Mainz. The doctrine of indulgences was the basis of the church's profitable traffic in "pardons," as they were sometimes called, remissions of the temporal penalties for sin. Although the doctrine was an outgrowth of the sacrament of penance, many churchmen were troubled by it. To Luther, the indulgences that had been bought across the border by some of his parishioners and the outrageous claims for their effectiveness that were being made by the indulgence preacher, the Dominican Johann Tetzel, seemed a surpassingly bad example of the concept of "works," especially in light of his own increasing conviction that works cannot work salvation in man—only faith "sola fides." In response to this

scandalous situation, Luther was led to propose his ninety-five theses
against indulgences. The document was dated October 31, 1517,
the most famous date in Protestantism. The theses were written in Latin,
intended for academic disputation, but somehow they were translated
into German and found their way into print. Despite their dry, scholarly
prose and formal organization they became a popular, even an
inflammatory manifesto. Ecclesiastical authorities, including the offended
Archbishop of Mainz, complained to Luther's superiors and eventually
to Rome. Luther was pressed to recant, but he refused. Instead, he
clung stubbornly not only to his basic position on indulgences but
to the ever more revolutionary implications of his belief in justification
by faith. Within three years, he had come to reject much of the
sacramental theory of the church, nearly all its traditions, and the
authority of the pope. In 1520 he defied Pope Leo X's bull of
condemnation; in the following year he defied the Emperor Charles V
in the famous confrontation at the Diet of Worms. The Lord's good
servant had become, in Charles' phrase, "that devil in the habit of a
monk." The Catholic Luther had become the Protestant Luther.

The Protestant Luther
MARTIN LUTHER

The image of Luther the Protestant results most directly, of course, from Luther's deeds—his successful act of defiance against established church and established state, his uncanny ability not only to survive but to build around him a new political-religious community vital enough to maintain itself. Luther's Protestant image is also based upon the incredible quantity of his writings—tracts and treatises, sermons, commentaries, translations, disputations, hymns, and letters—nearly a hundred heavy volumes in the standard modern edition. But his image also rests upon an elaborate Protestant tradition that can be traced to Luther himself.

Luther was a voluble and expansive man. Even his formal treatises are rich in anecdotes from his own experience and filled with autobiographical detail. These qualities carried over into his talk, and Luther loved to talk. As the Reformation settled into a political and social reality and Luther married—for he rejected clerical celibacy along with the other doctrines of the old church—his kitchen table became the center of the Protestant world. In addition to his own large family, there were always people visiting—friends and associates, wandering scholars and churchmen, professors and students, and religious refugees. After dinner, when the dishes were cleared and the beer steins passed around, they would talk, Luther usually taking the lead. He had opinions on practically everything—politics, people, theology, education, child raising—and he would reminisce about his own life as well.

Some of the guests took notes on these conversations, and a great many of them have been preserved—six volumes in the German Weimar edition—appropriately called the Tabletalk. *The following selections are from the* Tabletalk. *They are fragments of Luther's own recollections of his experience of monasticism, his inward struggle to gain a sense of justification, and his defiance of the old church.*

HE [MARTIN LUTHER] became a monk against the will of his father. When he celebrated his first mass and asked his father why he was angry about the step he took, the father replied reproachfully, "Don't you know that it's written, Honor your father and your mother" [Exod. 20:12]? When he excused himself by saying that he was so frightened by a storm that he was compelled to become a monk, his father answered, "Just so it wasn't a phantom you saw!" . . .

[Luther recalled] "later when I stood there during the mass and began the canon, I was so frightened that I would have fled if I hadn't been admonished by the prior. For when I read the words, 'Thee, therefore, most merciful Father,' etc., and thought I had to speak to God without a Mediator, I felt like fleeing from the world like Judas. Who can bear the majesty of God without Christ as Mediator? In short, as a monk I experienced such horrors; I had to experience them before I could fight them.". . . "I almost fasted myself to death, for again and again I went for three days without taking a drop of water or a morsel of food. I was very serious about it. I really crucified the Lord Christ. I wasn't simply an observer but helped to carry him and pierce [his hands and feet]. God forgive me for it, for I have confessed it openly! This is the truth: the most pious monk is the worst scoundrel. He denies that Christ is the mediator and highpriest and turns him into a judge."

"I chose twenty-one saints and prayed to three every day when I celebrated mass; thus I completed the number every week. I prayed especially to the Blessed Virgin, who with her womanly heart would compassionately appease her Son. . . ."

"When I was a monk I was unwilling to omit any of the prayers, but when I was busy with public lecturing and writing I often accumulated my appointed prayers for a whole week, or even two or three weeks. Then I would take a Saturday off, or shut myself in for as long as three days without food and drink, until I had said the prescribed prayers. This made my head split, and as a consequence I couldn't close my eyes for five nights, lay sick unto death, and went out of my senses. Even after I had quickly recovered and I tried again to read, my head went 'round and 'round. Thus our Lord God drew me, as if by force, from that torment of prayers. To such an extent had I been captive [to human traditions]. . . ."

"I wouldn't take one thousand florins for not having seen Rome because I wouldn't have been able to believe such things if I had been told by somebody without having seen them for myself. We were simply laughed at because we were such pious monks. A Christian was taken to be nothing but a fool. I know priests who said six or seven masses while I said only one. They took money for them and I didn't. In short, there's no disgrace in Italy except to be poor. Murder and theft are still punished a little, for they must do this. Otherwise no sin is too great for them." . . .

[As a young professor in Wittenberg] "the words 'righteous' and 'righteousness of God' struck my conscience like lightning. When I heard them I was exceedingly terrified. If God is righteous [I thought], he must punish.

But when by God's grace I pondered, in the tower [1] and heated room of this building, over the words, 'He who through faith is righteous shall live' [Rom. 1:17] and 'the righteousness of God' [Rom. 3:21], I soon came to the conclusion that if we, as righteous men, ought to live from faith and if the righteousness of God should contribute to the salvation of all who believe, then salvation won't be our merit but God's mercy. My spirit was thereby cheered. For it's by the righteousness of God that we're justified and saved through Christ. These words [which had before terrified me] now became more pleasing to me. The Holy Spirit unveiled the Scriptures for me in this tower." . . .

"That works don't merit life, grace, and salvation is clear from this, that works are not spiritual birth but are fruits of this birth. We are not made sons, heirs, righteous, saints, Christians by means of works, but we do good works once we have been made, born, created such. So it's necessary to have life, salvation, and grace before works, just as a tree doesn't deserve to become a tree on account of its fruit but a tree is by nature fitted to bear fruit. Because we're born, created, generated righteous by the Word of grace, we're not fashioned, prepared, or put together as such by means of the law or works. Works merit something else than life, grace, or salvation—namely, praise, glory, favor, and certain extraordinary things—just as a tree deserves to be loved, cultivated, praised, and honored by others on account of its fruit. Urge the birth and substance of the Christian and you will at the same time extinguish the merits of works insofar as grace and salvation from sin, death, and the devil are concerned."

"Infants who have no works are saved by faith alone, and therefore faith alone justifies. If the power of God can do this in one person it can do it in all, because it's not the power of the infant but the power of faith. Nor is it the weakness of the infant that does it, otherwise that weakness would in itself be a merit or be equivalent to one. We'd like to defy our Lord God with our works. We'd like to become righteous through them. But he won't allow it. My conscience tells me that I'm not justified by works, but nobody believes it. 'Thou art justified in thy sentence; against thee only have I sinned and done that which is evil in thy sight' [Ps. 51:4]. What is meant by 'forgive us our debts' [Matt. 6:12]? I don't want to be good. What would be easier than for a man to say, 'I am a sinful man' [Luke 5:8]? But thou art a righteous God. That would be bad enough, but we are our own tormentors. The Spirit says, 'Righteous art thou' [Ps. 119:137]. The flesh can't say this: 'Thou art justified in thy sentence' [Ps. 51:4]." . . .

"God led us away from all this in a wonderful way; without my quite being aware of it he took me away from that game more than twenty

---

[1] The tower was the "privy" of the cloister, and it was there that Luther suddenly saw the significance of justification by faith. Hence Lutheran scholarship refers to his *turmerlebnis,* or "tower experience."—ED.

years ago. How difficult it was at first when we journeyed toward Kemberg [2] after All Saints' Day in the year 1517, when I first made up my mind to write against the crass errors of indulgences! Dr. Jerome Schurff [3] advised against this: 'You wish to write against the pope? What are you trying to do? It won't be tolerated!' I replied, 'And if they have to tolerate it?' Presently Sylvester,[4] master of the sacred palace, entered the arena, fulminating against me with this syllogism: 'Whoever questions what the Roman church says and does is heretical. Luther questions what the Roman church says and does, and therefore [he is a heretic].' So it all began." . . .

"At the beginning of the gospel [5] I took steps only very gradually against the impudent Tetzel. Jerome, the bishop of Brandenburg, held me in esteem, and I exhorted him, as the ordinary of the place, to look into the matter and sent him a copy of my *Explanations* [6] before I published them. But nobody was willing to restrain the ranting Tetzel; rather, everybody ventured to defend him. So I proceeded imprudently while others listened and were worn out under the tyranny. Now that I got into the matter I prayed God to help me further. One can never pay the pope as he deserves."

The Catholic Luther
HARTMAN GRISAR

The traditional Catholic view of Luther is a hostile one. For Luther's Reformation set the new Protestantism against the old Catholicism with a bitterness and animosity that are apparent even to this day.

The following selection is from Martin Luther, His Life and Work, *by the German Jesuit scholar Hartmann Grisar (1845–1932), a shorter and somewhat more pointed work based upon his more famous,*

[2] A nearby monastery where, presumably, they were traveling on some routine parish business.—ED.

[3] A colleague of Luther's in the faculty of law.—ED.

[4] Sylvester Prierias, a papal official and a Dominican, the first dignitary in Rome to attack Luther.—ED.

[5] Luther often used this phrase for the beginning of the Reformation.—ED.

[6] The book Luther wrote explaining and defending his ninety-five theses.—ED.

six-volume Luther. *Although Grisar does abandon some of the more*
outrageous charges of the Catholic polemical tradition and displays an
awesome knowledge of the detail of his subject, he is still openly partisan
in his account and openly hostile in his interpretation. The passage
below focuses on the last years of Luther the Catholic, the years at
Wittenberg when Luther, as a young professor of theology, was struggling
toward his understanding of justification by faith. Grisar insists that
even then Luther was a "bad" Catholic. Instead of the frightened and
solitary figure striving against "the terror of the holy," we find a truculent
rebel, willfully distorting the rules of his own order and arrogantly
preferring his own interpretation of scripture and ecclesiastical tradition
to that of the church. Grisar makes Luther seem a selfish and overbearing
man, neglectful of his proper religious duties. He finds him misled
by his attraction to mysticism and excessive in his ascetic exercises.
In short, what Grisar builds is a case for Luther's suffering from
"a serious aberration."

THE YOUNG PROFESSOR of Sacred Scripture displayed a pronounced inclination towards mysticism. Mysticism had always been cultivated to a
certain extent in the religious orders of the Catholic Church. The reading
of Bonaventure had pointed Luther, even as a young monk, to the pious
union with God at which Mysticism aims. Toward the close of his lectures
on the Psalms, he became acquainted with certain works on Mysticism
which he imbibed with great avidity. They were the sermons of Tauler and
the tract *"Theologia deutsch."* They dominate his thoughts in 1515. Although these works were not designed to do so, they helped to develop
his unecclesiastical ideas. His lively experience of the weakness of the
human will induced him to hearken readily to the mystical voices which
spoke of the complete relinquishment of man to God, even though he did
not understand them perfectly. His opposition to good works opened his
mind to a fallacious conception of the doctrines of those books of the
mystical life. It appeared to him that, by following such leaders, his internal
fears could be dispelled by a calm immersion in the Godhead. . . . In
brief, he tried to transform all theology into what he called a theology of
the Cross. Misconstruing Tauler's doctrine of perfection he would recognize
only the highest motives, namely, reasons of the greatest perfection for
himself as well as for others. Fear of divine punishment and hope of divine
reward were to be excluded.

These were extravagances which could not aid him, but, on the contrary,
involved great danger to his orthodoxy; in fact, constituted a serious
aberration. But he trusted his new lights with the utmost self-confidence. . . .

In the spring of 1515, Luther was elected rural vicar by his fellow Augustinians.

At stated times he visited the monasteries thus entrusted to him. There were eleven of them, including Erfurt and Wittenberg. After the middle of April, 1516, he made a visitation of the congregations of the Order at Dresden, Neustadt on the Orla, Erfurt, Gotha, Langensalza, and Nordhausen. The letters written by him during his term of office as rural vicar, which normally lasted three years, contain practical directions and admonitions concerning monastic discipline and are, in part, quite edifying. Some of his visitations, however, were conducted with such astonishing rapidity that no fruitful results could be expected of them. Thus the visitation of the monastery at Gotha occupied but one hour, that at Langensalza two hours. "In these places," he wrote to Lang, "the Lord will work without us and direct the spiritual and temporal affairs in spite of the devil." At Neustadt he deposed the prior, Michael Dressel, without a hearing, because the brethren could not get along with him. "I did this," he informed Lang in confidence, "because I hoped to rule there myself for the half-year."

In a letter to the same friend he writes as follows about the engagements with which he was overwhelmed at that time: "I really ought to have two secretaries or chancellors. I do hardly anything all day but write letters. . . . I am at the same time preacher to the monastery, have to preach in the refectory, and am even expected to preach daily in the parish church. I am regent of the *studium* [*i.e.,* of the younger monks] and vicar, that is to say prior eleven times over; I have to provide for the delivery of the fish from the Leitzkau pond and to manage the litigation of the Herzberg fellows [monks] at Torgau; I am lecturing on Paul, compiling an exposition of the Psalter, and, as I said before, writing letters most of the time. . . . It is seldom that I have time for the recitation of the Divine Office or to celebrate Mass, and then, too, I have my peculiar temptations from the flesh, the world, and the devil."

The last sentence quoted above contains a remarkable declaration about his spiritual condition and his compliance with his monastic duties at that time. He seldom found time to recite the Divine Office and to say Mass. It was his duty so to arrange his affairs as to be able to comply with these obligations. The canonical hours were strictly prescribed. Saying Mass is the central obligation of every priest, especially if he is a member of a religious order. If Luther did not know how to observe due moderation in his labors; if he was derelict in the principal duties of the spiritual life; it was to be feared that he would gradually drift away from the religious state, particularly in view of the fact that he had adopted a false Mysticism which favored the relaxation of the rule. As rural vicar, it is probable that he did not sustain among the brethren the good old spirit which the zealous Proles had introduced into the society. Of the "temptations of the flesh" which he mentions we learn nothing definite. He was not yet in conflict with his vows. His wrestlings with the devil may signify the fears and terrors to which he was subject. . . . At times, in consequence either of a disordered affection of the heart or of overwork, he was so distressed that he could not eat or drink for a long time. One day he was found seemingly dead in his cell, so completely was he exhausted as a result of agitation and lack of food. . . .

Did Luther subject himself to extraordinary deeds of penance at any period of his monastic life, as he frequently affirmed in his subsequent conflict with the papacy and monasticism, when he was impelled by polemical reasons to describe himself as the type of a holy and mortified monk, one who could not find peace of mind during his whole monastic career? Holding then that peace of mind was simply impossible in the Catholic Church, he arbitrarily misrepresents monasticism, in order to exhibit in a most glaring manner the alleged inherent impossibility of "papistic" ethics to produce the assurance of God's mercy. "I tormented my body by fasting, vigils, and cold. . . . In the observance of these matters I was so precise and superstitious, that I imposed more burdens upon my body than it could bear without danger to health." "If ever a monk got to heaven by monkery, then I should have got there." "I almost died a-fasting, for often I took neither a drop of water nor a morsel of food for three days." . . .

The above picture of singular holiness is produced not by early witnesses, but by assertions which Luther made little by little at a later period of life. The established facts contradict the legend. Perhaps his description is based partly on reminiscences of his distracted days in the monastery, or on eccentric efforts to overcome his sombre moods by means of a false piety. His greatest error, and the one which most betrays him, is that he ascribes his fictitious asceticism to all serious-minded members of his monastery, yea, of all monasteries. He would have it that all monks consumed themselves in wailing and grief, wrestling for the peace of God, until he supplied the remedy. It is a rule of the most elementary criticism finally to cut loose from the distorted presentation of the matter which has maintained itself so tenaciously in Protestant biographies of Luther.

It may be admitted that, on the whole, Luther was a dutiful monk for the greatest part of his monastic life. "When I was in the monastery," he stated on one occasion, in 1535, "I was not like the rest of men, the robbers, the unjust, the adulterous; but I observed chastity, obedience, and poverty."

Yet, after his transfer to Wittenberg, and in consequence of the applause which was accorded to him there, the unpleasant traits of his character, especially his positive insistence on always being in the right, began to manifest themselves more and more disagreeably. . . . His opposition to the so-called doctrine of self-righteousness caused him to form a false conception of righteousness; instead of attacking an heretical error, he combated the true worth of good works and the perfections of the monastic life.

Voluntary poverty, as practiced by the mendicants, was one of the foundations of his Order. The inmates of monastic houses were to live on alms according to the practice introduced by the great Saint Francis of Assisi and for the benefactions received were to devote themselves gratis to the spiritual needs of their fellowmen. Many abuses, it is true, had attached themselves to the mendicant system; self-interest, avarice, and worldly-mindedness infected the itinerant mendicants. But in his explanation of the Psalms Luther attacks the life of poverty *per se:* "O mendicants! O mendicants! O mendicants!" he pathetically exclaims, "who can excuse you? . . . Look to it yourselves," etc. He places the practice of poverty in an unfavorable light. In his criticism of the "self-righteousness of his irksome enemies, he confronts them with the righteousness of the spirit that cometh from Christ. These people, whom he believed it his duty to expose, were guilty, in his opinion, of a Pharisaical denial of the true righteousness of Christ. His righteousness, and not our good works, effect our salvation; works generate a fleshly sense and boastfulness. These thought-processes evince how false mysticism, unclear theological notions, a darkening of the monastic spirit, and passionate obstinacy conspired in Luther's mind. . . .

The germ of Luther's reformatory doctrine is plainly contained in this species of Mysticism. Step by step he had arrived at his new dogma in the above described manner. The system which attacked the basic truths of the Catholic Church, was complete in outline. Before giving a fuller exposition of it, we must consider the individual factors which cooperated in its development in Luther's mind.

Confession and penance were a source of torturing offense to the young monk. Can one obtain peace with God by the performance of penitential works? He discussed this question with Staupitz [7] on an occasion when he sought consolation. Staupitz pointed out to him that all penance must begin and end with love; that all treasures are hidden in Christ, in whom we must trust and whom we must love. . . . Nor was Staupitz the man who could thoroughly free Luther from his doubts about predestination, although Luther says he helped him. His general reference to the wounds of Christ could not permanently set the troubled monk aright. . . . Recalling Staupitz's exhortations, he says, in 1532: We must stop at the wounds of Christ, and may not ponder over the awful mystery. The only remedy consists in dismissing from our minds the possibility of a verdict of damnation. "When I attend to these ideas, I forget what Christ and

---

[7] Johann Staupitz was a superior of Luther and one of his most trusted friends and confidants. Though Staupitz remained Catholic and in orders, they remained friends for many years.—ED.

God are, and sometimes arrive at the conclusion that God is a scoundrel.
. . . The idea of predestination causes us to forget God, and the *Laudate*
ceases and the *Blasphemate* begins." The part which these struggles had
in the origin of his new doctrine, is to be sought in Luther's violent efforts
to attain to a certain repose in the fact of his presumptive predestination.
. . . In his interpretation of the Epistle of St. Paul to the Romans, given
during the years 1515 and 1516, Luther completely unfolded his new
doctrine.

Luther Between Reform and Reformation
ERWIN ISERLOH

*A phenomenon of the last generation or so of Luther scholarship has been
the emergence of a new, more balanced, and more charitable Catholic
view of him. The polemical tone has almost disappeared, the shortcomings
of the old church have been recognized, and Luther himself is interpreted
in ways other than simply as a bad Catholic and a worse monk, led by
his own overweening hubris to an inevitable apostasy.*

*One of the best of the new Catholic critics is Erwin Iserloh, professor
of church history at the University of Münster in Germany. The following
selection is taken from his liveliest and most widely read book,* The Theses
Were Not Posted, Luther Between Reform and Reformation. *It is,
quite apart from its point of view, a stunning demonstration of how a
thoughtful scholar may use a precise event to reach a general conclusion.
The event in this case is the "primal image" of Luther nailing the ninety-five
theses to the door of the Castle Church in Wittenberg, thereby defiantly
proclaiming the beginning of his rebellion from the church. Iserloh
presents evidence that this treasured picture appeared only after Luther's
death, that it came not from Luther himself but from his younger associate
Philipp Melanchthon, and that Melanchthon had not even witnessed
the event. Iserloh goes on to point out that, far from an act of rebellion,
Luther's handling of the matter of the theses shows him to have been,
at this crucial point, both a good Catholic and a responsible theologian,*

in Iserloh's phrase, "an obedient rebel." Iserloh argues further that it
was not necessary for Luther to have been driven to rebellion; he might
well have been kept within the church to its great advantage, as well
as his own.

OUR INVESTIGATION of the sources and the reports concerning October 31, 1517, compels us to conclude that the drama of that day was notably less than what we would suppose from the jubilee celebrations which have been held since 1617 and from the Reformation Day festivals since their inception in 1668. In fact the sources rule out a public posting of the ninety-five theses.

Although October 31, 1517, lacked outward drama it was nevertheless a day of decisive importance. It is the day on which the Reformation began, not because Martin Luther posted his ninety-five theses on the door of the castle church in Wittenberg, but because on this day Luther approached the competent church authorities with his pressing call for reform. On this day he presented them with his theses and the request that they call a halt to the unworthy activities of the indulgence preachers. When the bishops did not respond, or when they sought merely to divert him, Luther circulated his theses privately. The theses spread quickly and were printed in Nürnberg, Leipzig, and Basel. Suddenly they were echoing throughout Germany and beyond its borders in a way that Luther neither foresaw nor intended. The protest that Luther registered before Archbishop Albrecht [8] and the inclusion of the theses with the letter eventually led to the Roman investigation of Luther's works.

Some will surely want to object: Is it not actually of minor importance whether Luther posted his theses in Wittenberg or not? I would answer that it is of more than minor importance. For October 31 was a day on which the castle church was crowded with pilgrims taking advantage of the titular feast of All Saints. Luther's theses on the door would have constituted a public protest. If Luther made such a scene on the same day that he composed his letter to Archbishop Albrecht, then his letter loses its credibility, even when we take into account its excessive protestations of submissiveness and humility as conventions of the time.

Above all, if Luther did post his theses, then for the rest of his life he knowingly gave a false account of these events by asserting that he only circulated his theses after the bishops failed to act.

If the theses were not posted on October 31, 1517, then it becomes all the more clear that Luther did not rush headlong toward a break with the church. Rather, as Joseph Lortz has never tired of repeating, and as Luther

[8] The Archbishop of Mainz, who had authorized the particular sale of indulgences.—ED.

himself stressed, he started the Reformation quite unintentionally. In the preface to an edition of his theses in 1538 Luther gave a detailed picture of the situation in 1517. It is as if he wanted to warn the Protestant world against dramatizing the start of the Reformation with false heroics. First he stresses how weak, reticent, and unsure he was; then he tells of his efforts to contact church authorities. This is something he knows his readers cannot appreciate, since they have grown used to impudent attacks on the broken authority of the pope. . . .

If Luther did turn first to the competent bishops with his protest, or better, with his earnest plea for reform, and if he did give them time to react as their pastoral responsibilities called for, then it is the bishops who clearly were more responsible for the consequences. If Luther did allow the bishops time to answer his request then he was sincere in begging the archbishop to remove the scandal before disgrace came upon him and upon the church.

Further, there was clearly a real opportunity that Luther's challenge could be directed to the reform of the church, instead of leading to a break with the church. But such reform would have demanded of the bishops far greater religious substance and a far more lively priestly spirit than they showed. The deficiencies that come to light here, precisely when the bishops were called on to act as theologians and pastors, cannot be rated too highly when we seek to determine the causes of the Reformation. These deficiencies had far more serious consequences than did the failures in personal morality that we usually connect with the "bad popes" and concubinous priests on the eve of the Reformation. Archbishop Albrecht showed on other occasions as well how indifferent he was to theological questions, and how fully incapable he was of comprehending their often wideranging religious significance. For example, he expressed his displeasure over the momentous Leipzig debate of 1519 where famous professors were, as he saw it, crossing swords over minor points of no interest for true Christian men. This same Albrecht sent sizable gifts of money to Luther on the occasion of his marriage in 1525 and to Melanchthon after the latter had sent him a copy of his commentary on Romans in 1532.

A whole series of objections might arise here: Do not the indulgence theses themselves mark the break with the church? Do they not attack the very foundations of the church of that day? Or, as Heinrich Bornkamm wrote, do they not decisively pull the ground from under the Catholic conception of penance? Was a reform of the church of that day at all possible by renewal from within? Is not the Luther of the ninety-five theses already a revolutionary on his way inevitably to the Reformation as a division of the church?

Our first question must be whether Luther's indulgence theses deny any binding doctrines of the church in his day. And even if this be true, we cannot immediately brand the Luther of late 1517 a heretic. This would be justified only if he became aware of holding something opposed to the teaching of the church and then remained adamant in the face of correction. It is especially important to recall this in view of Luther's repeated assertions that the theses do not express his own position, but that much in them is doubtful, that some points he would reject, and no single one out of all of them would he stubbornly maintain. . . .

Still, a truly historical judgment on the theses will not consider their precise wording only. We must further ask in what direction they are tending and what development is already immanent in them. Luther's theses can only be understood in the context of late medieval nominalism. This theology had already made a broad separation of divine and human activity in the church. For God, actions in the church were only occasions for his saving action, with no true involvement of the latter in the former. Regarding penance and the remission of punishment, Luther simply carries the nominalist separation of the ecclesiastical and the divine to the extreme in that he denies that ecclesiastical penances and their remission even have an interpretative relation to the penance required by or remitted by God. I see here one root of Luther's impending denial of the hierarchical priesthood established by God in the church.

The theological consequences of the ninety-five theses were not immediately effective. The secret of their wide circulation and their electrifying effect was that they voiced a popular polemic. Here Luther touched on questions, complaints, and resentments that had long been smouldering and had often been expressed already. Luther made himself the spokesman for those whose hopes for reform had often been disappointed in a period of widespread dissatisfaction.

Theses 81–90 list the pointed questions the laity ask about indulgences. If the pope can, as he claims, free souls from purgatory, why then does he not do this out of Christian charity, instead of demanding money as a condition? Why does he not forget his building project and simply empty purgatory? (82) If indulgences are so salutary for the living, why does the pope grant them to the faithful but once a day and not a hundred times? (88) If the pope is more intent on helping souls toward salvation than in obtaining money, why is it that he makes new grants and suspends earlier confessional letters and indulgences which are just as effective? (89) If indulgences are so certain, and if it is wrong to pray for people already saved, why are anniversary masses for the dead still celebrated? Why is the money set aside for these masses not returned? (83) Why does the pope not build St. Peter's out of his own huge wealth, instead of with the money of the poor? (86) These are serious and conscientious questions posed by laymen. If they are merely beaten down by authority, instead of being met with good reasons, then the church and the pope will be open to the ridicule of their enemies. This will only increase the misery of the Christian people. (90)

Here Luther's theses brought thoughts out into the open that all had more or less consciously found troublesome. . . .

The rapid dissemination of his theses was for Luther proof that he had written what many were thinking but, as in John 7:13, they would not speak out openly "out of fear of the Jews." (WBr 1, 152, 17)

Luther regretted the spread of the theses, since they were not meant for the public, but only for a few learned men. Furthermore, the theses contained a number of doubtful points. Therefore he rushed the "Sermon on Indulgences and Grace" into print in March 1518 (W 1, 239–46) as a popular presentation of his basic point on indulgences, and he wrote the *Resolutiones* (W 1, 526–628 and LW 31, 83–252) as an extensive theological explanation of the theses. . . .

[The] prefatory statements accompanying the explanations of the theses have been singled out for a remarkable combination of loyal submissiveness, prophetic sense of mission, and an almost arrogant conviction of their cause. Meissinger saw here the maneuverings of a chess expert. This does not strike me as an adequate analysis. I see rather the genuine possibility of keeping Luther within the church. But for this to have happened the bishops who were involved, and the pope himself, would have to have matched Luther in religious substance and in pastoral earnestness. It was not just a cheap evasion when Luther repeated again and again in 1517 and 1518 that he felt bound only by teachings of the church and not by theological opinions, even if these came from St. Thomas or St. Bonaventure. The binding declaration Luther sought from the church came in Leo X's doctrinal constitution on indulgences, *"Cum postquam"* (DS 1447ff.), on November 9, 1518. . . .

The papal constitution declares that the pope by reason of the power of the keys can through indulgences remit punishments for sin by applying the merits of Christ and the saints. The living receive this remission as an absolution and the departed by way of intercession. The constitution was quite reticent and sparing in laying down binding doctrine. This contrasts notably with the manner of the indulgence preachers and Luther's attackers. . . .

Silvester Prierias, the papal court theologian, exceeded his fellow Dominican Tetzel in frivolity. For him, a preacher maintaining the doctrines attacked by Luther is much like a cook adding seasoning to make a dish more appealing. Here we see the same lack of religious earnestness and pastoral awareness that marked the bishops' reaction to the theses.

This lack of theological competence and of apostolic concern was all the more freighted with consequences, in the face of Martin Luther's zeal for the glory of God and the salvation of souls in 1517–18. There was a real chance to channel his zeal toward renewal of the church from within.

In this context it does seem important whether Luther actually posted his theses for the benefit of the crowds streaming into the Church of All Saints in Wittenberg. It is important whether he made such a scene or whether he simply presented his ninety-five theses to the bishops and to some learned friends. From the former he sought the suppression of practical abuses, and from the latter the clarification of open theological questions.

I, for one, feel compelled to judge Luther's posting of the ninety-five theses a legend. With this legend removed it is much clearer to what a great extent the theological and pastoral failures of the bishops set the scene for Luther to begin the divisive Reformation we know, instead of bringing reform from within the church.

Suggestions for Further Reading

LUTHER WAS HIMSELF a voluminous and powerful writer, and students should sample his writings beyond the brief excerpt from the *Tabletalk* presented in this chapter. The standard English edition of his works is in many volumes and sets of volumes, each edited by several scholars, elaborately cross-indexed and with analytical contents so that individual works are easy to find. Of particular interest should be the set *Martin Luther, Career of the Reformer*, vols. 31–34 (Philadelphia: Muhlenberg Press, 1957–1960). Some of the same works will be found in another edition, Martin Luther, *Reformation Writings*, tr. Bertram L. Woolf, 2 vols. (New York: Philosophical Library, 1953–1956).

The career of the young Luther, which is emphasized in this chapter, has been of particular interest to Luther scholars. Heinrich Boehmer, *Road to Reformation, Martin Luther to the Year 1521*, tr. John W. Doberstein and Theodore S. Tappert (Philadelphia: Muhlenberg Press, 1946), is the standard work by a great German authority. The same ground is covered by Robert H. Fife, *The Revolt of Martin Luther* (New York: Columbia University Press, 1957). DeLamar Jensen, *Confrontation at Worms: Martin Luther and the Diet of Worms. With a Complete English Translation of the Edict of Worms* (Provo, Utah: Brigham Young University Press, 1973), gives a detailed look at the terminal event in young Luther's career. Erik H. Erikson, *Young Man Luther: A Study in Psychoanalysis and History* (New York: Norton, 1958), is a famous and controversial book that students find provocative.

Of the many works on Luther's theology and thought, two especially are recommended. Heinrich Bornkamm, *Luther's World of Thought,* tr. Martin H. Bertram (St. Louis: Concordia, 1958), is one of the most influential works of modern Luther literature. It is fundamentally a theological rather than an historical work and is difficult but also important. Of particular interest to the background of the young Luther is Bengt R. Hoffman, *Luther and the Mystics: A Re-examination of Luther's Spiritual Experiences and His Relationship to the Mystics* (Minneapolis: Augsburg Press, 1976).

Of the many general biographical works, James Atkinson, *Luther and the Birth of Protestantism* (Baltimore: Penguin, 1968), places emphasis on his theological development. Probably the best and most readable of all the Luther biographies is Roland H. Bainton, *Here I Stand: A Life of Martin Luther* (Nashville: Abingdon Press, 1950). Three books are recommended for the broader topic of Luther and his age. Two are very large and comprehensive: Ernest G. Schwiebert, *Luther and His Times, the Reformation from a New Perspective* (St. Louis: Concordia, 1950), and Richard Friedenthal, *Luther: His Life and Times,* tr. John Nowell (New York: Harcourt, Brace, 1970). The third, A. G. Dickens, *The German Nation and Martin Luther* (New York: Harper & Row, 1974), is really an attractive, authoritative extended essay.

For the still larger topic of Luther in relation to the Reformation, see A. G. Dickens, *Reformation and Society in Sixteenth-Century Europe* (New York: Harcourt, Brace, 1966); Lewis W. Spitz, *The Renaissance and Reformation Movements,* vol. 2 (Chicago: Rand McNally, 1971); and Harold J. Grimm, *The Reformation Era,* 2nd ed. (New York: Macmillan, 1973).

Elizabeth I, the Armada, and "The Black Legend"

"She had a sharp tongue, a vile temper, almost no feminine delicacy, and little or no feminine modesty. Of personal loyalty and affection she seems to have commanded little or none." [1] The lady thus so unflatteringly described was Elizabeth I, Queen of England; the describer, Conyers Read, the most eminent American scholar of Tudor England. And yet Read goes on to point out, as he did in a dozen other works, that Elizabeth was "Good Queen Bess" to the great bulk of her subjects and that she has held an unrivaled place in the affections of Englishmen since the end of the sixteenth century. Most other modern Elizabethan scholars would agree. They would also agree that despite their own learned assessments of the importance of one aspect or another of Elizabeth's reign—her management of the economy, her relations with Parliament, her domestic religious settlement—the most enduring of all Elizabethan traditions is that of Elizabeth and her England set against the Spain of Philip II, culminating in the dramatic English victory over the Spanish Armada in the late summer of the year 1588.

This hardy tradition has its origin in the Armada fight itself and in the events surrounding it. English hostility to Spain was growing for a number of reasons: sympathy for the beleaguered French Huguenots and the Protestants of Holland locked in their own desperate struggle with Philip; the undeclared sea war with Spain that English privateers and pirates had

[1] Conyers Read, "Good Queen Bess," *American Historical Review,* 31 (1926), 649.

already been carrying on for a generation; as well as the gnawing fear of a domestic fifth column of Spanish spies and English Catholics ready to betray their country for the sake of their religion. Holinshed's famous *Chronicle,* for example, quotes a speech given by one "Maister Iames "Dalton" in the year 1586 having to do with the designs of certain captive traitors and Spanish sympathizers, one of whom "vomited these prophane words out of his vncircumcised mouth; that it was lawfull for anie of worship in England, to authorise the vilest wretch that is, to séeke the death of hir highnese whose prosperous estate the italish préest and Spanish prince doo so maligne." Dalton goes on to decry "an inuasion long since pretended" and the popish threats "that would burne hir bones, and the bones of all such as loued hir, either alive or dead [and] that this was to de doone, when they held the sterne of gouernement; which shall be, when errant traitors are good subiects, and ranke knaues honest men." [2]

In the years immediately following the Armada, such sentiments were even more strongly voiced. Sir Walter Raleigh in his spirited account of "The Last Fight of the Revenge," written in 1591, spoke of "how irreligiously [the Spanish] cover their greedy and ambitious pretences with that veil of piety," and how they "more greedily thirst after English blood than after the lives of any other people of Europe, for the many overthrows and dishonours they have received at our hands, whose weakness we have discovered to the world, and whose forces at home, abroad, in Europe, in India, by sea and land, we have even with handfuls of men and ships over thrown and dishonoured." [3]

Thus by the end of the sixteenth century, the major elements of what modern Hispanic scholars have come to call "The Black Legend" were substantially formed: Spain was England's implacable enemy, cruel in victory, craven in defeat; Spaniards were treacherous and cowardly, made more so by their "popery"; and, though out-manned and out-gunned, English ships could either defeat Spanish ships or, if not, at least show how "beardless boys" could go to heroic death. The center of the legend was the Armada, which "more than any other event, implanted anti-Hispanism in the English consciousness." [4] And Queen Elizabeth became the exemplar of the virtues of her nation and the symbol of its hostility to Spain.

---

[2] *Holinshed's Chronicle* (London, 1808; rpt. New York: AMS Press, 1965), IV, 920.
[3] Sir Walter Raleigh, *Selected Prose and Poetry,* ed. Agnes M. C. Latham (London: University of London-Athlone Press, 1965), pp. 85, 87.
[4] William S. Maltby, *The Black Legend in England* (Durham, N.C.: Duke University Press, 1971), p. 84.

The Legendary Elizabeth
SIR FRANCIS BACON

Elizabeth's "Gloriana" image was a bit tarnished during the last years of her reign by grievances that had finally begun to surface, by the residue of unfulfilled hopes and unredeemed promises, and by a general restlessness after almost half a century of her rule. But the succession of her Stuart cousin James I shortly restored Elizabeth's luster. The Elizabethan Age and Elizabeth herself assumed heroic stature when compared with James I, "who feared his own shadow and manifested such unkingly habits as drivelling at the mouth, picking his nose, and closeting himself with pretty young men." [5] *Yet it was not his personal habits, no matter how offensive, not even his penchant for playing at "kingcraft" or the muddle he made of the religious settlement that most alienated James' English subjects; it was his resolution to abandon the tradition of hostility to Spain, indeed to court a Spanish-Catholic alliance.*

Sir Francis Bacon (1561–1626) was a functionary of James' court and one of the leading men of affairs in the new reign. But he had also been a figure of Elizabeth's court and a member of Parliament during the Armada. Though he had not advanced under Elizabeth as grandly as he thought his merits deserved, still, looking back to her reign, even the cold and analytical Bacon could not help being moved. In the summer of 1608, the year following his appointment by James as Solicitor General, Bacon wrote in Latin a memorial to Elizabeth that he titled "On the Fortunate Memory of Elizabeth Queen of England." He circulated the piece privately to a few friends but provided that it be published only after his death. Bacon was not only a stupendous genius: but also a good judge of his own advantage.

"On the Fortunate Memory of Elizabeth Queen of England" is of considerable interest because it is the mature reflection of one who had been close to the center of events. The memorial is equally important because it shows a renewed interest in "the heroic Elizabeth" in the light of her unheroic successor and the new foreign and religious policies he was already considering. Bacon was writing a memorial not only to Elizabeth but to an age of giants now sadly past.

[5] Lacey Baldwin Smith, *The Elizabethan World* (Boston: Houghton Mifflin, 1967), pp. 204–5.

I ACCOUNT . . . as no small part of Elizabeth's felicity the period and compass of her administration; not only for its length, but as falling within that portion of her life which was fittest for the control of affairs and the handling of the reins of government. She was twenty-five years old (the age at which guardianship ceases) when she began to reign, and she continued reigning till her seventieth year; so that she never experienced either the disadvantages and subjection to other men's wills incident to a ward, nor the inconveniences of a lingering and impotent old age. . . .

Nor must it be forgotten withal among what kind of people she reigned; for had she been called to rule over Palmyrenes or in an unwarlike and effeminate country like Asia, the wonder would have been less; a woman-ish people might well enough be governed by a woman; but that in England, a nation particularly fierce and warlike, all things could be swayed and controlled at the beck of a woman, is a matter for the highest admiration.

Observe too that this same humour of her people, ever eager for war and impatient of peace, did not prevent her from cultivating and maintaining peace during the whole time of her reign. And this her desire of peace, together with the success of it, I count among her greatest praises; as a thing happy for her times, becoming to her sex, and salutary for her conscience. . . .

And this peace I regard as more especially flourishing from two circumstances that attended it, and which though they have nothing to do with the merit of peace, add much to the glory of it. The one, that the calamities of her neighbours were as fires to make it more conspicuous and illustrious; the other that the benefits of peace were not unaccompanied with honour of war,—the reputation of England for arms and military prowess being by many noble deeds, not only maintained by her, but increased. For the aids sent to the Low Countries, to France, and to Scotland; the naval expeditions to both the Indies, some of which sailed all round the globe; the fleets despatched to Portugal and to harass the coasts of Spain; the many defeats and overthrows of the rebels in Ireland; —all these had the effect of keeping both the warlike virtues of our nation in full vigour and its fame and honour in full lustre.

Which glory had likewise this merit attached,—that while neighbour kings on the one side owed the preservation of their kingdoms to her timely succours; suppliant peoples on the other, given up by ill-advised princes to the cruelty of their ministers, to the fury of the populace, and to every kind of spoliation and devastation, received relief in their misery; by means of which they stand to this day.

Nor were her counsels less beneficent and salutary than her succours; witness her remonstrances so frequently addressed to the King of Spain that he would moderate his anger against his subjects in the Low Countries, and admit them to return to their allegiance under conditions not intolerable; and her continual warnings and earnest solicitations addressed to the kings of France that they would observe their edicts of pacification. That her counsel was in both cases unsuccessful, I do not deny. The common fate of Europe did not suffer it to succeed in the first; for so the ambition of Spain, being released as it were from prison, would have been free to spend itself (as things then were) upon the ruin of the kingdoms and commonwealths of Christendom. The blood of so many innocent persons, slaughtered with their wives and children at their hearths and in their beds by the vilest rabble, like so many brute beasts animated, armed, and set on by public authority, forbade it in the other; that innocent blood demanding in just revenge that the kingdom which had been guilty of so atrocious a crime should expiate it by mutual slaughters and massacres. But however that might be, she was not the less true to her own part, in performing the office of an ally both wise and benevolent.

Upon another account also this peace so cultivated and maintained by Elizabeth is matter of admiration; namely, that it proceeded not from any inclination of the times to peace, but from her own prudence and good management. For in a kingdom laboring with intestine faction on account of religion, and standing as a shield and stronghold of defence against the then formidable and overbearing ambition of Spain, matter for war was nowise wanting; it was she who by her forces and her counsels combined kept it under; as was proved by an event the most memorable in respect of felicity of all the actions of our time. For when the Spanish fleet, got up with such travail and ferment, waited upon with the terror and expectation of all Europe, inspired with such confidence of victory, came ploughing into our channels, it never took so much as a cockboat at sea, never fired so much as a cottage on the land, never even touched the shore; but was first beaten in a battle and then dispersed and wasted in a miserable flight with many shipwrecks; while on the ground and territories of England peace remained undisturbed and unshaken.

Nor was she less fortunate in escaping the treacherous attempts of conspirators than in defeating and repelling the forces of the enemy. For not a few conspiracies aimed at her life were in the happiest manner both detected and defeated; and yet was not her life made thereby more alarmed or anxious; there was no increase in the number of her guards; no keeping within her palace and seldom going abroad; but still secure and confident, and thinking more of the escape than of the danger, she held her wonted course, and made no change in her way of life.

Worthy of remark too is the nature of the times in which she flourished. For there are some times so barbarous and ignorant that it is as easy a matter to govern men as to drive a flock of sheep. But the lot of this Queen fell upon times highly instructed and cultivated, in which it is not possible to be eminent and excellent without the greatest gifts of mind and a singular composition of virtue. . . .

With regard to her moderation in religion there may seem to be a difficulty, on account of the severity of the laws made against popish subjects. But on this point I have some things to advance which I myself carefully observed and know to be true.

Her intention undoubtedly was, on the one hand not to force consciences, but on the other not to let the state, under pretence of conscience and religion, be brought in danger. Upon this ground she concluded at the first that, in a people courageous and warlike and prompt to pass from strife of minds to strife of hands, the free allowance and toleration by public authority of two religions would be certain destruction. Some of the more turbulent and factious bishops also she did, in the newness of her reign when all things were subject to suspicion,—but not without legal warrant—restrain and keep in free custody. The rest, both clergy and laity, far from troubling them with any severe inquisition, she sheltered by a gracious connivency. This was the condition of affairs at first. Nor even when provoked by the excommunication pronounced against her by Pius Quintus (an act sufficient not only to have roused indignation but to have furnished ground and matter for a new course of proceeding), did she depart almost at all from this clemency, but persevered in the course which was agreeable to her own nature. For being both wise and of a high spirit, she was little moved with the sound of such terrors; knowing she could depend upon the loyalty and love of her own people, and upon the small power the popish party within the realm had to do harm, as long as they were not seconded by a foreign enemy. About the twenty-third year of her reign however, the case was changed. And this distinction of time is not artificially devised to make things fit, but expressed and engraved in public acts.

For up to that year there was no penalty of a grievous kind imposed by previous laws upon popish subjects. But just then the ambitious and vast design of Spain for the subjugation of the kingdom came gradually to light. . . .

. . . It is true, and proved by the confessions of many witnesses, that from the year I have mentioned to the thirtieth of Elizabeth (when the design of Spain and the Pope was put in execution by that memorable armada of land and sea forces) almost all the priests who were sent over to this country were charged among the other offices belonging to their function, to insinuate that matters could not long stay as they were, that a new aspect and turn of things would be seen shortly, and that the state of England was cared for both by the Pope and the Catholic princes, if the English would but be true to themselves. . . .

. . . This so great a tempest of dangers made it a kind of necessity for Elizabeth to put some severer constraint upon that party of her subjects which was estranged from her and by these means poisoned beyond recovery, and was at the same time growing rich by reason of their immunity from public offices and burdens. And as the mischief increased, the origin of it being traced to the seminary priests, who were bred in foreign parts, and supported by the purses and charities of foreign princes, professed enemies of this kingdom, and whose time had been passed in places where the very name of Elizabeth was never heard except as that of a heretic excommunicated and accursed, and who (if not themselves stained with treason) were the acknowledged intimates of those that were directly engaged in such crimes, and had by their own arts and poisons depraved and soured with a new leaven of malignity the whole lump of Catholics, which had before been more sweet and harmless; there was no remedy for it but that men of this class should be prohibited upon pain of death from coming into the kingdom at all; which at last, in the twenty-seventh year of her reign, was done. Nor did the event itself which followed not long after, when so great a tempest assailed and fell with all its fury upon the kingdom, tend in any degree to mitigate the envy and hatred of these men; but rather increased it, as if they had utterly cast off all feeling for their country, which they were ready to betray to a foreign servitude. . . .

The "New" Elizabeth
JAMES ANTHONY FROUDE

James Anthony Froude (1818–1894), for all the criticism he received—his Oxford rival E. A. Freeman called him "the vilest brute that ever wrote a book" [6]*—was surely one of the most influential historians "that ever wrote a book." The book on which both his reputation and his influence most firmly rest is his massive, twelve-volume* History of England from the Fall of Wolsey to the Defeat of the Spanish Armada. *Froude began work on it about 1850, and it was published in two-volume installments roughly every other year between 1856 and 1870 to a rising chorus of popular acclaim. Ignoring the factual inaccuracies that bothered Froude's fellow scholars, the public was delighted by his preference for advocacy rather than objectivity. The people tended to agree with Froude that history proclaimed, or should proclaim, "the laws of right and wrong." Moreover, they agreed that right resided in the Church of*

---

[6] Quoted in F. Smith Fussner, *Tudor History and Historians* (New York: Basic Books, 1970), p. 55.

*England and wrong, more often than not, in the Church of Rome. If proof
was needed for their prejudices—or his—it was abundantly available in
the profusion of facts that crowded Froude's* History *and gave it an
unequalled sense of authenticity. For Froude was one of the first modern
British historians to go extensively to the original sources for his research;
he was aided by the fact that only in his lifetime was the great mass of
English public documents of the Tudor age at last being systematically
edited and published.*

*Froude considered the Tudor age to be the pivot of all English history.
The topical limits he set to his own great* History *display his thesis. The
fall of Wolsey and Henry VIII's break with Rome marked the start of the
English Reformation; the defeat of the Spanish Armada marked the
triumph of English Protestantism and the beginning of England's
supremacy in the modern world. Like his life-long friend Carlyle, Froude
was more impressed with people than with large economic or social
forces. Heroic men accomplish heroic deeds. Henry VIII was Froude's
hero, standing stalwart and unblinking at the beginning of his narrative.
At the other end stood the most heroic deed in English history, the defeat
of the Armada. Yet careful research revealed that Elizabeth, Henry's
daughter, was—at least by Froude's standards—considerably less than
heroic. Where Henry had been defiant, Elizabeth preferred to negotiate.
Where Henry had carried the fight to the enemy, Elizabeth was
suspicious of fighting and more than reluctant to throw her resources into
the great national effort against Spain. Even where the fight was
inevitable, she was stingy of her support and vacillating in her resolve.
Worst of all, Froude found her, at the most charitable, to be a guarded
and circumstantial Protestant, perhaps even a crypto-Catholic. If Henry
VIII was Froude's hero, Elizabeth was his burden. In order to reconcile
his low opinion of Elizabeth with the importance he attached to the
Armada, Froude made the triumph over the Armada a victory "in spite
of" Elizabeth, the product of the patient policy of her great Protestant
advisors and the selfless heroism of her seamen.*

*It may be charged that Froude, more than most historians, took his
conclusions to his sources and then found them there. But this failing is
surely not unique with him. Even his severest critics today admit that
Froude's* History *is "one of the great masterpieces of English historical
literature,"* [7] *that it is "a classic"* [8] *for its period, and that "more than
any other nineteenth-century English historian James Anthony Froude
set the nineteenth-century version of Tudor history."* [9] *An indispensable
part of that version was Froude's equivocal image of the "new"
Elizabeth.*

[7] Conyers Read, *Bibliography of British History, Tudor Period, 1485–1603*, 2nd ed.
(Oxford: Clarendon Press, 1959), p. 30.

[8] *Ibid.*

[9] Fussner, p. 55.

We turn now to the summation of Froude's account of Elizabeth and the Armada, from the conclusion of his History.

IT HAD BEEN my intention to continue this history to the close of Elizabeth's life. The years which followed the defeat of the Armada were rich in events of profound national importance. They were years of splendour and triumph. The flag of England became supreme on the seas; English commerce penetrated to the farthest corners of the Old World, and English colonies rooted themselves on the shores of the New. The national intellect, strung by the excitement of sixty years, took shape in a literature which is an eternal possession to mankind, while the incipient struggles of the two parties in the Anglican Church prepared the way for the conflicts of the coming century, and the second act of Reformation. But I have presumed too far already on the forbearance of my readers in the length to which I have run, and these subjects, intensely interesting as they are, lie beyond the purpose of the present work. My object, as I defined it at the outset, was to describe the transition from the Catholic England with which the century opened, the England of a dominant Church and monasteries and pilgrimages, into the England of progressive intelligence; and the question whether the nation was to pass a second time through the farce of a reconciliation with Rome, was answered once and for ever by the cannon of Sir Francis Drake. The action before Gravelines of the 30th of July, 1588, decided the largest problems ever submitted in the history of mankind to the arbitrement of force. Beyond and beside the immediate fate of England, it decided that Philip's revolted Provinces should never be reannexed to the Spanish Crown. It broke the back of Spain, sealed the fate of the Duke of Guise,[10] and though it could not prevent the civil war, it assured the ultimate succession of the King of Navarre.[11] In its remoter consequences it determined the fate of the Reformation in Germany; for had Philip been victorious the League must have been immediately triumphant; the power of France would have been on the side of Spain and the Jesuits, and the thirty years' war would either have never been begun, or would have been brought to a swift conclusion. It furnished James of Scotland with conclusive reasons for remaining a Protestant, and for eschewing for ever the forbidden fruit of Popery; and thus it secured his tranquil accession to the throne of England when Elizabeth passed away. Finally, it was the sermon which completed the conversion of the English nation, and transformed the Catholics into Anglicans. . . .

. . . The coming of the Armada was an appeal on behalf of the Pope to the ordeal of battle and the defeat of Spain with its appalling features,

10 The leader of the radical Catholic League in the French Wars of Religion.—ED.
11 The sometime leader of the French Protestant Huguenots who became King Henry IV in 1594.—ED.

the letting loose of the power of the tempests—the special weapons of the Almighty—to finish the work which Drake had but half completed, was accepted as a recorded judgment of heaven. The magnitude of the catastrophe took possession of the nation's imagination. . . . Had the Spanish invasion succeeded, however, had it succeeded even partially in crushing Holland and giving France to the League and the Duke of Guise, England might not have recovered from the blow, and it might have fared with Teutonic Europe as it fared with France on the revocation of the Edict of Nantes. Either Protestantism would have been trampled out altogether, or expelled from Europe to find a home in a new continent; and the Church, insolent with another century or two of power, would have been left to encounter the inevitable ultimate revolution which is now its terror, with no reformed Christianity surviving to hold the balance between atheism and superstition.

The starved and ragged English seamen, so ill furnished by their sovereign that they were obliged to take from their enemies the means of fighting them, decided otherwise; they and the winds and the waves, which are said ever to be on the side of the brave. In their victory they conquered not the Spaniards only, but the weakness of their Queen. Either she had been incredulous before that Philip would indeed invade her, or she had underrated the power of her people: or she discerned that the destruction of the Spanish fleet had created at last an irreparable breach with the Catholic governments. At any rate there was no more unwholesome hankering after compromise, no more unqueenly avarice or reluctance to spend her treasure in the cause of freedom. The strength and resources of England were flung heartily into the war, and all the men and all the money it could spare was given freely to the United Provinces and the King of Navarre. The struggle lasted into the coming century. Elizabeth never saw peace with Spain again. But the nation throve with its gathering glory. The war on the part of England was aggressive thenceforward. One more great attempt was made by Philip in Ireland, but only to fail miserably, and the shores of England were never seriously threatened again. Portugal was invaded, and Cadiz burnt, Spanish commerce made the prey of privateers, and the proud galleons chased from off the ocean. In the Low Countries the tide of reconquest had reached its flood, and thenceforward ebbed slowly back, while in France the English and the Huguenots fought side by side against the League and Philip. . . .

[Yet] for Protestantism Elizabeth had never concealed her dislike and contempt. She hated to acknowledge any fellowship in religion either with Scots, Dutch, or Huguenots. She represented herself to foreign Ambassadors as a Catholic in everything, except in allegiance to the Papacy. Even for the Church of England, of which she was the supreme governor, she affected no particular respect. She left the Catholics in her household so unrestrained that they absented themselves at pleasure from the Royal Chapel, without a question being asked. She allowed the country gentlemen all possible latitude in their own houses. The danger in which she had lived for so many years, the severe measures to which she was driven against the seminary priests, and the consciousness that the Protestants were the only subjects that she had on whose loyalty she could rely, had prevented her hitherto from systematically repressing the Puritan irregularities; but the power to persecute had been wanting rather than the inclination. The Bishops with whom she had filled the sees at her accession were chosen necessarily from the party who had suffered under her sister. They were Calvinists or Lutherans, with no special reverence for the office which they had undertaken; and she treated them in return with studied contempt. She called them Doctors, as the highest title to which she considered them to have any real right; if they disputed her pleasure she threatened to unfrock them; if they showed themselves officious in punishing Catholics, she brought them up with a sharp reprimand; and if their Protestantism was conspicuously earnest, they were deposed and imprisoned. . . .

To permit the collapse of the Bishops, however, would be to abandon the Anglican position. Presbytery as such was detestable to Elizabeth. She recognised no authority in any man as derived from a source distinct from herself, and she adhered resolutely to her own purpose. So long as her own crown was unsafe she did not venture on any general persecution of her Puritan subjects; but she checked all their efforts to make a change in the ecclesiastical system. She found a man after her own heart for the see of Canterbury in Whitgift; she filled the other sees as they fell vacant with men of a similar stamp, and she prepared to coerce their refractory "brethren in Christ" into obedience if ever the opportunity came.

On the reconciliation of the Catholic gentry, which followed on the destruction of the Spanish fleet, Elizabeth found herself in a position analogous to that of Henry IV of France. She was the sovereign of a nation with a divided creed, the two parties, notwithstanding, being at last for the most part loyal to herself.

Both she and Henry held at the bottom intrinsically the same views. They believed generally in certain elementary truths lying at the base of all religions, and the difference in the outward expressions of those truths, and the passionate animosities which those differences engendered, were only not contemptible to them from the practical mischief which they produced. On what terms Catholics and Protestants could be induced to live together peaceably was the political problem of the age. Neither of the two sovereigns shared the profound horror of falsehood, which was at the heart of the Protestant movement. They had the statesman's temperament, to which all specific religions are equally fictions of the imagination. . . .

To return to Elizabeth.

In fighting out her long quarrel with Spain and building her Church system out of the broken masonry of Popery, her concluding years passed away. The great men who had upheld the throne in the days of her peril dropped one by one into the grave. Walsingham died soon after the defeat of the Armada, ruined in fortune, and weary of his ungrateful service. Hunsdon, Knollys, Burghley, Drake, followed at brief intervals, and their mistress was left by herself, standing as it seemed on the pinnacle of earthly glory, yet in all the loneliness of greatness, and unable to enjoy the honours which Burghley's policy had won for her. The first place among the Protestant Powers, which had been so often offered her and so often refused, had been forced upon her in spite of herself. "She was Head of the Name," but it gave her no pleasure. She was the last of her race. No Tudor would sit again on the English throne. . . . She was without the intellectual emotions which give human character its consistency and power. One moral quality she possessed in an eminent degree: she was supremely brave. For thirty years she was perpetually a mark for assassination, and her spirits were never affected, and she was never frightened into cruelty. She had a proper contempt also for idle luxury and indulgence. She lived simply, worked hard, and ruled her household with rigid economy. But her vanity was as insatiable as it was commonplace. No flattery was too tawdry to find a welcome with her, and as she had no repugnance to false words in others, she was equally liberal of them herself. Her entire nature was saturated with artifice. Except when speaking some round untruth Elizabeth never could be simple. Her letters and her speeches were as fantastic as her dress, and her meaning as involved as her policy. She was unnatural even in her prayers, and she carried her affectations into the presence of the Almighty. . . .

Vain as she was of her own sagacity, she never modified a course recommended to her by Burghley without injury both to the realm and to herself. She never chose an opposite course without plunging into embarrassments, from which his skill and Walsingham's were barely able to extricate her. The great results of her reign were the fruits of a policy which was not her own, and which she starved and mutilated when energy and completeness were needed. . . .

But this, like all other questions connected with the Virgin Queen, should be rather studied in her actions than in the opinion of the historian who relates them. Actions and words are carved upon eternity. Opinions are but forms of cloud created by the prevailing currents of the moral air. Princes, who are credited on the wrong side with the evils which happen in their reigns, have a right in equity to the honour of the good. The greatest achievement in English history, the "breaking the bonds of Rome," and the establishment of spiritual independence, was completed without bloodshed under Elizabeth's auspices, and Elizabeth may have the glory of the work. Many problems growing out of it were left unsettled. Some were disposed of on the scaffold at Whitehall, some in the revolution of 1688; some yet survive to test the courage and the ingenuity of modern politicians.

Elizabeth and the "Invincible" Armada
GARRETT MATTINGLY

Twentieth-century Elizabethan scholarship has largely forsaken the "standard" view of Elizabeth that, more than anyone else, Froude helped to frame. Froude's Elizabeth is both too simple and too doctrinaire: Elizabeth was neither. There have been literally hundreds of special studies and monographs on various aspects of Elizabeth's reign and even a number of biographies. But despite this profusion of writing, there is not yet a comprehensive general interpretation of her for our time or an entirely satisfactory biography.

The same cannot be said, however, of the Armada, for that great and popular adventure found its definitive twentieth-century interpretation in the work of Garrett Mattingly, professor of history at Columbia University until his death in 1962. In addition to the sources that Froude had used to such advantage, Mattingly had access to even more and better British sources, for the process of editing and publishing the public documents of the Tudor age had continued and new archives and collections had been opened. French and Netherlandish archives were available to him, as well as collections in Italy and Spain. Thus Mattingly had the advantage of a rounded collection of materials that earlier scholars, whether English or Spanish, had not had. And he had the disposition to write a balanced account, free of the special pleading and the special point of view that were ultimately Froude's greatest flaws.

The following excerpt is taken not from Mattingly's slim and elegant masterpiece, The Armada,[12] *but from a carefully abbreviated account that he prepared for the Folger Shakespeare Library monograph series, entitled* The "Invincible" Armada and Elizabethan England. *It was his last work.*

Not surprisingly, the work deals primarily with the Armada rather than

12 (Boston: Houghton Mifflin, 1959).

with Elizabeth. But many elements of a contemporary view of Elizabeth
—even though that view has not entirely coalesced—can be discovered.
Mattingly admires Elizabeth's grasp of foreign policy, which reached
beyond a simplistic hostility to Spain. He admires her courage to resist
the opinions of her naval advisors that the war should be carried to
Spanish waters, opinions that she seemed to be almost alone in opposing.
The queen's courage was the greater when we realize, as Mattingly
points out, that she was already past "the peak of her popularity and
prestige." Finally, Mattingly admires the tenacity that enabled Elizabeth
to maintain the peace, no matter how tenuously, for thirty years and that
led her into war only when it could be fought on her terms. The victory
over the Armada was indeed Elizabeth's victory, and, in the words of
Froude, she may have the glory for it.

PROBABLY NO event in England's military history, not even the battles of
Trafalgar and Waterloo, not even the battle of Hastings, has been so
much written about, celebrated, and commented upon as the repulse of
the Spanish Armada by English naval forces after nine days of dubious
battle from the Eddystone to Gravelines in the summer of 1588. The
repulse foiled decisively, as it turned out, the Spanish plan to invade
England with the Duke of Parma's army of the Netherlands, covered and
supported by a Spanish fleet, and reinforced by the troop transports and
supply ships it convoyed. At first the significance of the repulse was by
no means clear. As it became clearer, the chroniclers of both combatants
tended to magnify, oversimplify, and distort the event. English writers,
pamphleteers, and historians hailed the victory, first as a sign of God's
favor to the champions of the Protestant cause, later as evidence of the
manifest destiny of an imperial people. . . .

. . . By now, through the efforts of two generations of historians,
Spanish and English, most of the mistakes about the Armada campaign
and the Anglo-Spanish naval war have been corrected and a more balanced emphasis restored. So far, however, no general account of the
correction has been drawn up. Let us attempt one here.

We shall have to begin with the long period of uneasy peace, cold war,
and "war underhand," undeclared and peripheral, before the actual outbreak of major hostilities. In general, historians both English and Spanish
have tended to assume that since war was coming anyway the sooner it
came the better, and that any policy that postponed its coming was feeble,
shortsighted, and mistaken. Most English historians have been certain
that Elizabeth should have unleashed her sea dogs against the Spanish
colossus long before she did and have blamed or excused her for feminine
weakness, gullibility at the hands of smooth Spanish diplomats, and
miserly reluctance to spend money. The chorus of blame begins in the
correspondence of the leading Puritans of her own day. They were always

bewailing to one another the Queen's vacillation, her stubborn refusal to subsidize Protestant leaders on the Continent as liberally as they would have liked to be subsidized, her obstinate belief that peace with the armies of Antichrist could still be preserved. The chorus of blame swelled through the centuries until it culminated in the thundering voice of James Anthony Froude, who could as little conceal his boundless, uncritical admiration for the male vigor of Henry VIII, who led England into one vainglorious, financially ruinous war after another, as he could his scorn for the feminine weakness of Henry's daughter Elizabeth, who preferred to save money and stay out of trouble. Since Froude, the chorus of blame has subsided somewhat, but its echoes are still distinctly audible. . . .

. . . Elizabeth . . . and her peace party had reasons more cogent (if any reasons can be more cogent) than prudence and economy. No ruler of this century was more sensitive to the economic interests of his subjects. She knew the importance of an outlet in the Netherlands—Antwerp for choice—for the vent of English cloth, on which, after agriculture, the prosperity of her realm depended. If there was a tradition of more than a hundred years of alliance with Spain, the tradition of alliance with Flanders, with "waterish Burgundy," was as old as any coherent English foreign policy at all. In Flanders, Zeeland, and Holland were the ports not only through which English goods could most cheaply and safely reach the Continent, but from which an invasion of England could be launched most quickly and easily. And on the frontier of Flanders lay France, divided for the moment by religious civil wars, but in area, population, productivity, and centralized power easily the greatest state in Europe. Somebody had to guard the Netherlands from France—if not Spain, then England.

Elizabeth preferred to have the Spanish bear the burden. . . .

There was still one tie between Elizabeth and Philip stronger than profitable trade, old alliances, or strategic necessities. That was the life of Mary Queen of Scots. For nearly twenty years Mary Stuart had been part guest, part prisoner of her cousin. Since she was a devout Catholic and the next in succession to the English throne, she had always been the center of plots by English Catholics. . . . But with each plot the outcry for Mary's life grew stronger, and at last Elizabeth could no longer resist the clamor. When in February, 1587, the ax fell, the die was cast. As soon as Philip heard the news and had taken his characteristic time to ponder the consequences, he began to put the creaky machinery of his painfully devised plans for the invasion of England into high gear.

His plans were further delayed by Drake's brilliant raid down the Spanish coast. On the whole that raid has been duly appreciated and well described, but perhaps for the sake of dramatic narrative the emphasis on its importance has been somewhat distorted. . . .

The real damage Drake did the Spaniards was afterward, by his operations off Cape St. Vincent. His mere presence there, though he found no one to fight with, kept the Spanish fleet from assembling. But more, he swept up along the coast a swarm of little coasting vessels, most of them laden with hoops and barrel staves ready to be made into casks for the food and drink of the invasion fleet. Without tight casks made of seasoned wood, provisions spoiled and wine and water leaked away. Drake burned the seasoned barrel staves. They were almost all the fleet at Lisbon was expecting, far more than it could ever collect again. This was the secret, mortal wound. Drake knew exactly what he was doing, but most of his biographers seem not to have appreciated it. . . .

After a description of the Spanish preparations for the Armada, Mattingly continues.

If Spanish historians have been too severe with their admiral and not critical enough of his sovereign, English historians have usually made the opposite mistake. From October, 1587, on, the English commanders by sea, Drake and Hawkins and finally even Lord Howard of Effingham, the Lord Admiral, had clamored to be let loose on the coast of Spain. If the smell of booty to be won by the sack of undefended Spanish towns had anything to do with their eagerness, they did not say so to the Queen. What they proposed was that they blockade the Spanish coast, fight the Spanish when they came out, perhaps prevent their sortie, or even destroy them in port. On the whole, English naval historians have warmly approved their plan and condemned the Queen for squelching it. Perhaps they were thinking of Nelson's ships, or Collingwood's. Elizabethan ships had not the same sea-keeping qualities. If they had taken station off Lisbon in November, by April they would have been battered and strained, sails and spars and rigging depleted, crews decimated or worse by ship's fever and scurvy, and provisions exhausted. Even if none of them had foundered, and such foundering was not unlikely, the English fleet would have been in no condition to face an enemy for weeks, perhaps for months. And the cost in pounds, shillings, and pence would have been staggering. Elizabeth, who had kept a wary eye on naval accounts for forty years, knew this. What she probably did not know was that had the fleets met off the Spanish coast and the English adopted the same tactics they later used off the Eddystone, as they surely would have done, they would have fired every shot in their lockers before they had done the Spanish any appreciable harm, and would have been obliged to scuttle home in search of more munitions, while the Spanish could have marched grandly into the Channel. Partly by prudence and partly by luck, Elizabeth's preference that the battle, if there had to be one, should be fought in home waters was a major contribution to English victory. . . .

. . . About the strength and composition of the two fleets there is actually very little doubt. The Armada sailed from Lisbon with 130 ships. . . . Opposing this force, English lists show 197 ships. Actually, not all of these saw action; some of them, though not so many nor such large ships as in the Spanish fleet, were mere supply ships, practically noncombatants, and a good many, a slightly higher percentage than in the Armada, were under a hundred tons, incapable of carrying guns heavier than a six-pounder and useful mainly for scouting and dispatch work. The first line of the English fleet was twenty-one Queen's galleons of two hundred tons and upward, roughly comparable in size and numbers with the ten galleons of Portugal and ten galleons of the Indian Guard which made up the Spanish first line, but tougher, harder hitting, and, on the whole, bigger.

The myth of the little English ships and the huge Spanish ones has long since been refuted by naval historians, without, of course, being in the least dispelled. Taking the official tonnage lists of the two first lines, the biggest ship in either fleet is English, and the rest pair off in what seems like rough equality. . . . We do know that in comparison with their English adversaries the Spanish were seriously undergunned. . . . In such guns, especially the culverin type, firing round shot of from four to eighteen pounds for three thousand yards or more, the English were superior by at least three to one. . . .

There follows a detailed description of the battle, the stiff Spanish discipline, the long-range gun battles that did little but deplete shot and powder supplies, and the crucial failure of Parma to "come out" with his barge-loads of soldiers to board the waiting fleet. They were blockaded by the Dutch in the tidal waters, safe from the deep-water Spanish fleet. Then came the English attack on the Armada mounted with fire ships and fire power and finally the famous storm in the channel that permitted the Armada to "escape" to the north and to its ultimate destruction, sailing around the British Isles in a desperate and futile attempt to return home.

When, on the thirtieth anniversary of her reign, the Queen went in state to St. Paul's, where the captured Spanish banners had been hung up, the kneeling, cheering throngs hailed her as the victorious champion of her kingdom and their faith. The next few years were probably those of Elizabeth's greatest popularity, at least around London, and this was almost certainly due to her having come forward at last as the open champion of the Protestant cause, to her gallant conduct in the months of danger, and to the victory, by divine intervention almost everyone believed, which crowned her efforts. It is probable, too, that the victory gave a lift to English morale. It may be that a good many Englishmen, like a good many other Europeans, though not like Elizabeth's sea dogs, had doubted that the Spanish could ever be beaten. Now they knew that they could. The thoughtful and the well-informed understood, however, that England had not won a war, only the first battle in a war in which there might be many more battles. England was braced for the struggle.

Suggestions for Further Reading

TO A CONSIDERABLE EXTENT, the central problem of Elizabethan scholarship has been to disentangle the historical Elizabeth from the Elizabeth of legend. This chapter is really about an aspect of that process, for the defeat of the Spanish armada was a powerful force in creating the Elizabeth legend. The historical Elizabeth still tends to elude scholars, but of all the books on her, the best modern work is still probably Sir John E. Neale, *Queen Elizabeth I* (London: J. Cape, 1961), reprinted a dozen times since its publication in 1934. Of the newer books on Elizabeth, the best by far is Lacey Baldwin Smith, *Elizabeth Tudor, Portrait of a Queen* (Boston: Little, Brown, 1975). But students may prefer Elizabeth Jenkins, *Elizabeth the Great* (New York: Coward, McCann and Geoghegan, 1958), a lively, personal-psychological biography, or the attractive, heavily illustrated Neville Williams, *The Life and Times of Elizabeth I* (New York: Doubleday, 1972). Two additional competent and straightforward biographies can also be recommended: Joel Hurstfield, *Elizabeth I and the Unity of England,* "Teach Yourself History Library" (New York: Macmillan, 1960), and Paul Johnson, *Elizabeth I, A Biography* (New York: Holt, Rinehart and Winston, 1974).

Among the great monuments of modern Tudor scholarship are studies of two of the men around Elizabeth by Conyers Read, *Mr. Secretary Walsingham and the Policy of Queen Elizabeth,* 3 vols. (Hamden, Conn.: Archon Books, 1967 [1925]), and *Mr. Secretary Cecil and Queen Elizabeth* (New York: Knopf, 1955) and its sequel *Lord Burghley and Queen Elizabeth* (New York: Knopf, 1960); these books are detailed and complex. Students may prefer the lighter and briefer Neville Williams, *All the Queen's Men, Elizabeth I and Her Courtiers* (New York: Macmillan, 1972). Two works on Elizabeth and her age are especially recommended: A. L. Rowse, *The England of Elizabeth, The Structure of Society* (New York: Macmillan, 1950), the first of two volumes on the Elizabethan age, the massive and lively work of a controversial and dynamic British scholar, and Lacey Baldwin Smith, *The Elizabethan World* (Boston: Houghton Mifflin, 1967). On the broader topic of Tudor England, the basic work is G. R. Elton, *England under the Tudors*, rev. ed. (London: Methuen, 1974); but students should see also A. J. Slavin, *The Precarious Balance; English Government and Society, 1450–1640* (New York: Knopf, 1973), an important revisionist study of the internal structure of Tudor England.

The standard work on the armada is Garrett Mattingly, *The Armada* (Boston: Houghton Mifflin, 1959), eminently readable and exciting. For more detailed diplomatic history background, the best work is probably R. B. Wernham, *Before the Armada: The Emergence of the English Nation, 1485–1588* (New York: Harcourt, Brace and World, 1966), and for a closer look at the technical-naval aspects of the armada, Michael A. Lewis, *The Spanish Armada* (New York: Crowell, 1960). For an account of the growth of the English anti-Spanish sentiment, see William S. Maltby, *The Black Legend in England, The Development of Anti-Spanish Sentiment, 1558–1660* (Durham, N.C.: Duke University Press, 1971). Finally, for Mary Queen of Scots, the diplomatic linchpin in the whole background of the armada, see the large and thoroughly readable biography by Antonia Fraser, *Mary, Queen of Scots* (New York: Delacorte Press, 1969).

Louis XIV:
"The Sun King"

In 1661, on the death of the regent Cardinal Mazarin, the personal reign of Louis XIV of France began. Though he was just twenty-three years old, Louis had already been nominally the king for almost twenty years. And he was to rule for more than another half century, through one of the longest, most brilliant, most eventful, and most controversial reigns in the history of modern Europe.

It had been the aim of Cardinal Richelieu, the great first minister of Louis' father, "to make the king supreme in France and France supreme in Europe." And to an extent Cardinal Richelieu, as well as his successor, Cardinal Mazarin, had been successful. France was the richest and most populous nation in Europe. Her army had surpassed that of Spain as Europe's most formidable military machine. And the two wily cardinals had gained for France a diplomatic ascendancy to match her military might. It remained for Louis XIV to complete their work. In the process he became the archetype of divine-right monarchical absolutism, justifying later historians' labeling of the age that he dominated as the "Age of Absolutism." Louis took the sun as his emblem, as he himself wrote, for its nobility, its uniqueness, and "the light that it imparts to the other heavenly bodies," and as "a most vivid and a most beautiful image for a great monarch." [1]

From the beginning of his personal rule, Louis XIV intended to make the other states of Europe—"the other heavenly bodies"—swing in the

[1] Louis XIV, . . . *Mémoires for the Instruction of the Dauphin,* Paul Sonnino, trans. (New York: Free Press, 1970), pp. 103–4.

279

orbit of his sun. In 1667 he began the so-called War of Devolution to claim the disputed provinces of the Spanish Netherlands for his Spanish wife. He fought a series of wars with Spain and the Empire, the Dutch, and the English, culminating in the great European conflict, the War of the Spanish Succession (1701–1714), to set his grandson on the throne of Spain and create a Bourbon "empire" to dominate the continent. In the course of these wars, he gained the hostility of most of Europe and was finally brought to terms in 1715 at the Peace of Utrecht. Even though Louis was reported on his deathbed to have said, "I have loved war too much," he had, nevertheless, come closer to making France supreme in Europe than any man before Napoleon.

Louis XIV disliked Paris. From early in his reign, he made increasing use of the royal estate of Versailles, some ten miles out of the city, as his principal residence and the locus of the court. Versailles grew in size and magnificence to become the most visible symbol of and the most enduring monument to Louis' absolutism. An English visitor, Lord Montague, sniffily called it "something the foolishest in the world," and thought Louis himself "the vainest creature alive." [2] But Versailles was far from foolish and, though vain indeed, Louis XIV was a consummate realist. Versailles was not simply a symbol of his absolutism; it was a working part of it. The function of Versailles was to help make the king supreme in France.

Royal supremacy was, in Louis' reign as before, most clearly threatened by the power and independence of the great nobility. On the very eve of Louis' personal rule, he, his mother, Mazarin, and the court had been faced with an uprising, called the Fronde, led by the great Princes of the Blood. Though it failed, Louis never forgot the Fronde. It became his deliberate policy to keep the great nobility at Versailles, separated from their provincial estates and the roots of their political power, and to redirect their interests and their energies. It may be argued that the elaborate court behavior that developed at Versailles with its perpetual spectacles and entertainments, its endless adulteries and affairs, its incredible tedium and banality—and its perpetual attendance upon the king—was really a device to neutralize the power of the great nobility while the king governed with the aid of a succession of ministers, appointed by him, answerable to him alone, and capable of being dismissed by him without question. It has been suggested by more than one scholar that Louis XIV was the archetype not only of the absolute monarch but of the "royal bureaucrat." The court life at Versailles was surely the most glittering side-show ever staged. But it was a show that fascinated the very people who played their parts in it; and it has fascinated—and distracted—observers ever since.

---

[2] Quoted in John C. Rule, "Louis XIV, Roi-Bureaucrate," in *Louis XIV and the Craft of Kingship,* ed. John C. Rule (Columbus: Ohio State University Press, 1969), p. 42.

The Memoirs

LOUIS, DUC DE SAINT-SIMON

*The sources for the reign of Louis XIV are an embarrassment of riches—
an enormous volume of public documents and official records, reports,
and inventories and such a mass of royal correspondence that it still has
not been completely edited. Many of the figures of the court wrote letters
as prodigiously as the king, and almost as many wrote memoirs as well.
Of these the most important are the memoirs of Louis de Rouvroy, Duc
de Saint-Simon.*

*Saint-Simon was born at Versailles in 1675 and lived there for the next
thirty years. Through much of that time—and throughout the rest of his
long life—he kept his memoirs with a compulsive passion. In one edition,
they run to forty-three volumes, and a complete text has yet to be
published. Saint-Simon's memoirs are important not only for their
completeness but also for the perspective they give on the age of Louis
XIV. Saint-Simon fancied himself a chronicler in the tradition of
Froissart or Joinville and saw his literary labor as preparing him in the
knowledge of "great affairs" "for some high office." But preferment
never came. Saint-Simon was never more than a minor figure of the
court, moving on the fringes of the affairs that his memoirs so carefully
record.*

*Saint-Simon blamed the king for his neglect—as he quite properly
should have, for nothing happened at Versailles without the wish of the
king, and the king simply disliked Saint-Simon. Saint-Simon also accused
the king of demeaning the old aristocracy to which Saint-Simon so self-
consciously belonged. This complaint is the nagging, insistent theme that
runs like a leitmotif through the memoirs. Saint-Simon believed that
Louis deliberately preferred "the vile bourgeoisie" to the aristocracy for
high office and great affairs. Although the claim is somewhat
exaggerated, it is indeed true that Louis preferred the lesser nobility for
his bureaucrats because they had no separate power base beyond the
king's preferment.*

*But while Saint-Simon hated his king, he was also fascinated by him,
for, like it or not, Louis was the center of the world in which Saint-Simon
lived. He set the fashion in dress, language, manners, and morals. Even
his afflictions inspired instant emulation: after the king underwent a
painful operation, no fewer than thirty courtiers presented themselves to
the court surgeon and demanded that the same operation be performed
on them.*

Saint-Simon hated Versailles nearly as much as he hated the king, and he described it with the same malicious familiarity—its size, its vulgarity, its inconvenience and faulty planning. But he also described the stifling, debasing, desperate style of life that it dictated for the court nobility so grandly imprisoned there.

One modern scholar has called Saint-Simon "at once unreliable and indispensable." [3] *We can correct his unreliability, however, by consulting other sources, and he remains indispensable for the picture he gives us of the "other side" of royal absolutism.*

We turn now to Saint-Simon at Versailles *for Saint-Simon's appraisal of Louis XIV.*

HE WAS A prince in whom no one would deny good and even great qualities, but he had many others that were petty or downright bad, and of these it was impossible to determine which were natural and which acquired. Nothing is harder to find than a well-informed writer, none rarer than those who knew him personally, yet are sufficiently unbiased to speak of him without hatred or flattery, and to set down the bare truth for good or ill.

This is not the place to tell of his early childhood. He was king almost from birth, but was deliberately repressed by a mother who loved to govern, and still more so by a wicked and self-interested minister, who risked the State a thousand times for his own aggrandisement. . . .

. . . After Mazarin's death, he had enough intelligence to realize his deliverance, but not enough vigour to release himself. Indeed, that event was one of the finest moments of his life, for it taught him an unshakable principle namely, to banish all prime ministers and ecclesiastics from his councils. Another ideal, adopted at that time, he could never sustain because in the practice it constantly eluded him. This was to govern alone. It was the quality upon which he most prided himself and for which he received most praise and flattery. In fact, it was what he was least able to do. . . .

. . . The King's intelligence was below the average, but was very capable of improvement. He loved glory; he desired peace and good government. He was born prudent, temperate, secretive, master of his emotions and his tongue—can it be believed?—he was born good and just. God endowed him with all the makings of a good and perhaps even of a fairly great king. All the evil in him came from without. His early training was so dissolute that no one dared to go near his apartments, and he would sometimes speak bitterly of those days and tell how they found him one night fallen into the fountain at the Palais Royal. He became very

[3] Peter Gay, in the introductory note to Louis, Duc de Saint-Simon, *Versailles, the Court, and Louis XIV*, ed. and trans. Lucy Norton (New York: Harper & Row, 1966), p. vii.

dependent on others, for they had scarcely taught him to read and write and he remained so ignorant that he learned nothing of historical events nor the facts about fortunes, careers, rank, or laws. This lack caused him sometimes, even in public to make many gross blunders.

You might imagine that as king he would have loved the old nobility and would not have cared to see it brought down to the level of other classes. Nothing was further from the truth. His aversion to noble sentiments and his partiality for his Ministers, who, to elevate themselves, hated and disparaged all who were what they themselves were not, nor ever could be, caused him to feel a similar antipathy for noble birth. He feared it as much as he feared intelligence, and if he found these two qualities united in one person, that man was finished.

His ministers, generals, mistresses, and courtiers learned soon after he became their master that glory, to him, was a foible rather than an ambition. They therefore flattered him to the top of his bent, and in so doing, spoiled him. Praise, or better, adulation, pleased him so much that the most fulsome was welcome and the most servile even more delectable. . . .

Flattery fed the desire for military glory that sometimes tore him from his loves, which was how Louvois [4] so easily involved him in major wars and persuaded him that he was a better leader and strategist than any of his generals, a theory which those officers fostered in order to please him. All their praise he took with admirable complacency, and truly believed that he was what they said. Hence his liking for reviews, which he carried to such lengths that he was known abroad as the "Review King," and his preference for sieges, where he could make cheap displays of courage, be forcibly restrained, and show his ability to endure fatigue and lack of sleep. Indeed, so robust was his constitution that he never appeared to suffer from hunger, thirst, heat, cold, rain, or any other kind of weather. He greatly enjoyed the sensation of being admired, as he rode along the lines, for his fine presence and princely bearing, his horsemanship, and other attainments. It was chiefly with talk of campaigns and soldiers that he entertained his mistresses and sometimes his courtiers. He talked well and much to the point; no man of fashion could tell a tale or set a scene better than he, yet his most casual speeches were never lacking in natural and conscious majesty.

He had a natural bent towards details and delighted in busying himself with such petty matters as the uniforms, equipment, drill, and discipline of his troops. He concerned himself no less with his buildings, the conduct of his household, and his living expenses, for he always imagined that he had something to teach the experts, and they received instruction from him as though they were novices in arts which they already knew by heart. To the King, such waste of time appeared to deserve his

---

[4] Michel Le Tellier, Marquis de Louvois (1641–1691), Louis' great minister of war.—ED.

constant attention, which enchanted his ministers, for with a little tact and experience they learned to sway him, making their own desires seem his, and managing great affairs of State in their own way and, all too often, in their own interests, whilst they congratulated themselves and watched him drowning amidst trivialities. . . .

From such alien and pernicious sources he acquired a pride so colossal that, truly, had not God implanted in his heart the fear of the devil, even in his worst excesses, he would literally have allowed himself to be worshipped. What is more, he would have found worshippers; witness the extravagant monuments that have been set up to him, for example the statue in the Place des Victoires, with its pagan dedication, a ceremony at which I myself was present, and in which he took such huge delight. From this false pride stemmed all that ruined him. We have already seen some of its ill-effects; others are yet to come. . . .

The Court was yet another device to sustain the King's policy of despotism. Many things combined to remove it from Paris and keep it permanently in the country. The disorders of the minority [5] had been staged mainly in that city and for that reason the King had taken a great aversion to it and had become convinced that it was dangerous to live there. . . .

The awkward situation of his mistresses and the dangers involved in conducting such scandalous affairs in a busy capital, crowded with people of every kind of mentality, played no small part in deciding him to leave, for he was embarrassed by the crowds whenever he went in or out or appeared upon the streets. Other reasons for departure were his love of hunting and the open air, so much more easily indulged in the country than in Paris, which is far from forests and ill-supplied with pleasant walks, and his delight in building, a later and ever-increasing passion, which could not be enjoyed in the town, where he was continually in the public eye. Finally, he conceived the idea that he would be all the more venerated by the multitude if he lived retired and were no longer seen every day. . . .

The liaison with Mme de La Vallière,[6] which was at first kept secret, occasioned many excursions to Versailles, then a little pasteboard house erected by Louis XIII when he, and still more his courtiers, grew tired of sleeping in a low tavern and old windmill, after long, exhausting hunts in the forest of Saint-Léger and still further afield. . . .

Gradually, those quiet country excursions of Louis XIV gave rise to a vast building project, designed to house a large Court more comfortably than in crowded lodgings at Saint-Germain, and he removed his residence there altogether, shortly before the death of the Queen.[7] Immense numbers of suites were made, and one paid one's court by asking for one,

[5] A reference to the Fronde.—ED.
[6] One of Louis' early mistresses.—ED.
[7] The Spanish princess Maria Theresa died in 1683.—ED.

whereas, at Saint-Germain, almost everyone had the inconvenience of lodging in the town, and those few who did sleep at the château were amazingly cramped.

The frequent entertainments, the private drives to Versailles, and the royal journeys, provided the King with a means of distinguishing or mortifying his courtiers by naming those who were or were not to accompany him, and thus keeping everyone eager and anxious to please him. He fully realized that the substantial gifts which he had to offer were too few to have any continuous effect, and he substituted imaginary favours that appealed to men's jealous natures, small distinctions which he was able, with extraordinary ingenuity, to grant or withhold every day and almost every hour. The hopes that courtiers built upon such flimsy favours and the importance which they attached to them were really unbelievable, and no one was ever more artful than the King in devising fresh occasions for them. . . .

. . . He took it as an offence if distinguished people did not make the Court their home, or if others came but seldom. And to come never, or scarcely ever, meant certain disgrace. When a favour was asked for such a one, the King would answer haughtily, "I do not know him at all," or, "That is a man whom I never see," and in such cases his word was irrevocable. . . .

There never lived a man more naturally polite, nor of such exquisite discrimination with so fine a sense of degree, for he made distinctions for age, merit and rank, and showed them in his answers when these went further than the usual *"Je verrai,"* [8] and in his general bearing. . . . He was sometimes gay, but never undignified, and never, at any time, did he do anything improper or indiscreet. His smallest gesture, his walk, bearing, and expression were all perfectly becoming, modest, noble, and stately, yet at the same time he always seemed perfectly natural. Added to which he had the immense advantage of a good figure, which made him graceful and relaxed.

On state occasions such as audiences with ambassadors and other ceremonies, he looked so imposing that one had to become used to the sight of him if one were not to be exposed to the humiliation of breaking down or coming to a full stop. At such times, his answers were always short and to the point and he rarely omitted some civility, or a compliment if the speech deserved one. The awe inspired by his appearance was such that wherever he might be, his presence imposed silence and a degree of fear. . . .

In everything he loved magnificently lavish abundance. He made it a principle from motives of policy and encouraged the Court to imitate him; indeed, one way to win favour was to spend extravagantly on the table, clothes, carriages, building, and gambling. For magnificence in such things he would speak to people. The truth is that he used this means

[8] "We shall see."—ED.

deliberately and successfully to impoverish everyone, for he made luxury meritorious in all men, and in some a necessity, so that gradually the entire Court became dependent upon his favours for their very subsistence. What is more, he fed his own pride by surrounding himself with an entourage so universally magnificent that confusion reigned and all natural distinctions were obliterated.

Once it had begun this rottenness grew into that cancer which gnaws at the lives of all Frenchmen. It started, indeed, at the Court but soon spread to Paris, the provinces, and the army where generals are now assessed according to the tables that they keep and the splendour of their establishments. It so eats into private fortunes that those in a position to steal are often forced to do so in order to keep up their spending. This cancer, kept alive by confusion of ranks, pride, even by good manners, and encouraged by the folly of the great, is having incalculable results that will lead to nothing less than ruin and general disaster.

No other King has ever approached him for the number and quality of his stables and hunting establishments. Who could count his buildings? Who not deplore their ostentation, whimsicality and bad taste? . . . At Versailles he set up one building after another according to no scheme of planning. Beauty and ugliness, spaciousness and meanness were roughly tacked together. The royal apartments at Versailles are beyond everything inconvenient, with back-views over the privies and other dark and evil-smelling places. Truly, the magnificence of the gardens is amazing, but to make the smallest use of them is disagreeable, and they are in equally bad taste. . . .

But one might be for ever pointing out the monstrous defects of that huge and immensely costly palace, and of its outhouses that cost even more, its orangery, kitchen gardens, kennels, larger and smaller stables, all vast, all prodigiously expensive. Indeed, a whole city has sprung up where before was only a poor tavern, a windmill and a little pasteboard château, which Louis XIII built so as to avoid lying on straw.

The Versailles of Louis XIV, that masterpiece wherein countless sums of money were thrown away merely in alterations to ponds and thickets, was so ruinously costly, so monstrously ill-planned, that it was never finished. Amid so many state rooms, opening one out of another, it has no theatre, no banqueting-hall, no ballroom, and both behind and before much still remains undone. The avenues and plantations, all laid out artificially, cannot mature and the coverts must continually be restocked with game. As for the drains, many miles of them still have to be made, and even the walls, whose vast contours enclose a small province of the gloomiest, most wretched countryside, have never been completely finished. . . . No matter what was done, the great fountains dried up (as they still do at times) in spite of the oceans of reservoirs that cost so many millions to engineer in that sandy or boggy soil.

A Rationalist View of Absolutism
VOLTAIRE

*Voltaire (1694–1778) was the preeminent figure of what modern scholars
call the Enlightenment, or the Age of Reason. He was also one of the
greatest and most influential of early modern historians. Among
Voltaire's most important books was* The Age of Louis XIV *(1751),
which he conceived as one of the earliest instances of what we would
nowadays call "cultural history." His intention in writing this book was
to illuminate the great achievements of Louis' "age"—as the title
announces—rather than the king himself. Indeed* The Age of Louis XIV
is usually published as part of his later Essay on the Morals and the
Spirit of Nations *(1756). But Louis the king was as impossible for
Voltaire to ignore as he had been for Saint-Simon, and as he has been
for historians of his age ever since.*

*Voltaire knew and cultivated many of the survivors of Louis' court,
some of them important figures. He collected their letters and memoirs
and those of other contemporaries—in short, he had much of the
equipment of modern historical research. Although Voltaire also had
strong and independent views on the past, as on most other subjects, his
portrait of Louis XIV is surprisingly balanced. He does not evade Louis'
faults, nor does he exploit them. Indeed, Voltaire seems rather to have
admired the king, both as a man and as a ruler. We must remember,
however, that, though a rationalist, Voltaire was not a revolutionary. He
thought highly of what has come to be called Enlightened Despotism. At
the time he completed* The Age of Louis XIV, *for example, Voltaire was
in Berlin as the guest, tutor, and "friend in residence" of Frederick the
Great of Prussia.*

*We must remember, too, that Voltaire was a French patriot who shared
Louis XIV's love for the glory of France. We do not even find him
denouncing Louis' militarism, so often the target of more recent
criticism. Voltaire was especially mindful of the unprecedented
domination of French culture in Europe during the age of Louis XIV and
of the extent to which Louis himself exemplified that culture. Voltaire
admired Louis' sound domestic economy and the diligence with which he
worked at his craft of kingship, and he had considerable sympathy for his
trials as a man. The picture that Voltaire gives us of Louis XIV is
altogether a very different one from that created by Saint-Simon.*

LOUIS XIV invested his court, as he did all his reign, with such brilliancy and magnificence, that the slightest details of his private life appear to interest posterity, just as they were the objects of curiosity to every court in Europe and indeed to all his contemporaries. The splendour of his rule was reflected in his most trivial actions. People are more eager, especially in France, to know the smallest incidents of his court, than the revolutions of some other countries. Such is the effect of a great reputation. Men would rather know what happened in the private council and court of Augustus than details of the conquests of Attila or of Tamerlane.

Consequently there are few historians who have failed to give an account of Louis XIV's early affection for the Baroness de Beauvais, for Mlle. d'Argencourt, for Cardinal Mazarin's niece, later married to the Count of Soissons, father of Prince Eugene; and especially for her sister, Marie Mancini, who afterwards married the High Constable Colonne.

He had not yet taken over the reins of government when such diversions occupied the idleness in which he was encouraged by Cardinal Mazarin, then ruling as absolute master. . . . The fact that his tutors had allowed him too much to neglect his studies in early youth, a shyness which arose from a fear of placing himself in a false position, and the ignorance in which he was kept by Cardinal Mazarin, gave the whole court to believe that he would always be ruled like his father, Louis XIII. . . .

In 1660, the marriage of Louis XIV was attended by a display of magnificence and exquisite taste which was ever afterwards on the increase. . . .

The king's marriage was followed by one long series of fêtes, entertainments and gallantries. They were redoubled on the marriage of *Monsieur,* the king's eldest brother, to Henrietta of England, sister of Charles II, and they were not interrupted until the death of Cardinal Mazarin in 1661.

The court became the centre of pleasures, and a model for all other courts. The king prided himself on giving entertainments which should put those of Vaux in the shade.

Nature herself seemed to take a delight in producing at this moment in France men of the first rank in every art, and in bringing together at Versailles the most handsome and well-favoured men and women that ever graced a court. Above all his courtiers Louis rose supreme by the grace of his figure and the majestic nobility of his countenance. The sound of his voice, at once dignified and charming, won the hearts of those whom his presence had intimidated. His bearing was such as befitted himself and his rank alone, and would have been ridiculous in any other. . . .

The chief glory of these amusements, which brought taste, polite manners and talents to such perfection in France, was that they did not for a moment detach the monarch from his incessant labours. Without such toil he could but have held a court, he could not have reigned: and had the magnificent pleasures of the court outraged the miseries of the people, they would only have been detestable; but the same man who gave these entertainments had given the people bread during the famine of 1662. He had bought up corn, which he sold to the rich at a low price, and which he gave free to poor families at the gate of the Louvre; he had remitted three millions of taxes to the people; no part of the internal administration was neglected, and his government was respected abroad. The King of Spain was obliged to allow him precedence; the Pope was forced to give him satisfaction; Dunkirk was acquired by France by a treaty honourable to the purchaser and ignominious to the seller; in short, all measures adopted after he had taken up the reins of government were either honourable or useful; thereafter, it was fitting that he should give such fêtes . . . that all the nobles should be honoured but no one powerful, not even his brother or *Monsieur le Prince*. . . .

Not one of those who have been too ready to censure Louis XIV can deny that until the Battle of Blenheim [9] he was the only monarch at once powerful, magnificent, and great in every department. For while there have been heroes such as John Sobieski and certain Kings of Sweden who eclipsed him as warriors, no one has surpassed him as a monarch. It must ever be confessed that he not only bore his misfortunes, but overcame them. He had defects and made great errors, but had those who condemn him been in his place, would they have equalled his achievements? . . .

. . . It was the destiny of Louis XIV to see the whole of his family die before their time; his wife at forty-five and his only son at fifty; but a year later we witnessed the spectacle of his grandson the Dauphin, Duke of Burgundy, his wife, and their eldest son, the Duke of Brittany, being carried to the same tomb at Saint-Denys in the month of April 1712, while the youngest of their children, who afterwards ascended the throne, lay in his cradle at death's door. The Duke of Berri, brother of the Duke of Burgundy, followed them two years later, and his daughter was carried at the same time from her cradle to her coffin.

These years of desolation left such a deep impression on people's hearts that during the minority of Louis XV I have met many people who could not speak of the late king's bereavement without tears in their eyes. . . .

The remainder of his life was sad. The disorganisation of state finances, which he was unable to repair, estranged many hearts. The complete confidence he placed in the Jesuit, Le Tellier, a turbulent spirit, stirred them to rebellion. It is remarkable that the people who forgave him all his mistresses could not forgive this one confessor. In the minds of the majority of his subjects he lost during the last three years of his life all the prestige of the great and memorable things he had accomplished. . . .

On his return from Marli towards the middle of the month of August

9 Marlborough's great victory (1704) for England and her allies in the War of the Spanish Succession.—ED.

1715, Louis XIV was attacked by the illness which ended his life. His legs swelled, and signs of gangrene began to show themselves. The Earl of Stair, the English ambassador, wagered, after the fashion of his country, that the king would not outlive the month of September. The Duke of Orleans, on the journey from Marli, had been left completely to himself, but now the whole court gathered round his person. During the last days of the king's illness, a quack physician gave him a cordial which revived him. He managed to eat, and the quack assured him that he would recover. On hearing this news the crowd of people that had gathered round the Duke of Orleans diminished immediately. "If the king eats another mouthful," said the Duke of Orleans, "we shall have no one left." But the illness was mortal. . . .

Though he has been accused of being narrow-minded, of being too harsh in his zeal against Jansenism,[10] too arrogant with foreigners in his triumphs, too weak in his dealings with certain women, and too severe in personal matters; of having lightly undertaken wars, of burning the Palatinate and of persecuting the reformers—nevertheless, his great qualities and noble deeds when placed in the balance eclipse all his faults. Time, which modifies men's opinions, has put the seal upon his reputation, and, in spite of all that has been written against him, his name is never uttered without respect, nor without recalling to the mind an age which will be forever memorable. If we consider this prince in his private life, we observe him indeed too full of his own greatness, but affable, allowing his mother no part in the government but performing all the duties of a son, and observing all outward appearance of propriety towards his wife; a good father, a good master, always dignified in public, laborious in his study, punctilious in business matters, just in thought, a good speaker, and agreeable though aloof. . . .

The mind of Louis XIV was rather precise and dignified than witty; and indeed one does not expect a king to say notable things, but to do them. . . .

Between him and his court there existed a continual intercourse in which was seen on the one side all the graciousness of a majesty which never debased itself, and on the other all the delicacy of an eager desire to serve and please which never approached servility. He was considerate and polite, especially to women, and his example enhanced those qualities in his courtiers; he never missed an opportunity of saying things to men which at once flattered their self-esteem, stimulated rivalry, and remained long in their memory. . . .

It follows from what we have related, that in everything this monarch loved grandeur and glory. A prince who, having accomplished as great

---

[10] A sect named after the Flemish theologian Cornelis Jansen that was, though Catholic, rather Calvinistic in many of its views. Jansenism was bitterly opposed by the Jesuits who finally persuaded Louis XIV to condemn it.—ED.

things as he, could yet be of plain and simple habits, would be the first among kings, and Louis XIV the second.

If he repented on his death-bed of having lightly gone to war, it must be owned that he did not judge by events; for of all his wars the most legitimate and necessary, namely, the war of 1701, was the only one unsuccessful. . . .

His own glory was indissolubly connected with the welfare of France, and never did he look upon his kingdom as a noble regards his land, from which he extracts as much as he can that he may live in luxury. Every king who loves glory loves the public weal; he had no longer a Colbert[11] nor a Louvois, when about 1698 he commanded each comptroller to present a detailed description of his province for the instruction of the Duke of Burgundy. By this means it was possible to have an exact record of the whole kingdom and a correct census of the population. . . .

The foregoing is a general account of what Louis XIV did or attempted to do in order to make his country more flourishing. It seems to me that one can hardly view all his works and efforts without some sense of gratitude, nor without being stirred by the love for the public weal which inspired them. Let the reader picture to himself the condition to-day, and he will agree that Louis XIV did more good for his country than twenty of his predecessors together; and what he accomplished fell far short of what he might have done. The war which ended with the Peace of Ryswick[12] began the ruin of that flourishing trade established by his minister Colbert, and the war of the succession completed it. . . .

. . . Nevertheless, this country, in spite of the shocks and losses she has sustained, is still one of the most flourishing in the world, since all the good that Louis XIV did for her still bears fruit, and the mischief which it was difficult not to do in stormy times has been remedied. Posterity, which passes judgment on kings, and whose judgment they should continually have before them, will acknowledge, weighing the greatness and defects of that monarch, that though too highly praised during his lifetime, he will deserve to be so for ever, and that he was worthy of the statue raised to him at Montpellier, bearing a Latin inscription whose meaning is *To Louis the Great after his death.*

---

11 Jean Baptiste Colbert, Louis' great minister of finance (d. 1683).—ED.
12 The War of the League of Augsburg (1688–1697).—ED.

Louis XIV and the Larger World
PIERRE GOUBERT

The historiography of Louis XIV is almost as vast as the original sources and almost as intimidating. Few figures in European history have been more variously or more adamantly interpreted. As W. H. Lewis has said, "To one school, he is incomparably the ablest ruler in modern European History; to another, a mediocre blunderer, pompous, led by the nose by a succession of generals and civil servants; whilst to a third, he is no great king, but still the finest actor of royalty the world has even seen." [13] *And such a list does not exhaust the catalog of Louis' interpreters.*

There is at least one contemporary revisionist school that has turned again to "the world of Louis XIV," not the limited world that Saint-Simon saw—the world of the court and the hated prison of Versailles— but the larger world of economic and social forces beyond the court. One of the best exponents of this school is the French historian Pierre Goubert, from whose Louis XIV and Twenty Million Frenchmen *the following selection is taken. Goubert is essentially an economic historian, occupied with such things as demographic trends, price and wage fluctuations, gross national products, and the like. In this book he is concerned with Louis XIV as an able bureaucratic manager rather than as strictly an autocrat; as a king whose foreign policy was often governed, not by his own absolutist theories, but by the realities of economics and whose domestic policies were limited by the dragging, inertial resistance to change of the inherited institutions of his own nation.*

AS EARLY AS 1661, as he declared in his *Mémoires,* Louis meant to have sole command in every sphere and claimed full responsibility, before the world and all posterity, for everything that should happen in his reign. In spite of constant hard work, he soon found he had to entrust the actual running of certain departments, such as finance or commerce, to a few colleagues, although he still reserved the right to take major decisions himself. There were, however, some aspects of his *métier de roi* to which he clung absolutely and persistently, although his persistence was not invariably absolute. Consequently, it is permissible to single out a kind of personal sphere which the king reserved to himself throughout his

[13] W. H. Lewis, *The Splendid Century, Life in the France of Louis XIV* (New York: Doubleday, 1957), p. 1.

reign, although this sphere might vary, while the rest still remained, as it were, under his eye.

As a young man, Louis had promised himself that his own time and posterity should ring with his exploits. If this had been no more than a simple wish, and not an inner certainty, it might be said to have been largely granted.

As a hot-headed young gallant, he flouted kings by his extravagant gestures and amazed them by the brilliance of his court, his entertainments, his tournaments and his mistresses. As a new Augustus he could claim, for a time, to have been his own Maecenas. Up to the year 1672, all Europe seems to have fallen under the spell of his various exploits and his youthful fame spread even as far as the "barbarians" of Asia. For seven or eight years after that, the armies of Le Tellier and Turenne [14] seemed almost invincible while Colbert's youthful navy and its great admirals won glory off the coast of Sicily. Then, when Europe had pulled itself together, Louis still showed amazing powers of resistance and adaptability. Even when he seemed to be ageing, slipping into pious isolation amid his courtiers, he retained the power to astonish with the spendours of his palace at Versailles, his opposition to the Pope and the will to make himself into a "new Constantine," and later by allying himself with Rome to "purify" the Catholic religion. When practically on his death bed, he could still impress the English ambassador who came to protest at the building of a new French port next door to the ruins of Dunkirk. . . .

For precisely three centuries, Louis XIV has continued to dominate, fascinate and haunt men's minds. "The universe and all time" have certainly remembered him, although not always in the way he would have wished. From this point of view, Louis' personal deeds have been a great success. Unfortunately, his memory has attracted a cloud of hatred and contempt as enduring as that which rises from the incense of his worshippers or the pious imitations of a later age.

In his personal desire to enlarge his kingdom, the king was successful. The lands in the north, Strasbourg, Franche-Comté and the "iron belt" [15] are clear evidence of success. In this way Paris was better protected from invasion. But all these gains had been made by 1681 and later events served only to confirm, rescue or reduce them. . . .

As absolute head of his diplomatic service and his armies, from beginning to end, he was well served while he relied on men who had been singled out by Mazarin or Richelieu but he often made a fool of himself by selecting unworthy successors. He was no great warrior. His father and his grandfather had revelled in the reek of the camp and the heady

[14] Le Vicomte Henri de Turenne (d. 1675), one of Louis' generals. A holdover from Louis' father's reign, Turenne was the French hero of the Thirty Years War and the war against Spain.—ED.

[15] A reference to the fortifications—the *frontiére de fer*—of the Marquis de Vauban (1663–1707), Louis' master military and seige engineer.—ED.

excitement of battle. His preference was always for impressive manoeuvres, parades and good safe sieges rather than the smoke of battle, and
as age grew on him he retreated to desk strategy. Patient, secretive and
subtle in constructing alliances, weaving intrigues and undoing coalitions,
he marred all these gifts by ill-timed displays of arrogance, brutality and
unprovoked aggression. In the last analysis, this born aggressor showed
his greatness less in triumph than in adversity but there was never any
doubt about his effect on his contemporaries whose feelings towards him
were invariably violent and uncompromising. He was admired, feared,
hated and secretly envied. . . .

More often than not, and permanently in some cases, administrative
details and the complete running of certain sectors of the administration
were left to agents appointed by the king and responsible to him. Louis
rarely resorted to the cowardly expedient of laying the blame for failure
on his subordinates. Not until the end of his life, and notably in the case
of the bishops, did he indulge in such pettiness. Everything that was done
during his reign was done in his name and Louis' indirect responsibility
in matters he had delegated was the same as his direct responsibility in
his own personal spheres. Moreover, the two sectors could not help but
be closely connected.

A policy of greatness and prestige demanded an efficient and effective
administration as well as adequate resources, both military and financial. . . .

In order to disseminate the king's commands over great distances and
combat the complex host of local authorities, a network of thirty intendants had been established over the country. These were the king's men,
dispatched by the king's councils and assisted by correspondents, agents
and *subdélégués* who by 1715 were numerous and well organized. By this
time the system was well-established and more or less accepted (even in
Brittany). It met with reasonable respect and sometimes obedience. Sometimes, not always, since we only have to read the intendants' correspondence to be disabused swiftly of any illusions fostered by old-fashioned
textbooks or history notes. The difficulties of communications, the traditions of provincial independence, inalienable rights and privileges and the
sheer force of inertia, all died hard. Lavisse used to say this was a period
of absolutism tempered by disobedience. In the depths of the country and
the remote provinces, the formula might almost be reversed. Nevertheless, there is no denying that a step forward had been made and that the
germ of the splendid administrative systems of Louis XV and of Napoleon was already present in the progress made between 1661 and 1715. . . .

In one adjacent but vital field, ministers and jurists laboured valiantly
to reach a unified code of French law, giving the king's laws priority over
local custom and simplifying the enormous tangled mass of statute
law. . . .

The navy, rescued from virtual oblivion by Colbert who gave it arsenals, shipwrights, gunners, talented designers, its finest captains and fresh personnel obtained by means of seaboard conscription, distinguished itself particularly from 1672 to 1690. . . .

The greatest of all the king's great servants were those who helped him to build up an army, which in size and striking force was for the most part equal to all the other armies of Europe put together. They were first Le Tellier and Turenne and later, Louvois and Vauban. Many others of less fame, such as Chamlay, Martinet, Fourilles and Clerville would also deserve a place in this unusually lengthy roll of honour if the historian's job were the awarding of laurels, especially military ones. The fighting strength was increased at least fourfold, discipline was improved, among generals as well as officers and men, and a civil administration superimposed, not without a struggle, on the quarrelsome, short-sighted and in many cases incompetent and dishonest military one. New ranks and new corps were introduced; among them the artillery and the engineers, as well as such new weapons as the flintlock and the fixed bayonet, and a new military architect, Vauban, all helped to make the army more efficient. Most important of all, the army at last possessed a real *Intendance* with its own arsenals, magazines, and regular staging posts. Uniforms became more or less general, providing employment for thousands of workers. The first barracks were an attempt to put an end to the notorious custom of billeting troops on civilian households. The Hôtel des Invalides [16] was built, on a grand scale. The instrument which these invaluable servants placed at their master's disposal was almost without parallel in their time, a genuine royal army, growing ever larger and more diversified, modern and disciplined. . . .

An ambition to astonish the world with magnificence and great armies is all very well so long as the world is prepared to be astonished.

At the beginning of his reign, when Louis surveyed the rest of Europe, he saw nothing but weakness and decline. Some of his observations, as regards Spain and Italy, were perfectly correct. In others, he was mistaken. He stupidly underestimated the United Provinces, as though a small, bourgeois and Calvinist population were an inevitable sign of weakness. Yet another observation was swiftly belied by the changes which occurred in two highly dissimilar entities; England and the Empire.

Louis XIV found himself baulked at every turn by the diplomacy and dogged courage, as well as by the seapower and the immense wealth of the United Provinces. It is no longer fashionable to believe that the "Golden Age" of the Dutch was over in 1661. For a long time after that, their Bank, their Stock Exchange, their India Company, their fleets and their florins remained as powerful as ever. The invasion of 1672 weakened them only temporarily and even in 1715 . . . their wealth, currency and bankers remained powerful and respected and often decisive. Their

16 Now a military museum and the site of Napoleon's tomb but originally intended as an old soldiers' home.—ED.

policy was not yet tied directly to England's. It was simply that they no longer enjoyed undivided supremacy: another nation's economy had reached the same level and was about to overtake them.

Louis XIV always did his best to ignore economic factors but they would not be denied and they took their revenge. . . .

Louis found other forces of opposition within the borders of his kingdom . . . the ancient, traditional and heavily calculated weight of inertia possessed by that collection of "nations," *pays, seigneuries,* fiefs and parishes which together made up the kingdom of France. Each of these entities was accustomed to living independently, with its own customs, privileges and even language, snug in its own fields and within sound of its own bells. The king consecrated at Rheims was a priest-king to be revered and almost worshipped, but from afar. . . .

If, dazzled by the splendours of Versailles, we let ourselves forget the constant presence of these seething undercurrents, we will have understood nothing of the France of Louis XIV and of the impossible task which the king and his ministers had set themselves, or of the massive inertia which made it so difficult. . . .

For some years now, younger historians of a certain school have tended to ignore the bustle of individuals and events in favour of what they call revealing, measuring, defining and illustrating the great dominant rhythms which move world history as a whole. These rhythms emerge as largely economic. . . . From 1600 onwards, the quantities of silver reaching Spain from America grew less and less until by 1650 the imports were only a fifth of what they had been in 1600. A probable revival of the mines of central Europe was insufficient to make up the deficit. First gold, and then silver, grew scarce, giving rise to hoarding. Copper from Sweden or Japan (via Holland) tended to take their place but it was a poor substitute. The whole age of Louis XIV was an age that Marc Bloch has called "monetary famine." . . .

Historians and economists have long been aware that the seventeenth century as a whole and the period from 1650-90 in particular, or even 1650-1730, was marked by a noticeable drop in the cost of basic foodstuffs as well as of a great many other things—a drop quite separate from annual "accidents." Landed incomes, offices and possible moneylending, all seem to have been affected by the same general reduction. . . .

There remains a strong impression that the period of Louis' reign was one of economic difficulties, suffering both from sudden, violent crises and from phases of stagnation and of deep depression. It is not easy to govern under such conditions especially when, like the king and most of his councillors, one is unaware of them. But what they tried to do and sometimes, despite such obstacles, achieved, remains nonetheless worthy of interest and even admiration.

It is possible, therefore, that France under Louis XIV may have been unconsciously subject to powerful economic forces which are still much disputed and not fully understood. Social, demographic, mental and other factors, wholly or partly incomprehensible to the rulers, may have played their part also. . . .

About the great mass of French society and its slow, ponderous development we know almost nothing, only a few glimmers here and there. . . .

It is true that Louis XIV, like most men who grew up between 1640 and 1660, was incapable of rising beyond the limits of his education, let alone of taking in, at one glance, the whole of the planet on which he lived, to say nothing of infinite space. A king to the depths of his being, and a dedicated king, he had a concept of greatness which was that of his generation: military greatness, dynastic greatness, territorial greatness and political greatness which expressed itself in unity of faith, the illusion of obedience and magnificent surroundings. He left behind him an image of the monarchy, admirable in its way, but already cracking if not outworn at the time of his death.

Suggestions for Further Reading

THE BEST BIOGRAPHY of Louis XIV is John B. Wolf, *Louis XIV* (New York: Norton, 1968), a comprehensive, analytical, and persuasive book. Another work, by an eminent French historian, Pierre Gaxotte, *The Age of Louis XIV,* tr. Michael Shaw (New York: Macmillan, 1970), can also be recommended, but it is not as readable as Nancy Mitford, *The Sun King* (New York: Harper & Row, 1966), a handsome book on Louis and the daily life at Versailles—the court intrigues and decisions of government— a lively and witty, if somewhat superficial, book by a popular British novelist and biographer. Two brief biographies can also be recommended: the older Maurice Ashley, *Louis XIV and the Greatness of France*, "Teach Yourself History Library" (New York: Macmillan, 1948), and the more recent and sympathetic Vincent Buranelli, *Louis XIV,* "Rulers and Statesmen of the World" series (New York: Twayne, 1966).

Louis XIV, no matter how he is judged, is the central figure in seventeenth-century Europe. Some works on that century and the age of Louis XIV are therefore necessary to an understanding of the Sun King. David Ogg, *Europe in the Seventeenth Century,* 8th rev. ed. (London: Macmillan,

1961), and G. N. Clark, *The Seventeenth Century,* 2nd ed. (Oxford, England: Clarendon Press, 1961), have long been the standard works of, respectively, the narrative and institutional history of the period. A famous interpretive book, somewhat like Clark, is W. H. Lewis, *The Splendid Century, Life in the France of Louis XIV* (New York: Doubleday, 1957 [1953]), but it is more lively and entertaining. More comprehensive and much more far-ranging in subject is Maurice Ashley, *The Golden Century, Europe 1598–1715* (New York: Praeger, 1969). Of the same sort, but more popular, is Ragnhild Hatton, *Europe in the Age of Louis XIV* (New York: Harcourt, Brace and World, 1969). J. B. Wolf, *Toward a European Balance of Power, 1620–1715* (Chicago: Rand McNally, 1970), deals almost entirely with the central role of Louis XIV's France in the evolution of that important political-diplomatic concept.

Through the last generation or so, seventeenth-century studies, and the study of Louis XIV, have passed through a major crisis of revision. One of the early works reflecting this is J. B. Wolf, *The Emergence of the Great Powers, 1685–1715,* "Rise of Modern Europe" series (New York: Harper & Row, 1951), a brilliant synthesis of narrative, analysis, and modern research. Students should read more extensively in the important work, Pierre Goubert, *Louis XIV and Twenty Million Frenchmen,* tr. Anne Carter (New York: Pantheon, 1970), excerpted in this chapter. There are three sets of readings that represent much of the newer research and interpretation of Louis XIV: *Louis XIV and the Craft of Kingship,* ed. John C. Rule (Columbus: Ohio State University Press, 1969), *Louis XIV and Absolutism,* ed. Ragnhild Hatton (Columbus: Ohio State University Press, 1976), and *Louis XIV and Europe,* ed. Ragnhild Hatton (Columbus: Ohio State University Press, 1976). Finally, students may be interested in an important thesis book on the so-called general crisis of the seventeenth century: Theodore K. Rabb, *The Struggle for Stability in Early Modern Europe* (New York: Oxford University Press, 1975), in which Rabb argues that the crisis was a search for a principle of authority.

Peter the Great and the Westernization of Russia

Peter the Great was six feet eight inches tall and so strong that he could break a horseshoe with his bare hands. He was practically indifferent to comfort, and he had a manic energy and a capacity for the most savage and destructive rage. In spite of an education so scant and faulty that he was virtually illiterate, he became a competent expert in more than a dozen technical crafts and a more than respectable amateur scientist. The enormous mass of laws, regulations, and edicts he framed have not even yet been completely edited. He was apt to invite anyone to eat or drink with him and was fond of stopping in the huts or shops of the humblest artisans to admire their skill or try his own and to chat with them. Yet Peter the Great sacrificed the lives of uncounted thousands of his peasants in the building of his new capital city of St. Petersburg—his "window on Europe"—in the desolate, disease-ridden marshes at the mouth of the Neva River on the Baltic. He could endure a slur to his own son made by a drunken companion, yet he rode rough-shod over the customs and sensibilities of his boyar court nobility, forcing them to set aside their old ways in favor of Western fashions in dress and education. He cut their beards himself and even demonstrated the new Western craft of dentistry on a few unfortunates among them. When a revolt of the *streltsy,* the imperial musketeers, forced him to return to Moscow from his first journey to the West, he disbanded the unit, personally saw to the torture and execution of more than a thousand of them, and displayed their corpses throughout the city as a lesson to other rebels. When, later in his reign, he suspected his weakling son Alexis of taking part in a conspiracy, Peter ordered his arrest and watched the boy be tortured to death.

Peter the Great is, in short, the most contradictory and intriguing figure in Russian history—as well as the most important. For no matter how it is interpreted, the reign of Peter the Great marks the most fundamental turning point in the history of his nation. And the central issue of this significant reign is Peter's policy of Westernization.

The offspring of the second marriage of Czar Alexis and third in the line of succession, Peter was raised by his mother away from the court in the so-called German suburb, where all the foreign residents of Moscow were compelled to live. Here Peter made friends among the Western merchants, artisans, technicians, and adventurers and developed his passion for Western ways. In 1697, after his succession to the throne, Peter made his celebrated first journey to the West, ostensibly to solicit support for a war against the Turks and also to sample for himself the wonders of Western technology. Peter traveled simply as a member of the party, disguised as Bombardier Peter Mikhailov. His true identity was discovered, however, and he was received at the courts of Brandenburg and Hanover, he met William of Orange and the Emperor Leopold, and he made friends with Augustus the Strong of Saxony, the king of Poland. On the whole, Peter's diplomatic initiative failed, but not so his technological mission. He visited iron foundries in Brandenburg. In Amsterdam he actually worked on the docks and in the shipyards as a ship's carpenter. In England he found the shipyards at Deptford and the Woolwich naval arsenal more interesting than London or the Parliament.

When the revolt of the *streltsy* forced him to cut short his visit to the West, Peter returned to Russia with the resolve to Westernize his nation. He not only imposed such seemingly trivial reforms as cleanshaven faces and Western clothing; he instituted the most fundamental changes in every aspect of Russian government and society. He reformed the judicial system and created a senate, whose members were appointed by him, to replace the old council of boyars. A series of ministries for public affairs was established; their directors were both Russians and foreigners. Peter recognized the chaotic system of local government, imposing upon it a structure of governorships responsible to him, and he drove the old conservative religious faction of the nobility out of the court. The power of the Patriarch over the Russian church was broken, and in its place an administrative system like the other ministries of the state was instituted. Peter forced Western-style education upon the boyars and created a new structure of nobility and a "Table of Ranks" based entirely on merit and service to the state. He reformed the system of taxation as well. He invited Western advisors and experts to Russia in unprecedented numbers and gave them unheard-of status and authority. At the same time, thousands of young Russians were sent to study and train in the West.

Peter the Great founded a merchant marine and opened up the vast resources of Russia to foreign trade. He created the Russian navy and completely reorganized the military establishment into Russia's first standing army. Never content to stand on the sidelines, Peter himself passed through all the ranks and grades in all the services of both the army and the navy. Even his foreign policy marked a fundamental turn to the West. The war against the Turks early in his career, was undertaken in the hope of gaining access to the Mediterranean through the Black Sea. And the major conflict of his reign, the Great Northern War (1700–1721), was waged to challenge Swedish supremacy in the Baltic and open Russia to the West. In the course of the war, he faced the greatest military genius of his age in Charles XII of Sweden; and, though defeated by him at Narva in 1700, Peter came back to defeat Charles at Poltava nine years later. In the treaty that ended the war at Nystadt, it was Peter's Russia that gained the lion's share of territory, and Peter gained his long hoped-for access to the West.

By the end of his reign in 1725, Peter the Great had changed the Russian monarchy into a Western absolutism; he had displaced Sweden as the dominant power in the Baltic; and he had thrust Russia as a new and powerful force into the family of European nations from which she would never again be excluded.

Panegyric to the Sovereign Emperor Peter the Great
MIKHAIL LOMONOSOV

Peter the Great not only had his detractors and opponents; he also had his champions, some of them men whom he had raised to high position and others, both contemporaries and near contemporaries, who shared Peter's vision of the future of their nation. One such defender was Mikhail Vasil'evich Lomonosov (1711–1765), as fanatic a champion of Russian cultural modernization as the great Czar himself and the author of "Panegyric to the Sovereign Emperor Peter the Great," from which the following selection is taken. The occasion for the panegyric was the coronation of Peter's daughter Elizabeth in 1741, and its purpose was clearly to remind the new empress of her father's policies. But the panegyric is important not only as a sympathetic retrospective survey of Peter's reign, but also as one of the first important contributions to the myth of Peter the Great, the founder of modern Russia, a man larger than life and altogether heroic. A contemporary of Lomonosov, P. N. Krekshyn, hailed the Czar in these terms, "Our father Peter the Great! Thou broughtest us from nothingness into existence!" [1]—a sentiment thoroughly compatible with Lomonosov's views.

. . . AS I EMBARK on this undertaking, with what shall I begin my discourse? With His bodily endowments? With the greatness of His strength? But it is manifest in his mastery of burdensome labors, labors without number, and in the overcoming of terrible obstacles. Shall I begin with His heroic appearance and stature combined with majestic beauty? But apart from the many who vividly call to mind an image of Him engraved in their memory, there is the witness of those in various states and cities who, drawn by His fame, flocked out to admire a figure appropriate to His deeds and befitting a great Monarch. Should I commence with His buoyancy of spirit? But that is proved by the tireless vigilance without which it would have been impossible to carry out deeds so numerous and great. Wherefore I do immediately proceed to present these deeds, knowing that it is easier to make a beginning than to reach the end and that

---

[1] Quoted in M. S. Anderson, *Peter the Great* (London: The Historical Association, 1969), p. 3.

this Great Man cannot be better praised than by him who shall enumerate His labors in faithful detail, were it but possible to enumerate them.

And so, to the extent that strength and the brevity of limited time will permit, we shall mention only His most important deeds, then the mighty obstacles therein overcome, and finally the virtues which aided Him in such enterprises.

As a part of His grand designs the all-wise Monarch provided as a matter of absolute necessity for the dissemination of all kinds of knowledge in the homeland, and also for an increase in the numbers of persons skilled in the higher branches of learning, together with artists and craftsmen; though I have given His paternal solicitude in this matter the most prominent place, my whole speech would not be long enough to describe it in detail. For, having repeatedly made the rounds of European states like some swift-soaring eagle, He did induce (partly by command and partly by His own weighty example) a great multitude of His subjects to leave their country for a time and to convince themselves by experience how great an advantage a person and an entire state can derive from a journey of inquiry in foreign regions. Then were the wide gates of great Russia opened up; then over the frontiers and through the harbors, like the tides in the spacious ocean, there did flow in constant motion, in the one direction, the sons of Russia, journeying forth to acquire knowledge in the various sciences and arts, and, in the other direction, foreigners arriving with various skills, books, and instruments. Then to the study of Mathematics and Physics, previously thought of as forms of sorcery and witchcraft, but now arrayed in purple, crowned with laurels, and placed on the Monarch's throne, reverential respect was accorded in the sanctified Person of PETER. What benefit was brought to us by all the different sciences and arts, bathed in such a glow of grandeur, is proved by the superabundant richness of our most varied pleasures, of which our forefathers, before the days of Russia's Great Enlightener, were not only deprived but in many cases had not even any conception. How many essential things which previously came to Russia from distant lands with difficulty and at great cost are now produced inside the state, and not only provide for our needs but also with their surplus supply other lands. There was a time when the neighbors on our borders boasted that Russia, a great and powerful state, was unable properly to carry out military operations or trade without their assistance, since its mineral resources included neither precious metals for the stamping of coins nor even iron, so needful for the making of weapons with which to stand against an enemy. This reproach disappeared through the enlightenment brought by PETER; the bowels of the mountains have been opened up by his mighty and industrious hand. Metals pour out of them, and are not only freely distributed within the homeland but are also given back to foreign peoples as if in repayment of loans. The brave Russian army turns against the enemy weapons produced from Russian mines and Russian hands.

In the establishment of the sizable army needed for the defense of the homeland, the security of His subjects, and the unhindered carrying out of important enterprises within the country, how great was the solicitude of the Great Monarch, how impetuous His zeal, how assiduous His search of ways and means! . . . The impossible was made possible by extraordinary zeal, and above all by an unheard-of-example. In former times the Roman Senate, beholding the Emperor Trajan standing before the Consul to receive from him the dignity of Consul, exclaimed: "Through this thou art the greater, the more majestic!" What exclamations, what applause were due to PETER the Great for His unparalleled self-abasement? Our fathers beheld their crowned Sovereign not among the candidates for a Roman consulship but in the ranks of common soldiers, not demanding power over Rome, but obedient to the bidding of His subjects. O you beautiful regions, fortunate regions which beheld a spectacle so wondrous! Oh, how you marveled at the friendly contest of the regiments of a single Sovereign, both commander and subordinate, giving orders and obeying them! Oh, how you admired the siege, defense, and capture of new Russian fortresses, not for immediate mercenary gain but for the sake of future glory, not for putting down enemies but to encourage fellow countrymen. Looking back at those past years, we can now imagine the great love for the Sovereign and the ardent devotion with which the newly instituted army was fired, seeing Him in their company at the same table, eating the same food, seeing His face covered with dust and sweat, seeing that He was no different from them, except that in training and in diligence He was superior to all. By such an extraordinary example the most wise Sovereign, rising in rank alongside His subjects, proved that Monarchs can in no other way increase their majesty, glory, and eminence so well as by such gracious condescension. The Russian army was toughened by such encouragement, and during the twenty years' war with the Swedish Crown, and later in other campaigns, filled the ends of the universe with the thunder of its weapons and with the noise of its triumphs. It is true that the first battle of Narva was not successful; but the superiority of our foes and the retreat of the Russian army have, through envy and pride, been exaggerated to their glorification and our humiliation, out of all proportion to the actual event. For although most of the Russian army had seen only two years' service and faced a veteran army accustomed to battle, although disagreement arose between our commanders, and a malicious turncoat revealed to the enemy the entire position in our camp, and Charles XII [of Sweden] by a sudden attack did not give the Russians time to form ranks—yet even in their retreat they destroyed the enemy's willingness to fight on to final victory. Thus the only reason the Russian Life Guard, which had remained intact, together with another sizable part of the army, did not dare to attack the enemy thereafter was the absence of its main leaders, who had been summoned by Charles for peace talks and detained as prisoners.

For this reason the Guards and the rest of the army returned to Russia with their arms and war chest, drums beating and banners flying. That this failure occurred more through the unhappy circumstances described than through any lack of skill in the Russian troops and that PETER's new army could, even in its infancy, defeat the seasoned regiments of the enemies, was proved in the next year and subsequently by many glorious victories won over them. . . .

Having covered Himself and His army with glory throughout the world by such famous victories, the Great Monarch finally proved that he had been at pains to establish His army mainly in the interests of our safety! For He decreed that it should never be dispersed, even in times of untroubled peace (as had happened under previous Sovereigns, frequently to no little loss of the country's might and glory), and also that it should always be kept in proper readiness. . . .

Having cast a quick glance over PETER's land forces, which came to maturity in their infancy and combined their training with victories, let us extend our gaze across the waters, my Listeners; let us observe what the Lord has done there, His marvels on the deep, as made manifest by PETER to the astonishment of the world.

The far-flung Russian state, like a whole world, is surrounded by great seas on almost every side and sets them as its boundaries. On all of them we see Russian flags flying. Here the mouths of great rivers and new harbors scarcely provide space for the multitude of craft; elsewhere the waves groan beneath the weight of the Russian fleet, and the sounds of its gunfire echo in the chasms of the deep. Here gilded ships, blooming like spring, are mirrored on the quiet surface of the waters and take on double beauty; elsewhere the mariner, having reached a calm haven, unloads the riches of faraway countries to give us pleasure. Here new Columbuses hasten to unknown shores to add to the might and glory of Russia; there a second Tethys dares to sail between the battling mountains; she struggles with snow, with frost, with everlasting ice, desirous to unite East and West. How did the power and glory of Russian fleets come to be spread over so many seas in a short time? Whence came the materials, whence the skill? Whence the machines and implements needed in so difficult and varied an enterprise? Did not the ancient giants tear great oaks from dense forests and lofty mountains and throw them down for building on the shores? Did not Amphion with sweet music on the lyre move the various parts for the construction of those wondrous fortresses which fly over the waves? To such fancies would PETER's wondrous swiftness in building a fleet truly have been ascribed if an exploit so improbable and seemingly beyond human strength had been performed in far-off ancient times, and if it had not been fixed in the memory of many eyewitnesses and in unexceptionably reliable written records. . . . From that very time when the contriving of a boat (which, though small in dimensions, was great in influence and fame) aroused in

PETER's unsleeping spirit the salutary urge to found a fleet and to show forth the might of Russia on the deep, He applied the forces of His great mind to every part of this important enterprise. As He investigated these parts, He became convinced that in a matter so difficult there was no possibility of success unless He Himself acquired adequate knowledge of it. But where was that to be obtained? What should the Great Sovereign undertake? . . .

. . . But greater still was the amazement that He aroused, greater the spectacle that He presented to the eyes of the whole world when, becoming convinced of the untold benefits of navigation—first on the small bodies of water in the Moscow area, then on the great breadth of Lake Rostov and Lake Kubensk, and finally on the expanse of the White Sea— He absented himself for a time from His dominions and, concealing the Majesty of His Person among humble workmen in a foreign land, did not disdain to learn the shipwright's craft. Those who chanced to be His fellow-apprentices at first marveled at the amazing fact that a Russian had not only mastered simple carpentering work so quickly, had not only brought Himself to the point where He could make with His own hands every single part needed in the building and equipping of ships, but had also acquired such skills in marine architecture that Holland could no longer satisfy His deep understanding. Then how great was the amazement that was aroused in all when they learned that this was no simple Russian, but the Ruler of that great state Himself who had taken up heavy labors in hands born and anointed to bear the Scepter and the Orb. But was it merely out of sheer curiosity or, at the most, for purposes of instruction and command, that He did in Holland and Britain attain perfection in the theory and practice of equipping a fleet and in navigational science? Everywhere the Great Sovereign aroused His subjects to labor, not only by command and reward, but also by His own example! I call you to witness, O great Russian rivers; I address myself to you, O happy shores, sanctified by PETER's footsteps and watered by His sweat. How many times you resounded with high-spirited and eager cries as the heavy timbers, ready for launching of the ship, were being slowly moved by the workmen and then, at the touch of His hand, made a sudden spurt toward the swift current, inspiring the multitude, encouraged by His example, to finish off the huge hulks with incredible speed. To what a marvelous and rousing spectable were the assembled people treated as these great structures moved nearer to launching! When their indefatigable Founder and Builder, now moving topside, now below, now circling round, tested the soundness of each part, the power of the machinery, and the precision of all the preparations and by command, encouragement, ingenuity, and the quick skill of His tireless hands, rectified the defects which He had detected. In this unflagging zeal, this invincible persistence in labor, the legendary prowess of the ancients was shown in PETER's day to have been not fiction but the very truth! . . .

I say nothing of the assistance afforded in this matter by other wise institutions, but will mention the increase of external revenues. Divine Providence aided the good designs and efforts of PETER, through His hand opening new ports of the Varangian [Baltic] Sea at towns conquered by His valor and erected by His own labors. Great rivers were joined for the more convenient passage of Russian merchants, duty regulations were established, and commercial treaties with various peoples were concluded. What benefit proceeded from the growth of this abundance within and without has been clear from the very foundation of these institutions, for while continuing to fight a burdensome war for twenty years Russia was free from debts.

What, then, have all PETER's great deeds already been depicted in my feeble sketch? Oh, how much labor still remains for my thoughts, voice, and tongue! I ask you, my Listeners, out of your knowledge to consider how much assiduous effort was required for the foundation and establishment of a judiciary, and for the institution of the Governing Senate, the Most Holy Synod, the state colleges, the chancelleries, and the other governmental offices with their laws, regulations, and statutes; for the establishment of the table of ranks and the introduction of decorations as outward tokens of merit and favor; and finally, for foreign policy, missions, and alliances with foreign powers. You may contemplate all these things yourselves with minds enlightened by PETER. . . .

Nothing can serve me so well to demonstrate the kindness and gentleness of His heart as His incomparable graciousness toward His subjects. Superbly endowed as He was, elevated in His Majesty, and exalted by most glorious deeds, He did but the more increase and adorn these things by His incomparable graciousness. Often He moved amongst His subjects simply, countenancing neither the pomp that proclaims the monarch's presence nor servility. Often anyone afoot was free to meet Him, to follow Him, to walk along with Him, to start a conversation if so inclined. In former times many Sovereigns were carried on the shoulders and heads of their slaves; graciousness exalted Him above these very Sovereigns. At the very time of festivity and relaxation important business would be brought to Him; but the importance did not decrease gaiety, nor did simplicity lessen the importance. How He awaited, received, and greeted His loyal subjects! What gaiety there was at His table! He asked questions, listened, answered, discussed as with friends; and whatever time was saved at table by the small number of dishes was spent in gracious conversation. Amid so many cares of state He lived at ease as among friends. Into how many tiny huts of craftsmen did He bring His Majesty, and heartened with His presence His most lowly, but skilled and loyal, servants. How often He joined them in the exercise of their crafts and in various labors. For He attracted more by example than He compelled by force. And if there was anything which then seemed to be compulsion, it now stands revealed as a benefaction. . . .

On the Corruption of Morals in Russia
PRINCE M. M. SHCHERBATOV

Lomonosov had proclaimed that the "compulsion" that had brought about Peter's reforms is "now revealed as a benefaction." To many, however, it continued to seem compulsion. One person who held this view was the conservative aristocrat Prince Mikhail Mikhailovich Shcherbatov (1733–1790). Shcherbatov belonged to one of the oldest and proudest families of the Russian traditional nobility, and throughout his life he was preoccupied with the status and the condition of the class to which he belonged. He was also a scholar and historian, one of the first to write a systematic, documentary history of his nation. Shcherbatov was commissioned by the Empress Catherine II to edit the private and public papers of Peter the Great. Thus, there was no man of his generation in a better position to assess Peter's accomplishments.

Shcherbatov was an admirer of Peter and even, to an extent, of Peter's Westernizing reforms. But, at the same time, he was alarmed by the consequences of those reforms, which he saw as undermining the position of the old aristocracy and corrupting the moral base that he considered to be fundamental to the greatness of Russia. These views are nowhere better or more succinctly expressed than in Shcherbatov's tract On the Corruption of Morals in Russia, *a work of his old age and a kind of summation of his reflections on the direction of Russian history. In Shcherbatov we have a cautious, even gloomy conservative to set beside Lomonosov, the euphoric enthusiast for Peter's reforms.*

PETER THE GREAT, in imitating foreign nations, not only strove to introduce to his realm a knowledge of sciences, arts and crafts, a proper military system, trade, and the most suitable forms of legislation; he also tried to introduce the kind of sociability, social intercourse and magnificence, which he first learnt from Lefort, and which he later saw for himself. Amid essential legislative measures, the organization of troops and artillery, he paid no less attention to modifying the old customs which seemed crude to him. He ordered beards to be shaved off, he abolished the old Russian garments, and instead of long robes he compelled the men to wear German coats, and the women, instead of the "telogreya" to wear bodices, skirts, gowns and "samaras," and instead of skull-caps, to adorn their heads with fontanges and cornettes. He established various assemblies where the women, hitherto segregated from the company of men, were present with them at entertainments. . . .

The monarch himself kept to the old simplicity of morals in his dress, so that apart from plain coats and uniforms, he never wore anything costly; and it was only for the coronation of the Empress Catherine Alexeevna, his wife, that he had made a coat of blue gros-de-tours with silver-braid; they say he also had another coat, grey with gold braid, but I do not know for what great occasion this was made.

The rest was all so plain that even the poorest person would not wear it today, as can be seen from such of his clothes as have remained, and are kept in the Kunst-Kamera at the Imperial Academy of Sciences.

He disliked cuffs and did not wear them, as his portraits attest. He had no costly carriages, but usually travelled in a gig in towns, and in a chaise on a long journey.

He did not have a large number of retainers and attendants, but had orderlies, and did not even have a bodyguard, apart from a Colonel of the Guard.

However, for all his personal simplicity, he wanted his subjects to have a certain magnificence. I think that this great monarch, who did nothing without farsightedness, had it as his object to stimulate trade, industries and crafts through the magnificence and luxury of his subjects, being certain that in his lifetime excessive magnificence and voluptuousness would not enthrone themselves at the royal court. . . .

As far as his domestic life was concerned, although the monarch himself was content with the plainest food, he now introduced drinks previously unknown in Russia, which he drank in preference to other drinks; namely, instead of domestic brandy, brewed from ordinary wine —Dutch aniseed brandy which was called "state" brandy, and Hermitage and Hungarian wine, previously unknown in Russia.

His example was followed by the grandees and those who were close to the court; and indeed it was proper for them to provide these wines; for the monarch was fond of visiting his subjects, and what should a subject not do for the monarch? . . . .

Closely copying him, as they were bound to do by their very rank, other leading officials of the Empire also kept open table, such as Admiral-of-the-Fleet, Count Fyodor Matveevich Apraxin, Field-Marshal-in-Chief, Count Boris Petrovich Sheremetev, the Chancellor, Count Gav-

rilo Ivanovich Golovkin, and the boyar, Tikhon Nikitich Streshnev, who
as first ruler of the Empire during Peter the Great's absence abroad, was
given estates in order to provide for such meals.

As these eminent men were copied by their inferiors, so the custom of
keeping an open table was now introduced in many homes. The meals
were not of the traditional kind, that is, when only household products
were used; now they tried to improve the flavor of the meat and fish with
foreign seasonings. And of course, in a nation in which hospitality has
always been a characteristic virtue, it was not hard for the custom of these
open tables to become a habit; uniting as it did the special pleasure of
society and the improved flavour of the food as compared with the traditional kind, it established itself as a pleasure in its own right. . . .

With this change in the way of life, first of the leading officials of state,
and then, by imitation, of the other nobles, and as expenditure reached
such a point that it began to exceed income, people began to attach themselves more and more to the monarch and to the grandees, as sources of
riches and rewards.

I fear someone may say that this, at any rate, was a good thing, that
people began to attach themselves more and more to the monarch. No,
this attachment was no blessing, for it was not so much directed to the
person of the monarch as to personal ends; this attachment became not
the attachment of true subjects who love their sovereign and his honour
and consider everything from the point of view of the national interest,
but the attachment of slaves and hirelings, who sacrifice everything for
their own profit and deceive their sovereign with obsequious zeal.

Coarseness of morals decreased, but the place left by it was filled by
flattery and selfishness. Hence came sycophancy, contempt for truth, be-
guiling of the monarch, and the other evils which reign at court to this
day and which have ensconced themselves in the houses of the grandees. . . .

But despite [his] love of truth and his aversion to flattery, the monarch
could not eradicate this encroaching venom. Most of those around him
did not dare to contradict him in anything, but rather flattered him,
praising everything he did, and never resisting his whims, while some
even indulged his passions. . . .

I said that it was voluptuousness and luxury that were able to produce
such an effect in men's hearts; but there were also other causes, stemming
from actual institutions, which eradicated resoluteness and good behaviour.

The abolition of rights of precedence (a custom admittedly harmful to
the service and the state), and the failure to replace it by any granting of
rights to the noble families, extinguished thoughts of noble pride in the
nobility. For it was no longer birth that was respected, but ranks and
promotions and length of service. And so everyone started to strive after
ranks; but since not everyone is able to perform straightforward deeds of
merit, so for lack of meritorious service men began to try and worm their

way up, by flattering and humouring the monarch and the grandees in
every way. Then there was the introduction of regular military service
under Peter the Great, whereby masters were conscripted into the ranks
on the same level as their serfs. The serfs, being the first to reach officer's
rank through deeds suited to men of their kind, became commanders over
their masters and used to beat them with rods. The noble families were
split up in the service, so that a man might never see his own kinsman.

Could virtue, then, and resolution, remain in those who from their
youth had gone in fear and trembling of their commanders' rods, who
could only acquire respect by acts of servility, and being each without any
support from his kinsmen, remained alone, without unity or defence,
liable to be subjected to violent treatment?

It is admirable that Peter the Great wished to rid religion of superstition,
for indeed, superstition does not signify respect for God and his Law, but
rather an affront. For to ascribe to God acts unbecoming to him is blas-
phemy.

In Russia, the beard was regarded as being in the image of God, and
it was considered a sin to shave it off, and through this, men fell into the
heresy of the Anthropomorphites.[2] Miracles, needlessly performed, manifestations of ikons, rarely proven, were everywhere acclaimed, attracted
superstitious idolatry, and provided incomes for dissolute priests.

Peter the Great strove to do away with all this. He issued decrees,
ordering beards to be shaved off, and by the Spiritual Regulation, he
placed a check on false miracles and manifestations and also on unseemly
gatherings at shrines set up at crossways. Knowing that God's Law exists
for the preservation of the human race, and not for its needless destruction, with the blessing of the Synod and the Ecumenical patriarchs, he
made it permissible to eat meat on fast-days in cases of need, and especially in the Navy where, by abstaining even from fish, the men were
somewhat prone to scurvy; ordering that those who voluntarily sacrificed
their lives by such abstinence, should, when they duly fell ill, be thrown
into the water. All this is very good, although the latter is somewhat
severe.

But when did he do this? At a time when the nation was still unenlightened, and so, by taking superstition away from an unenlightened people,
he removed its very faith in God's Law. This action of Peter the Great
may be compared to that of an unskilled gardener who, from a weak
tree, cuts off the water-shoots which absorb its sap. If it had strong roots,
then this pruning would cause it to bring forth fine, fruitful branches; but
since it is weak and ailing, the cutting-off of these shoots (which, through
the leaves which received the external moisture, nourished the weak tree)
means that it fails to produce new fruitful branches; its wounds fail to
heal over with sap, and hollows are formed which threaten to destroy the
tree. Thus, the cutting-off of superstitions did harm to the most basic

2 Attributing manlike qualities to God.—ED.

articles of the faith; superstition decreased, but so did faith. The servile fear of Hell disappeared, but so did love of God and his Holy Law; and morals, which for lack of other enlightenment used to be improved by faith, having lost this support began to fall into dissolution. . . .

And so, through the labours and solicitude of this monarch, Russia acquired fame in Europe and influence in affairs. Her troops were organized in a proper fashion, and her fleets covered the White Sea and the Baltic; with these forces she overcame her old enemies and former conquerors, the Poles and the Swedes, and acquired important provinces and sea-ports. Sciences, arts and crafts began to flourish there, trade began to enrich her, and the Russians were transformed—from bearded men to clean-shaven men, from long-robed men to short-coated men; they became more sociable, and polite spectacles became known to them.

But at the same time, true attachment to the faith began to disappear, sacraments began to fall into disrepute, resoluteness diminished, yielding place to brazen, aspiring flattery; luxury and voluptuousness laid the foundation of their power, and hence avarice was also aroused, and, to the ruin of the laws and the detriment of the citizens, began to penetrate the law-courts.

Such was the condition with regard to morals, in which Russia was left at the death of this great monarch (despite all the barriers which Peter the Great in his own person and by his example had laid down to discourage vice).

Peter the Great: A Modern View
NICHOLAS V. RIASANOVSKY

Modern historians of Russia, in their efforts to gain an objective view of Peter, have tried to uncover the real man behind the myth of Peter the Great. They have tried to strike a balance between the work of Peter's champions and the work of his detractors in order to put Peter's reign in proper perspective.

Their efforts have been complicated by the myths and prejudices not only of the eighteenth century but of the twentieth century as well. It is precisely on the issue of Peter's Westernization that the greatest difficulty arises. Through the late nineteenth century until the very eve of the revolution of 1917, one of the dominant themes of Russian intellectual life

*was Pan-Slav nationalism, with its extravagant praise of things Russian
and its almost paranoid suspicion of outside, non-Slavic influences. The
effect of such a point of view can be seen in the following conclusion of
Vasili Klyuchevsky, the greatest Russian historian of the generation just
before the revolution. "He was not a blind admirer of the West, on the
contrary, he mistrusted it, and was not deluded into thinking that he could
establish cordial relations with the West, for he knew that the West
mistrusted his country, and was hostile to it. . . . Thus for Peter
association with Europe was only a means to an end, and not an end
in itself."* [3]

*Russian hostility toward the West was only increased by the revolution
and by the events of Russian history ever since. The kindest treatment
Peter the Great has ever received at the hands of Soviet historians is a
kind of faint praise for his advancing of Russia's modernization. But even
that faint praise is no longer heard: Peter's Westernization is now simply
denounced as "cosmopolitanism,"* [4] *and work on the editing of the
documentary sources for Peter's reign has been halted indefinitely.*

*Despite such difficulties, a consensus view of Peter the Great is finally
beginning to appear among modern, non-Soviet Russian historians. That
view is represented in the following selection from* A History of Russia
*by the American scholar Nicholas V. Riasanovsky, considered by many
Russian historians to be the best general treatment of Russia's history.*

AFTER PETER took over the conduct of state affairs and began to reform
Muscovy, he found few collaborators. His own family, the court circles,
and the boyar duma [5] overwhelmingly opposed change. Because he discovered little support at the top of the state structure, and also because he
never attached much importance to origin or rank, the sovereign proceeded to obtain assistants wherever possible. Before long an extremely
mixed but on the whole able group emerged. . . .

Among foreigners, the tsar had the valuable aid of some of his old
friends, such as Patrick Gordon and the Swiss Francis Lefort, who
played a prominent role until his early death in 1699. Later such able
newcomers from Germany as the diplomat Andrew Ostermann and the
military expert Burkhard Münnich joined the sovereign's entourage. Some
of his numerous foreign assistants, for example, the Scot James Bruce
who helped with the artillery, mining, the navy and other matters, had
been born in Russia and belonged to the second generation of foreign
settlers in Muscovy.

Russian assistants to Peter ranged over the entire social gamut. . . .

[3] Vasili Klyuchevsky, *Peter the Great,* Liliana Archibald, (London: Macmillan,
1961), pp. 262–63.
[4] *Rewriting Russian History, Soviet Interpretations of Russia's Past,* ed. Cyril E.
Black, 2nd ed. (New York: Random House, 1962), p. 254.
[5] The old council of nobility.—ED.

War against Turkey was the first major action of Peter I after he took the government of Russia into his own hands in 1694, following the death of his mother.[6] In fighting Turkey, the protector of the Crimean Tartars and the power controlling the Black Sea and its southern Russian shore, the new monarch followed in the steps of his predecessors. However, before long it became apparent that he managed his affairs differently. The war began in 1695, and the first Russian campaign against Azov failed: supplied by sea, the fortress remained impregnable to the Muscovite army. Then, in one winter, the tsar built a fleet in Voronezh on the Don River. He worked indefatigably himself, as well as ordering and urging others, and utilized to the best advantage the knowledge of all available foreign specialists along with his own previously acquired knowledge. By displaying his tremendous energy everywhere, Peter the Great brought thirty sea-going vessels and about a thousand transport barges to Azov in May 1696. Some of the Russian fleet, it might be noted, had been built as far away as Moscow and assembled in Voronezh. This time besieged by sea as well as by land, the Turks surrendered Azov in July.

With a view toward a further struggle against Turkey and a continuing augmentation and modernization of the Russian armed forces, the tsar next sent fifty young men to study, above all shipbuilding and navigation, in Holland, Italy, and England. Peter dispatched groups of Russians to study abroad several more times in his reign. After the students returned, the sovereign often examined them personally. In addition to experts, the tsar needed allies to prosecute war against Turkey. The desire to form a mighty coalition against the Ottoman Empire, and an intense interest in the West, prompted Peter to organize a large embassy to visit a number of European countries and—a most unusual act for a Muscovite ruler—to travel with the embassy.

Headed by Lefort, the party of about 250 men set out in March 1697. The sovereign journeyed incognito under the name of Peter Mikhailov. His identity, however, remained no secret to the rulers and officials of the countries he visited or to the crowds which frequently gathered around him. The tsar engaged in a number of important talks on diplomatic and other state matters. But, above all, he tried to learn as much as possible from the West. He seemed most concerned with navigation, but he also tried to absorb other technical skills and crafts, together with the ways and manners and, in fact, the entire life of Europe as he saw it. As the so-called Grand Embassy progressed across the continent and as Peter Mikhailov also took trips of his own, most notably to the British Isles, he obtained some first-hand knowledge of the Baltic provinces of Sweden, Prussia, and certain other German states, and of Holland, England, and the Hapsburg Empire. From Vienna the tsar intended to go to Italy, but instead he rushed back to Moscow at news of a rebellion of the streltsy. Altogether Peter the Great spent eighteen months abroad in 1697–98.

[6] Who had served as his regent.—ED.

At that time over 750 foreigners, especially Dutchmen, were recruited to serve in Russia. Again in 1702 and at other times, the tsar invited Europeans of every nationality—except Jews, whom he considered parasitic—to come to his realm, promising to subsidize passage, provide advantageous employment, and assure religious tolerance and separate law courts.

The streltsy had already caused trouble to Peter and suffered punishment on the eve of the tsar's journey to the West—in fact delaying the journey. Although the new conspiracy—that was aimed at deposing Peter and putting Sophia [7] in power had been effectively dealt with before the sovereign's return, the tsar acted with exceptional violence and severity. After investigation and torture more than a thousand streltsy were executed, and their mangled bodies were exposed to the public as a salutary lesson. Sophia was forced to become a nun, and the same fate befell Peter's wife, Eudoxia, who had sympathized with the rebels.

If the gruesome death of the streltsy symbolized the destruction of the old order, many signs indicated the coming of the new. After he returned from the West, the tsar began to demand that beards be cut and foreign dress be worn by courtiers, officials, and the military. With the beginning of the new century, the sovereign changed the Russian calendar: henceforth years were to be counted from the birth of Christ, not the creation of the world, and they were to commence on the first of January, not the first of September. More important, Peter the Great rapidly proceeded to reorganize his army according to the Western pattern.

The Grand Embassy failed to further Peter the Great's designs against Turkey. But, although European powers proved unresponsive to the proposal of a major war with the Ottomans, other political opportunities emerged. Before long Peter joined the military alliance against Sweden organized by Augustus II, ruler of Saxony and Poland. . . .

In modern European history the Great Northern War was one of the important wars and Poltava one of the decisive battles. The Russian victory over Sweden and the resulting Treaty of Nystadt meant that Russia became firmly established on the Baltic, acquiring its essential "window into Europe," and that in fact it replaced Sweden as the dominant power in the north of the continent. Moreover, Russia not only humiliated Sweden but also won a preponderant position vis-à-vis its ancient rival Poland, became directly involved in German affairs—a relationship which included marital alliances arranged by the tsar for his and his half-brother Ivan V's daughters—and generally stepped forth as a major European power. . . .

In regard to internal affairs during the reign of Peter the Great, we find that scholars have taken two extreme and opposite approaches. On the one hand, the tsar's reforming of Russia has been presented as a series, or rather a jumble, of disconnected *ad hoc* measures necessitated by the exigencies of the moment, especially by the pressure of the Great Northern

[7] Peter's older half-sister.—ED.

War. Contrariwise, the same activity has been depicted as the execution of a comprehensive, radically new, and well-integrated program. In a number of ways, the first view seems closer to the facts. As Kliuchevsky pointed out, only a single year in Peter the Great's whole reign, 1724, passed entirely without war, while no more than another thirteen peaceful months could be added for the entire period. . . .

Yet a balanced judgment has to allow something to the opposite point of view as well. Although Peter the Great was preoccupied during most of his reign with the Great Northern War and although he had to sacrifice much else to its successful prosecution, his reforming of Russia was by no means limited to hectic measures to bolster the war effort. In fact, he wanted to Westernize and modernize all of the Russian government, society, life, and culture, and even if his efforts fell far short of this stupendous goal, failed to dovetail, and left huge gaps, the basic pattern emerges, nevertheless, with sufficient clarity. Countries of the West served as the emperor's model. We shall see, however, when we turn to specific legislation, that Peter did not merely copy from the West, but tried to adapt Western institutions to Russian needs and possibilities. The very number and variety of European states and societies offered the Russian ruler a rich initial choice. It should be added that with time Peter the Great became more interested in general issues and broader patterns. Also, while the reformer was no theoretician, he had the makings of a visionary. With characteristic grandeur and optimism he saw ahead the image of a modern, powerful, prosperous, and educated country, and it was to the realization of that image that he dedicated his life. Both the needs of the moment and longer-range aims must therefore be considered in evaluating Peter the Great's reforms. Other fundamental questions to be asked about them include their relationship to the Russian past, their borrowing from the West —and, concurrently, their modification of Western models—their impact on Russia, and their durability.

Peter the Great hit Muscovy with a tremendous impact. To many of his contemporaries he appeared as either a virtually superhuman hero or the Antichrist. It was the person of the emperor that drove Russia forward in war and reform and inspired the greatest effort and utmost devotion. It was also against Peter the Great that the streltsy, the Bashkirs, the inhabitants of Astrakhan, and the motley followers of Bulavin staged their rebellions, while uncounted others, Old Believers and Orthodox, fled to the borderlands and into the forests to escape his reach.[8] Rumor spread

---

[8] We have already noted the revolt of the *streltsy*. In Astrakhan an uprising took place in 1705–1707 against Western influence and was headed by a renegade member of the *streltsy* and a fanatic monk. Bulavin led a revolt of the Don Cossacks in 1707 over the same issue and again with religious overtones. The Bashkirs were Turkish subjects of Peter in the lower Volga area who rebelled against heightened Russian interference at about the same time. All these revolts were eventually put down. The Orthodox party and the Old Believers were conservative factions that were opposed to Peter's Westernization and often involved in revolt.—ED.

and legends grew that the reformer was not a son of Tsar Alexis, but a foreigner who substituted himself for the true tsar during the latter's journey abroad, that he was an imposter, a usurper, indeed the Antichrist. Peter himself contributed much to this polarization of opinion. He too saw things in black and white, hating old Muscovy and believing himself to be the creator of a new Russia. Intolerance, violence, and compulsion became the distinguishing traits of the new regime, and St. Petersburg—built in the extreme northwestern corner of the country, in almost inaccessible swamps at a cost in lives far exceeding that of Poltava—became its fitting symbol. The emperor's very size, strength, energy, and temperament intensified his popular image. . . .

. . . Scholarly investigations of the last hundred years, together with large-scale publication of materials on the reformer's reign, undertaken by a number of men from Golikov to Bogoslovsky, have established beyond question many close connections between Peter the Great and the Muscovite past. Entire major aspects of the reformer's reign, for example, foreign policy and social relations and legislation, testified to a remarkable continuity with the preceding period. Even the reformer's desire to curb and control ecclesiastical landholding had excellent Muscovite precedents. The central issue itself, the process of Westernization, had begun long before the reformer and had gathered momentum rapidly in the seventeenth century. In the words of a modern scholar, Peter the Great simply marked Russia's transition from an unconscious to a conscious following of her historical path.

Although in the perspective of Russian history Peter the Great appears human rather than superhuman, the reformer is still of enormous importance. Quite possibly Russia was destined to be Westernized, but Peter the Great cannot be denied the role of the chief executor of this fate. At the very least the emperor's reign brought a tremendous speeding up of the irreversible process of Westernization, and it established state policy and control, where formerly individual choice and chance prevailed.

Suggestions for Further Reading

THE HISTORIOGRAPHY OF Peter the Great divides along the line separating Rusian national scholars from Westerners. As we observed in the headnote to the Riasanovsky selection, above, this separation is a product not only of the Soviet revolution but of the earlier Pan-Slav movement with its deep suspicions of Western influence. Of this viewpoint of Russian nationalist historians, the best example is Vasily O. Kluchevsky, whose *A History of Russia,* tr. C. J. Hogarth, 5 vols. (New York: Russell and Russell, 1960), originally published in Russia between 1911 and 1931, is among the monuments of modern Russian historical writing. The section of Kluchevsky's history dealing with Peter has been separately published: *Peter the Great,* tr. Liliana Archibald (London: Macmillan, 1961). To some extent the views of Kluchevsky are seconded by M. T. Florinsky, *Russia: A History and an Interpretation,* 2 vols. (New York: Macmillan, 1953), which many admirers consider contains the best general account of Peter the Great. See also his *Russia: A Short History* (New York: Macmillan, 1965). For the Soviet views see the essay by C. E. Black, "The Reforms of Peter the Great" in *Rewriting Russian History, Soviet Interpretations of Russia's Past,* ed. Cyril E. Black, 2nd rev. ed. (New York: Random House, 1962).

In the Western tradition, probably the best full-scale biography of Peter is Ian Grey, *Peter the Great, Emperor of All Russia* (Philadelphia: Lippincott, 1960), while the two best brief accounts are B. H. Sumner, *Peter the Great and the Emergence of Russia,* "Teach Yourself History Library" (London: English Universities Press, 1950), and L. Jay Oliva, *Russia in the Era of Peter the Great* (Englewood Cliffs, N.J.: Prentice-Hall, 1969). Students may prefer the exciting popular biography by Harold Lamb, *The City and the Tsar: Peter the Great and the Move to the West, 1648–1762* (New York: Doubleday, 1948). For the interpretive problems of Peter, see *Peter the Great, Reformer or Revolutionary,* ed. Marc Raeff, rev. ed. (Boston: Heath, 1972).

For the role and setting of such figures as Lomonosov and Shcherbatov, see Hans Rogger, *National Consciousness in Eighteenth-Century Russia* (Cambridge, Mass.: Harvard University Press, 1960), and Marc Raeff, *Origins of the Russian Intelligentsia, the Eighteenth-Century Nobility* (New York: Harcourt, Brace and World, 1966).

Of brief general accounts of Russian history for the background to Peter the Great, the best is Nicholas V. Riasanovsky, *A History of Russia,* 2nd ed. (New York: Oxford University Press, 1969), excerpted in this chapter.

But students should also see the fine narrative history, George Vernadsky, *A History of Russia,* 6th rev. ed. (New Haven, Conn.: Yale University Press, 1971), and the exciting and readable James H. Billington, *The Icon and the Axe, An Interpretive History of Russian Culture* (New York: Knopf, 1966). For the role of Russia in Europe, see J. B. Wolf, *The Emergence of the Great Powers, 1685–1715,* cited for the preceding chapter.

Jean-Jacques Rousseau and the Spirit of Revolution

There was never a more unlikely harbinger of revolution than Jean-Jacques Rousseau nor, for that matter, a more unlikely subject for an enduring literary cult. Yet by the time of his death in 1778, his books were already famous, and scarcely more than a decade later, he was being celebrated as the godfather of the French Revolution.

Rousseau had practically no education. He was born in Geneva in 1712 and orphaned at an early age. Following his parents' deaths, friends and relatives took him in and apprenticed him to a number of crafts, including engraving and watchmaking. Succeeding at none of these, he gave them up for a wandering life that took him to Italy. After a time he returned to Switzerland, where, in Neuchâtel, he passed himself off as a composer and music teacher. In 1742 he departed for Paris with a harebrained scheme for a new system of musical notation he had invented—though he could not read a note of music!

Rousseau's musical notation system came to nothing, but while in Paris he was befriended by Denis Diderot, who allowed him to write some articles on music and political economy for the *Encyclopédie* that he was compiling. In 1749 Diderot encouraged Rousseau to submit an essay to a contest sponsored by the Academy of Dijon on the subject of whether the revival of the sciences and arts had been beneficial or detrimental to morals. Following Diderot's advice, Rousseau took the negative side. His essay won the prize, and Rousseau became an instant literary celebrity.

Despite the limitations of his background, Rousseau had a quick and retentive mind; a breathless, intense, personal style; and a passion for ideas. The Dijon prize essay, his *Discourse on the Sciences and Arts*, was the first of a series of discourses, treatises, articles, and books—each of which was a sensation in one way or another—that made Rousseau the most widely read author of his time, not excepting even the great Voltaire. In 1755 he published a revised and expanded version of his prize-winning essay, *A Discourse on the Origin and Foundations of Inequality*. Then, in the next five years, he wrote *Julie, or the New Héloïse*, a sentimental novel so popular that, as a result of it, Rousseau succeeded the Englishman Samuel Richardson as the leading spokesman for the cult of sensibility; a moral-political tract entitled *The Social Contract*; and, finally another novel, *Émile*, which was actually a treatise on education. The ideas that emerged from these writings were so important, the literary style so compelling, and the author himself so controversial that Rousseau's works gained almost universal popularity.

The framework of Rousseau's ideas began to take shape in the prize-winning essay of 1749, in which he argued that civilization, rather than having advanced human morality, had instead corrupted the inherent goodness of human nature. In his revision of the discourse, he expanded this argument, claiming that civilized society had introduced artificial distinctions of wealth and position that further corrupted the sublime equality and moral decency of the state of nature. *The Social Contract* opens with these famous words, "Man was born free, and he is everywhere in chains," and goes on to insist that, by the social contract through which primitive man surrendered his individual right to the collective society, he did not surrender his claim to practical equality and individual liberty. *Émile* begins with another famous sentence, "Everything is good as it leaves the hands of the Creator; everything degenerates in the hands of man." This novel demonstrates, through the account of its hero's education, how by proper instruction man could regain the happy state now denied him by civilized society and in the process become a free and responsible citizen. Rousseau called one of the sections of *Émile* "The Profession of Faith of the Savoyard Vicar," and he put into the mouth of his character a devastating attack upon both Protestantism and Catholicism for their part in the debasement of natural man.

Largely as a result of this attack, Rousseau was condemned by both the Catholic Sorbonne in Paris and the Calvinist Consistory in Geneva, and warrants for his arrest were issued in both cities. Public authorities were already suspicious of Rousseau because of his other radical ideas, for unlike most of his contemporaries, he insisted on publishing his works and proclaiming his ideas under his own name. But the publication of *Émile* was the last straw. Rousseau was forced to flee from one refuge to another across Europe, even stopping briefly in England in 1766, where he was the guest of the historian and philosopher David Hume.

By this time, Rousseau's health had begun to fail, and he suffered from a number of ailments. His actual ailments, real enough, began to blend with others that existed only in his troubled mind. He shunned society and fled from his legion of admirers—in one of his residences, he even had a trap door to the cellar into which he would dart at the approach of a stranger. He quarreled with most of his friends and benefactors, including Hume and Diderot, and accused them of plotting against him. His last years were devoted to attempts to justify his life, his work, and his ideas. The *Confessions* were part of this effort, and, though the book was not published until after his death, he would read from the manuscript in any salon where he could find an audience. Rousseau died in 1778, convinced that he was a failure.

It was Voltaire's opinion that Rousseau was quite mad. This judgment, however, was neither charitable nor entirely correct. Rousseau was certainly a spectacular eccentric, but it was not his eccentricity that bothered critics like Voltaire. Most of them were among the leaders of the broad philosophical and literary movement that dominated the eighteenth century—the Enlightenment. This period is often called the Age of Reason, and with considerable justice, for its leading motif was a belief in reason. The men of the Enlightenment tended to believe that the capacity for reason belonged not to the great mass of the people but to an intellectual elite. They tended not only to accept monarchy but to extol as the best form of government a monarchy committed to reason, the so-called enlightened despotism. They tended to be hostile to religiosity and contemptuous of organized religion, but they were also optimistic about the future of mankind and had a sublime confidence in the inevitability of human progress. In spite of the fact that Rousseau shared many of the ideas of the Enlightenment, he did not really belong to it. He was as suspicious of reason as his friends were of religion, and he was as profoundly, if erratically, religious as they were skeptical. Rousseau was an uncompromising democrat and egalitarian, but, at the same time, he was bitterly pessimistic about the future of humanity. His friends and enemies alike simply did not understand him. They rejected his often-proclaimed sincerity as hypocrisy and were convinced that his intense personalism was only self-serving. Voltaire maliciously observed to d'Alembert that "Jean-Jacques would be delighted to be hanged, provided his name was mentioned." [1] Even Hume, in the end, found little to praise in Rousseau except his eloquence, and he doubted gravely that eloquence alone could support the extravagance of Rousseau's ideas.

Yet those very ideas, so alien to the men of the Enlightenment, were

---

[1] Quoted in Lester G. Crocker, *Jean-Jacques Rousseau, The Prophetic Voice (1758–1778)* (New York: Macmillan, 1973), p. 244.

the wave of the future. A modern scholar has called them "the most radical and comprehensive social criticism ever formulated up to his time, a criticism whose impact on modern society was and remains incalculably great." [2] Rousseau's criticism of society was to be the bridge between the Age of Reason and the Age of Revolution. In *Émile* he wrote, "We are approaching a state of crisis and a century of revolutions." The philosopher Ernst Cassirer, in a famous essay on Rousseau, observed that although "Rousseau, the outcast and the eccentric, shied away from the turmoil of the market place and the noise of battle . . . the truly revolutionary impetus emanated from him, not from the men who represented and dominated the public state of mind of contemporary France." [3]

[2] J. Christopher Herold, "The Solitary Wanderer," *Horizon,* 5, no. 3 (1964), 95.
[3] Ernst Cassirer, *The Question of Jean-Jacques Rousseau,* ed. and trans. Peter Gay, (New York: Columbia University Press, 1954), p. 69.

The Social Contract

JEAN-JACQUES ROUSSEAU

*The revolutionary impetus of Rousseau's ideas emanated, more than
from any of his other works, from the little treatise he wrote in 1762 called*
The Social Contract. *Considered by one modern authority to be the
"capstone" of Rousseau's system of thought,* The Social Contract *was
to be the most enduring, the most controversial, and the most influential
of his works. It was also to become the manifesto of the French
Revolution. Despite its faulty history and naive anthropological
constructs, it clearly proclaimed such ideas as popular sovereignty, the
general will, the inevitable corruption of princely power, and, of course,
the idea of the primal contract among men that is the only possible basis
of human society and government—the contract that, at least by
inference, the existing governments of Europe had violated.*

We turn now to sample this famous work.

MAN WAS BORN free, and he is everywhere in chains. Those who think
themselves the masters of others are indeed greater slaves than they.
How did this transformation come about? I do not know. How can it be
made legitimate? That question I believe I can answer.

If I were to consider only force and the effects of force, I should say:
"So long as a people is constrained to obey, and obeys, it does well; but
as soon as it can shake off the yoke, and shakes it off, it does better; for
since it regains its freedom by the same right as that which removed it,
a people is either justified in taking back its freedom, or there is no
justifying those who took it away." But the social order is a sacred right
which serves as a basis for all other rights. And as it is not a natural right,
it must be one founded on covenants. The problem is to determine what
those covenants are. . . .

I assume that men reach a point where the obstacles to their preservation in a state of nature prove greater than the strength that each man has
to preserve himself in that state. Beyond this point, the primitive condition cannot endure, for then the human race will perish if it does not change
its mode of existence.

Since men cannot create new forces, but merely combine and control
those which already exist, the only way in which they can preserve themselves is by uniting their separate powers in a combination strong enough
to overcome any resistance, uniting them so that their powers are directed
by a single motive and act in concert.

Such a sum of forces can be produced only by the union of separate men, but as each man's own strength and liberty are the chief instruments of his preservation, how can he merge his with others' without putting himself in peril and neglecting the care he owes to himself? This difficulty, which brings me back to my present subject, may be expressed in these words:

"How to find a form of association which will defend the person and goods of each member with the collective force of all, and under which each individual, while uniting himself with the others, obeys no one but himself, and remains as free as before." This is the fundamental problem to which the social contract holds the solution.

The articles of this contract are so precisely determined by the nature of the act, that the slightest modification must render them null and void; they are such that, though perhaps never formally stated, they are everywhere the same, everywhere tacitly admitted and recognized; and if ever the social pact is violated, every man regains his original rights and, recovering his natural freedom, loses that social freedom for which he exchanged it.

These articles of association, rightly understood, are reducible to a single one, namely the total alienation by each associate of himself and all his rights to the whole community. Thus, in the first place, as every individual gives himself absolutely, the conditions are the same for all, and precisely because they are the same for all, it is in no one's interest to make the conditions onerous for others.

Secondly, since the alienation is unconditional, the union is as perfect as it could be, and no individual associate has any longer any rights to claim; for if rights were left to individuals, in the absence of any higher authority to judge between them and the public, each individual, being his own judge in some causes, would soon demand to be his own judge in all; and in this way the state of nature would be kept in being, and the association inevitably become either tyrannical or void.

Finally, since each man gives himself to all, he gives himself to no one; and since there is no associate over whom he does not gain the same rights as others gain over him, each man recovers the equivalent of everything he loses, and in the bargain he acquires more power to preserve what he has.

If, then, we eliminate from the social pact everything that is not essential to it, we find it comes down to this: "Each one of us puts into the community his person and all his powers under the supreme direction of the general will; and as a body, we incorporate every member as an indivisible part of the whole."

Immediately, in place of the individual person of each contracting party, this act of association creates an artificial and collective body composed of as many members as there are voters in the assembly, and by this same act that body acquires its unity, its common *ego*, its life and its will. The public person thus formed by the union of all other persons was once called the *city*, and is now known as the *republic* or the *body politic*. In its passive role it is called the *state*, when it plays an active role it is the *sovereign*; and when it is compared to others of its own kind, it is a *power*. Those who are associated in it take collectively the name of *a people*, and call themselves individually *citizens*, in so far as they share in the sovereign power, and *subjects*, in so far as they put themselves under the laws of the state. . . .

As soon as the multitude is united thus in a single body, no one can injure any one of the members without attacking the whole, still less injure the whole without each member feeling it. Duty and self-interest thus equally oblige the two contracting parties to give each other mutual aid; and the same men should seek to bring together in this dual relationship, all the advantages that flow from it.

Now, as the sovereign is formed entirely of the individuals who compose it, it has not, nor could it have, any interest contrary to theirs; and so the sovereign has no need to give guarantees to the subjects, because it is impossible for a body to wish to hurt all of its members, and, as we shall see, it cannot hurt any particular member. The sovereign by the mere fact that it is, is always all that it ought to be. . . .

Hence, in order that the social pact shall not be an empty formula, it is tacitly implied in that commitment—which alone can give force to all others—that whoever refuses to obey the general will shall be constrained to do so by the whole body, which means nothing other than that he shall be forced to be free; for this is the condition which, by giving each citizen to the nation, secures him against all personal dependence, it is the condition which shapes both the design and the working of the political machine, and which alone bestows justice on civil contracts—without it, such contracts would be absurd, tyrannical and liable to the grossest abuse. . . .

Suppose we draw up a balance sheet, so that the losses and gains may be readily compared. What man loses by the social contract is his natural liberty and the absolute right to anything that tempts him and that he can take; what he gains by the social contract is civil ilberty and the legal right of property in what he possesses. . . .

If the state, or the nation, is nothing other than a legal person the life of which consists in the union of its members and if the most important of its cares is its own preservation, it must have a universal and compelling power to move and dispose of each part in whatever manner is beneficial to the whole. Just as nature gives each man an absolute power over all his own limbs, the social pact gives the body politic an absolute power over all its members; and it is this same power which, directed by the general will, bears, as I have said, the name of sovereignty.

However, we have to consider beside the public person those private persons who compose it, and whose life and liberty is naturally independent of it. Here we have to distinguish clearly the respective rights of the citizens and of the sovereign, and distinguish those duties which the citizens have as subjects from the natural rights which they ought to enjoy as men.

We have agreed that each man alienates by the social pact only that part of his power, his goods and his liberty which is the concern of the community; but it must also be admitted that the sovereign alone is judge of what is of such concern.

Whatever services the citizen can render the state, he owes whenever the sovereign demands them; but the sovereign, on its side, may not impose on the subjects any burden which is not necessary to the community. . . .

The world has seen a thousand splendid nations that could not have accepted good laws, and even those that might have accepted them could have done so only for short periods of their long history. Nations, like men, are teachable only in their youth; with age they become incorrigible. Once customs are established and prejudices rooted, reform is a dangerous and fruitless enterprise; a people cannot bear to see its evils touched, even if only to be eradicated; it is like a stupid pusillanimous invalid who trembles at the sight of a physician.

I am not denying that just as certain afflictions unhinge men's minds and banish their memory of the past, so there are certain violent epochs and revolutions in states which have the same effect on peoples that psychological shocks may have on individuals; only instead of forgetting the past, they look back on it in horror, and then the state, after being consumed by civil war, is born again, so to speak, from its own ashes, and leaps from the arms of death to regain the vigour of youth. Such was the experience of Sparta at the time of Lycurgus, of Rome after the Tarquins, and, in the modern world, of Holland and Switzerland after the expulsion of the tyrants.

But such events are unusual; they are exceptional cases to be explained by the special constitution of the states concerned. It could not even happen twice to the same people; because although a people can make itself free while it is still uncivilized, it cannot do so when its civil energies are worn out. Disturbances may well destroy a civil society without a revolution being able to restore it, so that as soon as the chains are broken, the state falls apart and exists no longer; then what is needed is a master, not a liberator. Free peoples, remember this maxim: liberty can be gained, but never *regained*. . . .

We have seen that the legislative power belongs, and can only belong, to the people. On the other hand, it is easy to see . . . that executive power cannot belong to the generality of the people as legislative or sovereign, since executive power is exercised only in particular acts which are outside the province of law and therefore outside the province of the sovereign which can act only to make laws.

The public force thus needs its own agent to call it together and put it into action in accordance with the instructions of the general will, to serve also as a means of communication between the state and the sovereign, and in a sense to do for the public person what is done for the individual by the union of soul and body. This is the reason why the state needs a government, something often unhappily confused with the sovereign, but of which it is really only the minister.

What, then, is the government? An intermediary body established between the subjects and the sovereign for their mutual communication, a body charged with the execution of the laws and the maintenance of freedom, both civil and political. . . .

Just as the particular will acts unceasingly against the general will, so does the government continually exert itself against the sovereign. And the more this exertion increases, the more the constitution becomes corrupt, and, as in this case there is no distinct corporate will to resist the will of the prince and so to balance it, sooner or later it is inevitable that the prince will oppress the sovereign and break the social treaty. This is the inherent and inescapable defect which, from the birth of the political body, tends relentlessly to destroy it, just as old age and death destroy the body of man. . . .

From these explanations, it follows . . . that the act which institutes the government is not a contract but a law, and that the holders of the executive power are not the people's masters but its officers; and that the people can appoint them and dismiss them as it pleases; and that there is no question of their contracting, but of obeying; and that in discharging the functions which the state imposes on them, they are only doing their duty as citizens, without having any sort of right to argue terms.

Thus when it happens that the people institutes a hereditary government, whether monarchical in one family, or aristocratic in a class of citizens, it does not enter into any undertaking; hereditary government is simply a provisional form that it gives to the administration until such time as it pleases to arrange it differently.

It is true that such changes are always dangerous, and that one should never touch an established government unless it has become incompatible with the public welfare; but such circumspection is a precept of politics and not a rule of law; and the state is no more bound to leave civil authority to its magistrates than military authority to its generals. . . .

In the end, when the state, on the brink of ruin, can maintain itself only in an empty and illusory form, when the social bond is broken in every heart, when the meanest interest impudently flaunts the sacred name of the public good, then the general will is silenced: everyone, animated by secret motives, ceases to speak as a citizen any more than as if the state had never existed; and the people enacts in the guise of laws iniquitous decrees which have private interests as their only end.

Does it follow from this that the general will is annihilated or corrupted? No, that is always unchanging, incorruptible and pure, but it is subordinated to other wills which prevail over it. . . .

Rousseau and the Tyrannical Majority
J. L. TALMON

Rousseau has always been a figure of controversy. As we have seen, he was almost deified by the early leaders of the French Revolution. Not surprisingly, he was hated by its enemies with equal intensity. The Englishman Edmund Burke called him "the insane Socrates of the National Assembly." This controversy has continued in the enormous mass of recent criticism, theorizing, and speculation about Rousseau and especially about his theories of government and society. One of the most influential modern interpretations of Rousseau is that of the distinguished Israeli historian J. L. Talmon, contained in his The Origins of Totalitarian Democracy. *Like many Jewish scholars, Talmon has been interested in discovering the sources of the totalitarianism that produced the Jewish holocaust of Hitler's Germany. He has found at least one source in what he calls the "totalitarian democracy" that had its origin in the eighteenth century and its first historic demonstration in the French Revolution. He sees Rousseau as its prophet.*

Talmon views Rousseau as a "tormented paranoiac," a shattered personality whose prescriptions for society—despite their noble intentions—are as contradictory as the man himself. Those prescriptions, in Talmon's opinion, add up to the most dangerously paradoxical of all modern political notions—totalitarian democracy, the tyranny of the majority. In defense of Rousseau, Talmon notes that we cannot expect an eighteenth-century man to express twentieth-century ideas and that the absolutist nature of his theories, both of man and of society, belongs generally to the intellectual order of the eighteenth century. Nevertheless, he claims, Rousseau was the principal architect of the theoretical structure that, in its justification of the tyranny of the majority

and the dehumanization of the individual, ultimately produced, in the
twentieth century, the fearful tyranny of the right in Nazi Germany and
the equally fearful tyranny of the left in Soviet Russia.
    Here is Talmon's analysis.

A MOTHERLESS vagabond starved of warmth and affection, having his
dream of intimacy constantly frustrated by human callousness, real or
imaginary, Rousseau could never decide what he wanted, to release
human nature or to moralize it by breaking it; to be alone or a part of
human company. He could never make up his mind whether man was
made better or worse, happier or more miserable, by people. Rousseau
was one of the most ill-adjusted and egocentric natures who have left a
record of their predicament. He was a bundle of contradictions, a recluse
and anarchist, yearning to return to nature, given to reverie, in revolt
against all social conventions, sentimental and lacrimose, abjectly self-
conscious and at odds with his environment, on the one hand; and the
admirer of Sparta and Rome, the preacher of discipline and the submergence of the individual in the collective entity, on the other. The secret
of this dual personality was that the disciplinarian was the envious dream
of the tormented paranoiac. *The Social Contract* was the sublimation of
the *Discourse on the Origins of Inequality.* . . . Rousseau, the teacher of
romantic spontaneity of feeling, was obsessed with the idea of man's
cupidity as the root cause of moral degeneration and social evil. Hence
his apotheosis of Spartan ascetic virtue and his condemnation of civilization in so far as civilization is the expression of the urge to conquer, the
desire to shine and the release of human vitality, without reference to
morality. He had that intense awareness of the reality of human rivalry
peculiar to people who have experienced it in their souls. Either out of
a sense of guilt or out of weariness, they long to be delivered from the
need for external recognition and the challenge of rivalry. . . .
    It was of vital importance to Rousseau to save the ideal of liberty,
while insisting on discipline. He was very proud and had a keen sense
of the heroic. Rousseau's thinking is thus dominated by a highly fruitful
but dangerous ambiguity. On the one hand, the individual is said to obey
nothing but his own will; on the other, he is urged to conform to some
objective criterion. The contradiction is resolved by the claim that this
external criterion is his better, higher, or real self, man's inner voice, as
Rousseau calls it. Hence, even if constrained to obey the external
standard, man cannot complain of being coerced, for in fact he is merely
being made to obey his own true self. He is thus still free; indeed freer
than before. For freedom is the triumph of the spirit over natural, elemental instinct. It is the acceptance of moral obligation and the disciplining
of irrational and selfish urges by reason and duty. The acceptance of the

obligations laid down in *The Social Contract* marks the birth of man's personality and his initiation into freedom. Every exercise of the general will constitutes a reaffirmation of man's freedom. . . .

Ultimately the general will is to Rousseau something like a mathematical truth or a Platonic idea. It has an objective existence of its own, whether perceived or not. It has nevertheless to be discovered by the human mind. But having discovered it, the human mind simply cannot honestly refuse to accept it. In this way the general will is at the same time outside us and within us. Man is not invited to express his personal preferences. He is not asked for his approval. He is asked whether the given proposal is or is not in conformity with the general will. "If my particular opinion had carried the day, I should have achieved the opposite of what was my will; and it is in that case that I should not have been free." For freedom is the capacity of ridding oneself of considerations, interests, preferences and prejudices, whether personal or collective, which obscure the objectively true and good, which, if I am true to my true nature, I am bound to will. What applies to the individual applies equally to the people. Man and people have to be brought to choose freedom and if necessary to be forced to be free.

The general will becomes ultimately a question of enlightenment and morality. Although it should be the achievement of the general will to create harmony and unanimity, the whole aim of political life is really to educate and prepare men to will the general will without any sense of constraint. Human egotism must be rooted out, and human nature changed. "Each individual, who is by himself a complete and solitary whole, would have to be transformed into part of a greater whole from which he receives his life and being." Individualism will have to give place to collectivism, egoism to virtue, which is the conformity of the personal to the general will. The Legislator "must, in a word, take away from man his resources and give him instead new ones alien to him, and incapable of being made use of without the help of other men. The more completely these natural resources are annihilated, the greater and the more lasting are those which he acquires, and the more stable and perfect the new institutions, so that if each citizen is nothing and can do nothing without the rest, and the resources acquired by the whole are equal or superior to the aggregate of the resources of all individuals, it may be said that legislation is at the highest possible point of perfection." As in the case of the materialists, it is not the self-expression of the individual, the deployment of his particular faculties and the realization of his own and unique mode of existence, that is the final aim, but the loss of the individual in the collective entity by taking on its colour and principle of existence. The aim is to train men to "bear with docility the yoke of public happiness," in fact to create a new type of man, a purely political creature, without any particular private or social loyalties, any partial interests, as Rousseau would call them.

Rousseau's sovereign is the externalized general will, and, as has been said before, stands for essentially the same as the natural harmonious order. In marrying this concept with the principle of popular sovereignty, and popular self-expression, Rousseau gave rise to totalitarian democracy. The mere introduction of this latter element, coupled with the fire of Rousseau's style, lifted the eighteenth-century postulate from the plane of intellectual speculation into that of a great collective experience. It marked the birth of the modern secular religion, not merely as a system of ideas, but as a passionate faith. Rousseau's synthesis is in itself the formulation of the paradox of freedom in totalitarian democracy in terms which reveal the dilemma in the most striking form, namely, in those of will. There is such a thing as an objective general will, whether willed or not willed by anybody. To become a reality it must be willed by the people. If the people does not will it, it must be made to will it, for the general will is latent in the people's will.

Democratic ideas and rationalist premises are Rousseau's means of resolving the dilemma. According to him the general will would be discerned only if the whole people, and not a part of it or a representative body, was to make the effort. The second condition is that individual men as purely political atoms, and not groups, parties or interests, should be called upon to will. Both conditions are based upon the premise that there is such a thing as a common substance of citizenship, of which all partake, once everyone is able to divest himself of his partial interests and group loyalties. In the same way men as rational beings may arrive at the same conclusions, once they rid themselves of their particular passions and interests and cease to depend on "imaginary" standards which obscure their judgment. Only when all are acting together as an assembled people, does man's nature as citizen come into active existence. It would not, if only a part of the nation were assembled to will the general will. They would express a partial will. Moreover, even the fact that all have willed something does not yet make it the expression of the general will, if the right disposition on the part of those who will it was not there. A will does not become general because it is willed by all, only when it is willed in comformity to the objective will.

Exercise of sovereignty is not conceived here as the interplay of interests, the balancing of views, all equally deserving a hearing, the weighing of various interests. It connotes the endorsement of a truth, self-identification on the part of those who exercise sovereignty with some general interest which is presumed to be the fountain of all identical individual interests. Political parties are not considered as vehicles of the various currents of opinion, but representatives of partial interests, at variance with the general interest, which is regarded as almost tangible. It is of great importance to realize that what is to-day considered as an essential concomitant of democracy, namely, diversity of views and interests, was far from being regarded as essential by the eighteenth-century fathers of democracy. Their original postulates were unity and unanimity. The affirmation of the principle of diversity came later, when the totalitarian implications of the principle of homogeneity had been demonstrated in Jacobin dictatorship.

This expectation of unanimity was only natural in an age which, starting with the idea of the natural order, declared war on all privileges and inequalities. The very eighteenth-century concept of the nation as opposed to estates implied a homogeneous entity. Naïve and inexperienced in the working of democracy, the theorists on the eve of the Revolution were unable to regard the strains and stresses, the conflicts and struggles of a parliamentary democratic régime as ordinary things, which need not frighten anybody with the spectre of immediate ruin and confusion. . . .

Like the Physiocrats [4] Rousseau rejects any attempt to divide sovereignty. He brands it as the trick of a juggler playing with the severed limbs of an organism. For if there is only one will, sovereignty cannot be divided. Only that in place of the Physiocratic absolute monarch Rousseau puts the people. It is the people as a whole that should exercise the sovereign power, and not a representative body. An elected assembly is calculated to develop a vested interest like any other corporation. A people buys itself a master once it hands over sovereignty to a parliamentary representative body.

Now at the very foundation of the principle of direct and indivisible democracy, and the expression of unanimity, there is the implication of dictatorship, as the history of many a referendum has shown. If a constant appeal to the people as a whole, not just to a small representative body, is kept up, and at the same time unanimity is postulated, there is no escape from dictatorship. This was implied in Rousseau's emphasis on the all-important point that the leaders must put only questions of a general nature to the people, and moreover, must know how to put the right question. The question must have so obvious an answer that a different sort of answer would appear plain treason or perversion. If unanimity is what is desired, it must be engineered through intimidation, election tricks, or the organization of the spontaneous popular expression through the activists busying themselves with petitions, public demonstrations, and a violent campaign of denunciation. This was what the Jacobins and the organizers of people's petitions, revolutionary *journées*, and other forms of direct expression of the people's will read into Rousseau.

Rousseau demonstrates clearly the close relation between popular sovereignty taken to the extreme, and totalitarianism. . . . In the predemocratic age Rousseau could not realize that the originally deliberate creation of men could become transformed into a Leviathan, which might

---

[4] A school of eighteenth-century economic philosophers who held that land and agriculture were the only true sources of a nation's wealth (thus opposing the mercantilists) and that taxation should be assessed only on land values. They also supported royal absolutism.—ED.

crush its own makers. He was unaware that total and highly emotional absorption in the collective political endeavour is calculated to kill all privacy, that the excitement of the assembled crowd may exercise a most tyrannical pressure, and that the extension of the scope of politics to all spheres of human interest and endeavour, without leaving any room for the process of casual and empirical activity, was the shortest way to totalitarianism. Liberty is safer in countries where politics are not considered all-important and where there are numerous levels of non-political private and collective activity, although not so much direct popular democracy, than in countries where politics take everything in their stride, and the people sit in permanent assembly.

The Utopian Rousseau
LESTER G. CROCKER

To some scholars, Talmon's interpretation of Rousseau is as controversial as Rousseau himself. The British historian Alfred Cobban, for example, characterizes Talmon's view simply as an "onslaught" on Rousseau that trims the subject to fit Talmon's own preconceptions.[5] On the other hand, Lester G. Crocker, in his Jean-Jacques Rousseau, The Prophetic Voice (1758–1778), *the most recent major general treatment of Rousseau, agrees—although somewhat reluctantly—with Talmon's thesis. Crocker maintains, like Talmon, that Rousseau was a man of his time and that he cannot be held responsible for the uses that the future would make of his ideas. He even defends Rousseau's motives as essentially moral and humanitarian. But he also argues that the utopianism inherent in Rousseau's political theory—for all its brilliance, rationalism, and originality—when applied to human affairs makes freedom the inevitable victim.*

The Social Contract is the capstone of Rousseau's rationalistic pyramid. It is one segment of a single sociopolitical system, carefully worked out in his mind and reflecting the needs of his personality, a system designed

---

[5] Alfred Cobban, *Rousseau and the Modern State* (London: Allen & Unwin, 1964), pp. 29-31.

to make men virtuous and happy. The theoretical mode of political institutions it contains corresponds to the architectonics of his broader
plan, his grand plan, to fashion a man and a society "according to his
heart." . . .

. . . The most seminal of eighteenth-century writers, he is also the
most debated. It has been said that he was "the revolutionary thinker
who first inscribed on the political banners of modern times the opposing
slogans both of democratic and totalitarian government." "Liberal" would
be a better word than "democratic." . . . [Yet] it is obvious that both
words, "liberal" and "totalitarian," are partly anachronistic when applied
to Rousseau. He did, however, have a clear idea or model, in his beloved
Sparta, of a totalitarian collectivity. In any event, the appropriateness of
words cannot affect the appropriateness of recognizing clear tendencies.
Eighteenth-century thinkers, living in an archaic social and political structure that was out of tune with the economics and ideologies of a new stage
in Western culture, were groping for ways to reorganize society on a
rational basis and to solve the unending problem of the relation of the
individual to the group. . . .

In the *Discourse on Inequality*, Rousseau had painted a vivid picture
of a competitive society as one whose values are perverted by a false
notion of "progress" and "good," one in which men have every interest
in hating each other and in hurting each other. He saw that Western
civilization espouses a Christian ethic of brotherhood, but practices a cut-
throat, exploitative way of life.

Rousseau's apparent "primitivism" had a powerful appeal to his contemporaries, as well as to men of later times. Some followed the logic of
his *Discourse* to its obvious end, dreaming of an egalitarian, communistic
society, or even of an anarchistic social state. But Rousseau himself, as
he turned to the constructive part of his work and sought a way out of
man's dilemma, rejected primitivism. While he urged a simple way of
living and abjured none of his criticisms of society, he realized that the
simplistic solutions of "abolition" were pure fantasy. There can be no
return to innocence. Evolution is an irreversible process.

For Rousseau, society is the original sin, but it is also the testing place,
as earthly life is in the Christian tradition. The direction man must take
is not a "return to nature"—neither to the hypothetical, metaphysical
nature of "natural man," nor to the empirical laws of nature. We must
leave all this behind and forge a new destiny, unknown to nature, one
that is truly man's own. . . .

However complex and intricate Rousseau's theorizing may become in
The Social Contract, it rests on this set of simple assumptions. To him
they have all the self-evidence and certitude of Descartes' "clear ideas."

Ever since Pascal, the search for happiness and emotional security has
been an increasingly important problem in Western civilization. Rousseau
was not concerned with men's basic irrationality or the lack of purpose

in human existence. He had no feeling of the absurd, of cosmic alienation. Like some other millenarian theorists, he believed that the human problem could be solved in human terms, by the true society.

The Social Contract opens with a famous first sentence: "Man was born free, and everywhere he is in chains." It would be wrong to take these words as a protest. They are only the statement of a fact, that man in society no longer enjoys the freedom of "'natural man." The prime purpose of Rousseau's inquiry, as he says immediately afterwards, will be to determine what conditions justify this civil status; in other words, what are the foundations of a legitimate political society. Here he breaks with most other thinkers of his time, who, like Montesquieu, were seeking to found the body politic on natural laws, or else on a rational "Natural Law." Following his view that society is not natural to man, he looks elsewhere, to artificial and deliberate conventions. In this, Hobbes' influence was doubtless great. In nature, argues Rousseau, there is only force. In society, men create right, which, though using force, supersedes it. Force under law is quite different from force without law. Right comes into being by the convention of the social compact.

Rousseau's version of the social contract theory is brilliantly original. For him, as for Hobbes,[6] it terminates the state of nature, with its natural freedom and equality. But a legitimtae political society gives men, in their stead, something new and far more precious: political liberty (as Rousseau understands it) and civil equality. The compact is the one unanimous act that obviates the need for further unanimity in voting. It creates the obligation to submit to the will of the majority: legally, since the individual has agreed to its rule; morally, since he is still obeying his true will, which is that the general will shall rule. Rousseau shows in detail what is lost forever on accepting the compact, and the gains which, point by point, are substituted for the losses. Possession, for instance, a usurpation which is limited only by strength, becomes property, a right which is both secured and limited by the community. Further, society is assumed, in Rousseau's theory, to be prior to government. The consequence is revolutionary. The so-called rulers of men have no part in the contract; they are only the instruments and servants of the people, in whom all sovereignty inalienably resides, and they may be dispossessed by the simple will of sovereign citizens.

This summary points to the two great problems of *The Social Contract* that have exercised the minds of countless commentators. The first is the expression of the will of the community, which is to be the determinant of justice and social control. This involves Rousseau's famous notion of

---

[6] Like many of his ideas, the idea of the social contract was not unique with Rousseau. Indeed, it enjoyed a kind of general currency in the eighteenth century, having originated (in all likelihood) with the English political theorist Thomas Hobbes in the previous century. It was first popularized by John Locke, but Rousseau gave the concept its most familiar form.—ED.

the "general will." The general will is to be ascertained or formulated by the process of majority vote, that is, a process of cancellation, in accordance with what Rousseau considered to be the workings of the mathematical laws of probability. But we must not err, as many commentators do, by confusing the nature of the general will with this positivistic process of its expression. The "general will" is essentially a rationalistic notion and involves the same type of hypothesis as "natural man" or the "state of nature." Rousseau does not deny what we might call "empirical man," man as he is, fighting primarily for his own interest. But beyond this he assumes a rational unity among all men, consisting of what their reason would desire if all individual passions and desires could be stilled. This is the "general will." It is questionable whether in majority rule Rousseau has found a procedure that would realize it, or whether he was really convinced that he had. It is on the general will, and on the participation of each citizen in the voting process, that he bases his theory that political and civil liberty consist not in doing what we as individuals want, but in doing what this hypothetical or metaphysical "general will" wants. . . .

Scholars have puzzled over the seeming contradiction between the individualism and spirit of rebellion in the *Discourse on Inequality* and the ideal of submissiveness and docility to the univocal will of an organic society in *The Social Contract*. Rousseau himself denied any real contradiction in his writings, and in this regard, at least, there is none. Rousseau's individualism, like his exaltation of the individual conscience, applies only to existing societies, which are corrupt, unjust, and exploitative. It is in the true society of which he dreams, where men are socialized, that the new, emergent conscience of the community, the "general will," supersedes individual conscience and individual will.

The second difficult problem, the new relationship of the individual citizen to the State, is the inevitable sequel. Is Rousseau's thought totalitarian or liberal? A remarkable quantity of ink has flowed in the attempt to prove it one or the other. Rousseau of course was not thinking in such terms. He wanted only to secure men's happiness, through a just, legitimate, political society. This could not be done without sacrifice and control. If we are to make a successful transition from a natural state of force to a civil state of right, we must think of men as citizens who have become part of a greater whole, and not as independent, self-centered individuals. The mutuality of the sacrifice, the application of laws to all, the respecting of others as we wish them to respect us, the limitation of the sacrifice by the sovereign people itself—this is the theoretical justification.

In the working out of Rousseau's plan, however, both individual dissent and political groupings are excluded. Not only are there no minority rights; there cannot even be minorities. Rousseau constantly uses the word "liberty," but for him it does not have the same meaning as for us. Liberty, for him, is first of all the independence or sovereignty of the

State. Second, it is the independence of any individual from all others, or from group pressures. It is the prevention of exploitation, either by individuals or by groups. This goal is achieved by the complete dependence of all on the collective self—an impersonal, inflexible force like that of nature in the original state of nature. Third, liberty is law self-given, or consented to—in other words, the sovereignty of the people as expressed in the general will. . . .

When we realize what kind of society Rousseau is dreaming of, we can better understand the function of the political processes outlined in *The Social Contract*. Sovereignty belongs to all the citizens and cannot be alienated or limited. This "democratic" doctrine turns out to be an absolutist doctrine. The sovereign power is in effect unlimited, even if it is (supposedly) held by an all-powerful general will rather than a despot. In fact, the potential tyranny is greater, because it is to take on a different coloration, that of impersonal necessity. Oppression by the State becomes, by definition, impossible; no self can want to hurt itself, Rousseau argues. It thereby tends to become unlimited. Rousseau's expressed intention is to reach beyond overt conformity and to "capture wills." . . .

Democracy and totalitarianism are not exclusive terms. Democracy is rule by the people. Totalitarianism is the attempt to impose a single pattern upon the thought, feelings, and actions of a community. The opposite of totalitarianism is not democracy, but the pluralistic society, in which people are free to differ and to judge the law itself, one in which complete conformity is not the test of good citizenship. Obedience to law is one thing; submergence into a "higher unity," surrender of one's judgment and will are quite different. We are inclined to cry out with the other Rousseau, the *romantic* Rousseau, "I am I, a sacred I. Thus far do I surrender myself, thus far do I *belong*, but no further." The libertarian will not accept Rousseau's "people's democracy." The general will belongs to the realm of myth; in the realm of reality, it can be expressed only by an individual or a group that speaks in its name and exercises the real power. It is difficult not to conclude that this is what Rousseau really intended, with his "Lawmakers" and his "guides," and all the mechanisms of control of thought and behavior.

In the ideal society Rousseau so ardently longed for, men are made to be happy, because in each man a harmony is created between wish and possibility, and a harmony among all men by the elimination of exploitation and aggressive, self-centered competition. It will also be a just society. Justice will never come from individual conscience or Natural Law, which are simply useless. They could never form the kind of *social* man of whom he was thinking. In their place he put the general will, a juridical, not a moral phenomenon, one that concerns the general welfare. . . .

Utopianism leads to rigorism, for all other ways are wrong. History shows utopianism to be conducive to cruelty and fanaticism, since its theories ignore the persistent refractory elements of human nature. Rousseau expressly favors fanaticism. Ultimately, then, unlimited control of individuals is implied, because that is what is required to make them act in a fashion consonant with utopianism. Most often, as in Rousseau, a utopian myth serves to rationalize coercion. To be sure, his political theory in *The Social Contract* is an attempt to transcend experience and is unrelated to action. However, when theory is ruthlessly applied to human affairs, freedom is its victim. . . .

Whether or not we like Rousseau's "new society," we feel his incomparable candor and the courage he drew from absolute conviction. In one sense, his message is one of hope. Neither society nor human nature is beyond the reach of man's will and rational powers; under certain conditions, both can be turned in new directions. Rousseau thought he had pointed out the paths toward a more human existence.

The *Discourse on Inequality* tells us what men may have been, in their remote origins, or what they still are in their fundamental substructure, and what has happened to them because of social experience. *The Social Contract*, a purely theoretical work, indicates a new direction. It tells us how to overcome and transform this "natural man" within us. It tells us what men may become—or rather, what Rousseau thought they must become, if the unique *human* experiment in a *natural* universe is to succeed and to survive.

Was he "a false prophet," as Irving Babbitt once called him? We cannot, at this point in history, say that he was wrong. His criticisms of our kind of society have surely lost none of their validity. And in such matters, only history can pronounce the verdict.

Suggestions for Further Reading

ROUSSEAU WAS ONE of the most popular and influential writers of the eighteenth century. Students are encouraged to read further in his most important work, *The Social Contract,* beyond the brief excerpt in this chapter. If not as important, his *Confessions* were even more popular. See *The Confessions of Jean-Jacques Rousseau* . . . ed. A. S. B. Glover (New York: Heritage Press, 1955). Students may also find interesting *Jean-Jacques Rousseau, Citizen of Geneva: Selections from the Letters* . . . ed. Charles W. Hendel (New York and London: Oxford University Press, 1937), *The*

First and Second Discourses, ed. Roger D. Masters (New York: St. Martin's, 1964), *Julie, or, The New Eloise* . . . tr. and abridged by Judith H. McDowell (University Park: Pennsylvania State University Press, 1968), or *The Émile of Jean-Jacques Rousseau,* tr. and ed. William Boyd (New York: Columbia University Press, 1971).

Both because of his influence and because of his slippery, contradictory character, there is an enormous biographical and critical literature on Rousseau. The standard major work is Lester G. Crocker, *Jean-Jacques Rousseau, Vol. 1, The Quest, 1712–1758, Vol. 2, The Prophetic Voice, 1758–1778* (New York: Macmillan, 1968–1973), the second volume excerpted in this chapter. Students may also be interested in Crocker's *Rousseau's Social Contract: An Interpretive Essay* (Cleveland: Case Western Reserve University Press, 1968), in which he goes even further toward an endorsement of J. L. Talmon's controversial views, which students may also wish to examine in greater detail in *The Rise of Totalitarian Democracy* (Boston: Beacon, 1952). As part of the same controversy, students may be interested in William H. Blanchard, *Rousseau and the Spirit of Revolt, A Psychological Study* (Ann Arbor: University of Michigan Press, 1967), a work of psycho-history which examines the conflicting sentiments of tyrant and rebel in Rousseau. Jakob H. Huizinga, *Rousseau: The Self-Made Saint* (New York: Grossman, 1976), is a brilliantly written debunking biography, and Ernst Cassirer, *The Question of Jean-Jacques Rousseau,* ed. and tr. Peter Gay (New York: Columbia University Press, 1954), is a standard work of interpretation by a great contemporary philosopher.

Although something of an anti-Enlightenment figure, Rousseau always figures in works on the Enlightenment. A good, brief, introductory essay is Frederick B. Artz, *The Enlightenment in France* (Kent, Ohio: Kent State University Press, 1968), but the most important modern work is Peter Gay, *The Enlightenment, An Interpretation,* 2 vols. (New York: Knopf, 1966–1969), and it is immensely readable. Norman Hampson, *A Cultural History of the Enlightenment* (New York: Pantheon, 1968), is a work that can bear comparison with Gay. Two of the early classic works on the Enlightenment can still be read with profit: Ernst Cassirer, *The Philosophy of the Enlightenment,* tr. Fritz C. A. Koelln and James P. Pettegrove (Princeton, N.J.: Princeton University Press, 1951 [1932]), because it is still the best analytical work on its subject; and Carl L. Becker, *The Heavenly City of the Eighteenth Century Philosophers* (New Haven, Conn.: Yale University Press, 1932), because of its wisdom and urbanity. For the more recent critique of Becker, see *Carl Becker's Heavenly City Revisited,* ed. Raymond O. Rockwood (Hamden, Conn.: Archon Books, 1968).

Leo Gershoy, *From Despotism to Revolution, 1763–1789,* "Rise of Modern Europe" (New York: Harper, 1944), is still one of the best histories of the time of Rousseau, and Joan McDonald, *Rousseau and the French Revolution, 1762–1791* (London: University of London, Athlone Press, 1965), is an important revisionist work dealing with the often noted impact of Rousseau on the revolution.

Napoleon: Child or Betrayer of the Revolution?

Was Napoleon the child of the French Revolution? Napoleon himself felt that he was. And in one sense at least, the assertion is undeniably true. The Revolution had broken the caste system of the old military order, just as it had broken the social order of the Old Regime generally. In the struggling revolutionary republic, threatened with invasion and armed reprisal from every side, any man who showed the ability and the willingness to serve could advance in the military—even such an apparently unpromising officer as the young Napoleon Bonaparte, with his heavy Italian accent, his mediocre record as a military cadet and a junior officer, and his consuming interest in the politics of his native Corsica, which seemed to preclude any involvement in the great events that had been shaking France since 1789.

But Napoleon was not indifferent to those events. As early as 1791, he had become a member of the Jacobin Club in his garrison town of Valence, in the south of France, and was an outspoken advocate of Jacobin radicalism. His political views, rather than any proven military ability, secured for him his first important commission as commander of artillery at the siege of Toulon against the royalists and the British. Napoleon was successful, and he caught the eye of the military commissioner Augustin Robespierre, who praised the young officer in a letter to his brother Maximilien, then at the zenith of his political career in Paris. Napoleon was appointed commandant of artillery in the army of Italy. But Robespierre and his faction soon fell from power, and

345

Napoleon, deprived of his command, was arrested. After a brief imprisonment, he departed for Paris to try to rescue his fortunes.

In 1795 the National Convention, its tenure running out, submitted to referendum the so-called Constitution of the Year III,[1] with its accompanying decree that two-thirds of the convention's members must be returned to the new legislative assembly. The royalists, enraged at this attempt to insure continued radical domination of the government, rose in revolt. Someone remembered that the young radical Napoleon was in Paris, and he was given effective command of the defense of the convention. As the rebels marched on 13 Vendémiaire, Year IV (October 5, 1795), Napoleon had already positioned his artillery and coolly ordered it to fire. The famous "whiff of grapeshot" carried the day—though there is no record that Napoleon used the phrase—and friends and enemies alike began to call him "Général Vendémiaire." He was now a force to be reckoned with in the politics of the Revolution.

When the new government was formed, headed by a Directory, Napoleon was its military adviser. Within a year, he was given command of the army of Italy. The Italian campaign was at that time verging on failure, but Napoleon turned it around. He gained the loyalty of his troops —largely by authorizing them to live off the land they conquered in lieu of the pay their republic had failed to provide—and he won battles. Within less than a year, Napoleon was the master of Italy. Far exceeding his authority, he set up a series of Italian republics and forced the Austrians out of Italy entirely. Then Napoleon returned to Paris once more to engineer the Treaty of Campo Formio with the defeated Austrians. Although the Directory was far from pleased, Napoleon was fast becoming a popular hero.

Britain, with its formidable sea power and its wealth and industry, was clearly France's most dangerous enemy, and the Directory had formulated a plan for an invasion of England from across the channel. Napoleon was placed in command of the operation. After a cursory inspection, he rejected the plan, arguing instead for a strike at the British lifeline to India—a campaign in Egypt. Napoleon was able to overcome the Directory but not the British sea power and the squadrons of Lord Nelson. The Egyptian campaign was a disaster. But rather than admit defeat, Napoleon returned to France and proclaimed a victory when in fact there was none. The French people believed him.

In 1799 Napoleon, with Abbé Sieyès, an ambitious member of the Directory, engineered a coup d'état. The coup, which took place on 18–19 Brumaire, Year VIII (November 9–10, 1799), was successful, and the Directory was replaced by a Consulate of three men, one of them

---

[1] The early leaders of the Revolution had proclaimed a new calendar dating from the overthrow of the Old Regime. Napoleon would later return France to the common usage.

Napoleon. Within a matter of weeks, a new "Constitution of the Year
VIII" was proclaimed, making Napoleon First Consul and the
government of France a military dictatorship. It is true that the
constitution was overwhelmingly approved by plebescite, after the fact.
It is true that under its authority Napoleon launched far-reaching reforms,
moving the nation in the direction of order and stability. But it is also true
that the French nation had succumbed to the myth of Napoleon, a myth
that was ultimately founded upon his military invincibility and—at least
in Napoleon's mind——upon continued military victories.

In 1802 Europe might well have had peace. Even Britain had agreed
to the Treaty of Amiens. For achieving this diplomatic coup, Napoleon
was granted lifetime tenure as First Consul, but even this did not satisfy
his ambition. Napoleon demanded an empire and he got it: on May 18,
1804, he was proclaimed Emperor of the French. In the years that
followed, Napoleon compiled an incredible list of military victories: he
defeated the Austrians at Ulm and the Austrians and Russians at
Austerlitz in the winter of 1805, the Prussians at Jena and Auerstädt in the
fall of 1806, and the Russians alone at Eylau and Friedland in the spring
and summer of 1807. By this time, Napoleon had redrawn the map of
western Europe, and his own relations sat on half a dozen thrones. His
plan was to organize the Continent against the stubborn British; to this
end, he signed an agreement with the new Russian emperor, Alexander I,
dividing Europe between them.

In 1810 Napoleon, standing at the apex of his power, decided to
disregard his agreement with Alexander and invade Russia. It was a
disastrous miscalculation, and it proved to be the crucial turning point in
Napoleon's career. Out of the almost half a million men who had massed
on the banks of the Neman in the summer of 1812, fewer than ten
thousand remained after the winter's march back from Moscow. The
myth of Napoleon was shattered, and the powers of Europe rose up
against him. Not only had he defeated and humiliated them, but he had
brought them the Revolution. Even if he had subverted the Revolution
in France, he had, nevertheless, exported its principles along with his
conquests. To the Old Regime of Europe, this was Napoleon's greatest
insult, the ultimate betrayal that they could not forgive. But it was also
perhaps Napoleon's most enduring claim to having been one of the
makers of the Western tradition, for, whatever his motives, Napoleon
introduced the Age of Revolution that persisted on the Continent, in one
guise or another, through most of the nineteenth century and that
fundamentally changed the nature of European government and society.

Napoleon was forced to abdicate and was exiled to the Mediterranean
island of Elba. But even as the victors were gathering to undo his work
and the Bourbons were returning to France, Napoleon escaped from
Elba. This was the beginning of his Hundred Days. As Napoleon, with

an escort of grenadiers, approached Grenoble, he met the first battalion
sent to intercept him. His secretary, the Marquis de Las Cases, described
the scene:

> The commanding officer refused even to parley. The Emperor
> without hesitation, advanced alone, and one hundred of his
> grenadiers marched at some distance from him, with their arms
> reversed. The sight of Napoleon, his costume, and in particular his
> grey military great coat, produced a magical effect on the soldiers,
> and they stood motionless. Napoleon went straight up to a veteran
> whose arm was covered with *chevrons*, and very unceremoniously
> seizing him by the whisker, asked him whether he would have the
> heart to kill his Emperor. The soldier, his eyes moistened with tears
> immediately thrust the ramrod into his musquet, to show that it was
> not loaded, and exclaimed, "See, I could not have done thee any
> harm: all the others are the same." Cries of *Vive l'Empereur!*
> resounded on every side. Napoleon ordered the battalion to make
> half a turn to the right, and all marched on to Paris.[2]

With every mile resistance melted, and cries of *Vive l'Empereur* swelled
up from the throngs that lined the roads and from garrison troops and
militia. Napoleon had returned and France was his. Even after the
catastrophe at Waterloo, an officer lying in the mud with a shattered thigh
cried out, "He has ruined us—he has destroyed France and himself—yet
I love him still." [3]

But what of the Revolution? The old veteran on the road to Grenoble
and the wounded officer on the field of Waterloo wept for their emperor,
not for the lost cause of the Revolution. Thousands unquestionably
shared their views. But many thousands more were convinced that,
despite the terrible cost of Napoleon's search for glory, he had carried
the Revolution to its proper, even to its inevitable conclusion. Napoleon
himself wrote:

> I purified a revolution, in spite of hostile factions. I combined all
> the scattered benefits that could be preserved; but I was obliged to
> protect them with a nervous arm against the attacks of all parties;
> and in this situation it may be truly said that the public interest, *the
> State, was myself.*[4]

The wheel had come full circle. Napoleon "the child of the Revolution"
echoed the words often ascribed to Louis XIV, "I am the state."

---

[2] The Count de Las Cases, *Memoirs of the Life, Exile, and Conversations of the
Emperor Napoleon,* new ed. (New York: Eckler, 1900), III, 295.
    [3] Louis Antoine Fauvelet de Bourrienne, *Memoirs of Napoleon Bonaparte,* ed. R. W.
Phipps (New York: Scribners, 1891), IV, 204.
    [4] Las Cases, *Memoirs,* III, 255-56.

Napoleon's Memoirs
THE COUNT DE LAS CASES

When, after Waterloo, Napoleon was sent into exile again, this time to the tiny, distant island of St. Helena in the south Atlantic, he was only forty-five years old, apparently in the prime of life. Might he not escape once more, even against all odds? Might he even be called back by one or another of the victorious allies, already beginning to quarrel among themselves? Might not France even summon her emperor again? Napoleon was planning for any eventuality, as carefully and methodically as he might plan a military campaign.

Napoleon had, of course, some limited contact with the Bonapartists in France, but this was restricted by the tight control over the island. He was able to carry on some correspondence, though much of it consisted of complaints to the British government about the conditions of his exile. But mainly Napoleon devoted himself to his memoirs, which he dictated to his secretary, the Marquis de Las Cases. Las Cases carefully transcribed the material, and then Napoleon read and corrected it himself.

Memoirs of the Life, Exile, and Conversations of the Emperor Napoleon is a vast and complicated work—four volumes in its final published form. In addition to Napoleon's own recollections of events, discourses, and opinions, it contains comments, reflections, and interpolations by Las Cases. It details Napoleon's bitter, petty, continuing controversy with the authorities on the island whose task it was to maintain his captivity. But primarily the book is Napoleon's own apologia, the justification for his policies and his career, directed to his own French people, to the allies, and to the tribunal of history. To Napoleon, the book was his final weapon.

It is in this work, more than in any other place, that we see the precise terms in which Napoleon considered himself the child, the inheritor, the "purifier" of the Revolution.

"THE FRENCH REVOLUTION was not produced by the jarring interests of two families disputing the possession of the throne; it was a general rising of the mass of the nation against the privileged classes." . . . The principal object of the Revolution was to destroy all privileges; to abolish signorial jurisdictions, justice being an inseparable attribute of sovereign authority; to suppress feudal rights as being a remnant of the old slavery of the people; to subject alike all citizens and all property to the burdens of the state. In short, the Revolution proclaimed equality of rights. A citizen might attain any public employment, according to his talent and the chances of fortune. The kingdom was composed of provinces which had been united to the Crown at various periods: they had no natural limits, and were differently divided, unequal in extent and in population. They possessed many laws of their own, civil as well as criminal: they were more or less privileged, and very unequally taxed, both with respect to the amount and the nature of the contributions, which rendered it necessary to detach them from each other by lines of custom-houses. France was not a state, but a combination of several states, connected together without amalgamation. The whole had been determined by chance and by the events of past ages. The Revolution, guided by the principle of equality, both with respect to the citizens and the different portions of the territory, destroyed all these small nations: there was no longer a Brittany, a Normandy, a Burgundy, a Champagne, a Provence, or a Lorraine; but the whole formed a France. A division of homogeneous territory, prescribed by local circumstances, confounded the limits of all the provinces. They possessed the same judicial and administrative organization, the same civil and criminal laws, and the same system of taxation. The dreams of the upright men of all ages were realized. The opposition which the Court, the Clergy, and the Nobility, raised against the Revolution and the war with foreign powers, produced the law of emigration and the sequestration of emigrant property, which subsequently it was found necessary to sell, in order to provide for the charges of the war. A great portion of the French nobility enrolled themselevs under the banner of the princes of the Bourbon family, and formed an army which marched in conjunction with the Austrian, Prussian, and English forces. Gentlemen who had been brought up in the enjoyment of competency served as private soldiers; numbers were cut off by fatigue and the sword; others perished of want in foreign countries; and the wars of La Vendée and of the Chouans, and the revolutionary tribunals, swept away thousands. Three-fourths of the French nobility were thus destroyed; and all posts, civil, judicial, or military, were filled by citizens who had risen from the common mass of the people. The change produced in persons and property by the events of the Revolution, was not less remarkable than that which was effected by the principles of the Revolution. A new church was created; the dioceses of Vienne, Narbonne, Féjus, Sisteron, Rheims, &c., were superseded by sixty new dioceses, the boundaries of which were circumscribed, in Concordat,[5] by new Bulls applicable to the present state of the French territory. The suppression of religious orders, the sale of convents and of all ecclesiastical property, were sanctioned, and the clergy were pensioned by the State. Everything that was the

___

[5] The agreement (1801) between Napoleon and Pope Pius VII that restored Catholicism to France, though largely on Napoleon's terms.—ED.

result of the events which had occurred since the time of Clovis, ceased to exist. All these changes were so advantageous to the people that they were effected with the utmost facility, and, in 1800, there no longer remained any recollection of the old privileges and sovereigns of the provinces, the old parliaments and bailiwicks, or the old dioceses; and to trace back the origin of all that existed, it was sufficient to refer to the new law by which it had been established. One-half of the land had changed its proprietors; the peasantry and the citizens were enriched. The advancement of agriculture and manufactures exceeded the most sanguine hopes. France presented the imposing spectacle of upwards of thirty millions of inhabitants, circumscribed within their natural limits, and composing only a single class of citizens, governed by one law, one rule, and one order. All these changes were conformable with the welfare and rights of the nation, and with the justice and intelligence of the age.

The five members of the Directory were divided. Enemies to the Republic crept into the councils; and thus men, hostile to the rights of the people, became connected with the government. This state of things kept the country in a ferment; and the great interests which the French people had acquired by the Revolution were incessantly compromised. One unanimous voice, issuing from the plains of France and from her cities and her camps, demanded the preservation of all the principles of the Republic, or the establishment of an hereditary system of government, which would place the principles and interests of the Revolution beyond the reach of factions and the influence of foreigners. By the constitution of the year VIII the First Consul of the Republic became Consul for ten years, and the nation afterwards prolonged his magistracy for life: the people subsequently raised him to the throne, which it rendered hereditary in his family. The principles of the sovereignty of the people, of liberty and equality, of the destruction of the feudal system, of the irrevocability of the sale of national domains, and the freedom of religious worship, were now established. The government of France, under the fourth dynasty, was founded on the same principles as the Republic. It was a moderate and constitutional monarchy. There was as much difference between the government of France under the fourth dynasty and the third, as between the latter and the Republic. The fourth dynasty succeeded the Republic, or, more properly speaking, it was merely a modification of it.

No Prince ever ascended a throne with rights more legitimate than those of Napoleon. The crown was not presented to him by a few Bishops and Nobles; but he was raised to the Imperial throne by the unanimous consent of the citizens, three times solemnly confirmed.[6] Pope Pius VII, the head of the Catholic religion, the religion of the majority of the French

---

[6] A reference to the successive plebiscites that Napoleon used to gain approval of his modifications in the government. The last sanctioned his assumption of the imperial title.—ED.

people, crossed the Alps to anoint the Emperor with his own hands, in the presence of the Bishops of France, the Cardinals of the Romish Church, and the Deputies from all the districts of the Empire.[7] The sovereigns of Europe eagerly acknowledged Napoleon: all beheld with pleasure the modification of the Republic, which placed France on a footing of harmony with the rest of Europe, and which at once confirmed the constitution and the happiness of that great nation. Ambassadors from Austria, Russia, Prussia, Spain, Portugal, Turkey, and America, in fine, from all the powers of Europe, came to congratulate the Emperor. England alone sent no ambassador: she had violated the treaty of Amiens, and had consequently again declared war against France. . . .

The English declaration of war (1803) precipitated the imperial phase of Napoleon's career, during which, in victory after victory, he defeated the great powers of Europe. He hoped to complete his plans for Europe and for himself in the attack upon Russia. Here he reflects upon those plans and upon the Russian war.

. . . "That war should have been the most popular of any in modern times. It was a war of good sense and true interests; a war for the repose and security of all; it was purely pacific and preservative; entirely European and continental. Its success would have established a balance of power and would have introduced new combinations, by which the dangers of the present time would have been succeeded by future tranquillity. In this case, ambition had no share in my views. In raising Poland,[8] which was the key-stone of the whole arch, I would have permitted a King of Prussia, an Archduke of Austria, or any other to occupy the throne. I had no wish to obtain any new acquisition; and I reserved for myself only the glory of doing good, and the blessings of posterity. Yet this undertaking failed, and proved my ruin, though I never acted more disinterestedly, and never better merited success. As if popular opinion had been seized with contagion, in a moment, a general outcry, a general sentiment, arose against me. I was proclaimed the destroyer of kings—I, who had created them! I was denounced as the subverter of the rights of nations—I, who was about to risk all to secure them! And people and kings, those irreconcileable enemies, leagued together and conspired against me! All the acts of my past life were now forgotten. I said, truly, that popular favour

---

[7] Though the pope was present, Napoleon placed the crown on his own head, as depicted in the famous painting of the occasion by the court painter Jacques-Louis David.—ED.

[8] His creation of an independent Poland was an indignity Russia would not endure. It was over this matter that the Russian campaign actually began.—ED.

would return to me with victory; but victory escaped me, and I was ruined. . . ."

The ruin brought upon him by the Russian war was purely fortuitous, claims Napoleon, and in no way can obscure his true accomplishments.

"I closed the gulf of anarchy and cleared the chaos. I purified the Revolution, dignified Nations and established Kings. I excited every kind of emulation, rewarded every kind of merit, and extended the limits of glory! This is at least something! And on what point can I be assailed on which an historian could not defend me? Can it be for my intentions? But even here I can find absolution. Can it be for my despotism? It may be demonstrated that the Dictatorship was absolutely necessary. Will it be said that I restrained liberty? It can be proved that licentiousness, anarchy, and the greatest irregularities, still haunted the threshold of freedom. Shall I be accused of having been too fond of war? It can be shown that I always received the first attack. Will it be said that I aimed at universal monarchy? It can be proved that this was merely the result of fortuitous circumstances, and that our enemies themselves led me step by step to this determination. Lastly, shall I be blamed for my ambition? This passion I must doubtless be allowed to have possessed, and that in no small degree; but at the same time, my ambition was of the highest and noblest kind that ever, perhaps, existed—that of establishing and of consecrating the empire of reason, and the full exercise and complete enjoyment of all the human faculties! And here the historian will probably feel compelled to regret that such ambition should not have been fulfilled and gratified!" Then after a few moments of silent reflection: "This," said the Emperor, "is my whole history in a few words."

On Politics, Literature, and National Character
MADAME DE STAËL

There were many who, like one hostile critic, regarded Napoleon simply as "the Corsican ogre." But there were other, more thoughtful critics who, though they condemned Napoleon, tried to understand why they did so. One of these was Madame de Staël (1766–1817). She was the daughter of the Swiss banker Jacques Necker, who, as Minister of Finance to Louis XVI, had tried without much success—and without much imagination—to rescue France from fiscal chaos on the eve of the Revolution. Madame de Staël had grown up in the highest circles of the French aristocracy and the court, marrying the Swedish ambassador to France, Eric Magnus de Staël-Holstein, in 1786. She lived through the Revolution and knew most of its leading figures, as she did Napoleon and the men of the counterrevolution.

But Madame de Staël was more than simply another fashionable, aristocratic woman. She was one of the last great luminaries of the Age of Enlightenment and one of the most important European writers of her time. She was also one of Napoleon's most perceptive and persistent critics. Though Madame de Staël was a passionate champion of liberty and an outspoken French patriot, she was no friend of the Revolution. But then, she observed, neither was Napoleon! He was, in her view, nothing less than its most sinister subverter. Napoleon tried first to moderate her views, then to persuade her of his good intentions, but he failed altogether to understand the basis of her hostility. Finally, he sent her into exile, and from Switzerland, Germany, Russia, and England she continued to observe and to write about the unfolding of the events she had foreseen. We turn now to Madame de Staël, On Politics, Literature, and National Character, and her account of the rise and fall of Napoleon, so different in every way from his own.

THE DIRECTORY was not inclined to peace, not because it wished to extend French rule beyond the Rhine and the Alps but because it believed war useful for the propagation of the republican system. Its plan was to surround France with a belt of republics. . . .

General Bonaparte was certainly less serious and less sincere than the

Directory in the love of republican ideas, but he was much more shrewd in estimating a situation. He sensed that peace would become popular in France because passions were subsiding and people were weary of sacrifices; so he signed the Treaty of Campo Formio with Austria.

General Bonaparte distinguished himself as much by his character and mind as by his victories, and the imagination of the French was beginning to attach itself to him strongly. A tone of moderation and nobility prevailed in his style, which contrasted with the revolutionary gruffness of the civil leaders of France. The warrior spoke like a magistrate, while the magistrates expressed themselves with martial violence. . . .

It was with this feeling, at least, that I saw him for the first time in Paris. I could find no words of reply when he came to me to tell me that he had sought my father at Coppet and that he regretted having passed through Switzerland without having seen him. But when I was somewhat recovered from the confusion of admiration, a very strong sense of fear followed. Bonaparte at that time had no power; he was even believed to be somewhat threatened by the jealous suspicions of the Directory. So the fear he inspired was caused only by the extraordinary effect of his person upon nearly all who approached him. I had seen men worthy of respect, and I had seen fierce men: there was nothing in the impression Bonaparte produced upon me that recalled either the former or the latter. I very quickly saw, in the various occasions I had to meet him during his stay in Paris, that his character could not be defined by the words we ordinarily use; he was neither good, nor fierce, nor gentle, nor cruel, like others we know. Such a being, having no equals, could neither feel nor arouse any sympathy: he was more than a human being or less than one. His appearance, his mind, and his speech were foreign in nature—an added advantage for subjugating the French.

Far from being reassured by seeing Bonaparte more often, I was made increasingly apprehensive. I had a vague feeling that no emotions of the heart could influence him. He considers a human being a fact or a thing, not a fellow man. He does not hate nor does he love. For him, there is nothing but himself; all others are ciphers.

Every time I heard him speak I was struck by his superiority: yet it had no resemblance to that of men educated and cultivated by study or by social intercourse, such as may be found in England or France. But his speech showed a feeling for the situation, like the hunter's for his prey. . . .

General Bonaparte, at this same time, the end of 1797, sounded public opinion regarding the Directors; he realized that they were not liked but that republican sentiment made it as yet impossible for a general to take the place of civilian officials. The Directory proposed to him the assault upon England. He went to examine the coasts, and, quickly seeing that this expedition was senseless, returned resolved to attempt the conquest of Egypt.

Bonaparte has always sought to seize the imagination of men and, in this respect, he knows well how one must govern when one is not born to the throne. An invasion of Africa, the war carried to an almost fabulous country like Egypt, must make an impression upon every mind. . . .

But in his climb to power, Napoleon depended not only upon his growing military reputation.

The most potent magic that Bonaparte used to establish his power was the terror the mere name of Jacobinism inspired, though anyone capable of reflection knew perfectly well that this scourge could not reappear in France. People readily pretend to fear defeated parties in order to justify harsh measures. Everyone who wants to promote the establishment of despotism forcefully reminds us of the terrible crimes of demagogy. It is a very simply technique. So Bonaparte paralyzed every form of resistance to his will by the words: *Do you want me to hand you over to the Jacobins?* And France bowed down before him, no man bold enough to reply to him: *We shall be able to fight the Jacobins and you.* In short, even then he was not liked, only preferred. He almost always presented himself in competition with another cause for alarm, in order to make his power acceptable as a lesser evil. . . .

We cannot watch too attentively for the first symptoms of tyranny; when it has grown to a certain point, there is no more time to stop it. One man sweeps along the will of many individuals of whom the majority, taken separately, wish to be free but who nevertheless surrender because people fear each other and do not dare to speak their thoughts freely. . . .

General Bonaparte decreed a constitution in which there were no safeguards. Besides, he took great care to leave in existence the laws announced during the Revolution, in order to select from this detestable arsenal the weapon that suited him. The special commissions, deportations, exiles, the bondage of the press—these steps unfortunately taken in the name of liberty—were very useful to tyranny. To adopt them, he sometimes advanced reasons of state, sometimes the need of the times, sometimes the acts of his opponents, sometimes the need to maintain tranquillity. Such is the artillery of phrases that supports absolute power, for "emergencies" never end, and the more one seeks to repress by illegal measures the more one creates disaffected people who justify new injustices. The establishment of the rule of law is always put off till tomorrow. This is a vicious circle from which one cannot break out, for the public spirit that is awaited in order to permit liberty can come only from liberty itself. . . .

It was particularly advantageous to Bonaparte's power that he had to manage only a mass. All individual existence was annihilated by ten years

of disorder, and nothing sways people like military success; it takes great
power of reason to combat this tendency instead of profiting from it. No
one in France could consider his position secure. Men of all classes,
ruined or enriched, banished or rewarded, found themselves one by one
equally, so to speak, in the hands of power. Bonaparte, who always
moved between two opposed interests, took very good care not to put an
end to these anxieties by fixed laws that might let everyone know his
rights. To one man he returned his property, while another he stripped
of his forever. The First Consul reserved to himself the power of determining, under any pretext, the fate of everything and everyone.

Those Frenchmen who sought to resist the ever-increasing power of
the First Consul had to invoke liberty to struggle against him successfully. But at this word the aristocrats and the enemies of the Revolution
cried "Jacobinism," thus supporting the tyranny for which they later
sought to blame their adversaries. . . .

I sensed more quickly than others—and I pride myself on it—Bonaparte's tyrannical character and intentions. The true friends of liberty are
in this respect guided by an instinct that does not deceive them. But my
position, at the outset of the Consulate, was made more painful by the
fact that respectable society in France thought it saw in Bonaparte the
man who had saved them from anarchy or Jacobinism. They therefore
vigorously condemned the spirit of opposition I displayed toward
him. . . .

*Madame de Staël's opposition led to her exile. But even in exile she
continued to comment upon Napoleon and upon the rise and finally the
decline of his military and political fortunes. In 1813, following the
Russian disaster, the allies invaded France, heading for Paris.*

From the moment the Allies passed the Rhine and entered France it
seemed to me that the prayers of the friends of France must undergo a
complete change. I was then in London, and one of the English Cabinet
Ministers asked me what I wished for. I ventured to reply that my desire
was to see Bonaparte victorious and slain. The English had enough
greatness of soul to make it unnecessary for me to conceal this French
sentiment from them. Yet I was to learn, in the midst of the transports
of joy with which the city of the conquerors reverberated, that Paris was
in the power of the Allies. At that moment I felt there was no longer a
France: I believed Burke's prediction realized and that where France had
existed we should see only an abyss. The Emperor Alexander, the Allies,
and the constitutional principles adopted through the wisdom of Louis
XVIII banished this gloomy presentiment.

There was, nevertheless, something of grandeur in Napoleon's farewell to his troops and to their eagles, so long victorious. His last campaign had been long and skillful: in short, the fatal magic that bound France's military glory to him was not yet destroyed. Thus the conference at Paris must be blamed for having made his return possible. . . .

Many people like to argue that Bonaparte would still be emperor if he had not attempted the expeditions against Spain or Russia. This opinion pleases the supporters of despotism, who insist that so fine a government could not be overthrown by the very nature of things but only by an accident. I have already said, what observation of France will confirm, that Bonaparte needed war to establish and maintain absolute power. A great nation would not have supported the dull and degrading burden of despotism if military glory had not ceaselessly moved or exalted the public spirit. . . .

I shall never forget the moment when I learned, from one of my friends the morning of March 6, 1815, that Bonaparte had landed on the French coast. I had the misfortune to foresee at once the consequences of that event—as they have since taken place—and I thought the earth was about to open under me. I said, "There will be no liberty if Bonaparte wins and no national independence if he loses." Events, it seems to me, have borne out this sad prediction only too well. . . .

. . . Enlightened men could see in Bonaparte nothing but a despot, but by a rather fatal conjunction of circumstances this despot was presented to the nation as the defender of its rights. All the benefits achieved by the Revolution, which France will never willingly give up, were threatened by the endless rashness of the party that wants to repeat the conquest of Frenchmen, as if they were still Gauls. And that part of the nation that most feared the return of the Old Regime thought they saw in Bonaparte a way to save themselves from it. The most fatal association that could overwhelm the friends of liberty was that a despot should join their ranks—should, so to speak, place himself at their head—and that the enemies of every liberal idea should have a pretext for confusing popular violence with the evils of despotism and thus make tyranny appear to be the result of liberty itself. . . . If it was criminal to recall Bonaparte, it was silly to try to disguise such a man as a constitutional monarch. . . .

Whether Napoleon lives or perishes, whether or not he reappears on the continent of Europe, only one reason moves me to speak of him: the ardent wish that the friends of liberty in France completely separate their cause from his and beware of confusing the principles of the Revolution with those of the Imperial *régime*. I believe I have shown that there is no counter-revolution so fatal to liberty as the one he made.

A Modern Napoleon
GEORGES LEFEBVRE

*Napoleon has been the most enduringly fascinating figure in modern
history, the subject of literally thousands of books—more than 200,000 by
some estimates. Recent opinion has tended to divide along precisely the
lines that appeared in Napoleon's own time—as suggested in the first two
selections of this chapter—either "for" or "against" him, to borrow from
the title of a famous book on the Napoleonic tradition.⁹ The following
selection is from* Napoleon, From 18 Brumaire to Tilsit 1799–1807, *by the
distinguished French historian Georges Lefebvre, considered by many
competent critics to have been the best modern scholar of the Napoleonic
age. But Lefebvre was also a great authority on the French Revolution,
and so we turn to him for his view on the relationship of Napoleon to the
Revolution and his answer to the question of whether Napoleon was its
child or its betrayer. It is the opinion of Lefebvre that the Revolution had
betrayed itself long before Napoleon became its conscious heir; that only
in the most elementary sense of its giving him the opportunity to rise to
power could Napoleon be considered its offspring; that—as Madame de
Staël argued—Napoleon was always the same, from the beginning to the
end of his career, an autocrat; and that he did not purify the Revolution
but rather manipulated it.*

THAT THE FRENCH Revolution turned to dictatorship was no accident; it
was driven there by inner necessity, and not for the first time either. Nor
was it an accident that the Revolution led to the dictatorship of a general.
But it so happened that this general was Napoleon Bonaparte, a man
whose temperament, even more than his genius, was unable to adapt to
peace and moderation. Thus it was an unforeseeable contingency which
tilted the scale in favour of "la guerre éternelle."

For a long time the republicans had wanted to strengthen the central
authority. One need only look at the constitutions they gave to the vassal
states: in Holland, the members of the Directory controlled the treasury;
in Switzerland, they appointed government officials; in Rome, they appointed judges as well. In the Helvetic and Roman Republics every
department already possessed a "prefect." All this is not to mention the

⁹ Pieter Geyl, *Napoleon, For and Against*, Olive Renier, trans. (New Haven: Yale
University Press, 1949).

Cisalpine Republic, which was Bonaparte's personal fief. . . . The coup d'état of 18 Fructidor had provided the occasion sought by Sieyès, Talleyrand, and Bonaparte, but they let the opportunity slip. In Year VII, however, they hoped to bring about a new one. Without realizing it, the republicans were giving way to a tendency which, ever since the start of the civil and foreign wars, was pushing the Revolution in the direction of a permanent and all-powerful executive, that is to say toward dictatorship. It was this social revolution that drove the dispossessed nobility far beyond insurrection. Subsidized by enemy gold, it exploited the wartime hardships—that inexhaustible source of discontent —and particularly the monetary and economic crisis, thereby intending to turn the people against the government. The French did not want a return to the Old Regime, but they suffered and they held their leaders responsible for it. At every election the counter-revolution hoped to regain power. It was awareness of this danger that led the Mountain [10] in 1793 to declare the Convention in permanent session until the peace. The Thermidorians had intended to restore elective government, but they immediately returned to Jacobin expediency by passing the Decree of the Two-Thirds. Next, the Directory, overwhelmed by the elections of 1797, re-established the dictatorship on 18 Fructidor. Yet as long as the Constitution of Year III continued to exist, this dictatorship, put to the test each year, required a host of violent measures and could never be brought into working order. So it was still necessary to revive the principle of 1793 and invest it with permanence until such time as peace, settled once and for all, would persuade the counter-revolution to accept the new order. It was in this respect that Napoleon's dictatorship became so much a part of the history of the French Revolution. No matter what he may have said or done, neither he nor his enemies were ever able to break this bond, and this was a fact which the European aristocracy understood perfectly well.

In 1799, as in 1793, the Jacobins wished to establish a democratic dictatorship by relying on the Sans-culottes[11] to push it through the councils. Taking advantage of the crisis preceding the victory at Zurich, they succeeded in forcing the passage of several revolutionary measures: a compulsory loan, the abolition of exemptions from military service, the law of hostages, a repeal of assignments on public revenues which had been granted to bankers and government contractors, withholdings on the rente and on salaries, and finally, requisitions. These measures constituted a direct attack on bourgeois interests and brought that class to action. Thus it was symbolic that assignments on public revenues were restored the very night of 19 Brumaire. The Idéologues who gathered around Madame de Condorcet at Auteuil or in the salon of Madame de

---

[10] The popular name given to the radical faction in the Convention.—Ed.
[11] Another popular name for the urban proletariat, especially of Paris, who tended to support Jacobin radicalism.—Ed.

Staël wanted neither a democratic dictatorship nor even a democracy. . . . Madame de Staël expressed their desire: to devise a representative system of government which would assure power to the moneyed and talented "notables." Sieyès, who had become a Director, took his inspiration from the Decree of the Two-Thirds. Together with his friends he wanted to select the membership of the newly constituted bodies which would then expand themselves by co-optation, leaving to the nation only the role of electing candidates. Furthermore, those already in office saw in this plan the chance to keep themselves in power.

The people having been eliminated as an obstacle to the dictatorship of the bourgeoisie, only the army remained. The Directory had already sought its help on 18 Fructidor, Year V, and had managed to keep the upper hand, despite serious incursions. Now, however, the situation was very different in that steadfast republicans, not royalists, were to be driven out. Only a popular general could have carried it through, and Bonaparte's sudden return destined that it should be he. The will of the nation which was invoked to justify 18 Brumaire played no part in the event. The nation rejoiced at the news that Bonaparte was in France because it recognized an able general; but the Republic had conquered without him, and Masséna's victory [12] had bolstered the reputation of the Directory. Consequently, the responsibility for 18 Brumaire lies on that segment of the republican bourgeoisie called the Brumairians, whose leading light was Sieyès. They had no intention of giving in to Bonaparte, and they chose him only as an instrument of their policy. That they propelled him to power without imposing any conditions, without even first delimiting the fundamental character of the new regime, betrays their incredible mediocrity. Bonaparte did not repudiate the notables, for he too was not a democrat, and their collaboration alone enabled him to rule. But on the evening of 19 Brumaire, after they had hurriedly slapped together the structure of the Provisional Consulate, they should not have harboured any more illusions. The army had followed Bonaparte, and him alone. He was complete master. Regardless of what he and his apologists may have said, his rule was from its origins an absolute military dictatorship. It was Bonaparte alone who would decide the questions on which the fate of France and Europe hinged.

What sort of a man was he? His personality evolved in so singular a manner that it defies portrayal. He appeared first as a studious officer full of dreams, garrisoned at Valence and Auxonne. As a youthful general, on the eve of the battle of Castiglione, he could still hold a council of war. But in the final years as Emperor, he was stupefied with his own omnipotence and was infatuated with his own omniscience. And yet distinctive traits appear throughout his entire career: power could do no more than accentuate some and attenuate others.

Short-legged and small in stature, muscular, ruddy, and still gaunt at

[12] At Zurich over the Russians.—ED.

the age of thirty, he was physically hardy and fit. His sensitivity and steadiness were admirable, his reflexes quick as lightning, and his capacity for work unlimited. He could fall asleep at will. But we also find the reverse: cold humid weather brought on oppression, coughing spells, dysuria; when crossed he unleashed frightful outbursts of temper; over-exertion, despite prolonged hot baths, despite extreme sobriety, despite the moderate yet constant use of coffee and tobacco, occasionally produced brief collapses, even tears. His mind was one of the most perfect that has ever been: his unflagging attention tirelessly swept in facts and ideas which his memory registered and classified; his imagination played with them freely, and being in a permanent state of concealed tension, it never wearied of inventing political and strategic motifs which manifested themselves in unexpected flashes of intuition like those experienced by poets and mathematicians. This would happen especially at night during a sudden awakening, and he himself referred to it as "the moral spark" and "the after midnight presence of the spirit." This spiritual fervour shone through his glittering eyes and illuminated the face, still "sulphu-ric" at his rise, of the "sleek-haired Corsican." This is what made him unsociable, and not, as Hippolyte Taine would have us think, some kind of brutality, the consequence of a slightly tarnished *condottiere* being let loose upon the world in all his savagery. He rendered a fair account of himself when he said, "I consider myself a good man at heart," and indeed he showed generosity, and even kindness to those who were close to him. But between ordinary mortals, who hurried through their tasks in order to abandon themselves to leisure or diversion, and Napoleon Bonaparte, who was the soul of effort and concentration, there could exist no common ground nor true community. Ambition—that irresistible impulse to act and to dominate—sprang from his physical and mental state of being. . . .

Ever since his military school days at Brienne, when he was still a poor and taunted foreigner, timid yet bursting with passion, Napoleon drew strength from pride in himself and contempt for others. Destined to become an officer, his instinct to command without having to discuss could not have been better served. Although he might on occasion have sought information or opinion, he alone was master and judge. Bona-parte's natural propensity for dictatorship suited the normal practice of his profession. In Italy and in Egypt he introduced dictatorship into the government. In France he wanted to put himself forward as a civilian, but the military stamp was indelibly there. He consulted often, but he could never tolerate free opposition. More precisely, when faced with a group of men accustomed to discussion, he would lose his composure. This explains his intense hatred of the Idéologues. The confused and undisci-plined, yet formidable masses inspired in him as much fear as contempt. Regardless of costumes and titles, Bonaparte took power as a general, and as such he exercised it. . . .

. . . Having entered into a life of action, he still remained a thinker. This warrior was never happier than in the silence of his own study, surrounded by papers and documents. In time he became more practical, and he would boast that he had repudiated "ideology." Nevertheless, he was still a typical man of the eighteenth century, a rationalist, a philosophe. Far from relying on intuition, he placed his trust in reason, in knowledge, and in methodical effort. . . .

He seemed to be dedicated to a policy of realism in every way, and he was, in fact, a realist in execution down to the slightest detail. . . . And yet he was a realist in execution only. There lived in him an alter-ego which contained certain features of the hero. It seems to have been born during his days at the military academy out of a need to dominate a world in which he felt himself despised. Above all he longed to equal the semi-legendary heroes of Plutarch and Corneille. His greatest ambition was glory. "I live only for posterity," he exclaimed, "death is nothing, but to live defeated and without glory is to die every day." His eyes were fixed on the world's great leaders: Alexander, who conquered the East and dreamed of conquering the world; Caesar, Augustus, Charlemagne—the creators and the restorer of the Roman Empire whose very names were synonymous with the idea of a universal civilization. From these he did not deduce a precise formulation to be used as a rule, a measure, or a condition of political conduct. They were for him examples, which stimulated his imagination and lent an unutterable charm to action. . . . That is why it is idle to seek for limits to Napoleon's policy, or for a final goal at which he would have stopped: there simply was none. . . .

That a mind so capable of grasping reality in certain respects should escape it in others . . . can only be due to Napoleon's origins as much as to his nature. When he first came to France, he considered himself a foreigner. Until the time when he was expelled from Corsica by his compatriots in 1791, his attitude had been one of hostility to the French people. Assuredly he became sufficiently imbued with their culture and spirit to adopt their nationality; otherwise he could never have become their leader. But he lacked the time to identify himself with the French nation and to adopt its national tradition to the point where he would consider its interests as a limitation upon his own actions. Something of the uprooted person remained in him; something of the déclassé as well. He was neither entirely a gentleman nor entirely common. He served both the king and the Revolution without attaching himself to either. This was one of the reasons for his success, since he could so easily place himself above parties and announce himself as the restorer of national unity. Yet neither in the Old Regime nor in the new did he find principles which might have served as a norm or a limit. . . .

What about moral limits? In spiritual life he had nothing in common with other men. Even though he knew their passions well and deftly turned them to his own ends, he cared only for those that would reduce men to dependence. He belittled every feeling that elevated men to acts of sacrifice—religious faith, patriotism, love of freedom—because he saw in them obstacles to his own schemes. Not that he was impervious to these sentiments, at least not in his youth, for they readily led to heroic deeds; but fate led him in a different direction and walled him up within himself. In the splendid and terrible isolation of the will to power, measure carries no meaning.

Suggestions for Further Reading

NAPOLEON IS LINKED inescapably with both the French Revolution that created him and with the nineteenth-century age of revolution that he created. Thus, the first category of books to be recommended for Napoleon and his age are those which treat this large topic. The best general work is probably Erich J. Hobsbawm, *The Age of Revolution: Europe 1789–1848* (Cleveland: World, 1962); it is a book of ideas rather than a factual survey, and the author is interested in the continuing social and cultural trends of the revolutionary age, in which he includes the topic of England and her industrial revolution. Of the same sort is Norman Hampson, *The First European Revolution, 1776–1850* (New York: Harcourt, Brace and World, 1969), a brief, attractive survey and analysis which plays down the role of Napoleon in favor of the continuity of the idea of revolution. George Rudé, *Revolutionary Europe, 1783–1815* (New York: Harper & Row, 1966), is a good summary, while somewhat more comprehensive is Franklin L. Ford, *Europe, 1780–1830* (London: Longman, 1970); both are excellent, straightforward accounts.

The outstanding modern work on the French Revolution itself is Georges Lefebvre, *The French Revolution*, 2 vols., Vol. 1, tr. Elizabeth M. Evanson (New York: Columbia University Press, 1962), Vol. 2, tr. John Hall Stewart and James Friguglietti (New York: Columbia University Press, 1964), along with Lefebvre's brilliant analytical work, *The Coming of the French Revolution, 1789,* tr. R. R. Palmer (Princeton, N.J.: Princeton University Press, 1947). R. R. Palmer, *The World of the French Revolution* (New York: Harper & Row, 1969), is a highly interpretive, brief, readable, analytical survey, while M. J. Sydenham, *The French Revolution* (New

York: Putnam, 1965), is a brief, largely political history. Alfred Cobban, *The Social Interpretation of the French Revolution* (Cambridge, England: Cambridge University Press, 1964), is a major critical work, revising much of the sociological theorizing about classes that had marked a generation of revolutionary studies. Cobban argues that the land-owning class eventually triumphed in revolutionary France and that in the course of the French Revolution the shift from title to property as the basis for social status was finally made. Norman Hampson, *A Social History of the French Revolution* (Toronto: Toronto University Press, 1963), is a briefer and more balanced treatment of the same themes.

Georges Lefebvre is the most important authority on Napoleon, as he is on the Revolution. See his *Napoleon,* 2 vols., Vol. 1 *Napoleon from 18 Brumaire to Tilsit, 1799–1807,* tr. H. F. Stockhold, Vol. 2 *Napoleon from Tilsit to Waterloo, 1807–1815,* tr. J. E. Anderson (New York: Columbia University Press, 1969) (the first volume is excerpted in this chapter). J. C. Herold, *The Age of Napoleon* (New York: Harper & Row, 1963), is not only a lush and beautiful book but an interpretive study; Herold is not an admirer of Napoleon and considers him at the best an ungrateful child of the Revolution. On the other hand, Robert B. Holtman, *The Napoleonic Revolution* (Philadelphia: Lippincott, 1967), sees Napoleon as a dramatic and important innovator in a score of fields, thus preserving the best gains of the Revolution. Felix M. Markham, *Napoleon and the Awakening of Europe,* "Teach Yourself History Library" (New York: Macmillan, 1954), and his *Napoleon I, Emperor of the French* (New York: New American Library, 1964) are good short biographies. Several special studies are also recommended. For military history see the good, comprehensive, straightforward account in David G. Chandler, *The Campaigns of Napoleon* (New York: Macmillan, 1966), and the detailed study by Christopher L. Hibbert, *Waterloo: Napoleon's Last Campaign* (New York: New American Library, 1967). A related work is the dramatic and exciting Edith Saunders, *The Hundred Days* (New York: Norton, 1964). An extremely interesting work on a subtopic of Napoleon is J. Christopher Herold, *Bonaparte in Egypt* (New York: Harper & Row, 1962). Pieter Geyl, *Napoleon, For and Against,* tr. Olive Renier (New Haven, Conn.: Yale University Press, 1949), is a famous book of Napoleonic historiography. Finally, highly recommended is the luminous biography by J. Christopher Herold, *Mistress to an Age: A Life of Madame de Staël* (Indianapolis: Bobbs-Merrill, 1958).

Byron:
Lord of Paradox

The great cultural vogue of the early nineteenth century was Romanticism
—in art, in music, in fashions and tastes and foibles, and especially in
literature. And the darling of Romantic Europe was the English poet
George Gordon Lord Byron (1788–1824). More than any other figure,
Lord Byron seemed to exemplify the confused and contradictory passions
of Romanticism, its "phrensy" and its melancholy, its bursting sunlight
and gloomy darkness, its blend of the bizarre, the exotic, and the
wildly creative.

Byron was, from the very beginning, almost doomed to be a Romantic,
even "Byronic," hero. The son of "a handsome, dissolute father and a
foolish, ill-educated, violent-tempered mother," [1] he was a strikingly
beautiful child but was born with a club foot, a flawed angel. He was
seduced by a lubricious chambermaid at the age of nine, the beginning
of an incredible odyssey of sexual adventures and stormy romantic liaisons
that would shock, scandalize, and enthrall his contemporaries—including
dark rumors of incest with his half-sister Augusta Leigh, his "Dear
Augusta"; a celebrated adultery with the fashionable and beautiful Lady
Caroline Lamb; and later in Italy a series of affairs with women, at least
in the estimate of his friend Shelley, of such low character that they

---

[1] *Byron: A Self-Portrait, Letters and Diaries, 1798–1824*, ed. Peter Quennell (London: Murray, 1950), I, ix.

367

"do not scruple to avow practices which are not only not named but I believe seldom even conceived in England." [2]

Byron's earliest years were spent in poverty, in the slums of Aberdeen, with his neurotic and possessive mother, constantly in debt and hiding from creditors. Then, when he was ten years old, he came into his title on the death of an uncle, "the wicked lord" Byron of Rochdale. But his inheritance was as rundown as its desolate seat at Newstead Abbey in Nottinghamshire, on the edge of Sherwood Forest, a ruined Gothic pile,

> . . . fast-falling, once resplendent dome . . .
> Proudly majestic frowns thy vaulted hall,
>   Scowling defiance on the blasts of fate.

Newstead Abbey was almost uninhabitable, its roof fallen in and its furnishings hauled away for debts. Nearly every asset of the barony was encumbered. But it was a great lordly inheritance, nonetheless, and a source of financial credit. Byron would be careless, even profligate, with money all his life.

But while he cared little about money, he cared much about fame. From Harrow, where he was placed at the urging of the family lawyer, he wrote his mother, "I can, I will cut myself a path through the world or perish in the attempt." [3] The process of cutting his path through the world really began in 1809, when he set out for a tour of the Continent with his lifelong friend, John Cam Hobhouse. He had already left Cambridge with a degree but with a totally undistinguished record. There is no hint that he ever attended a single lecture. But it should perhaps be noted that he kept in his rooms a girl casually disguised as a page and that, when he discovered university regulations forbade him to keep dogs, he bought a tame bear. He also ran up debts of £12,000. He had taken his hereditary seat in the House of Lords and rather extravagantly espoused a number of unpopular causes. And he had published the first small collections of his poetry. They were almost uniformly disliked by such critics as Southey, Scott, Wordsworth, and Coleridge. Byron attacked them in another poem, a savage satire called *English Bards and Scotch Reviewers*.

But the lure of the Continent lay ahead. Byron and Hobhouse visited Portugal and Spain, then Sardinia, Malta and Albania, Turkey and Greece —which completely won his heart, as its ruins dazzled him and its cruel subjugation to the Turks choked him with rage. He kept notebooks of his adventures and amatory conquests which became the basis for his first great poem, *Childe Harold's Pilgrimage*. The first two cantos were published in 1812, and Byron was instantly famous.

Again the critics tended to dislike the book. But the public adored it, not so much for its literary merits—which were considerable, despite

    [2] *Byron, The Critical Heritage,* ed. Andrew Rutherford (New York: Barnes and Noble, 1970), p. 156.
    [3] Quennell, I, ix.

contemporary critics—as for its exotic settings, its theme of travel and adventure, its gothic imagery, and especially because it was so obviously autobiographical. The scandalous young nobleman protested that he did not describe himself. But his readers knew that the youthful hero of "Albion's isle" was Byron. Who else had

> . . . spent his days in riot most uncouth,
> And vex'd with mirth the drowsy ear of
>   Night.
> Ah me! in sooth he was a shameless
>   wight.
>   Sore given to revel and ungodly glee;
>   Few earthly things found favour in his
>   sight
>   Save concubines and carnal companie,
> And flaunting wassailers of high and low
>   degree.

Poems continued to flow from Byron's pen, each more exotic and adventurous than the last—*The Giaour, The Bride of Abydos, The Corsair*. His notoriety increased with every poem and with every affair. Then he decided to marry. His unlikely choice of a bride was an aristocratic, cool young woman—Annabella Milbanke, whose main attraction seemed to be that she did not care for him! He pursued her tirelessly, and they were married in 1815. It was a disaster, only made worse by the birth of a daughter. Annabella left him and sued for permanent separation. She was a limited and literal-minded woman who failed utterly to understand her husband's extravagant flights of language, his drunken rages, his melancholy—to which she contributed—and his flippancy that seemed so cruel to her, and likely was. In a later canto of *Childe Harold* Byron spread the story of their separation before the world. She never forgave him this indignity. Indeed, she tried to get a physician to declare him insane. She was not alone in her suspicions. Byron had long admitted his own emotional instability and now was convinced he was going mad. Wordsworth pronounced him "somewhat cracked," and Shelley later wrote to a friend, "Lord Byron is an exceedingly interesting person and, as such, is it not to be regretted that he is a slave to the vilest and most vulgar prejudices, and as mad as a hatter?" [4]

In the spring of 1816 Byron left England again, never to return. He visited Brussels and the field of Waterloo, Cologne, and then Switzerland, where he met an English party including Shelley who, after the initial shock wore off, became Byron's warm friend—though he never really understood him. Shelley and his party departed, and Byron went to Italy.

4 *Byron, The Critical Heritage*, p. 37.

Byron fell in love with Italy, its sun, its landscapes, its history, its people, its women. Some degree of serenity at last came into his life, in good part because of his passion for a young Italian girl, Teresa Guiccioli, the wife of an aging and eccentric nobleman. He began work on what was to be his most famous book, *Don Juan*. The first two cantos were published in England in 1819, the next two in 1821. Others followed to cantos XV by the spring of 1823; the two final cantos were published after his death. It was again a tale of romantic wanderings and adventures, again strongly autobiographical and more scandalous than *Childe Harold*. John Murray, his publisher, pleaded with him to revise the manuscript; Byron refused. Again the critics attacked him. Wordsworth wrote, "I am persuaded that *Don Juan* will do more harm to the British character than anything of our time." [5] Southey, the Poet Laureate, called it "a foul blot on the literature of his country, an act of high treason on English poetry." [6]

In Italy, meanwhile, Byron followed Teresa and her husband from one city to another. He grew close to her family, especially her father and brother, who were deeply involved in the secret society of the Carbonari, one of several underground revolutionary groups dedicated to Italian independence. It was a thoroughly dangerous business, and Byron relished both the cause and the danger.

But he had never forgotten his passion for Greece. In 1822 word reached him of the outbreak of the Greek war for independence. He promptly joined the cause and threw himself into the work of supplying the rebels with money and support—without really understanding the sordid factionalism or the accumulation of petty local and personal causes of which the great cause of Greek independence was comprised. He was dazzled by the ideal, and with Byron in the forefront, Romantic Europe was too. The Greek war for independence was, in Byron's phrase, a "thorn in my couch." He rallied supporters, raised money, recruited troops, and even designed their uniforms. In the late summer of 1823 he himself went to Greece. He met several of the leaders of the revolt and joined a military contingent he had helped finance, training at Missolonghi on the Greek west coast. The climate did not agree with him and, as the rainy season came on, he was too energetic in his exertions. He suffered from recurring fevers. One day in April, 1824, despite his weakness, he insisted on riding in the driving rain. The fever set in again, and on the evening of April 19 he died. He was thirty-six years old.

[5] *Ibid.*, p. 164.
[6] *Ibid.*, p. 179.

The Character of Byron
THOMAS MOORE

The news of Byron's death caused shock, surprise, and grief across Europe. In England the young Tennyson scratched into a sandstone bank the words, "Byron is dead! Byron is dead!" There was a flurry of sentimental and heroic tributes, many of them in verse. The following lines from one by the Reverend W. L. Bowles is typical:

> *So ends Childe Harold his last pilgrimage!—*
> *Upon the shores of Greece he stood, and cried*
> *"Liberty!" and those shores, from age to age*
> *Renown'd, and Sparta's woods and rocks, replied*
> *"Liberty!" But a Spectre, at his side,*
> *Stood mocking;—and its dart, uplifting high,*
> *Smote him:—he sank to earth in life's fair pride.*

There was an immediate clamor for biographical accounts of Byron— which were not hard to come by, considering his celebrity, the obviously autobiographical strain running through virtually all his poetry, his hundreds of letters (among the most candid and charming of any English man of letters), his critical essays and notebooks, and the recollections of the host of people who knew him. But the task was harder than it seemed. For Byron was one of the most contradictory of men. Despite his endless love affairs, he was contemptuous of women, even of love. But he loved his daughter tenderly and was fiercely loyal to his friends. He was improvident and generous. He was mean and he was fine-spirited. People who met him in one of his gay and talkative moods could not believe he was the brooding, saturnine, often melancholy hero of Childe Harold. *He was capable of the most profound melancholy and self-hatred, but it could flash in an instant into mocking flippancy. He could be totally cynical about himself and about the Byron legend he had labored to create, and he loved to puncture that legend with great bursts of what would nowadays be called black humor.*

Among all the rest of the Byron material there was, however, an authentic and substantial autobiographical memoir, written some years earlier in Italy and given to his friend, the Irish poet Thomas Moore, to do with as he pleased. At the time of Byron's death, Moore had already sold the rights to the manuscript to the Longman publishing firm and was preparing to edit it for publication. But Byron's friend Hobhouse and his old publisher, John Murray, resolved to get hold of the manuscript and destroy it, in Hobhouse's words, "to lose no time in doing my duty by preserving all that was left to me of my friend, his fame." [7] *Hobhouse had not even read it! It was perhaps enough that Murray had declared it "horrid and disgusting." In any event, Hobhouse and Murray purchased back the rights to the manuscript from Longman (dragging Moore reluctantly along with them), had the necessary legal papers drawn up and signed, and in Murray's office they burned the memoir.*

In 1830 the same Thomas Moore wrote a biography of Byron in the form of an edition of Byron's letters and journals, along with "Notices of his Life." Hobhouse and many of Byron's other friends and admirers never forgave Moore for this "betrayal." Thomas Love Peacock, in reviewing the book, was unsparing of Moore's "querulous egotism" and "scaturient vanity bubbling up in every page," of his violation of "all the confidences of private life," and of what he considered Moore's malicious intent toward his subject. [8] *Most modern critics are kinder; indeed, they tend to regard Moore's biography as the best of the early lives of Byron, the most sensitive, perceptive, and accurate.*

In spite of his best efforts, however, Moore could not resolve the paradox of Byron's nature. In the end, he made it the central quality of that nature and of Byron's character.

IT MUST HAVE BEEN observed, throughout these pages, and by some, perhaps, with disappointment, that into the character of Lord Byron, as a poet, there has been little, if any, critical examination; but that, content with expressing generally the delight which, in common with all, I derive from his poetry, I have left the task of analyzing the sources from which this delight springs to others. In thus evading, if it must be so considered, one of my duties as a biographer, I have been influenced no less by a sense of my own inaptitude for the office of critic than by recollecting with what assiduity, throughout the whole of the poet's career, every new rising of his genius was watched from the great observatories of Criticism, and the ever-changing varieties of its course and splendour tracked out and recorded with a degree of skill and minuteness which has left but little for succeeding observers to discover. It is, moreover, into the character and conduct of Lord Byron as a man, not distinct from, but forming, on the contrary, the best illustration of his character as a writer, that it has been the more immediate purpose of these volumes to inquire; and if, in the course of them, any satisfactory clew has been afforded to those anomalies, moral and intellectual, which his life exhibited,—still more, should it have been the effect of my humble labours

---

[7] Quoted in Doris Langley Moore, *The Late Lord Byron* (New York: Lippincott, 1961), p. 14.
[8] *Ibid.,* p. 499.

to clear away some of those mists that hung round my friend, and show him, in most respects, as worthy of love as he was, in all, of admiration, then will the chief and sole aim of this work have been accomplished.

Having devoted to this object so large a portion of my own share of these pages, and, yet more fairly, enabled the world to form a judgment for itself, by placing the man, in his own person, and without disguise, before all eyes, there would seem to remain now but an easy duty in summing up the various points of his character, and, out of the features, already separately described, combining one complete portrait. The task, however, is by no means so easy as it may appear. There are few characters in which a near acquaintance does not enable us to discover some one leading principle or passion consistent enough in its operations to be taken confidently into account in any estimate of the disposition in which they are found. . . .

In Lord Byron, however, this sort of pivot of character was almost wholly wanting. Governed as he was at different moments by totally different passions, and impelled sometimes, as during his short access of parsimony in Italy, by springs of action never before developed in his nature, in him this simple mode of tracing character to its sources must be often wholly at fault; and if, as is not impossible, in trying to solve the strange variances of his mind, I should myself be found to have fallen into contradictions and inconsistencies, the extreme difficulty of analyzing, without dazzle or bewilderment, such an unexampled complication of qualities must be admitted as my excuse.

So various, indeed, and contradictory were his attributes, both moral and intellectual, that he may be pronounced to have been not one, but many; nor would it be any great exaggeration of the truth to say that out of the mere partition of the properties of his single mind a plurality of characters, all different and all vigorous, might have been furnished. It was this multiform aspect exhibited by him that led the world, during his short wondrous career, to compare him with that medley host of personages, almost all differing from each other, which he thus playfully enumerates in one of his Journals:—

I have been thinking over, the other day, on the various comparisons, good or evil, which I have seen published of myself in different journals, English and foreign. This was suggested to me by accidentally turning over a foreign one lately,—for I have made it a rule latterly never to *search* for anything of the kind, but not to avoid the perusal if presented by chance.

To begin, then: I have seen myself compared personally or poetically, in English, French, *German* (*as* interpreted to me), Italian, and Portuguese, within these nine years, to Rousseau, Goethe, Young, Aretine, Timon of Athens, Dante, Petrarch, 'an alabaster vase, lighted up within,' Satan, Shakespeare, Buonaparte, Tiberius, Æschylus, So-

phocles, Euripides, Harlequin, the Clown, Sternhold and Hopkins, to
the phantasmagoria, to Henry the Eighth, to Chenier, to Mirabeau, to
young R. Dallas (the schoolboy), to Michael Angelo, to Raphael, to a
petit-maitre, to Diogenes, to Childe Harold, to Lara, to the Count in
Beppo, to Milton, to Pope, to Dryden, to Burns, to Savage, to Chatter-
ton, to 'oft have I heard of thee, my Lord Biron,' in Shakespeare, to
Churchill the poet, to Kean the actor, to Alfieri, &c. &c. &c. . . .

It would not be uninteresting, were there either space or time for
such a task, to take a review of the names of note in the preceding
list, and show, in how many points, though differing so materially among
themselves, it might be found that each presented a striking resemblance
to Lord Byron. . . .
    By the extract just given from his Journal, it will be perceived that,
in Byron's own opinion, a character which, like his, admitted of so
many contradictory comparisons, could not be otherwise than wholly
undefinable itself. It will be found, however, on reflection, that this very
versatility, which renders it so difficult to fix, "ere it change," the fairy
fabric of his character is, in itself, the true clew through all that fabric's
mazes,—is in itself the solution of whatever was most dazzling in his
might or startling in his levity, of all that most attracted and repelled,
whether in his life or his genius. A variety of powers almost boundless,
and a pride no less vast in displaying them,—a susceptibility of new impressions and impulses, even beyond the usual allotment of genius, and
an uncontrolled impetuosity, as well from habit as temperament, in
yielding to them,—such were the two great and leading sources of all
that varied spectacle which his life exhibited; of that succession of victories achieved by his genius, in almost every field of mind that genius
ever trod, and of all those sallies of character in every shape and direction
that unchecked feeling and dominant self-will could dictate. . . .
    The quality which I have here denominated versatility, as applied
to *power*, Lord Byron has himself designated by the French word
"mobility," as applied to *feeling* and *conduct;* and, in one of the Cantos
of Don Juan, has described happily some of its lighter features. After
telling us that his hero had begun to doubt, from the great predominance
of this quality in her, "how much of Adeline was *real*," he says,—

> "So well she acted, all and every part,
>   By turns,—with that vivacious versatility,
> Which many people take for want of heart.
>   They err—'tis merely what is call'd mobility,
> A thing of temperament and not of art,
>   Though seeming so, from its supposed facility;
> And false—though true; for surely they're sincerest,
> Who are strongly acted on by what is nearest."

That he was fully aware not only of the abundance of this quality in his own nature, but of the danger in which it placed consistency and singleness of character, did not require the note on this passage, where he calls it "an unhappy attribute," to assure us. The consciousness, inneed, of his own natural tendency to yield thus to every chance impression, and change with every passing impulse, was not only for ever present in his mind, but,—aware as he was of the suspicion of weakness attached by the world to any retraction or abandonment of long-professed opinions,—had the effect of keeping him in that general line of consistency, on certain great subjects, which, notwithstanding occasional fluctuations and contradictions as to the details of these very subjects, he continued to preserve throughout life. A passage from one of his manuscripts will show how sagaciously he saw the necessity of guarding himself against his own instability in this respect.

> The world visits change of politics or change of religion with a more severe censure than a mere difference of opinion would appear to me to deserve. But there must be some reason for this feeling;—and I think it is that these departures from the earliest instilled ideas of our childhood, and from the line of conduct chosen by us when we first enter into public life, have been seen to have more mischievous results for society, and to prove more weakness of mind than other actions, in themselves more immoral.

The same distrust in his own steadiness, thus keeping alive in him a conscientious self-watchfulness, concurred not a little, I have no doubt, with the innate kindness of his nature, to preserve so constant and unbroken the greater number of his attachments through life;—some of them, as in the instance of his mother, owing evidently more to a sense of duty than to real affection the consistency with which, so creditably to the strength of his character, they were maintained.

But while in these respects, as well as in the sort of task-like perseverance with which the habits and amusements of his youth were held fast by him, he succeeded in conquering the variableness and love of novelty so natural to him, in all else that could engage his mind, in all the excursions, whether of his reason or his fancy, he gave way to this versatile humour without scruple or check,—taking every shape in which genius could manifest its power, and transferring himself to every region of thought where new conquests were to be achieved.

It was impossible but that such a range of will and power should be abused. It was impossible that, among the spirits he invoked from all quarters, those of darkness should not appear, at his bidding, with those of light. And here the dangers of an energy so multifold, and thus luxuriating in its own transformations, show themselves. To this one great object of displaying power,—various, splendid, and all adorning power,—every other consideration and duty were but too likely to be sacrificed. Let the advocate but display his eloquence and art, no matter what the cause;—let the stamp of energy be but left behind, no matter with what seal. *Could* it have been expected that from such a career no mischief would ensue, or that among these cross-lights of imagination the moral vision could remain undisturbed? *Is* it to be at all wondered at that in the works of one thus gifted and carried away, we should find,— wholly, too, without any prepense design of corrupting on his side,—a false splendour given to Vice to make it look like Virtue, and Evil too often invested with a grandeur which belongs intrinsically but to Good?

Among the less serious ills flowing from this abuse of his great versatile powers,—more especially as exhibited in his most characteristic work, Don Juan,—it will be found that even the strength and impressiveness of his poetry is sometimes not a little injured by the capricious and desultory flights into which this pliancy of wing allures him. . . . But, on the whole, favourable as was all this quickness and variety of association to the extension of the range and resources of his poetry, it may be questioned whether a more select concentration of his powers would not have afforded a still more grand and precious result. . . . If Lord Byron had not been so actively versatile, so totally under the dominion of

> A fancy like the air, most free,
> And full of mutability,

he would not have been less wonderful, perhaps, but more great.

Nor was it only in his poetical creations that this love and power of variety showed itself;—one of the most pervading weaknesses of his life may be traced to the same fertile source.

The Romantic Revolutionary
WILFRED S. DOWDEN

Romanticism was as much the child of the French Revolution as Napoleon was, perhaps more so. For the Romantics—painters like Delacroix, composers like Verdi and Rossini, even Beethoven, and an endless stream of writers—continued to burn with the passion of revolutionary causes right on through the early nineteenth century. In this

*important connection, as in virtually every facet of Romanticism, Byron
led the way. The heroes of his works were all, in one way or another,
champions of fettered liberty, and throughout his life he identified with
popular and revolutionary causes.*

*Yet even in the cause of revolution and liberty, the paradoxical
element in Byron was not entirely absent. Sir Walter Scott took him
to task for his sentimentalizing of Napoleon's defeat at Waterloo—
"this place of skulls," "the grave of France"—when Byron had earlier
ranted against Napoleon's tyranny in Spain. And his readings of the
history of tyranny and freedom, especially in Italy, were often as muddled
as they were passionate. There is evidence that he was becoming
disillusioned with the sorry state of the Greek war for independence
in the months before his death and as he saw the war at first hand.*

*In the following selection, Wilfred S. Dowden takes the position that
"Byron's consistency was not in politics," in which he was often wrong,
but in the social doctrine that lay beneath the surface of political action;
that Byron was not paradoxical in his love of liberty but consistent.*

IF WE WERE to apply Emerson's maxim of the foolish consistency to the
mind of Lord Byron, we should find that it was neither small nor plagued
with hobgoblins. His lordship was nothing if not inconsistent. His career
bears witness to this fact, for his life was full of radical changes. His
poetry, too, is inconsistent. For example, he experimented with many
metrical forms, trying established measures of his own country (such
as the heroic couplet of the school of Pope), as well as measures formerly
used almost exclusively by foreign poets (such as the ottava rima of
Pulci). In content, too, this inconsistency is manifest. His habit of changing, within a single paragraph or stanza, from a mood of high seriousness
to one of light banality cannot be overlooked by even the most casual
reader of his poetry. Yet, there was one point on which he never varied
in his thinking.

In a recent study of Byron, Professor Paul Trueblood explains that
the poet's medium was satire and that he began his career with satirical
verse, turned from it to sentiment in *Childe Harold* and other poems,
and finally returned to it in *Don Juan, The Vision of Judgment,* and
works of the later period. He also explains that Byron became increasingly
serious in political and social doctrines from December, 1820, when he
broke off the composition of *Don Juan* after completing his fifth canto, to
June, 1822, when he took up the poem again. He says, too, that there is
evidence in the last eight cantos of *Don Juan* of revolutionary indoctrination, which was not apparent earlier.

There can be no doubt that Byron exhibited maturity and found his
poetic medium in the satire of *Don Juan, The Irish Avatar,* and other
of these later poems. In them he could attack cant, religious, political,

and moral, as he had never been able to attack it in verses of the *Childe Harold* type. His nature was basically satirical, and he returned to that form of verse as a natural consequence of this nature.

If, however, he turned away from satire in the poems of the middle period, he did not turn away from the principles of his satiric verse, or from the abuses at which he directed it. He did not wield the cudgel so effectively in sentimental verse as in satire, but he wielded it, nevertheless, against the same enemy which he attacked in the later cantos of *Don Juan*.

This consistency in Byron's social doctrine is indicated best, I think, by an entry in his journal on January 16, 1814:

> As for me, by the blessing of indifference, I have simplified my politics into an utter detestation of all existing governments; and, as it is the shortest and most agreeable and summary feeling imaginable, the first moment of an universal republic would convert me into an advocate for single and uncontradicted despotism. The fact is, riches are power, and poverty is slavery all over the earth, and one sort of establishment is no better nor worse for a *people* than another. . . . I have no consistency, except in politics; and that probably arises from my indifference on the subject altogether.

After we have loosed this statement from its tangle of Byronic facetiousness, one fact is clear: Byron's consistency was not in his politics, as he maintained. His interest in government was in what it would do for a people, and his consistent theme in his poetry, as in his life, was a relentless fight against oppression and for freedom. He was no more serious in thought and purpose in this respect in 1823 than he was in 1812. . . .

The opportunity of devoting himself to the cause of freedom came in the last few years of his career, during the Italian and Greek struggles for independence; but throughout his life he seemed to be seeking some cause on which to expend his energy. Had the opportunity presented itself earlier, there is little doubt that he would have flung himself into the fight then as wholeheartedly as he did in 1823. . . .

But Byron was first of all a poet; so it will be well for us to turn our attention from his brief and stormy political career in order to examine his literary productions. We look first at *Childe Harold,* because it is, I think, a key poem. In the first place, it covers a large part of Byron's creative period. He began work on it early in his career and did not finish it until 1818, six years before his death; and his mind was occupied with it during much of that time. In the second place, it contains many ideas on the subject of liberty, which he developed more fully in other poems and dramas. It is, therefore, a kind of catch-all and carry-all of Byron's thoughts on social doctrine.

It is a significant fact, I think, that Byron returns again and again

to the love of freedom in his description of each of the places Childe
Harold visits. This fact is true, not only of the first two cantos, published
in 1812, but also of cantos three and four, published in 1816 and 1818
respectively. In Lisbon, for example, he notes with horror the poverty
and slavery which abound there. In Spain he sees that Seville is free but
must soon fall to the tyrant. The history of Spain indicates that the fight
for freedom has been a long one, and he regrets that the tree of liberty
is not yet planted in Spanish soil. . . .

He also laments for Greece when he compares her present state with
her past glory. He regrets that Greece is a "sad relic of departed worth."
He laments the fact that the people are slaves from birth to death, and
that every "carle can lord it o'er the land." He dreams that the hour is
near which shall give Greece back the heritage that is hers—her lost
liberty. "What spirit," he asks, "shall call thee from the tomb?" The
Greeks themselves cry for foreign arms and aid. But he calls indignantly
to these hereditary bondsmen: Do they not know that they who would
be free must strike the blow themselves? Help from outside may "lay
their despoilers low," but that will *not* win freedom's flame. He ends this
plea by calling on Greece to change her lords; her "glorious day is o'er,
but not [her] years of shame."

We are not surprised by the first significant fact exhibited in this
passage. Byron shows here a deep love for liberty. He had shown that
in the first canto and in some early poems and letters as well. We note,
however, that in calling upon the hereditary bondsmen of Greece to rid
themselves of their present lords, and in admonishing them that they
alone can achieve the freedom they deserve, he is anticipating revolutionary indoctrination, which, as Mr. Trueblood points out, is part of
the essence of the latter cantos of *Don Juan.* Byron was indoctrinated
with revolutionary fervor a good while before the appearance of the
great satires of the later period, or, for that matter, before appearance
of *Childe Harold,* Canto IV, in 1818. Had he found a more suitable
means of expression in his earlier career, he would have raised a stronger
voice on behalf of these principles.

Revolution, Byron would say, is the means by which a country might
rid itself of tyrants and achieve the freedom it deserves. The idea of
revolution versus tyranny was much on his mind, and the thought of one
seemed to lead to an expression of the other. Thus there are several discussions of each in *Childe Harold.* . . .

The tendency toward revolution is expressed in a letter to Tom Moore,
dated April 20, 1814. Byron explains that he refused to see Louis XVIII
make his triumphal entry into London; but, he says, "in some coming year
of Hegira, I should not dislike to see the place where he *had* reigned,
shortly after the second revolution and a happy sovereignty of two months,
the last six weeks being civil war."

The "Ode to Napoleon Buonaparte," which was published in 1814, is in keeping with the spirit of this letter. . . . Napoleon had the opportunity of being something other than a tyrant, but he had to don the purple and tyrannize, as had those whom he conquered. Thus, he was doomed to failure. . . . Byron's thesis that tyrants are conquered only by tyrants, [is expressed] later in *Childe Harold.* . . .

The poet is led to a brief discussion of the French Revolution, and herein lies much of Byron's philosophy of "revolution in the right cause." The French people made themselves a fearful monument, the wreck of old opinions. They went too far and overthrew good with evil; hence they left ruins and only the foundations upon which to renew dungeons and thrones. In short, tyrants were conquered by tyrants. . . .

The cause of liberty and laments for its loss are no less ardent in the last canto of the poem than they had been in the first three. Italy is the object of the poet's description, and he leads off with an account of his impressions of Venice. After a few introductory remarks he returns to his old theme. He regrets that Venice, after thirteen hundred years of freedom, is now in submission to foreign foes. . . .

The Prophecy of Dante was not published until April 12, 1821; but since Byron first mentions it early in 1820, we may assume that it was on his mind the year before. If this assumption is correct, then, the composition of the poem was not far removed in time from that of the last canto of *Childe Harold,* and would naturally contain many of the ideas expressed in the earlier work.

The theme of the *Prophecy* is the unification and freedom of Italy. . . . The history of Italy is . . . presented as if it were being prophesied by Dante. Italy, he says, will succumb to each tyrant who invades her. She has already fallen to the Goth and German; Frank and Hun are yet to come. But Italy still has "hearts, and hands, and arms" with which to fight oppression. . . .

The consistency in Bryon's social doctrine is exemplified in his dramas as well as in his poetry. On April 9, 1820, he wrote to Murray that he had begun work on *Marino Faliero, Doge of Venice.* The drama was completed in July, 1820, and published with *The Prophecy of Dante* the following year. He found the story in Marin Sanuto's *Lives of the Doges.* . . .

These three works on Italian history, all of which dealt with the problem of Italian freedom, were published at a time when unification was the primary question and the Carbonari were secretly active. They could not have escaped official notice. Byron's letters to friends in England at this time are full of allusions to the situation in Italy and of his own active participation in these affairs. He harbored the ammunition and arms of the liberals in his home, offered to defend any who were in danger of arrest by the authorities, offered his house as a kind of fort to be used by the liberals until the countryside could be aroused. . . .

The part Byron played in the Greek fight for independence is too well known and too complex to be discussed here. Suffice it to say that we now know that he did not go to Greece out of any feeling of boredom or philhellenic enthusiasm. Richard Edgecumbe and Harold Nicholson, in their studies of Byron's activities in Greece, did away with that misconception long ago. Indeed, some of his contemporaries realized the importance of his part in the Greek fight for liberty, as witness this statement taken from an article in *The Gentleman's Magazine* for June, 1824:

> Lord Byron had succeeded . . . in stirring up among the people of the part of Greece in which he resided, an almost inconceivable enthusiasm. His exertions were incessant in their cause, and the gratitude of the people was proportioned to them. His influence was not lessened by being employed often to procure humane, even kind treatment towards the Turkish captives.

But if we are to understand Byron, we have to take, not glimpses, but an over-all view of the man and the poet. Such a view will reveal to us one who never wavered in the pursuit of his objective. He began his career with expressions of hope for the freedom of man. He continued to express this hope, which is a dominant element in most of his poetry, and he ended his days striving, successfully, to instill that hope and love of liberty in the hearts of a suffering people.

The Poetic Self-Image
ELIZABETH FRENCH BOYD

We have already noted that one of the most characteristic features of Byron's poetry was its autobiographical content. Certainly it was its most popular feature, as his readers thrilled to each veiled revelation of scandal and outrageous escapade and every declaration of revolutionary principle. As one modern scholar has put it, "It is Byron and Byron's idea of himself

which held his work together, just as that idea enthralled Europe." Byron
was his own "raw material to be satanized."[9]

   The following selection is taken from a study of Byron's Don Juan *by*
Elizabeth French Boyd and applies the autobiographic thesis to the greatest
of his poetic works. The argument turns on the point that the poem was
never finished. Here again, we meet with the paradoxical nature of Byron.
The last canto he wrote—he took the notes with him to Greece—finds
his hero in an English castle inhabited by an ancient clerical ghost. But
neither his encounter with this spirit nor his more fleshly encounter with
the lovely mistress of the castle is ever resolved. The poem simply ends:
"I leave the thing a problem, like all things." Was the specter a premonition
of Byron's own end? Was the lady a symbol of life and the ghost a symbol
of death? What did the lady's final enigmatic smile really mean? One
modern critic has said of Don Juan, *"The poem is identifiable with Byron's*
mature life, and excludes nothing vital in that life, and so could not be
finished until Byron was." [10] *Boyd essentially agrees "that he had carried*
Juan's story as far as he could on the basis of his present positive
knowledge and belief," that he "left the word and took up the deed: he
completed Don Juan *in action."*

THE CONFLUENCE IN *Don Juan* of literary motifs from every age and clime
of European literature gives the poem the richness of its texture and the
universality of its appeal. Here is the evidence that the mind of Byron,
brooding on his own strange fortunes and explaining himself in the story
of Don Juan, is the mind of a true poet. Imprisoned like every human
being in the mystery of life on this planet, and that imprisonment made
doubly bitter for him by the peculiarities of his physical nature and by
his errors which he interpreted fatalistically, he could nevertheless give
voice for common human nature to the mystery and the bitterness. That
Byron the poet rose with such urbanity and such triumph over the limitations of Byron the man is the final act in the drama, the act which makes
the drama a tragedy in the true sense. . . .

   . . . In spite of his stormy and disrupted career, books were Byron's
constant companions. They instructed him, steadied him, comforted him,
fed his imagination, and enlarged his intellectual horizon. The role of
books in his life is extremely important, though secondary to his intense
personal experience.

   To be a little fanciful, we might say that he behaved toward books as
he did toward his friends and enemies, though more cavalierly, without

   [9] *Byron, A Collection of Critical Essays,* ed. Paul West (Englewood Cliffs, N.J.:
Prentice-Hall, 1963), p. 2.
   [10] Harold Bloom, *The Visionary Company: A Reading of English Romantic Poetry*
(New York: Doubleday, 1961), p. 251.

the polish and restraint of manners. He trusted books rather naïvely, but he was rough with them. As Leigh Hunt recollected, the fiercely creased, double and triple dog-ears in books which Byron had read were symbolic of Byron's attitude toward them. Books were tools to be used, servants to supply the overwhelming needs of that amalgam of thought and feeling that was Byron's mind. The same arrogance, ruthlessness, and absorbing egotism are demonstrated here as in Byron's other relationships. But on the other hand, we find likewise the same awe, genuine admiration of excellence, envy and emulation of a recognized superior, the same tenderness, passionate opinionated loyalty, and hard commonsense.

Useful, informational reading appealed to Byron, but, as with most of us, to a less degree than the reading of poetry and fiction. Byron's commonsense told him how to acquire information by means of short cuts. He relied on historical and biographical dictionaries and on "epitomes of information" like Burton's *Anatomy* and Aulus Gellius' *Attic Nights,* and on rich historical surveys like Gibbon and Mitford. But the power generated by such reading and rereading was certainly not secondary to what a lesser mind might have accomplished by more painful study. The drudgery of study Byron usually avoided, though he undertook it from time to time, when his mind "needed something craggy to break itself on," or when he had a definite purpose of composition in view.

In poetry and fiction, the range, the catholicity, one might almost say the tastelessness, of his choice of favorites reflect faithfully the division of direction in his own poetic productions. Lucian, Juvenal, Lucretius, Ariosto and Tasso, Pope and Scott, Rousseau and Voltaire—the mind which could embrace all these at once was bound to be a divided mind and to produce a mixed poetry. Byron's mind was autocratic and incapable of receiving a single decisive influence. Even Shelley, who had the most far-reaching effect on him, could teach him only temporarily and by indirection. Byron's intellectual integrity was stubborn; he learned from opposition, from the pressure of circumstances, and from the long percolation of ideas derived from books, colleagues, and personal experience. But his catholicity of taste was only an extreme case of romantic eclecticism. Byron's library and his poetic principles and practice demonstrate the clash of systems and tastes in all the world of thought and of creative art at the meeting of the eighteenth and nineteenth centuries. Some poets and some thinkers were removed farther to the right or to the left of the clash. Byron was squarely at its center. He stayed there through his career, feeding on conflict, achieving poise in the midst of opposing forces.

Byron read with intense vitality and awareness. He defined the chief value of living as the feeling of being alive, and this full liveliness appears in the contemporaneity of his viewpoint toward books. He had a strong sense of the past, enlarging as his studies went on to include archaeology and geology. But he judged all the past, even the most remote, in the light of the present. To him, everything was vivid, near, and personally applicable even in the most ancient books. What came out of the presses from modern authors might be disappointingly inferior, but it was immediately compared with all the literature of the past. For Byron there is no division between poets, the great dead and the mere living. The race of poets goes on uninterrupted; there is a tradition to preserve, a right and wrong to uphold or to combat, a future to poetry.

The sense of competition increased Byron's urgency to know everything new. His avid interest in contemporary literature contains a degree of amusing furtiveness and shame, which, however, a less candid nature than Byron's would never have revealed. In his mind, the hierarchy of the great, the near great, the passable average, and the unworthy is constantly ranged to join the similar hierarchy of past poets. He thought he knew where he belonged in that grouping—on a fairly low level, though he was ambitious to rise. One of his methods of rising was to exhibit himself publicly and associate himself privately with what he considered the best, the aristocracy of poets. But he did not deny himself the pleasure of absorbing what he thought the second- and third-rate too. . . . In this, his practice was like Shakespeare's and many another English poet's.

Byron once confessed that his mind was a fragment, and that it was no wonder he produced fragments of poetry. Lord Ernle has called *Don Juan* "the least incomplete portrait of Byron himself," and perhaps its gigantic fragmentariness is the most characteristic feature of the portrait.

Why did Byron not complete this poem? Had he lost interest in it, or said all that he had to say? Had he lost interest in writing anything in the face of the call to action in Greece? My conviction is that he had carried Juan's story as far as he could on the basis of his present positive knowledge and belief. The introduction of the supernatural was a brake on his creative momentum, for it brought him up sharply against his inhibiting skepticism.

For sixteen cantos, skepticism had been held in suspense in the ruminative digressions, while the story marched on in positive conviction. But at the end of Canto XVI, Byron was confronted with a choice that he still did not feel ready to make: he had either to show Juan drifting toward disaster, as he had drifted in similar circumstances, or he had to show him maturing in character to make a heroic stand against circumstances, so that he might survive for his destined role as a hero of liberty. Juan's maturity could be based only on a conviction of the value of moral action, and that could spring either from "principles" or from experience. Juan had no principles, and very little experience of moral action; sudden maturity would be a rather too surprising development in his character. Byron's "principles," on the other hand, were unsettled by the chaotic state of his philosophic and religious thinking, and he had had less experience than he craved in positive moral action. I picture him as coming to the point in Juan's story over which his forecasting mind had been painfully hesitating for years, and having to postpone the completion of the poem until he had acquired more experience and a greater degree of certainty. He might have carried on the *satire* of *Don Juan* indefinitely, but the direction of the *story* required positive rather than antagonistic or oppugnant views.

Over and above this intellectual dilemma lay the terrifying emotional tangle. To go back in memory and merely to recount the conflicts and the bitter passions and remorse would have been a self-punishment not to be endured. But to attempt to extract their essence, to resolve the tangle, perhaps to blame himself by implication, to confess and repent publicly—Byron could not objectify that story, not in poetry.

Don Juan, for all its negations, is fundamentally an affirmative poem. . . . [Byron's] earliest aim, a poem "to giggle and make giggle" (a phrase he borrowed from Ginguené's description of Pulci), persisted, but it was the comedian's method of conveying grave truths.

Like his master Pope, Byron felt a primary and almost exclusive concern with human nature and human society. Though he dabbled unceasingly in metaphysical speculation, he postponed defining and elaborating abstractions, from a hard-headed conviction that he could know only what came to him through his senses. He cared supremely for reality, and in one sense, the outward show of things is the only reality for him; but he knew that in a truer sense, there must be abstract reality behind the outward show. This was what he was searching for and what he partially found. For there are abstract conceptions at the back of his individualizing. While the behavior of human beings is the important object of his observation, abstract morality is the center of his universe. His cynicism, if at bottom he has any, springs from his ideal of perfection in human nature which he sees everywhere betrayed by frailty and ignorance. He has the preternaturally clear sight and just sense of proportion that belong to the satirist and the humorist, and also to the perfectionist.

Paradoxically for a poet, and especially for one who affirmed the power of the word, Byron distrusted verbiage. Verbal explanations and systematizations may satisfy some minds, but action is what counts. Life, for him, is made up of the action of feelings and the action of deeds, and manifests itself in a pageant of tangible effects. Time and change subdue all these appearances ("all things are a show"), but the mind of man, the source of feeling and action, is eternal and unchangeable. The mind with its innate feelings is for Byron the manifestation of a central, unshakable Godhead, the reason that, for all his skepticism, he could and did frequently affirm his belief in God, in truth, in right, and in immortality. God is a moral being, and man is his image.

With this scale of value Byron measured mankind and the world with a just proportion. The denials of value or of constancy in the temporary show of things passed in review through *Don Juan* are the repeated answers of the perfectionist forced to comment on an imperfect world.

They should be read in the light of Byron's subsequent behavior in the imperfect world of Greek revolution and political skullduggery as much as in his surrender to imperfection of life in Venice and London. For, as Lord Ernle has pointed out, Byron had one solitary conviction on the value of moral action, that bridged the hiatus between his abstract beliefs and his practice: through courageous moral action, the world will achieve the ideal of liberty.

The history of Byron's intellectual skepticism is the drama of the opposing tendencies in his nature toward participation and toward isolation. He is a skeptic who would like to persuade himself that he is perfectly poised in his skepticism, but who is really so uncomfortable in it that he is constantly launching out on a new, though hopeless, struggle toward belief. He longs to believe and shrinks from believing because he thinks himself incurably solitary and independent at the center of opposing systems. During most of his life he is unwilling to commit himself, either in poetry or in action. Nature and fate have made him solitary and an outsider. He cannot give himself wholly to anything, to an individual, a social group, a party, or a system of belief. He is the Pilgrim of Eternity. Yet he longed to submit and to be absorbed. The glory of Byron's life is that at last he did commit himself in the cause of Greek liberty. It does not do to explain away this last decided commitment by references to his ambition, to his boredom, and to all the other motives for the Greek expedition which were most undoubtedly and compellingly present. The fact of heroic self-sacrifice remains. Byron was right when he said that we should not dig for motives and causes and thereby destroy the value of a good deed and a good effect:

> 'T is sad to hack into the root of things,
>   They are so much intertwisted with the earth;
> So that the branch a goodly verdure flings,
>   I reck not if an acorn gave it birth.

He begged Colonel Stanhope to judge him by his actions and not by his words. This final commitment was what Byron was working out for himself in *Don Juan,* explaining his origin and his history, not in any crassly objective autobiography, but in the deepest sense, in the mirror of poetry. Don Juan was to have died for human freedom. Byron left the word and took up the deed: he completed *Don Juan* in action.

Suggestions for Further Reading

ALTHOUGH ROMANTIC POETRY is no longer much in fashion, students should sample Byron, especially the autobiographical *Childe Harold's Pilgrimage* and *Don Juan*, which so titillated his contemporaries. There are many editions of Byron's works—his poems, his essays, his letters, diaries, even his conversations. Two convenient, well-edited selections are *Byron: A Self-Portrait, Letters and Diaries, 1798 to 1824*, ed. Peter Quennell, 2 vols. (London: Murray, 1950), and *Byron, Selections from Poetry, Letters, and Journals*, ed. Peter Quennell (London: Nonesuch Press, 1949). One of the most useful collections of Byron criticism is *Byron, The Critical Heritage*, ed., Andrew Rutherford (New York: Barnes and Noble, 1970), a massive, carefully selected sampling largely of contemporary critical comment on Byron and his work. The best guide to Byron's work and one of the best works on Byron himself is by the eminent biographer and editor of Byron, Leslie A. Marchand, *Byron's Poetry: A Critical Introduction* (Boston: Houghton Mifflin, 1965). There are two good collections of modern Byron criticism: *Byron, A Collection of Critical Essays*, ed. Paul West (Englewood Cliffs, N.J.: Prentice-Hall, 1963), and *Twentieth Century Interpretations of Don Juan*, ed. Edward E. Bostetter (Englewood Cliffs, N.J.: Prentice-Hall, 1969). Two additional basic studies of *Don Juan* can also be recommended: Paul G. Trueblood, *The Flowering of Byron's Genius: Studies in Byron's Don Juan* (New York: Russell and Russell, 1962 [1945]), and Elizabeth French Boyd, *Byron's Don Juan, A Critical Study* (London: Routledge and Kegan Paul, 1958 [1946]), excerpted in this chapter.

The great modern definitive work on Byron is Leslie A. Marchand, *Byron: A Biography*, 3 vols. (New York: Knopf, 1957), but students may prefer his *Byron: A Portrait* (New York: Knopf, 1970), the best brief biography. Another good brief biography is Paul G. Trueblood, *Lord Byron*, rev. ed. (New York: Twayne, 1977), and there are two good introductory works on Byron and his age: John D. Jump, *Byron* (London and Boston: Routledge and Kegan Paul, 1972), and Derek Parker, *Byron and His World* (New York: Viking, 1969). There are also a number of special studies that can be recommended. Bernard D. Grebanier, *The Uninhibited Byron: An Account of His Sexual Confusion* (New York: Crown, 1970), deals with another aspect of the Byron paradox, which is the theme of this chapter. This is also the central theme of a first-rate historical novel, Frederic Prokosch, *The Missolonghi Manuscript* (New

York: Farrar, Straus, 1967). John Buxton, *Byron and Shelley: The History of a Friendship* (New York: Harcourt, Brace and World, 1958), traces this famous friendship in a kind of dual biography. David A. Howarth, *The Greek Adventure: Lord Byron and Other Eccentrics in the War of Independence* (New York: Atheneum, 1976), is a lively, often hilarious book about a war at once silly and horrible and its enormous appeal to such Romantic adventurers as Byron. Doris Langley Moore, *The Late Lord Byron: Posthumous Dramas* (Philadelphia: Lippincott, 1961), is a striking account of the scandalous scramble over Byron, his literary estate, and his reputation following his death.

Byron is part and parcel of the linkage between Romanticism and revolution. Thus, works on this general topic will be germane to further study of Byron. Some of the works listed in the previous chapter regarding Byron's political era also apply here. More specifically, Romanticism is dealt with in a good collection of readings, *Romanticism: Problems of Definition, Explanation, and Evaluation*, ed. John B. Halsted (Boston: Heath, 1965), and Ronald W. Harris, *Romanticism and the Social Order, 1780–1830* (London: Blandford, 1969), a survey of the principal British literary figures, including Byron, and their social and political views. Finally, two important revisionist works can be recommended: J. L. Talmon, *Romanticism and Revolt: Europe 1815–1848* (New York: Harcourt, Brace and World, 1967), advances the thesis that Romanticism was the product of the cultural disruption caused by the French Revolution; and Howard Mumford Jones, *Revolution and Romanticism* (Cambridge, Mass.: Harvard University Press, 1974), argues that Romanticism was not so much the child of the Revolution as its most important survivor.

Charles Darwin and the Evolutionary Revolution

Charles Darwin (1809–1882), the man whose name is indelibly associated with the revolutionary theory of biological evolution, was the son of a prosperous Shropshire physician. His grandfather Erasmus Darwin had been not only a physician but an amateur scientist of some note and an early advocate of evolutionary theory. From the beginning, Darwin was destined for the family profession. At sixteen he was enrolled in the great medical school of the University of Edinburgh but was a dismal failure. He hated the work and could not stand the sight of blood. Darwin's father was convinced that it was a matter not of disposition but of indifference. "You care for nothing but shooting, dogs and rat-catching," he said, "and you will be a disgrace to yourself and all your family." [1] There was more than a little truth in his father's angry charge: Darwin's only real enthusiasms were for hunting and natural history.

The decision was made to send him to Christ's College, Cambridge, to prepare for a career in the church. His academic record at Cambridge was only slightly less dismal than it had been at Edinburgh, and he scraped through his degree finally with a bare "pass" in 1831. In the years at Cambridge, however, Darwin continued his passion for natural history and collecting. It was not an unusual interest, for science was much the vogue in the early nineteenth century and tied in with the generally

[1] Quoted in J. W. Burrow, "Makers of Modern Thought: Charles Darwin," *Horizon*, 8, no. 4 (Autumn 1966), 42.

accepted notions of natural theology, that is, the conviction that the phenomena of nature were the specific evidences of God's wonderfully reasonable order of creation. The intellectual world in which Charles Darwin grew up was smug, orderly, and comfortable.

While at Cambridge, Darwin met two great teachers, the biologist John Stevens Henslow and the geologist Adam Sedgwick. Both men took the young naturalist with them on collecting trips, and Henslow, in particular, made him a kind of protégé. He invited Darwin to the famous Friday evening discussions at his home; he gently urged him to take this course or hear that lecture; he recommended books, encouraged his interests, and taught him the value of patient, careful, minute observation. It was Henslow who recommended Darwin for the job that he himself had reluctantly had to turn down, as unpaid naturalist aboard HMS *Beagle,* about to set out in 1831 on a scientific and mapping voyage to the Southern Hemisphere.

Darwin was offered the position, and, barely overcoming the reluctance of his father, he accepted. As a parting gift, Henslow gave him a copy of the recently published first volume of Charles Lyell's *Principles of Geology,* the work that was to revolutionize geology in the same way— and amid the same furor—that Darwin's would revolutionize biology. For Lyell contended, in contradiction to the accepted biblical chronology, that the earth had not been created in a few thousand years by catastrophic change but rather was millions of years old. It is worth noting that Henslow, while he admired Lyell's method, was unalterably opposed to his conclusions, as he would later be to Darwin's. The captain of the *Beagle,* Robert FitzRoy, confided to Darwin that he hoped that his collections and observations would prove, once and for all, the literal truth of God's creation as set forth in the Bible. At this point, Darwin found nothing strange in such a notion. But in the course of the five-year voyage, his work led him not toward that notion but away from it. The voyage of the *Beagle* was the turning point in Darwin's life.

On his return to England, Darwin was elected a Fellow of the Royal Society, worked briefly for the Geographical Society, and came to know Sir Charles Lyell, whose works he had long admired. Then in 1839 he married his cousin Emma Wedgwood and three years later bought "a good, very ugly house with 18 acres" [2] at Down in Kent, where he spent the rest of his life. Amid the "quiet gladness" of his family, in his study and library and at his modest window-ledge laboratory, Darwin worked out the theories that had begun to emerge in the notebooks and jottings he had made during his voyage half-way around the world. In 1856, as he was preparing the abstract for a paper that would present those theories, he received a communication from another scientist, Alfred Russel Wallace, with a sketch of a paper setting out exactly the same views. In

[2] Quoted in Walter Karp, *Charles Darwin and the Origin of Species* (New York: Harper & Row, 1968), p. 85.

spite of the fact that Wallace's work was almost entirely theoretical while
his own rested upon a mass of detailed scientific observations and data,
the modest Darwin was ready to withdraw from the field. But his friend
Lyell intervened, brought the two men together, and arranged for their
work to appear as a joint paper, "On the Tendency of Species to Form
Varieties; and on the Perpetuation of Varieties and Species by Natural
Means of Selection." The paper was read before the Linnaean Society
in 1858 and published in the journal of the society for the same year. It
caused no stir at all.

But this was not the case when, in the following year, Darwin published
his *On the Origin of Species by Means of Natural Selection, or the
Preservation of Favoured Races in the Struggle for Life.* The book was
a sensation: the first printing sold out in a single day. The theory of
evolution was at last before the public essentially in its modern form.

To a considerable extent, the theory of evolution was an idea whose
time had come. It had been speculated upon since antiquity, and the
theory itself, in broad and general terms, had been revived by the
freethinkers and rationalists of the late eighteenth century, including
Diderot and Buffon in France and Darwin's own grandfather in England.
The work of the French zoologist Lamarck, though theoretically faulty,
had clearly anticipated Darwin's. Work in parallel fields, such as Lyell's
in geology, was available to support a breakthrough in biological theory.
Moreover, the rapidly accumulating data of scientific observation—
geological stratification, fossils, the enormous variation in plant and
animal species—put an increasing strain upon accepted beliefs. Strain
reached the breaking point with the publication of *The Origin of Species.*

And yet Darwin was as modest about his contributions as he was
about his abilities. At the end of his autobiography (1876) he wrote:

My success as a man of science, whatever this may have amounted to,
has been determined, as far as I can judge, by complex and diversified
mental qualities and conditions. Of these the most important have been
—the love of science—unbounded patience in long reflecting over my
subject—industry in observing and collecting facts—and a fair share of
invention as well as of common-sense. With such moderate abilities as I
possess, it is truly surprising that thus I should have influenced to a
considerable extent the belief of scientific men on some important
points.[3]

In one sense, Darwin was correct in this self-effacing assessment.
His great contribution was not the originality of the idea of evolution—
as he himself readily admitted. Rather, he gave the theory a solid basis
in scientific fact and explained how the mechanisms of evolution really
worked.

[3] *The Autobiography of Charles Darwin (1809–1882)*, ed. Nora Barlow (New York: Harcourt, Brace, 1958), pp. 144-45.

While Darwin had enthusiastic supporters, such as the great zoologist T. H. Huxley, the botanist Sir Joseph Hooker, and, of course, Sir Charles Lyell, he had equally zealous opponents. These included both his adored teachers Henslow and Sedgwick and a number of other important scientists, led by Sir Richard Owen, the brilliant and unscrupulous curator of paleontology for the British Museum. His enemies, of course, also included a significant number of important members of the clergy and lay spokesmen for outraged biblical literalism. But whether scientists or clergymen, the bitterness of these opponents—often approaching fanaticism—can be largely attributed to two things: Darwin's work had completely upset the whole comfortable system of natural theology and it had made untenable the notion of special creation. It was "the crime" of Darwin to demythologize man, to set him down like every other being with "no pedigree or armorial bearings," a creature of nature in nature's order rather than in God's image.

The Origin of Species
CHARLES DARWIN

*Darwin himself took little part in the controversies that surrounded him.
His health was rapidly failing and there was no time to spare from his
work. In 1868 his* The Variation of Animals and Plants under
Domestication *appeared, followed by* The Descent of Man, Selection in
Relation to Sex *(1871),* The Expression of the Emotions in Men and
Animals *(1872), a host of technical notes and papers, an enormous
correspondence, and endless revisions of* The Origin of Species *until his
death in 1882.*

Despite the greater notoriety of The Descent of Man—*with all the
clamor over men and apes—his most important book remained* The
Origin of Species, *for it contained the basic assertions of his work in their
clearest form. He revised the book tirelessly, incorporating changes
arising not only from his own further work and reflection but from the
criticism of other scientists. The final version of this most prized of his
works contains the "Recapitulation and Conclusion" from which the
following excerpt is taken.*

I HAVE NOW recapitulated the facts and considerations which have thoroughly convinced me that species have been modified, during a long
course of descent. This has been effected chiefly through the natural
selection of numerous successive, slight, favourable variations; aided in
an important manner by the inherited effects of the use and disuse of
parts; and in an unimportant manner, that is in relation to adaptive
structures, whether past or present, by the direct action of external
conditions, and by variations which seem to us in our ignorance to arise
spontaneously. . . .

It can hardly be supposed that a false theory would explain, in so
satisfactory a manner as does the theory of natural selection, the several
large classes of facts above specified. It has recently been objected that
this is an unsafe method of arguing; but it is a method used in judging of
the common events of life, and has often been used by the greatest natural
philosophers. The undulatory theory of light has thus been arrived at; and
the belief in the revolution of the earth on its own axis was until lately
supported by hardly any direct evidence. It is no valid objection that
science as yet throws no light on the far higher problem of the essence
or origin of life. Who can explain what is the essence of attraction of

gravity? No one now objects to following out the results consequent on this unknown element of attraction; notwithstanding that Leibnitz formerly accused Newton of introducing "occult qualities and miracles into philosophy."

I see no good reason why the views given in this volume should shock the religious feelings of anyone. It is satisfactory, as showing how transient such impressions are, to remember that the greatest discovery ever made by man, namely the law of the attraction of gravity, was also attacked by Leibnitz, "as subversive of natural, and inferentially of revealed, religion." A celebrated author and divine has written to me that "he has gradually learnt to see that it is just as noble a conception of the Deity to believe that He created a few original forms capable of self-development into other and needful forms, as to believe that He required a fresh act of creation to supply the voids caused by the action of His laws." . . .

Although I am fully convinced of the truth of the views given in this volume under the form of an abstract, I by no means expect to convince experienced naturalists whose minds are stocked with a multitude of facts all viewed, during a long course of years, from a point of view directly opposite to mine. It is so easy to hide our ignorance under such expressions as the "plan of creation," "unity of design," etc., and to think that we give an explanation when we only re-state a fact. Anyone whose disposition leads him to attach more weight to unexplained difficulties than to the explanation of a certain number of facts will certainly reject the theory. A few naturalists, endowed with much flexibility of mind, and who have already begun to doubt the immutability of species, may be influenced by this volume; but I look with confidence to the future,—to young and rising naturalists, who will be able to view both sides of the question with impartiality. Whoever is led to believe that species are mutable will do good service by conscientiously expressing his conviction; for thus only can the load of prejudice by which this subject is overwhelmed be removed. . . . When we no longer look at an organic being as a savage looks at a ship, as something wholly beyond his comprehension; when we regard every production of nature as one which has had a long history; when we contemplate every complex structure and instinct as the summing up of many contrivances, each useful to the possessor, in the same way as any great mechanical invention is the summing up of the labour, the experience, the reason, and even the blunders of numerous workmen; when we thus view each organic being, how far more interesting,—I speak from experience,—does the study of natural history become!

A grand and almost untrodden field of inquiry will be opened, on the causes and laws of variation, on correlation, on the effects of use and disuse, on the direct action of external conditions, and so forth. The study of domestic productions will rise immensely in value. A new variety raised by man will be a more important and interesting subject for study than one more species added to the infinitude of already recorded species. Our classifications will come to be, as far as they can be so made, genealogies; and will then truly give what may be called the plan of creation. The rules for classifying will no doubt become simpler when we have a definite object in view. We possess no pedigrees or armorial bearings; and we have to discover and trace the many diverging lines of descent in our natural genealogies, by characters of any kind which have long been inherited. Rudimentary organs will speak infallibly with respect to the nature of long-lost structures. Species and groups of species which are called aberrant, and which may fancifully be called living fossils, will aid us in forming a picture of the ancient forms of life. Embryology will often reveal to us the structure, in some degree obscured, of the prototypes of each great class.

When we can feel assured that all the individuals of the same species, and all the closely allied species of most genera, have within a not very remote period descended from one parent, and have migrated from some one birth-place; and when we better know the many means of migration, then, by the light which geology now throws, and will continue to throw, on former changes of climate and of the level of the land, we shall surely be enabled to trace in an admirable manner the former migrations of the inhabitants of the whole world. Even at present, by comparing the differences between the inhabitants of the sea on the opposite sides of a continent, and the nature of the various inhabitants on that continent in relation to their apparent means of immigration, some light can be thrown on ancient geography.

The noble science of Geology loses glory from the extreme imperfection of the record. The crust of the earth with its embedded remains must not be looked at as a well-filled museum, but as a poor collection made at hazard and at rare intervals. The accumulation of each great fossiliferous formation will be recognised as having depended on an unusual concurrence of favourable circumstances, and the blank intervals between the successive stages as having been of vast duration. But we shall be able to gauge with some security the duration of these intervals by a comparison of the preceding and succeeding organic forms. We must be cautious in attempting to correlate as strictly contemporaneous two formations, which do not include many identical species, by the general succession of the forms of life. As species are produced and exterminated by slowly acting and still existing causes, and not by miraculous acts of creation; and as the most important of all causes of organic change is one which is almost independent of altered and perhaps suddenly altered physical conditions, namely, the mutual relation of organism to organism,—the improvement of one organism entailing the improvement or the extermination of others; it follows that the amount of organic change in the fossils of consecutive formations probably serves as a fair measure of the relative, though not actual lapse of time. A number of species, however, keeping in a body might remain for a long period unchanged, whilst within the same period, several of these species, by migrating into new countries and coming into competition with foreign associates, might become modified; so that we must not overrate the accuracy of organic change as a measure of time. . . .

Authors of the highest eminence seem to be fully satisfied with the view that each species has been independently created. To my mind it accords better with what we know of the laws impressed on matter by the Creator, that the production and extinction of the past and present inhabitants of the world should have been due to secondary causes, like those determining the birth and death of the individual. When I view all beings not as special creations, but as the lineal descendants of some few beings which lived long before the first bed of the Cambrian system was deposited, they seem to me to become ennobled. Judging from the past, we may safely infer that not one living species will transmit its unaltered likeness to a distant futurity. And of the species now living very few will transmit progeny of any kind to a far distant futurity; for the manner in which all organic beings are grouped, shows that the greater number of species in each genus, and all the species in many genera, have left no descendants, but have become utterly extinct. We can so far take a prophetic glance into futurity as to foretell that it will be the common and widely spread species, belonging to the larger and dominant groups within each class, which will ultimately prevail and procreate new and dominant species. As all the living forms of life are the lineal descendants of those which lived long before the Cambrian epoch, we may feel certain that the ordinary succession by generation has never once been broken, and that no cataclysm has desolated the whole world. Hence we may look with some confidence to a secure future of great length. And as natural selection works solely by and for the good of each being, all corporeal and mental endowments will tend to progress towards perfection.

It is interesting to contemplate a tangled bank, clothed with many plants of many kinds, with birds singing on the bushes, with various insects flitting about, and with worms crawling through the damp earth, and to reflect that these elaborately constructed forms, so different from each other, and dependent upon each other in so complex a manner, have all been produced by laws acting around us. These laws, taken in the largest sense, being Growth with Reproduction; Inheritance which is almost implied by reproduction; Variability from the indirect and direct action of the conditions of life, and from use and disuse: a Ratio of Increase so high as to lead to a Struggle for Life, and as a consequence to Natural Selection, entailing Divergence of Character and the Extinction of less-improved forms. Thus, from the war of nature, from famine and death, the most exalted object which we are capable of conceiving, namely, the production of the higher animals, directly follows. There is

grandeur in this view of life, with its several powers, having been originally breathed by the Creator into a few forms or into one; and that, whilst
this planet has gone cycling on according to the fixed law of gravity, from
so simple a beginning endless forms most beautiful and most wonderful
have been, and are being evolved.

Darwin and the Beagle
ALAN MOOREHEAD

*From the rumination of a sick and weary old man contemplating the
meaning of his life's work, we turn now to the engaging picture of the
vigorous young Darwin in the midst of his preparation for that work,
serving as naturalist aboard the* Beagle. *The basis of any account of that
epochal voyage is, of course, Darwin's own voluminous notebooks,
letters, and records. They have been used by Alan Moorehead for his
crackling narrative* Darwin and the Beagle, *from which the following
selection is excerpted.*

ONE OF THE fascinating things about Charles Darwin is that he really does
seem to have been one of those men whose careers quite unexpectedly
and fortuitously are decided for them by a single stroke of fortune. For
twenty-two years nothing much happens, no exceptional abilities are
revealed; then suddenly a chance is offered, things can go either this way
or that, but luck steps in, or rather a chain of lucky events, and away he
soars into the blue never to return. It all looks so inevitable, so predes-
tined; yet the fact is that in 1831 no one in England, certainly not Darwin
himself, had the slightest inkling of the extraordinary future that lay ahead
of him, and it is next to impossible to recognize in the brooding, ailing
figure of the later years this blithe young extrovert on the brink of his
greatest adventure—the voyage of the *Beagle*.

Events moved so quickly that he could hardly take in what was happening. On 5 September 1831 he was summoned to London to meet Robert
FitzRoy, captain of HMS *Beagle*, a ship which the Admiralty was sending off on a long voyage round the world, and the suggestion was that
Darwin should be offered the post of naturalist on the voyage. It was an

astonishing idea. He was only twenty-three years old, he had never met Captain FitzRoy, and a week ago he had never even heard of the *Beagle*. His youth, his inexperience, even his background, seemed all against him; yet against all these odds he and FitzRoy got on famously and the offer was made.

The *Beagle*, FitzRoy explained, was a small ship, but a good one. He knew her well; he had taken over the command of her previous voyage to South America, and had brought her back to England. Now she was being entirely refitted at Plymouth and she had a splendid crew, many of whom had sailed in her before and had volunteered for this new voyage. They had two missions: first they were to continue the charting of the South American coast, and secondly they were to get a more accurate fixing of longitude by carrying a chain of chronological reckonings round the world. The ship would set off in a matter of weeks; they would be away more than two years, perhaps even three or four, but Darwin would be free to leave the ship and return home whenever he chose to do so. He would have ample opportunities for getting ashore, and in the course of the voyage they would be doing many exciting things, exploring unknown rivers and mountains, calling at coral islands in the tropics and sailing far down towards the frozen south. Oh, it was all wonderful. "There is indeed a tide in the affairs of men," Darwin wrote to his sister Susan, "and I have experienced it." . . .

After frustrating delays, the Beagle *sailed, not "in a matter of weeks" but at the end of December 1831—bound across the Bay of Biscay for the Madeiras and the Atlantic. Darwin was wretchedly seasick until they made a first landfall at the Cape Verde Islands. Things began to improve —though Darwin never became a good sailor—as the ship slanted across the Atlantic to the coast of South America. In the spring of 1832, Darwin experienced, for the first time, the richness and variety of tropical forests (and saw the horrors of slavery). As they coasted south toward the tip of the continent, he not only continued his collecting of living specimens but discovered great prehistoric fossil remains along the escarpment of the desolate Patagonian coast.*

What then had exterminated so many species? "Certainly no fact in the long history of the world is so startling as the wide and repeated extermination of its inhabitants." He ruled out the possibility that changes in climate might have caused this exterminaion, and after considering many theories came to the conclusion that the isthmus of Panama might once have been submerged. He was right. For seventy million years there was no isthmus of Panama, South America was an island, and these great animals evolved in isolation. When the isthmus arose and North America was joined to South America the fate of these curious and largely helpless beasts was sealed.

When Darwin took his specimens back on board the *Beagle* Wickham [4] was disgusted at the "bedevilment" of his clean decks and railed against "the damned stuff." FitzRoy later on recalled "our smiles at the apparent rubbish he frequently brought on board." But to Darwin this was no light matter, and it must have been about this time that he first began to argue with FitzRoy about the authenticity of the story of the Flood. How had such enormous creatures got aboard the Ark? FitzRoy had an answer. Not *all* the animals had managed to get aboard the Ark, he explained; for some divine reason these had been left outside and drowned. But, Darwin protested, *were* they drowned? There was much evidence—the seashells, for example—to prove that the coast here had risen above the sea, and that these animals had roamed across the Pampas in much the same way as the guanacos did at the present time. The land had *not* risen, FitzRoy contended; it was the sea that had risen and the bones of these drowned animals were an additional proof of the Flood.

At this early stage of the voyage Darwin was not prepared to put his arguments too forcibly; he was puzzled, he needed more evidence, more time for thought. He was even willing to be persuaded that these new and disturbing ideas that were stirring in his mind were wrong. Certainly he had no wish to deny the truth of the Bible: "No one can stand in these solitudes [the great forests] unmoved," he had written, "and not feel there is more in man than the mere breath of his body." It was just a matter of interpreting its words in the light of modern science. . . .

After a perilous passage "around the Horn" and a difficult session of mapping and charting, the Beagle *began to beat northward along the coast of Chile, with the majestic Andes in sight.*

. . . By now (the spring of 1833), [Darwin] knows the ropes, the last remnants of his hesitancy and inexperience drop away and he becomes a very useful member of the expedition. The idea of his entering the church grew fainter and fainter, and natural history possessed him entirely. "There is nothing like geology," he wrote to Catherine [5]; "The pleasure of the first day's partridge shooting or the first day's hunting cannot be compared to finding a fine group of fossil bones, which tell their story of former times with almost a living tongue . . . I collect every living creature which I have time to catch and preserve." In his journals which he kept up faithfully day by day one can see his confidence steadily in-

---

[4] The first mate.—ED.
[5] Another sister of Darwin.—ED.

creasing; his ideas form patterns and speculations begin to harden into theories. . . .

But it is the geology of the mountains that engrosses him, and he makes two discoveries that rivet his attention: at 12,000 feet he comes on a bed of fossil seashells, and then somewhat lower down a small forest of snow-white petrified pine trees with marine rock deposits round them. Now at last the "marvellous story" was beginning to unfold. These trees had once stood on the shores of the Atlantic, now 700 miles away; they had been sunk beneath the sea, then raised 7000 feet. Clearly all this part of the South American peninsula was once submerged beneath the sea, and in quite recent geological times had been elevated again. As the Andes were pushed upwards they became at first a series of wooded islands and then a continuous chain of mountains whose cold climate killed off the vegetation as they rose. This movement had been accompanied by earthquakes and volcanic eruptions which acted like safety valves. . . .

By the time the Beagle *reached the Galapagos Islands, Darwin's convictions were becoming more fixed. The great natural laboratory of these fascinating islands, astride the equator off the western coast of South America, was to provide the clinching certainty for his emerging theories.*

Apart from their practical uses there was nothing much to recommend the Galapagos; they were not lush and beautiful islands like the Tahiti group, they were (and still are) far off the usual maritime routes, circled by capricious currents, and nobody lived in them then except for a handful of political prisoners who had been stranded there by the Ecuador government. The fame of the islands was founded upon one thing; they were infinitely strange, unlike any other islands in the world. No one who went there ever forgot them. For the *Beagle* this was just another port of call in a very long voyage, but for Darwin it was much more than that, for it was here, in the most unexpected way—just as a man might have a sudden inspiration while he is travelling in a car or a train—that he began to form a coherent view of the evolution of life on this planet. To put it into his own words: "Here, both in space and time, we seem to be brought somewhat near to that great fact—that mystery of mysteries—the first appearance of new beings on this earth."

But the *Beagle* could not linger, much as Darwin longed to. "It is the fate of most voyagers, no sooner to discover what is [of] most interest in any locality, than they are hurried from it." Back on board he began to sort out his specimens, and was soon struck by an important fact: the majority of them were unique species which were to be found in these islands and nowhere else, and this applied to the plants as well as to the reptiles, birds, fish, shells and insects. It was true that they resembled other species in South America, but at the same time they were very different. "It was most striking," Darwin wrote later, "to be surrounded by new birds, new reptiles, new shells, new insects, new plants, and yet by innumerable trifling details of structure, and even by the tones of voice and plumage of the birds, to have the temperate plains of . . . Patagonia, or the hot dry deserts of northern Chile, vividly brought before my eyes."

He made another discovery: the species differed from island to island, even though many of the islands were only fifty or sixty miles apart. His attention was first drawn to this by comparing the mocking-thrushes shot on various islands, but then Mr. Lawson, an Englishman who was acting as vice-governor of the archipelago, remarked that he could tell by one look at a tortoise which island it came from. Thus the tortoises of Albemarle Island had a different sort of shell from those on Chatham, and both differed again from those on James.

With the little finches these effects were still more marked. The finches were dull to look at, and made dreary unmusical sounds; all had short tails, built nests with roofs, and laid white eggs spotted with pink, four to a clutch. Their plumage varied within limits: it ranged from lava black to green, according to their habitat. (It was not only the finches that were so dully feathered; with the exception of a yellow-breasted wren and a scarlet-tufted flycatcher none of the birds had the usual gaudy colouring of the tropics.) But it was the number of different species of finch, and the variety of their beaks, that so amazed Darwin. On one island they had developed strong thick beaks for cracking nuts and seeds, on another the beak was smaller to enable the bird to catch insects, on another again the beak was adjusted to feeding on fruits and flowers. There was even a bird that had learned how to use a cactus spine to probe grubs out of holes.

Clearly the birds had found different foods available on different islands, and through successive generations had adjusted themselves accordingly. The fact that they differed so much among themselves as compared with other birds suggested that they had got to the Galapagos islands first; for a period, possibly quite a long one, they were probably without competitors for food and territory, and this had allowed them to evolve in directions which would otherwise have been closed to them. For instance, finches do not normally evolve into woodpecker-like types because there are already efficient woodpeckers at work, and had a small mainland woodpecker already been established in the Galapagos it is most unlikely that the woodpecker finch would ever have evolved. Similarly the finch which ate nuts, the finch which ate insects, and the finch which fed on fruit and flowers, had been left in peace to evolve their best method of approach. Isolation had encouraged the origin of new species.

Somewhere here a great principle was involved. Naturally Darwin did not grasp the full implications of it all at once; for instance, he makes little

mention of the finches in the first published edition of his Journal, yet the
subject of their diversity and modification later became one of the great
arguments in his theory of natural selection. But by this time he must have
realised that he was on the edge of a remarkable and disturbing discovery.
Until this point he had never openly objected to the current belief in the
creation of unchangeable species, though he may well have had secret
doubts. But now here on the Galapagos, faced with the existence of different forms of mocking-birds, tortoises and finches on different islands,
different forms of the same species, he was forced to question the most
fundamental contemporary theories. Indeed, it was more than that; if
the ideas that were now buzzing round in his head were proved correct
then all the accepted theories of the origin of life on this earth would have
to be revised, and the Book of Genesis itself—the story of Adam and Eve
and the Flood—would be exposed as nothing more than a superstitious
myth. It might take years of research and investigation to prove anything,
but in theory at least all the pieces of the jig-saw seemed to be coming
together.

Darwin and "The Origin of Species" Today
GAVIN DE BEER

*The pieces of the jigsaw did indeed come together, as we have seen, to
make Darwin the father of modern evolutionary theory and the
publication of his* The Origin of Species *one of the crucial turning points
in the history of ideas. It is the judgment of Sir Julian Huxley and
H. B. D. Kettlewell that Darwin "changed the whole framework of human
thought, substituting a dynamic and progressive vision of existence for
the traditional view" and that "in the process he made important
discoveries in geology, botany, paleontology, genetics, reproduction,
behaviour, and general natural history; virtually created the new sciences
of ecology and ethnology, laid the foundations for a scientific taxonomy;
and prepared the way for a rational anthropology."* [6]
   *But is Darwin's work of only historical importance today? One answer
is that given by Sir Gavin de Beer, the distinguished British scientist, man*

---

[6] Julian Huxley and H. B. D. Kettlewell, *Charles Darwin and His World* (New
York: Viking, 1965), pp. 127-28.

of letters, and former director of natural history at the British Museum.
The following excerpt is taken from an article that he wrote for Natural
History *entitled* "Darwin's 'Origin' Today."

ON JANUARY 16, 1869, Charles Darwin wrote to his friend Sir Joseph
Dalton Hooker: "It is only about two years since the last edition of the
Origin, and I am fairly disgusted to find how much I have to modify and
how much I ought to add." On January 22 he continued, "If I lived
twenty more years and was able to work, how I should have to modify
the *Origin*, and how much the views on all points will have to be modified."

At that time Darwin was seriously troubled by two lines of attack on
the *Origin* that appeared to be dangerous and damaging. One was a
criticism brought forward by Fleeming Jenkin, who objected that the
chances of single variations (that is, mutations) becoming incorporated in
a population were infinitesimally small because of the infrequency (in the
then current state of knowledge) with which two similar variants could
be expected to meet. He also said it was virtually certain that such
variants would be swamped and obliterated by interbreeding with the rest
of the population.

Jenkin's criticism increased the difficulty under which Darwin was
already laboring to account for a supply of variation sufficient for natural
selection to work on. Darwin admitted to Alfred Russel Wallace on
January 22, 1869: "F. Jenkins argued . . . against single variations ever
being perpetuated, and has convinced me." In the new (5th) edition of
the *Origin* then in preparation, Darwin did the best he could, which was
to lean more heavily on the position that variation was produced as the
result—then supposedly inherited—of acquired characters, of the use and
disuse of different portions of the anatomy, and of environmental action.

The other attack that Darwin had to meet was from Sir William Thomson, afterward Lord Kelvin, who claimed that the rate of cooling of the
earth proved that its age could not be estimated at more than forty million
years. This was extremely damaging to the theory that evolution was
caused by the natural selection of random variations, and was "opportunistic" because the time available would have been insufficient to allow for
the evolution of all organisms from the primordial germ, unless design and
direction had been at work. This was a basic and a direct threat to
Darwin's constant aim to keep the subject of evolution on a strictly
scientific basis, free from metaphysical or theological concepts of provi-
dential guidance, which would, of course, have involved supernatural
interference with the laws of nature.

That Darwin was shaken by this second blow is shown by a letter he
wrote on January 31, 1869. "I am greatly troubled at the short duration
of the world according to Sir W. Thomson for I require for my theoretical

views a very long period before the Cambrian formation." But Darwin himself as a geologist had devoted prolonged attention to the length of time that must have been involved in the deposition of sedimentary rocks, and he felt justified in writing to Hooker on July 24, 1869, "I feel a conviction that the world will be found rather older than Thomson makes it."

From this standpoint Darwin has been triumphantly vindicated by the discoveries of radioactivity. Today the age of the habitable earth is estimated at some three thousand million years—ample for what Darwin called "wasteful blundering" and blind action of natural selection to have produced what it has. Darwin's fears on that score can be removed.

The manner in which Jenkin's attack has been parried may be introduced by quoting a passage in the *Origin* in which Darwin wrote: "The laws governing inheritance are for the most part unknown." Even the 6th edition, published in 1872, contains this passage, which, had Darwin (and everyone else) known it, was already overtaken by events. On February 8 and March 8, 1865, G. J. Mendel had delivered the famous lectures in which he laid down the foundations of the science of genetics, based on his work with generations of garden peas. Mendel's work remained unknown until 1900, when it was unearthed and confirmed, but even then the biologists of the day failed to appreciate its significance. Because the character differences then known to obey Mendel's laws were clearcut, the opposition to Darwin's view of gradual and infinitesimal variation saw in Mendel's work a stick with which to beat Darwin.

It remained for Ronald Fisher in 1930 to show the real importance of Mendel's discovery, which was that inheritance is particulate—which means that variance is preserved instead of being "swamped," as had been assumed under the false notion of blending inheritance. Darwin, of course, never knew this, but he need not have worried on either of the scores that troubled him so greatly in 1869. The amount by which the *Origin* has had to be modified to keep it abreast of the present state of knowledge is much less than Darwin thought, from the point of view of theory, and there is much more evidence now available that confirms, extends, and refines its arguments.

Confirmation of the validity and reality of the principle of natural selection comes from two sources, genetic and paleontological. Taking the genetic evidence first, it was shown by Fisher that the phenotypic effects of a gene are subject to control by the other genes of the gene complex, and that as the gene complex is reshuffled in every generation by the segregation and recombination of the genes, the resultant individuals show variation of the effects of the gene in question. These effects can be *gradually* enhanced or diminished, according to which gene complex provides the most efficient adaptation of the organism to its environment.

This is why some advantageous genes have become dominant, and others have become recessive and even suppressed. E. B. Ford showed about 25 years ago that a given gene in the currant moth can be made to become dominant or recessive according to the direction of the selection exerted on different lineages. In other words, there is incontrovertible evidence for selection at the heart of genetics. The phenotypic effects of a gene, clear-cut or not, are themselves the result of selection, and this selection gradually produces results—which is exaclty what Darwin claimed.

Heredity is particulate, but this does not mean that evolution is discontinuous or "jerky." In other words, Mendelian genetics and the chromosome mechanism provide exactly what is required to explain evolution by natural selection. A new edition of the *Origin* would say, therefore, that the laws governing inheritance are now known, and that heritable variation arises from the random recombination of segregated, previously mutant genes. . . .

From the paleontological side George Gaylord Simpson has shown that the rate of evolution is not correlated with variability, nor with the number of years occupied by a single generation. Furthermore, in the evolutionary history of such animals as horses, there has been no straight program at all. From the Eocene onward, the trends have zigzagged— first in the direction of many-toed browsers, then of many-toed grazers, and lastly of one-toed grazers. Those lineages that lingered and persisted too long in any of the previous trends of horse evolution paid the penalty of extinction. This, together with the demonstrable adaptation of successful lineages to changed ecological conditions, as revealed by geologic and climatological data, shows that natural selection has been the governing factor in directing evolution. By comparing related marine and terrestrial animals it can likewise be shown that it is natural selection that determines whether evolution takes place rapidly, slowly, or remains stuck, because genetic mechanism can produce either variability or stability—the former because genes can mutate, segregate, and cross over in their chromosomes; the latter because genes mutate only infrequently, they never blend, and they can be linked together in their chromosomes.

It is because natural selection is Darwin's personal contribution to science that his credit remains unblemished. It has sometimes been suggested that as he frequently spoke of "survival" as the prize of victory in selection, he was more interested in longevity than in reproductive capacity; and it has even been held that reproductive selection is "non-Darwinian." This is, however, unjustifiable, for by survival Darwin meant ability "to propagate their kind in larger numbers than the less well adapted." David Lack's demonstration that the *optimum* number of offspring for species survival is not equivalent to the *maximum* is relevant here.

Toward the end of his life, Darwin told his son Leonard that he expected evidence on natural selection to be available in about fifty years.

As Fisher's and Simpson's work shows, this estimate was remarkably accurate, and the evidence now available is formidable and constantly increasing. . . .

. . . The theory of evolution by natural selection of heritable variation is [now] established on an experimental basis to an extent that Darwin himself would hardly have imagined possible. Here, then, the *Origin* can be confirmed in theory, expanded in detail, explained in mechanism, and clarified. The same can be said of the fossil record, which by now has provided close series of lineages—in Jurassic ammonites, Cretaceous sea urchins, and Tertiary horses, camels, and elephants—and has also revealed forms that are indicators of the precursors of various classes of vertebrates and of the evolutionary stages intermediate between them.

Advances made in comparative anatomy and embryology since Darwin's day would fill in many chapters in a hypothetical new version of the *Origin*. . . .

To bring the *Origin* truly up to date, however, new chapters would have to be provided discussing branches of science that were not even dreamed of in Darwin's day. Here belong serology and immunology, which provide means of measuring the chemical divergence between the bloods and body fluids of different groups of related animals. Biochemistry shows that the affinities of animals can be revealed by the chemical substances built into their systems. Chromosome studies are another new field in which the minute investigation of translocations has enabled T. Dobzhansky to unravel the genealogy of some species of the fruit fly *Drosophila*. . . .

Another topic that would have to be covered in a new *Origin* relates to population studies that may represent, as Ernst Mayr says, the most important recent revolution in biological concepts. In one sense, Darwin himself introduced population thinking, because instead of regarding a species as a "type," he stressed the variability of individuals within a species—"individual differences . . . frequently observed in the individuals of the same species inhabiting the same confined locality." But he slipped back into thinking of populations as types when discussing varieties and species. It is now necessary to realize that the product of evolution is a population with an adapted pattern of genetic inequality.

Sexual selection is a subject that received only brief mention in the *Origin* and, as Julian Huxley showed, it is in need of revision because some of the cases in which the sexes differ in structure, appearance, and behavior are not attributable to sexual selection, which benefits the reproductive capabilities of individuals of one sex, but to natural selection, which benefits the whole species.

Finally, to bring the *Origin* up to date, a new edition would contain a chapter of agenda for the solution of chief outstanding problems; which are certainly no less numerous than when the first edition appeared. Such an agenda would necessarily include adequate theories of fitness, of sex-ratio control, of variation, and of how the effect of genes is under the control of other genes in the gene complex. This last problem will probably be worked out by the microbiologists—F. Jacob and J. Monod have already found that through chemically interrelated enzymes genes can collaborate to produce a controlling system that responds to changes in conditions. Most important, of course, would be the recognition that evolution must be considered as "dynamic" and not simply as "dynastic."

Suggestions for Further Reading

AS THE EXCERPTED PASSAGE from *The Origin of Species* demonstrates, Darwin's own works are both readable and comprehensible to nonscientists. Students are encouraged to read further in them. *The Origin of Species* is available in several editions, including *The Origin of Species, A Variorum Text*, ed. Morse Peckham (Philadelphia: University of Pennsylvania Press, 1959), logging the thousands of changes Darwin made throughout many editions of this work. There are also good modern editions of *The Descent of Man, The Expression of the Emotions in Man and Animals, The Variation of Animals and Plants under Domestication*, and *The Different Forms of Flowers on Plants of the Same Species. Charles Darwin's Diary of the Voyage of H.M.S. "Beagle"*, ed. from the manuscript by Nora Barlow (Cambridge, England: Cambridge University Press, 1933), is the best edition of this work. His scientific papers are now available in *The Collected Papers of Charles Darwin*, ed. Paul H. Barrett, 2 vols. (Chicago: University of Chicago Press, 1977). His autobiography is available in two editions, one by his son, the other by his granddaughter: *Charles Darwin's Autobiography, with his Notes and Letters Depicting the Growth of The Origin of Species*, ed. Francis Darwin (New York: Schuman, 1950), and *Charles Darwin. Autobiography . . .* , ed. Nora Barlow (New York: Harcourt, Brace and World, 1958). His son also prepared *The Life and Letters of Charles Darwin . . .* ed. Francis Darwin, 2 vols. (New York: Appleton, 1899). An important collection of the correspondence is *Darwin and Henslow: The Growth of an Idea: Letters 1831–1860*, ed. Nora Barlow (Berkeley: University of California Press, 1967). Students, however, may prefer *The Darwin Reader*, ed. Marston Bates and

Philip S. Humphrey (New York: Scribners, 1956), or *Darwin for Today, The Essence of his Works*, ed. Stanley E. Hyman (New York: Viking, 1963). For the storm of controversy caused by Darwin, students should see two excellent books: Peter J. Vorzimmer, *Charles Darwin: The Years of Controversy: The Origin of Species and Its Critics, 1859–1882* (Philadelphia: Temple University Press, 1970), and *Darwin and His Critics: The Reception of Darwin's Theory of Evolution by the Scientific Community*, ed. David L. Hull (Cambridge, Mass.: Harvard University Press, 1973).

G. R. deBeer, *Charles Darwin: Evolution by Natural Selection* (New York: Doubleday, 1963), is probably the best brief introduction to Darwin and his work, but also recommended are Walter Karp, *Charles Darwin and The Origin of Species* (New York: Harper & Row, 1968), and Julian Huxley and H. B. D. Kettlewell, *Charles Darwin and His World* (New York: Viking, 1965). Alan Moorehead, *Darwin and the Beagle* (New York: Harper & Row, 1969), excerpted in this chapter, is an exciting account. Equally exciting on another subject is William Irvine, *Apes, Angels, and Victorians: The Story of Darwin, Huxley, and Evolution* (New York: McGraw-Hill, 1955). There are two important books setting Darwin and his ideas in their own time: John C. Greene, *The Death of Adam: Evolution and Its Impact on Western Thought* (Ames: Iowa State University, 1959), and Loren Iseley, *Darwin's Century: Evolution and the Men Who Discovered It* (New York: Doubleday, 1958). There are two more good books dealing largely with the impact of Darwinism: Gertrude Himmelfarb, *Darwin and the Darwinian Revolution* (New York: Doubleday, 1959), and Paul B. Sears, *Charles Darwin: The Naturalist as a Cultural Force* (New York: Scribners, 1950). Finally, students will enjoy Jacques Barzun, *Darwin, Marx, Wagner: Critique of a Heritage*, rev. 2nd ed. (New York: Doubleday, 1958), a brilliant work in which Barzun considers these three men as the revolutionary influences in the making of the modern world.

Bismarck:
The Iron Chancellor

The history of Continental Europe—indeed, of much of the world—
in the second half of the nineteenth century was overshadowed by the
Empire of Germany. And Germany was overshadowed by the massive,
brooding figure of Otto Eduard Leopold von Bismarck, Minister-
President of Prussia and Chancellor of the Empire for almost thirty
years, the mastermind and creator of modern Germany. The question
of the nature of Bismarck's policies is a crucial one—whether he
sought German hegemony of Europe to secure the peace (as he claimed)
or to satisfy the motives of power, whether he was a great statesman
or simply one more German tyrant. For how we answer this question
will tend to determine how we look at the history of the world in our
own fateful century following hard upon Bismarck's death in 1898.
It is almost impossible, in the backwash of two world wars that undeniably
stemmed from German aggression, not to regard the question as rhetorical
and consequently to condemn both Bismarck the man and Bismarck the
statesman. And yet, in the years immediately following World War II,
many "good Germans" both in Germany and abroad looked back to
the age of Bismarck as a kind of golden age when Germany could
have prestige without dishonor, greatness without cruelty, and empire
without genocide. The historian Friedrich Meinecke, though he knew
very well to what disaster Prussian militarism had led, could still recall
how "free and proud" "we Germans often felt in the mightily flourishing

413

Empire of 1871." [1] And Hajo Holborn, himself an exile from German
tyranny, could still argue that Bismarck's empire was founded not only
upon naked force but upon German philosophic idealism and the
traditions of German Protestantism.

The beginning of the German Empire, regardless of how we view its
end, is to be found in Germany's legitimate search for national security.
Prussia, the major state among the scattering of German principalities,
was nevertheless the smallest and weakest of the so-called great powers
that had finally defeated Napoleon. But in the years following the
Napoleonic wars, Prince Metternich (1773–1859), architect of France's
containment and of the Concert of Europe, kept Prussia subordinated
to his own Austria. When the Metternichian Concert began to become
unstrung by revolts and revolutions and, after mid-century, to be
replaced by the direct competition of the great powers, the Prussian King
William I, with some reservation, in 1862 appointed Otto von Bismarck
Minister-President of the Kingdom of Prussia.

Bismarck by this time was an experienced diplomat and politician.
He had learned to hate the arrogance of Austria as the Prussian envoy
to the Federal Diet in 1851. He had been ambassador to Russia from
1859 to 1862 and had gained considerable respect for that great
Eastern bear. In 1862 he had been briefly ambassador to Napoleon III
of France for whom he had only contempt. But Bismarck reserved his
choicest contempt for the notions of popular government and for the
abortive Frankfort Parliament of 1849 that had tried in vain to bring
the blessings of revolutionary liberalism to Germany. He judged liberalism
to be as weak as the "weak men" of Frankfort who advocated it.
Indeed, the whole idea of personal liberty—at the heart of the liberal
creed—seemed to him not only unattainable but selfish to the point of
indecency. Man lives for the state, for duty, service, order—not for
himself. Bismarck was a conservative through and through, and an
autocrat. Shortly after his appointment as chief minister, appearing
before the Budget Commission of the Prussian Diet, he delivered his
most famous speech. He spoke of the prestige that Prussia enjoyed
among the other German states, a prestige that flowed from her power
and resolve, not from her liberalism. He spoke of Prussia's need to
collect her forces and look to her "natural" frontiers. And he ended,
"Not by speeches and majorities will the great questions of the day be
decided—that was the mistake of 1848 and 1849—but by iron and
blood." [2]

What Bismarck sought in this famous speech was a dramatic increase

[1] Quoted in W. N. Medlicott, *Bismarck and Modern Germany* (London: English
Universities Press, 1965), p. 183.
[2] Quoted in Louis L. Snyder, *The Blood and Iron Chancellor, A Documentary-
Biography of Otto von Bismarck* (New York: Van Nostrand, 1967), p. 127.

in the military budget. The Diet refused to authorize the necessary taxes. Bismarck levied them anyway, collected them, and used them to enlarge and reorganize the already substantial Prussian army and to supply it with the most modern equipment. Liberals in the Diet charged that the government was acting unconstitutionally; neither Bismarck nor the Prussian people seemed to mind. Prussia, indeed all of Germany, was prospering. The Industrial Revolution was in full swing. The modern world was opening up, and the great majority of Prussians shared Bismarck's views. Order, discipline, and military power seemed more likely to guarantee their future in that brave new world than outworn parliamentarianism.

Bismarck's first opportunity to employ his new army came quickly, in the Schleswig-Holstein dispute of 1863. These two north German provinces were claimed by Denmark and about to be annexed. The German Federal Diet, as sensitive on this question as Bismarck himself, clamored for war. But Bismarck was not a German nationalist, he was a Prussian. And he wanted no part of a war in which Prussian arms would contribute to the prestige of the hated federation. He wanted a Prussian victory for Prussia. To that end, he joined with Austria in 1864 in a war against Denmark, which was quickly defeated. Prussia took Schleswig, and Austria, Holstein.

But the Austrians were not welcome in Holstein, and frictions developed. Bismarck encouraged them. Austria complained to the Federal Diet. Bismarck denied its jurisdiction, accused Austria of aggression, and occupied Holstein. The Diet supported Austria, and in 1866 Austria and most of the rest of the federated states declared war on Prussia. Again Bismarck and the Prussian army were ready. The war lasted just seven weeks and was an unqualified Prussian victory. Then Bismarck simply declared the federal union dissolved, annexed the majority of its northern member states, and organized them into a North German Confederacy, clearly subordinate to Prussia. The North German Confederation was also clearly a half-way house to a Prussian empire.

The powers of Europe were stunned and unsettled by these developments in Germany—none more so than France, justly alarmed at the growth of Prussian power on her border and disillusioned with the failures of Napoleon III. There was almost universal talk of a Franco-Prussian war in the offing. Bismarck hoped that Napoleon III would attempt it on the chance of rescuing his policies at home by military success abroad. For Bismarck was convinced that no such French victory would ensue. And he was also convinced that a Franco-Prussian war would force the remaining south German states, already linked to him by defensive alliances, to unify with Prussia.

In the summer of 1870, on a trivial diplomatic pretext cleverly escalated by Bismarck, Napoleon III did declare war on Prussia. His own folly had robbed him of allies, and Bismarck contrived to make the war seem a wanton French aggression. In any event, it was again a short war and again a decisive Prussian victory. Bismarck caused the issues of the war to be settled and the new German Empire to be proclaimed in the famed Hall of Mirrors of the Palace at Versailles—a dramatic gesture never to be forgotten by the French.

The other German states, except Austria—as Bismarck anticipated— had joined Prussia in the war. They now capitulated to their powerful ally, the North German Confederation was dissolved, and the King of Prussia was transformed into the Emperor of Germany—ruler of what had become overnight the mightiest state in Europe.

France was humiliated, saddled with an enormous indemnity, and forced to give up the rich industrialized border provinces of Alsace and Lorraine. Bismarck's task now became the prevention of a French war of vengeance; it continued to be the preoccupation of his foreign policy. He spread an increasingly complex web of alliances, understandings, secret treaties, and secret protocols of published agreements across Europe —meanwhile proclaiming that he sought only peace. For example, in 1878 he offered his services in the crisis precipitated by a Russian attack on the rotting Turkish Empire that threatened to upset the balance of Western interests in the "Eastern question." At the resulting Congress of Berlin, Bismarck expansively posed, in his phrase, as "the honest broker." Alone among the great powers, Germany refused to make any territorial demands upon Turkey, which nevertheless was effectively partitioned by the agreements reached. Bismarck wanted only peace— and the continued isolation of France.

In the following year he formed a military pact with Austria, which Italy was permitted to join in 1882. Thus was formed the Triple Alliance, the basic alliance of the so-called Central Powers that would carry into World War I. Austria and Italy were thus safely removed from a possible French alliance. England, long averse to continental alliances, was moreover in sharp conflict with France over colonial issues. Only Russia remained a possibility, and a remote one at that, for there seemed no common ground between backward, autocratic Russia and the French Third Republic. But to be careful, Bismarck approached the Russians. Indeed, he had cultivated them since his days as ambassador to St. Petersburg. He had supported Russia in a Polish insurrection in 1863 and prevented Austrian interference. Russia had been induced to remain neutral in the Franco-Prussian war. But Bismarck was blamed by some Pan-Slav extremists for his part in the Congress of Berlin and the consequent thwarting of Russian victory over the Turks. And now, to approach Russia with any kind of proposal in the face of his alliance with Austria, Russia's great foe in the Balkans, took all Bismarck's nerve and skill. He proposed a secret League of the Three Emperors—

of Germany, Russia, and Austria—directed precisely to the preservation of both Austrian and Russian interests in the Balkans and Turkey. But though the parties agreed, the agreement was never implemented; in 1881 Czar Alexander II was assassinated by a terrorist bomb. But Bismarck persevered and in 1887 finally signed with Russia the famous Reinsurance Treaty, a further "insurance" against a possible Franco-Russian alliance. In 1888 Bismarck stood at the zenith of his career; he appeared to be the master of Europe.

The Speech for the Military Bill
of February 6, 1888
OTTO VON BISMARCK

*At the very moment that he seemed to hold Europe in his hand,
Bismarck paradoxically appealed to the Reichstag twice within two
months for extraordinary increases in German armaments—on
December 9, 1887, and on January 31, 1888. It was in connection with
these proposals that he spoke before the Reichstag on February 6, 1888.
It was a speech second in fame only to the "Blood and Iron" speech
at the beginning of his career. In one respect, it is its superior. For it is
—to quote one of Bismarck's most perceptive modern critics—
among his "most important and comprehensive" expositions of his
foreign policy, "a majestic survey of German policy in the past, present,
and future" that "makes this speech a historical document of great
value."* [3] *We excerpt it below.*

WHEN I SAY that we must constantly endeavor to be equal to all con-
tingencies, I mean by that to claim that we must make greater exertions
than other powers in order to attain the same result, because of our geographical position. We are situated in the middle of Europe. We have at
least three fronts of attack. France has only its eastern frontier, Russia
only its western frontier, on which it can be attacked. We are, moreover,
in consequence of the whole development of the world's history, in consequence of our geographical position, and perhaps in consequence of the
slighter degree of internal cohesion which the German nation as compared
with others has thus far possessed, more exposed than any other people
to the risk of a coalition. God has placed us in a situation in which we
are prevented by our neighbors from sinking into any sort of indolence
or stagnation. He has set at our side the most warlike and the most restless
of nations, the French; and he has permitted warlike inclinations, which in
former centuries existed in no such degree, to grow strong in Russia. Thus
we get a certain amount of spurring on both sides, and are forced into
exertions which otherwise perhaps we should not make. The pikes in the
European carp pond prevent us from becoming carps, by letting us feel
their prickles on both our flanks; they constrain us to exertions which

---

[3] Joseph Vincent Fuller, *Bismarck's Diplomacy at Its Zenith* (New York: Fertig,
1967), p. 310.

perhaps we should not voluntarily make; they constrain us Germans also to a harmony among ourselves that is repugnant to our inmost nature: but for them, our tendency would rather be to separate. But the Franco-Russian press in which we are caught, forces us to hold together, and by its pressure it will greatly increase our capacity for cohesion, so that we shall reach in the end that state of inseparableness which characterizes nearly all other nations, and which we still lack. But we must adapt ourselves to this decree of Providence by making ourselves so strong that the pikes can do no more than enliven us. . . .

The bill gives us an increase in troops trained to arms—a possible increase: if we do not need it, we need not call for it; we can leave it at home. But if we have this increase at our disposal, and if we have the weapons for it, . . . then this new law constitutes a reinforcement of the guarantees of peace, a reinforcement of the league of peace, that is precisely as strong as if a fourth great power with an army of 700,000 men— and this was formerly the greatest strength that existed—had joined the alliance. This powerful reinforcement will also, I believe, have a quieting effect upon our own countrymen, and lessen in some degree the nervousness of our public opinion, our stock-market, and our press. I hope it will act upon them as a sedative when they clearly comprehend that from the moment at which this law is signed and published the men are there. The armament, too, may be said to be ready, in the shape of what is absolutely necessary: but we must procure a better, for if we form an army of triarians of the best human material that we have,—of the men above thirty, the husbands and fathers,—we must have for them the best weapons there are. We must not send them into the fight with an outfit that we do not regard as good enough for our young troops of the line. The solid men, the heads of families, these stalwart figures that we can still remember from the time that they held the bridge of Versailles,—these men must have the best rifles on their shoulders, the completest armament, and the amplest clothing to protect them from wind and weather. We ought not to economize there.

But I hope it will tranquilize our fellow citizens, if they are really thinking of the contingency (which I do not expect to occur) of our being attacked simultaneously on two sides,—of course, as I have pointed out in reviewing the events of the last forty years, there is always the possibility of any sort of coalition,—I hope it will tranquilize them to remember that if this happens, we can have a million good soldiers to defend each of our frontiers. At the same time we can keep in the rear reserves of half a million and more, of a million even, and we can push these forward as they are needed. I have been told, "That will only result in the others going still higher." But they cannot. They have long ago reached their limits. . . . In numbers they have gone as high as we, but in quality they cannot compete with us. Bravery, of course, is equal among all civilized nations; the Russian and the Frenchman fight as bravely as the German:

but our men, our 700,000 new men, have seen service; they are soldiers who have served their time, and who have not yet forgotten their training. Besides—and this is a point in which no people in the world can compete with us—we have the material for officers and under-officers to command this enormous army. It is here that competition is excluded, because it involves a peculiarly broad extension of popular culture, such as exists in Germany and in no other country. . . .

There is a further advantage that will result from the adoption of this law: the very strength at which we are aiming necessarily makes us peaceful. That sounds paradoxical, but it is true. With the powerful machine which we are making of the German army no aggression will be attempted. If I saw fit—assuming a different situation to exist from that which in my conviction does exist—to come before you here today and say to you, "We are seriously menaced by France and Russia; the prospect is that we shall be attacked: such at least is my conviction, as a diplomatist, on the basis of the military information that we have received; it is to our advantage to defend ourselves by anticipating the attack, and to strike at once; an offensive war is a better one for us to wage, and I accordingly ask the Imperial Diet for a credit of a milliard or half a milliard, in order to undertake today the war against our two neighbors,"—well gentlemen, I do not know whether you would have such confidence in me as to grant such a request. I hope not. But if you did, it would not be enough for me.

If we in Germany desire to wage a war with the full effect of our national power, it must be a war with which all who help to wage it, and all who make sacrifices for it—with which, in a word, all the nation —must be in sympathy. It must be a people's war; it must be a war that is carried on with the same enthusiasm as that of 1870, when we were wickedly attacked. I remember still the joyful shouts that rang in our ears at the Cologne station; it was the same thing from Berlin to Cologne; it was the same thing here in Berlin. The waves of popular approval bore us into the war, whether we liked it or not. So it must be, if a national force like ours is to be brought fully into operation. It will be very difficult, however, to make it clear to the provinces, to the federal states and to their people, that a war is inevitable, that it must come. It will be asked: "Are you so sure of it? Who knows?" If we finally come to the point of making the attack, all the weight of the imponderables, which weigh much more than the material weights, will be on the side of our antagonist whom we have attacked. "Holy Russia" will be filled with indignation at the attack. France will glisten with weapons to the Pyrenees. The same thing will happen everywhere. A war into which we are not borne by the will of the people—such a war will of course be carried on, if in the last instance the established authorities consider and have declared it to be necessary. It will be carried on with energy and perhaps victoriously, as soon as the men come under fire and have seen blood; but there will not be back of it, from the start, the same dash and heat as in a war in which we are attacked. . . .

I do not believe—to sum up—that any disturbance of the peace is an immediate prosepct; and I ask you to deal with the law that lies before you, independently of any such idea or apprehension, simply as a means for making the great force which God has lodged in the German nation completely available in the event of our needing it. If we do not need it, we shall not call for it. We seek to avoid the chance of our needing it. This effort on our part is still, in some degree, impeded by threatening newspaper articles from foreign countries; and I wish to address to foreign countries especially the admonition to discontinue these threats. They lead to nothing. The threat which we receive, not from the foreign government, but in the press, is really a piece of incredible stupidity, if you think what it means—that by a certain combination of words, by a certain threatening shape given to printer's ink, a great and proud power like the German Empire is assumed to be capable of intimidation. This should be discontinued; and then it would be made easier for us to assume a more conciliatory and obliging attitude toward our two neighbors.

Every country is responsible in the long run, somehow and at some time, for the windows broken by its press; the bill is presented some day or other, in the ill-humor of the other country. We can easily be influenced by love and good will,—too easily perhaps,—but most assuredly not by threats. We Germans fear God, but nothing else in the world; and it is the fear of God that makes us love and cherish peace. But whoever, despite this, breaks it, will find that the warlike patriotism that in 1813, when Prussia was weak, small, and exhausted by plunder, brought her whole population under her banners, has today become the common heritage of the whole German nation; and whoever attacks the German nation will find it united in arms, and in every soldier's heart the firm faith "God will be with us."

Bismarck and the Failure of Realpolitik
JOSEPH VINCENT FULLER

*The same critic, Joseph Vincent Fuller, who declared the speech for
the military bill of 1888 one of the "most important and comprehensive"
expositions of Bismarck's foreign policy sees it at the same time
not as the ringing defiance it seems to be but a desperate admission
that Bismarck and his foreign policy had failed. This, he argues,
explains the paradox of Bismarck's appeal for increased military
expenditures in the face of apparent diplomatic victory: the victory had
already slipped away.*

This is the thesis of Fuller's book, Bismarck's Diplomacy at Its
Zenith. *The book dates from the early 1920s and is surely in part a
result of the author's experience as an attaché to the American delegation
at the Paris Peace Conference of 1919, where so much of the tangle
of European diplomacy was laid bare, along with the treachery and
cynicism of the master diplomats who had done so much to bring
about World War I—Bismarck above all. But whatever its inception,
the book remains the classic condemnation of Bismarck as the great
exponent of* Realpolitik, *the "practical" politics of ruthless
opportunism and military power. Fuller believes that the failure of
Bismarck's policies was predictable, even inevitable.*

*He focuses special attention upon the 1888 speech as the key
revelation of Bismarck's failure. Following is his analysis.*

THE SPEECH OF February 6, 1888, is probably the most notable in
Bismarck's career. Although he was so ill that only recourse to stimulants
enabled him to speak at all, and he was obliged to deliver most of his
address while seated, he spoke with a power and appeal which brought
him a popular triumph unsurpassed in even his brilliant experience. His
majestic survey of German policy in the past, present, and future makes
this speech a historical document of great value. Next to the *Gedanken
und Erinnerungen,*[4] it is the most important and comprehensive exposition of the Chancellor's views on foreign policy which he has handed
down. The aspects of it chiefly considered here will be those bearing upon
the events of the two or three preceding years.

Bismarck was careful to begin by saying that he undertook his exposi-

[4] "Thoughts and Recollections," the title Bismarck gave to his memoirs, published after his forced retirement in 1890.—ED.

tion less for the sake of convincing the Reichstag of the need for the
proposed law than for that of convincing Europe that its passage implied
no threat to peace. The events of the recent past were represented as having reached, on the whole, a satisfactory outcome. The interpretation of
them was, naturally, calculated to give the impression of German policy
which Bismarck wished to produce upon the world—regardless of the
deep-lying facts of the case. . . . Yet the Chancellor must justify a
proposal to augment her military forces by 700,000 men—the equivalent
of a fourth ally.

"I do not anticipate any immediate disturbance of the peace," ran his
argument, "and I ask that you treat the proposed law independently of
such considerations and anxieties." But he had stipulated beforehand:
"The fact that I hold these for the moment unfounded is far from leading
me to the conclusion that we need no increase in our armed forces—quite
the contrary." And why? Because, after all is said and done, the war on
two fronts looms in the future; and Germany must neglect no preparations
to face it. His words were impressive and yet reassuring: "I hope our
fellow citizens will take comfort in the thought that, if we should be
attacked from two sides at once—which I do not anticipate, though the
events of the past forty years show that all sorts of coalitions are still
possible—we could have a million good soldiers for the defence of each
of our frontiers. And we can raise, besides, a half-million, or even a
million, reservists in the interior to send forward where needed." This
picture of power and security should suffice to convince his hearers of
the wisdom of voting as they were asked to do.

But Germany and the world at large must have no idea that this great
force would ever be turned to the uses of aggression. The possibility that
Germany should have any ends of expansion to achieve was not even
considered. But Bismarck did feel called upon to dispel the suspicion that
she might sometime undertake a "preventive war." Upon the fantastic
assumption that her Chancellor should ever conceive such a project, he
ventured to hope that the Diet would withhold its support; and he expressed confidence that the nation would not rise to the occasion. All
this was merely persiflage. Had Bismarck desired a "preventive war," he
would have found German public opinion the least of his obstacles. On
the several occasions when he had appeared to be preparing for a new
war, national sentiment outran him if anything; it was the failure of his
ostensible occasions to develop properly that averted the explosions.

Such empty considerations brought the speaker round to his dramatic
peroration. He had painted a picture of Germany, strong in her own
might and in the consciousness of following ever the path of honor—a
Germany misunderstood and maligned, standing between jealous neighbors who constituted always a potential threat to peace. Firm in her own
peaceful intentions, she would arm to meet that threat in the most dangerous shape it could take. So Bismarck came to the rhetorical flourish

which will ring forever in the hearts of his countrymen: "We Germans fear God, but nothing else in the world!"

Leaving rhetoric and misrepresentation aside, what was the situation of Germany as pictured by Bismarck in the great speech of 1888? Certainly it was far different from the situation of three years before, when the German Empire had stood at the centre of a system of alliances and understandings embracing the whole continent of Europe. The year 1888 found that system crumbling to ruin, the friendship with France destroyed and the alliance with Russia undermined. In 1885 Germany was fearlessly challenging England's supremacy in distant colonial fields: in 1888 she was preoccupied with the defence of her own frontiers and dependent upon England's help for preserving the remains of her structure of alliances. In 1885 Germany's diplomacy brilliantly sufficed for the attainment of her most ambitious ends: three years later she was straining every nerve to keep up a military establishment that would enable her to remain mistress of her own destiny. Bismarck's sounding phrases are a confession of the breakdown of his policy. The problem of assuring Germany's future had got so far beyond the resources of his diplomacy that he had nothing left to recommend but reliance on her own brute force. Another formidable military bill hardly a year after the preceding one—such was the culmination of Bismarck's diplomacy in the eventful year 1887. And such was the international situation which Bismarck left as heritage to his successors; for it had changed but little when they took it over two years later.

The only dependable diplomatic resource he left to them was the Austrian alliance, which they correctly appraised as the most solid element in his international system. . . . From the day of its conclusion, the Austrian alliance had been the cornerstone of Bismarck's system; and he had taken care to promote Austrian interests as far as the limits of caution allowed. His successors overstepped those limits in the end; but it is questionable if Bismarck himself could have kept within them indefinitely. His mask of duplicity had slipped so far aside in 1887 that Russia could never again have any real confidence in his professions as "honest broker." The League of the Three Emperors as a complement to the Austrian alliance had definitely ceased to exist.

Its other complement, the Triple Alliance, remained; but Bismarck had never set great store by the friendship of Italy. He rated Italy's material value to his system hardly above that of the Balkan satellites of Austria, and he realized fully the unreliability of her engagements. . . . Bismarck had, it is true, made extensive commitments on Germany's behalf in renewing the alliance, but he never meant to go out of his way to fulfil them. He had made them during a crisis, when there had appeared an especial need for assuring himself of Italy's rôle with regard to both France and the Eastern Question. In the latter connection, he had skilfully contrived to make Italy and England influence each other. He had drawn England into his system by way of an understanding with Italy, and at the same time induced her to share Germany's burden of satisfying Italy's claims of support for her own interests. Masterly as had been the accomplishment of February, 1887, however, it was a *tour de force* of momentary, rather than permanent, significance.

By his dealings with England, Bismarck appeared to have secured a new addition to his international system, making up for the defection of France and the weakening of the Russian connection. But it was a compensation far from satisfactory in his own mind. His lack of confidence in the straightforwardness and continuity of English foreign policy prevented his ever regarding England's friendship as a permanent asset. He had made no serious effort to attach England directly to Germany by any formal bond. He was fully conscious of the fact that, in dealing with her at all, he was only taking advantage of a temporarily favorable situation for temporary ends. His utilization of England was, in reality, inconsistent with even the slight remnant of his old political system, which he had no idea of altering fundamentally. Germany's own relations with Russia, which Bismarck still valued highly, despite the ill services he had rendered her, would necessarily suffer through Germany's intimacy with England.[5] Moreover, the agreement between England and Germany's two allies, brought about in 1887, had practically fulfilled its purpose when Russia abandoned her designs on Bulgaria. Deprived of its immediate object, the bonds of the agreement must slacken, following Bismarck's own theory that England's support could be counted upon only where English interests were pressingly involved.

Pursuing the consequences of the settlement of 1888 still further, they could entail only an increasing alienation of England from the Central Empires. She had nothing to gain through the replacement of Russian influence in the Balkan Peninsula by the Austrian penetration which followed the opening of the railways to Salonica and Constantinople. She was still less gratified by the diversion of Russia's expansive forces into the Far East which accompanied the development of the Trans-Siberian line. And both these tendencies would necessarily have at least the moral approval of even Bismarck's Germany. The weakening of England's connection with Bismarck's international system, therefore, began with the moment the connection was established. It was essentially self-destructive. Its disappearance would inevitably undermine Italy's position in the Triple Alliance. Italy's connection with England was of more importance to her than that with the Central Empires: once England had broken away from them, the Triple Alliance was practically dissolved. So the new Triple Alliance and the Austro-Italian entente with England were legacies of doubtful value at the best.

---

[5] Because of the hostility lingering between Russia and England from the Crimean War.—ED.

The most perplexing of Bismarck's diplomatic legacies was the Re-insurance Treaty with Russia. His heirs cannot be greatly blamed for renouncing their title to it. His most bitter criticisms of their policy arose from this action; yet it is doubtful if even in his hands this bond of alliance would ever have proved more than a rope of sand. His regard for the Russian connection was beyond question sincere, but it was a regard which embraced only Germany's interest in maintaining it. He was perpetually cut off from a proper appreciation of Russia's interest by his overweening solicitude for the greatness of Austria. He wished to retain the friendship of Russia as a check upon Austria; yet he could not em-ploy it indefinitely as a mask behind which to contrive the balking of all Russia's designs running counter to Austria's. Perhaps he was not con-sciously striving to injure Russia; but, supposing he believed himself to be acting for her own good, he could not expect her always to accept his definition of her reasonable and salutary expectations. . . . The con-sequence could only be the acceleration of Russia's drift toward France. The renewal of the Reinsurance Treaty in 1890 could have checked that tendency only if it had been accompanied by a radical change in German policy, such as Bismarck had shown no signs of bringing about. The re-sults of his conduct were inevitable, whether they took shape immediately in the binding and loosing of formal diplomatic ties or not. The diverting of Russia into the Far East, accompanied by a refusal of the means to develop her projects, brought on the Franco-Russian alliance. That al-liance gave Russia a partner in the West to reach her a hand for the return to Europe when those projects were undone by a military defeat in the East.

France's action in these developments was no more dependent upon formal agreements than was Russia's. The Reinsurance Treaty alone could not keep Russia away from France: a treaty with Russia was not necessary to assure France's cooperation against Germany. It was less necessary than ever, after the events of 1887. Whatever progress Bismarck had previously made toward a reconciliation with France had been an-nulled by his conduct in that critical year. The blame for the revival of enmity between France and Germany rests even more clearly on his shoulders than does that for the estrangement between Germany and Russia. . . . The crises of 1887 demonstrated very clearly to France a positive malevolence against which she would do well to provide. Looked at from the western side, then, the Franco-Russian alliance appears again as the fruit of Bismarck's diplomacy. It would have taken more than his mere continuance in office, more than a simple renewal of the Reinsurance Treaty, to prevent this eventual alliance of hatred and suspicion.

Many tributes have been paid to Bismarck's personality, to his im-pressive renown, to his unequalled grasp of affairs and sureness of touch, as the essential elements in his policy, impossible to transmit to any successor. Such explanations of the failure of his successors needlessly obscure the shortcomings of the policy they inherited. Of the critical period in which Bismarck's diplomacy put its final touches on Germany's destiny, Robertson has written: "The years 1887 and 1888 were . . . the severest touchstones of a German statesman's statecraft. Bismarck's performance was, when we appreciate the complex difficulties, a consummate one. The master proved his mastery." The eulogy bears almost an ironic interpretation when examined in the light of the situation in which Bismarck's statecraft had placed his country. His performance, "consummate" in duplicity and brutality, left the main problem of the period regulated by a one-sided settlement which only entailed new difficulties. It left Germany between two potential foes about to join hands across her frontiers. It left her with but one dependable alliance amid a set of unstable combinations. It left her frankly dependent upon a vast military establishment as the main reliance for her future. Could the "master" himself have found a safe way out of this situation? If Bismarck's successors were to fall below his level in resourcefulness, the outlook was dark indeed! . . .

Without calling Bismarck's early, fundamental achievements into question—which is beyond the scope of this study—it is not possible to indicate what better courses could have been followed. It is at least clear, however, that his diplomacy contained no priceless and unique key to imperial Germany's future, irrecoverable once wantonly thrown away. Rather, it may be maintained that Bismarck's diplomacy, at the zenith of his power, contained all the causes of his Empire's downfall.

Bismarck the Statesman
GORDON A. CRAIG

After World War II, as after World War I, there were scholars who charged that that worldwide catastrophe was the ultimate fruit of the Bismarckian tradition of Realpolitik. Erich Eyck, for example—whose three-volume work, published outside Germany in the closing years of World War II, is the most comprehensive biography of Bismarck (see the suggested readings at the end of this chapter)—characterizes him as a ruthless demagogue who stifled German domestic development and involved his nation in the fatal net of his diplomacy. On the other hand, there were, as we observed above, the "good Germans" who chose to separate the Hitler era from the earlier tradition of German statecraft and erected the figure of an idealized Bismarck as a symbol of the good old Germany. Between these two extremes, there is a continuum of opinion and judgment.

The following selection is chosen in part because of its moderate position and in part because of the eminence of its author: Gordon A. Craig, one of the best modern historians of Germany, whose The Politics of the Prussian Army, 1640–1945 *is the standard work on its subject. The selection below, however, comes from a broad, reflective series of lectures which he delivered in the Albert Shaw Lectures on Diplomatic History at Johns Hopkins University (1958), entitled* From Bismarck to Adenauer: Aspects of German Statecraft. *The purpose of the series is to explain the tragic experience of German statecraft in the past century, and it is essentially sympathetic. Craig's reviewer in the* American Historical Review,[6] *the late John L. Snell, while generally favorable toward the book, ends his review with the caution that he, and he suspects others, would like to have Bismarck "share more of the responsibility for the tragedies [of German statecraft] than Craig assigns him."*

Controversy thus continues to follow "the Iron Chancellor" in history as in his lifetime.

IN HIS FAMOUS essay on "Politics as a Vocation," Max Weber asks: "What kind of a man must one be if he is to be allowed to put his hand on the wheel of history?"; and he answers his own question by saying: ". . . three pre-eminent qualities are decisive for the politician: passion, a feeling of responsibility, and a sense of proportion." Although he never mentions him in the course of his essay, Weber might just as well have been describing Otto von Bismarck.

When I speak here of passion I do not mean the sort of thing one flies into, or the sultry emotion that the Hays Office used to try to keep from the cinema screen, but rather the quality that enables men to escape the fate of the Laodiceans whom Dante found confined in the dark plain of limbo: the quality of wholehearted devotion and total commitment to something. This kind of passion Bismarck possessed in full measure; and the something to which he brought his devotion was his profession: the office he held and the duties he was called upon to perform in the service of his King. . . .

It was a devotion to the job that excluded personal vanity and prejudice. This is not, of course, meant to imply that Bismarck as a private person was immune to the baser passions, for he was not. It is well known that in his personal relationships he was often swept by gusts of jealousy and rage,

[6] LXIV (1958–1959), 712.

that he could admit to having lain awake all night hating, and that he could permit his personal antipathies to degenerate into vindictiveness and persecution. Yet the very violence of these internal fires makes more impressive the fact that he generally kept them in check while conducting foreign policy. Bülow the elder wrote to his more famous son, the future Chancellor: "Prince Bismarck is in the habit of saying that indignation and rancor are conceptions foreign to diplomacy. The diplomat is neither a preacher of penitence, nor a judge in a criminal court, nor a philosopher. His sole and exclusive concern must be the real and downright interest of his country." Bismarck himself in a well-known passage in one of his letters to Leopold von Gerlach makes the same point with greater force and clarity.

> Sympathies and antipathies with respect to foreign Powers and persons I cannot justify to my sense of duty to the foreign service of my country, either in myself or in others. Therein lies the embryo of disloyalty toward one's master or the land one serves. And especially when one undertakes to arrange one's current diplomatic connections and the maintenance of friendly relations in peacetime in accordance with those things, one ceases in my opinion to conduct politics and begins to act according to personal caprice. In my view, not even the King has the right to subordinate the interests of the fatherland to personal feelings of love and hate toward the foreigner.

Otto Vossler is certainly correct in saying that no one can read this passage, with its emphatic use of terms like "justify," "duty," "service," "disloyalty," "caprice," and "right," without being impressed by its moral and ethical earnestness. Certainly it leaves little doubt that Bismarck's passionate devotion to his office was animated by something more than the interest and importance of the work or even the patriotism that he felt as a Prussian officer and servant of his King. Behind it there was a deep sense of responsibility, which had its roots in Bismarck's religious faith.

Ludwig Bamberger once wrote: "Prince Bismarck believes firmly and deeply in a God who has the remarkable faculty of always agreeing with him." This is, perhaps, clever; but it should not be allowed to throw doubt on the genuineness of Bismarck's faith or its importance in his statecraft. . . .

"I am God's soldier," he wrote to Johanna when he first learned that he was to be sent to Frankfurt, "and where he sends me there must I go, and I believe that he does send me and that he shapes my life as he needs it." This has sometimes been taken merely as an ingratiating plea to a devout wife who did not want to have to move her family and furniture to another city; and it might be accepted as such if it stood alone. But it is one of many statements that show that Bismarck did not regard diplomacy as a mere job, but as a *vocatio,* an office to which he had been called by God. "I didn't ask for the royal service," he wrote to Gerlach in May 1860, "or search for personal honor in it, at least in a premeditated way . . . God set me unexpectedly in it." And if it was God's will that he do this job, then doing it as well as he could was both an expression of obedience and an act of service. "I believe that I am obeying God when I serve my King," he said on one occasion; and, again, "It is precisely my living evangelical and Christian faith that lays upon me the duty—in behalf of the land where I was born and for whose service God created me and where high office has been entrusted to me—to guard that office against all sides." Here, of course, we hear echoes of Luther's concept of *Beruf,* or vocation, as the work specifically assigned by God to the individual so that in performing it he might at one and the same time do his duty to God and to his fellow men.

Bismarck's faith also helped him bear the burdens that went with the authority of his office, especially the heavy weight of decisions that could bring war, and even defeat, upon his country. . . . "If it hadn't been for me," Bismarck said once, "there wouldn't have been three great wars, 80,000 men would not have died and parents, brothers, sisters and widows would not be mourning. But that I have had to settle with God." . . .

It is clear from all this that the decisiveness and sureness of touch so much admired by Bismarck's followers were not merely the products of a dynamic personality or of professional virtuosity, but had other roots; and one can understand more easily now the passion Bismarck brought to his vocation and the confidence with which he performed his duties. Nevertheless, the belief that one is a chosen instrument of God can be, and often has been, a dangerous belief, leading to *hubris* and megalomania. What prevented Bismarck from treading this same path? Here we come to the third of the qualities mentioned by Max Weber: a sense of proportion.

In one of the many essays written in Germany about Bismarck since 1945, Franz Schnabel has described the Chancellor as "the last great representative in the line of classical diplomats," "a 'member of the guild' with Choiseul, Kaunitz, Talleyrand and Metternich," and one who believed, like them, that "politics was . . . an exact science concerned with calculable magnitudes." About this claim two things must be said. First, it is dangerous to seek to classify Bismarck, and to make him a Kaunitzian does even more injustice to the character of his statecraft than to describe him—as some writers have done recently—as a Bonapartist. Second, and more important, it is simply not true that Bismarck believed politics to be "an exact science concerned with calculable magnitudes." On the contrary, he always described it as an art rather than a science; he repeatedly and specifically denied that it was either exact or logical; and, throughout his career, he was conscious of the limitations imposed upon the man who practiced it. If he did not actually say that politics is "the art of the possible," he certainly believed it; and it was this belief that lent proportion and perspective to his statecraft.

There is no doubt that Bismarck would have accepted the proposition that the first law of politics—and especially of foreign politics—is that one can rarely do exactly what one would like to do. The course that theory would define as the best in a given contingency, circumstances usually render impracticable; and the statesman finds himself compelled to settle for the least harmful of a number of unpleasant alternatives. Bismarck never forgot this, and, from hard experience, he came to know the factors that, in given cases, could, and generally did, limit his freedom of choice and action.

Prussian, and later German, foreign policy was, for one thing, limited in its freedom by the nation's geographical position. This made a vigilant and active foreign policy essential, for, as Bismarck wrote in 1857, "a passive lack of planning, which is content to be left alone, is not for us, situated as we are in the middle of Europe." On the other hand, it forbade adventures in exotic and exciting areas remote from the nation's main sphere of interest, activity, and danger. Thus, Bismarck could say to a colonial enthusiast in the 1880's, "Your map of Africa is very beautiful, but my map of Africa is in Europe. Here is Russia and here is France, and here we are in the middle. That is my map of Africa."

Germany's policy was limited also by her power at any given moment, and Bismarck's appreciation of this—so dramatically illustrated during the years of the constitutional conflict—need not be elaborated, except to note that—unlike some later statesmen in his own and other countries—he never took too restricted a view of power and always recognized that it included both a nation's actual and potential military and economic strength, and its reputation as well. . . .

And there were other limitations that had to be observed. The freedom of Prusso-German diplomacy was always limited by the nature of its international setting. Opportunities like those that were offered to it when the European concert was riven by dissension, as in the years from 1856 to 1870, were not likely to recur in times when there was a consensus among the powers, and a wise statesman had to adjust his policy accordingly. At any given moment, moreover, Germany's freedom to act was limited by the groupings of the powers, the strength and reliability of allies, and other facts of international life. It was equally affected by the nature of its domestic constitutional arrangements; and, while Bismarck did not have to reckon with anything like democratic control of foreign policy, he could never completely ignore public opinion; and even his relative freedom in this respect was balanced by the way in which he was limited, and his policy disrupted, by the prerogatives and prejudices of his sovereign, to say nothing of those forays into politics by military and other irresponsible agencies that were so much a part of the Prusso-German system. Finally, German diplomacy was limited by the effectiveness of its representatives, who, despite their schooling at Bismarck's hands, remained subject to human frailties, and by the nature of the problems with which they, and he, had to deal—some of which (the problem of Austro-Russian rivalry in the Balkans, for example) were not susceptible of easy solution, if, indeed, they were soluble at all.

If Bismarck had refused to recognize any of these limitations—and he did not—he would still have been held back from *hubris* by one more that he never forgot. Diplomatic plans, like all human designs, are always subject to the intervention of chance or providence. . . .

Bismarck is generally described in the textbooks as the first *Realpolitiker;* but unfortunately so much has been written about *Realpolitik* that its meaning has become obscure and mixed up with blood and iron and incitement to war by the malicious revision of royal telegrams. This is neither the place nor the time to correct what has become a traditional view. Even so, it may be permissible to suggest that the essence of Bismarck's realism was his recognition of the limitation of his craft, and that it was this, coupled with the passion and the responsibility that he brought to his vocation, that made him a great statesman.

Suggestions for Further Reading

BISMARCK PROVOKED STRONG REACTIONS, both in his own lifetime and in the critical works on the man and his policies since that time. And those works, even the best of them, tend to divide along the lines represented by the selections from Fuller and Craig presented in this chapter. The stronger tradition is that hostile to Bismarck, and its classic formulation in modern scholarship is Joseph Vincent Fuller, *Bismarck's Diplomacy at Its Zenith* (New York: H. Fertig, 1967 [1922]). Fuller's views are shared even by the greatest German authority on Bismarck, whose massive three-volume biography has been scaled down in a one-volume English abridgement: Erich Eyck, *Bismarck and the German Empire* (New York: Macmillan, 1950). This is also the case with the work of Werner Richter, *Bismarck*, tr. Brian Battershaw (New York: Putnam, 1964), a revisionist book directed against the revival of the old patriotic German myth of Bismarck. A. J. P. Taylor, the great British diplomatic historian, tends to be negative toward Bismarck in his *Bismarck, the Man and the Statesman* (New York: Knopf, 1954), as in his more substantial and scholarly works.

Gordon A. Craig, *From Bismarck to Adenauer: Aspects of German State-craft* (Baltimore: Johns Hopkins University Press, 1958), is in the best tradition of historical revision and attempts to present a somewhat more balanced—and favorable—view of Bismarck in this attractive, well-written, and reflective book. Another extremely interesting work—while not on Bismarck himself—tends to exculpate him from many of the charges leveled against him. It is the last work of the great German historian Friedrich Meinecke, *The German Catastrophe: Reflections and Recollections*, tr. Sidney B. Fay (Boston: Beacon, 1964), originally appearing in German in 1946 and an attempt to appraise the events of World War II in historical perspective. The most moderate and even-handed account of Bismarck is probably William N. Medlicott, *Bismarck and Modern Germany*, "Teach Yourself History Library" (London: English Universities Press, 1965), along with Eyck's book the two best brief biographies of him. Louis L. Snyder, *The Blood and Iron Chancellor, A Documentary-Biography of Otto von Bismarck* (Princeton, N.J.: Van Nostrand, 1967), is useful in providing a wide sampling of readings on Bismarck from both sources and secondary works. See also *Otto von Bismarck: A Historical Assessment*, ed. Theodore S. Hamerow, rev. ed. (New York: Harper & Row, 1973).

Bismarck's imperial diplomacy is one of the key subjects of modern European diplomatic history and is therefore treated in any general work on that broad and prolific topic. One of the standard works is William L. Langer, *European Alliances and Alignments, 1871–1890*, 2nd rev. ed. (New York: Knopf, 1950). While somewhat harsher and more anti-German in tone, the brilliant and stylish A. J. P. Taylor, *The Struggle for Mastery in Europe, 1848–1914* (Oxford, England: Clarendon Press, 1954), is the best work since Langer. Of the same sort is the massive, authoritative work of E. Malcolm Carroll, *Germany and the Great Powers, 1866–1914* (New York: Archon Books, 1966 [1938]). Of the broader and more general surveys Norman Rich, *The Age of Nationalism and Reform, 1850–1890* (New York: Norton, 1970), is a good synthesis, as is the more far-ranging classic, Carlton J. H. Hayes, *A Generation of Materialism, 1871–1900*, "Rise of Modern Europe" series (New York: Harper & Bros., 1941). Two final works on German history are also recommended: Hajo Holborn, *A History of Modern Germany*, Vol. 3, 1840–1945 (New York: Knopf, 1969), broad gauge and reflective and likely to become a standard work on German history; and A. J. P. Taylor, *The Course of German History: A Survey of the Development of Germany since 1815* (New York: Coward-McCann, 1946), a highly personal interpretive sketch, full of harsh, decisive judgments and interesting to compare with the reflections of Friedrich Meinecke.

Cecil Rhodes and the Dream of Empire

If the history of Europe in the second half of the nineteenth century was dominated by Bismarck's German Empire, that of the rest of the world was dominated by the imperial England of Queen Victoria. For in that half century the British Empire reached its greatest extent, and England became the model colonial power of the modern world.

The process had begun centuries before, with the expansion of Europe at the end of the Middle Ages, with the age of exploration and the creation of the first great colonial empires of Portugal and Spain. They were followed by the Dutch, the French, and the British. Colonial rivalries became issues between the major European powers in the seventeenth and eighteenth centuries. But with the coming of the Industrial Revolution, the nature of colonialism was dramatically altered, along with nearly everything else in the modern world.

Interest in underdeveloped areas had formerly been largely commercial and mercantile; it now became exploitative. The Western industrial nations needed raw materials for their factories—rubber, petroleum, copra, hemp, jute, cotton, lumber, copper. European populations demanded vast quantities of meat and grain and such products as coffee, tea, and tobacco. At the same time, the backward peoples of the world represented a new market for industrial goods—for many of which the need itself had to be fabricated as well as the goods.

The industrialized nations turned not only to the colonies they already had but to the entire area now popularly called the Third World. They

invested enormous amounts of capital, which was to be protected by the
military forces of the mother country. Colonial policy became an extension
of national economic policy. When necessary, both political and economic
interests manipulated native political naïveté and exploited native labor,
usually with the greedy collusion of native political leaders. Colonialism
and all its practices were justified as bringing the blessings of civilization
to the less fortunate peoples of the world. By most civilized people this was
regarded not only as an opportunity but an obligation, to "take up the
white man's burden." Part of that burden was, of course, the responsibility
of bringing God's word to the savage places and heathen populations now
beginning to become known. Throngs of missionaries went out to establish
schools, hospitals, and churches. They were often spectacularly successful.
But they were sometimes killed, and when this happened, their martyrdom
became the provocation for further extension of colonial control. Even the
ideas of Darwin were converted into a social gospel and used to justify
the supremacy of the Western industrial nations over the poor, the ignorant,
the "less favored" and usually more pigmented peoples of the world.

As Great Britain was the leading industrial power of modern Europe,
she was also the leading colonial power. But even imperial Britain was
not without rivals in the competition for colonies and spheres of colonial
influence—in China, the East Indies, and Southeast Asia, in the Middle
East, in Persia, in the lands of the rotting Ottoman Empire, and along the
borders of British India. But it was in Africa that the most savage scramble
for colonies took place. Even Bismarck's Germany belatedly entered the
race.

This was the scene upon which Cecil John Rhodes came in 1870. He
was only seventeen years old, the son of a poor Hertfordshire parson. He
had been diagnosed as suffering from incipient tuberculosis and had
decided to join his older brother in South Africa for his health. Shortly
after Rhodes' arrival there, the great Kimberley diamond strike was made.
Rhodes gained his first fortune in this enterprise, and multiplied it many
times over by his business acumen. He consolidated existing claims,
refinanced bankrupt operations, bought others, and opened new ones. By
1887 his holdings were second only to those of the main Kimberley mine,
held by a rough and ready diamond merchant and financial genius named
Barnett "Barney" Barnato. With backing from the Rothschild Bank,
Rhodes bought out his larger rival the following year for more than five
million pounds. Thus, he secured absolute control of South African
diamond production for his De Beers Consolidated Mines Ltd., the name
retained from a former company he had taken over. At the same time, he
was deeply involved in gold and had formed the powerful Gold Fields of
South Africa Company.

At intervals between making fortunes and between bouts of recurring
illness, Rhodes had managed to return to England for several periods of
residency at Oxford, where he was graduated in 1881. In that same year, he

stood successfully for the Cape Parliament, and his political career began. Politics to Rhodes was simply business by other means, and he was equally successful at it. He quickly became a dominant figure in South African public life. But Rhodes was a British imperialist to the bone. And as he looked to the north, he envisioned British dominion from Cape Colony not only across the Zambezi River to the great lakes of central Africa but to the Sudan and eventually Cairo—to "paint the map of Africa red," as he put it.

Immediately to the north of Cape Colony lay a vast land controlled by native chieftains. The most important of them was Lobengula, King of the Matabele. Rhodes negotiated with him, at the same time hoping to persuade either the Cape government or the British to support his negotiation. Neither was prepared. So Rhodes formed another company, the British South Africa Company, secured a charter for it, and carried through his own negotiations. As a result, he gained virtually sovereign control over the area that would become modern Rhodesia.

Rhodes' further plans were blocked by the opposition of the Boers. The word "boer" means farmer, and the Boer language is an old dialect of Dutch. For the Boers had been Dutch colonists, largely farmers and religious refugees, who had settled in South Africa in the seventeenth century. When the English took control of the Cape following the Napoleonic wars, the Boers had made their "great trek," an epic journey almost a thousand miles to the north. There, they settled in two small republics, the Transvaal and the Orange Free State. They continued to farm, to practice their religion, and to live by a stern, archaic moral code. Their spokesman was Paul Kruger, Prime Minister of the Transvaal. Kruger became Rhodes' most implacable enemy. He disliked Rhodes' plans for British imperial expansion—after all, it was precisely because of such a threat the Boers had fled from the Cape. He distrusted Rhodes' proposal for federation with the other South African states, suspecting that it was no more than a ploy—which it was not. And more generally, like most Boers, Kruger did not care for foreigners—"uitlanders"—money men and mining speculators. Indeed, the Transvaal government did everything to discourage such men, including placing high duties on goods crossing its frontiers and ruinous rail tariffs. The situation reached crisis proportions in 1895 after the discovery of further gold and diamond deposits in the Transvaal "on the Rand." Kruger still refused to consider joining a South African federation, stepped up economic resistance, and even sought support from the German imperial government.

Since 1890, Rhodes had been Prime Minister of Cape Colony. He now entered into a conspiracy to overthrow the Kruger government in the Transvaal. He organized a raiding party under the command of a friend, Dr. J. S. Jameson. The Jameson Raid was a military fiasco, and Rhodes' complicity in it was revealed. Such behavior by a head of state was intolerable both for the Cape Colony government and the British. Rhodes was stripped of his office and his seat in Parliament and censured by the British House of Commons, whose inquiry into the matter stopped just short of implicating high officials in the British Colonial Office. Rhodes would never totally recover his influence in South Africa, and the Jameson Raid would become a key incident leading to the Boer War. Rhodes himself died in 1902, not yet fifty years old.

Cecil Rhodes was the most obvious example of nineteenth-century British colonialism. He exemplified all its economic rapacity and political ambition, its chauvinism and its parternalism, its racism and bigotry. He also exemplified the untrammeled gospel of wealth. In a time of robber barons on a worldwide scale—Cornelius Vanderbilt, J. P. Morgan, Andrew Carnegie, John D. Rockefeller, Baron Krupp, and Lord Rothschild— Rhodes was the greatest both in resources and in vision. There was nothing, he thought, that could not be bought, no one who could not be bribed. He used his wealth to gain political ends and political power to further his fortune. And he dreamed dreams of empire that other men might applaud or condemn but, for their scope and daring, few could match.

Contemporary Recollections
SIDNEY LOW

*While Cecil Rhodes was a doer and a talker of imperial proportions, he
was no writer or formal speechmaker. Thus his ideas are not readily
found in his own writings. He kept no journal, his letters are of the most
routine sort, and he did not live long enough to indulge in the fancy of a
memoir—which he would probably have disdained anyhow. But his views
were far from unknown. He would and did talk with anybody, often to
the disadvantage of his image, his reputation, even his business enterprises.
The following excerpt is thus not from Rhodes himself but from the
recollections of an exceptionally able journalist, Sidney Low, who knew
him well, who interviewed him many times, and who can report the man
and his views better, in this instance, than the man himself. The following
piece was written on the occasion of Rhodes' death in 1902 for the British
popular magazine* The Nineteenth Century and After.

MY FIRST INTERVIEW with Rhodes dates back nearly ten years. It occurred
on the 10th of December 1892. Up to that time the managing director of
the Chartered Company had been to me a vague, and not altogether a sympathetic, figure. I had followed South African affairs with some attention,
and I was far from enthusiastic over the methods and constitution of Mr.
Rhodes's Company. I recognised the importance of keeping open the road
from Cape Colony to the north, and was prepared to admit that the countries of the Matabele and the Mashona should be placed within the British
sphere of influence, if only to exclude the possibility of foreign interference.
But I held that if the work of conquest or annexation were worth doing, it
should be done directly, with a full assumption of responsibility, by the
Imperial Government itself. The delegation of the duty to a body of private
adventurers, aiming primarily at their own profit, seemed to me a doubtful
expedient; and the Chartered Company, with its mixture of high politics
and Stock Exchange speculation, I regarded with some distrust. What I
could gather of the financial arrangements of the concern did not increase
my confidence. . . .

I happened, shortly before the date mentioned, to meet a person much
interested in the Chartered enterprise, who attempted, not very successfully, to convert me to a more favourable opinion of the project. He urged
me to see Rhodes, and arranged a meeting. At the appointed time I presented myself at the Burlington Hotel. My credentials were duly passed by

some members of the little court of secretaries and retainers, whom Rhodes always had about him. He was simple enough in his personal habits, but there was something regal in his dependence upon his suite. He required his trusted favourites and henchmen to be constantly at hand, and he could scarcely write a letter without the assistance of one or other member of his private Cabinet. Eventually I found myself at the end of a large room, in front of a large man, standing before a large fire. Size was the first external impression you received of Cecil Rhodes. In whatever company you met him he seemed the biggest man present. Yet, though tall and broadly built, his stature was not really phenomenal; but there was something in the leonine head, and the massive, loose pose, which raised him to heroic proportions. He received me with a cordial smile and an invitation to sit down in one of the two comfortable arm-chairs, which flanked the fireplace. After a question or two to break the ice, he began to talk, and he went on for an hour almost without intermission. Sometimes I put in a word or two to open the points, and switch him from one track to another; but in the main it was a monologue by Rhodes, or perhaps I should say a lecture on the future of South Africa. As he sat up in his crumpled tweed suit, with his left foot twisted round his right ankle, I lay back in my arm-chair and listened, amazed and fascinated, while the rapid sentences poured out of the broad chest in curiously high notes, that occasionally rose almost to a falsetto. Rhodes's voice was peculiar. It was uneven and apparently under no control. Sometimes it would descend abruptly, but as a rule when he was moved it reached the upper part of the register in odd, jerky transitions. But if it had been full of music and resonance it could have had no more effect upon the listener. I never heard Rhodes make a speech in public, and I am told he was no orator. But a talker he was, of more compelling potency than almost anyone it had been my lot to hear. Readiness, quickness, an amazing argumentative plausibility, were his: illustrations and suggestions were touched off with a rough happy humour of phrase and metaphor: he countered difficulties with a Johnsonian ingenuity: and if you sometimes thought you had planted a solid shot into his defences, he turned and overwhelmed you with a sweeping Maxim-fire of generalisation. Yet in all the intellectual accomplishments of conversation and debate he was inferior to many men one has known. Wittier talkers, more brilliant, far better read, infinitely closer and more logical in argument, it would be easy to name. But these men produced no such impression as Rhodes. It was the personality behind the voice that drove home the words—the restless vivid soul, that set the big body fidgeting in nervous movements, the imaginative mysticism, the absorbing egotism of the man with great ideas, and the unconscious dramatic instinct, that appealed to the sympathies of the hearer. One must add a smile of singular and most persuasive charm. It would break over the stern brickdust-coloured face like the sun on a granite hill, and gave to the large features and the great grey eyes a feminine sweetness that was irresistible. . . .

I came away from my first interview with Rhodes rather fascinated than convinced. It was the character more than the mind one admired. Then, and subsequently, it seemed to me that Rhodes's weakness was on the intellectual side. He was not a clear reckoner or a close thinker, but rather —so he himself admitted—a dreamer of dreams, vague, mighty, somewhat impalpable. Nor did it seem to me that he was an originator of ideas, but one who took up the conceptions of others, expanded them, dwelt upon them, advertised them to the world in his grandiloquent fashion, made them his own. Of late years he has been taken as the typical Imperialist. But in 1892 he seemed to me not an Imperialist at all, in the sense in which we then understood the term. He had risen to power at the Cape, it must be remembered, as the opponent of direct Imperial rule, and of all that was known as "Downing Street." His alliance with the Afrikander Bond was based on joint antipathy against the Colonial Office. When he talked of eliminating the Imperial factor he may have used a casual phrase, with no very precise meaning; but in fact that was what he wanted, though of course he did not mean to eliminate the British flag as well. His ideal was South Africa for the Afrikanders *utriusque juris*. Colonists of both races were to be worked together and federated to form an Afrikander nation, just as the Australians have formed an Australian, and the people of the Dominion a Canadian, nation. To some of us in 1892 the notion of bringing about this result by means of the Dutch, whose hostility to England and the English was well known, seemed dangerous. I asked Mr. Rhodes if the end would not be a secession and the conversion of the Federation to an independent Republic. "Are you going to be the Bismarck or the Washington of South Africa?" I said. Rhodes had his full share of vanity, and was delighted at being linked with these great names; but he hesitated, in order to ponder the question, and then replied with much seriousness, "Oh, Bismarck for choice of course." I suggested that his alliance with the Dutch Nationalists might really involve a danger of separation. He denied it emphatically. He said that he had joined Mr. Hofmeyr, in order to bring the Dutch into Cape constitutional politics and to prepare the way for a United South Africa, able to manage its own affairs, which it had a perfect right to do. "You people at home," he said, "don't understand us." But he laughed at the notion of secession, and he declared that neither Hofmeyr nor any other Dutchman would really want to get rid of English supremacy. "We must have the British Navy behind us," he said, "to keep away foreigners. We all know that." . . .

. . . Rhodes sometimes spoke of England and the English with that kind of irritation which many energetic colonists and Americans feel for this comfortable old country, with its innate conservatism, its arrogant belief in itself, its indifference to new ideas, and its absorption in controversies which, to the pushing new man from beyond the seas, seem time-worn and threadbare. Mr. Kipling's line "What do they know of England who only England know?" had not been written at the date of my first meeting with

Rhodes; but the sentiment it conveyed was shared by him to the full. He thought of the British Isles as a few crowded specks of European territory, whose swarming millions should be given room for expansion in the vacant lands of the ampler continents. He was possessed—I had almost said obsessed—by the fear that if we neglected our chances, they would be taken from us by others, and the English people would be throttled for lack of breathing-space. This work seemed to him of such paramount importance that everything else in politics sank into insignificance beside it. He believed sincerely that the service he had rendered the nation by securing Rhodesia as a field for British colonisation could hardly be over-estimated, and he was astonished that the public took the gigantic benefaction so calmly. . . .

. . . The domestic affairs of some forty millions of people seemed to him hardly worth considering when any question of territorial or colonial expansion was in the balance. Lord Salisbury once recommended the use of "large maps" as a corrective to groundless political alarms. Rhodes was fond of large maps too, but they had a different effect upon him. He would gaze upon the great polygon between the Transvaal and the Zambesi which he had coloured red, and expatiate upon the vastness of the country; then he would run his finger northward, and explain how Africa was to be linked up and thrown open by his Cape-to-Cairo telegraph and railway. It was in my first conversation with him that I heard Rhodes mention this project, which was a novel one to me. I hinted some doubts—whether anyone would want to use the through route, whether the native chiefs and slave traders would not interfere with the poles and wires. Rhodes took up the latter point with one of his touches of cynical humour: "The slavers! Why, before my telegraph had been running six months they would be using it to send through their consignment of slaves." Something was said about the Khalifa, and the obvious difficulty of constructing a railway through the Equatorial Provinces, then in the hands of fanatical barbarians. "You ask me," said Rhodes, in words which, I believe, he afterwards repeated in public, "how I am going to get the railway through the Soudan; well, I don't know. But I tell you, when the time comes we shall deal with the Mahdi in one way or another. If you mean to tell me that one man can permanently check an enterprise like this, I say to you it is not possible." This was very characteristic of Rhodes in two ways. He had a profound belief in destiny and in the power of world-movements to fulfil their ends. And he had also a conviction that almost any man could be "dealt with," if you knew the right way to go to work with him. It was based, I suppose, on his own experience, for he had been singularly successful in manipulating and moulding men to his own purposes. From the keen-eyed speculators in Kimberley to the suspicious savages in the Matoppo caves, there were few with whom he had failed to come to terms when he desired to make them his instruments or allies. Partly I am sure that this was due to the mere personal influence, the "magnetism," to which I have already referred. But Rhodes was always a believer in the arts of bargain and management. He held that most people have their price, though the currency is not always notes or cheques or shares. By appealing to a person's vanity, his patriotism, his ideals, or his cupidity, you can generally contrive to get him to do what you want. It was part of the piquancy of Rhodes's character that he mingled the practical shrewdness of the diamond mart and the gambling table wtih his prophetic visions and imaginative enthusiasms. . . .

Whatever inconsistency there may have been in his actions, his opinions, so far as I could perceive, did not vary. In fact, he repeated himself a good deal, having a kind of apostolic fervour in expatiating on the broad simple tenets of the Rhodesian religion. His cardinal doctrines I should say were these: First, that insular England was quite insufficient to maintain, or even to protect, itself without the assistance of the Anglo-Saxon peoples beyond the seas of Europe. Secondly, that the first and greatest aim of British statesmanship should be to find new areas of settlement, and new markets for the products that would, in due course, be penalised in the territories and dependencies of all our rivals by discriminating tariffs. Thirdly, that the largest tracts of unoccupied or undeveloped lands remaining on the globe were in Africa, and therefore that the most strenuous efforts should be made to keep open a great part of that continent to British commerce and colonisation. Fourthly, that as the key to the African position lay in the various Anglo-Dutch States and provinces, it was imperative to convert the whole region into a united, self-governing, federation, exempt from meddlesome interference by the home authorities, but loyal to the Empire, and welcoming British enterprise and progress. Fifthly, that the world was made for the service of man, and more particularly of civilised, white, European men, who were most capable of utilising the crude resources of nature for the promotion of wealth and prosperity. And, finally, that the British Constitution was an absurd anachronism, and that it should be remodelled on the lines of the American Union, with federal self-governing Colonies as the constituent States. . . .

. . . He had a reverence such as is more common now among Americans than Englishmen, for enterprise on an extensive scale. Man in his view was clearly an active animal. He was made to do "big" things, and to do them in a modern, scientific, progressive manner. With the obstructionist, who clogged the wheels of the machine, whether from indolence, ignorance, or an exaggerated regard for the past, he had no patience. Some months before the opening of the South African War I was dining with him and a number of his friends, who were mostly interested in one way or other in Rhodesian or Transvaal affairs. The conversation turned on the condition of Johannesburg, the grievances of the Uitlanders, and the possible attitude of Great Britain. "If I were in the position of the British Government," said Rhodes, "I should say to old Kruger, 'Mr. Kruger, you are interfering with business, and you will have to get out of the way.' " The little speech was characteristic; so, by the way, was the pronunciation of the ex-President's name. Rhodes, as I have said, had no mastery of detail. In his thirty years in South Africa he had not learned how Dutch words should be spoken. He called his ancient enemy "old Krooger," like the man in the street.

My most interesting talk with Rhodes occurred in the early days of February 1896, after the shattering collapse of Jameson's failure, when the deeply compromised Cape Premier hastened to England to "face the music." I was anxious to see him. Knowing that he was an early riser, I thought I should have the best chance of catching him disengaged if I went before most other callers were out of bed. So on the second morning after his arrival, at about eight o'clock, I sent in my name at the Burlington Hotel. My access to Rhodes on this occasion, when few but intimate friends were allowed to approach him, was facilitated by the fact that he had been reading some articles of mine on the events of the preceding month. I was no apologist for the Raid, nor have I ever been able to regard Rhodes's participation in the plot against the Transvaal Republic as anything but an unpardonable breach of trust and a monstrous abuse of the exceptional powers and privileges which had been conferred upon him. But if I did not excuse his conduct, I thought it was possible to explain it; and, as it happened, my explanations were very much on the lines of those which he himself would have framed. On this morning—the 6th of February 1896—I was taken up to Rhodes in his bedroom. He had risen, but was not quite dressed, and as he talked he walked feverishly up and down the room, awkwardly completing his toilet. He had been dining out the evening before; the dress clothes he had worn were scattered in disorder about the room; the large, rather bare, hotel apartment seemed strangely cold and friendless in the chilly light of the grim London morning; and the big man, with the thatch of grey-brown hair, who paced up and down in his shirt-sleeves, was a pathetic, almost a desolate figure. He was much changed by these few bitter weeks of suspense and suffering. Through the ruddy bronze of the sea wind and the veldt breezes his cheeks showed grey and livid; he looked old and worn. He asked me to sit down while he finished dressing; and presently he began to talk about the Raid and the conspiracy. I had felt some diffidence in approaching the subject; but he was full of it—too full to keep silence. He was, as I have said, always candid; but on this occasion, considering the circumstances in which he stood and my own comparatively slight acquaintance with him, I was amazed at his freedom. I thought, indeed, that he was saying too much, and more than once I tried to check him and rose to go; but he evidently wanted to talk—I suppose to ease his mind after a sleepless night—and he begged me to remain till he had finished his story. . . .

. . . From his very candid exposition of his own motives and expectations, I derived a strong, and, I think, perfectly correct impression that Rhodes's intervention in the Johannesburg conspiracy was due quite as much to fear of the Uitlanders as to animosity against Mr. Kruger. Rhodes disliked the reactionary Dutch oligarchy at Pretoria; but he also rather despised it, and believed that it was bound to fall before long by its inherent weakness, which he greatly over-estimated. He was, however, possessed by a genuine apprehension that it might be succeeded by a Republican Government which might be anti-Imperialist and perhaps anti-British. He knew that among the leading reformers at Johannesburg there were Americans, many Australians and Cape Afrikanders, some Germans and other foreigners. They objected to the Krugerite *régime,* which dipped into their pockets and shackled their enterprise; but they had no liking for Downing Street and many of them had even a very qualified affection for the Union Jack. Rhodes put it somewhat in this way:

I knew that in five years there would be 250,000 white settlers on the Rand. In ten years there might be half a million or more. Now, that large European population, with its enormous wealth and industry, would inevitably become the political centre of all South Africa. If we left things alone, the Uitlanders were certain, sooner or later, to turn out Kruger and his lot, to get possession of the Transvaal administration, and to make the Republic a modern, financial, progressive State, which would draw all South Africa after it. But they would have done it entirely by their own efforts. They would owe no gratitude to England, and, indeed, they might feel a grudge against the Home Government for having left them in the lurch so long. They would take very good care to retain their independence and their flag, with perhaps a leaning towards some foreign power, and all the Afrikander world would grad- ually recognise their leadership. So that, in the end, instead of a British Federal Dominion, you would get a United States of South Africa, with its capital on the Rand, and very likely it would be ruled by a party that would be entirely opposed to the English connection. In fact, you would lose South Africa, and lose it by the efforts of the English-speaking minority in the Transvaal, who are at present anti-British as well as anti-Kruger. I saw that if left to itself this section would become predominant when the Dutch oligarchy was expelled. That was why I went into the movement. I joined with the wealthy men who were ready to give their money to overthrow Kruger, so that we might be able to turn the revolu- tion in the right direction at the right time. You may say, 'Rhodes should have left it alone; it was no business of his.' Yes; and if I had done so, there was the certainty that the revolution would have been attempted— perhaps not just now, but in two years, three years, or five years—all the same; that it would have succeeded; and then the money of the capitalists, the influence of the leading men in Johannesburg, would have been used in favour of this new and more powerful Republican Govern- ment, which would have drifted away from the Empire and drawn all South Africa—English as well as Dutch—after it.

I had much more talk with Rhodes on the subject, both on this day and subsequently. But the passage I have reproduced, as nearly as possible in his own words, has always seemed to me the gist of Rhodes's whole defence of his action in 1895.

A South African View of Rhodes
STUART CLOETE

The opinions about Rhodes available in South Africa are, of course, as varied as the political extremes of that troubled region. Most white Rhodesians regard him not only as the founding father of their country but as the patron of their way of life. Even the descendants of the South African Boers share many of his views, in particular his racial views. Most black South African intellectuals regard him as the fountainhead of their own present discontent. Stuart Cloete is a native-born white South African who, in a string of highly successful novels, has essayed the hard task of espousing a middle course on the many questions faced by South Africa today. He is a moderate in a land increasingly dominated by extremists. In his assessment of Rhodes he is as moderate as in his other writings, recognizing at once the blight that Rhodes and his sort laid upon South Africa but still able to see the man behind the symbol. The following selection is from his Against These Three, A Biography of Paul Kruger, Cecil Rhodes, and Lobengula, Last King of the Matabele.

RHODES WAS A MAN who parodied his own virtues, whose whole life was a paradox of Machiavellian simplicity. An expatriate who devoted his life to the aggrandizement of the country he had left, and all but ruined the Africa he loved. Hero to some. Murderer to others. The godless man whom men worshipped almost as a god. The Colossus with lungs of clay. The great cynic, the great idealist. The financier who was always in debt. The imperialist who shares with Simón Bolívar the liberator the honor of having a great country named after him. The man who chose a mountain for a tomb. The only white man who ever received the Zulu royal salute of "Bayete" from the very people he had destroyed; and who, exposing another facet of his character, left uncompleted the greatest deal of his life to go to the deathbed of a friend. The maker of a million settlers' homes who had none, in the real sense, of his own. The uncrowned king of half a continent. The man, to whom hundreds of women offered themselves in concubinage or as wives, who never touched a woman. The student of history who forgot men were not bloodless pawns. . . .

He was not a man who lived by rote or thought in terms of precedent. His idea was to force on a reluctant Africa a federation resembling the American federation of states. But he went beyond this. He wanted to get America back and said—"Even from an American point of view, just picture what they have lost." At another time he wrote to Stead, "Fancy the charm to young America to share in a scheme to take the government of the world."

This was Rhodes's master plan—the orderly government of the world by a superstate. The limited plan he came near to achieving was the African federation.

The race for Africa was now really on. The preliminary canter was over. The Belgians were in the Congo—led by Stanley, the explorer; the French were in the Congo—led by another explorer, de Branza. Germans were everywhere hunting, prospecting as engineers for gold, as missionaries for souls. The silences of the great rivers were broken by the shots of the hunters and the hymns of the ministers. Soon they were to echo under the crack of the kiboko and the cries of natives being thrashed for failing to produce their quota of rubber. Portugal was claiming more rights. Germany had established her colonies. France was creeping down the Niger. England must make her way up from the Limpopo and join the Cape to Egypt. Is it wonderful, therefore, that the Boers were afraid? That they sought protection, that they wanted an outlet of their own to the sea? That they, who to live, needed farms so large that they could live by the increase of their herds alone, felt themselves hemmed in? Above all they hated and feared England, and England guided by Rhodes was on the march. "I look upon this territory of Bechuanaland as the Suez Canal of the trade of this country," Rhodes said, ". . . the key of its road to the interior. Some honorable members," he went on, "may say this is immorality. The lands they may say belong to the chief, Mankoroane. . . . Now I have not these scruples. I believe the natives are bound gradually to come under the control of Europeans. . . ." Here Rhodes paraphrased Darwin. He knew what he had to do. He felt conquest his duty—not merely to England, but to the world. . . .

Rhodes always looked older than he was, thirty when he was twenty; forty when he was thirty. He is described as thick and heavy—square, with big hands, a double chin, a sensual mouth, and a high falsetto voice. Bismarck, the maker of Germany and competitor for Africa, another big man, had a similar voice.

Rhodes, the so-called solitary—this is part of the fiction that has been built up about him—hated even to have a meal by himself. He loved to surround himself by friends and if friends were not available enemies would do. He had to talk, he had to have an audience. And often, when he had done talking, his enemies became his friends. He hated loafers and, like many childless men, had definite ideas about education. A good education he felt was essential. "Then kick all the props away. If they are worth anything the struggle will make them better men; if they are not, the sooner they go under the better for the world." Here we get the theory of the survival of the fittest introduced into family life. . . . He investigated God factually and gave God his chance—a fifty per cent chance. He decided that Charles Darwin was the best interpreter of God's work, which in terms of fact appeared to be that "dog eats dog": the bigger dog destroying the lesser. It remained merely for man to follow this lead and God's will was done.

God's finest product, according to Rhodes, was the Englishman. Here was the one race which had true ideals of justice, peace, and liberty without any suggestion of equality. . . .

Rhodes's attitude to the natives varied with the political wind. At one time he said—this was when he wanted the natives on his side—"I do not believe they are different from ourselves." But he also said on other occasions, "The natives are children." On the native question at least Rhodes and the Boers had no quarrel. It was their one and lowest common denominator. Rhodes said, "I am no negrophilist"—a superfluous assertion, since he threw so much emphasis on pigmentation. All that was Nordic blond was good to him—in which conclusion he agreed perfectly with the thoughts of Nietzsche, whom he had never seen.

He has been described as overbearing and ruthless. And he was. But he was also reasonable and conciliatory, colloquial; and explanatory when it was worth his while. He was for a time—and not a short time either—successful in being all things to all men. Whether he fooled them or fooled himself, or whether he thought circumstance itself would come to his aid, it seems impossible to determine. He did not believe with Kruger that "alles sal regt kom"—that all would come right; but appears to have thought that he could make things come right if he had control.

Rhodes's charm was undeniable. Barnato said, "You can't resist him." Hofmeyr said, "We had a talk and were friends ever afterwards." The Matabele whom he destroyed said, "You have come again and now all things are clear, we are your children." General Gordon said, "Stay and work with me." Then he asked him to come and help "smash the Mahdi." Rhodes's reply was typical. He would not fight the Mahdi, "but deal with him." To "deal" or to "square" were pleasant euphemisms for bribing: a simpler and a cheaper method of settling difficulties than war. Rhodes is even supposed to have said to Parnell, when he said owing to his divorce, the priests were against him, "Can't you square the Pope?" Nothing daunted Rhodes. After getting Barney Barnato into the Kimberley Club, "to make a gentleman of him" and bring him onto his side of the diamond fence, Barney said, "But your crowd will never leave me in. They will turn me out in a year or two."

"Then we'll make you a life governor," was Rhodes's answer.

This final act of amalgamation took place in Doctor Jameson's cottage. Rhodes and Biet were on one side. On the other were Woolf Joel and Barnato. The stakes were for millions and none of the men concerned was yet thirty-six years old. The argument went on till dawn, Rhodes talking, Rhodes exhorting, cajoling, threatening. Rhodes's high voice stringing out long estimates of costs and profits. Rhodes getting up and sitting down. The room was filled with smoke. The men were drinking as they talked. Someone would lean forward to adjust the light of the lamp, turning the wick up or down. "If you have an idea and it's a good idea, if you will only stick to it, you will come out all right," was Rhodes's argument, and the amalgamation of the diamond fields and consolidation of diamond interests was a good idea. And then, as the sky began to pale, Rhodes threw in his final argument: he promised Barney Barnato a seat in Parliament. That finished it. Barney gave in. Life governor of the Kimberley Club and the right to put the magic letters M.P. after his name.

Ambition. Rhodes's was endless. He even wanted the stars, he said. "These stars that you see overhead at night, these vast worlds which we can never reach. I would annex the planets if I could. I often think of that. It makes me sad to see them so clear and so far away." This takes us back to the story of the old Boer who said there were no minerals in the moon because if there were the British would have taken possession of it long ago.

But what chance had men like Lobengula, and the others who were against him, with Rhodes? The man who wanted the stars, whose thoughts were so big that men were less than ants. Perhaps he saw them as ants toiling to make the world red for England. . . . Rhodes's sense was of the future, always the future; the present meant little to him. Today was no more to Rhodes than the rung which he must climb to attain tomorrow.

An example of Rhodes's sense of timing is given by Fitzpatrick when he describes his negotiations for the sale of a parcel of diamonds worth half a million sterling. What he wanted was a cash offer for the whole lot made on behalf of all the buyers present. They could agree among themselves afterwards as to the proportions they would take, and how the payment should be made, but he alone, acting for the de Beers shareholders, would decide whether the offer they made was adequate or not. The diamonds were laid out on sheets of paper exactly fitting a teak trough twelve inches wide. The sheets overlapped each other like the tiles of a roof and the diamonds on each sheet were carefully sorted and graded by the de Beers experts—the work, perhaps, in a parcel of this size, of several months. The diamonds in each little heap were identical.

The first offer made was not enough and Rhodes said so. He said, "I know the value as well as you do," and, turning to Brink, said, "That's not good enough."

A few minutes later, the buyers agreed to a much higher price which Rhodes accepted.

At this time the diamond market "was in a very nervous condition and it was realized that the sale, releasing of a mass of stones, would have a very serious effect upon prices." Everyone knew this, but the buyers each thought that he would be first in the field and resell quickly. All knew the enormous advantage of buying well-classified stones. Rhodes, when he signed the contract, had said, "I can make no contract with you binding you to hold these stones off the market. . . ." "The buyers were all rivals and none believed that everybody would exercise this restraint or comply with Rhodes's wishes . . . After all, business is business," Harris says. However, all agreed with Rhodes and there was a little chaff about his idealistic touch. Everything was now signed. The lawyers were finished and Rhodes said, casually: "All right, you will get the stones tomorrow when payment is made. They will be here in the de Beers office. Brink will take care of them for you. . . . Come along, Brink, put them away . . . and you understand, delivery tomorrow morning against payment.

"For a moment everyone was happy. Then Rhodes strolled across the room to speak to Brink from the head of the long trough where the diamonds lay grouped on their white paper. A wooden bucket was at the other end of the trough, and as Rhodes told Brink to put them away, he raised the head of the teak trough and shot the whole in a cataract into the bucket. He did it with the most natural movement, just as indifferently as one would toss an old newspaper onto the table. He did not say a word to those round him; was seemingly quite unconscious of what he had done and strolled out of the room without showing any sign of what had happened.

"Believe me, the faces of our people were a treat . . . the whole work of sorting was wiped out in one second and for six or eight months the entire output was kept off the market at surely as if it had been locked in the de Beers' safe. Someone said, 'My God, we have not a word in the contract about the grading or classifying. We just bought the output. . . .' Then someone else said, 'How the Christian beat the Jews!' and there was a roar of laughter such as you would only get from a gathering of Jews, who can, after all, enjoy a story at their own expense. And mind you, Rhodes was perfectly right. Our stones were locked up, but when we could sell them we realized a much better price than we could possibly have done at the time. His judgment was completely justified."

Rhodes and the Twentieth Century
JOHN FLINT

Cecil Rhodes has continued to fascinate not only those whose lives are somehow still touched by his imperial dreams but academic scholars as well, who have brought to their studies both a commitment to impartiality and a distance conducive to perspective. One of the best of these is the Canadian historian John Flint, from whose recent biography of Rhodes the following selection is excerpted. Flint, as one of his reviewers has pointed out,[1] is the first biographer of Rhodes to bring to his task an authentic expert knowledge of black Africa. What is perhaps more important, Flint is an authority on the British Chartered Companies. He sees Rhodes, therefore, not so much as an imperialist who was a businessman as a businessman who intended to use imperialism for his own ends. In this view and in the linkage Flint makes between Rhodes' immediate aims and his darker fancies, he contributes significantly to the modern understanding of this colossal and paradoxical figure.

THE STOCK IMAGE of Rhodes was the one he invented for himself, and the one all his biographers have perpetuated even when critical of his actions: Rhodes the archetype of imperialism, the patriot of empire, embodying in his person the vigor of British individualism and will to expand. The image was also the basis of his popularity in Britain during the last years of his life; it was the Rhodes of the music-hall stage and the Rhodes in the minds of bus drivers and cabbies who hailed him on the streets. No other imperial figure of his day could stand in quite the same unqualified way as "the man of empire." . . .

Rhodes posthumously deluded both his admirers and his critics, for in reality he was by no means a typical figure of the late-Victorian imperialist movement. In the true sense he was not an imperialist at all, for his career and policies had been largely concerned with resisting the metropolitan authority of Britain, with limiting the *imperium* in British imperialism. Rhodes used and exploited British imperialism for his own distinct ends and aims, which did not encompass the extension of direct British power and authority in southern Africa. To him the "imperial factor" was remote, meddling, and dangerously color-blind on racial

---

[1] "The Duty of an Anglo-Saxon," *Times Literary Supplement* (Nov. 19, 1976), p. 1461.

issues. It could be manipulated where necessary, but it must be a symbolic authority, a majesty to warn off foreigners but not to rule him or his people. The British flag, he told a meeting of De Beers shareholders four days after the relief of Kimberley, was "the best commercial asset in the world." Those who were close to the heart of imperial policies, and especially those with wider experiences of British Imperial questions, seemed to sense Rhodes' propensity to manipulate Imperial symbols; and they distrusted him. Imperial statesmen like Salisbury, Chamberlain or Rosebery kept Rhodes at a certain formal distance, even before the Jameson Raid. The really "typical" figures of British late-Victorian imperialism were the proconsular governors and administrators of the newly acquired or older territories, . . .

Such men, whatever their faults, possessed a certain sense of the awesomeness of the British Imperial system and a feeling for justice and impartial rule, however much some of them at times traduced these principles. Rhodes was too much the white South African, too "colonial," to share such sentiments. If anything he must be described as a colonialist, not an imperialist, in that he dedicated himself to the expansion of the white race in southern Africa. Even the pursuit of this goal was upon his own terms: the whites must expand in his way and to his profit and power. In the last Rhodes' ambitions were ambitions for Rhodes. . . .

The image of Rhodes as the archimperialist, held by admirers and critics alike, has indeed helped to obscure some of his most creative achievements. Politically his dreams evaporated and his schemes collapsed. His major practical political goal, the creation of a South African federation (to include Rhodesia) controlled by an Afrikaner-English alliance under the British flag collapsed under the impact of the Jameson Raid fiasco. Today South Africa has realized Kruger's, not Rhodes' ideas, and is an independent republic outside the British Commonwealth. Even his beloved Rhodesia flies its own green and white flag and is a republic. Rhodes' most original and lasting achievements were economic rather than political. The De Beers company was a multinational corporation, with worldwide shareholding, and a world outlook on the marketing of its product. Though not as dominant in gold mining, the Consolidated Gold Fields company likewise became an international conglomerate. In mining Rhodes was a pioneer innovator in the exploitation of new techniques, and he brought the best of American engineers to South Africa to improve and develop the means of mineral extraction. This determination to develop the means of production in Africa was not confined to minerals. His private and official initiatives in practice established prosperous agriculture in the Cape, where the creation of fruit-growing and the wine industry, also with the help of much American expertise, were major achievements. Joseph Chamberlain has often been credited with initiating economic development in British Africa with his concepts of "developing the Imperial estate." But Rhodes, by directly supervising the application of capital and

technology, by stressing planning and pilot schemes, expanded production
in actual rather than theoretical terms. . . .

. . . His mystic obsession with his "idea," which was never clearly
enunciated, seemed to anticipate the stress on the Leader's intuition in
later fascism and Nazism. His companies, like the later fascist parties,
operated as states within the formal state; the British South Africa Company openly, the others clandestinely. De Beers had its own police and
detective force, ostensibly to curb diamond thefts and illicit diamond
buying, but it kept dossiers on prominent South Africans who had little
or nothing to do with the diamond business. Rhodes bought into the press,
in South Africa and England, to control opinion in his favor and to
suppress criticism of his own affairs and information about them. He was
never scrupulous in the means he employed to secure his ends, and he
thought most men easily corruptible. Like Mussolini after him, Rhodes
felt himself Roman. He fancied he bore a likeness to the emperor Hadrian,
commissioned dozens of busts and statues of himself, and even arranged
for his own funeral to be like that of an emperor. Rhodes' views on race,
though not particularly anti-Semitic or unusual for his time, also seemed
congenial to extreme right-wing thought in the years between the wars.
For Rhodes the achievements of the British were the result of an inner
dynamism contained in the "British race"; all other peoples, except the
Germanic, were in varying degrees inferior. . . .

In South Africa Rhodes' memory has been cherished best among English-
speakers, where there still exists a popular tradition of Rhodes as a heroic
figure who might have unified southern Africa with a white colonial regime
under the Union Jack had it not been for the impetuous Jameson's tragic
mistake in 1895. Many such people would still claim to accept in theory
Rhodes' dictum of "Equal rights for all civilized men" while demonstrating
in successive elections their increasing willingness to vote Nationalist and
support *apartheid* in practice.

Suggestions for Further Reading

THE POWERFUL, complex, and enigmatic figure of Cecil Rhodes continues
to elude his biographers, and the definitive, critical biography remains to
be written. Sarah Gertrude Millin, *Cecil Rhodes* (New York and London:

Harper & Bros., 1933), is, to an extent, the standard work on him, a colorful and exciting account by an experienced novelist and biographer. Both Felix Gross, *Rhodes of Africa* (New York: Praeger, 1956), and John Marlowe, *Cecil Rhodes: The Anatomy of Empire* (London: Elek, 1972), are superficial popular works. Even J. G. Lockhart and C. M. Woodhouse, *Cecil Rhodes: Colossus of Southern Africa* (New York: Macmillan, 1963), though based more fully on documents than any previous study, is timid and indecisive. John Flint, *Cecil Rhodes* (Boston and Toronto: Little, Brown, 1974), excerpted in this chapter, although a very small book, is probably the best general treatment of him. There are, however, three special studies that can be recommended: John S. Galbraith, *Crown and Charter: The Early Years of the British South Africa Company* (Berkeley: University of California Press, 1974), tells the dramatic story of the founding of Rhodesia and of Rhodes at the height of his power, with an interesting focus on the internal affairs of the company and its dealings; Brian Roberts, *Cecil Rhodes and the Princess* (London: Hamilton, 1969), is an intriguing account of a bizarre incident in Rhodes' life, as exciting as an espionage thriller; and Jeffrey Butler, *The Liberal Party and the Jameson Raid* (Oxford, England: Clarendon Press, 1968), is a fine study of the political ramifications of a famous incident.

Rhodes was, of course, the quintessential figure of British economic imperialism, and the enormous literature of that subject almost invariably deals with him. The definitive work on a key aspect of imperialism is W. L. Langer, *The Diplomacy of Imperialism,* 2nd ed. (New York: Knopf, 1968 [1950]). A smaller book but broader in scope is Heinz Gollwitzer, *Europe in the Age of Imperialism, 1880–1914,* tr. Adam and Stanley Baron (New York: Harcourt, Brace and World, 1969). Raymond F. Betts, *The False Dawn: European Imperialism in the Nineteenth Century* (Minneapolis: University of Minnesota Press, 1975), and *The "New Imperialism": Analysis of Late Nineteenth Century Expansion,* ed. H. M. Wright, rev. ed. (Boston: Heath, 1975), both deal with the theories and arguments about imperialism.

With respect to British imperialism, the best survey is Ronald Hyam, *Britain's Imperial Century 1815–1914: A Study of Empire and Expansion* (New York: Barnes and Noble, 1976). A briefer and more lively book dealing with some of the same matter is Bernard Porter, *The Lion's Share: A Short History of British Imperialism, 1850–1970* (New York: Longman, 1975). *British Imperialism: Gold, God, and Glory,* ed. Robin W. Winks (New York: Holt, Rinehart and Winston, 1963), deals with some of the controversies about the nature and motives of British imperialism, as does Richard Faber, *The Vision and the Need: Late Victorian Imperialist Aims* (New York: Humanities Press, 1966). L. H. Gann and Peter Duignan, *Burden of Empire, An Appraisal of Western Colonialism in Africa South of the Sahara* (New York: Praeger, 1967), also deals with the nature and motives of imperialism in Africa; it is a respected cautionary book, asserting that the benefits of colonialism may have outweighed its more publicized disadvantages for all concerned. A shorter book of readings, *The Scramble for Africa: Causes and Dimensions of Empire*, ed. Raymond F. Betts, rev. 2nd ed. (Boston: Heath, 1972), deals with some of the same issues. The fundamental revisionist monograph on the causes and motives of African imperialism is Ronald Robinson and John Gallagher, *Africa and the Victorians: The Climax of Imperialism in the Dark Continent* (New York: St. Martin's, 1961), but students may prefer *Imperialism: The Robinson and Gallagher Controversy*, ed. William R. Louis (New York: New Viewpoints, 1976). Recommended finally is R. Hallett, *Africa Since 1875* (Ann Arbor: University of Michigan Press, 1974), with its focus upon Africa rather than Europe.

Lenin:
Anatomy of a Revolutionary

The factual outline of Lenin's biography is well known. He was born Vladimir Ilyich Ulyanov in 1870, the son of a superintendent of public schools for the province of Simbirsk on the Volga and a member of the lesser nobility that provided most of the minor officialdom of Czarist Russia. Vladimir was a bright student. After high school, he went to study law at the regional university of Kazan. His political activities and growing radicalism led to his arrest, and for a year he was under police surveillance. He was soon arrested again, however, and in 1897 was exiled to Siberia. During his exile, he turned away from the tradition of populism, as the native Russian radicalism was called, and became an ardent Marxist. Later, he was to be the principal force in the unlikely task of applying the doctrines of Marx to vast, peasant Russia.

Returning from exile in 1900, Lenin fled Russia for Western Europe. It was at this time that he began writing under the name Lenin. He became active in the underground of radical émigrés and exiles; published a shoestring newspaper, *Iskra (The Spark);* and began to build a group of disciples who would become the inner circle of his revolutionary party. In 1902 he wrote his first major prescription for revolution, a book entitled *What Is To Be Done?* The following year he seized the leadership of the majority of delegates—the Bolsheviks—to the conventions of the tiny, splintered Russian Social-Democratic Workers Party, meeting in London and Brussels. He hurried back to Russia when the Revolution of 1905 broke out. But the Revolution failed, and Lenin returned to his self-imposed exile in the West. When World War I came, he watched anxiously from Geneva as revolution again broke out in Russia under the stress of war.

Lenin was soon approached by the German government. Would he and his radical followers return to Russia under German safe conduct? The Germans, of course, hoped that Lenin would further radicalize the revolution already under way in Russia, paralyze the government, and destroy military resistance. Lenin agreed, and in what is surely one of the most bizarre incidents in modern history, Lenin and his party were put aboard a train, granted extraterritorial rights to pass through Germany and shipped across Germany to the Baltic and to Petrograd. They arrived at the Finland Station in mid-April 1917.

Lenin quickly became involved in the Revolution and soon was its leading figure. By November he had organized his faction and driven the hopeless Provisional Government of Alexander Kerensky out of power. After the fall of Kerensky, Lenin was elected chairman of the new Council of People's Commissars. He was now, in fact, the head of a new state, ready to implement his theoretical ideas by direct political action. "Not a single problem of the class struggle has ever been solved in history except by violence," he told the Third All-Russian Congress of Soviets on January 24, 1918.

Lenin had already made the bold and controversial decision to take Russia out of "the imperialist World War," not to please the Germans— though it did—but to preserve his revolution and to save his country from sure defeat. The war had been useful as a "powerful accelerator to overturn the filthy and bloodstained cart of the Romanov monarchy," [1] but it served no further useful purpose. Lenin accepted the German peace terms at Brest-Litovsk on March 3, 1918. He called it not so much a surrender as a "compromise" with the "bandits of German imperialism," which would enable the imperialists to do whatever they wished while he and his comrades consolidated their revolution.[2]

The treaty of Brest-Litovsk, however, did not signify the end of war for the Russians. Between the collapse of the old Czarist government and a secure new revolutionary government lay years of civil war and invasion by Russia's former allies, outraged at the surrender at Brest-Litovsk and frightened by the apparent success of the Revolution. Lenin later recalled, "Our Red Army did not exist at the beginning of the war. . . . Nevertheless, we conquered in the struggle against the world-mighty Entente" and did so with "the alliance between the peasants and the workers, under the leadership of the proletarian state." [3] They indeed did conquer, and by the early 1920s modern Soviet Russia was a reality. Lenin had worked ruthlessly and tirelessly. In 1918 he had been seriously

[1] V. I. Lenin, *Selected Works* (New York: International Publishers, 1943), VI, 5.
[2] *Ibid.*, X, 75-76.
[3] *Ibid.*, IX, 246.

wounded in an assassination attempt from which he never fully
recovered. Then in 1922 he suffered a stroke, followed by another that
partially paralyzed him. In 1924 he died.

Lenin was the most famous man in Russia and one of the most famous
in the world. As "The Father of the Revolution," his picture looked
benignly down from giant posters over Red Square, and countless
photographs of him appeared in the Western Press. But the man behind
the picture was almost unknown—in Russia as well as in the West. Lenin
was obsessively secretive about himself. In all his vast collected works,
in page after page of mind-boggling theories and bitter polemics, there are
no more than a handful of brusque personal anecdotes. When his friends
inquired too closely into aspects of his personal life, his tastes, his likes
and dislikes, he shoved their questions aside as "trivial" and
"unimportant." The cause, the work, the Revolution—these were the
things that mattered.

It became almost an obsession with those closest to him to penetrate
the "secret corner of his life," that "special room completely to himself,"
as Lenin called it,[4] in order to understand Lenin the man and to know
what made and moved Lenin the leader and revolutionary. His friend the
historian M. N. Pokrovsky found the key to Lenin "his tremendous
political courage." "Among revolutionaries," Pokrovsky wrote, "there
has been no lack of brave people unafraid of the rope and the gallows or
of Siberia. But these people were afraid of taking upon themselves the
burden of great political decisions." Not so Lenin, "no matter how
weighty the decisions." [5] The novelist Maxim Gorky asked a friend,
"what, in his opinion, was Lenin's outstanding feature. 'Simplicity! He's
as simple as the truth,' he answered without hesitation, as though
reiterating a long established fact." [6] Lenin was not simple, of course, and
Gorky did not find him so. On the other hand, he never did succeed in
identifying to his own satisfaction Lenin's "outstanding feature."

At least two others succeeded somewhat better. And they also isolated
what they regarded as the causes that moved Lenin to be the man he was.
We turn now to the first of these, Leon Trotsky.

[4] Quoted in N. V. Volsky, *Encounters with Lenin* (London: Oxford University
Press, 1968), p. 43.
[5] Quoted in Tamara Deutscher, ed., *Not by Politics Alone—the Other Lenin* (London: Allen & Unwin, 1973), p. 71.
[6] Quoted in George Hanna, ed., *About Lenin,* J. Guralsky, trans. (Moscow:
Progress Publishers, n.d.), p. 30.

The Young Lenin
LEON TROTSKY

Like Lenin, Trotsky was both a radical revolutionary intellectual and an exile. He opposed Lenin in the split of the Russian Social-Democratic Congress in 1903 and took a middle position between Lenin's Bolsheviks and the Menshevik "minority." Unlike Lenin, Trotsky was one of the heroes of the unsuccessful Revolution of 1905, after which he was imprisoned. In the successful Revolution of 1917, however, he joined forces with Lenin, and his brilliance, audacity, and organizational ability contributed mightily to its success.

In the power struggle following Lenin's death, Trotsky lost out to Stalin and in 1929 was exiled from Russia. Finally, in 1940, he was assassinated in Mexico, allegedly by Stalinist agents. While in exile, as earlier, Trotsky was a prolific writer, and he continued both his struggle against Stalin and his self-justification in his many books and articles. But he often came back to the subject of Lenin and wrote about him extensively, for example, in his My Life *(1930) and his three-volume* History of the Russian Revolution *(1936). In many ways, the most interesting of Trotsky's works on Lenin is* The Young Lenin, *from which the following selection is taken. The book was written in the early 1930s as the first of two volumes on Lenin's life. The second volume was never finished, delayed by other projects and ultimately by Trotsky's death. The work as it stood was translated by the American journalist and publicist Max Eastman, who had translated Trotsky's other works. Then the manuscript was lost, and it did not turn up again until the late 1960s.* The Young Lenin *was at last published in 1972, almost forty years after it was written.*

More interesting than the curious history of the manuscript is the book's insightful treatment of Lenin's early years, very nearly unique among the memoirs and recollections of other Lenin intimates—including the Reminiscences *of Lenin's wife, which reveal almost nothing about him. Especially intriguing is the importance Trotsky attaches to a series of tragic incidents that occurred at the end of Lenin's adolescence. Trosky finds in these tragedies of Lenin the boy the key to understanding Lenin the man—and the revolutionary.*

"HAPPY FAMILIES are all alike," says Tolstoy. "Each unhappy family is unhappy in its own way." The Ulyanov family had lived a happy life for almost twenty-three years, and been like other harmonious and fortunate families. In 1886 the first blow fell, the death of the father. But misfortunes never come singly. Others followed swiftly: the execution of Alexander, the arrest of Anna. And beyond these there were more, and still more, misfortunes to come. Henceforth everybody, both strangers and intimates, began to consider the Ulyanovs an unhappy family. And they had truly become unhappy, though in their own way. . . .

When Ilya Nikolayevich had completed twenty-five years of service, the ministry retained him for but one supplementary year, and not five as was usual with important government officials. . . . In 1884, simultaneously with the new university constitution, new rules were issued for parish schools. Ilya Nikolayevich was opposed to this reform—not out of hostility to the church, of course, for he zealously saw to it that religion was regularly taught in *zemstvo* schools—but out of loyalty to the cause of education. As the winds of reaction grew strong, the Simbirsk superintendent of public schools, by the very fact that he felt concerned for the cause of literacy, willy-nilly found himself opposing the new course. What had formerly been considered his merit had now, it seemed, become a fault. He was compelled to retreat and adapt himself. His whole life's work was under attack. When an occasion presented itself, Ilya Nikolayevich was not averse to pointing out to his older children the disastrous consequences of revolutionary struggle, and how instead of progress it produced reaction. This was the mood of the majority of peaceful educators of the time.

A Simbirsk landowner, Nazarycv, in sending in his regular dispatch to the editor of the liberal journal *Vestnik Yevropy,* wrote to him confidentially about Ulyanov; "He is not in the good graces of the ministry, and is far from doing well." Ilya Nikolayevich took to heart the government's attack upon the elementary schools, although he obeyed the new policy. His former buoyancy had vanished. His last years were poisoned with uncertainty and anxiety. He fell sick suddenly in January 1886, while preparing his annual report. Alexander was in Petersburg, wholly immersed in his zoology term paper. Vladimir, only a year and a half away from high-school graduation, must have been thinking already about the university. Anna was at home for the Christmas holidays. Neither the family nor the physician took Ilya Nikolayevich's illness seriously. He continued to work on his report. His daughter sat reading some papers to him until she noticed that her father was becoming delirious. The next morning, the twelfth, the sick man did not come to the table, but only came to the dining room door, and looked in—"as though he had come to say good-by," remembered Maria Alexandrovna. At five o'clock the mother, in alarm, called Anna and Vladimir. Ilya Nikolayevich lay dying on the sofa which served him for a bed. The children saw their father shudder twice and go still forever. He was not yet fifty-five years old. The physician described the cause of his death—"hypothetically although with overwhelming probability," to quote his own words—as a cerebral hemorrhage. Thus the first heavy blow fell upon the Ulyanov family. . . .

Anna remained in Simbirsk for a time in order to be near her mother. It was at that time that the elder sister and Vladimir grew close to each other. The winter walks together date from that time, and the long conversations in which her brother revealed himself to her as a rebel and nonconformist, the embodiment of protest—so far, however, only in relation to "high-school authorities, high-school studies, and also to religion." During the recent summer vacation, these moods had not yet existed.

The death of the father had suddenly destroyed the lulling flow of life in a family whose well-being had seemed sure to go on indefinitely. How can we avoid assuming that it was this blow that imparted a new critical direction to Vladimir's thoughts? The answers of the church catechism to questions of life and death must have seemed to him wretched and humiliating, confronted with the austere truth of nature. Whether in reality he threw his cross into the garbage, or whether, as is more likely, Krzhizhanovsky's memory converted a metaphorical expression into a physical gesture, one thing is beyond doubt: Vladimir must have broken with religion abruptly, without long hesitation, without attempts at an eclectic reconciliation of truths with lies, with that youthful courage which was here for the first time spreading its wings.

Alexander was staying up nights engrossed in his work when the unexpected news came of his father's death. "For several days he dropped everything," relates a fellow student at the university, "pacing his room from corner to corner as though wounded." But wholly in the spirit of the family, in which strong feelings went hand in hand with discipline, Alexander did not leave the university, and did not hasten to Simbirsk. He pulled himself together and went back to work. After a few weeks his mother received a letter, brief as always: "I have received a gold medal for my zoological study of annelids." Maria Alexandrovna wept with joy for her son and with grief for her husband. . . .

. . . Life was beginning to move again in its new, narrower channel, when a totally unexpected blow, and a double blow at that, descended upon the family: Both son and daughter were involved in a trial for an attempted assassination of the tsar. It was dreadful even to breathe those words!

Anna was arrested on March 1 in her brother's room, which she had entered while a search was in progress. Shrouded in dreadful uncertainty, the girl was locked up in prison in connection with a case in which she had no part. This, then, is what Sasha was busy with! They had grown up side by side, played together in their father's study with sealing wax and magnets, often fallen asleep together to their mother's music, studied together in Petersburg—and yet how little she knew him! The older Sasha grew, the more he withdrew from his sister. Anna remembered bitterly how, when she visited him, Alexander would tear himself from his books with evident regret. He did not share his thoughts with her. Each time he heard of some new vileness of the tsarist authorities his face would darken, and he would withdraw more deeply into himself. "A penetrating observer could have predicted even then his future course. . . ." But Anna was no penetrating observer. During the last year, Alexander had refused to share an apartment with her, explaining to his companions that he did not want to compromise his sister, who showed no desire for public activity. During that winter Anna saw Alexander with some strange objects in his hands. How far she was from the thought of bombs! . . .

A Petersburg relative of the Ulyanovs wrote of the arrest of Alexander and Anna to a former teacher of the children, asking her to prepare the mother cautiously. Narrowing his young brows, Vladimir stood silent a long time over the Petersburg letter. This lightning stroke revealed the figure of Alexander in a new light. "But this is a serious thing," he said. "It may end badly for Sasha." He evidently had no doubt of Anna's innocence. The task of preparing the mother fell to him. But she, sensing tragedy in the first words, demanded the letter, and immediately began to prepare for a journey.

There was still no railroad from Simbirsk; one had to travel by horse and wagon to Syzran. For the sake of economy and for safety on the journey, Vladimir sought a companion for his mother. But the news had already spread through the town. Everyone turned away fearfully. No one would travel with the mother of a terrorist. Vladimir never forgot this lesson. The days that followed were to mean much in the forming of his character and its direction. The youth became austere and silent, and frequently shut himself up in his room when not busy with the younger children left in his charge. So that is what he was, this tireless chemist and dissector of worms, this silent brother so near and yet so unknown! When compelled to speak with Kashkadamova of the catastrophe, he kept repeating: "It means Alexander could not have acted otherwise." The mother came back for a short time to see the children and told them of her efforts and her dream of a life sentence to hard labor for Sasha. "In that case I would go with him," she said. "The older children are big enough and I will take the younger with me." Instead of a chair at a university and scholarly glory, chains and stripes now became the chief object of the mother's hopes. . . . She was admitted to sessions of the court. In his month and a half of confinement, Alexander had grown more manly; even his voice acquired an unfamiliar impressiveness. The youth had become a man. "How well Sasha spoke—so convincingly, so eloquently." But the mother could not sit through the whole speech; that eloquence would break her heart. On the eve of the execution, still hoping, she kept repeating to her son through the double grating: "Have courage!" On May 5, on her way to an interview with her daughter, she learned from a leaflet given out on the street that Sasha was no more. The feelings that the bereaved mother brought to the grating behind which her daughter stood are not recorded. But Maria Alexandrovna did not bend, did not fall, did not betray the secret to her daughter. To Anna's questions about her brother, the mother answered: "Pray for Sasha." Anna did not detect the despair behind her mother's courage. How respectfully the prison authorities, who knew already of the execution of Alexander, admitted this severe woman in black! The daughter did not yet guess that the mourning for her father had become a mourning for her brother.

Simbirsk was fragrant with all the flowers of its orchards when news came from the capital of the hanging of Alexander Ulyanov. The family of a full state counselor, until then respected on every side, became overnight the family of an executed state criminal. Friends and acquaintances, without exception, avoided the house on Moscow Street. Even the aged schoolteacher who had so often dropped in for a game of chess with Ilya Nikolayevich no longer showed his face. Vladimir observed with a keen eye the neighbors around them, their cowardice and disloyalty. It was a precious lesson in political realism.

Anna was set free some days after the execution of her brother. Instead of sending her to Siberia, the authorities agreed to have her restricted, under police surveillance, to the village of Kokushkino, the home of her mother. . . .

What ideas and moods captivated Vladimir in the summer of 1886, on the eve of his last year at high school? In the preceding winter, according to Anna Yelizarova, he had begun "rejecting authority in the period of his first, so to speak, negative formation of personality." But his criticisms, for all their boldness, still had limited scope. They were directed against high-school teachers, and to some extent against religion. "There was nothing definitely political in our conversations." On her return from the capital, Vladimir did not put any questions to his sister about revolutionary organizations, illegal books, or political groupings among the students. Anna adds: "I am convinced that with our relations being what they were at that time, Volodya would not have concealed such interests from me," had he had any. . . . Vladimir remained completely untouched politically and did not show the slightest interest in those economics books that filled Alexander's shelf in their common room. The name of Marx meant nothing to this young man whose interests were almost exclusively in *belles lettres*. Moreover, he gave himself up to literature with passion. For whole days he drank in the novels of Turgenev, page by page, lying on his cot and carried away in his imagination into the realm of "superfluous people" and idealized maidens under the linden trees of aristocratic parks. Having read through to the end, he would begin all over again. His thirst was insatiable. . . .

Some years later, the Social Democrat Lalayants questioned Lenin about the affair of March 1. Lenin answered: "Alexander's participation in a terrorist act was completely unexpected for all of us. Possibly my sister knew something—I knew nothing at all." As a matter of fact, the sister knew nothing either. The testimony of Lalayants fully corroborates Anna's story and coincides with what we know on this subject from Krupskaya's *Recollections*. In explaining this fact, Krupskaya refers to the difference in their ages, which wholly destroys her own account of the closeness of the brothers. But this reference, inadequate to say the least, does not alter the fact itself. Lenin's grief for his brother must have been colored with bitterness at the thought that Alexander had concealed from him what was deepest and most important. And with remorse over his own lack of attentiveness toward his brother and his arrogant assertions of his own independence. His childish worship of Sasha must have returned now with tenfold strength, sharpened by a feeling of guilt and a consciousness of the impossibility of making amends. His former teacher who handed him the fateful letter from Petersburg, says: "Before me sat no longer the carefree cheerful boy but a grown man buried in thought. . . ." Vladimir went through his final high-school experiences with his teeth clenched. There exists a photograph evidently made for the high-school diploma. On the still unformed but strongly concentrated features with the arrogantly pushed-out lower lip, lay the shadow of grief and of a first deep hatred. Two deaths stood at the beginning of the new period of Vladimir's life. The death of his father, convincing in its physiological naturalness, impelled him to a critical attitude toward the church and the religious myth. The execution of his brother awakened bitter hostility toward the hangmen. The future revolutionary had been planted in the personality of the youth and in the social conditions that formed him. But an initial impulse was needed. And this was provided by the unexpected death of his brother. The first political thoughts of Vladimir must inevitably have arisen out of a twofold need: to avenge Sasha and to refute by action Sasha's distrust.

Lenin the Revolutionary
NIKOLAY VALENTINOV

Like Trotsky and so many of Lenin's other early intimates, N. V. Volsky (d. 1964)—who wrote under the name of Nikolay Valentinov—was fascinated by Lenin even though they broke over philosophical disagreements while Lenin was still in exile, long before the Revolution of 1917. But Volsky's recollections of Lenin remained vivid and became the subject of Encounters with Lenin, *the book from which the following excerpt is taken. In a long chapter entitled "My Attempts to Understand Lenin," Volsky described a singular incident when Lenin dropped his "oriental mask" and allowed a handful of friends into "the secret room of his life." What he revealed was not a moving personal tragedy such as Trotsky relates but a passionate intellectual advocacy for a book whose ideas, Volsky was convinced, made Lenin a revolutionary. The book was* What Is to Be Done? *by Nikolai Chernyshevsky (d. 1889). It is not insignificant, as Lenin himself admitted, that he used this title for the first major proclamation of his own revolutionary program, for Chernyshevsky's book was programmatic. The author had been a leading figure in native Russian radicalism and highly regarded by many Russion radicals before the time of Lenin, though hardly known in the West then or later. But what is perhaps more important than the program of Chernyshevsky was Lenin's passion for the book, a clear indication of the debt he owed to its influence. It is also significant that there existed a bridge between the emotional experience that Trotsky saw as Lenin's center and the intellectual experience described by Volsky. Lenin's dead brother Alexander had loved Chernyshevsky's book. Clearly, young Lenin had read at least one of the books on the shelf in their common room.*

DURING MY ATTEMPTS to understand Lenin, I made some "discoveries" which agreeably surprised me (his love of nature or his attitude to Turgenev, for example), but I also made others which simply nonplussed me. I shall now describe one of these.

At the end of January 1904 I ran into Lenin, Vorovsky, and Gusev in a small café near the square of the Plaine de Plainpalais in Geneva. As I arrived later than the others I did not know how the conversation between Vorovsky and Gusev had started. I only heard Vorovsky mention some literary works which had been very successful in their day but had quickly "dated," and now aroused only boredom and indifference. I remember that he included in this category Goethe's *Werther,* some pieces by George Sand, Karamzin's "Poor Liza," and other Russian works, including Mordovtsev's *A Sign of the Times.* I butted in to say that since he had mentioned Mordovtsev, why not Chernyshevsky's *What is to be Done?* too? "One is amazed," I said, "how people could take any interest or pleasure in such a thing. It would be difficult to imagine anything more untalented, crude and, at the same time, pretentious. Most of the pages of this celebrated novel are written in unreadable language. Yet when someone told him that he lacked literary talent, Chernyshevsky answered arrogantly: 'I am no worse than those novelists who are considered great.' "

Up to this moment Lenin had been staring vacantly into space, taking no part in the conversation. But when he heard what I had just said, he sat up with such a start that the chair creaked under him. His face stiffened and he flushed around the cheek-bones—this always happened when he was angry.

"Do you realize what you are saying?" he hurled at me. "How could such a monstrous and absurd idea come into your mind—to describe as crude and untalented a work of Chernyshevsky, the greatest and most talented representative of socialism before Marx! Marx himself called Chernyshevsky a great Russian writer."

"It wasn't *What is to be Done?* that made Marx call him a great writer. Marx probably didn't read the book," I said.

"How do you know that Marx didn't read it? I declare that it is impermissible to call *What is to be Done?* crude and untalented. Hundreds of people became revolutionaries under its influence. Could this have happened if Chernyshevsky had been untalented and crude? My brother, for example, was captivated by him, and so was I. *He completely transformed my outlook.* When did you read *What is to be Done?*? It is no good reading it when one is still a greenhorn. Chernyshevsky's novel is too complex and full of ideas to be understood and appreciated at an early age. I myself started to read it when I was 14. I think this was a completely useless and superficial reading of the book. But, after the execution of my brother, I started to read it properly, as I knew that it had been one of his favourite books. I spent not days but several weeks reading it. Only then did I understand its depth. This novel provides inspiration for a lifetime: untalented books don't have such an influence."

"So," Gusev asked, "it was no accident that in 1902 you called your pamphlet *What is to be Done?*"

"Is this so difficult to guess?," was Lenin's answer.

Of the three of us I attached the least importance to Lenin's words. On the other hand, Vorovsky became very interested. He began to ask Lenin when he had become acquainted with Chernyshevsky's other works besides *What is to be Done?*, and, in general, which writers had had a particularly strong influence on him before he had become familiar with Marxism. Lenin did not usually speak about himself—this in itself distinguished him from most people. However, on this occasion he broke his rule, and answered Vorovsky's question in great detail. The result was a page of autobiography which has never been recorded in print. In 1919 Vorosky, who was chairman of the Gosizdat (State Publishing House) for a short time, wanted to reconstruct and write down what Lenin said on this occasion. . . .

Vorovsky's reconstruction of Lenin's words throws new light on Lenin's intellectual and political development. I have to admit that it was only very much later that I realized this. It might have been thought that

Vorovsky's transcript would be published in the USSR, where even the most worthless scraps of paper connected with Lenin are carefully preserved. However, I have not been able to find it anywhere in the Soviet literature available to me. There is no mention of it whatsoever. What can the explanation be? The point is that Vorovsky records Lenin as saying, in his own words, that he had been "transformed" by Chernyshevsky, and that under his impact he had become a revolutionary before his introduction to Marxism. It is thus impossible, unless one gives credence to a wanton misconception, to believe that Lenin was shaped only by Marx and Marxism. By the time he came to Marxism, Lenin, under Chernyshevsky's influence, was already forearmed with certain revolutionary ideas which provided the distinctive features of his specifically "Leninist" political make-up. All this is extremely important and sharply contradicts both the party canons and Lenin's official biographers. It is very probable that this is the reason why Vorovsky's transcript has not been published. . . .

. . . This is the gist of what Lenin said: "During the year that followed my banishment from Kazan, I used to read greedily from early morning till late at night. I think this was the most intensive period of reading in my whole life, not excluding my time in prison in Petersburg and my exile in Siberia. On the assumption that I might soon be permitted to return to the university, I read my university textbooks. I read a great deal of fiction, I became a great admirer of Nekrasov; what is more, my sister and I used to compete to see who could learn the greater number of Nekrasov's poems by heart. However, I read mainly articles which had once been published in the periodicals *Sovremennik* (Contemporary), *Otechestvennye Zapiski* (Fatherland Notes), and *Vesnik Europy* (Herald of Europe). These periodicals included the best and most interesting social and political writings of the previous decades. Chernyshevsky was my favorite author. I read and reread everything he had published in the *Sovremennik*. Chernyshevsky introduced me to philosophical materialism. It was again Chernyshevsky who first gave me an indication of Hegel's role in the development of philosophical thought, and I got the concept of dialectical method from him; this made it much easier for me to master the dialectic of Marx later on. I read Chernyshevsky's magnificent essays on aesthetics, art, and literature from cover to cover, and Belinsky's revolutionary figure became clear to me. I read all Chernyshevsky's articles on the peasant problem and his notes on the translation of Mill's *Political Economy*. Chernyshevsky's attack on bourgeois economics was a good preparation for my later study of Marx. I read with particular interest and profit Chernyshevsky's surveys of life abroad, which were remarkable for their intellectual depth. I read him pencil in hand, and made long excerpts and abstracts of what I was reading. I kept these notes for a long time. Chernyshevsky's encyclopedic knowledge, the brilliance of his revolutionary views, and his ruthless polemical talent captivated me. I even found out his address and wrote a letter to him; I was very pained when I did not receive any answer, and I was greatly distressed when I heard the news of his death in the following year. Chernyshevsky was hampered by the censorship and could not write freely. Many of his views could only be conjectured at; nevertheless, if one reads his articles carefully for a long time, as I did, one acquires the key to the complete decipherment of his political views, even of those which are expressed allegorically or by means of allusions. It is said that there are musicians with perfect pitch: one could say that there are also people with perfect revolutionary flair. Marx and Chernyshevsky were such men. You can't find another Russian revolutionary who understood and condemned the cowardly, base, and perfidious nature of every kind of liberalism with such thoroughness, acumen, and force as Chernyshevsky did. In the magazines I read there may have been a few things on Marxism too—for example, Mikhaylovsky's and Zhukovsky's articles. I can't say with any certainty whether I read them or not. One thing is certain—they did not attract my attention until I read the first volume of Marx's *Capital* and Plekhanov's book, *Our Differences,* although thanks to Chernyshevsky's articles I had begun to take an interest in economic questions, particularly in Russian rural life. This interest was prompted by essays of Vorontsov, Glep Uspensky, Engelhardt, and Skaldin. Only Chernyshevsky had a real, overpowering influence on me before I got to know the works of Marx, Engels, and Plekhanov, and it started with *What is to be Done?* Chernyshevsky not only showed that every right-thinking and really honest man must be a revolutionary, but he also showed—and this is his greatest merit—what a revolutionary must be like, what his principles must be, how he must approach his aim, and what methods he should use to achieve it. This compensates for all his shortcomings which, in fact, were not so much his fault as a consequence of the backwardness of social relations in his day. . . ."

After this conversation with Lenin, on our way back to the hotel, Gusev said laughingly:

"Ilyich could have scratched your eyes out for your disrespectful attitude to Chernyshevsky. Our old man has apparently not forgotten him to this very day. Still, I would never have believed the extent to which Chernyshevsky turned his head when he was a young man."

I found it even more difficult to believe. Lenin's infatuation with Chernyshevsky was quite incomprehensible and bewildering to me. It seemed strange that such a dreary, tedious, and feeble book as *What is to be Done?* could "transform his whole outlook" and provide "inspiration for a lifetime." It had never occurred to me that there was a special and hidden, yet strongly revolutionary, ideological, political, and psychological line running from Chernyshevsky's *What is to be Done?* to Lenin's

What is to be Done?, and that there was more to it than the identity of titles. I had to admit that I had not understood an apparently very important part of Lenin's way of thinking.

The Lenin of History
ROBERT V. DANIELS

Western scholars of modern Russian history have also been fascinated by Lenin, the man who, more than any other, made the most significant revolution of the modern world. One of the best of these scholars is the American historian Robert V. Daniels, whose book Red October *provides a detailed account of the opening phase of the Revolution of 1917. Daniels' analysis of Lenin is central to his account, and it is an analysis unobscured by either commitment to or disillusionment with one or another revolutionary ideology. Daniels sees the motives of Lenin—the center of the man—in his ruthless drive for personal power and his cynical manipulation of the very dialectic that he mastered and that has been enshrined in Communist methodology since Lenin's time.*

It would be rash to conclude that Daniels' view of Lenin is more "true" than the views of his earlier comrades or of the current crop of Marxian admirers. But it at least has the virtue of a kind of objectivity we cannot expect from those closer either in time or spirit to Lenin.

THE RUSSIAN Social Democratic Workers Party (of Bolsheviks) had never known any leader but Lenin. It was his personal political creation, starting as a devoted little group of twenty-two Russian *émigrés* (counting Lenin, his wife, and his sister) who met in Geneva in 1904. Their aim was to keep alive his side of the controversy that had split the Russian Marxist movement the year before. . . . Lenin had been adroit enough to seize the label "Bolsheviks"—"Majority men"—for his faction, even though he won only one of the numerous votes that turned around the "hard" political philosophy that he represented. . . .

Lenin had worked out his personal version of Marxist revolutionary philosophy between 1897 and 1900 while serving a sentence of Siberian exile for his revolutionary agitation among the St. Petersburg workers. In 1902, soon after he had left Russia for Western Europe, he published his propositions in the celebrated book, *What Is To Be Done?* Like practically everything Lenin ever said or wrote, the book was couched in the form of a polemic—in this case against the "Economists" because they put the economic progress of the workers ahead of political revolution. "The history of all countries," Lenin insisted, "shows that the working class, exclusively by its own effort, is able to develop only trade union consciousness." What would make them revolutionary, then? "Socialist ideology" and "class political consciousness" that could be "brought to the workers *only from without,* that is, from outside of the economic struggle." By whom? By the Social Democratic Party, and more specifically, "a small compact core of the most reliable, experienced and hardened activists . . . , an organization . . . chiefly of people professionally engaged in revolutionary activity."

Unlike the Mensheviks, who kept to the Marxist doctrine that a bourgeois revolution and capitalism had to precede the proletarian revolution, Lenin took the position that the Russian middle class was too cowardly to revolt, and that the proletariat—led by Lenin—should seize power directly and rule with the peasantry as its "allies." But this revolution would never occur of its own accord. Contrary to Marx, and more in keeping with the tradition of Russian revolutionary conspiracy, Lenin insisted that the proletarian revolution had to be accomplished by the deliberate action of a tightly organized conspiratorial party. He did not trust spontaneous mass movements, and at several crucial moments—in 1905 and in July, 1917—opposed the "adventurism" of Bolsheviks who wanted to exploit a popular outburst. In the fall of 1917, when it seemed as though the proletarian revolution might roll to victory almost as spontaneously as the bourgeois revolution of February, Lenin was beside himself. He was desperate then to demand that his party impose itself by force, to prove its own necessity and keep alive for himself the chance of ruling alone. . . .

Between Lenin and the Mensheviks the basic difference was more temperamental than doctrinal. The Mensheviks, like many earlier critics of Russian injustice, were idealists driven by sympathy for the masses but disinclined to conspire and fight; they admired Western democratic socialism and hoped for a peaceful and legal path to social reform once the Russian autocracy was overthrown. They were appalled by Lenin's elastic political morality and the philosophy they termed "dictatorship over the proletariat."

It is impossible to escape the very strong suspicion that Lenin's deepest motive was the drive for personal power, however he might have rationalized it. Like practically every politician Lenin had a philosophy about the welfare of the people—in his case it was the entire world proletariat—but the philosophy also said or implied that power for him and him alone was the only way this goal could be achieved. Lenin had an inordinate dislike of any sort of political cooperation or compromise, not because it might fail, but because it might succeed, and leave him with less than the whole loaf of power. He never worked honestly under or alongside anyone else, but only as the sole and unquestioned leader of his own forces, even if they had to be whittled down to meet his conditions. He was fascinated by armed force, and did not believe that any revolution worthy of the name could come about without it. "Major questions in the life of nations are settled by force," he wrote when he was a spectator to the Revolution of 1905. "The bayonet has really become the main point on the political agenda . . . , insurrection has proved to be imperative and urgent—constitutional illusions and school exercises in parliamentarism become only a screen for the bourgeois betrayal of the revolution. . . . It is therefore the slogan of the dictatorship of the proletariat that the genuinely revolutionary class must advance."

Many attempts, none very successful, have been made to explain Lenin's psychology. His childhood environment and youthful experiences, hardly exceptional for a family of the nineteenth-century Russian intelligentsia, offer only the sketchiest explanations of the demon that soon came to possess him. He was born in 1870 to a family of the lesser nobility—to be sure, the principal seedbed of the Russian revolutionary movement. His father, Ilya Ulyanov, was the Superintendent of Schools in the Volga city of Simbirsk, also the hometown, interestingly enough, of Alexander Kerensky. Lenin had some traumatic experiences—the untimely death of the father he esteemed; the execution of his older brother Alexander for complicity in an attempt on Tsar Alexander III; and his own expulsion from Kazan University because of a student demonstration. But the most abnormal thing about Lenin was his lack of abnormality among the typically eccentric and extremist Russians. He combined his natural brilliance and energy with an utterly un-Russian rigor and self-discipline which gave him an untold advantage in every political confrontation of his career. "Lenin is sheer intellect—he is absorbed, cold, unattractive, impatient at interruption," wrote John Reed's wife when she met the Bolshevik chief just after the Revolution. In another society Lenin would have risen to Grand Vizier or Corporation Counsel. In fact he did start a legal career in St. Petersburg, in 1893, before the encounter with a circle of Marxist agitators including his future wife Nadezhda Krupskaya finally committed him to the Marxist revolutionary movement.

Most people were either repelled or spellbound by Lenin. He was endowed with an extraordinary force of personality, along with an unbelievably vituperative vocabulary, that made most mortals helpless to opposed him within his own camp—they yielded or left. His extremism attracted many revolutionary romantics of independent mind but none of them were at ease in what Trotsky once called the "barrack regime" of the Bolshevik Party. Lenin hated liberalism and softness and the "circle spirit" of impractical discussion. "Nothing was so repugnant to Lenin," Trotsky recalled, "as the slightest suspicion of sentimentality and psychological weakness." Lenin hated the "spontaneity" of social movements without conscious leadership, and he hated the "opportunism" and "tail-end-ism" of people who went along with such movements. His life was consumed with hatred, and hatred of his rivals for the future of Russia almost more than the old regime. He wrote scarcely anything that was not aimed immediately to abuse an opponent, and usually a democratic and socialist opponent at that.

It is something of a puzzle that young Russian revolutionaries like Lenin embraced the philosophy of Marxism. Literally interpreted, Marx's doctrine of the change of society by deep-seated economic forces held out for an underdeveloped country such as Russia only the prospect of capitalism and middle-class rule for generations—the last thing that the radical intelligentsia wanted. Nor did they plump for Marxism for lack of an alternative philosophy, for the Russian revolutionaries since the 1850's had worked out a substantial body of socialist doctrine—"Populism," it was later termed—based on revolution by the peasants under the direction of the intelligentsia. The conspiratorial methods which so attracted the Russian extremists were an integral part of the Populist philosophy, whereas they were quite foreign to Western Marxism. In short, Marxism did not fit either the way the Russian revolutionaries wanted to work or the goals they wanted to work for, yet they flocked to its banner in ever-increasing numbers. They seem to have been attracted to Marxism because it gave them the secure sense of scientific inevitability and more especially because it stressed the role of the people who were obviously becoming the most vigorous, if small, revolutionary force in Russia, the industrial workers in the big cities. . . .

The stark truth about the Bolshevik Revolution is that it succeeded against incredible odds in defiance of any rational calculation that could have been made in the fall of 1917. The shrewdest politicians of every political coloration knew that while the Bolsheviks were an undeniable force in Petrograd and Moscow, they had against them the overwhelming majority of the peasants, the army in the field, and the trained personnel without which no government could function. Everyone from the right-wing military to the Zinoviev-Kamenev Bolsheviks judged a military dictatorship to be the most likely alternative if peaceful evolution failed. They all thought—whether they hoped or feared—that a Bolshevik attempt to seize power would only hasten or assure the rightist alternative.

Lenin's revolution, as Zinoviev and Kamenev pointed out, was a wild gamble, with little chance that Bolsheviks' ill-prepared followers could prevail against all the military force that the government seemed to have, and even less chance that they could keep power even if they managed to seize it temporarily. To Lenin, however, it was a gamble that entailed little risk, because he sensed that in no other way and at no other time would he have any chance at all of coming to power. This is why he demanded so vehemently that the Bolshevik Party seize the moment and hurl all the force it could against the Provisional Government. Certainly the Bolshevik Party had a better overall chance for survival and a future political role if it waited and compromised, as Zinoviev and Kamenev wished. But this would not yield the only kind of political power—exclusive power—that Lenin valued. He was bent on baptizing the revolution in blood, to drive off the fainthearted and compel all who subscribed to the overturn to accept and depend on his own unconditional leadership.

To this extent there is some truth in the contentions, both Soviet and non-Soviet, that Lenin's leadership was decisive. By psychological pressure on his Bolshevik lieutenants and his manipulation of the fear of counterrevolution, he set the stage for the one-party seizure of power.

Suggestions for Further Reading

LENIN'S OWN VOLUMINOUS WRITINGS, although they do not illuminate his life, nevertheless reveal his ideas and policies and the scathing declamatory style of virtually everything he wrote. The standard English-language edition is his *Collected Works,* 44 vols. (Moscow: Progress Publishers, 1960–1970), but most students will prefer either his *Collected Works,* rev. and annotated, 3 vols. published in 5 vols. (New York: International Publishers, 1927–   ), or the one-volume *Selected Works* (New York: International Publishers, 1971). There is also a separate edition of *The Letters of Lenin,* tr. and ed. Elizabeth Hill and Doris Mudie (London: Chapman and Hall, 1937), and of his important revolutionary pamphlet, *What Is to Be Done? Burning Questions of our Movement,* ed. V. J. Jerome, tr. J. Fineberg and G. Hanna (New York: International Publishers, 1969).

Lenin was endlessly fascinating to his own close associates—magnetic, harsh, demanding, domineering, but fascinating all the same. This, added to the fame of Lenin the man and Lenin the symbol, has brought into print a steady stream of memoirs and recollections of uneven quality and usefulness. Two of these are excerpted in this chapter: Trotsky's *The Young Lenin,* tr. Max Eastman (New York: Doubleday, 1972) and Valentinov's

Encounters with Lenin, tr. Paul Rosta and Brian Pearce (London and New York: Oxford University Press, 1968). Both works are valuable and interesting, as is another work by Trotsky, *Lenin: Notes for a Biography,* tr. Tamara Deutscher (New York: Putnam, 1971), a new translation of a work first published in 1925. Valentinov, *The Early Years of Lenin,* tr. R. H. W. Theen (Ann Arbor: University of Michigan Press, 1969), is part of the same memoir as his *Encounters with Lenin,* but its hostility destroys much of its usefulness. Angelica Balabanoff, *Impressions of Lenin,* tr. Isotta Cesari (Ann Arbor: University of Michigan Press, 1964), is the memoir of another early socialist colleague of Lenin. N. K. Krupskaia, *Reminiscences of Lenin,* tr. Bernard Isaacs (Moscow: Foreign Language Publishing House, 1959), is the recollections of Lenin's wife, but it is more political polemic than domestic memoir. *About Lenin,* ed. George Hanna, tr. J. Guralsky (Moscow: Progress Publishers, n.d.), is a series of readings from fellow revolutionaries and colleagues, published for "official" purposes and carefully sanitized of all unorthodoxy. Much more interesting and useful is *Not by Politics Alone—the Other Lenin,* ed. Tamara Deutscher (London: Allen and Unwin, 1973), an excellent collection of readings from Lenin himself and many of his contemporaries, about his views on a broad range of topics and revealing Lenin as casual and informal as he ever was.

The same fascination with Lenin that prompted the many recollections of those who knew him has created a flood of biographies. The best and most definitive is Louis F. Fischer, *The Life of Lenin* (New York: Harper & Row, 1964). Two straightforward, unbiased, workmanlike shorter biographies are Harold Shukman, *Lenin and the Russian Revolution* (New York: Putnam, 1967), and Robert Conquest, *V. I. Lenin* (New York: Viking, 1972). Isaac Deutscher, *Lenin's Childhood* (London and New York: Oxford University Press, 1970), is the separately published first chapter of a proposed definitive biography by a great authority; it can be favorably compared with Trotsky's *The Young Lenin.* Another work on Lenin's youth and the influences that formed him is R. H. W. Theen, *Lenin: Genesis and Development of a Revolutionary* (Philadelphia: Lippincott, 1973). A classic piece of exciting history and biography is Bertram D. Wolfe, *Three Who Made a Revolution, A Biographical History,* 4th rev. ed. (New York: Dell, 1964), the interconnected story of Lenin, Trotsky, and Stalin. More interesting and informative than her own memoirs is Robert H. McNeal, *Bride of the Revoltuion: Krupskaya and Lenin* (Ann Arbor: University of Michigan Press, 1972).

Robert V. Daniels, *Red October* (New York: Scribners, 1967), excerpted in this chapter, is an excellent account of the actual outbreak of the Russian Revolution. Another key event is detailed in J. W. Wheeler-Bennett, *Brest-Litovsk, The Forgotten Peace, March 1918* (London: Macmillan, 1956 [1938]), a brilliant, now classic account. Two important works on the theoretical-intellectual background to Lenin and the revolution must also be recommended: Franco Venturi, *Roots of Revolution: A History of the*

Populist and Socialist Movements in Nineteenth-Century Russia, tr. Francis Haskell (New York: Knopf, 1960), is the definitive work on its subject, and Edmund Wilson, *To the Finland Station: A Study in the Writing and Acting of History,* rev. ed. (New York: Farrar Straus, 1972 [1940]), is probably the classic work of the great American social and literary critic, a kind of intellectual history of socialist radicalism ending with Lenin and the outbreak of the Russian Revolution. Finally, Robert V. Daniels, *Russia* (Englewood Cliffs, N.J.: Prentice-Hall, 1964), is an excellent brief book, specifically intended as an introduction to Russia in the twentieth century.

Adolf Hitler:
Nightmare of Our Century

In the early 1920s, the Bavarian city of Munich was a gathering place for the most militant and dissatisfied groups of German war veterans. They despised the weak government of the postwar Weimar Republic; they hated the allies who had defeated Germany in World War I and now seemed bent upon destroying her in peace; and they were desperate in the face of German economic collapse, unemployment, and runaway inflation. In this kind of setting, with a weak and harassed central government far away and the Bavarian state authorities—already distrustful of the national government and disposed to separatism—unwilling or unable to threaten them, a rash of splinter political parties flourished. These parties fought bitterly for support among the veterans and among the equally dissatisfied and hard-pressed working classes from which the bulk of the veterans came. At one extreme were the Communists; at the other a cluster of right-wing extremist groups, which, though they battled each other for supporters, shared a hatred for the Communists and for the Jews, who were a handy—and hated—minority to seize upon. One of these right-wing parties was the National Socialist German Workers' Party—*Nationalsozialistische Deutsche Arbeiterpartei*—Nazi for short. Since 1921 its leader was Adolf Hitler.

In November 1923, Hitler and his party command conceived a plan for a *Putsch,* an armed uprising to capture the leaders of the Bavarian state government and force them to proclaim a revolution against the Weimar Republic. It was to be the beginning of a new Germany. Hitler had gained the cooperation of General Erich von Ludendorff, one of Germany's war heroes and a right-wing, nationalist fanatic himself, and he was confident that Ludendorff's presence would prevent the military's intervening against the coup. He was also sure that he could count on the Bavarian government's growing hostility toward the government in Berlin. On the evening of November 8, the Bavarian authorities announced a rally and meeting to be held in a Munich beer hall. Hitler and his fellow party leaders—supported by a considerable force of private military police and strong-arm hoodlums already known as stormtroopers—broke into the meeting. They hustled the government officials at gunpoint into a side room and forced them to proclaim a German revolution with Hitler as dictator. As soon as the officials were released, however, they repudiated their action. On the following morning, when the rebels attempted to march on the War Ministry building, they were met by the police. A skirmish ensued and sixteen Nazis were killed. Two days later, Hitler was arrested. The "beer hall *Putsch*" had been a total failure.

The apparently ruined politician who was so ignominiously handled by the Munich police in those autumn days of 1923 had been born in nearby Austria, just across the Bavarian border, in the little town of Braunau, in 1889. The details of his early life are sketchy and contradictory. Hitler's own later accounts of his youth differed as the circumstances demanded, and he generally preferred to remain somewhat mysterious.

His father had been an older man, a retired customs official, stern and domineering. His mother was much younger, usually dominated—if not brutalized—by her husband and idolized by her son. Her death in 1907 was a crushing blow to Hitler. Soon after his mother's death, with his undistinguished career in high school completed, Hitler went to Vienna, hoping to be admitted to the state school of art. He failed the entrance examination twice and then drifted into the Viennese underworld of poverty and crime, often near starvation, though he occasionally found work as a sign and postcard painter.

Hitler then went to Munich, and there, with the outbreak of World War I, he joined the German army. Despite a relatively undistinguished military record—he rose only to corporal's rank—the war was the high point in Hitler's life. He belonged at last to a substantial, honored organization engaged in a noble and desperately contested cause. In 1918, as the war was ending, Hitler was hospitalized as the result of a gas attack, and, though not seriously injured, he suffered temporary blindness and loss of speech.

After the war, Hitler joined the obscure political party he was later to lead, and he found a new cause in politics—the obvious end for him being the restoration of the German glory that had come to ruin in 1918. By the time of the failure of the "beer hall *Putsch*," Hitler was a known figure in German radical politics. He should have been finished by the fiasco of the *Putsch*, but he was not. In 1923 his career was only just beginning.

Mein Kampf
ADOLF HITLER

*At the instance of the Bavarian authorities, Hitler and the other leaders
of the* Putsch *were tried, not in the federal court, but a provincial
Bavarian court and given the minimum sentence of five years—of which
Hitler served less than nine months—in nearby Landsberg prison. In
prison he was treated more like an exiled head of state than a common
criminal, with exemption from work details, extended visiting hours for
the streams of political dignitaries that came to see him, and other special
privileges. Despite the failure of his uprising, Hitler still commanded
several thousand irregular stormtroopers, even though they were
scattered throughout Bavaria. And no one knew how many members his
party had, nor the exact extent of his influence. It was in Landsberg
prison that his secretary, Rudolf Hess, suggested to Hitler the title*
der Fuehrer *(the leader). Hitler liked it and adopted it. It was also in prison
that he wrote the book "frequently asked of me" by his followers, which
he intended to be "useful for the Movement."* [1] *He called it* Mein Kampf
(My Struggle).*

*The title suggests an autobiography, and in part it is an autobiography,
though with much falsification of fact. It is also a political polemic
against communism and a distorted vision of history, rife with the most
savage and hate-filled racism. But most of all,* Mein Kampf *is a vision
of the future as Hitler intended it to be under the domination of his party
—the Movement. In this respect, the book is both a political manifesto
and an incredible, step-by-step prescription for what he planned to do.
One of the most thoughtful modern scholars of* Mein Kampf, *Werner
Maser, has observed that "from 1925 until his suicide in April 1945, Hitler
clung faithfully to the ghastly doctrine set out in* Mein Kampf," *and, even
more amazingly, despite the notoriety of his doctrine, "he was able to
seize power, to consolidate it and to carry the German people with him
into the abyss."* [2]

*The passage excerpted below is from the first chapter of the second
volume of* Mein Kampf, *written in 1927 after Hitler's release from prison.
In it he recalls "the first great public demonstration" of the Movement
in Munich in 1920. This was the eve of Hitler's takeover of the Nazi
party, which was already committed to his ideas. These ideas—world*

[1] Adolf Hitler, *Mein Kampf* (New York: Stackpole, 1939), p. 11.
[2] Werner Maser, *Hitler's Mein Kampf, An Analysis*, R. H. Barry, trans. (London:
Faber and Faber, 1970), pp. 11-12.

conquest, brutal direct action, glorification of power, Aryan racial supremacy, anti-Semitism, and anticommunism—show up starkly in the selection that follows.

ON FEBRUARY 24, 1920, the first great public demonstration of our young movement took place. In the festsaal of the Munich Hofbräuhaus the twenty-five theses of the new party's program were submitted to a crowd of almost two thousand and every single point was accepted amid jubilant approval.

With this the first guiding principles and directives were issued for a struggle which was to do away with a veritable mass of old traditional conceptions and opinions and with unclear, yes, harmful aims. Into the rotten and cowardly bourgeois world and into the triumphant march of the Marxist wave of conquest a new power phenomenon was entering, which at the eleventh hour would halt the chariot of doom.

It was self-evident that the new movement could hope to achieve the necessary importance and the required strength for this gigantic struggle only if it succeeded from the very first day in arousing in the hearts of its supporters the holy conviction that with it political life was to be given, not to a new *election slogan*, but to a new *philosophy* of fundamental significance. . . .

Since with all parties of a so-called bourgeois orientation in reality the whole political struggle actually consists in nothing but a mad rush for seats in parliament, in which convictions and principles are thrown overboard like sand ballast whenever it seems expedient, their programs are naturally tuned accordingly and—inversely, to be sure—their forces also measured by the same standard. They lack that great magnetic attraction which alone the masses always follow under the compelling impact of towering great ideas, the persuasive force of absolute belief in them, coupled with a fanatical courage to fight for them.

At a time when one side, armed with all the weapons of a philosophy, a thousand times criminal though it may be, sets out to storm an existing order, the other side, now and forever can offer resistance only if it clads itself in the forms of a new faith, in our case a political one, and for a weak-kneed, cowardly defensive substitutes the battle cry of courageous and brutal attack. . . .

In the first volume I have dealt with the word "folkish," in so far as I was forced to establish that this term seems inadequately defined to permit the formation of a solid fighting community. All sorts of people, with a yawning gulf between everything essential in their opinions, are running around today under the blanket term "folkish." Therefore, before I proceed to the tasks and aims of the National Socialist German Workers' Party, I should like to give a clarification of the concept "folkish," as well as its relation to the party movement.

The concept *"folkish"* seems as vaguely defined, open to as many interpretations and as unlimited in practical application as, for instance, the word "religious. . . ." In it, too, there lie various basic realizations. Though of eminent importance, they are, however, so unclearly defined in form that they rise above the value of a more or less acceptable opinion only if they are fitted into the framework of a political party as basic elements. *For the realization of philosophical ideals and of the demands derived from them no more occurs through men's pure feeling or inner will in themselves than the achievement of freedom through the general longing for it. No, only when the ideal urge for independence gets a fighting organization in the form of military instruments of power can the pressing desire of a people be transformed into glorious reality.*

Every philosophy of life, even if it is a thousand times correct and of highest benefit to humanity, will remain without significance for the practical shaping of a people's life, as long as its principles have not become the banner of a fighting movement which for its part in turn will be a party as long as its activity has not found completion in the victory of its ideas and its party dogmas have not become the new state principles of a people's community. . . .

This transformation of a general, philosophical, ideal conception of the highest truth into a definitely delimited, tightly organized political community of faith and struggle, unified in spirit and will, is the most significant achievement, since on its happy solution alone the possibility of the victory of an idea depends. From the army of often millions of men, who as individuals more or less clearly and definitely sense these truths, and in part perhaps comprehend them, *one* man must step forward who with apodictic force will form granite principles from the wavering idea-world of the broad masses and take up the struggle for their sole correctness, until from the shifting waves of a free thought-world there will arise a brazen cliff of solid unity in faith and will.

The general right for such an activity is based on necessity, the personal right on success.

If from the word "folkish" we try to peel out the innermost kernel of meaning, we arrive at the following:

Our present political world view, current in Germany, is based in general on the idea that creative, culture-creating force must indeed be attributed to the state, but that it has nothing to do with racial considerations, but is rather a product of economic necessities, or, at best, the natural result of a political urge for power. This underlying view, if logically developed, leads not only to a mistaken conception of basic racial forces, but also to an underestimation of the individual. For a denial of the difference between the various races with regard to their general culture-creating forces must necessarily extend this greatest of all errors to the judgment of the individual. The assumption of the equality of the races then becomes a basis for a similar way of viewing peoples and finally individual men. And hence international Marxism itself is only the transference, by the Jew, Karl Marx, of a philosophical attitude and conception, which had actually long been in existence, into the form of a definite political creed. Without the subsoil of such generally existing poisoning, the amazing success of this doctrine would never have been possible. Actually Karl Marx was only the *one* among millions who, with the sure eye of the prophet, recognized in the morass of a slowly decomposing world the most essential poisons, extracted them, and, like a wizard, prepared them into a concentrated solution for the swifter annihilation of the independent existence of free nations on this earth. And all this in the service of his race.

His Marxist doctrine is a brief spiritual extract of the philosophy of life that is generally current today. And for this reason alone any struggle of our so-called bourgeois world against it is impossible, absurd in fact, since this bourgeois world is also essentially infected by these poisons, and worships a view of life which in general is distinguished from the Marxists only by degrees and personalities. The bourgeois world is Marxist, but believes in the possibility of the rule of certain groups of men (bourgeoise), while Marxism itself systematically plans to hand the world over to the Jews.

In opposition to this, the folkish philosophy finds the importance of mankind in its basic racial elements. In the state it sees on principle only a means to an end and construes its end as the preservation of the racial existence of man. Thus, it by no means believes in an equality of the races, but along with their difference it recognizes their higher or lesser value and feels itself obligated, through this knowledge, to promote the victory of the better and stronger, and demand the subordination of the inferior and weaker in accordance with the eternal will that dominates this universe. Thus, in principle, it serves the basic aristocratic idea of Nature and believes in the validity of this law down to the last individual. It sees not only the different value of the races, but also the different value of individuals. From the mass it extracts the importance of the individual personality, and thus, in contrast to disorganizing Marxism, it has an organizing effect. It believes in the necessity of an idealization of humanity, in which alone it sees the premise for the existence of humanity. But it cannot grant the right to existence even to an ethical idea if this idea represents a danger for the racial life of the bearers of a higher ethics; for in a bastardized and niggerized world all the concepts of the humanly beautiful and sublime, as well as all ideas of an idealized future of our humanity, would be lost forever.

Human culture and civilization on this continent are inseparably bound up with the presence of the Aryan. If he dies out or declines, the dark veils of an age without culture will again descend on this globe.

The undermining of the existence of human culture by the destruction of its bearer seems in the eyes of a folkish philosophy the most execrable crime. Anyone who dares to lay hands on the highest image of the Lord commits sacrilege against the benevolent creator of this miracle and contributes to the expulsion from paradise.

And so the folkish philosophy of life corresponds to the innermost will of Nature, since it restores that free play of forces which must lead to a continuous mutual higher breeding, until at last the best of humanity, having achieved possession of this earth, will have a free path for activity in domains which will lie partly above it and partly outside it. . . .

. . . Not until the international world view—politically led by organized Marxism—is confronted by a folkish world view, organized and led with equal unity, will success, supposing the fighting energy to be equal on both sides, fall to the side of eternal truth.

A philosophy can only be organizationally comprehended on the basis of a definite formulation of that philosophy, and what dogmas represent for religious faith, party principles are for a political party in the making.

Hence an instrument must be created for the folkish world view which enables it to fight, just as the Marxist party organization creates a free path for internationalism.

This is the goal pursued by the National Socialist German Workers' Party.

That such a party formulation of the folkish concept is the precondition for the victory of the folkish philosophy of life is proved most sharply by a fact which is admitted indirectly at least by the enemies of such a party tie. Those very people who never weary of emphasizing that the folkish philosophy is not the "hereditary estate" of an individual, but that it slumbers or "lives" in the hearts of God knows how many millions, thus demonstrate the fact that the general existence of such ideas was absolutely unable to prevent the victory of the hostile world view, classically represented by a political party. If this were not so, the German people by this time would have been bound to achieve a gigantic victory and not be standing at the edge of an abyss. What gave the international world view success was its representation by a political party organized into storm troops; what caused the defeat of the opposite world view was its lack up to now of a unified body to represent it. Not by unlimited freedom to interpret a general view, but only in the limited and hence integrating form of a political organization can a world view fight and conquer.

Therefore, I saw my own task especially in extracting those nuclear ideas from the extensive and unshaped substance of a general world view and remolding them into more or less dogmatic forms which in their clear delimitation are adapted for holding solidly together those men who swear allegiance to them. In other words: *From the basic ideas of a general folkish world conception the National Socialist German Workers' Party takes over the essential fundamental traits, and from them, with due consideration of practical reality, the times, and the available human*

material as well as its weaknesses, forms a political creed which, in turn,
by the strict organizational integration of large human masses thus made
possible, creates the precondition for the victorious struggle of this world
view.

Hitler and His Germany
ERNST NOLTE

In spite of the fact, as Maser reminds us, that the German people had
Hitler's plan before them in Mein Kampf, *they followed him anyway.*
Why? The answer may be, to some extent, that they did not take him
seriously. There were, after all, other leaders of lunatic rightist
movements in Germany in the 1920s, plumping for German nationalism,
spouting anti-Semitic and anti-Communist slogans while the Communists
shouted back. But to a greater extent, the German people did take Hitler
seriously. He preached his doctrine of hatred for the Jews and fear of the
Communists, of rabid, militant nationalism more effectively, more
tirelessly, more virulently than his competitors—and the German people
listened. What Hitler said was crude, but it had a powerful appeal. The
Nazi party grew stronger every year, until by the elections of 1932 it was
the second most powerful party in Germany. Hitler courted the military
establishment, the one great indispensable Germany national institution,
as carefully as he had courted old General Ludendorff in the early 1920s.
And he cultivated the economic baronage. Germany's desperate plight
was worsened by the world depression of the early 1930s, and the
captains of industry, always conservative and disposed to right-wing
politics, now frightened by the threat of trade unionism and the
Communists, sought a financial-political alliance with Hitler.

In 1933 the aged President Paul von Hindenburg was compelled by the
political situation to name Hitler as chancellor. Hitler persuaded
Hindenburg to call for new elections in an effort to achieve a Nazi
majority in the Reichstag. Then, on February 27, 1933, a spectacular fire
gutted the Reichstag building. It was a case of arson—the arsonist, a
Dutch radical, was arrested and confessed—but the fire and the sinister
rumors that the Nazis spread of Communist plots provided the excuse for
an emergency declaration. In this atmosphere of tension, the Nazis

polled a working parliamentary majority in the elections. Upon Hindenburg's death the following year, the offices of chancellor and president were merged for Hitler. The Fuehrer was made. Germany was recovering economically, and part of it was the result of Hitler's military spending that created a vast public debt but also jobs and prosperity. Part of it, too, was the beginning of worldwide recovery. But no matter. Hitler claimed the credit. More Germans supported him, and those who did not were intimidated by open terrorism. Jews had already begun to stream out of Germany.

Hitler was now ready to implement his foreign policy. In 1935 the Rhineland was reclaimed by plebescite and the following year remilitarized. In 1938 Austria was united with Germany; Czechoslovakia was surrendered to Germany; and on September 1, 1939, Poland was invaded. World War II had begun.

That Hitler was a dangerous psychopath is virtually a cliché of modern European historical studies, and every book that deals seriously with Hitler or his age must come to terms with it and venture a diagnosis. A more interesting question than what particular aberration Hitler suffered from is why the German people were willing to follow a madman, in Werner Maser's phrase, "into the abyss." It is a much more difficult question, a more essential one, and one to which the answers are more diverse. German scholars of the postwar era have been especially preoccupied with this question.

In a now famous essay, Three Faces of Fascism: Action Française, Italian Fascism, National Socialism, *the German historian Ernst Nolte gives his analysis. Although he subjects Hitler to penetrating study and finds him "infantile," "monomaniacal," and "mediumistic," Nolte is unwilling to set him down simply as a madman. Rather, he argues that these very aberrant qualities enabled him to exemplify the experience of his more normal fellow countrymen. Hitler told the German people in a passionate and oversimplified way what they themselves wanted to hear, and for this reason he came for a brief time "to be lord and master of his troubled era."*

We turn now to Nolte's analysis.

THE DOMINANT trait in Hitler's personality was infantilism. It explains the most prominent as well as the strangest of his characteristics and actions. The frequently awesome consistency of his thoughts and behavior must be seen in conjunction with the stupendous force of his rage, which reduced field marshals to trembling nonentities. If at the age of fifty he built the Danube bridge in Linz down to the last detail exactly as he had designed it at the age of fifteen before the eyes of his astonished boyhood friend, this was not a mark of consistency in a mature man, one who has learned and pondered, criticized and been criticized, but the stubbornness of the child who is aware of nothing except himself and his mental image and to whom time means nothing because childishness has not been broken and forced into the sober give-and-take of the adult world. Hitler's rage was the uncontrollable fury of the child who bangs the chair because the chair refuses to do as it is told; his dreaded harshness, which nonchalantly sent millions of people to their death, was much closer to the rambling imaginings of a boy than to the iron grasp of a man, and is therefore intimately and typically related to his profound aversion to the cruelty of hunting, vivisection, and the consumption of meat generally.

And how close to the sinister is the grotesque! The first thing Hitler did after being released from the Landsberg prison was to buy a Mercedes for twenty-six thousand marks—the car he had been dreaming of while serving his sentence. Until 1933 he insisted on passing every car on the road. In Vienna alone he had heard *Tristan and Isolde* between thirty and forty times, and had time as chancellor to see six performances of *The Merry Widow* in as many months. Nor was this all. According to Otto Dietrich he reread all Karl May's boys' adventure books during 1933 and 1934, and this is perfectly credible since in *Hitler's Table Talk* he bestowed high praise on this author and credited him with no less than opening his eyes to the world. It is in the conversations related in *Hitler's Table Talk* that he treated his listeners to such frequent and vindictive schoolboy reminiscences that it seems as if this man never emerged from his boyhood and completely lacked the experience of time and its broadening, reconciling powers.

The monomaniacal element in Hitler's nature is obviously closely related to his infantilism. It is based largely on his elemental urge toward tangibility, intelligibility, simplicity. In *Mein Kampf* he expressed the maxim that the masses should never be shown more than *one* enemy. He was himself the most loyal exponent of this precept, and not from motives of tactical calculation alone. He never allowed himself to face more than one enemy at a time; on this enemy he concentrated all the hatred of which he was so inordinately capable, and it was this that enabled him during this period to show the other enemies a reassuring and "subjectively" sincere face. During the crisis in Czechoslovakia he even forgot the Jews over Beneš.[3] His enemy was always concrete and personal, never merely the expression but also the cause of an obscure or complex event. The Weimar system was caused by the "November criminals," the predicament of the Germans in Austria by the Hapsburgs, capitalism and bolshevism equally by the Jews.

A good example of the emergence and function of the clearly defined

[3] Eduard Beneš, the heroic president of Czechoslovakia who resisted Hitler's schemes and the machinations of the other great powers. He escaped to the United States in 1938. Later, in Britain, he was the head of the Czech government in exile. At the end of the war, he returned to become president of Czechoslovakia once more until his death in 1948.—ED.

hate figure, which took the place of the causal connection he really had in mind, is to be found in *Mein Kampf*. Here Hitler draws a vivid picture of the miseries of proletarian existence as he came to know it in Vienna— deserted, frustrated, devoid of hope. This description seems to lead inevitably to an obvious conclusion: that these people, if they were not wholly insensible, were bound to be led with compelling logic to the socialist doctrine, to their "lack of patriotism," their hatred of religion, their merciless indictment of the ruling class. It should, however, have also led to a self-critical insight: that the only reason he remained so aloof from the collective emotions of these masses was because he had enjoyed a different upbringing, middle-class and provincial, because despite his poverty he never really worked, and because he was not married. Nothing of the kind! When he was watching spellbound one day as the long column of demonstrating workers wound its way through the streets, his first query was about the "wirepullers." His voracity for reading, his allegedly thorough study of Marxist theories, did not spur him on to cast his gaze beyond the frontier and realize that such demonstrations were taking place in every city in Europe, or to take note of the "rabble-rousing" articles of a certain Mussolini, which he would doubtless have regarded as "spiritual vitriol" like those in the *Arbeiterzeitung*.[4]

What Hitler discovered was the many Jewish names among the leaders of Austrian Marxism, and now the scales fell from his eyes—at last he saw who it was who, beside Hapsburgs, wanted to wipe out the German element in Austria. Now he began to preach his conclusions to his first audiences; now he was no longer speaking, as until recently he had spoken to Kubizek, to hear the sound of his own voice: he wanted to convince. But he did not have much success. The management of the men's hostel looked on him as an insufferable politicizer, and for most of his fellow inmates he was a "reactionary swine." He got beaten up by workers, and in conversations with Jews and Social Democrats he was evidently often the loser, being no match for their diabolical glibness and dialectic. This made the image of the archenemy appear all the more vivid to him, all the more firmly entrenched. Thirty years later the most experienced statesmen took him for a confidence-inspiring statesman after meeting him personally; hard-bitten soldiers found he was a man they could talk to; educated supporters saw in him the people's social leader. Hitler himself, however, made the following observations in the presence of the generals and party leaders around his table: though Dietrich Eckart had considered that from many aspects Streicher [5] was a fool, it was impossible to conquer the masses without such people, . . . though Streicher was criticized for his paper, *Der Stürmer*; in actual fact Streicher

---

[4] A labor newspaper.—ED.

[5] Julius Streicher was the publisher of a radical, anti-Semitic newspaper, *Der Stürmer,* and one of Hitler's earliest supporters. He continued to be a functionary of the party, survived the war, and was convicted of war crimes at Nürnberg.—ED.

idealized the Jew. The Jew was far more ignoble, unruly, and diabolical than Streicher had depicted him.

Hitler rose from the gutter to be the master of Europe. There is no doubt that he learned an enormous amount. In the flexible outer layer of his personality he could be all things to all men: a statesman to the statesmen, a commander to the generals, a charmer to women, a father to the people. But in the hard monomaniacal core of his being he did not change one iota from Vienna to Rastenburg.

Yet if his people had found that he intended after the war to prohibit smoking and make the world of the future vegetarian it is probable that even the SS would have rebelled. There are thousands of monomaniacal and infantile types in every large community, but they seldom play a role other than among their own kind. These two traits do not explain how Hitler was able to rise to power.

August Kubizek tells a strange story which there is little reason to doubt and which sheds as much light on the moment when Hitler decided to enter politics as on the basis and prospects of that decision. After a performance of *Rienzi* in Linz, Kubizek relates, Hitler had taken him up to a nearby hill and talked to him with shining eyes and trembling voice of the mandate he would one day receive from his people to lead them out of servitude to the heights of liberty. It seemed as if another self were speaking from Hitler's lips, as if he himself were looking on at what was happening in numb astonishment. Here the infantile basis is once again unmistakable. The identification with the hero of the dramatic opera bore him aloft, erupted from him like a separate being. There were many subsequent occasions testifying to this very process. When Hitler chatted, his manner of talking was often unbearably flat; when he described something, it was dull; when he theorized, it was stilted; when he started up a hymn of hate, repulsive. But time and again his speeches contained passages of irresistible force and compelling conviction, such as no other speaker of his time was capable of producing. These are always the places where his "faith" finds expression, and it was obviously this faith which induced that emotion among the masses to which even the most hostile observer testified. But at no time do these passages reveal anything new, never do they make the listener reflect or exert his critical faculty: all they ever do is conjure up magically before his eyes that which already existed in him as vague feeling, inarticulate longing. What else did he express but the secret desires of his judges when he declared before the People's Court: "The army we have trained is growing day by day, faster by the hour. It is in these very days that I have the proud hope that the hour will come when these unruly bands become battalions, the battalions regiments, the regiments divisions, when the old cockade is raised from the dust, when the old flags flutter again on high, when at last reconciliation takes place before the eternal Last Judgment, which we are prepared to face."

His behavior at a rally has often been described: how, uncertain at first, he would rely on the trivial, then get the feel of the atmosphere for several minutes, slowly establish contact, score a bull's-eye with the right phrase, gather momentum with the applause, finally burst out with words which seemed positively to erupt through him, and at the end, in the midst of thunderous cheering, shout a vow to heaven or, amid breathless silence, bring forth a solemn Amen. And after the speech he was as wet as if he had taken a steambath and had lost as much weight as if he had been through a week's strict training.

He told every rally what it wanted to hear—yet what he voiced was not the trivial interests and desires of the day but the great universal, obvious hopes: that Germany should once again become what it had been, that the economy should function, that the farmer should get his rights, likewise the townsman, the worker, and the employer, that they should forget their differences and become one in the most important thing of all—their love for Germany. He never embarked on discussion, he permitted no heckling, he never dealt with any of the day-to-day problems of politics. When he knew that a rally was in a critical mood and wanted information instead of *Weltanschauung*,[6] he was capable of calling off his speech at the last moment.

There should be no doubt as to the mediumistic trait in Hitler. He was the medium who communicated to the masses their own, deeply buried spirit. It was because of this, not because of his monomaniacal obsession, that a third of his people loved him long before he became chancellor, long before he was their victorious supreme commander. But mediumistic popular idols are usually simpletons fit for ecstasy rather than fulfillment. In the turmoil of postwar Germany it would have been *impossible* to love Hitler had not monomaniacal obsession driven the man on and infantile wishful thinking carried him beyond the workaday world with its problems and conflicts. Singly, any one of these three characteristics would have made Hitler a freak and a fool; combined, they raised him for a brief time to be lord and master of this troubled era.

A psychological portrait of Hitler such as this must, however, give rise to doubts in more ways than one. Does the portrait not approach that overpolemical and oversimplified talk of the "madman" or the "criminal"? There is no intention of claiming that this represents a clinical diagnosis. It is not even the purpose of this analysis to define and categorize Hitler as an "infantile mediumistic monomaniac." What has been discussed is merely the existence of infantile, mediumistic, and monomaniacal traits. They are not intended to exhaust the nature of the man Hitler, nor do they of themselves belong to the field of the medically abnormal. Rather do they represent individually an indispensable ingredient of the exceptional. There can be few artists without a streak of infantilism, few ideological politicians without a monomaniacal element in their make-up.

[6] "World view."—ED.

It is not so much the potency of each element singly as the combination of all three which gives Hitler his unique face. Whether this combination is pathological in the clinical sense is very doubtful, but there can be no doubt that it excludes historical greatness in the traditional sense.

A second objection is that the psychological description prevents the sociological typification which from the point of view of history is so much more productive. Many attempts have been made to understand Hitler as typical of the angry petit bourgeois. The snag in this interpretation is that it cannot stand without a psychologizing adjective and almost always suggests a goal which is obviously psychological as well as polemical. What this theory tries to express is that Hitler was "actually only a petit bourgeois," in other words, something puny and contemptible. But it is precisely from the psychological standpoint that the petit bourgeois can best be defined as the normal image of the "adult": Hitler was exactly the reverse. What is correct, however, is that, from the sociological standpoint, bourgeois elements may be present in an entirely nonbourgeois psychological form. It remains to be shown how very petit bourgeois was Hitler's immediate reaction to Marxism. However, it was only by means of that "form" which cannot be deduced by sociological methods that his first reaction underwent its momentous transformation.

The third objection is the most serious. The historical phenomenon of National Socialism might be considered overparticularized if it is based solely on the unusual, not to say abnormal, personality of one man. Does not this interpretation in the final analysis even approach that all too transparent apologia which tries to see in Hitler, and only in him, the "*causa efficiens* of the whole sequence of events"? But this is not necessarily logical. It is only from one aspect that the infantile person is more remote from the world than other people; from another aspect he is much closer to it. For he does not dredge up the stuff of his dreams and longings out of nothing; on the contrary, he compresses the world of his more normal fellow men, sometimes by intensifying, sometimes by contrasting. From the complexity of life, monomaniacal natures often wrest an abstruse characteristic, quite frequently a comical aspect, but at times a really essential element. However, the mediumistic trait guarantees that nothing peripheral is compressed, nothing trivial monomaniacally grasped. It is not that a nature of this kind particularizes the historical, but that this nature is itself brought into focus by the historical. Although far from being a true mirror of the times—indeed, it is more of a monstrous distortion—nothing goes into it that is pure invention; and what does go into it arises from certain traits of its own. Hitler sometimes compared himself to a magnet which attracted all that was brave and heroic; it would probably be more accurate to say that certain extreme characteristics of the era attracted this nature like magnets, to become in that personality even more extreme and visible. Hence from now on there will be little mention of Hitler's psyche, but all the more of the conditions, forces, and trends of his environment to which he stood in some relationship. For whether he merely interpreted these conditions or intervened in them, whether he placed himself on the side of these forces or opposed them, whether he let himself be borne along by these trends or fought them: something of this force or this trend never failed to emerge in extreme form. In this sense Hitler's nature may be called a historical substance.

Hitler: A Study in Tyranny
ALAN BULLOCK

Not only German scholars, as we have seen, but other scholars of modern European history have been intrigued with the question of why and how Hitler rose to power. The most widely respected of these is Alan Bullock, whose most important work is Hitler: A Study in Tyranny. *Bullock tends to share Nolte's opinion about Hitler's infantilism— though he does not use the term. Stressing the fact that Hitler was incapable of real growth or change, Bullock finds him at the end of his career the same as at its beginning, unwilling to admit the possibility of his own error and seeing everyone's faults but his own. But even with such serious flaws of character and personality, Bullock, again like Nolte, is unwilling to dismiss Hitler as a madman. He sees him rather as the possessor of gifts amounting to political genius, evil genius admittedly but genius nonetheless. And he sees Hitler as using those gifts to secure a wholly personal tyranny over Germany. On the question of why Germany followed Hitler, Bullock diverges sharply from Nolte and from many other German scholars. He finds the explanation, not in the terrible German experience of defeat in World War I and depression in the postwar era, but more deeply rooted in German history, in German nationalism, militarism, and authoritarianism—of which Hitler's tyranny was the "logical conclusion."*

We pick up Bullock's account of Hitler at its last moment, late in April 1945, in the chancellery bunker in Berlin. While Russian artillery crashes above him, shattering what remains of his capital, he dictates to his secretary, Frau Junge, his will and his political testament. Hitler is on the point of committing suicide.

FACING DEATH and the destruction of the régime he had created, this man who had exacted the sacrifice of millions of lives rather than admit defeat was still recognizably the old Hitler. From first to last there is not a word of regret, nor a suggestion of remorse. The fault is that of others, above all that of the Jews, for even now the old hatred is unappeased. Word for word, Hitler's final address to the German nation could be taken from almost any of his early speeches of the 1920s or from the pages of *Mein Kampf*. Twenty-odd years had changed and taught him nothing. His mind remained as tightly closed as it had been on the day when he wrote: "During these years in Vienna a view of life and a definite outlook on the world took shape in my mind. These became the granite basis of my conduct. Since then I have extended that foundation very little, I have changed nothing in it." . . .

In the course of Sunday, the 29th, arrangements were made to send copies of the Fuehrer's Political Testament out of the bunker, and three men were selected to make their way as best they could to Admiral Doenitz's and Field-Marshal Schoerner's headquarters. One of the men selected was an official of the Propaganda Ministry, and to him Goebbels entrusted his own appendix to Hitler's manifesto. At midnight on 29 April another messenger, Colonel von Below, left carrying with him a post-script which Hitler instructed him to deliver to General Keitel. It was the Supreme Commander's last message to the Armed Forces, and the sting was in the tail:

> The people and the Armed Forces have given their all in this long and hard struggle. The sacrifice has been enormous. But my trust has been misused by many people. Disloyalty and betrayal have undermined resistance throughout the war. It was therefore not granted to me to lead the people to victory. The Army General Staff cannot be compared with the General Staff of the First World War. Its achievements were far behind those of the fighting front.

The war had been begun by the Jews, it had been lost by the generals. In neither case was the responsibility Hitler's and his last word of all was to reaffirm his original purpose:

> The efforts and sacrifice of the German people in this war [he added] have been so great that I cannot believe they have been in vain. The aim must still be to win territory in the east for the German people. . . .

He now began to make systematic preparations for taking his life. He had his Alsatian bitch, Blondi, destroyed, and in the early hours of Monday, 30 April, assembled his staff in the passage in order to say farewell. Walking along the line, he shook each man and woman silently by the hand. Shortly afterwards Bormann sent out a telegram to Doenitz, whose headquarters was at Ploen, between Lübeck and Kiel, instructing him to proceed "at once and mercilessly" against all traitors. . . .

In the course of the early afternoon Erich Kempka, Hitler's chauffeur, was ordered to send two hundred litres of petrol to the Chancellery Garden. It was carried over in jerricans and its delivery supervised by Heinz Linge, Hitler's batman.

Meanwhile, having finished his lunch, Hitler went to fetch his wife from her room, and for the second time they said farewell to Goebbels, Bormann and the others who remained in the bunker. Hitler then returned to the Fuehrer's suite with Eva and closed the door. A few minutes passed while those outside stood waiting in the passage. Then a single shot rang out.

After a brief pause the little group outside opened the door. Hitler was lying on the sofa, which was soaked in blood: he had shot himself through the mouth. On his right-hand side lay Eva Braun, also dead: she had swallowed poison. The time was half past three on the afternoon of Monday, 30 April, 1945, ten days after Hitler's fifty-sixth birthday.

Hitler's instructions for the disposal of their bodies had been explicit, and they were carried out to the letter. Hitler's own body, wrapped in a blanket, was carried out and up to the garden by two S.S. men. The head was concealed, but the black trousers and black shoes which he wore with his uniform jacket hung down beneath the covering. Eva's body was picked up by Bormann, who handed it to Kempka. They made their way up the stairs and out into the open air, accompanied by Goebbels, Guensche and Burgdorf. The doors leading into the garden had been locked and the bodies were laid in a shallow depression of sandy soil close to the porch. Picking up the five cans of petrol, one after another, Guensche, Hitler's S.S. adjutant, poured the contents over the two corpses and set fire to them with a lighted rag.

A sheet of flame leapt up, and the watchers withdrew to the shelter of the porch. A heavy Russian bombardment was in progress and shells continually burst on the Chancellery. Silently they stood to attention, and for the last time gave the Hitler salute; then turned and disappeared into the shelter. . . .

In this age of Unenlightened Despotism Hitler has had more than a few rivals, yet he remains, so far, the most remarkable of those who have used modern techniques to apply the classic formulas of tyranny.

Before the war it was common to hear Hitler described as the pawn of the sinister interests who held real power in Germany, of the Junkers or the Army, of heavy industry or high finance. This view does not survive examination of the evidence. Hitler acknowledged no masters, and by 1938 at least he exercised arbitrary rule over Germany to a degree rarely, if ever, equalled in a modern industrialized State.

At the same time, from the re-militarization of the Rhineland to the invasion of Russia he won a series of successes in diplomacy and war which established an hegemony over the continent of Europe comparable with that of Napoleon at the height of his fame. While these could not have been won without a people and an Army willing to serve him, it was Hitler who provided the indispensable leadership, the flair for grasping opportunities, the boldness in using them. In retrospect his mistakes appear obvious, and it is easy to be complacent about the inevitability of his defeat; but it took the combined efforts of the three most powerful nations in the world to break his hold on Europe.

Luck and the disunity of his opponents will account for much of Hitler's success—as it will of Napoleon's—but not for all. He began with few advantages, a man without a name and without support other than that which he acquired for himself, not even a citizen of the country he aspired to rule. To achieve what he did Hitler needed—and possessed— talents out of the ordinary which in sum amounted to political genius, however evil its fruits.

His abilities have been sufficiently described in the preceding pages: his mastery of the irrational factors in politics, his insight into the weaknesses of his opponents, his gift for simplification, his sense of timing, his willingness to take risks. An opportunist entirely without principle, he showed considerable consistency and an astonishing power of will in pursuing his aims. Cynical and calculating in the exploitation of his histrionic gifts, he retained an unshaken belief in his historic role and in himself as a creature of destiny.

The fact that his career ended in failure, and that his defeat was preeminently due to his own mistakes, does not by itself detract from Hitler's claim to greatness. The flaw lies deeper. For these remarkable powers were combined with an ugly and strident egotism, a moral and intellectual cretinism. The passions which ruled Hitler's mind were ignoble: hatred, resentment, the lust to dominate, and, where he could not dominate, to destroy. His career did not exalt but debased the human condition, and his twelve years' dictatorship was barren of all ideas save one—the further extension of his own power and that of the nation with which he had identified himself. Even power he conceived of in the crudest terms: an endless vista of military roads, S.S. garrisons and concentration camps stretching across Europe and Asia.

The great revolutions of the past, whatever their ultimate fate, have been identified with the release of certain powerful ideas: individual conscience, liberty, equality, national freedom, social justice. National Socialism produced nothing. . . .

The view has often been expressed that Hitler could only have come to power in Germany, and it is true—without falling into the same error of racialism as the Nazis—that there were certain features of German historical development, quite apart from the effects of the Defeat and the Depression, which favored the rise of such a movement.

This is not to accuse the Germans of Original Sin, or to ignore the other sides of German life which were only grossly caricatured by the Nazis.

But Naziism was not some terrible accident which fell upon the German people out of a blue sky. It was rooted in their history, and while it is true that a majority of the German people never voted for Hitler, it is also true that thirteen millions did. Both facts need to be remembered.

From this point of view Hitler's career may be described as a *reductio ad absurdum* of the most powerful political tradition in Germany since the Unification. This is what nationalism, militarism, authoritarianism, the worship of success and force, the exaltation of the State and *Realpolitik* lead to, if they are projected to their logical conclusion.

There are Germans who will reject such a view. They argue that what was wrong with Hitler was that he lacked the necessary skill, that he was a bungler. If only he had listened to the generals—or Schacht—or the career diplomats—if only he had not attacked Russia, and so on. There is some point, they feel, at which he went wrong. They refuse to see that it was the ends themselves, not simply the means, which were wrong: the pursuit of unlimited power, the scorn for justice or any restraint on power; the exaltation of will over reason and conscience; the assertion of an arrogant supremacy, the contempt for others' rights. As at least one German historian, Professor Meinecke, has recognized, the catastrophe to which Hitler led Germany points to the need to re-examine the aims as well as the methods of German policy as far back as Bismarck.

The Germans, however, were not the only people who preferred in the 1930s not to know what was happening and refused to call evil things by their true names. The British and French at Munich; the Italians, Germany's partners in the Pact of Steel; the Poles, who stabbed the Czechs in the back over Teschen; the Russians, who signed the Nazi-Soviet Pact to partition Poland, all thought they could buy Hitler off, or use him to their own selfish advantage. . . .

Hitler, indeed, was a European, no less than a German phenomenon. . . . The conditions and the state of mind which he exploited, the *malaise* of which he was the symptom, were not confined to one country, although they were more strongly marked in Germany than anywhere else. Hitler's idiom was German, but the thoughts and emotions to which he gave expression have a more universal currency.

Hitler recognized this relationship with Europe perfectly clearly. He was in revolt against "the System" not just in Germany but in Europe, against that liberal bourgeois order, symbolized for him in the Vienna which had once rejected him. To destroy this was his mission, the mission in which he never ceased to believe; and in this, the most deeply felt of his purposes, he did not fail. Europe may rise again, but the old Europe of the years between 1789, the year of the French Revolution, and 1939, the year of Hitler's War, has gone for ever—and the last figure in its history is that of Adolf Hitler, the architect of its ruin. "*Si monumentum requiris, circumspice*"—"If you seek his monument, look around."

Suggestions for Further Reading

STUDENTS ARE ENCOURAGED to read further in Hitler's revealing *Mein Kampf*, beyond the brief passage excerpted in this chapter. The understanding of *Mein Kampf* will be greatly enhanced by reading Werner Maser, *Hitler's Mein Kampf, An Analysis*, tr. R. H. Barry (London: Faber, 1970). Maser, an eminent German authority on Hitler, has also edited *Hitler's Letters and Notes*, tr. Arnold Pomerans (New York: Harper & Row, 1974). Also important for insights into Hitler is *Hitler: Secret Conversations, 1941–1944*, tr. N. Cameron and R. H. Stevens (New York: Octagon, 1972 [1953]), conversations with Hitler's intimates that he himself preserved.

The two best biographies of Hitler are the classic Alan Bullock, *Hitler: A Study in Tyranny*, rev. ed. (New York: Harper & Row, 1962), excerpted in this chapter, and Joachim C. Fest, *Hitler*, tr. Richard and Clara Winston (New York: Harcourt Brace Jovanovich, 1974), which adds some material not available to Bullock. This is the case also with Werner Maser, *Hitler: Legend, Myth and Reality*, tr. Peter and Betty Ross (New York: Harper & Row, 1973). John Toland, *Adolf Hitler* (New York: Doubleday, 1976), is a massive, definitive work on Hitler, based on every shred of material available, but students may still prefer the more interpretive and readable works listed above. There are three interesting psycho-historical works: Walter C. Langer, *The Mind of Adolf Hitler: The Secret Wartime Report* (New York: Basic Books, 1972), the fascinating account of how a team of psychiatrists and psychologists built up a strategic psychological profile of Hitler during World War II; Rudolf Binion, *Hitler Among the Germans* (New York: Elsevier, 1976), a psycho-history of Hitler and his Germany; and Robert G. Waite, *The Psychopathic God: Adolf Hitler* (New York: Basic Books, 1977), more decidedly and professionally psychoanalytic than Binion and more up-to-date than Langer. Two special studies are also recommended: Bradley F. Smith, *Adolf Hitler: His Family, Childhood and Youth* (Stanford: Hoover Institute, 1967), and Harold J. Gordon, *Hitler and the Beer Hall Putsch* (Princeton, N.J.: Princeton University Press, 1972), the definitive study of this incident so important to the rise of Hitler.

In addition to Ernst Nolte's *Three Faces of Fascism*, tr. Leila Vennewitz (New York: Holt, Rinehart and Winston, 1965), students are urged to read H. R. Kedward, *Fascism in Western Europe, 1900–1945* (London: Blackie, 1969), or F. L. Carsten, *The Rise of Fascism* (Berkeley: University of California Press, 1967). On German fascism, one of the most complete and comprehensive works is K. D. Bracher, *The German Dictatorship: The Origins, Structure, and Effects of National Socialism*, tr. J. Steinberg (New

York: Praeger, 1970). Probably the best general survey of political, social, and cultural history is Raymond J. Sontag, *A Broken World, 1919–1939* "Rise of Modern Europe" series (New York: Harper & Row, 1971), but the most readable and exciting popular history is William L. Shirer, *The Rise and Fall of the Third Reich, A History of Nazi Germany* (New York: Simon and Schuster, 1960), A. J. P. Taylor, *From Sarajevo to Potsdam* (New York: Harcourt, Brace and World, 1966), is a vigorous, witty, highly personal interpretive history. Hannah Vogt, *The Burden of Guilt, A Short History of Germany, 1914–1945,* tr. Herbert Strauss (New York: Oxford University Press, 1964), is especially interesting in that it was specifically written for the instruction of post-World War II German young people. Finally, two important books on the German army must be recommended: John W. Wheeler-Bennett, *The Nemesis of Power: The German Army in Politics, 1918–1945* (New York: St. Martin's, 1954), and Robert J. O'Neill, *The German Army and the Nazi Party, 1933–1939* (London: Cassell, 1968).

Albert Einstein and the Atomic Age: A Question of Responsibility

By the early 1930s, Albert Einstein was the most famous scientist in the world. Indeed, he had become a kind of symbol for the abstruseness of modern science itself, an expert in a branch of theoretical physics so remote and lofty that—at least according to the popular press—only a dozen other people could even understand his theories, much less explain them.

Long before this time, Einstein had established the fundamental direction of his work. As early as 1905, at the age of twenty-six, he had published very important papers, among them his theory of relativity, his work on statistical mechanics, and the quantum theory of radiation. When these first papers were published, Einstein was working as a patent clerk in Berne since he could not find an academic position, but by 1914 he held a professorship at the University of Berlin and was director of the Institute of Physics in the Kaiser Wilhelm Society for the Development of Sciences and a member of the Royal Prussian Academy of Sciences. In 1916 he published the fundamental paper on the general theory of relativity that established his worldwide fame, and in 1921 he received the Nobel Prize for Physics.

Although Einstein's main interest through the late 1920s was in the development of what came to be called his general field theory, other developments far removed from the abstractions of science had begun to crowd in upon his world. Hitler was on the rise in Germany, and Einstein was a Jew. In 1933 Einstein resigned his academic appointments, severed the associations of a lifetime, and joined the thousands of Jews,

501

humble and famous, who had already begun to flee Hitler's Germany. An honored position was created for him at the Institute for Advanced Study at Princeton University, and there he remained for the rest of his life.

Einstein maintained contact with other brilliant refugee physicists who had fled the tyrannies of Europe, among them his old friend Max Born in England, the Hungarian Leo Szilard in the United States, and dozens of other scholars. These men, through their ties with what remained of the old international community of physicists, began to hear troubling rumors in the mid 1930s of experimental work being done in Europe in the field of atomic energy. Then in 1939 Niels Bohr brought word that Hahn and Strassman of the Kaiser Wilhelm Society in Berlin had actually produced nuclear fission. An atomic bomb was now a practical possibility. The work that Bohr reported and the work that would subsequently be done in Germany, England, and the United States was based, in the last analysis, upon Einstein's theories.

Twenty years before, Einstein had argued in his special theory of relativity that, as an object approached the speed of light, its acceleration would tend to produce not only increased speed but increased mass. He explained the process in the elegantly simple equation $E = mc^2$, in which the potential energy (E) of an object is equal to its mass (m) multiplied by the square of the speed of light (c^2). The enormous product of energy that would result from even the most infinitesimal transformation of mass —with the speed of light computed at 186,000 miles per second—was quite beyond anything but mathematical comprehension and even theoretically possible in terrestrial physics only at the atomic level. Now, working with unstable, heavy elements and apparently quite by accident, German scientists had produced a nuclear chain reaction, the instantaneous transformation of one element into another with exactly the incredible release of energy that Einstein's equation had described. As Leo Szilard would later write, "The dream of the alchemists came true. . . . But while the first successful alchemist was undoubtedly God, I sometimes wonder if the second successful alchemist may not have been the Devil himself." [1]

If German scientists had discovered the secret of atomic fission, it would probably not be long before the German government would have an atomic bomb. This prospect brought Leo Szilard and Eugene Wigner to Einstein. As a result of their discussion, Einstein immediately agreed to take action and eventually signed the now famous letter to President Roosevelt urging government support of research on nuclear chain reactions. Now, with the alarming news from Germany and the push from Einstein, work on the Manhattan Project seriously began, and with it the chain of events leading to the explosions over Hiroshima and Nagasaki in August 1945.

[1] "Creative Intelligence and Society," in *Collected Works of Leo Szilard* . . . , ed. B. T. Feld and G. W. Szilard (Cambridge, Mass.: M.I.T. Press, 1972), I, 189.

The Complaint of Peace
ALBERT EINSTEIN

Technology is older than science, but through the centuries the two have always been linked together, technology adapting the theoretical findings of science to the practical uses of society. Sad to say, these uses, more often than not, have been military. With "the bomb," society at last had the ultimate weapon, the doomsday machine capable of destroying not only one's enemies but all mankind.

With the bomb there also came the difficult question of the scientists' moral responsibility for the application of their theoretical and experimental work. One of the most troubled by this question was Albert Einstein. In December 1945, within months of the explosions over Japan, Einstein addressed the Nobel Anniversary Dinner in New York, speaking of the parallel between Alfred Nobel and his desire to atone for the invention of "an explosive more powerful than any then known" and the physicists "who participated in producing the most formidable weapon of all time" and who "are harassed by a similar feeling of responsibility, not to say guilt." But, he continued, their choice was as clear as their anguish was real. "We helped create this new weapon in order to prevent the enemies of mankind from achieving it first. . . . The war is won, but the peace is not." [2]

The persistent theme of all Einstein's public statements and the principal concern of the last decade of his life was the creation of a supranational organization to make sure that the bomb would never again be used. Some of Einstein's friends were exasperated with him for his continued refusal to advocate the surrender of the bomb to the United Nations, then in its confident infancy. But Einstein perceived the essential weakness of that organization, later to be so tragically demonstrated: it was not capable of keeping the peace. But his own proposal—the establishment of a world government—was even more unrealistic.

Einstein stated his views in an interview-article with Raymond Swing that originally appeared in the Atlantic Monthly *in November 1945. A slightly revised version of this article, from* Einstein on Peace, *is reprinted below in its entirety. Einstein's statements tended to be brief and simple. But in this piece, it is not his arguments that are striking; rather, it is the tension between his belief that pure science is essentially unmanageable*

[2] *Einstein on Peace*, ed. Otto Nathan and Heinz Norden (New York: Schocken Books, 1968), p. 355.

and his profound sense of the scientist's moral responsibility in the realm of human affairs.

THE RELEASE of atomic energy has not created a new problem. It has merely made more urgent the necessity of solving an existing one. One could say that it has affected us quantitatively, not qualitatively. As long as there are sovereign nations possessing great power, war is inevitable. This does not mean that one can know when war will come but only that one is sure that it will come. This was true even before the atomic bomb was made. What has changed is the destructiveness of war.

I do not believe that the secret of the bomb should be given to the United Nations Organization. I do not believe it should be given to the Soviet Union. Either course would be analogous to a man with capital who, wishing another individual to collaborate with him on an enterprise, starts by giving him half his money. The other man might choose to start a rival enterprise, when what is wanted is his co-operation. The secret of the bomb should be committed to a world government, and the United States should immediately announce its readiness to do so. Such a world government should be established by the United States, the Soviet Union and Great Britain, the only three powers which possess great military strength. The three of them should commit to this world government all of their military resources. The fact that there are only three nations with great military power should make it easier, rather than harder, to establish a world government.

Since the United States and Great Britain have the secret of the atomic bomb and the Soviet Union does not, they should invite the Soviet Union to prepare and present the first draft of a Constitution for the proposed world government. This would help dispel the distrust of the Russians, which they feel because they know the bomb is being kept a secret chiefly to prevent their having it. Obviously, the first draft would not be the final one, but the Russians should be made to feel that the world government will guarantee their security.

It would be wise if this Constitution were to be negotiated by one American, one Briton and one Russian. They would, of course, need advisers, but these advisers should serve only when asked. I believe three men can succeed in preparing a workable Constitution acceptable to all the powers. Were six or seven men, or more, to attempt to do so, they would probably fail. After the three great powers have drafted a Constitution and adopted it, the smaller nations should be invited to join the world government. They should also be free not to join and, though they should feel perfectly secure outside the world government, I am sure they will eventually wish to join. Naturally, they should be entitled to propose changes in the Constitution as drafted by the Big Three. But the Big

Three should go ahead and organize the world government, whether or not the smaller nations decide to join.

Such a world government should have jurisdiction over all military matters, and it need have only one other power. That is the power to interfere in countries where a minority is oppressing the majority and, therefore, is creating the kind of instability that leads to war. For example, conditions such as exist today in Argentina and Spain should be dealt with. There must be an end to the concept of non-intervention, for to abandon non-intervention in certain circumstances is part of keeping the peace.

The establishment of a world government should not be delayed until similar conditions of freedom exist in each of the three great powers. While it is true that in the Soviet Union the minority rules, I do not believe that the internal conditions in that country constitute a threat to world peace. One must bear in mind that the people in Russia had not had a long tradition of political education; changes to improve conditions in Russia had to be effected by a minority for the reason that there was no majority capable of doing so. If I had been born a Russian, I believe I could have adjusted myself to this situation.

It should not be necessary, in establishing a world government with a monopoly of authority over military affairs, to change the internal structure of the three great powers. It would be for the three individuals who draft the Constitution to devise ways for collaboration despite the different structures of their countries.

Do I fear the tyranny of a world government? Of course I do. But I fear still more the coming of another war. Any government is certain to be evil to some extent. But a world government is preferable to the far greater evil of wars, particularly when viewed in the context of the intensified destructiveness of war. If such a world government is not established by a process of agreement among nations, I believe it will come anyway, and in a much more dangerous form; for war or wars can only result in one power being supreme and dominating the rest of the world by its overwhelming military supremacy.

Now that we have the atomic secret, we must not lose it, and that is what we would risk doing if we gave it to the United Nations Organization or to the Soviet Union. But, as soon as possible, we must make it clear that we are not keeping the bomb a secret for the sake of maintaining our power but in the hope of establishing peace through world government, and that we will do our utmost to bring this world government into being.

I appreciate that there are persons who approve of world government as the ultimate objective but favor a gradual approach to its establishment. The trouble with taking little steps, one at a time, in the hope of eventually reaching the ultimate goal, is that while such steps are being taken, we continue to keep the bomb without convincing those who do not have the bomb of our ultimate intentions. That of itself creates fear and suspicion, with the consequence that the relations between rival countries deteriorate to a dangerous extent. That is why people who advocate taking a step at a time may think they are approaching world peace, but they actually are contributing by their slow pace to the possibility of war. We have no time to waste in this way. If war is to be averted, it must be done quickly.

Further, we shall not have the secret of the bomb for very long. I know it is being argued that no other country has money enough to spend on the development of the atomic bomb and that, therefore, we are assured of the secret for a long time. But it is a common mistake in this country to measure things by the amount of money they cost. Other countries which have the raw materials and manpower and wish to apply them to the work of developing atomic power can do so; men and materials and the decision to use them, and not money, are all that is needed.

I do not consider myself the father of the release of atomic energy. My part in it was quite indirect. I did not, in fact, foresee that it would be released in my time. I only believed that it was theoretically possible. It became practical through the accidental discovery of chain reaction, and this was not something I could have predicted. It was discovered by Hahn in Berlin, and he himself at first misinterpreted what he discovered. It was Lise Meitner who provided the correct interpretation and escaped from Germany to place the information in the hands of Niels Bohr.[3]

In my opinion, a great era of atomic science cannot be assured by organizing science in the way large corporations are organized. One can organize the application of a discovery already made, but one cannot organize the discovery itself. Only a free individual can make a discovery. However, there can be a kind of organization wherein the scientist is assured freedom and proper conditions of work. Professors of science in American universities, for instance, should be relieved of some of their teaching so as to have more time for research. Can you imagine an organization of scientists making the discoveries of Charles Darwin?

I do not believe that the vast private corporations of the United States are suitable to the needs of the times. If a visitor should come to this country from another planet, would he not find it strange that, in this country, private corporations are permitted to wield so much power without having to assume commensurate responsibility? I say this to stress my conviction that the American government must retain control of atomic energy, not because socialism is necessarily desirable but because atomic energy was developed by the government; it would be unthinkable to turn over this property of the people to any individual or group of

---

[3] Einstein is in error on a minor point. . . . Lise Meitner did not "escape from Germany to place the information [about atomic fission] in the hands of Niels Bohr." She was already in Sweden at the time.

individuals. As for socialism, unless it is international to the extent of producing a world government which controls all military power, it might lead to wars even more easily than capitalism because it represents an even greater concentration of power.

To give any estimate as to when atomic energy might be applied for peaceful, constructive purposes is impossible. All that we know now is how to use a fairly large quantity of uranium. The use of small quantities, sufficient, say, to operate a car or an airplane, is thus far impossible, and one cannot predict when it will be accomplished. No doubt, it will be achieved, but no one can say when. Nor can one predict when materials more common than uranium can be used to supply atomic energy. Presumably, such materials would be among the heavier elements of high atomic weight and would be relatively scarce due to their lesser stability. Most of these materials may already have disappeared through radioactive disintegration. So, though the release of atomic energy can be, and no doubt will be, a great boon to mankind, this may not come about for some time.

I myself do not have the gift of explanation which would be needed to persuade large numbers of people of the urgency of the problems that now face the human race. Hence, I should like to commend someone who has this gift of explanation: Emery Reves, whose book *The Anatomy of Peace* is intelligent, clear, brief, and, if I may use the absurd term, dynamic on the topic of war and need for world government.

Since I do not foresee that atomic energy will prove to be a boon within the near future, I have to say that, for the present, it is a menace. Perhaps it is well that it should be. It may intimidate the human race into bringing order to its international affairs, which, without the pressure of fear, undoubtedly would not happen.

Einstein and the Bomb
OTTO NATHAN AND HEINZ NORDEN

Einstein clearly did not consider himself to be the father of the bomb. Indeed, as he stated in the preceding article, he felt his role to be quite indirect. How Einstein came to be involved in the American effort to construct the atomic bomb is a fascinating story, especially in light of the fact that as late as 1939 he did not seem to be very optimistic about practical applications of nuclear fission. But international events finally prompted Einstein to advise President Roosevelt and the American government to undertake the work that became the Manhattan Project and ultimately produced the bomb. The circumstances leading to Einstein's action are described by Otto Nathan, one of Einstein's confidants and the executor of his Last Will, and Heinz Norden in Einstein on Peace, *from which the following selection is excerpted.*

IT WAS ONLY . . . in the early summer of 1939 that Einstein, through Szilard, became involved in the efforts to experiment with the construction of atomic bombs. It would appear that, several years before, Einstein had been very doubtful about the possibility of splitting the atom. At the winter session of the American Association for the Advancement of Science in Pittsburgh in January 1935, reporters asked Einstein whether he thought that scientists would ever be able to transmute matter into energy for practical purposes. In the subsequent newspaper account, which should be considered with caution, Eistein is reported to have replied that he felt almost certain it would not be possible, and to have referred to the vast amount of energy required to release energy from a molecule. "It is," he is reported to have added, "something like shooting birds in the dark in a country where there are only a few birds."

It is possible that Einstein may have learned early in 1939 about the Hahn-Strassmann-Meitner-Frisch work as well as about subsequent publications concerning these developments. It does not appear, however, that he was very optimistic regarding the possibility of a practical application of the new scientific discoveries at an early date. In a statement made in reply to a question submitted to him on the occasion of his sixtieth birthday, March 14, 1939, and published in *The New York Times,* Einstein made the following remarks:

> The results gained thus far concerning the splitting of the atom do not justify the assumption that the atomic energy released in the process could be economically utilized. Yet, there can hardly be a physicist with so little intellectual curiosity that his interest in this important subject could become impaired because of the unfavorable conclusion to be drawn from past experimentation.

Szilard's first contact with Einstein in the matter of nuclear fission took place several months later. When he first considered consulting with Einstein about the new scientific discoveries and their implications, he did not contemplate any approach to the United States Government. Szilard recalls that he and Wigner had by this time become very perturbed by the thought that Germany might obtain large quantities of uranium from the Belgian Congo, the chief source of the material. Germany might thus be greatly helped in her research on atomic energy and ultimately in the production of atomic bombs. Szilard and Wigner felt that the Belgian Government should be advised of these eventualities in order that uranium exports to Germany might be halted if Belgium so desired. Szilard knew that Einstein had for years been on friendly terms with Queen Elizabeth of Belgium. When he and Wigner decided to visit Einstein at Nassau Point, Peconic, Long Island, where Einstein was spending the summer, it was, as Szilard has reported, their intention to suggest to Einstein that he communicate with Queen Elizabeth. It is one of the dramatic aspects of the whole atomic development that this visit, with a relatively modest and probably inconsequential purpose, led to events of completely different and, eventually, momentous import. The visit took place around July 15, 1939.

Szilard recalls that Einstein, when told about the possibility of producing a chain reaction, exclaimed, *"Daran habe ich gar nicht gedacht!"* (That never occurred to me.) Szilard reports that Einstein immediately recognized the implication of Germany's access to uranium in the Congo and declared he would be prepared to assist in informing the Belgian Government accordingly. Several approaches to the problem were discussed by the three scientists. Wigner apparently emphasized not only the desirability of advising the Belgian Government through the Queen or the Belgian Ambassador in Washington of the dangers involved in uranium exports to Germany but also the need for large imports of uranium into the United States. Whether recommendations were made as to how to secure such imports or who might be approached on the matter is not known. Einstein is reported to have favored a suggestion, apparently also offered by Wigner, to submit to the State Department a draft of a projected letter to the Queen of Belgium. The letter would be mailed to the Queen only if no objection were raised by the State Department. There is no information available as to whether, at this original meeting, Einstein, Szilard and Wigner considered advising the American Government of the implications of the new scientific discoveries with a view to engaging its interest in promoting or subsidizing further research in the atomic field.

Even before his visit to Einstein, Szilard had discussed the entire problem with a New York friend in the financial world; he had felt that the financial resources of the physics department of Columbia University would not suffice for the additional research contemplated by Fermi and himself and that outside funds would therefore be necessary. Upon Szilard's return to New York from his visit to Einstein, the finance expert informed him that he had consulted with Dr. Alexander Sachs, a well-known economist connected with the New York banking house of Lehman Brothers and sometimes one of President Roosevelt's unofficial advisers. When it was suggested to Szilard that he communicate with Dr. Sachs, he did so, apparently without delay. It was undoubtedly Sachs who recognized the magnitude and significance of the problem and realized that, to obtain results, the matter should be brought to the attention of the White House. He, therefore, suggested to Szilard that Einstein's letter be addressed to President Roosevelt rather than to the Belgian Queen or the Belgian Ambassador. Sachs offered to see to it that the letter would reach the President personally. Writing to Einstein on July 19, 1939, Szilard stated that, although he had seen Sachs only once in his life and had not been able to form an opinion of him, he nonetheless recommended accepting the course of action outlined by him. Szilard added that this recommendation was also supported by Professor Edward Teller, then guest professor at Columbia University, with whom he had consulted. Szilard further suggested that Einstein's projected letter be entrusted to Sachs since he believed that Sachs was in a position to do as he had promised. Szilard enclosed a draft of the letter. Since Sachs was to play an important role during the ensuing months, and since Einstein's letter to Roosevelt was to release a "chain reaction" which possibly no move by any other individual could have effected at that time, Szilard's casually arranged meeting about an all-important matter with a person completely unknown to him, his subsequent confidence in that person on the basis of a single meeting, and Sachs's perception of Roosevelt's capacity for bold decisions are startling incidents in the drama that was to unfold.

While it is not possible to reconstruct all the developments during the two weeks following Szilard's meeting with Sachs, it is known that, during this period, Szilard once again called on Einstein at his Long Island summer home. Since Wigner was out of town, Szilard was accompanied on his second visit by Edward Teller. At this meeting with Szilard and Teller, if not before by phone or mail, Einstein accepted Sachs's suggestion to bring the matter to the attention of the President and to have a letter to Roosevelt transmitted through Sachs. Einstein dictated to Teller the draft of a letter in German which is preserved in his files. This draft contains some of the main points of the history-making communication to Roosevelt that Einstein was eventually to sign. . . .

Einstein's draft is an indication of how, in possibly less than a week, the initial modest proposition to write a letter to the Belgian Queen had developed into a meaningful and highly suggestive approach to the President of the United States. Whether Einstein's dictated draft was inspired by the draft which Szilard had prepared after his meeting with Sachs and had mailed to Einstein before his second visit cannot be ascertained. On August 2, 1939, Szilard wrote to Einstein that, in his discussions with Sachs about additional recommendations, K. T. Compton, Bernard Baruch and Charles Lindbergh had been suggested for the position of liaison man between the government and the atomic scientists, the position recommended in Einstein's draft and also in his final letter to Roosevelt. Szilard added that Lindbergh was the "favorite" at the time of writing.

On the basis of Einstein's German draft, Szilard prepared, after a further meeting with Sachs, two English versions of a letter to the President, which he forwarded to Einstein in his letter of August 2, 1939. Einstein favored the shorter of the two Szilard drafts. The letter actually sent to Roosevelt and dated August 2, 1939, reads as follows:

Albert Einstein
Old Grove Road
Nassau Point
Peconic, Long Island
August 2, 1939

F. D. Roosevelt
President of the United States
White House
Washington, D.C.

Sir:

Some recent work by E. Fermi and L. Szilard, which has been communicated to me in manuscript, leads me to expect that the element uranium may be turned into a new and important source of energy in the immediate future. Certain aspects of the situation seem to call for watchfulness and, if necessary, quick action on the part of the Administration. I believe, therefore, that it is my duty to bring to your attention the following facts and recommendations.

In the course of the last four months it has been made probable—through the work of Joliot in France as well as Fermi and Szilard in America—that it may become possible to set up nuclear chain reactions in a large mass of uranium, by which vast amounts of power and large quantities of new radium-like elements would be generated. Now it appears almost certain that this could be achieved in the immediate future.

This new phenomenon would also lead to the construction of bombs, and it is conceivable—though much less certain—that extremely powerful bombs of a new type may thus be constructed. A single bomb of this type, carried by boat or exploded in a port, might very well destroy the whole port together with some of the surrounding territory. However, such bombs might very well prove to be too heavy for transportation by air.

The United States has only very poor ores of uranium in moderate quantities. There is some good ore in Canada and the former Czechoslovakia, while the most important source of uranium is the Belgian Congo.

In view of this situation you may think it desirable to have some permanent contact maintained between the Administration and the group of physicists working on chain reactions in America. One possible way of achieving this might be for you to entrust with this task a person who has your confidence and who could perhaps serve in an unofficial capacity. His task might comprise the following:

   a) To approach Government Departments, keep them informed of the further developments, and put forward recommendations for Government action, giving particular attention to the problem of securing a supply of uranium ore for the United States.

   b) To speed up the experimental work which is at present being carried on within the limits of the budgets of University laboratories, by providing funds, if such funds be required, through his contacts with private persons who are willing to make contributions for this cause, and perhaps also by obtaining the cooperation of industrial laboratories which have the necessary equipment.

   I understand that Germany has actually stopped the sale of uranium from the Czechoslovakian mines which she has taken over. That she should have taken such early action might perhaps be understood on the ground that the son of the German Under-Secretary of State, von Weizsäcker, is attached to the Kaiser Wilhelm Institute in Berlin, where some of the American work on uranium is now being repeated.

Yours very truly,

A. Einstein

   This letter, addressed by the then greatest living scientist to one of the most important political leaders of the world, bearing on dramatically important scientific and military developments and suggesting crucial moves by the American Government, was actually not submitted to President Roosevelt for over two months, during which period the Germans might have made much progress in the search for a nuclear chain reaction. The available documents in Einstein's files and all other sources of information fail to provide an adequate explanation for the delay in transmitting Einstein's communication. In a letter of September 27, 1939, Szilard conveyed to Einstein his impression that the letter "had already been in Washington for some time." But in another letter, dated October 3, 1939, Szilard reported that he and Wigner had called on Sachs, and Sachs admitted still having Einstein's letter in his possession; Sachs explained that he had gained the impression from several telephone conversations with Roosevelt's secretary that it was advisable to see the President at a later time since he was overburdened with work. In his testimony of November 27, 1945, before the Special Committee on Atomic Energy of the United States Senate, Sachs stated that he had not wanted to accept an appointment with the President as long as the President was involved in revising the existing neutrality legislation. However, the neutrality legislation did not become an acute issue until the war broke out in Europe on September 1, 1939, which was more than four weeks after Einstein had signed the letter.

   In his letter to Einstein of October 3, 1939, Szilard remarked that he and Wigner had begun to wonder whether it might not become necessary to entrust another person with the mission Dr. Sachs had volunteered to perform. But Sachs did finally see President Roosevelt on October 11, 1939, and submitted to the President Einstein's letter, a more technical memorandum by Szilard, as well as considerable background material. The Szilard memorandum stated that, if fast neutrons could be used, "it would be easy to construct extremely dangerous bombs . . . with a destructive power far beyond all military conceptions." Sachs also submitted to the President a written statement of his own in which he summarized the main problems involved and listed the steps which he thought should be taken by the United States in the matter of further exploring the problem of nuclear fission.

President Roosevelt acted at once. He appointed an "Advisory Committee on Uranium," which was to report to him as soon as possible; a few days later, he addressed the following letter to Einstein:

The White House
Washington

October 19, 1939

My dear Professor,

I want to thank you for your recent letter and the most interesting and important enclosure.

I found this data of such import that I have convened a board consisting of the head of the Bureau of Standards and a chosen representative of the Army and Navy to thoroughly investigate the possibilities of your suggestion regarding the element of uranium.

I am glad to say that Dr. Sachs will co-operate and work with this committee and I feel this is the most practical and effective method of dealing with the subject.

Very sincerely yours,
Franklin D. Roosevelt

. . . The further history of the many stages in the development of the atomic bomb is recorded in other publications and need not be repeated. What is of interest here are the few instances when Einstein again intervened.

After the first meeting of the Advisory Committee, other scientists were invited to participate in subsequent consultations. Sachs continued to play a very important role as the representative of the President and, as he himself frequently emphasized, as the individual who maintained contact with Einstein: he consulted with Einstein and presented Einstein's opinions and suggestions to the President or the committee orally or in writing, as circumstances would dictate. . . .

Although the Advisory Committee continued to operate, Szilard and

Sachs were perturbed at its relatively slow progress and, in February 1940, they decided once again to secure Einstein's intervention. It took the form of another letter from Einstein, dated March 7, 1940.

In this letter, Einstein reviewed the rapid development of atomic research—Szilard's and Fermi's continuing work, for example, and the likelihood that similar work was going forward in Europe, especially in Germany.

On March 15, 1940, Sachs brought Einstein's second letter to the attention of the President, who, on April 5, 1940, proposed an enlarged meeting of the Advisory Committee on Uranium which would include Einstein and others whom Einstein might suggest. Briggs, the chairman of the committee, invited Einstein to participate in such a meeting. Since Einstein was unable to accept the invitation, he addressed, on April 25, 1940, the following letter to Briggs:

I thank you for your recent communication concerning a meeting of the Special Advisory Committee appointed by President Roosevelt.

As, to my regret, I shall not be able to attend this meeting, I have discussed with Dr. Wigner and Dr. Sachs particularly the questions arising out of the work of Dr. Fermi and Dr. Szilard. I am convinced as to the wisdom and the urgency of creating the conditions under which that and related work can be carried out with greater speed and on a larger scale than hitherto. I was interested in a suggestion made by Dr. Sachs that the Special Advisory Committee submit names of persons to serve as a board of trustees for a nonprofit organization which, with the approval of the government committee, should secure from governmental or private sources, or both, the necessary funds for carrying out the work. It seems to me that such an organization would provide a framework which could give Dr. Fermi and Dr. Szilard and co-workers the necessary scope. The preparation of the large-scale experiment and the exploration of the various possibilities with regard to practical applications is a task of considerable complexity, and I think that given such a framework and the necessary funds, it could be carried out much faster than through a loose co-operation of university laboratories and government departments.

As far as can be established, Einstein had no further connection either with the work that preceded the atomic bomb project or with the project itself. The Advisory Committee did not continue much longer as such. When, in June 1940, Roosevelt created the National Defense Research Committee, which was to develop into a very significant organization with regard to America's military preparations, he asked that the Advisory Committee be reorganized, again under the chairmanship of Dr. Briggs, as a subcommittee of the newly created National Defense Research Committee. The President specifically assigned to the new committee the responsibility for research on nuclear problems. "This meant," Professor Karl T. Compton, a member of the new committee, remarked, "reviewing and acting upon the recommendations of Dr. Briggs's committee."

Viewed in historical perspective, it would appear that the decision to use Einstein's unique authority in the attempt to obtain the government's direct participation and financial assistance in atomic research may well have been decisive, since his intervention succeeded in securing the attention of President Roosevelt. The Advisory Committee on Uranium was organized by the President as an immediate result of Einstein's intervention and was the germinal body from which the whole huge atomic effort developed. Whether, without Einstein's intervention, similar developments would have taken place around the same period, and whether the atomic bomb would still have been produced around the time it was produced—that is, before the end of the war—are legitimate questions. . . .

. . . We shall never know with any degree of certainty what would have happened if Szilard had not called on Einstein in July 1939, or if Einstein, in turn, had not been immediately willing to lend his authority to supporting a request to the President of the United States that was partly based on scientific assumptions and speculations.

From the Camp of the Enemy
WERNER HEISENBERG

In the last years of his life, as we have seen, Einstein appealed to scientists around the world to join him in the common cause of peace. And there were many scientists who shared his fears, though not always his precise prescriptions. Leo Szilard, whose own work had been so instrumental in the bomb's development, had argued against its use, insisting that an open demonstration of its terrible destructive power would be fully as persuasive as its actual military employment. Einstein's friend Max Born, who had steadfastly refused to work on the British bomb project, returned to Germany after the war. He wrote to Einstein, "I felt it to be my duty to continue the task of enlightenment about the dangers of nuclear war and other developments and the fight against war and militarism." ⁴ Otto Hahn, the discoverer of atomic fission, and other German physicists petitioned the postwar Federal Republic against atomic rearmament.

One of the most outspoken of the German nuclear scientists was Werner Heisenberg. Heisenberg won the Nobel Prize for physics in 1932 and in 1941 was appointed to the directorship of the Institute of Physics in the Kaiser Wilhelm Society, the post Einstein had held until 1933. In the early 1930s, Heisenberg had seriously considered fleeing Germany for the United States, where he had traveled and lectured widely, but he decided to remain in his own country. There he worked for the government as director of what the German scientists called "the uranium club," Germany's war effort to build an atomic bomb.

There is now substantial evidence that Heisenberg and his colleagues, if they did not actually sabotage the German atomic effort, at least "dragged their feet" and consistently reported to their government that the project was not feasible. Perhaps they even believed that it was not, for they were completely surprised by the news that the United States had exploded the bomb.

The following selection, from "The Responsibility of the Scientist (1945–1950)," is a graphic recollection of the impact upon Heisenberg and his colleagues of the news of Hiroshima. He and other German nuclear scientists had been captured at the end of the war in Europe and were interned in England when the news came. It is instructive to see the American effort through the eyes of a German scientist and to note the parallels between the reactions of Heisenberg and those of Einstein, their views, and their arguments about the ultimate responsibility of scientists for their work and for humanity.

AFTER BRIEF STOPS in Heidelberg, Paris and Belgium my captors finally took me to Farm Hall, where I was reunited with a few old friends and young collaborators of the uranium club. They included Otto Hahn, Max von Laue, Walther Gerlach, Carl Friedrich von Weizsäcker and Karl Wirtz. Farm Hall lies at the edge of Godmanchester, some twenty-five miles from the old English university city of Cambridge, and I was familiar with the landscape from earlier visits to the Cavendish Laboratory. This time there were ten of us, and we all came to look upon Otto Hahn, whose attractive personality and quiet, reflective attitude in a difficult position we greatly admired, as our obvious spokesman. He

---

⁴ *The Born-Einstein Letters* . . . , Irene Born, trans. (London: Macmillan, 1971), pp. 201-2.

would negotiate with our captors whenever it was necessary, and this was not very often; the officers in charge of us did their job with extraordinary tact and humanity, so that after only a short while our relationship became one of complete mutual trust. We had been asked very little about our atomic researches, and we thought it rather odd that they should take so little interest in our work and yet guard us so carefully and prevent us from making even the slightest contact with the outside world. When I asked whether the American and the British had also been studying the uranium problem, I was told by the American physicists who had been sent to interrogate us that, unlike us, Allied scientists had devoted all their attention to tasks connected with the immediate war effort. This seemed quite plausible, in view of the fact that throughout the war there had been not the slightest hint of American work on nuclear fission.

On the afternoon of August 6, 1945, Karl Wirtz suddenly rushed in to tell me about a special news flash: an atom bomb had been dropped over Hiroshima. At first I refused to believe it, for I was convinced that the construction of atom bombs involved enormous technical efforts and probably the expenditure of many thousands of millions of dollars. I also found it psychologically implausible that scientists whom I knew so well should have thrown their full weight behind such a project. Under the circumstances, I was much more inclined to believe the American physicists who had interrogated us than some radio announcer who had perhaps been ordered to broadcast some sort of propaganda story. Moreover, Wirtz had told me that the word "uranium" had not been mentioned in the bulletin; this seemed to suggest that if any bombs had been dropped, they could not have been "atom bombs" in the sense that I used that term. But later in the evening, when the newscaster described the gigantic technical efforts that had been made, I had reluctantly to accept the fact that the progress of atomic physics in which I had participated for twenty-five long years had now led to the death of more than a hundred thousand people.

Worst hit of all was Otto Hahn. Uranium fission, his most important scientific discovery, had been the crucial step on the road toward atomic power. And this step had now led to the horrible destruction of a large city and its population, of a host of unarmed and mostly innocent people. Hahn withdrew to his room, visibly shaken and deeply disturbed, and all of us were afraid that he might do himself some injury. That night we said many ill-considered things, and it was not until next morning that we managed to put some order into our confused thoughts.

Behind Farm Hall, an old red-brick building, was a somewhat neglected lawn on which we used to play fist ball. Between the lawn and the ivy-covered wall that was our boundary lay an elongated rose garden, tended chiefly by Gerlach. It was surrounded by a path which we used much as medieval monks must have used the cloister. It was just the place for serious tête-à-têtes. On the morning after the terrifying news Carl

Friedrich and I walked up and down in it for hours, thinking and talking. We began by voicing our anxiety about Otto Hahn, and Carl Friedrich then expressed the thought that was oppressing all of us:

"It is easy to see why Hahn should be dejected. His greatest scientific discovery now bears the taint of unimaginable horror. But should he really be feeling guilty? Any more guilty than any of us others who have worked in atomic physics? Don't all of us bear part of the responsibility, a share of his guilt?"

"I don't think so," I told him. "The word 'guilt' does not really apply, even though all of us were links in the causal chain that led to this great tragedy. Otto Hahn and all of us have merely played our part in the development of modern science. This development is a vital process, on which mankind, or at least European man, embarked centuries ago—or, if you prefer to put it less strongly, which he accepted. We know from experience that it can lead to good or to evil. But all of us were convinced —and especially our nineteenth-century rationalist predecessors with their faith in progress—that with growing knowledge good would prevail and evil could be kept under control. The possibility of constructing atom bombs never seriously occurred to anyone before Hahn's discovery; nothing in physics at the time pointed in that direction. To have played a part in so vital a scientific endeavor cannot possibly be considered a form of guilt."

"There will, of course, be quite a few," Carl Friedrich remarked, "who will contend that science has gone far enough. They will argue that there are far more important social, economic and political tasks to be done. They may, of course, be right, but all those who think like them fail to grasp that, in the modern world, man's life has come to depend on the development of science. If we were to turn our backs on the continuous extension of knowledge, the number of people inhabiting the earth in the fairly near future would have to be cut down radically. And that could only be done by means as horrible as the atom bomb or perhaps even worse.

"And then knowledge is power. As long as power struggles continue on earth—and at the moment their end is not even in sight—we must also fight for knowledge. Perhaps one day we may have a world government— and let us hope that it will be as free as possible—under which the search for further scientific knowledge does not have to be quite so frantic. But that is not our problem today. For the present, the development of science is a vital need of all mankind, so that any individual contributing toward it cannot be called guilty. Our task, now as in the past, is to guide this development toward the right ends, to extend the benefits of knowledge to all mankind, not to prevent the development itself. Hence the correct question is: What can the individual scientist do to help in this task; what are the precise obligations of the scientific research worker?"

"If we look upon the development of science as an historical process on a world scale," I replied, "your question reminds me of the old problem of the role of the individual in history. It seems certain that in either field the individual is replaceable. If Einstein had not discovered relativity theory, it would have been discovered sooner or later by someone else, perhaps by Poincaré or Lorentz. If Hahn had not discovered uranium fission, perhaps Fermi or Joliot would have hit upon it a few years later. I don't think we detract from the great achievement of the individual if we express these views. For that very reason, the individual who makes a crucial discovery cannot be said to bear greater responsibility for its consequences than all the other individuals who might have made it. The pioneer has simply been placed in the right spot by history, and has done no more than perform the task he has been set. As a result, he may possibly be able to exert just a little extra influence on the subsequent progress of his discovery, but that is all. In fact, Hahn invariably made a point of speaking out in favor of the exclusive application of uranium fission to peaceful purposes; in Germany he was loud in his warnings and counsels against any attempts to use atomic energy in war. Of course, he had no influence on developments in America."

"What is more," Carl Friedrich continued, "we must probably make a clear distinction between the discoverer and the inventor. As a rule, the former cannot predict the practical consequences of his contribution before he actually makes it, the less so as many years may go by before it can be exploited. Thus Galvani and Volta could have had no conception of the subsequent course of electrical engineering, nor can the slightest responsibility be attached to them for the uses and abuses of subsequent developments. Inventors seem to be in quite a different position. They have a definite, practical goal in view, and ought to be able to judge its merits. Hence we can apparently hold them answerable for their contributions. Yet it is precisely the inventor who can be seen to act not so much on his own behalf as for society at large. The inventor of the telephone, for instance, knew that society was anxious to speed up communication. In much the same way the inventor of firearms may be said to have acted on the orders of a society desirous of increasing its military strength. Hence no more than partial blame can be attached to him either, the less so as neither he nor society can foresee all the consequences of his invention. A chemist, for instance, who discovers an agricultural pesticide can tell you no more than the farmer what the ultimate consequences will be in regard to changes in the insect population due to his intervention. In short, we can ask no more of the individual than that he should try to set his own objectives in a wider context, that he should not thoughtlessly endanger the many for the sake of the few. All we can really ask of the individual is that he pay careful and scrupulous attention to the wider framework into which all scientific and technical progress must fit, even when this does not seem to further his immediate interests."

"If you draw a line between invention and discovery, where precisely do you put the atom bomb, the most recent and terrifying product of technical progress?"

"Hahn's fission experiments were a discovery, the manufacture of the atom bomb an invention. The physicists who built the bomb in America were inventors; they were not acting on their own behalves but on the overt or implicit orders of a warring group anxious to obtain the maximum striking power for its army. You once said that, for purely psychological reasons, you could not imagine that American physicists would put their whole hearts into the production of the atom bomb. Only yesterday you were still reluctant to accept the truth of the Hiroshima story. What do you think of our colleagues in America now?"

"Perhaps U.S. physicists were afraid that Germany might be the first to produce atom bombs. And understandably so, for, after all, uranium fission was discovered by Hahn, and atomic physics had reached a very high standard in Germany before Hitler drove out so many of our most capable physicists. A Nazi victory with the atom bomb must have seemed so ghastly a threat that anything seemed justified to stop it, even an atom bomb of one's own. I don't think any of us could really object to that, particularly if we consider what happened in the concentration camps. After the end of the war in Europe, no doubt, many American physicists advised against the use of this terrible weapon, but by that time they no longer had a decisive say. In this respect, too, we cannot really criticize them, for which one of us was able to prevent any of the revolting crimes our own government has committed? The fact that we did not know the full extent of these crimes is no excuse, for we ought to have made greater efforts to find out.

"The worst thing about it all is precisely the realization that it was all so unavoidable. Throughout history, people have acted on the principle that right must be defended by might. Or in more evil and blatant form: that the end justifies the means. And what alternative could we put up against that attitude?"

Suggestions for Further Reading

EINSTEIN'S OWN STATEMENTS about the atomic bomb and scientific responsibility were as brief and often cryptic as were his public statements on other subjects. His most substantial one is the interview with Raymond Graham Swing reproduced in this chapter ("Einstein on the Atomic Bomb," *Atlantic Monthly,* 176, No. 5 [Nov. 1945], 43–45), but some parallel statements are to be found in his *Out of My Later Years* (New York: Philosophical Library, 1950), especially the section "Science and Life." These, as well as nearly all his other related statements, are reprinted and edited in *Einstein on Peace,* ed. Otto Nathan and Heinz Norden (New York: Simon and Schuster, 1960). Some of his concern comes through in *The Born–Einstein Letters: Correspondence between Albert Einstein and Max and Hedwig Born from 1916–1955,* commentary by Max Born, tr. Irene Born (London: Macmillan, 1971), but this book is much more revealing of Born's anguish. The same sentiment is expressed throughout the world community of nuclear physicists, as the excerpt from Werner Heisenberg, *Physics and Beyond: Encounters and Conversations,* tr. A. J. Pomerans (New York: Harper & Row, 1971) demonstrates, as well as Otto Hahn, *My Life . . . ,* tr. E. Kaiser and E. Wilkins (New York: Herder and Herder, 1970). The same sorts of views are expressed in the United States by J. Robert Oppenheimer in *The Flying Trapeze: Three Crises for Physicists* (London: Oxford University Press, 1964), especially the third crisis dealing with the atomic bomb and the moral responsibility of scientists; and in *The Open Mind* (New York: Simon and Schuster, 1955).

Most of the books about Einstein deal with his scientific and technical work: Lincoln Barnett, *The Universe and Dr. Einstein,* 2nd rev. ed. (New York: W. Sloane, 1957), or Jeremy Bernstein, *Einstein* (New York: Viking, 1973), for example. But the best and most comprehensive book on him, Ronald W. Clark, *Einstein: The Life and Times* (New York: World, 1971), does focus on the political and social implications of his work rather than strictly on the work itself. To a somewhat lesser extent, this is the case with Banesh Hoffman, *Albert Einstein, Creator and Rebel* (New York: Viking, 1972). Antonina Vallentin, *Einstein, A Biography,* tr. M. Budberg (London: Weidenfeld and Nicolson, 1954), is interesting in that it deals more fully than any other book with the intimacies, family relations, and day-to-day affairs of Einstein.

Lansing Lamont, *Day of Trinity* (New York: Atheneum, 1965), is a fascinating account of the making and employment of the atomic bomb. The implications of that employment are dealt with in three important books: Herbert Feis, *The Atom Bomb and the End of the War in the Pacific*, rev. ed. (Princeton, N.J.: Princeton University Press, 1966), Martin J. Sherwin, *A World Destroyed: The Atomic Bomb and the Grand Alliance* (New York: Knopf, 1975), and Gar Alperovitz, *Atomic Diplomacy: Hiroshima and Potsdam; The Use of the Atomic Bomb and the American Confrontation with Soviet Power* (New York: Simon and Schuster, 1965). These issues and others are conveniently presented in a book of readings, *The Atomic Bomb: The Critical Issues*, ed. Barton J. Bernstein (Boston: Little, Brown, 1975).